LAW'S ALABAMA BRIGADE

in the

War Between the Union and the Confederacy

By

J. Gary Laine & Morris M. Penny

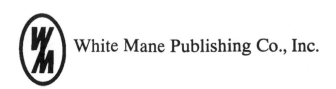 White Mane Publishing Co., Inc.

This White Mane Publishing Company, Inc. publication was printed by
Beidel Printing House, Inc.
63 West Burd Street
Shippensburg, PA 17257 USA

In respect for the scholarship contained herein, the acid-free paper used in this book meets the guidelines for permanence and durability of the Committee on Production Guidelines for Book Longevity of the Council on Library Resources.

For a complete list of available publications please write:
White Mane Publishing Company, Inc.
P.O. Box 152
Shippensburg, PA 17257-0152 USA

Library of Congress Cataloging-in-Publication Data

Laine, J. Gary.
    Law's Alabama Brigade in the war between the Union and the
Confederacy / J. Gary Laine & Morris Penny.
        p.   cm.
    Includes bibliographical references (p.   ) and index.
    ISBN 1-57249-024-1 (alk. paper)
    1. Confederate States of America. Army. Law's Alabama Brigade.
2. Alabama--History--Civil War, 1861–1865--Regimental histories.
3. United States--History--Civil War, 1861–1865--Regimental
histories. 4. Law, Evander McIver, 1836–1920. I. Penny, Morris,
1942–   . II. Title.
E547.L39L35   1997   96-44654
973.7'4761--dc20   CIP

Dedication

This book is dedicated to the memory of three members of Law's Brigade.

Riley Penny
William Penny
Salathiel Clements

Riley and William Penny were brothers of coauthor Morris Penny's great grandfather. Riley and William gave their lives for a cause as it exited the world stage. Salathiel Clements was the great grandfather of coauthor Gary Laine. Sal Clements survived the war and left his devastated Alabama for Texas.

Table of Contents

Dedication iii

Illustrations vii

Maps ix

Acknowledgments xii

Introduction xiv

Abbreviations xix

   1. Law Earns His Commission 1

   2. The Alabamians 19

   3. The Siege of Suffolk 45

   4. The Route to Gettysburg 66

   5. Attack on the Federal Left 78

   6. Farnsworth's Charge 112

   7. On the Rappahannock 127

   8. Fighting along the Chickamauga 138

   9. Charge through the Federal Center 157

  10. Affair in Lookout Valley 176

  11. Campaigning in East Tennessee 201

  12. Fighting Alone in the Wilderness 230

  13. On the Confederate Right at Spotsylvania 255

  14. A Bloody Day at Cold Harbor 266

  15. Richmond and Petersburg Besieged 280

  16. Guarding the Roads to Richmond 299

  17. Appomattox and Home 326

Epilogue 340

Appendix A: Brigade Field and Staff 346

Appendix B: Regimental Organization 347

Appendix C: Roster of Officers 353

Appendix D: Brigade Statistics 365

Appendix E: Battles and Skirmishes 367
Appendix F: Casualties from Selected Battles 369
Appendix G: The Resignation of E. M. Law 371
Notes 372
Bibliography 417
Index 435

Illustrations

1. Brigadier General Evander McIver Law 41
2. Colonel James Lawrence Sheffield, 48th Alabama 42
3. Colonel Pinckney Downey Bowles, 4th Alabama 42
4. Lieutenant Mims Walker, Aide-de-Camp, Law's Staff 42
5. Colonel Egbert J. Jones, 4th Alabama 42
6. Colonel James Cantey, 15th Alabama 43
7. Sergeant William C. Hester, Company E, 4th Alabama 43
8. Lieutenant Colonel Owen Kenan McLemore, 4th Alabama 43
9. Major William McKendre Robbins, 4th Alabama 43
10. Captain Nathaniel H. R. Dawson, Company C, 4th Alabama 44
11. Sergeant John C. Dinson, Company B, 44th Alabama 44
12. Adjutant Robert Thompson Coles, 4th Alabama 44
13. Captain Lewis Lindsay, Company K, 4th Alabama 44
14. Brigadier General William Flack Perry 225
15. Colonel William Calvin Oates, 15th Alabama 226
16. Lieutenant Colonel William Houston Scruggs, 4th Alabama 226
17. Adjutant Henry Stokes Figures, 48th Alabama 226
18. Lieutenant Colonel Isaac Ball Feagin, 15th Alabama 226
19. Captain James H. Young, Company K, 4th Alabama 227
20. Private John Anderson, Company K, 48th Alabama 227
21. Captain Reuben Vaughan Kidd, Company A, 4th Alabama 227
22. First Lieutenant Erwin Foster Rice, Company K, 48th Alabama 227
23. Captain Major Dowell Sterrett, Company C, 4th Alabama 228
24. Captain John W. Purifoy, Company C, 44th Alabama 228
25. First Lieutenant Alvin O. Dickson, Company A, 48th Alabama 228

26. Captain John B. Fondren, Company K, 4th Alabama 228

27. Second Lieutenant William A. Beaty, Company K, 44th Alabama 229

28. Captain David L. Bozeman, Company A, 44th Alabama 229

29. Private Anderson Walker, Company B, 4th Alabama 229

30. Private James David King, Company K, 48th Alabama 229

Maps

For clarity, only the Confederate and Federal Units essential to the understanding of the tactical situation with Law's Brigade are shown on the maps.

1. The 4th Alabama at First Manassas, Virgina - July 21, 1861 7

2. Law Charges the Federal Line, Battle of Gaines's Mill, Virginia - June 27, 1862 12

3. The Alabamians at the Battle of Second Manassas, Virginia - August 29–30, 1862 15

4. The 4th Alabama at the Battle of Sharpsburg, Maryland - September 17, 1862 17

5. Alabama Counties Where the Regiments of Law's Brigade Were Raised 22

6. The 4th and 15th Alabama at the Battle of Sharpsburg, Maryland - September 17, 1862 26

7. The 44th Alabama at the Battle of Sharpsburg, Maryland - September 17, 1862 30

8. The 47th and 48th Alabama at the Battle of Cedar Run, Virginia - August 9, 1862 33

9. The 47th and 48th Alabama at the Battle of Sharpsburg, Maryland - September 17, 1862 36

10. Area of Operations, Suffolk, Virginia - April–May 1863 49

11. Law's Brigade Travels North - May–June 1863 69

12. The Route to Gettysburg, Pennsylvania - June–July 1863 73

13. Hood Launches His Assault - July 2, 1863 86

14. Law Moves Across Plum Run Valley - July 2, 1863 89

15. Law Begins His Assault on the Federal Left - July 2, 1863 92

16. The Fight for the Federal Left - July 2, 1863 97

17.　Final Assault on Little Round Top - July 2, 1863 102

18.　Farnsworth's Charge North through the Plum Run Valley - July 3, 1863 115

19.　Law Breaks the Cavalry Charge - July 3, 1863 117

20.　Return to Virginia - July 1863 .... 124˙

21.　Travel in Virginia - July–August, 1863 135

22.　Virginia to Georgia - August–September 1863 140

23.　Law's Position - 3:00 p.m. - September 19, 1863 147

24.　Law's Position - 3:30 p.m. - September 19, 1863 150

25.　William Perry's Map Detailing Movements of the 44th Alabama -
　　　September 19–20, 1863 153

26.　Law's Position - 4:45 p.m. - September 19, 1863 155

27.　Situation about 11:00 a.m. - September 20, 1863 160

28.　Longstreet Charges the Federal Gap - September 20, 1863 163

29.　The Breakthrough Is Achieved - September 20, 1863 165

30.　The Artillery Is Overrun - September 20, 1863 169

31.　Troop Deployment, Night Engagement at Wauhatchie, Tennessee -
　　　October 28, 1863 187

32.　Smith Attacks Law, Night Engagement at Wauhatchie, Tennessee -
　　　October 28, 1863 192

33.　East Tennessee Campaign, Area of Operations - 1863–1864 203

34.　Battle of Campbell's Station - November 16, 1863 207

35.　Gordonsville to the Wilderness, Virginia - May 4–6, 1864 233

36.　Situation on the Plank Road - 7:30–8:00 a.m., May 6, 1864 239

37.　Situation North of the Plank Road - 8:00–9:00 a.m., May 6, 1864 242

38.　Situation North of the Plank Road - 9:30–10:30 a.m., May 6, 1864 249

39.　Wilderness to Spotsylvania, Virginia - May 7–8, 1864 256

40.　Situation Midmorning, Spotsylvania, Virginia - May 8, 1864 259

41.　Law's Brigade, Spotsylvania, Virginia - May 9–12, 1864 264

42.　Spotsylvania to Hanover Junction, Virgina - May 23–24, 1864 268

43.　Initial Attack on Law's Brigade, Battle of Second Cold Harbor, Virginia -
　　　June 3, 1864 273

44.　Area of Operations - Vicinity of Richmond and Petersburg, Virginia -
　　　June 1864–April 1865 285

45. Battle of Fussell's Mill or Second Deep Bottom, Virginia -
     August 16, 1864 294
46. First Battle of Darbytown Road, Virginia - October 7, 1864 306
47. Second Battle of Darbytown Road, Virginia - October 13, 1864 311
48. The Route from Richmond to Appomattox, Virginia - April 1865 331

Acknowledgements

Many individuals contributed to the preparation of this history, including the late Colonel Harold B. Simpson who encouraged us to get started as early as 1987. Dozens of others, in libraries, archives and historical and genealogical societies listed in the bibliography whose names we do not know and who are not mentioned, also helped.

Above all, special acknowledgement is given to Lynda Lasswell Crist and Mary Seaton Dix, editors of the Papers of Jefferson Davis. They furnished valuable research citations, read parts of the manuscript and offered criticisms regarding it. Most of all, they offered wise counsel and friendship. Great appreciation is due Jane Law Norvell, who provided Law's resignation and important facts about the Law family. A very special thanks goes to James E. Coleman for his support through the long years of research and for editing the material that appears in this book.

Geographer Lawrence W. Erickson, Huntsville, Alabama, researched and prepared the maps, most of which are to scale. He converted several very rough drafts into excellent maps.

Charlotte M. Timmons, Long Beach, Mississippi, performed valuable photocopy work.

Several historians volunteered valuable advice, and we are grateful for their assistance. They are Robert K. Krick, Chief Historian at the Fredericksburg and Spotsylvania National Military Park, who provided sources, encouragement and sound advice; Bryce A. Suderow, Washington, D.C., who shared citations and his unpublished manuscript on the Battle of Second Deep Bottom, offered advice, and treated us to a walking tour of the battlefield at Fussell's Mill; William Glenn Robertson of Leavenworth, Kansas, gave many suggestions regarding the Battle of Chickamauga; William G. Piston, Southwest Missouri State University, provided material not included in his biography of James Longstreet; John Michael Priest, Boonesboro, Maryland, offered his resources on the Battle of the Wilderness and made critical suggestions on our manuscript; Jeffrey D. Wert, Centre Hall, Pennsylvania, provided an obscure nineteenth century address; Joseph T. Glatthaar, University of Houston, shared sources; Kenneth H. Williams, assistant editor of the Papers of Jefferson Davis furnished several newspaper articles; Gary R. Baker, Columbia, South Carolina, located newspaper articles of value; Henry L. Nelson, Richmond, Virginia, convinced farmers to let us visit Fort Holly and inspect the remaining breastworks nearby.

This study could not have been accomplished without the extensive assistance of the scholars and students of history that follow: Richard J. Sommers, the U.S. Army Military History Institute, Carlisle Barracks, Pennsylvania; the late Sarah Jackson and Michael P.

Musick of the National Archives; Robert E. L. Krick, Petersburg National Military Park, Petersburg, Virginia; Glenn LaFantasie, Senior Program Officer, Council on Library Resources; William C. Davis, Mechanicsburg, Pennsylvania; Horace Rudisill, Darlington Historical Commission, Darlington, South Carolina; Clark Center, W. Stanley Hoole Special Collections Library, University of Alabama; Iva Jean Maddox, Historical Center of York County, York, South Carolina; Herbert J. Hartsook, South Caroliniana Library, University of South Carolina, Columbia, South Carolina; Albert Young, Burtonsville, Maryland; the late L. H. Purcell, Lakeland, Florida; Richard A. Shrader and John White, Southern Historical Collection, University of North Carolina, Chapel Hill, North Carolina; Elizabeth Alexander and Pamela Williams, Yonge Library, University of Florida, Gainesville, Florida; the late Alice Rains Trulock, Indianapolis, Indiana; Norwood A. Kerr, Alabama Department of Archives and History, Montgomery, Alabama; William E. Simpson, Wallace State Community College, Hanceville, Alabama; Jan Earnest, Anniston Public Library, Anniston, Alabama; Linda McCurdy and Phillip Shiman, Duke University, Durham, North Carolina; Peggy Fox, the late Harold B. Simpson, Confederate Research Center, Hill College, Hillsboro, Texas; Jane Yates and Major Rick Mill, The Citadel, Charleston, South Carolina; J. Michael Miller, U.S. Marine Corps History Center, Washington Navy Yard, Washington, D.C.; Ellen Nemhauser, Emory University; Kathleen Georg and Paul M. Shevchuk, Gettysburg National Military Park, Gettysburg, Pennsylvania; Chris Daw, Chapel Hill, North Carolina; Annewhite T. Fuller and Ranée Pruitt, Huntsville Madison-County Public Library, Huntsville, Alabama; Marvin Y. Whiting, Birmingham Public Library, Birmingham, Alabama; David L. Coles, Florida State Archives, Tallahassee, Florida; Bernard F. Pasqualini, Free Library of Philadelphia, Philadelphia, Pennsylvania; Jim Baldwin, Greenville, South Carolina.

Grateful acknowledgment is also given to the following individuals for their varied contributions of time and source material: Jim and Linda Taylor, Columbia, South Carolina; Delores A. Bentke, Hillendahl Library, Houston, Texas; Peggy Bailey, Clayton Library, Houston, Texas; Robert Mackintosh, J. Tracy Power and Elmer O. Parker, South Carolina Department of Archives and History, Columbia, South Carolina; Jack Thompson, Overlook Publishing, Albertville, Alabama; Larry Joe Smith, Jacksonville State University, Jacksonville, Alabama; Judge Bobby Junkins, Gadsden, Alabama; AnnMarie F. Price and H. W. Cole, Virginia Historical Society; Mike Wisener, Holly Pond, Alabama; Dr. M. S. Brasfield, Demopolis, Alabama; Mr. and Mrs. George McKee, Faunsdale, Alabama; Jane M. Rouse, Henderson, North Carolina; Richard F. Law, Fairfax, Virginia; Don D. Beaty, Kress, Texas; George Jones, Princeton, New Jersey and Charles Rice, Huntsville, Alabama.

We must also mention the valuable contributions of the staffs at the Alabama Department of Archives and History, Montgomery, Alabama; Anniston Public Library, Anniston, Alabama; Department of Archives and History, Auburn University, Auburn, Alabama; Birmingham Public Library, Birmingham, Alabama; Chickamauga and Chattanooga National Military Park, Fort Oglethorpe, Georgia; Gettysburg National Military Park, Gettysburg, Pennsylvania; Houston Public Library, Houston, Texas; Iuka Public Library, Iuka, Mississippi; Jacksonville State University, Jacksonville, Alabama; Library of Congress, Manuscripts Division, Washington, D.C.; and Western Reserve Historical Society, Cleveland, Ohio.

Appreciation is also due to the photo archivists and photo collectors who helped so much with this volume: Michael J. Winey, the U.S. Army Military History Institute, Carlisle Barracks, Pennsylvania; Gregg D. Gibbs, Austin, Texas.

Introduction

"God bless the Alabamians," exclaimed Robert E. Lee. Only minutes before, Lee had attempted to lead the Texas brigade into battle in the famous Lee-to-the-rear incident at the Battle of the Wilderness. His fighting blood still up, Lee now rode Traveler back and forth along the column as Law's Brigade of Alabamians filed onto the battlefield, encouraging them to halt the Federal breakthrough. Law's Brigade delivered the third hammer blow against the Federal II and V Corps north of the Plank Road, following the Texans and Georgians. After the Confederate collapse was repaired, the Alabama brigade remained the only Southern unit north of the road for more than two hours, stubbornly fighting to a draw elements of four Union divisions. This resolute fighting spirit was the hallmark of Law's Brigade.

This aggressive brigade was led by Brigadier General Evander McIver Law, a courageous twenty-six-year-old graduate of the Citadel. Law was the first born son of a South Carolina plantation owner and the grandson of a Revolutionary War soldier. He was slightly built and wore a goatee to cover his youthful countenance. His men proudly referred to themselves as Law's Brigade, a testimonial to his charisma and leadership on the battlefield. By war's end, the brigade was officially known as Perry's Brigade, after Law's successor, William Flake Perry, who actually commanded the brigade longer than Law. Respect and adoration was so ingrained for their little chieftain, however, that brigade members continued to call themselves Law's Brigade.

The men who served in the brigade were a cross section of antebellum Alabama. The 4th and 15th Alabama regiments were organized in 1861. The 4th, its ranks filled with clergy, lawyers, planters and physicians, won distinction and official thanks from the Alabama Legislature for their remarkable display of cohesion and fighting ability at First Manassas.[1] These first volunteers left their homes for adventure and glory, convinced the Yankee could be easily beaten. The 15th earned praise in Stonewall Jackson's "foot cavalry" in the Valley Campaign. The 44th, 47th and 48th Alabama regiments formed in 1862 just before Confederate conscription went into effect when the fortunes of war were turning against the Confederacy and its armies were in desperate need of manpower. These three units were known to the veteran regiments as the "Fortykins." By law, they had the status of volunteer units, including the right to bounties but they did not enjoy that status in the eyes of the 4th and 15th Alabama regiments until they had proven themselves. The fighting ability of these new arrivals proved to be equal to that of the veterans. When called to fight, to use a phrase from the era, "They did their duty."

The officers of Law's Brigade, including its commander, were ambitious and competitive. William Calvin Oates carried out a running feud over rank with Alexander A. Lowther of the 15th Alabama which lasted virtually the entire war. After serving as the regiment's colonel for over a year, Oates found himself without a command and reduced in rank to major. Oates gained command of another regiment with the help of President Jefferson Davis. When a majority became available in the 4th Alabama, two captains lobbied for the rank. When Thomas K. Coleman got the job, E. Jones Glass resigned his commission over the insult to his honor. Law tried to have Major James McDonald Campbell removed as a field officer of the 47th Alabama for cause. This quarrel consumed months and included a board of inquiry which twice failed to reach a decision, the fortunes of war finally settling the controversy. Law quarreled with the colonel of the 44th Alabama over the colonel's conduct on the field at Chickamauga. In addition, Law resented the colonel's position in relation to Law's quarrel with Longstreet. Law also placed under arrest the colonel of the 4th Alabama for reasons now unknown and waged an aggressive campaign to block the promotion of the major of the 47th Alabama.

More serious was Law's quarrel with Lieutenant General James Longstreet and Brigadier General Micah Jenkins. Law had earned a solid reputation as a brigade commander at Gaines's Mill, Second Manassas, and Sharpsburg. When the five Alabama regiments came together in January 1863 as Law's Alabama Brigade, Law was a rising star in the Confederacy, but he ran afoul of Longstreet in 1863 when his career looked most promising. It may be that Law fell into disfavor with "Old Pete" in April when two companies of his brigade were captured, along with a battery of artillery at Suffolk, Virginia. But Law's aide-de-camp, an eccentric Englishman named John Cussons, dates the problem between the two men to the Battle of Gettysburg. Cussons claimed Longstreet considered Law insubordinate when the junior officer "firmly insisted that the road to victory lay around the unguarded left of the Federal army." The staff officer felt Longstreet overreacted and forgot the contributions made by Law, "...whose skill and daring had added luster to Longstreet's name on every field from Cold Harbor to Gettysburg."[2] In late 1863, Law's rigid code of honor was offended by Longstreet, his commanding officer, which led to his refusal to serve under that officer's command. This estrangement also involved Lee, Davis and other Confederate officers. Unfortunately, Longstreet and Law never reconciled their differences.

Friction between Law and Jenkins predated the war. Both South Carolinians, graduates of the Citadel and members of the faculty of Kings Mountain Preparatory Military School, Law and Jenkins were natural rivals. Their estrangement may have begun in 1858, at the Fourth of July celebration held at the tiny South Carolina community of Bullock's Creek. There were several speeches and toasts to George Washington, John C. Calhoun, the soldiers of 1812 and even to the "Emerald Isle." A newspaper report of the festivities counted four speeches, eleven regular toasts and a volunteer toast to the military school. In response to the toast to the school, Law delivered the final remarks of the day. The newspaper story did not quote from Law's speech, only saying that "...propriety demands that the writer should forbear to speak of the address."[3]

After the war began, Jenkins became Longstreet's protégé, who did all he could to advance the younger man's career. While commanding a division at Gettysburg, Major General John Bell Hood's left arm was all but severed by an artillery burst. This gave Longstreet the opportunity to both further Jenkins's career and have the South Carolinian serve in his corps. Jenkins was denied immediate command of Hood's Division when Hood cut short his rehabilitation to accompany his troops to the Battle of Chickamauga. Hood's biographer asserts the officers of his division asked Hood to go with them to Georgia to prevent Jenkins from assuming command of the division.[4] Hood's continued bad luck proved fortunate for Jenkins as the division commander was again struck down in battle, this time losing a leg. Jenkins assumed command of the division, and Law was passed over. As Davis predicted to Longstreet, trouble in his command was inevitable.

A continuous thread through the history of the Alabama brigade was the problem of finding and keeping effective commanders. The 4th Alabama lost many officers at its reorganization in the spring of 1862 because some felt they had done their duty by serving for the year they signed up to serve, and felt no obligation to stay longer. Others left their companies when their men refused to reelect them upon the reorganization, claiming that their honor demanded they return to Alabama. The officer ranks of the 4th and 15th regiments were badly depleted in the fighting of 1861 and 1862. First Manassas, Gaines's Mill, Second Manassas and particularly, Sharpsburg, badly depleted the officers of the 4th and 15th Alabama regiments. The officers of Law's Brigade learned command in combat, a method of study high in attrition. Combat resulted in death and disabling wounds, but also quickly weeded out the unqualified. The realities of this war required officers to lead by example, to demonstrate their courage to their command. Before the Battle of First Manassas, the officers of the 4th Alabama wanted Colonel Egbert J. Jones removed from command but his coolness and courage under fire along the banks of Bull Run earned him the deepest respect of his regiment. A half a century after the fight at Cold Harbor, a Texas soldier could not forget the fearless image of Law standing in the open on the Confederate breastworks as the Federals attacked.[5]

Combat for the Alabamians was up close and personal. At Gettysburg, Brown's Ferry, and the Battle of Wauhatchie the fighting was hand-to-hand. At Chickamauga, Cold Harbor, and Spotsylvania they engaged in fire fights within 100 yards of their enemy. At the Wilderness, Fussell's Mill and the three fights on the Darbytown Road in the fall of 1864, the brigade fought to within steps of the Federals. The Alabama brigade displayed an aggressive attitude, initiating charges in seven of their ten major engagements throughout 1863–64.[6] Morale remained remarkably stable despite the ever present attrition during the course of the war, and shortages of basic necessities. On three occasions— following Chickamauga, with Longstreet in East Tennessee, and during the winter of 1864–65— they endured shortages of food, clothing, and shoes with resolute patriotism.[7]

The brigade's finest hour came in May 1864 in that dark forest known as The Wilderness. The Alabamians followed the Texans and Georgians into the fight when Longstreet's timely arrival saved the Army of Northern Virginia from defeat. G. Moxley Sorrel, on the staff of Longstreet, believed forming battle lines in the dense undergrowth of the Wilderness, while under fire and with A. P. Hill's men retreating through its ranks was the best demonstration during the war of the discipline and courage of the First Corps.[8] For two hours, Law's Brigade was the only Confederate unit in action north of the Plank Road. By early afternoon, the Alabamians were fought out. When attacked by superior numbers and flanked, the veterans knew to get out of harm's way. The day of their most splendid fighting was also the only day that Law's Brigade was driven from the field.

The officers who commanded Law's Brigade were indifferent to report writing. Law noted he filed no report on Gettysburg because he received reports from the brigade commanders just prior to his command's detachment to Georgia and the Battle of Chickamauga. After that battle he admitted the report was simply not written.[9] Law commanded Hood's Division at Gettysburg and Chickamauga yet we have no report to tell us where he was and what he did during these very important battles. It would be useful to read his account of the discussions regarding a move around the Federal left at Gettysburg, for example.

Fortunately, reports of the operations of Law's Brigade exist in the form of three histories of the 15th Alabama, written by Oates, William C. Jordan and William Augustus

McClendon. Robert Thompson Coles compiled a history of the 4th Alabama at the turn of the century. Though not as comprehensive, writings by Joseph Quarterman Burton and Theophilus F. Botsford of the 47th Alabama, Rufus Hollis, the 4th Alabama, and Henry H. Sturgis, the 44th Alabama, offer valuable insights into the activities of these units. Between these documents, a reasonably clear picture can be drawn of the brigade's service. These are augmented by letters and diaries of members of the five regiments. Contemporary newspapers provide additional material, most notably casualty reports from members of the brigade in the form of letters to hometown editors. Post–war publications, such as the *National Tribune*, the Philadelphia *Weekly Press*, various Alabama newspapers, the *Confederate Veteran*, the papers of the *Southern Historical Society* and regimental histories furnish a rich collection of eyewitness accounts of brigade experiences during the war. For any volume on the war between the Union and the Confederacy, the *War of the Rebellion: A Compilation of the Official Records of the Union and Confederate Armies*, generally known as the Official Records, is an indispensable source. This book relies heavily on these records.

In addition to muster rolls in the National Archives, many Alabama regiments had historical muster rolls compiled during the last winter of the war by a representative of the state of Alabama. William Henry Fowler was elected Secretary of the Secession Convention, served as captain in the 5th Alabama, and organized "Fowler's Battery" before accepting the assignment as Alabama Superintendent of Army Records. His task was to collect the names of Alabamians who mustered into Confederate service, particularly those who died, whether from disease or in battle. By order of the legislature, these names were to be recorded and "preserved among the archives of the state as a token of respect to their memories." Fowler took blank rolls to Law's Brigade, headquartered at the McKenzie farm near Richmond, to record for posterity the names of all Alabamians who served in the brigade. Fowler gave us the most contemporary total of killed, wounded and deserters, although some will quarrel with his count of deserters.

Chapter One introduces General Law, one of the many gallant commanders who served ably during the war, but who are virtually unknown today. Although biographical material on Law is scanty, a picture emerges which reveals how he proved himself an able brigade commander and gained promotion for himself. Chapter Two, "The Alabamians," gives a short history of the five Alabama regiments before they came together as Law's Brigade. Their organization and first battle are given. The personalities which play major roles in the brigade history are introduced. The colorful but serious intramural conflicts which began during this period often remained throughout the war. The remaining chapters are the brigade history from early 1863 through the surrender at Appomattox.

Units of both armies are designated by contemporary terminology. Northern corps were known by roman numerals but Confederate corps of the Army of Northern Virginia were usually designated by the words first, second and third. Federal divisions and brigades were numbered (thus, First Brigade, First Division, IX Corps). Confederate divisions and brigades were normally named for their official commander, as in Law's Brigade, Hood's Division, First Corps. As the war wore on and the Confederacy lost more and more of its capable officers, many brigades were under command of someone other than the commander for whom it was named. In such cases, brigade is not capitalized. An example of this is Bowles's brigade or Law's Brigade, Colonel Bowles commanding. Law was the official commander of the Alabama brigade, and it was called Law's Brigade even when he was not present, until Perry was officially given command in February 1865, at which time the brigade became Perry's Brigade.[10]

There was great early enthusiasm for the war in both the North and the South. There was real animosity for the opponent in the early stages of the fighting which did not exist later in the conflict. Animosity gave way to respect when the adversaries saw the courage of his opponent on the battlefield.[11] The greatest difference for the Alabama brigade in the later stages of the war was the terrible losses among its bravest officers and men. By the summer of 1864, most Alabama soldiers in the Army of Northern Virginia realized the cause was lost but their honor and personal courage kept them in the field. Many of their best officers were dead or disabled. The war had become grim. Looking at the American Civil War after more than a century and a quarter, it may again seem an adventure. Law, however, offered a different point of view. "War may be glorious at a distance," he wrote in 1887, "and its fruits may sometimes be the only nutriment of Liberty, but a sight of the harvest which it gathers upon the battlefield is anything but inspiring."[12]

Abbreviations

A	Acting
ACS	Assistant Commissary
ADAH	Alabama Department of Archives and History
ADC	Aide-de-Camp
Adj	Adjutant
A&IG	Adjutant and Inspector General
AGC	Alabama Governors' Correspondence, May, 1863–April, 1864, ADAH
AL	Alabama
ANV	Army of Northern Virginia
AP	Edward Porter Alexander Papers, Southern Historical Collection
APJSU	"The Correspondence of John M. Anderson, Private, CSA", JSU
AQM	Assistant Quartermaster
Brig. Gen., BG	Brigadier General
B&L	*Battles and Leaders of the Civil War*
BPDU	Beauregard Papers, Duke University
BPL	Birmingham Public Library
Brgd	Brigade
BS	Brigade Staff
BSF	Bulger, Surname File, Alabama Department of Archives and History
CAH	Center for American History, Austin, Texas
Capt	Captain
Cav	Cavalry
CCNMP	Chickamauga, Chattanooga National Military Park
CGP	Cedar Grove Plantation Papers, Birmingham Public Library
CGSO	Compiled Service Records, Confederate Generals and Staff Officers, and Nonregimental Enlisted Men, National Archives
CMH	*Confederate Military History*
Co	Company
Col	Colonel
CSR	Compiled Service Records
CSS	Confederate States Ship
CV	*Confederate Veteran*
CWTI	*Civil War Times Illustrated*

DC	Dartmouth College
DCSU	Letters of James Barrett Daniel, Samford University
DU	Duke University
ECP	Ezra Ayers Carman Papers, New York Public Library
ECPLC	Ezra Ayers Carman Papers, Library of Congress
EU	Emory University
FC	Figures Collection, Huntsville–Madison County Public Library
FS	Field and Staff
GA	Georgia
GNMP	Gettysburg National Military Park
GO	Compiled Service Records, General Officers, National Archives
HC	Confederate Research Center, Hillsboro College
HMCPL	Huntsville-Madison County, Alabama Public Library
HM	Historical Memoranda
HMR	Historical Muster Rolls
HQ	Headquarters
IL	Illinois
IN	Indiana
Inf	Infantry
JPCL	James Preston Crowder Letters, Emory University
JSU	Jacksonville State University
KY	Kentucky
LC	Library of Congress
LRCAI	Letters Received by the Confederate Adjutant and Inspector General
Lt	Lieutenant
LTCAIG	Letters/Telegrams sent by the Confederate Adjutant and Inspector General
Lt Col	Lieutenant Colonel
M	Microfilm
MA	Massachusetts
Maj	Major
MD	Maryland
MDAH	Mississippi Department of Archives and History
ME	Maine
MHC	Michigan Historical Collection
MHSM	Military Historical Society of Massachusetts
MI	Michigan
MJP	Micah Jenkins Papers, Duke University
ML	John V. McKee Letters
MN	Minnesota
MOLLUS	Military Order of the Loyal Legion of the U.S.
MPSCL	Samuel W. Melton Papers, South Carolina Library
MPSHC	McLaws Papers, Southern Historical Collection
MS	Mississippi
n	Number
NA	National Archives
NDP	N. Dawson Papers, Southern Historical Collection
NHHS	New Hampshire Historical Society
NJ	New Jersey

NC	North Carolina
NOR	**[Spell out Abbreviation]**
NY	New York
NYPL	New York Public Library
OC	Oates Corrspondence, Gettysburg National Military Park
OH	Ohio
OR	*Official Records*
ORA	Atlas of the OR
ORN	*Official Records of the Navies*
OROC	Official Register of the Offices and Cadets
PA	Pennsylvania
PACS	Provisional Army of the Confederate States
Pt	Part
QM	Quartermaster
RC	Regimental Command
REC	Record of Event Cards
Regt	Regiment
RFP	Rayburn Family Papers
RG	Record Group
RPSHC	Robbins Papers, Southern Historical Collection
RS	Regimental Staff
RU	Rice University
SC	South Carolina
SCDAH	South Carolina Department of Archives and History
SCL	South Carolinian Library
Sec	Second
SHC	Southern Historical Collection
SHSP	*Southern Historical Society Papers*
SU	Samford University
TAHS	*Transactions of the Alabama Historical Society*
TN	Tennessee
TX	Texas
UA	University of Alabama
USAMHI	U.S. Army Military History Institute, Carlisle Barracks, Pennsylvania
USS	United States Ship
v, Vol	Volume
VA	Virginia
VHS	Virginia Historical Society
WAGL	William Alexander Griffin Letters
WFPP	William F. Perry Papers, War Department Collection of Confederate Records, General and Staff Officers, Box 227, National Archives
WRHS	Western Reserve Historical Society
WWL	Watson D. Williams Letters, Confederate Research Center, Hillsboro College

Chapter 1

Law Earns His Commission

The election of Abraham Lincoln to the presidency in 1860 created an intense emotional reaction throughout Alabama. The legal profession, major newspapers and dominant churches, the Baptists and Methodists, clamored for secession. These two denominations represented most of the state's citizens and the Methodists, meeting in conference in Montgomery, published a resolution declaring that Lincoln's election amounted to a declaration of war. The Baptists, at their state convention in Tuskegee, approved a resolution stating that they were prepared to defend the sovereignty and independence of the state.[1]

Nine months earlier the state legislature had already declared that Alabama had the right to secede and appropriated $200,000 for military needs. On December 6, 1860, Governor Andrew B. Moore, acting under authority granted by the legislature's resolution, called a convention to consider secession. One hundred delegates were elected on Christmas Eve and gathered at the state capital in Montgomery on January 7, 1861, dividing into two groups, Secessionists and Cooperationists.[2] Secessionists argued for immediate withdrawal from the Union while the Cooperationists favored a more cautious approach. The Cooperationists' strength lay in central and north Alabama where a large number of citizens opposed secession under any conditions.[3]

The debate over secession required just four days to reach a decision. By a vote of 61 to 39 the State of Alabama, on January 11, 1861, seceded from the United States. The huge crowd assembled in the capitol rotunda burst into joyful celebration with the announcement, and a group rushed into the meeting room and unfurled a magnificent flag on the floor.[4]

Among the delegates opposing the Ordinance of Secession were Michael Jefferson Bulger of Tallapoosa County and James Lawrence Sheffield of Marshall County. They believed an action as important as secession should be put before the people of Alabama for a vote. Bulger had moved to Alabama in 1823 as a seventeen-year-old apprentice to a gin maker. He prospered in his adopted state, becoming a planter and later serving in the legislature in 1851 and 1857.[5] He told his fellow delegates that secession was "unwise and impolitic and not a remedy for any wrong of which we complain in the Union," but he found it "immediate and separate without reference to the people for their ratification or rejection (and) a foregone conclusion."[6] Bulger refused to vote for secession. He was threatened by a mob for his stand, but when he sent word to the ruffians to do their worst to any man who did not vote the wishes of his constituents, they decided they had misjudged him.[7] Bulger, at the advanced age of 56, then raised a company and went on to serve as lieutenant colonel of the 47th Alabama Regiment until wounds took him out of the war.

Jim Sheffield described himself as a Union man upon constitutional principles, but believed in secession if Alabama's rights were denied in the Union. Nonetheless, in an impassioned speech to the convention, Sheffield warned of the consequences of secession. "In my judgment, its (Union) dissolution is a calamity, and upon its preservation, perhaps not only depended our own happiness, but that of countless generations yet to come."[8] Joining others who saw passage of the secession ordinance as inevitable, he finally voted in favor of the ordinance. Sheffield vowed to the other delegates to defend his state if she were threatened and made good his promise with service in the 9th and 48th Alabama Regiments.

In response to the threat posed to the state, volunteer military companies sprang up throughout Alabama. One such company was the Tuskegee Zouaves, later Company B of 4th Alabama Regiment, organized by Evander McIver Law, principal of the Tuskegee Military High School, who had come to the state from South Carolina. This self-confident young man of twenty-four years, with a military education and a gift for oratory, put aside his teaching career to answer the call of his adopted state. For the next four years his occupation was soldier.

McIver[9] Law was the first son of Ezekiel Augustus Law and Sarah Elizabeth McIver of Society Hill, South Carolina. Judge Gus Law was a graduate of Yale Law School, member of the legislature, and for many years Chancellor in Equity.[10] The Laws lived a comfortable plantation life where McIver enjoyed the gentlemanly pursuits of riding and hunting. He attended the Common School and St. John's Academy at Darlington.[11]

On the first of January 1853, at age sixteen, Law entered the Arsenal Academy at Columbia for a year. He was a lean five feet eight and half inches tall and had black hair and blue eyes.[12] He then transferred to the Citadel Academy at Charleston for three years. The two schools were together known as the South Carolina Military Academy and governed by a single board. The course of study at the Citadel was patterned after West Point, with one month of each session devoted to military training. Twice a year the cadets went into the field with musket and knapsack to live the life of the soldier. The cadets lived in tents and learned to construct field fortifications, serve on guard duty, and drill by Scott's *Infantry Tactics* and Hardee's *Manual*.[13]

Law joined one of the two literary societies at the Citadel, the Polytechnic, becoming, during his fourth year, the "Society Orator." On February 22, 1856, Hugh S. Thompson, future governor of South Carolina, rose in the salon of the Citadel to read Washington's farewell address. Next, Law spoke for 45 minutes to the crowd of 400. The Charleston (South Carolina) *Evening News* noted the audience held many ladies "who are uniform admirers of the brave young soldier and never fail to cheer him." The paper reported Law gave an excellent address, "distinguished alike for the chasteness of diction and the ease and grace of its delivery." Cadet Law finished with remarks on the volatile political situation in the United States. "Upon the whole," continued the article, "it was just such an address as the occasion required and one which reflected credit alike on the head and heart of the young patriotic orator."[14]

At graduation, Law ranked fourth in his class and had earned firsts in English Literature, Constitutional Law, and two in Elocution. In Military Engineering and Tactics he ranked a respectable seventh and fifth. His standing in conduct was fourteenth out of his class of fifteen.[15]

Though his marks in conduct were never better than average, Law's poor standing his last year was due primarily to one reprimand. On July 7, 1856, nominations for the next year's July Fourth speaker led to bad blood among several cadets. Law had wanted to "bring to account" H. D. Moore for previous remarks and Moore's comments on this occasion put him over the edge. Law and cadets John Frances Lanneau, R. M. Sims and J. A. Scott called on Moore, each wishing to fight him first. Scott demanded an apology, Moore refused and they were quickly into a fight. The brawling students were arrested, and Law was charged with interfering with the arrest. Law's challenge to the charge was dismissed and he received a reprimand.[16]

Law's overall standing, together with his leadership ability, earned him promotion to third lieutenant as well as assistant teacher in Belles Letters for the second session of his senior year. Law gave the salutatory address at the Citadel commencement ceremony on November 2, 1856. He was the last minute replacement for the address when the assigned student had to leave hurriedly after his father's death. With only one day to prepare his talk, Law, by his cousin's appraisal, eclipsed the other speakers "His soft, melodious voice was very pleasant to the ear after hearing those of the others," was Tom Law's diary entry for the day.[17]

The military education Law acquired at the well-respected South Carolina Military Academy was a solid foundation for a Confederate officer.[18] He was a member of that small cadre in the army who knew the officer's profession. This was crucial for the soldiers who served under Law's command. Most Confederate officers received their military training in camp by reading military manuals such as Hardee and with separate officer drill. Officers of the 4th Alabama and Law's Brigade used these methods as well but they also had the advantage of command by a military instructor.[19]

After graduation, Law took a position at the Kings Mountain Preparatory Military School at Yorkville, South Carolina, as Professor of Belles Letters.[20] This school was founded by two classmates of Law and 1854 graduates of the Citadel, Micah Jenkins and Asbury Coward. Jenkins had graduated first in the class of 1854. While employed at the school, Law lived at the Rose Hotel in town.[21] Beginning in 1858, he began reading law in the office of W. B. Wilson of Yorkville.[22] Before completing his law study, Law moved to Alabama in September 1860 to act as principal of the Tuskegee Military High School, which he co-founded.[23]

Because of his military education, Law believed it was his duty to answer Alabama's call for volunteers. "Without political antecedent, of any kind, having never taken part in public affairs," Law wrote to President Andrew Johnson in 1865, "I entered the army on principle, and during my continuance in the service, simply discharged my duties as a soldier."[24] He offered the services of the "Tuskegee Zouaves" to Governor Moore on January 7, 1861. The state command immediately ordered the company to Pensacola, Florida, as part of the contingent of Alabama troops sent to help Florida militia occupy Federal forts. Law received a commission as captain in the Alabama forces on January 12. The Confederates occupied Fort Barrancas and the Navy Yard on the mainland. Across Pensacola Bay, on an east-west strip of sand, the Union forces had established a strong position at Fort Pickens. The Confederates had to cross open water to dislodge the Federals. The result was a standoff. Law, in a letter to a South Carolina friend, suggested Fort Pickens could be taken but only at the cost of many Southern lives. Although he offered his opinion that the Alabama and Florida soldiers would count it an honor to die at Fort Pickens, no assault was ordered. Law and his Macon County men returned home on February 14.[25]

Another Alabama militia company went to Florida during the crisis. After its first formation, the "Conecuh Guards," later Company E, 4th Alabama, marched to Pensacola only to find its services were not needed.[26] Among the privates of the Conecuh Guards was twenty-five-year-old Pinckney Downey Bowles, an attorney from Sparta, Alabama. He had attended the Citadel for two years, one while Law was a student at the prestigious school, but resigned after one year when his health failed. Entering the junior class at the

University of Virginia in the fall of 1855, he proved an exceptional student, graduating with honors in 1857.[27] Bowles made such an impression on his fellow soldiers that, after their return from Florida, his company elected him its captain. During the four years of the war, he would succeed his Citadel classmate to command of both the 4th Alabama and Law's Brigade.

Many Southerners considered it a joyous occasion to go to war in the early spring of 1861. A sense of chivalry prevailed in defending the country, along with a certain mystique associated with the glory of combat. Young ladies' hearts beat faster when they thought of their young men achieving victory on the battlefield. For young men eager to engage the Yankee soldier, the horrors of war lay in the future. Their only frame of reference to judge warfare were stories of the Mexican War or tales of the Revolutionary War. The coming war was viewed by the typical Southerner as a very noble cause. Many referred to the anticipated event as the Second War for Independence. Volunteers were eager to reach the front because they feared the fighting would be over in a few months. Most of the first volunteers literally thought that one Southern soldier was worth ten Yankees.

4th Alabama Infantry

Ten companies of Alabama volunteers left in late April 1861 for Dalton, Georgia, to organize the 4th Alabama. Citizens sent company after company off with much fanfare. Townspeople presented flags to company officers at receptions and the ceremonies given in their honor with the gala events were usually accompanied by patriotic speeches and singing. The "Marion Light Infantry," received a blue silken banner, the gift from a bride of less than three months who made the flag from her wedding dress. A local politician gave a farewell speech at the courthouse, followed by the young ladies from Judson College who sang an appropriate song. The company then marched to the depot where, with much fanfare, a special train waited for the men to board "the cars" and rumble off to war.[28]

Similar scenes were repeated throughout the state. The "Canebrake Rifles" carried a flag showing a cotton plant in bloom, under which lay a coiled rattlesnake and a shield with the motto *Nol: Me Tangere*. The other side was emblazoned with the Alabama State seal.[29] The "Magnolia Cadets" were presented a flag adorned with the likeness of a beautiful magnolia wreath on one side. A cross with eight stars was embroidered on the reverse side. Each company officer was presented a bouquet of flowers. Every member of the company received a Bible with the charge to learn not only their duty to country, but how to fight the great moral battle of life. To take care of their medical needs a large medicine chest was donated.[30] As the "Governor's Guards" prepared to board the train, a young admirer rushed up to Sergeant Reuben Vaughan Kidd and placed a small silken Confederate flag in his hand.[31] At the railroad depot at Sparta, Alabama, the Ladies Aid Society presented the "Conecuh Guards" with a beautiful flag to accompany them to war.[32]

Eight of the ten companies were in Dalton, Georgia, by May 1 where the grateful residents put on a May Day celebration to welcome the Alabamians. The "North Alabamians" arrived last, reaching Dalton on May 2.[33] Election of field officers began immediately, with a spirited contest for colonel developing between former Governor John A. Winston and Captain Egbert J. Jones of Huntsville, Alabama. Winston was favored by the south Alabamians because they felt his political connections and his character would secure an advantageous battlefield position for the 4th Alabama. Winston did have military credentials, having been elected a field officer of a volunteer regiment in the war with Mexico.[34] Jones drew support from the four companies raised in North Alabama. Winston's nomination was supported by the "Governor's Guards," "Tuskegee Zouaves," "Magnolia Cadets" and "Conecuh Guards." The "Canebrake Rifles" planned to cast a symbolic vote for Governor

Moore on the first ballot, then on the second vote for Winston. Companies from the southern part of the state understood the "Marion Light Infantry" planned to do the same. Through some last minute political maneuvering, however, members of the "Marion Light Infantry" threw their support to Jones, who was elected by 11 votes on the first ballot. Captain Robert McFarland of the "Lauderdale Guards" opposed Law for lieutenant colonel. When the votes were cast at 3 p.m. Law was unanimously elected on the first ballot, and Charles Lewis Scott was elected major on the second ballot.[35]

Earlier, Scott had moved to California during the height of the gold rush and remained long enough to be elected to the U.S. Congress. He returned to Alabama and enlisted as a private in the 4th Alabama. Scott married a cousin of the Civil War diarist Mary Chestnut.[36]

Jones's election caused considerable disappointment among the companies from the southern part of the state. Those who knew Jones assured the doubters the new colonel's qualifications were solid. In contrast to Jones, everyone had great confidence in Law's leadership. It made little difference that he lacked combat experience and field command. He was considered an accomplished officer and a gentleman by the 4th Alabama, and that was sufficient. It was known by everyone that Scott was unfamiliar with military procedures. Most apparently considered that a minor problem. Scott was considered a man with above average intelligence. His men believed he would acquire the knowledge to command the gallant troops from Alabama.[37]

Virginia Bound

The new regiment departed Dalton Friday, May 3, for Lynchburg, Virginia, arriving there in a rainstorm on May 6. The 4th Alabama was inducted into Confederate service May 7 and departed by train for Strasburg, Virginia, on May 11. From Strasburg, the men marched through the Shenandoah Valley to Winchester. Enthusiastic crowds, including ladies waving handkerchiefs and flags, welcomed the weary Alabamians as they marched through town. After a day's rest the regiment moved upstate to Harpers Ferry.[38]

The 4th Alabama joined Brigadier General Joseph E. Johnston's Army of the Shenandoah and was attached to Brigadier General Barnard E. Bee's Third Brigade.[39] For the Alabamians, camp life during the months of May and June was an enjoyable experience, but then a drastic change took place when the regiment fell into a rigorous and unwanted routine of daily drills and fatigue details. Reveille sounded at 4 a.m. each morning with regimental drill lasting from 4:30 until 7 a.m. General inspection was held at 8 a.m., with company drill in progress from 9 until 12 noon. Following mid-day break, another drill session began at 2:30 and lasted until 5:30 p.m., with a dress parade immediately following. Supper was at 6:30, roll call at 9 p.m. and tattoo at 9:30 when all lights were extinguished.[40] Many of the Alabamians grew restless and irritated with the repetitious, boring schedule. The discipline imposed by Jones became the focus of their irritation. They had ventured north from Alabama to fight the Yankees and resented the monotony of camp life. The regiment soon developed new concern over Jones's lack of fighting experience from the Mexican War. They decided he was unqualified to lead the gallant 4th.[41] Talk around camp led to a petition requesting Jones's resignation. Officers and men from six companies signed the paper and presented it to Jones on May 27. Seven captains sent word through a friend of Jones that the regiment's best interest would be served by his resignation. Jones immediately placed the matter before Johnston, who advised him to return the papers and inform the regiment to either draft a formal complaint or drop the issue. Nothing was submitted, but the unrest continued. By this time Jones was thought to be thoroughly incompetent to discharge the duties of colonel.[42] Jones settled the affair by assembling the regiment where he expressed regret at not giving satisfaction and not meeting the men's expectations, adding that he anticipated a battle in the near future. He ended his speech by promising to resign after the battle if the regiment still thought him unqualified.[43]

Daily drill routines began to show improvement. Some of the officers gradually recognized the value of discipline and conceded the 4th was well drilled.[44] Law's standing and popularity with the regiment increased daily. By late June 1861, the regiment was rapidly making itself ready for combat.

Initiation into Battle

The 4th Alabama arrived at Manassas Junction at approximately 9 a.m. on July 20 and marched about two miles north of the junction, bivouacking near Ball's Ford.[45] Shortly after sunrise on July 21, the booming of cannon announced the opening of the Battle of First Manassas. The 4th accompanied Bee to counter a Federal flanking maneuver, their first action coming at an eminence known as Buck Hill. The 4th Alabama's line of battle, just east of the hill, placed the regiment's left in a cornfield adjacent to a skirt of wood, the center and right resting in an open field. When the Federals appeared, the Alabamians began firing at will. To protect his men, Jones ordered the regiment to lie down under cover of the hill's crest. Jones, appearing very calm, sat on his big bay horse the men had dubbed Old Battalion. Jones positioned a leg casually across the saddle's pommel as he surveyed the Federal movements.[46] On his signal the men of the 4th rose, delivered a volley and then on his signal fell back to cover under the hill.[47] In this manner the 4th fought well over an hour with its flanks supported only by artillery. Private John Lamar of Lowndes County said bullets were flying all around them like hail, and men were falling like leaves from trees as the men of the 4th repulsed four Federal charges.[48] Private Frank Haralson, Company A, also of Lowndes, thought he could fire his musket more often if he remained standing. During one Federal charge Haralson saw a mounted officer leading a regiment and judged him an easy target. Ignoring orders to take cover with the regiment, Haralson knelt down to take better aim. He pressed the stock against his shoulder to steady his rifle and calmly told a comrade, "Watch how nicely I can take that officer off his horse." Before Haralson could fire, a Federal ball penetrated his head near his nose, scattering his brains on the field.[49] Old Battalion was wounded, forcing Jones to dismount and direct the regiment's fire on foot.[50]

The 4th Alabama was finally flanked and as the regiment retired Jones went down, seriously wounded in both legs. Law was now in command of the regiment which retired in relatively good order and began forming a new line of battle. Captain Edward Dorr Tracey wanted to go back for Jones and asked for volunteers to assist him, but Captain Thomas Jefferson Goldsby saw the futility and restrained Tracey.[51] Off to their right a body of troops, dressed in gray uniforms, stood in a tightly packed battle line. Believing them to be Confederates, Law ordered the 4th Alabama to form in their rear, but when the 4th Alabama's color bearer unfurled the regimental flag, fire erupted from the supposed friendly ranks, disabling Major Scott with a serious leg wound. After a sharp exchange of fire at close range the 4th fell back in disorder.[52] Law did his best to rally the Alabamians but he was soon wounded, his left arm shattered at the elbow by a minie ball.

Two hundred dejected Alabamians wearily tried to regroup while Tracey stepped to the front, delivered a patriotic speech and implored the men to do their duty. Bee rode up, excitedly waving his sword and asked their identity. Someone responded: "Why General don't you know your own troops, the 4th Alabama?" Bee said the regiment was the only part of his command he could find.[53] When Bee reached for the flag to lead the regiment forward Sergeant Robert R. Sinclair, Company B, resisted: "General, I cannot give you my flag, but I will place it wherever you command!"[54] Bee looked over the 4th Alabama and

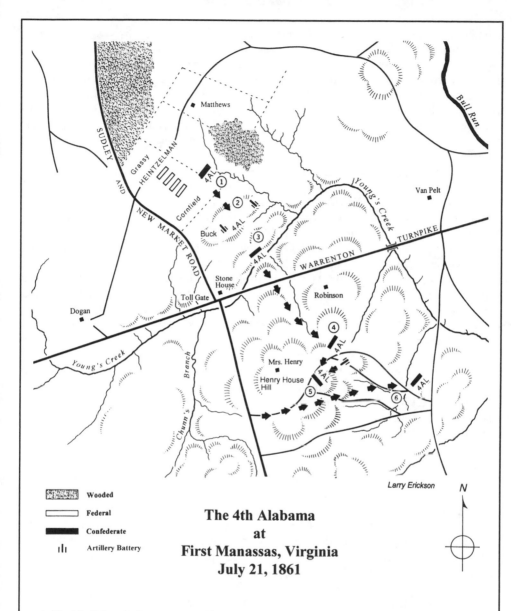

The 4th Alabama
at
First Manassas, Virginia
July 21, 1861

Larry Erickson

Legend:
- Wooded
- Federal
- Confederate
- Artillery Battery

1. The 4th Alabama's first encounter with the Federals occurs at Buck Hill. Colonel Jones places the 4th Alabama just over the crown of Buck Hill to protect it from the Federal fire.
2. From a position atop Buck Hill Jones observes the Federals. On his signal the 4th Alabama rises and fires into the Federal line. Four successive attacks on the 4th Alabama are repulsed in 1 1/2 hours.
3. The 4th Alabama is finally flanked and forced to fall back. A Federal regiment, believed to be Confederate by the 4th Alabama, suddenly fires into the 4th Alabama's ranks.
4. The 4th Alabama retires across the Warrenton Turnpike where it encounters General Bee.
5. General Bee starts toward the left with the 4th Alabama; but an artillery battery cuts through the 4th Alabama, causing considerable confusion in the ranks.
6. After receiving Federal fire the 4th Alabama retires to its final position of the day.

pointed in the direction of Colonel Thomas J. Jackson's brigade. To those around him he said: "Let us go yonder and support Jackson. See he stands like a stone wall."[55] As the regiment moved left an artillery battery cut through the regiment's ranks, separating the right most company and Bee from the main body. Bee and the company obliqued right while the rest of the regiment moved forward to a wooded area. Unable to distinguish friend from foe as bullets whizzed about them, the 4th retired to await orders.[56] Their fighting was over for the day. By 5 p.m. the tide of battle turned and the Federal army quit the field. In the first major engagement of the war the 4th Alabama had taken part in driving a Federal army from the field.[57]

Four officers and 36 men were killed in the regiment's baptism of fire. The wounded numbered six officers and 151 men.[58] Adjutant Coles reported the 4th Alabama carried about 600 into the battle. Based on this number the percentage in losses were about 33 percent, but by later standards of the war the Battle of First Manassas was a mere skirmish. However, in terms of percentages the 4th Alabama's casualties were comparable to those the regiment would sustain in the battles of Gettysburg, Chickamauga and The Wilderness.

Private James Jackson, Company H, lay on the field barely alive. Before enlisting Jackson owned a plantation, known as "The Sinks," near Florence, Alabama. The dapper thirty-nine-year-old with gray eyes and graying hair listed his occupation as planter and gentleman.[59] He was a world traveler and well known breeder and racer of fine horses. On a trip abroad he had purchased a watch with precision works to time his horses and carried the prized possession into the battle. Jackson fell early in the battle with a shot through a lung, and was left behind when the 4th Alabama retired. Sometime later a Federal soldier approached. Jackson begged for water, and as the Federal bent over Jackson's prostrate form he noticed the watch and chain tucked in the wounded man's vest pocket. It was obvious that Jackson was not long for this world and so the Federal proposed to send the watch to the wounded man's family. Jackson suspected the Federal had other intentions and quickly made a counterproposal. The watch would belong to the Federal if he pulled Jackson into the shade and filled his canteen with water. A few minutes later Jackson was lying under a shade tree and the Federal owned a fine Liverpool watch. Jackson lay on the field almost 24 hours before he was found and carried to a field hospital. He survived and later declared the trade of the watch for water was the best deal he ever made. Jackson was discharged on September 25 and returned home to Florence, Alabama.[60]

The Alabamians rested in their bivouac that night and reflected over the day's events. They were very dejected over their performance. Most felt they had disgraced the regiment for showing their backs to the Yankees."[61] One private said the 4th Alabama fought off separate assaults by four Federal regiments because they "considered it disgraceful to be whipped by a single regiment."[62] It was not until the next day that they realized what they had accomplished. Praise of their 90-minute stand came from many sources. Governor Moore gave a speech before the state legislature lauding the accomplishments of the Alabamians.[63]

The 4th Alabama quickly became heroes to the Southern cause. They were said to be the best drilled regiment in the army. Suddenly the grumbling about Jones ceased and his popularity soared. There was an outpouring of sentiment from the regiment for their fallen leader which Reuben Kidd expressed when he wrote home: "He is one of the best colonels in the field from our state, although we thought when he was elected that he did not know enough to take charge of the regiment."[64] Unfortunately Jones was not in camp to bask in the glory and enjoy the pleasure of acceptance by his men. After the battle, he was removed to a hospital at Orange Court House.[65] Personal messages went from individual members, and a resolution expressing the regiment's sentiment was also sent the colonel's bedside.

Doctor Josiah Nott, a physician and noted "racial theorist" from Mobile spent the night of July 20 in the tent of future brigadier Zachariah C. Deas, his brother-in-law. Nott was friends with Pierre T. G. Beauregard and Johnston and rode with Beauregard during the fighting of July 21. He returned to Richmond on the 22nd, but received a telegram requesting him to attend to Jones. He traveled to Orange Court House to treat the wounded colonel, but his efforts were not enough to save Jones.⁶⁶ Jones's condition steadily deteriorated and he died on September 3, 1861. Old Battalion recovered from his wound and was placed aboard the same train with his master's body and returned to Huntsville, Alabama, arriving Friday, September 6, 1861. After a large crowd gathered at the Madison County Courthouse to bid the fallen soldier goodbye, Jones went to his final resting place with full military honors in Maple Hill Cemetery.⁶⁷

Law was still on wounded leave when the 4th Alabama held an election to fill the vacancy created by Jones's death. Law won easily, receiving 643 votes in a race that proved no contest.⁶⁸ In early November, five candidates ran to fill the lieutenant colonel's office vacated by Law. The aspirants were Major Owen Kenan McLemore, Captains Pinckney Bowles and Nathaniel H. R. Dawson, Adjutant Joseph Hardee, and Lieutenants George D. Johnston and Thomas K. Coleman. Dawson's efforts resulted in only the votes of his own company and the "Governor's Guards." The other candidates were able to do little better than carry their own companies. Hardee and McLemore dropped out after the second ballot and Dawson on the third. Because a plurality was required, the election was deadlocked after the first day. During the morning of November 6 Captain Goldsby was put forward as a compromise candidate, receiving a majority of the votes on the next ballot to became the 4th Alabama's second lieutenant colonel. Sergeant Reuben Kidd was later elected captain to replace Goldsby. Kidd received 43 votes to Hardee's six.⁶⁹

The war entered its second year with Major General George B. McClellan in command of the Federal army and preparing to advance on Richmond. McClellan began assembling his army and its supplies near Hampton. His plan was to advance up the Peninsula and lay siege to Richmond from the southeast. Johnston countered by moving his army to Yorktown, reaching there on the last of April 1862.

Because its one-year enlistment expired the 4th Alabama reorganized and elected officers on April 21. Law was easily reelected colonel. In a close contest McLemore was selected lieutenant colonel over Goldsby, and Charles Scott was elected major.⁷⁰ The 4th experienced a major shake-up in the company officers' ranks. Twenty-five officers either resigned or were turned out of office. After the election was over only four captains retained their office, while 24 men from the ranks were issued commissions.

Captain Porter King resigned when he was not elected during the reorganization, and returned to his plantation near Uniontown, Alabama, where he became a circuit judge in 1863. At home King petitioned directly to President Jefferson Davis to exempt his overseer from military service, explaining that he had nearly 100 slaves on his plantation and his widowed sister had nearly 70 on her nearby estate.⁷¹ Nathaniel Dawson also resigned after his one-year enlistment expired. He served in the Alabama legislature for many years, beginning in 1863. He gained the powerful post of Speaker of the House in 1880.⁷²

Law Assumes Brigade Command

Law's first brigade command was as temporary replacement for Brigadier General William H. C. Whiting, who, in turn, was temporary commander of a division of his own and Hood's Texas Brigade. Whiting's Third Brigade was comprised of the 11th Mississippi, 2nd Mississippi, 6th North Carolina and the 4th Alabama.⁷³ Lieutenant Colonel McLemore was elevated to temporary command of the 4th Alabama. None of the parties involved at the time knew it, but once Law assumed command of Whiting's brigade he would not relinquish it.

Law was an ambitious young man. He wanted higher command and as quickly as possible. During the winter and spring of 1862, Law developed close personal relationships with Brigadier Generals Louis T. Wigfall and John Bell Hood. Wigfall was a politician turned general and, for a time, commander of the Texas Brigade. In February 1862 he resigned his commission to take a seat in the senate. Wigfall became Law's political ally. After Wigfall's departure, Hood was given command of the Texans. The good relationship between Hood and Law was not surprising because both shared similar traits. They were both fearless in battle, and their basic battlefield philosophy was the charge. Each quickly gained the complete confidence of their men, and both came to the Confederate service with military training. Hood was destined to command a Confederate army. He became Law's champion within the military.

Law made the most of the opportunity afforded him, immediately exhibiting the skill of a veteran politician by gaining support from influential politicians and military associates. After submitting an application for a brigadier's commission to Senator Wigfall, he enlisted a number of influential Alabama politicians to lobby President Davis and the War Department on his behalf. In a letter dated April 17, 1862, William Lowndes Yancey, distinguished orator, senator, and fiery secession advocate from Alabama, recommended Law's appointment to brigadier general. Yancey took the liberty to enclose an endorsement from Wigfall. Five days later Law wrote Confederate Attorney General Thomas H. Watts seeking his recommendation as brigadier and asking Watts to petition Davis on his behalf.[74] On June 6, regimental and company officers from Whiting's brigade petitioned Davis requesting Law's appointment to command the brigade.[75] Davis forwarded the petition, with his endorsement, to Secretary of War William Randolph. However, General Robert E. Lee wasn't ready to promote Law. He explained that, although Law was competent, Law's promotion would leave Whiting without a command. Davis let the matter drop, but, not without a mild rebuke directed at Lee. The president noted that "Gen. Lee overlooks the evil complained of, that the brigade is without a brigadier in command. A remedy might be found in distributing the regiments to the brigades of their several states."[76] Law, as colonel, remained in temporary command of the Whiting's brigade.

The 4th Alabama participated in the Peninsula Campaign where it saw little action until the Battle of Seven Pines on May 29, 1862. Davis placed Lee in command of the army on June 1. Lee was an unknown quantity to the soldiers which led to a great deal of speculation regarding his leadership qualities. Law saw the army's new commander for the first time a day or two after that and observed him with considerable interest. Except for a neatly trimmed mustache Law saw a man with a clean-shaven face. Lee was neatly dressed in a uniform befitting his rank, and wore a felt hat and top boots that reached the knees. He sat astride the horse as if his home were the saddle.[77] Law adopted a wait and see attitude about the new commanding general.

Law Excels in the Summer and Fall of 1862

Law more than vindicated Davis's confidence in his abilities by his superb handling of the brigade during the summer and fall of 1862. The Battle of Gaines's Mill may have been his finest hour. Late in the afternoon of June 27, Whiting's division (Law's brigade and Hood's brigade) charged a fortified Federal position that was three lines deep. Law's brigade advanced in two lines, the 11th Mississippi and the 4th Alabama forming the first. The 6th North Carolina and 2nd Mississippi made up the second. Law gained the crest of a rise fronting the Federal position as Hood passed rapidly across Law's rear with the 4th

Texas and 18th Georgia and came up on Law's right. The 1st and 5th Texas remained on Law's left. Major General Ambrose Powell Hill's men lay on the crest, exhausted after a bloody repulse. Whiting ordered his division not to stop or exchange fire during the advance, but to push right up to the Federal works.[78] As the 4th Alabama approached the crest, McLemore went to the front of the line. Walking backwards so that he faced the 4th Alabama, McLemore called the cadence. His commands rang out in a loud clear voice: "Guide center, keep in step, one, two, three four; one, two, three four."[79] The 4th Alabama responded as if it was on dress parade. Whiting gave the order to charge as his line passed Hill's men. In an extraordinary demonstration of passage of lines Whiting's men skillfully passed through Hill's exhausted ranks. Then with Law and Hood in front, the Southerners plunged into the killing zone between the lines.[80] Law's brigade charged at the double quick time, with trail arms and without firing. The entire division broke into a trot as it moved down the slope of a ravine. Federal artillery blasted great holes in the lines, but despite the heavy toll of casualties, Law remembered, "There was no confusion and not a step faltered as the two gray lines swept silently and swiftly on."[81]

Whiting's line immediately closed toward the center and maintained its formation. Neither the charging Confederate line or the defending Federal infantry had as yet fired a shot. The pace became more rapid as the line approached the Federal breastworks. The Federal infantry unleashed their first volley when the Confederates came within 30 yards. More holes appeared in Whiting's line but his men responded with a yell and rushed for the works. At 10 paces from the works, the Federal front line broke and fled up the ravine carrying the second line with it. Whiting's men fired on the retreating Federals with great effect.[82]

Jesse Harrison, Company D, 4th Alabama, raced ahead of the main line and jumped into the breastworks, landing among a group of startled Federals. He shot the nearest Federal in the chest, then quickly drew his pistol and demanded the others to surrender. Without hesitation a captain and 22 privates became prisoners, the captain promptly turning over his sword and pistol to Harrison. In the style later made famous by Sergeant Alvin York in World War I, Harrison led the captain and privates to the Confederate rear. That task complete, he returned to his company.[83]

The Confederates scrambled up the hillside before the Federal artillery could be removed and captured 14 pieces. The Federal line was cut in two and retreated in disorder. After Whiting's line overran the batteries supporting the infantry several batteries farther back began blasting away. The 4th Texas, 11th Georgia, 4th Alabama, and 11th Mississippi continued toward the batteries. A Federal cavalry charge attempted to turn back the thrust, but was easily repulsed with considerable loss.

Although they had suffered terrible losses, Hood and Law achieved a remarkable breakthrough, rewarding Lee with his first victory. When Law's soldiers saw the open ground they had to traverse under rifle and artillery fire and the formidable Federal position, some of the line hesitated, but Law encouraged his men forward with: "Forward boys! Charge them!" And the line surged ahead into the storm of enemy fire.[84] It was a textbook example of shock tactics, frequently attempted during the war, but rarely as successful as Whiting's charge at Gaines's Mill. Stonewall Jackson lavished rare praise on Hood and Law for the success achieved by their brigades.[85]

The Confederate army lay before Richmond, taking a well-earned rest during July and early August. During this time, Whiting had became embroiled in a controversy over the idea of state brigades. Davis was an ardent supporter of the concept, but some of his commanders were not. However, most were not as vocal in their opposition as Chase Whiting. He considered the concept of state brigades an idea that was exceedingly foolish, declaring

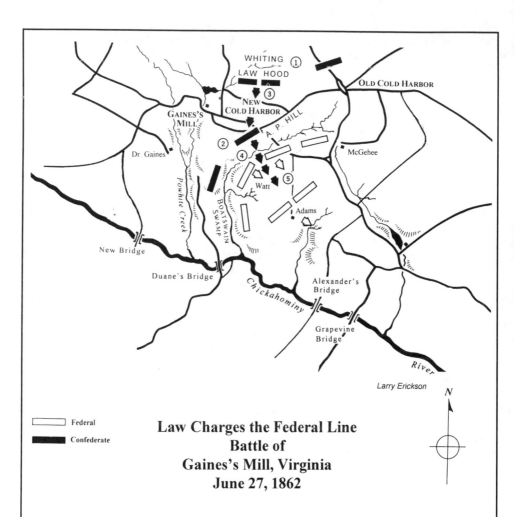

Law Charges the Federal Line
Battle of
Gaines's Mill, Virginia
June 27, 1862

1. Whiting arrives on the field in rear of A. P. Hill's line.
2. A. P. Hill's men are lying down, having fought themselves out in previous fighting.
3. Whiting orders Law and Hood forward.
4. Law and Hood rush through Hill's line and into the swampy area in front of the Federal line.
5. The charge breaks the Federal line, sending it reeling backward in confusion.

his intention not to submit to any system which, in his words, was "...devised solely for the advancement of logrolling, humbugging politicians."[86] By July 1862 Whiting was out of favor with Davis, but as the movement for state brigades gained momentum, Whiting bluntly informed the Richmond authorities he did not wish to lead a Mississippi brigade.[87] The once highly respected general was later removed from the Army of Northern Virginia and sent to Wilmington, North Carolina, where he developed Fort Fisher.[88] Whiting's departure paved the way for Law's promotion to brigadier, which was just a matter of time.

In August Law led his brigade north with the remainder of Lee's army. After the battles before Richmond, Lee, on his own authority, reorganized the army into two commands. Major General James Longstreet was given one corps, and Major General Thomas Jackson the other. Lee's reorganized army also had a new name, the Army of Northern Virginia. Hood was given command of Whiting's division. Whiting's Third Brigade, under the command of Law, was placed in Hood's division, Longstreet's corps. By the Battle of Sharpsburg, Maryland, Whiting's brigade would be known as Law's brigade.

The Battle of Second Manassas took place on August 29–30, 1862. During the height of the fighting of the first day, Law's men witnessed a determined assault on Jackson's right which was beaten off by the men of Brigadier General William E. Starke's brigade.[89] After repulsing the assault Starke moved forward and captured a gun, at which time Hood immediately advanced until he drew even with Starke's line.[90] Around 6 p.m. a Federal force consisting of an artillery battery and infantry advanced to within 400 yards of Law's brigade. The battery was barely unlimbered on the crest of a small ridge and in position to fire when Hood ordered the division forward. Law's brigade first came under artillery fire, then musketry. Law's men delivered several volleys as they advanced. The Federals quickly limbered three guns and hurried them off the field before Law's men arrived. But one remained, its gunners rapidly firing the piece toward the advancing infantrymen. When the Confederates reached the base of the ridge, the Federal gunners were no longer able to depress the guns to fire on the front line. Bent over to avoid the gun blast, several of Law's soldiers raced up the ridge for the gun. The first men over the crest received powder burns from the muzzle blast as the gunners fired their last shot.[91]

After wresting the gun from its defenders, a flanking fire came from Federal infantry moving on Law's right and rear. Law formed the 2nd Mississippi along the Warrenton Turnpike, and sending that regiment forward, forced the enemy infantry to retire out of range. The 2nd Mississippi, together with the Texas brigade, then moved forward and cleared stragglers from an open field. In the meantime Law, with the 4th Alabama, 11th Mississippi, 6th North Carolina and 23rd South Carolina, in support, advanced and drove the Federal force eastward. Law halted a half mile in advance of his original position and remained until midnight.[92] The afternoon proved very profitable in terms of a trophy count. Law's men proudly counted three flags to go along with their captured Federal field piece.[93]

Daylight of August 30 brought skirmishing along Law's front, which continued until about 3 p.m. At that time a Federal division made a determined assault on Jackson's right. Longstreet's artillery was posted on a rise about 200 yards to Law's left and rear. Law's men viewed some of the heaviest fighting that day, as Jackson's men repulsed repeated Federal charges. When Jackson requested reinforcements, Longstreet decided his artillery firing enfilade would be more effective. In less than ten minutes the attack on Jackson's right was broken. Longstreet then threw his entire line forward in a counterattack.[94]

Retreating Federal brigades fell back, about faced, fired a volley and fell back again. Law advanced a considerable distance, then halted to support a battery. Hood ordered Law's brigade to the left of the Texas brigade. On reaching a slight rise on his front, Law failed to see the Texas brigade. He did see a Federal force getting into position to support a battery, and decided to attack. The 4th Alabama and 6th North Carolina were placed in a skirt of pines. The 2nd Mississippi was sent to the left and to the foot of a rise. The 11th Mississippi was supposed to move on the battery from the left, but because there was confusion regarding the orders they moved instead to the right and became engaged. While Law waited for the 11th Mississippi to get in position a body of infantry appeared. A volley from the 4th Alabama and 6th North Carolina drove the Federals back. Law decided to charge the battery without the 11th Mississippi. The Federal infantry, however, managed to buy enough time for the battery to limber up and escape. Law came away with a few wounded and several prisoners for his efforts. The action essentially ended Law's fighting for the day, but his brigade continued to advance until Longstreet halted his line for the night.[95] Law's brigade suffered 56 killed and 264 wounded during the fighting at Second Manassas. Losses in the 4th Alabama were 19 killed and 44 wounded. There were no missing or captured to report.[96]

After Second Manassas, Law's brigade followed Lee into Maryland where Lieutenant Colonel McLemore was mortally wounded in an engagement against the Federals at Boonsboro Gap. Before the fall campaign began a friend had remarked: "Don't let the Yankees get you." Holding up his sword in his right hand the young officer had replied: "Never will they get over this." He was carried from the field on a stretcher and transported to Shepherdstown, Virginia. Unfortunately his sword was left behind to become a trophy for an unknown Federal.[97] Law moved on to Sharpsburg, arriving there early in the afternoon of September 16.

The Battle of Sharpsburg opened on September 17 with skirmishing at 3 a m. and serious fighting getting under way at daylight. Breakfast was still cooking when Brigadier General Alexander R. Lawton requested Hood to come to his relief. One and a half hours after the fighting began Hood's men stormed out of the woods surrounding the Dunker Church, crossed the Hagerstown Turnpike and charged into a large open area of pasture land with a large cornfield about 250 yards to the north.[98] A Federal battery deployed in the north end of the pasture belched forth missiles of destruction. An enemy battle line of two regiments rested in the pasture about halfway between the cornfield and the Dunker Church.[99] When Law entered the field he saw very few Confederates and they appeared to be in considerable confusion. Law's brigade continued to advance, with the Texas brigade on its left.

The 4th Alabama was on the brigade's extreme right and moved along the Smoketown Road in column of fours. After entering the pasture, the 5th Texas was ordered to Law's right flank.[100] The 4th Alabama and 5th Texas then advanced into the East Woods, both regiments forming at right angles to the main battle line along the Hagerstown Road. Captain Lawrence Houston Scruggs, commanding the regiment, received a foot wound as the 4th Alabama entered the woods, leaving Captain William McKendre Robbins in command. After the line entered the East Woods, a battalion from the 21st Georgia joined the 4th Alabama and advanced on its right.[101] The 4th Alabama, 5th Texas and the 21st Georgia battalion then fought their way to the northeast corner of the East Woods.

Law's left remained in the pasture and drove the Federal line beyond its battery support. Law pressed up to the face of the guns only to be forced back by a new and determined Federal line. After a determined struggle which ebbed back and forth Law's men were forced to resupply themselves with cartridges from wounded comrades. The appearance of more Federal infantry which extended the Federal line and enveloped Law's left flank caused him to fall back.[102] Law then reformed with the Texas brigade around the Dunker Church.

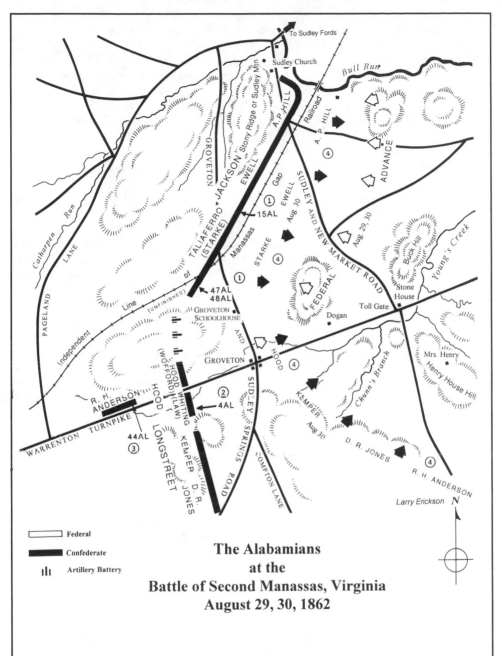

The Alabamians
at the
Battle of Second Manassas, Virginia
August 29, 30, 1862

Federal

Confederate

Artillery Battery

1. The 15th, 47th, and 48th Alabama fight behind the unfinished railroad August 29, 30. Their portion of the line sees some of the severest fighting both days.
2. Whiting's brigade, Law commanding, goes into line near noon on August 29. Later in the afternoon Hood's two brigades charge forward.
3. The 44th Alabama, in Wright's Brigade, arrives on the field early on August 30.
4. Late in the afternoon of August 30 the entire Confederate line charges forward. The 44th Alabama, on the Confederate extreme right, sees its first action after arriving in Virginia.

After almost two hours, in which time they fought the stubborn 10th Maine and 111th Pennsylvania, the 4th Alabama, 5th Texas and the 21st Georgia were driven from the East Woods. The 4th retreated under a withering fire. Captain Robbins was so sure he would be hit by the intense Federal fire that he walked backwards to keep from being found with a wound in his back.[103] Major General Lafayette McLaws's Division was moving in to relieve Hood's division when the 4th Alabama came off the field.

Law's brigade had performed well in a fight that Hood described as "...the most terrible clash of arms by far that has occurred during the war."[104] Law skillfully handled the brigade and had charged unflinchingly into the pasture under heavy fire from a Federal battery and a strong infantry line. He retired only after his ammunition was depleted and he was confronted by a vastly superior force.

Law's brigade moved to the right later in the afternoon and managed to get a good sleep during the night of September 17. Casualties from the day's fight came to seven killed and 37 wounded.[105] During the night of September 18 Law's brigade quietly folded its blankets, marched to the Potomac River and crossed into Virginia. The brigade arrived at Bunker Hill on September 20, remained until September 27, then moved onto Winchester. Lieutenant Colonel McLemore, wounded earlier at Boonsboro Gap, died at Winchester September 30.[106] A native of Alabama, he ranked 39th out of 49 cadets in his class at West Point, graduating July 1, 1856 and receiving commission as second lieutenant in the infantry. Serving first with the 6th and then the 8th United States Infantry, the young officer traveled throughout much of the Midwest and Pacific regions. Resigning his commission April 8, 1861, at San Francisco after Alabama seceded, he reached the east coast through New York City and made his way to Alabama, though at some peril to himself because he still wore his officer's uniform. Once in his native state McLemore immediately offered his services to the governor and was given the assignment of recruiting and enlisting volunteers in the 14th Alabama Infantry. McLemore was then appointed major of that regiment September 1, 1861 and was serving in that capacity when assigned to the 4th Alabama by the Provisional Congress. Of the five members of his class who later became members of Confederate armies, he was the only one to die in service.[107]

Law Becomes a Brigadier General

During the summer and fall of 1862 Law's supporters continued their efforts to secure his promotion to brigadier. From Tuskegee, Alabama, Congressmen David Clopton and Edmund S. Dargan wrote President Davis with their endorsement of Law for brigadier.[108] Thomas Watts followed up with his own recommendation to the secretary of war.[109] Hood offered his support in a letter to Randolph, stating in part:

> *"I have the honor to recommend for promotion Col. E. M. Law of the 4th Ala. I have served with him since Nov. last and have had the best of opportunities to judge of his qualifications as an officer, both in the camp and on the battlefield. And I take great pleasure in stating I know of no other officer more worthy of promotion than Col. Law."*[110]

About September 1, officers of Law's brigade submitted their second petition requesting his promotion. This time the petition was submitted to Secretary of War Randolph.[111] A third petition, also to Randolph, followed on September 20. In requesting Law's promotion the officers stated that Law "has led us victoriously through all engagements up to the 20th of September."[112] Finally, Law's application for a brigadier's commission was confirmed by Congress while Lee's army rested in its camps after the Battle of Sharpsburg. His rank

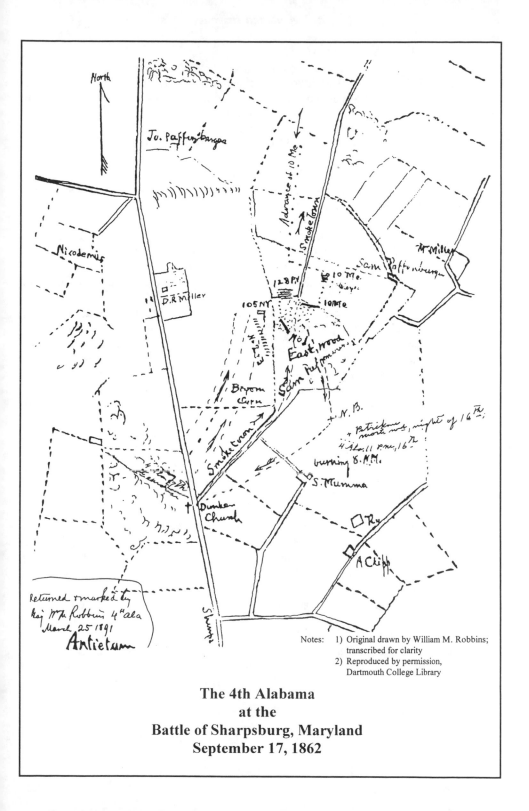

The 4th Alabama
at the
Battle of Sharpsburg, Maryland
September 17, 1862

Notes: 1) Original drawn by William M. Robbins;
transcribed for clarity
2) Reproduced by permission,
Dartmouth College Library

as brigadier dated from October 3, 1862.[113]

The adjutant general's office conducted an inspection of Lee's army as it rested near Winchester. Colonel Edwin J. Harvie, on November 7, found Hood's camps in tolerable order. Discipline was noted as good, but clothing and arms were barely acceptable. Arms in the 4th Alabama were found to be mixed, though serviceable. Fifty men were found in need of clothing and shoes, with two of the men without shoes. The Alabamians were better equipped than the North Carolinians and Texans. Seventy men in the 6th North Carolina were barefoot; the 1st Texas had 60 men in the same condition and the 4th Texas, 75. Assistant Adjutant General Robert Hall Chilton commended Hood for his management, but suggested companies of the same regiment have the same caliber arms.[114] There is no record that Hood complied with the suggestion.

The summer and fall campaigns dealt harshly with the 4th Alabama's field officers. Deaths, promotions, hardships of military life in the field, and sickness created 11 officers' vacancies in the 4th Alabama. Six were discharged by resignation, four were killed in battle, and one died of battlefield wounds.[115] Charles Scott resigned July 7, citing disability. Many of the senior captains were absent during the fiercest fighting in Northern Virginia and Maryland.

After Law's promotion Pinckney Bowles became colonel. His successor as lieutenant colonel was Lawrence Scruggs, a twenty-eight-year-old merchant from Huntsville, Alabama.[116] Scruggs's vacancy created a conflict when Captains Thomas Coleman and E. Jones Glass became involved in a bitter dispute over seniority, each claiming he was entitled to be promoted. The issue was finally settled in Coleman's favor by Longstreet's headquarters.[117] Glass resigned and joined the cavalry service. Coleman was destined to lead the regiment at the Battles of Gettysburg and Chickamauga.[118]

The Army of Northern Virginia lay along a line between the Potomac and Winchester, Virginia until late October. Then by a series of marches and maneuvers the Federal and Confederate armies began concentrating around Fredericksburg, Virginia. Longstreet's command left Winchester and took up the line of march for Culpeper, arriving there November 2. On November 5 Longstreet departed for Fredericksburg. As his men approached the city, they met women, children, and old men on the way out.[119] Some were riding in wagons while others plodding on foot along the muddy roads.[120]

After the army's return from Maryland, Lee began the task of reorganizing the Army of Northern Virginia. In June, Lee, on his own authority, replaced the clumsy division system. At that time the army was divided into two corps. But, it was not until September 18, 1862, that Davis signed an act of the Confederate Congress authorizing corps and the rank of lieutenant general to command them.[121] James Longstreet was selected to command the First Corps and Thomas Jackson the Second, and Hood was elevated to major general.[122] On November 26, 1862, Lee reassigned the 44th Alabama from Wright's Brigade to Law's command, the second Alabama regiment assigned to Law.[123]

The Battle of Fredericksburg was fought on December 13, 1862, on a bitterly cold day with snow on the ground. Law's Brigade saw little action but was the target of artillery fire in which the 4th Alabama sustained 22 casualties—four killed and 18 wounded.[124]

Chapter 2

The Alabamians

While the real war raged on the battlefields, another conflict over the issue of state brigades was being waged between Confederate army commanders and civilian government leaders. The idea to group Confederate soldiers by state was an old one and a favorite of President Davis. As early as July 23, 1861, Major General Pierre G. T. Beauregard had organized his regiments into state brigades at the expressed desire of the president. In an exchange of letters in the fall, Beauregard told Davis he was still reserving judgment on state brigades but was opposed to state divisions. Beauregard feared the great loss which could befall a state if a division was cut up or captured.[1] Davis believed strongly that state brigades fostered better morale than mixed brigades and would enhance volunteerism in the Confederacy. Also, he was pressed by politicians who wanted brigades organized by states and commanded by generals of the same states. Davis answered their demands with his promise that such changes would be made. As commander-in-chief, Davis was confident that his promises were on firm constitutional ground. He noted in a letter, written in October 1861, "The authority to organize regiments into brigades and the latter into divisions is by law conferred only on the president."[2] Some of his field commanders resisted the president's control of their troop organization, forcing him to issue direct orders to them to organize their armies into state brigades.[3] On May 6, 1862, Davis referred a letter to Lee which he had received from the officers of the 16th Mississippi Regiment asking for reassignment to a brigade of Mississippi regiments or a transfer to the Army of the Valley of the Mississippi. Addressing the army commander simply as General Lee, the president of the Confederacy reminded him that, "Special orders were given months ago to have the Mississippi regiments put in brigades together." Davis further reminded Lee that the morale of the 16th Mississippi was suffering and the enclosed petition was only a new manifestation of this low morale. Davis closed his letter to Lee with an admonition: "Reiterate the order." The president was perhaps irritated at this point because this was the second letter he had received in April from a regiment of his state with the same complaint. He dealt with the first by sending it to the secretary of war with his opinion that the issue of state brigades had been "settled by law." For added emphasis, Davis included his order that "Generals commanding armies will be required to observe the rule."[4] Lee was opposed to state brigades, but, he realized the importance Davis attached to the idea, and regiments were finally organized into state brigades in the fall of 1862.[5]

Since Law was recognized as an Alabama brigadier it was natural to modify the makeup of his brigade to reflect the president's desire. On January 19, 1863, Lee, in Special Order 19, ordered the North Carolina regiments transferred from Law's Brigade.[6] They were replaced by the 15th, 47th and 48th Alabama regiments from Jackson's Second Corps. Captain William Oates, 15th Alabama, was among those opposed to the idea of the reorganization. Oates considered Longstreet's First Corps a fine force but he was reluctant to leave Stonewall Jackson's command. As he put it, the men of the 15th Alabama had never known defeat under Jackson. Captain Noah Baxter Feagin, commanding Company B of the same regiment, shared Oates's sentiments.[7] He, like Oates, was disappointed at having to separate from Jackson's leadership, but accepted the change. In a letter written in late January, Feagin expressed regret at leaving the Second Corps because he, like every other soldier under Jackson, believed the command superior to all others in the Confederacy. It was with considerable pride that Jackson's men referred to themselves as Jackson's Foot Cavalry. But, in recognition of Jackson's penchant for rapid marching, Feagin suggested the new assignment was "better for our health and more consoling to our muscular apparatus."[8] Brigadier General William B. Taliaferro assembled the 47th and 48th Alabama one last time to bid the regiments farewell. In an address, typical of its day, Taliaferro expressed his appreciation of the two regiments:

> *The Brigadier General commanding, in taking leave of the 47th and 48th Alabama regiments, cannot refrain from expressing his high admiration of soldierly bearing and conspicuously gallant conduct in the battles of Cedar Run and Manassas, in which it was his pleasant duty to command. And his taking leave of such men he feels sure that in the new command to which you are about to be transferred, should occasion require, you will gain fresh honors and never sully the good name you have already won by your heroic courage in battle, patience of privations, and cheerful obedience to orders and discipline. With regret at thus being compelled to part, I bid you adieu.[9]*

There was some irritation in the 47th Alabama ranks, brought on more than anything else, by the inconvenience of the move. Winter quarters had just been completed, and the transfer meant giving up their comfortable living conditions. A rumor around the 47th Alabama's camps had it that the brigade might be sent to its home state. So the men left their little huts and tents with the anticipation of soon returning home and seeing loved ones for the first time after a long absence.[10]

Law's views on the subject of state brigades are not known, but after the success enjoyed by his old brigade he surely experienced some uneasiness about gaining more glory with the new brigade. After all, the exploits of the Alabamians, Mississippians, and Georgians at First and Second Manassas, Gaines's Mill, and Sharpsburg had earned the young general his brigadier's commission. Fortunately for Law, the replacement regiments were seasoned veterans of the 1862 campaigns in Virginia, having participated in some of the severest fighting of the war to that time. The five Alabama regiments that made camp the first time on the Catharpin Road near Fredericksburg, Virginia, remained an Alabama brigade until Appomattox.[11]

15th Alabama Infantry

One hundred and twenty-one young men, in the care of Captain Oates, left Abbeville, Alabama, on July 27, 1861. The group sported new homemade gray uniforms with red trim. Before their departure Oates assured his men they would be home for the fall harvesting. Their orders were to join nine other companies at Fort Mitchell, Alabama, to organize the 15th Alabama Regiment. The company marched to Franklin, on the Chattahoochee River and boarded a steamboat to Jackson, and from there traveled on to Fort Mitchell.[12] Oates and his company arrived after the election of colonel and lieutenant colonel had been held. James Cantey was elected colonel without opposition. Cantey was a prominent planter from Fort Mitchell and veteran of the war with Mexico where he was recognized for bravery.[13]

Captains Benjamin Gardner and John Fletcher Treutlen were rivals for the office of lieutenant colonel. Because none of the candidates could garner a plurality of votes from the companies in camp, each visited the camps of the companies still in their counties. Gardner was a large man with gruff manners who promised the men his orders would be obeyed. Treutlen was just the opposite, made no such promises, and was easily elected.[14]

John Wilhite Lewis Daniel was elected major, and looked every bit the military man in his new uniform. He carried himself well, was an excellent horseman, and his physique gave him a splendid appearance. A strong advocate of secession, Daniel was a member of the Secession Convention and proudly voted for the ordinance in January 1861.[15]

All commissions for the 15th Alabama were dated July 3, 1861. There was a question, however, of seniority since each captain's commission carried the same date. Cantey proposed the order of seniority be determined by company designation. When put to a vote all captains, except Oates and Lieutenant William H. Strickland, representing Captain Gardner, favored the proposal. Sufficient Mississippi Rifles had been procured to arm only two companies. Cantey assigned the rifle companies to Captains Alexander A. Lowther and Isaac Ball Feagin. Their companies were to be on the right and left and carry the designations A and B. Lowther and Feagin then decided that Lowther's company be designated A and Feagin's B. The remaining company designations were determined by drawing lots. Some thought this a bit unusual, but said nothing. At this stage of the war the inexperienced captains knew little, if any, of the rules of the military. They certainly knew little of the value of seniority, and since all were eager to go to war they would have agreed to almost anything.[16] No one seriously objected in July 1861, but Cantey's method of determining seniority was to have a profound effect on the career of Captain Oates.

The 15th Alabama left the state the first week of August 1861. Cantey's new soldiers had not learned the value of traveling light. There was so much baggage that a single train could not transport the regiment. Upon arrival in Richmond the 15th Alabama went into camp on the north side of the James River. About August 18 they traveled to Manassas Junction by rail, and from there the regiment marched about five miles to a camp at Pageland. Captain Gardner, shaded by a large umbrella, marched at the head of his company. Gardner was a large man, fifty-two years old and, after many years of working in an office, needed protection from the sun. Oates remembered the affair as ludicrous.[17]

Ill feelings quickly developed between Cantey and Daniel. Cantey's style of command caused Daniel to chafe and pout. It was said by those who knew him that Daniel was very sensitive, and as his relationship with Cantey deteriorated, he grew weary of military camp life and resigned his commission, effective October 24, 1861.[18] Daniel returned home and raised a company for Hilliard's Legion, and was later given a captain's commission and placed in the conscript department.

With Daniel gone the question of his successor arose. The regiment wanted to hold an election, but Cantey did not. He was presented a petition requesting an election which was forwarded to the brigade commander, Brigadier General Isaac R. Trimble. Cantey claimed an election would "play hell with his regiment." Trimble was from the old army and did not subscribe to the idea of electing officers. After Trimble returned the petition with no

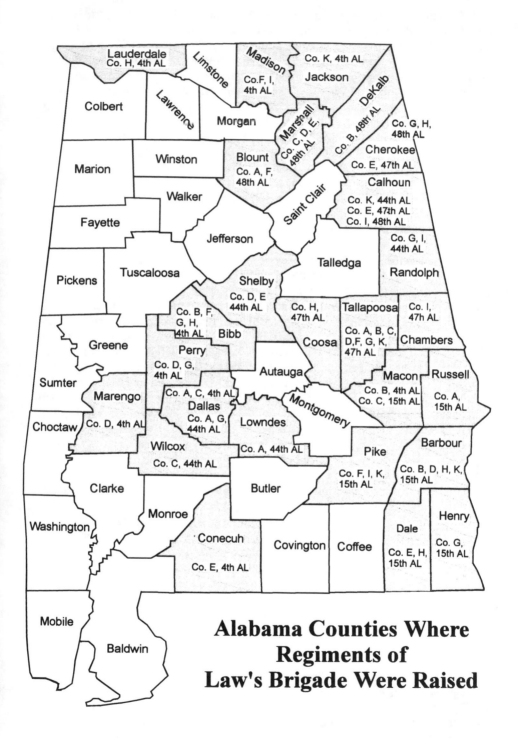

Alabama Counties Where Regiments of Law's Brigade Were Raised

recommendation, Cantey put the petition in his desk drawer and appointed Lowther to the rank of major, claiming Lowther was entitled to promotion by reason of seniority. He neglected to publish orders announcing the promotion and also failed to formally apply to the War Department for Lowther's appointment.[19] Apparently there was some feeling among the captains that Cantey exceeded his authority, or at least, did not follow commonly practiced procedures for volunteer regiments. As at Fort Mitchell, none of the captains choose to pursue the issue further. In his later years Oates was sure he would have been elected major had an election been held.[20] Regardless, Lowther was recognized as the regiment's major by his superiors and was obeyed as major by the rest of the regiment.[21] In all respects he was accorded the status and privilege due the rank of major.

The 15th Alabama left its winter camps at Manassas Junction on the first of March 1862 and marched to the Rappahannock River. The 15th came under fire for the first time as its men were tearing up railroad tracks near the river. Company L joined the regiment at this time. Doctor Robert H. Hill's "Pike Sharpshooters" were mustered into service March 15, 1862, and became the eleventh company. Its men arrived in Virginia in late March and joined the 15th Alabama at Brandy Station. Unfortunately, the company arrived in the field during exceptionally bad weather. Life in the raw conditions of camp brought considerable discomfort to men who had just left the comfort of warm homes in Alabama.[22]

The regiment traveled to Gordonsville where the 15th became part of Jackson's command in the Valley Campaign in the spring of 1862, with its first significant fighting at Cross Keys.[23] The day began with skirmishing as Cantey formed the 15th in line of battle on a slight hill with an open field on its front. A wooded area lay 100 yards ahead, and when a Federal skirmish line emerged from the wooded area anxious Alabamians quickly prepared to receive their first charge. All along the line came the sound of "click," "click," "click" as muskets were made ready to fire. Before the regiment could deliver a volley, Cantey moved back about a mile. The Federal skirmish line gave chase as Cantey's men retired. Here, Second Lieutenant Wesley B. Mills became the 15th Alabama's first officer to die in battle.[24] The 15th joined Trimble's line of battle behind a fence. A field of buckwheat, about 150 yards wide, lay on their front, and woods lay on either side. When a Federal line appeared, the 15th unleashed a volley before Cantey could restrain the men.[25] The Federal force attempted to turn Trimble's right, and Trimble countered by ordering the 15th Alabama to extend his line. Trimble then divided the 15th into two battalions. The left, under Treutlen, advanced against a Federal regiment resting on a hill while the right, under Cantey, moved forward to capture a battery. Cantey found the battery supported in strength by infantry and withdrew. Treutlen was engaged about 20 minutes, and as his men began withdrawing the battalion was momentarily seized by panic. Officers rallied the men and both battalions reunited and joined the main line. That night the 15th lay on its arms and watched Federal campfires flickering in the cold night air. The Alabamians were so close that conversations between Federal soldiers could be heard. At dawn the 15th moved on to Fort Republic where it was able to observe fighting from a high hill which overlooked the town.[26]

On July 12, 1862, Lowther tendered his resignation, citing ill health and extreme fatigue.[27] His resignation was routinely forwarded for processing. However, in an unusual move on Trimble's part, Lowther remained in command of the 15th Alabama. Even though the 15th did little more than observe the fighting from the lower slopes of Cedar Mountain during the Battle of Cedar Run on August 9. Lowther's commanding officers heaped lavish praise on him for distinguished service and conduct. A short time later, Trimble successfully lobbied to have Lowther's resignation revoked.

The 15th Alabama accompanied Jackson on his march around the Federal army commanded by Major General John Pope. Major General Richard S. Ewell's Division captured Bristoe Station about 9 p.m. on August 26. The 15th ate like royalty at Manassas Junction, where on August 27, a large quantity of Federal supplies had been captured. Oates saw a pile of bacon that looked the size of a small house. There were numerous delicacies such as pickled oysters, lobster salad, sardines, fresh fruit and canned meats. A large quantity of new shoes was found and distributed.[28] Each man was permitted to help himself to whatever he could carry. Many of the men remembered the want of rations on the march to Manassas and helped themselves to more than they could carry for any distance. With haversacks full the 15th departed Manassas Junction late in the afternoon of August 27. It wasn't long before the weight of the ample supply of foodstuff became a burden that was too heavy to carry. After a mile or two the roadside was littered with full and partially empty boxes of crackers and slabs of bacon.[29]

At the Battle of Second Manassas the 15th Alabama fought for two days behind an unfinished railroad cut. During one assault on August 29 a Federal major on horseback led a regiment against the 15th, and Captain Francis Key Shaaff shot the Federal major from his horse. After the fighting died down, Captain Isaac Feagin chastised Shaaff for shooting such a brave individual. Stonewall Jackson was nearby, and on hearing Feagin's rebuke, corrected the captain with instructions to kill the brave ones because they lead the others. During an assault on August 30 the opposing lines in the vicinity of the 15th Alabama were so close the battle flags almost touched. At the height of the fighting the 15th fired to the right oblique and assisted an adjacent brigade in repelling an attack. Oates watched Brigadier William E. Starke's Virginians fight with rocks after their ammunition ran out.[30]

The 15th participated in the siege of Harpers Ferry, then marched to Sharpsburg on September 16 and stacked arms near the Dunker's Church. Lowther was absent sick, leaving Feagin in command. About 10 p.m. the brigades of Trimble and Lawton relieved Hood's Division. Trimble's Brigade replaced Law.[31] They were on Jackson's right when the fighting opened at sunrise September 17.[32] The 15th Alabama's ammunition was nearly exhausted and its losses heavy when Hood's Division relieved Trimble and Lawton. Fire had slowed in their sector and the 15th waited for more ammunition to be brought forward. Feagin was collecting cartridges from the wounded when Major General Daniel H. Hill rode up. Hill asked the regiment's identity and the name of its commander. When directed to Feagin, Hill found the captain behind a haystack searching through a cartridge box. When Feagin identified himself and his regiment, Hill was said to have exclaimed, "My God, is this an Alabama regiment lying here?" Rejecting the excuse that they had no ammunition, he reportedly suggested the Alabamians use bayonets and then rocks to attack the enemy. Angry voices from the 15th ranks encouraged Feagin to ignore Hill's order. Hill assumed Feagin was acting cowardly and made a mental note to press charges. The two officers looked at each for a moment without speaking. A disgusted Hill then rode away.[33]

The 15th Alabama returned to Virginia with no field officers. Feagin had been wounded at Boteler's Mill and was put out of action for several months, leaving Oates in command. Feagin had been the only regimental commander in Trimble's Brigade not killed or wounded at Sharpsburg.[34] Oates led the 15th at the Battle of Fredericksburg, where it was under fire but not actively engaged. Many of the men were without shoes and suffered grievously from the cold. Oates saw two of his men, both barefoot, waiting for a mortally wounded Federal to die. On further investigation he found the pair arguing over possession of the dying man's shoes. The issue was settled by Oates taking the dying man's shoes for his own use and giving his old pair away.[35]

Cantey transferred from the 15th Alabama January 8, 1863, his promotion to brigadier general ranking from that date.[36] He went to the western army and later commanded a brigade in the Atlanta Campaign. Cantey accompanied Hood into Tennessee in late 1864 and surrendered in North Carolina. After the war he returned to Alabama and died on his plantation near Fort Mitchell in 1874.[37] John Treutlen was promoted to colonel but was absent much of the time because of ill health.[38] Early in December Lowther departed for Alabama on 30 days' leave and did not return for six months. This may have been a contributing factor in the delay to fill the vacancy for lieutenant colonel. No immediate action was taken to fill that post. On Lowther's departure Isaac Feagin, the regiment's senior captain, was on convalescent leave. Oates, the next senior in rank of those present, assumed command of the 15th Alabama.

44th Alabama Infantry

Southerners volunteered in great numbers in 1861, but volunteerism slowed after the initial period of excitement. As the twelve-month enlistments expired in the spring of 1862, the Confederacy faced the prospect that its army would go home, and to hold it together the Confederate Congress passed the first conscript act in American history in April 1862. A short waiting period was granted to allow men to volunteer and avoid the stigma attached to conscription. Each recruit was exempt from a conscript status and given a bounty. The 44th, 47th and 48th Alabama Regiments were organized during this grace period, all in May 1862. Many in the 4th and 15th regiments, expecting to do their bit and return home, felt betrayed by the draft law. Their one-year terms expired and many felt they were being coerced to reenlist.[39] Others objected to conscription on principle. Men from the 4th and 15th Alabama, discussing the newer Alabama regiments, frequently referred to them as the "Fortykins" because of their double-digit regiment numbers starting with the number four.[40]

The 44th Alabama was organized at Selma, Alabama, on May 16, 1862, and elected James Kent, a physician from Selma, as its colonel.[41] The men voted Charles Alexander Derby, a Virginia Military Institute graduate and Episcopal minister, lieutenant colonel.[42] They chose William Perry, a Jackson County, Georgia native as major.

While in camp of instruction, Kent was dismayed by his men's zealous use of alcohol. A number of prescriptions from unknown physicians were issued for liquor, supposedly for medicinal purposes. In an attempt to eliminate alcohol from his camp, Kent appealed to the local saloonkeepers and druggists to refrain from selling liquor to the 44th. When that failed, Kent issued a notice to Selma druggists and liquor dealers that a physician's prescription for liquor must be approved by his personal signature.[43] The affair turned into a mental chess game between Kent and the men of the 44th as shown by a brief article published by the Selma *Reporter* on May 30, describing the battle of wits between Kent and his thirsty soldiers.

> *A few days since Colonel Kent became painfully conscious that his paper blockade upon plain liquor, mint juleps, brandy, cocktails, etc., was lamentably inefficient, and to stay the tide of evil published a card in the Reporter declaring that a physician's order hereafter would not be valid unless countersigned by himself. How this expedient is to succeed we know not. It is evident however that orders for the much coveted*

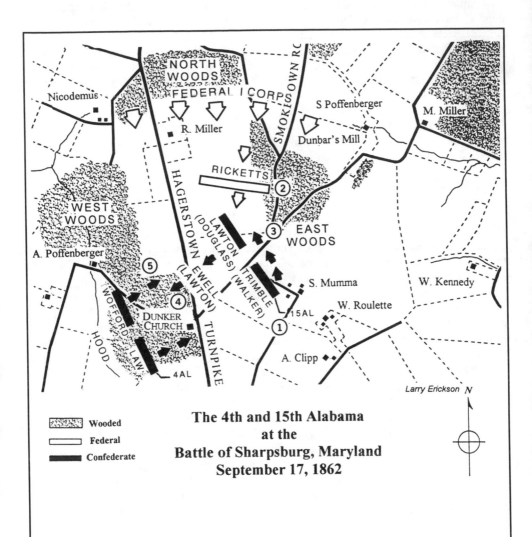

The 4th and 15th Alabama
at the
Battle of Sharpsburg, Maryland
September 17, 1862

Larry Erickson N

Wooded
Federal
Confederate

1. The 15th Alabama is on the extreme right of Trimble's Brigade, south of the Smoketown Road, when the fighting begins.
2. Ricketts' Second Division drives through the cornfield and attacks Lawton's position.
3. Trimble's Brigade advances to join the fight in the cornfield.
4. Lawton's Division is driven from its position in the cornfield.
5. Hood, with Law and the Texas Brigade under Wofford, drives forward from the woods west of the Dunker Church, enters the cornfield and pushes the Federals from the field.

article can be forged as we understand has been done heretofore. Where
there is a will there is a way, in most undertakings; and we have no
reason to believe that this case will be an exception to the general rule.
Colonel Kent is to be praised, however, for his vigilance and evident
determination to put a stop to drunkenness among his soldiers, a few of
whom have been tight under the license of a physician's order for liquor.
Let those who sail under this coast with bottles in their pockets, look out
for breakers, since there is many a slip between cup and lip.

The regiment received a splendid send off when it departed Selma on June 17. The affair was a festive occasion as the regiment, led by a brass band, marched down Broad Street.[44] Local citizens lined the street and cheered as the companies passed. Accompanied by a large number of local citizens the 44th marched to the landing and boarded steamboats for Montgomery. From there the regiment traveled by rail to Richmond, Virginia by way of Atlanta and Augusta, Georgia; Columbia, South Carolina; then on to Charlotte, Raleigh, and Weldon, North Carolina.[45] Kent's Alabamians found the citizens of Charlotte an inhospitable lot who refused care to the sick and were unwilling to sell rations to the Alabama soldiers. Fortunately for the 44th, the citizens of Raleigh extended considerable kindness to the Alabamians by sharing food and treating the sick. From Weldon, they traveled to Petersburg where they could hear the ominous cannonading before Richmond. The night of June 24 was spent in open boxcars while a downpour thoroughly drenched the men. William Alexander Griffin, Company K, was still feeling the effects of the exposure two days later when he wrote his wife: "I am nearly past going on account of it."[46] The regiment finally arrived at Richmond on June 25 at about 10 p.m.

Because it was a new regiment and unarmed when it arrived in the Confederate capital, the 44th Alabama did not participate in the battles around Richmond.[47] It marched to entrenchments below Richmond June 28 and from then until July 1 camped on the Charles City Road where its primary duties were supporting batteries defending the city. Nearly half of the men were sick in camp.[48] The 44th Alabama was assigned to Brigadier General Ambrose R. Wright's Brigade of Major General Richard H. Anderson's Division, Longstreet's Corps.[49] On July 5 the regiment went into camp at Falling Creek, remaining there until August 18. It was here that the 44th received weapons and its first instruction in the manual of arms with real muskets.

The 44th traveled north with Longstreet's Corps when Lee moved to confront Pope, who had moved south of the Rapidan. The first leg of the trip was made by a march to Richmond where cars were boarded for Louisa Court House. The remainder of the journey, which ended at Manassas Junction, was on foot by way of Jefferson and Salem.[50] At the Rapidan, Joab Goodson paused to watch Longstreet's column wade the river and was awed by the splendor of the scenery around him. The majestic Blue Ridge swerved as a spectacular backdrop for the column which with battle flags waving in the breeze made its way across luxurious fields of clover and corn.[51] On August 25, Corporal Charles T. Dexter, Company E, 44th Alabama, became one of the first of Law's Alabamians to go over to the enemy when he swam the Rapidan and entered the Federal lines. Dexter cooperated freely with the enemy, supplying information on Lee's movement. He reported the Confederate army was large, which he estimated to be of 100,000 strong, though poorly fed.[52] The 44th's Alabama's first action came August 30 at the Battle of Second Manassas. The previous day Anderson's Division lay in support of Longstreet's main line. In late afternoon the 44th participated in the final Confederate assault of the day, losing one fifth of its number engaged. [53]

James Kent resigned his commission as colonel, effective September 1, 1862, citing disability caused by failing health. Derby moved up to Kent's position, and Perry was promoted to lieutenant colonel. Captain John Archibald Jones became the regiment's major. Kent underwent medical treatment at Petersburg, and eventually returned to Selma to resume his medical practice.[54]

Jones was a native of Fayetteville, North Carolina, whose family had moved to Alabama when he was quite young. He graduated from the University of Alabama in 1855, and for the next two years stayed there to teach Latin and Greek. He went to Tuskegee where he taught mathematics at the Central Female College in Tuskegee from 1857 through 1858. In 1859, he relocated to Bibb County, Alabama, where he farmed and served as a corporate officer of the cotton mill at Scottsville.[55]

The 44th fought in the Confederate center at the Battle of Sharpsburg, carrying 149 men and 13 officers into the battle. When D. H. Hill's line in Bloody Lane became severely threatened, the 44th charged into the fighting on the right of Wright's Brigade. During the charge the color bearer was severely wounded, leaving the colors lying on the ground. Sergeant Winns P. Becker retrieved the fallen colors, raised the standard and charged into the smoke amid a hail of bullets.[56] He lived to become captain of Company G. Though it fought only a short time before falling back, casualties from the fighting at Sharpsburg were almost 47 percent. Two officers lay dead on the field, Lieutenant Colonel Derby, the former Episcopal minister, and Junior Second Lieutenant Augustus Ray of Company I.

William Perry's commission as colonel of the 44th Alabama was dated September 17, 1862. He became a teacher at age 20, and from 1848 through 1853 he served as principal at a school in Talladega, Alabama. After studying the law under Judge Chilton at Tuskegee, he was admitted to the Alabama Bar in 1854, though he did not practice law. In the same year he was appointed Alabama's first state superintendent of education, serving in that capacity until 1858. Perry returned to private life and became principal of the East Alabama Female Institute in Tuskegee, Alabama, and served in that capacity until the war started.[57]

Perry took some time to process the paper work for his new lieutenant colonel, and it was almost three months before John Jones's appointment to the post was confirmed on January 1, 1863.[58] Perry would wait until the late spring of 1863 to fill the position of major.

47th Alabama Infantry

The 47th Alabama came into existence at the small rail stop of Loachapoka, just west of Auburn, Alabama. Its organization took place May 22, 1862, with James McCarthy Oliver, a lawyer from Dadeville, Alabama, elected colonel.[59] The men elected James Washington Jackson as lieutenant colonel and John Y. Johnston, a thirty-year-old physician, as major.[60]

Jackson, a Georgia native, attended a military academy in Greenville, Georgia and studied medicine in New York City. Before the war he practiced medicine at Lafayette, Alabama and was instrumental in raising and drilling a volunteer company known as the "Lafayette Guards." Jackson was a strong secessionist, and as soon as Alabama seceded from the Union, offered the company's services to the governor. The company was accepted and became Company A of the 7th Alabama. Unfortunately, after several months in the field, Jackson's health began to fail and he resigned his captain's commission October 29, 1861 and returned to Lafayette. He was still in ill health when he began raising a company of volunteers that was assigned to the 47th Alabama. At Loachapoka he was very sick, but still ran for lieutenant colonel. A wave of protest rose from the ranks when he was elected, a large number of disgruntled privates and officers openly expressing their opinion the regiment had elected a dead man. Friends defended the choice, declaring Jackson was their man dead or alive.[61]

48th Alabama Infantry

After Alabama seceded, Jim Sheffield worked to raise a volunteer company which became Company K of the 9th Alabama. Sheffield was elected the original first lieutenant and later captain. The 9th Alabama did little more than picket duty in the summer and fall of 1861. During this period of relative inactivity, Sheffield became convinced that his property in Alabama suffered greatly from want of attention, and by November he was extremely anxious to return to Alabama. His personal affairs were in a shambles, he was extremely homesick, and he threatened to resign if unable to obtain a furlough.[62] After exhausting all avenues to gain a furlough, he turned to the idea of raising a regiment.[63] He was encouraged to pursue this endeavor by Captain Abner A. Hughes, a forty-four-year-old farmer from DeKalb County, Alabama. Hughes promised support in raising several companies from his county.

John Rayburn, a young member of Sheffield's company, wrote to his father, Samuel K. Rayburn, a wealthy citizen of Marshall County, with statewide influence, about Sheffield.[64] Young Rayburn said that Sheffield wanted to raise a regiment from his home district, and believed he could raise seven or eight companies on his own. The younger Rayburn suggested that Sheffield could succeed in raising a regiment with S. K. Rayburn's influence with the Confederate secretary of war. To convince his father, Rayburn reminded him that the Confederacy needed men in the field.[65]

John Rayburn matter-of-factly summed up Sheffield's leadership qualities by stating his great weakness was instilling discipline in the ranks. As far as his general qualifications, the young man believed there were others inferior to Sheffield. Rayburn wrote his father that he would serve in Sheffield's new regiment, except he was tired of raw recruits.[66]

By the end of February 1862, Sheffield was back in North Alabama, his plan to raise a regiment in full swing.[67] He put his considerable political skills to work to raise companies in Marshall, Blount and DeKalb counties, using nearly $60,000 of his own money to outfit the regiment.[68] In mid–May, ten companies were ordered to Auburn to organize into a regiment.

Samuel K. Rayburn raised a company to serve in Sheffield's command as Company E, but resigned about a month later, due to his advanced age.[69] John Rayburn wrote home that Law wanted to make room in his regiment for S. K. Rayburn's Company, but Rayburn stayed with the regiment from Marshall County.[70]

Captain Moses Lee's Company departed Mount Polk in Calhoun County for Auburn on May 18, 1862. Lee and the company marched to the Alabama and Tennessee Railroad at Jacksonville, Alabama and from there they traveled south through central Alabama to Selma and then east to Auburn to join the companies gathering to form the 48th Alabama. Times were different from the departing scenes the previous year when food and shelter were freely offered along the way. Lee's men were instructed to carry sufficient rations to last until the company reached Montgomery.[71]

The 48th Alabama was organized May 22, 1862 at Auburn, the same day as the 47th. These two were later known as the twin regiments. Both were always in the same brigade and fought side by side during the war, the history of one evolving as the history of the other. Sheffield became the regiment's colonel. Abner Hughes was elected lieutenant colo-

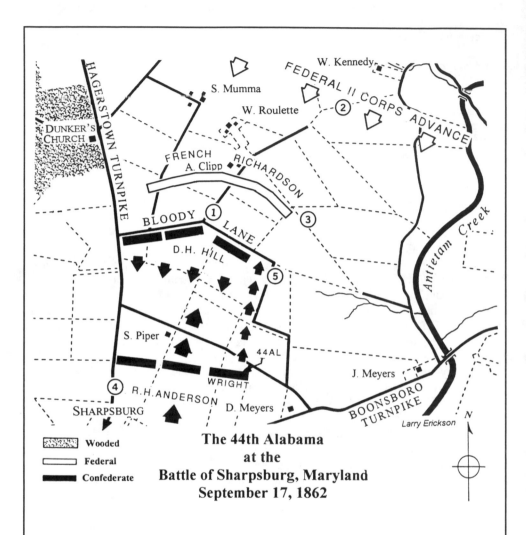

The 44th Alabama
at the
Battle of Sharpsburg, Maryland
September 17, 1862

Larry Erickson

Wooded
Federal
Confederate

1. D. H. Hill's Division, in the Confederate center, is deployed along the Sunken Road.
2. Sumner's II Corps sweeps westward south of the Dunker Church.
3. Hill's line is severely pressed by French's and Richardson's divisions.
4. R. H. Anderson's Division arrives on the field shortly after mid morning and are sent to support D. H. Hill's Division in line along the Sunken Road.
5. The 44th Alabama, in Wright's Brigade, moves into the Sunken Road on Hill's extreme right. A few minutes later Hill's right collapses and the entire line falls back.

nel, and Enoch Alldredge was elected major.

Sheffield was born December 5, 1819, at Huntsville, the same year Alabama became a state. He attended the local schools and at age 18, moved to Claysville in Marshall County, Alabama, where he clerked in a store and served as deputy sheriff from 1844–1847. Sheffield then became a planter, and through hard work and good fortune was able to accumulate considerable wealth. In the 1860 census enumeration of Marshall County, Sheffield listed his occupation as retired farmer. He was active in Marshall County politics and served in the state legislature from 1852–1855.[72]

Enoch Alldredge, at age 53, was an early settler in North Alabama. A native of Bledsoe County in the Sequachie Valley of East Tennessee, he moved to Alabama as a young man and entered farming. He was a veteran of the Indian Wars and Alabama politics, having served 26 sessions in the state legislature.[73]

Bound for Virginia

On June 20, 1862 the 47th and 48th Alabama reached Richmond, arriving about 5 p.m. and marched to the fairgrounds, then known as Camp Lee.[74] As the regiments marched through the city, citizens came to front doors and inquired as to the new arrivals' identities. When told they were from Alabama loud cheers greeted the ranks. The regiments did not participate in the fighting around Richmond. They were assigned to Stonewall Jackson's command and attached to Brigadier General William Taliaferro's Third Brigade. In addition to the 47th and 48th Alabama, the brigade consisted of the 10th, 23rd and 37th Virginia.[75] In mid-August Taliaferro's brigade moved to Gordonsville where Colonel Oliver resigned August 2, citing disability due to face and scalp neuralgia caused by a chronic liver disease. James Jackson was later promoted to colonel with his commission dated to rank from August 2, 1862.[76]

The first battlefield experience for the 47th and 48th regiments came at Cedar Run on August 9, 1862. They left their camps near Gordonsville on Friday evening, marching nearly all night and most of the next day.[77] It was 4 p.m. when the first artillery shells began bursting over the 47th Alabama's leading companies while they were south of the Cedar Run battlefield.[78] Jackson was still lieutenant colonel, though in command of the 47th Alabama. The Alabamians marched the next mile with shells exploding around them. Because of their line of march, most of the men in the 47th failed to recognize the signs of impending fighting. Taliaferro's brigade halted in line under cover of woods on the left of the Orange-Gordonsville Road while Brigadier General Jubal A. Early's line of battle lay several yards to the right and perpendicular to Taliaferro's. The Alabamians were deployed before they realized their first encounter with the Federal army was close at hand.[79] At first, shells bursting over their heads caused confusion in the ranks of the 47th Alabama. However, a few minutes later the men began to settle down and forty minutes later the 47th had yet to sustain casualties.[80]

Taliaferro's brigade was first ordered across the road to form line of battle in a wheat field on the east side of the road, but before the line could be established orders came to recross the road. The distinctive roll of musket fire came from the west, rapidly intensifying and spreading along the Confederate line. This was the beginning of an attack by the Federals on Lieutenant Colonel Thomas S. Garnett's brigade.[81] A few minutes later Taliaferro's men were sent across the road a second time.[82]

The 10th Virginia deployed on the left side of the road, and to the right of the road, from left to right, the order of deployment was the 47th Alabama, 48th Alabama, 37th Virginia, and 23rd Virginia. The 47th Alabama's left rested on the road.[83] There was a gap between the 47th and the 10th Virginia as the brigade advanced about 20 yards to a fence, which it crossed and moved onto the crest of a slight rise. Before them was the Federal line in three columns.[84] The opposing lines exchanged fire for 20 to 30 minutes.

Meanwhile on the left side of the road, the Federals entered the woods and turned Garnett's left flank, causing the men to fall back in disorder. The line of the 10th Virginia, resting in the woods, was protected from the Federal breakthrough, however, the Federals emerged from the woods on the left of the road and attacked the gap between the 10th Virginia and 47th Alabama. Jackson was unaware of the break until Federal infantry was already in his rear, and from about 40 paces the Federals began to pour a destructive fire into the 47th Alabama's left flank and rear.[85]

Jackson attempted to maneuver his left to face the new threat, giving an order to about face. The right obeyed, but the left turned directly into a flanking fire, which quickly resulted in the loss of three captains. Captain Albert Menefee, Company D, fell, mortally wounded. Captain James Campbell, Company E, was severely wounded, and Captain Michael Bulger, Company A, received a nasty arm wound, which he bound tightly and continued to lead his men. A short while later he took a ball in the leg, cutting an artery. Soldiers produced two corn cobs and a set of suspenders to fashion a crude tourniquet.[86] By now Bulger was so weakened from shock and loss of blood he was unable to stand. Fellow soldiers carried him to a farmhouse, and miraculously, he slowly recovered and lived to fight again.

The flanking fire became too destructive for the men of the 47th to bear and its left gave way. The men retreated in considerable disorder, recrossed the fence, and moved to the cover of the ridge. Captain Henry C. Lindsay looked toward the road and was amazed to see members of the 47th Alabama jumping the fence, with the Federals giving chase. The right of the 47th became confused by the disorderly retreat of its left and it, too, fell back.[87] Because the left of the 48th Alabama was uncovered, all but one company quickly followed suit. Company K, commanded by Moses Lee, remained in the open sometime before dropping back.[88] When the 48th Alabama retreated the left of the 37th Virginia was uncovered and it too departed the firing line. Major H. C. Wood, in his report of the action, was quick to point out that the 37th Virginia "would have been able to maintain its position had the 47th and 48th Alabama been able to maintain theirs."[89]

Once the 47th broke it became impossible to stop the retreat, and Jackson could do nothing more than follow his troops to safety. The 47th Alabama finally stopped behind a fence which ran near a farmhouse. The color bearer had the presence of mind to remain near the ridge's crest, providing a rallying point for the anxious Alabamians. The sight of their colors waving on the crest gave the men some sense of security, and a few began to rally and reform.[90]

A short time later, the 47th, its line in much disarray, began advancing toward its original position. Jackson was weak from exertion and exhausted to the point of collapse, and was having trouble maintaining effective command over the regiment. He had to content himself with urging the stragglers forward and preventing them from firing into the front line. When those in the front moved a few yards, the rear followed suit. In this manner the 47th was able to move back within 200 yards of the Federal line and return the enemy fire.[91]

The Federal attack had not only stalled, but the Federal line was now outnumbered, as a reinforced Confederate line drove the Federals from the woods. The tide of battle was rapidly turning, but suddenly a new threat appeared. From the woods across the wheat field, Federal cavalry in column of fours rushed toward the road. The charging Federals cheered loudly, but accurate Confederate fire quickly emptied many saddles. The charge

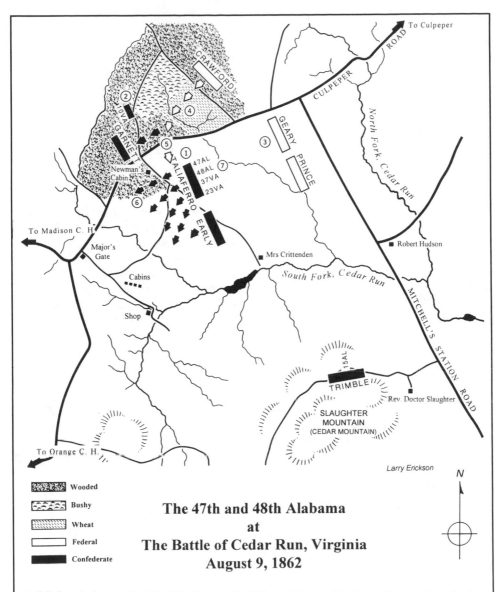

The 47th and 48th Alabama
at
The Battle of Cedar Run, Virginia
August 9, 1862

Larry Erickson

Legend:
- Wooded
- Bushy
- Wheat
- Federal
- Confederate

1. Taliaferro deploys on the right of the Culpeper Road. Garnet is deployed in the woods across the road and forward of Taliaferro.
2. The 10th Virginia, initially in position on Taliaferro's extreme left, is sent across the road, leaving the 47th Alabama to occupy the brigade's extreme left.
3. Taliaferro's regiments, on the right of the road begin exchanging fire with Geary's brigade.
4. Crawford attacks across the wheat field and turns Garnett's left, throwing the brigade into disorder and causing it to retreat.
5. Elements of Crawford's brigade cross the Culpeper Road and get into the rear of Taliaferro's brigade. The 47th Alabama receives fire from its left flank and rear, killing and wounding many of its soldiers.
6. The 47th Alabama retreats in considerable confusion, uncovering the left of the 48th Alabama which also falls back. The 37th and 23rd Virginia follow suit.
7. Taliaferro's regiments rally and return to the original position where they once again engage the Federal line across Cedar Run.

died in front of Taliaferro's brigade, and a short time later the entire Federal line began to retire.[92]

The reinvigorated Confederate line, advancing at the double quick, drove the Federal line a considerable distance. The 47th and 48th Alabama advanced in line with the rest of the brigade. Green Alabama troops, who had been routed a short time before, now became victors. The Confederate pursuit continued until dark when the exhausted survivors lay down and slept in place. The Battle of Cedar Run was over by 9 p.m. [93]

Major John Y. Johnston resigned under a cloud of disgrace. His resignation, dated August 18, 1862, was based on a surgeon's certificate of disability, but officers of the 47th Alabama saw the situation differently. They were unanimous in recommending that Jackson accept his resignation on the grounds of cowardly and disgraceful behavior at Cedar Run.[94]

While on leave recovering from his arm and leg wounds, Bulger was promoted to lieutenant colonel. He had come to the 47th Alabama after a lengthy association with the militia. His duty in the Indian wars and service as brigadier general had served him well.[95]

Campbell, who was also absent on convalescent leave, was elected major. He received very little formal education, but early in life decided his calling was the ministry. When Alabama left the Union, Campbell resigned his ministry and joined the troops gathering at Pensacola. He eventually became chaplain of the First Georgia Regiment and accompanied that regiment to Virginia in the summer of 1861. During the winter of 1861–62, the regiment found itself stationed in the mountains of western Virginia, primarily performing picket duty. Not only were the Virginia mountains miserably cold, but his duties as chaplain left him with considerable time on his hands and the minister did a lot of soul searching and meditating to determine if his duty lay with his country or the ministry. He penned frequent letters to a brother in Cherokee County, Alabama, asking about regiments that might be forming in the area. He discovered that an old friend and minister, Francis Thomas Jefferson Brandon, planned to recruit and organize a company from the vicinity of his home. Campbell settled on a decision to leave the ministry and become a soldier. It was not an easy decision, for his life's work was devoted to peace on earth and the pursuit of sending men's souls to heaven. On the other hand Campbell was an able-bodied man and in the end he felt his place was to actively participate in the defense of his country.[96]

Brandon promised Campbell the position of first lieutenant in his new company, the only problem being that the same position had been promised to Robert Russell Savage. Brandon solved the problem by proposing Campbell as captain, Savage first lieutenant, himself second lieutenant, and Joseph Nathaniel Hood the third, or junior second lieutenant. All were elected and the two Methodist ministers went to war with the 47th Alabama.

Campbell first came to prominence within the regiment after a nasty encounter with Colonel Oliver who was given to frequent cursing. He thought the best way to maintain discipline was with liberal doses of verbal abuse. After a particularly bad drill, Oliver singled out Campbell's company for its mistakes. An irate Oliver faced the company, cursing and yelling at the men. Campbell stepped between Oliver and his company and boldly confronted the colonel. Lack of skill at drill was one thing, but hurling profanity at his men would not be tolerated. The two men stood nose to nose angrily shouting at each other. Oliver eventually backed down and the men took note that Campbell was concerned for them.[97] The former minister was elected major when that position became vacant.

The 47th and 48th Alabama next saw fighting at Groveton on August 28. The regiments then fought from behind an unfinished railroad cut at the Battle of Second Manassas on August 29–30. Starke ascended to division command when Taliaferro was wounded at Groveton. During the fighting of August 30, the 47th and 48th Alabama participated in fighting off a division.[98] Opposing lines were so close the battle lines virtually touched each other. When their ammunition ran out, Starke's men resorted to throwing rocks at their assailants. At the height of the fighting, the 15th Alabama on the immediate left of Starke fired to the right oblique and assisted one of Starke's brigades in repelling an attack.[99] After the Federal assault was broken, the 47th and 48th Alabama joined in a spirited charge against a Federal battery, resulting in the death of Captain Moses Lee, Company K, 48th Alabama.[100]

The 47th and 48th followed Robert E. Lee into Maryland, participated in the siege of Harpers Ferry and reached Sharpsburg, Maryland late in the afternoon of September 16.[101] The 47th Alabama carried 147 men into battle under Jackson.[102] The 48th did a little better, mustering a strength of 163 officers and men but with no field officers present. Sheffield was still suffering from the effects of his wound received at Cedar Run and was making his way to the regiment. He arrived on the field on September 18 with several stragglers, recovered wounded, and sick. Lieutenant Colonel Hughes was in the hospital, recovering from chronic fatigue and poor health.[103] Major Enoch Alldredge was still on leave because of a wound, leaving Captain Robert C. Golightly to lead the 48th Alabama. Jackson was the lone field officer present in the 47th Alabama.

Taliaferro's brigade was in the second line on the division's extreme right. Its right rested on the Hagerstown Pike, when fighting commenced on the Confederate left at sunrise. Fighting was vicious and intense and casualties mounted rapidly, and Jackson ascended to brigade command. When the first line was shattered by the enemy, the second line was called on to drive a Federal line from the cornfield east of the Hagerstown Pike. The 47th and 48th participated in a charge to the fence bordering the road which checked and halted the progress of an advancing Federal line. Taliaferro's men came under a murderous fire as they attempted to cross the fence. After slugging it out at close range his brigade grudgingly gave ground and fell back to the West Wood.[104]

Though the 47th and 48th Alabama were forced to retire in the face of superior numbers, both regiments fought well at Sharpsburg. After Groveton and Manassas they were no longer the green troops the Virginians accused of fleeing in the face of the enemy at Cedar Run. They paid a heavy price for their bravery at Sharpsburg as the 47th lost nine killed and 25 wounded, a number estimated to be 23 percent of the number engaged. The 48th Alabama fared little better, suffering six killed and 30 wounded, or about 22 percent of its force.[105] Golightly was the lone officer killed, leaving Junior Second Lieutenant Columbus B. St. John as the senior officer present when the 48th mustered September 18.[106]

The 47th was badly scattered about the battlefield and those only slightly wounded were still in the rear. Only 15 men under a sergeant answered the roll call September 18.[107] The trip into Maryland remained forever in the memories of the men from the 47th. It was beset with extreme hardships brought on by hard marching and scanty rations. Fighting at Sharpsburg was the worst yet and particularly upsetting, since the 47th had been literally cut to pieces. Private James B. Daniel, Company H, 47th, was so distraught by the ordeal that he found it difficult to write home to his wife. This was unusual as the young Alabamian wrote home every time the chance arose.[108]

The 47th and 48th Alabama recrossed the Potomac and marched to Martinsburg. While Jackson's command camped at Martinsburg, the 47th concentrated on tearing up the track and bridges of the Baltimore and Ohio Railroad during the week of October 24. They placed sections of rails on huge stacks of crossties which were set afire. The fire rendered the iron rails twisted and unusable. The men also burned trestles, destroyed bridges, water towers and took down telegraph lines.[109]

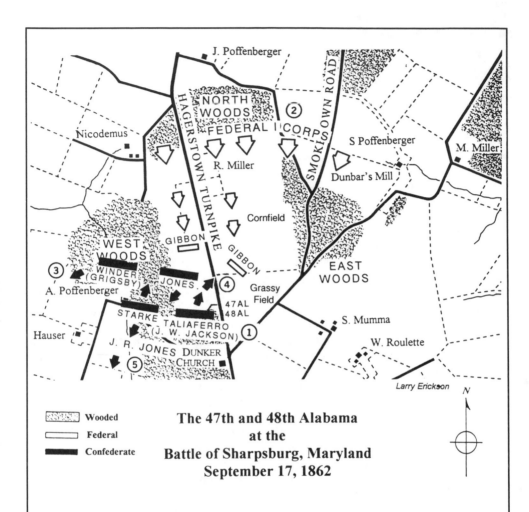

The 47th and 48th Alabama
at the
Battle of Sharpsburg, Maryland
September 17, 1862

Larry Erickson

- Wooded
- Federal
- Confederate

1. The 47th and 48th Alabama are deployed on the right side of Taliaferro's brigade on September 17, 1862. Colonel James W. Jackson, 47th Alabama, commands Taliaferro's brigade.
2. The Federal I Corps advances south toward the Dunker Church at first light. Doubleday's First Division moves along the Hagerstown Road.
3. Jones's front line is crushed by the Federal onslaught and gives way.
4. Starke's and Taliaferro's brigades charge toward the Hagerstown Turnpike where they engage in a bloody fight with Gibbon's Iron Brigade.
5. Starke and Taliaferro are caught in a cross fire from Federal artillery and infantry and fall back to the south and west of the Dunker Church.

While the regiments rested in their camps, a fervent interest developed in religious matters, particularly in Jackson's Corps. Soldiers broke into groups and held gospel meetings in one of the camps nearly every night.[110] Campbell and Brandon conducted frequent religious services for the 47th Alabama, and on several occasions conducted religious services for other regiments of the brigade.

Enoch Alldredge resigned September 29, 1862, citing disability caused by wounds received at Cedar Run. In a lengthy letter to the secretary of war, Alldredge told how he entered the service with five sons and two sons-in-law.[111] One son died from disease, one was killed at Second Manassas, and Lieutenant Colonel Jesse J. Alldredge was shot through both legs at Manassas. His wounds would lead to retirement from the service.[112] The elder Alldredge returned to Alabama and served the latter part of the war on the governor's staff.[113]

Lieutenant Colonel Abner Hughes resigned October 15, suffering from chronic rheumatism.[114] Jesse Alldredge, thirty-year-old son of Enoch Alldredge, succeeded Hughes as lieutenant colonel of the 48th. Before entering the army, Alldredge was a merchant at Summit, Alabama.[115]

William McTyiere Hardwick, originally from Jasper County, Georgia, succeeded Enoch Alldredge as major. His commission was dated to rank from September 29. Before the war Hardwick resided at Cedar Bluff in Cherokee County, Alabama, where he worked as a carpenter. He first saw service as a private with Company C, 7th Alabama Infantry. Hardwick became first lieutenant of Company H, 48th Alabama at its organization. He was captured at Sharpsburg and sent to Fort McHenry in Baltimore, Maryland, and was later exchanged in November 1862 after being transported to Fort Monroe, Virginia[116]

The 47th and 48th Alabama took up the line of march for Fredericksburg on November 14. Many men left the camp barefoot as a cold rain fell, causing the roads to turn into mud and icy slush as the temperature dropped. Later that afternoon a frigid wind blew from the north adding to the men's misery. Sheffield went to brigade headquarters and confronted Colonel E. T. H. Warren, brigade commander. An irate Sheffield issued Warren an ultimatum: "Colonel, I have many men in my regiment barefooted. I don't have the ambulances to haul them, and before I will see them march over frozen ground without shoes, I will build winter quarters here and remain until spring. Therefore, if you wish us to remain with your brigade you must send transportation for my barefooted men." Warren immediately made wagons available to transport Sheffield's barefoot men.[117]

The 47th and 48th were under fire at Fredericksburg, but were not actively engaged. Weather in the area remained terribly cold, and since winter quarters were not constructed, the men suffered from exposure to the elements. Private James Daniel, Company H, 47th Alabama, informed his wife that dogs fared better than the men in the field did because a "dog could sleep under the house." He related that times were bad and predicted they were likely to get worse. The monotony was broken when the 47th was ordered to the Rappahannock River for picket duty and to prepare siege gun emplacements. Yankee fires were clearly visible at night across the river, and for the moment both sides were content to simply watch each other.[118] Yankee and Confederate pickets were soon on friendly terms. One Bluecoat walked along the river and jokingly asked the 47th pickets if they were on guard duty. When they replied yes, the Yankee responded that he was duck hunting. He offered the opinion that shooting ducks was a lot more useful than firing across the river at the Confederates.[119]

Winter brought an end to marching and fighting, and none too soon for the Alabama regiments who had been on the move virtually nonstop in active campaigning in 1862. The change was welcome, because it reduced the duties of the Alabama soldiers to roll call, occasional drill and on some days, dress parade.[120] Serving as pickets twice a week was the only duty required of the 15th Alabama from the middle of December 1862 until joining Law's Brigade in January.[121]

Construction on winter quarters began in late December. The 15th and 47th regiments camped near Port Royal. Their shelters ranged from traditional log cabins with mud filling the cracks between the logs, to tents, often with chimneys, to holes dug in the ground, covered with boards and dirt.[122] Construction was equally varied in the camp of the 4th near Hamilton's Crossing, the 48th at Skinker's Neck and the 44th near the city of Fredericksburg.[123] After becoming Law's Alabama Brigade in January, the regiments established a new camp along the Catharpin Road, south of Fredericksburg, making it necessary to construct winter quarters a second time.

Law's Brigade remained in camp southwest of Fredericksburg about a month after the reorganization. At that time smallpox broke out among the Alabamians. A rumor making its way through camp was that Sergeant John P. Walke of Company D, 4th Alabama, brought the disease to camp on his return from furlough. Supposedly his entire family had died of the disease while he was with them.[124] Actually Walke was not the culprit. The Alabamians' bout with the disease came at the end of an epidemic which had struck the Army of Northern Virginia in October and had nearly run its course by mid-February.

A particularly heavy snowfall in the latter part of January 1863 provided an ample quantity for a snowball fight. The Texas brigade started the affair which came to be known as the Great Snowball Fight. The Texans fought among themselves and then attacked Brigadier General George Thomas "Tige" Anderson's Georgia Brigade.[125] After a couple hours fighting the Georgians, the Texans returned to camp and went after the 47th and 48th Alabama regiments. The Alabamians were quickly overpowered and driven from their camps. The 15th Alabama came to the relief of their fellow Alabamians, but found them in a foul mood after the thrashing delivered at the hands of their previous opponents. The 47th and 48th combined to turn on the 15th and after a spirited contest, the flag of the 15th Alabama was wrested from the color bearer and victory declared.[126] Hood's Division then went after Major General Lafayette McLaws's Division.[127] Men on horseback were generals. Handkerchiefs served as battle flags. Deafening yells erupted as opposing lines clashed. Snowballs filled the air, as the fighting became furious. When one side faltered, mounted officers cheered the men. Flag bearers waved their banners and called the men to rally on the flag. The combatants stood and fought until one side or the other gave way. The victorious side would then charge at the double quick and "then such running you never saw," noted Captain Joab Goodson, commanding Company B, 44th Alabama.[128] A South Carolina colonel, on horseback, was surrounded, unhorsed and rolled in the snow, as someone removed the saddle from his horse.[129] In the end Hood's Division managed to prevail in the struggle, then after a good-natured exchange of pleasantries both divisions returned to quarters.[130] The South Carolina colonel was forced to return to quarters riding his horse bareback.[131]

One witness claimed it was as exciting as real combat. Generals and their staffs led as they did in battle, riding among the men and receiving a storm of snowballs. They endured courageously, though they shed real blood.

Law led his brigade three miles to make a surprise attack on Jenkins's South Carolina brigade. The Alabamians planned ahead by preparing snowballs the night before. These were frozen solid by morning. "Jenkins and his men were right badly used up," remembered an observer. The tables were turned the next morning, however. Jenkins led his South Carolinians against Law as the Alabamians prepared breakfast. Even though the drums beat out the long roll and the men rallied under Law and his officers, they had no ammunition and were soundly beaten. The attack took place near Lee's headquarters and as he came outside to watch he, too, received a barrage of snowballs.[132]

During this inactive time some of the brigade were lucky enough to receive orders taking them away from Fredericksburg. One officer and one enlisted man from each company of the 47th and 48th regiments were detailed to return to Alabama to arrest deserters and enlist volunteers to replenish their ranks.[133]

Resting in winter quarters gave the brigade a chance to catch up on its administrative work, especially handling a backlog of court-martial cases and promotions that had accumulated during the fall campaign. Officers of the regiments were detailed to serve on the courts. D. H. Hill charged Captain Isaac Feagin, Company B, 15th Alabama, with conduct unbecoming an officer.[134] Feagin was unaware of the charges until he returned from leave in Alabama. A court was convened in Trimble's Brigade camp because Feagin was attached to that brigade when the offense, the so-called "haystack episode," allegedly occurred.[135] Oates, commanding the 15th Alabama, served as judge advocate of the court that heard Feagin's case. Colonel James Walker, Feagin's commanding officer at Sharpsburg, had mentioned the incident between Feagin and Hill in his report of the battle and described it as a misunderstanding. The report, written in October 1862, explained that Feagin's orders were to move his command to the rear after it had exhausted its ammunition.[136] After all the facts were laid before the court Feagin was, in the language of the court, "most honorably acquitted." The court went on to say that "being acquitted, Captain Feagin will resume his sword."

Three other officers of Law's Brigade were tried at this time, all three being convicted. William Randolph, first lieutenant of Company E, 44th Alabama, resigned in December 1862, and two days later he withdrew the resignation and returned to his company. But in the early spring he failed to return from a furlough granted February 4, 1863, and the court found him guilty of being absent without leave and ordered him dismissed from the service on April 14, 1863.[137] The court convicted Albert Garmon, lieutenant in Company E, 48th Alabama, of cowardice and had him cashiered. In the case of Garmon, the court decreed "his crime, his name and place of abode and his punishment be published as the Articles of War require."[138] Captain Albert Towles, Company I, 47th Alabama, was dismissed from the service by sentence of court-martial February 19, 1863.[139]

Enlisted men were tried on a variety of charges, including two privates of the 48th who were caught in the act of "taking a chicken without the consent of the proper owner." Both were sentenced to a diet of bread and water for several days. When examined by the review board, however, the findings and sentences of their cases were disallowed because the court had neglected to swear in the witnesses. Other Alabama volunteers were tried for "drunkenness," conduct prejudicial to good order and military discipline, and mistreatment of a private citizen. More serious charges were filed against two privates of the 44th regiment: cowardice and desertion. Both pleaded guilty. S. Pratt Kornegay, Company H, was sentenced to walk before his regiment for three days with a placard on his back labeling him a coward. Then, for 30 successive days, he had to walk a 50 foot circle, on alternate hours, from reveille to retreat, while carrying a thirty pound weight. The sentence of the court for convicted deserter James Smith was the same, with the added burden of fifty pounds and the forfeiture of pay for two months.[140]

As the winter wore on Law's Brigade regained its strength as men returned from leave, and a few recruits joined the ranks. A number of promotions were necessary to fill vacancies caused by death and resignations. From August 1, 1862 until February 28, 1863, seventy-eight officers were separated from their regiments. Two were dropped from the rolls, 53 were discharged, five died of disease, 12 died in action, and three died from wounds received in battle. Three officers transferred from the brigade.[141] During the same time frame, 208 men were promoted to higher positions, fifty-six of these were promotions from the ranks. As the brigade prepared for the spring campaign, there were many new faces in the regimental field and staff. In fact, only three field officers—Perry, 44th Alabama; Jackson, 47th Alabama; and Sheffield, 48th Alabama—counted themselves among the original officers who led their regiments from Alabama.

A full contingent of field officers were present in the 4th Alabama, all seasoned veterans of the previous year's fighting. Perry and Jones, both solid officers, were the only two field officers in the 44th Alabama. No field officers were on the rolls of the 15th Alabama, and the office of lieutenant colonel was still vacant. All three field officers were present in the 47th Alabama, Jackson and Campbell being veterans of the summer and fall campaigns while Bulger had participated in only one battle. Two field officers were present in the 48th Alabama, Colonel Sheffield and Major Hardwick, the least experienced of the brigade field officers.

Law faced a dilemma with the staff of the 15th Alabama. Cantey was in Alabama actively seeking a brigadier's commission. Lowther had been absent sick in Alabama since early December and he was not held in high regard by Law. He would not return until early spring. Law had yet to decide on a course of action to fill the lieutenant colonel's position. Though he was not the senior captain present, Oates was in command and showed excellent leadership qualities. Discipline was good, and Law apparently liked what he saw at 15th Alabama headquarters.

Law had reason to be concerned with the situation in the 47th Alabama. Though he always managed to be present when the regiment entered a fight, Jackson was frequently absent. He continued to suffer from serious health problems which had plagued his military career but the 47th Alabama had, under his leadership, matured into a good fighting unit. Bulger had been in only one engagement and had only recently returned from extended convalescent leave. Though he had little formal training in military tactics, Bulger led by example and exhibited considerable courage under fire. Law noticed that discipline in the regiment was somewhat lax. It was reported to him that men tended to straggle on marches, more so than in the other regiments of the brigade. Since Jackson was absent frequently, Law turned his attention to Campbell, whom he decided to observe closely in the months ahead.

The 48th Alabama was the real unknown. Sheffield had led the regiment in only one battle, Cedar Run, and only briefly then and had not yet proven himself a good disciplinarian and able field commander.[142] Alldredge was absent wounded and destined to resign before the spring was over. Hardwick was untried at field command, his experience limited to fighting at Cedar Run and Manassas.

In spite of apparent weaknesses in the command structure, Law's Brigade, in the spring of 1863, was a solid fighting unit. At age twenty-six, Law was one of Lee's youngest brigadiers. He was also recognized as one of Lee's most promising young generals, and if all went well in the campaigns of 1863 Law could reasonably expect to earn his major general's commission. 1863 promised to be a very good year for Law and his Alabama brigade.

Brigadier General Evander McIver Law

Courtesy Virginia Historical Society

42

**Colonel James Lawrence Sheffield,
48th Alabama**

*Courtesy Katherine M. Duncan and Larry Smith,
Duncan,* Marshall County, *51*

**Colonel Pinckney Downey Bowles,
4th Alabama**

Courtesy ADAH

**Lieutenant Mims Walker,
Aide-de-Camp, Law's Staff**

*Courtesy Gregg D. Gibbs
Austin, Texas*

**Colonel Egbert J. Jones,
4th Alabama**

Courtesy ADAH

**Colonel James Cantey,
15th Alabama**

Courtesy ADAH

**Sergeant William C. Hester,
Company E, 4th Alabama**

Courtesy USAMHI

**Lieutenant Colonel Owen Kenan
McLemore, 4th Alabama**

Courtesy ADAH

**Major William McKendre Robbins,
4th Alabama**

Courtesy ADAH

**Captain Nathaniel H. R. Dawson,
Company C, 4th Alabama**

Courtesy ADAH

**Sergeant John C. Dinson, Company B,
44th Alabama**

Courtesy USAMHI

**Adjutant Robert Thompson Coles,
4th Alabama**

Courtesy ADAH

**Captain Lewis Lindsay,
Company K, 4th Alabama**

Courtesy USAMHI

Chapter 3

The Siege of Suffolk

During the idle months before the expected spring campaign, Lee corresponded with Davis and Secretary of War James A. Seddon about possible moves of the Federal army.[1] Davis and Seddon felt confident of the line held by Lee along the Rappahannock, but worried about a Federal advance against Richmond by way of the Peninsula.[2] Lee received intelligence on February 14, 1863, that the Federal IX Corps was moving south to Newport News, Virginia with the ultimate destination of Suffolk.[3] This Federal troop transfer seemed to justify the fears of Davis and Seddon. To counter this move, which threatened the Confederate capital, Lee ordered Major General George E. Pickett to march his division to Richmond. He also ordered Hood to ready his division to follow Pickett, if necessary.

To allay the fears of President Davis and the War Department for the safety of the capital, Lee ordered Hood's Division to move on February 16 from Phillips Crossing to Hanover Junction, less than 15 miles from Richmond and at the juncture of the Richmond, Fredericksburg & Petersburg, and Virginia Central Railroads.[4] This would put Hood in position to reinforce Pickett if the Federals moved on Richmond or, in the event of an offensive against Lee, to hurry back to the Army of Northern Virginia.

Snow began to fall, as if on cue, when the order arrived for Law's Brigade to prepare to march, and temperatures plummeted during the night of February 16. The snowfall continued throughout the next day, coming down so heavily at times that it was difficult to see more than a hundred yards ahead. To make matters worse, a cold rain fell during the third day's march, turning the road into a knee deep combination of slush and mud.[5] This was the most severe march the Alabamians had made to date, for the brigade, like most Confederate units, was ill-equipped for marching in such weather.[6] They had left with three days' rations, which were gone in two. Another day's march in knee deep snow and mud was to be endured before food was available.[7] Weary men were forced to pile up brush and logs for crude beds to keep from sleeping on the ground.[8]

Seddon, however, believed a Federal offensive from the southeast posed a danger to Richmond and wanted both of Longstreet's divisions south of the capital.[9] Orders were changed and Hood's Division, including Law's command, marched beyond Hanover Junction, passing through Richmond on Saturday, February 21, and encamped south of the city alongside the Richmond and Petersburg Railroad. Ragged as they were, the veteran fighting men of Hood's Division gave the citizens of Richmond confidence in their own safety.[10] Despite their hardships the men were in high spirits, sure of their fighting ability. Richmond residents who lined the streets to witness the passage of the division were amazed at the vigor and spirit of soldiers who had marched from Fredericksburg in a snowstorm. One officer on the march believed the civilians pitied the troops marching past, but he felt sure the soldiers in their filthy uniforms cared nothing for the sympathy of non-combatants.[11] The lean and ragged soldiers were proud of their accomplishments and felt an intense esprit de corps which those outside their ranks could not understand.

Private James Daniel, 47th Alabama, suffered on the march as much as any soldier in his regiment. As they entered Richmond, Daniel was detailed at the rear of his regiment to push along stragglers. The first night in their camp near the city, Daniel was on guard duty all night in the heavy snowstorm. The next night, Daniel was ordered into Richmond to round up Alabamians who left camp for the comfort of the city. He walked through town in the deep slush looking for his missing companions. In a letter home, he complained that he nearly froze to death those three nights. He hoped they could be transferred to Savannah or any other place but Virginia.[12]

Despite the discomfort of the inclement weather, their new campsite near the railroad offered some diversion for the soldiers of Law's Brigade until they moved to Suffolk in April. Lieutenant Paul Turner Vaughan of the 4th Alabama recorded in his diary the practice of granting daily passes to two privates in every company and two officers from each of the five regiments. The camp's location on the railroad to Richmond provided free transportation to town. The closeness to Richmond was a strong temptation to some who went without authorization and, when caught, had to suffer the punishment of marking time.[13] As an officer, Vaughan perhaps felt constrained not to mention the raucous behavior of some soldiers while in Richmond. James Daniel felt no such restraint in his letters home, in which he described his fellow soldiers as wild men whose pursuit of whiskey and women was furious. He thought it would be better if they moved from the vicinity of Richmond.[14]

Vaughan noted the inflated prices of wartime in Richmond and saw many well-dressed officers, who, he was sure, had "never done any fighting nor seen any hard sacrifice." He also visited Drewry's Bluff, observing the fortifications there—impregnable, he felt—and got his first look at an ironclad ship.[15]

During another snowstorm, orders were issued in the early morning hours of March 18 to prepare to march in a half hour.[16] Within the hour, Hood's Division was on the turnpike back to Richmond. Most assumed their destination was Lee's army, a suspicion encouraged by newsboys who met the soldiers on the road to Richmond and gave accounts of the Federal crossing of the Rappahannock.[17] Near the city, the division paraded before Hood, who spoke to each brigade, telling them they were to meet the Federals who had crossed the river, and a severe march lay before them. Hood said he knew they had no breakfast but urged them to save their flour until they could cook it that night. The men gave him three cheers and the division marched through the streets of Richmond accompanied by the martial sounds of the drum and fife.[18] It was a forced march, witnessed by a diarist in the capital who wrote that "the division of Hood defiled through the streets, at a quick pace, marching back to Lee's army."[19]

While marching through the deep snow, a soldier in the 15th Alabama discharged his weapon, taking off one of his toes. The soldier claimed the amputation was accidental but Captain Frank Park reported to Oates his belief that it was deliberate. Oates sided with the captain, a physician from Orion, Alabama, and ordered Private O. J. Motes to march all day with the regiment before he reluctantly sent him to the hospital.[20] Park's accusation was suspect, as Motes returned from the hospital and faithfully performed his duties until severely wounded at Knoxville.[21]

Hood's Division was indeed bound for Lee's army but as the columns reached Ashland on March 18, after a twenty-four mile march in terrible conditions, Lee notified Longstreet that the crossing was only a cavalry raid and his division would not be needed after all.[22] The troops were ordered back to their camps below Richmond. It was bitterly cold and the snowfall of March 1863 was of record proportions.[23]

Law's Brigade bivouacked near Ashland the night of March 18, sleeping in the snow without tents. In groups of twos and threes, the men wrapped themselves in their blankets and slept under the snow, making little mounds from which small clouds of vapor would rise as they breathed.[24]

During the night, the large fires built in the camp were extinguished by snowfall and the Alabamians had difficulty reigniting them.[25] The men were exhausted on March 19 and were allowed to stay in camp all day to rest. They resumed the march toward Richmond the next day and many thought it the worst marching of the war.[26] Exhausted from plodding along nearly impassable roads, the Alabamians passed through Richmond again en route to camp south of the capital and crowds of civilians once more lined the streets to watch. This time, the perfectly dressed rear echelon soldiers with "bomb proof" government jobs irritated a private of the 4th Alabama who challenged one of them to a fist fight. Private Dump Sterling, after describing the well-dressed young man as a "bird," offered to catch him a "worm" if he would march with the column to the outskirts of town.[27] When the Alabamians reached their old camp, they found their camp equipment, with the exception of two tents, had been sent to the brigade depot in Richmond.[28] Friday night was the third consecutive night they slept in the snow.

To Fill the Commissary Wagons

The Confederate high command sent Longstreet to Richmond to join his detached divisions, numbering nearly 16,000 men. Besides the divisions of Hood and Pickett, Longstreet had Major General Samuel G. French's two-brigade division. The detached force also had two regiments of cavalry and four batteries of artillery. Longstreet's first independent command had two primary objectives: he was to protect the seat of government from attack from the south,[29] and to gather foodstuffs from the southside for shipment to Lee's ill-fed army on the Rappahannock.[30] Seddon wished Longstreet to take on yet another task: the capture of the Federal garrison at Suffolk.[31] This idea was much discussed by Seddon, Longstreet and Lee in March and April. In the end, it was Longstreet's decision that the gain did not warrant the cost.[32] Without a doubt he would have preferred destroying the Federal force at Suffolk, but he did not believe he had sufficient numbers and was unable to obtain reinforcements. Longstreet made a demonstration against Suffolk of sufficient strength to hold the Federal garrison immobile while the bountiful foodstuffs of southeastern Virginia and North Carolina were gathered for shipment to Lee's army. This was not a true siege, however, since the Federal commander at Suffolk had two railroads connecting Norfolk and Suffolk, giving him open lines of communications and reinforcements upon call. By mid-April Longstreet's command would grow to encompass the area from Richmond to the Cape Fear River. This included the Department of Richmond, under command of Brigadier General Arnold Elzey; the Department of Southern Virginia, commanded by French; and Major General Harvey Hill's Department of North Carolina, eventually reaching a total of 40,000 men.[33]

During April, Longstreet pushed the Federals into the works at Suffolk and held them there while his trains were filled with provisions by the First Corps commissary officers. Law's Alabamians left their camp on the railroad near Richmond on April 2, as part of Longstreet's besieging force, making camp three miles south of Petersburg on April 4.[34] The march to Suffolk was resumed on April 8, this leg on the Jerusalem Plank Road, which made for good marching.[35]

Law went back to Richmond on April 4 to bring his new bride to the camp south of Petersburg. She had joined him at Richmond only hours before orders came to march to Petersburg. Law had married Jane Elizabeth Latta in Columbia, South Carolina, less than a month before on March 9, 1863.[36] Known as Jennie, Law's new bride was the nineteen-year-old daughter of William A. Latta, a wealthy merchant and planter from York County.[37] He was obviously much in love, telling his officers of the virtues of wedded life and advising them to marry as soon as possible.[38] Even before Law's officers met his young wife, they knew of her because Law wrote to her often and had shown her picture to several of them.[39] As Law's fiancee, Jennie had come to Virginia in 1861 with her mother to nurse Law back to health after the wound he received at First Manassas.

Even though Longstreet had by then decided not to attempt to attack the Federal fortifications at Suffolk, one of the rumors in camp was that such an assault was planned. "It is supposed that our intention is to attack the Federal force now at Suffolk," was how Vaughan saw it on April 9.[40] Mims Walker, of the 4th Alabama, reported in a letter home on April 4 that some said they would transfer to Tennessee. Walker wished the military authorities would let the veterans in Hood's Division replace the garrison troops in and around Petersburg, a town he found more to his liking than Richmond, with its "spirit of speculation." He knew it was only a dream, however, for he believed Hood's men would always be posted near the enemy. Walker attributed this to Hood's ambition to become a lieutenant general.[41]

At the Blackwater River, named for the dark coloring imparted to the water by the juniper trees growing in that swampy area, the 4th Alabama halted to bivouac near where a group of slaves from a nearby plantation were seining the river for mullet.[42] Lieutenant Colonel Scruggs paid the superintendent of the work party ten dollars to catch a load of the fish for the regiment. According to Lieutenant Robert Coles, adjutant of the 4th, "fresh fish was quite a treat to us, [and] the men remained up late in the night cooking and eating fish."[43]

Law's Brigade was within three miles of Suffolk by the night of April 11. The men were issued ammunition and it was expected that they would be in battle the next day. The morning of the 11th was bright and clear and Vaughan, anticipating combat at any moment, knelt with Thomas K. Beatty to pray that they would be spared in the expected fighting. He asked, too, for more prayer and less profanity from the soldiers. Vaughan was impressed that the enlisted men, perhaps only minutes away from an assault against the Federal fortifications, were "as careless as if nothing of importance was on hand."[44]

Located about 20 miles east of the Blackwater River, Suffolk was a sleepy Southern town at the head of the Nansemond River. Federal troops captured and heavily fortified the town in 1862. By 1863, the town was ringed by Federal forts and artillery batteries. The Nansemond River flowed north until a tributary known as the Western Branch flowed into it, widening the stream considerably on its way to Hampton Roads.

By nightfall of April 12, Law's men were pressing against the Federal fortifications at Suffolk. Longstreet approached Suffolk by the South Quay Road. Hood's Division was in the lead, taking up position on the Confederate left, from near Suffolk to the Western Branch. French held the center of the line, in front of the town, while Pickett held the segment from Suffolk to the Dismal Swamp south of town. The Alabamians had patrolled the roads in their sector west of Suffolk right to the town, capturing a few prisoners, until they reached the cleared area in front of a Federal battery, positioned on an elevation behind a water mill.[45] This was probably Battery Rosecrans with its guns overlooking Savage's Mill Pond and the clearing west of the pond. They held this position under the fire of the battery behind the mill until April 15, when they were moved north of Suffolk,

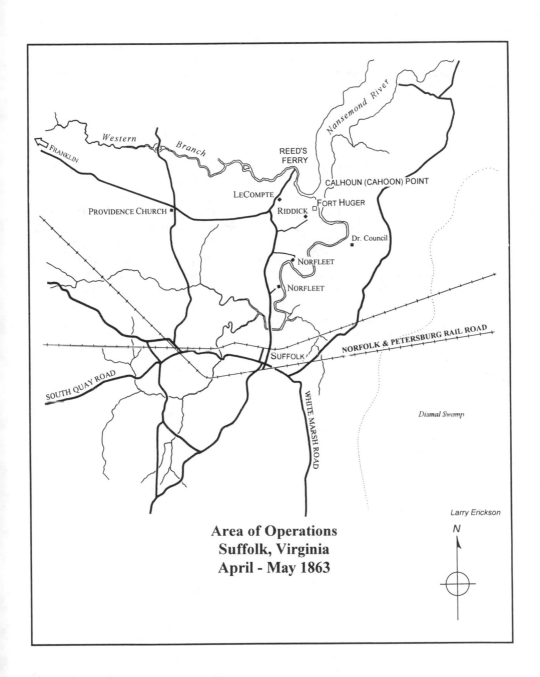

**Area of Operations
Suffolk, Virginia
April - May 1863**

Larry Erickson

N

replacing Brigadier General Tige Anderson's Georgia brigade along the river.[46]

Duty on the Nansemond

Hood's Division took up positions along the Nansemond River with its lines facing east from the left bank of the river, north from the right bank of the Western Branch and south into Suffolk. Law's Brigade went to work constructing fortifications along their lines, building an impressive line of breastworks in a stand of pine trees on the left bank of the Nansemond.[47]

Along the upper Nansemond, the Confederates began constructing earthworks to secure their exposed left flank. Even before crossing the Blackwater, Longstreet had requested aid from the navy to provide additional firepower for his left wing, asking for vessels that were able to pass the Confederate obstructions blocking the James River.[48] The secretary of the navy suggested the ironclad gunboat *Richmond* be used, but naval engineers informed him his plan was unworkable.[49]

In addition to newly constructed works, Longstreet had the use of old Fort Huger, a redoubt built in 1861 at Hill's Point by the Confederates when they occupied Suffolk. The earthwork was named for Brigadier General Benjamin Huger, then commander at Norfolk. Fort Huger was constructed to command the Nansemond and its Western Branch where they converged, seven miles north of Suffolk by the narrow Upper Nansemond, about four-and-a-half miles by road.[50] Its gun embrasures were separated by earthen traverses which restricted the guns' field of fire so only one gun could fire directly across the Upper Nansemond.[51] This narrow field of fire would prove an embarrassment to the Confederates in only a few days. Lee suggested Longstreet use Fort Huger to control the navigation on the river. Lee offered advice, but did not send the additional troops requested by Longstreet.[52]

Law's Alabamians spent most of April in the newly constructed fortifications around Suffolk under constant artillery and rifle fire. The entry for the Suffolk campaign in the Record of Events for Company A, 4th Alabama read, "Since our arrival here we have been detailed on picket doing constant duty in the trenches."[53] Thus, the Alabamians were introduced to trench warfare, an experience they would come to know well in the summer of 1864 when they went into the trenches at besieged Petersburg. Although cooking camps and headquarters were behind the fortifications and out of range of the Federal batteries, the regimental camps remained within gun range and picket duty along the river meant nearly constant exposure to sharpshooters on the opposite bank. Most activities took place in the darkness of night. The Alabama soldiers did fatigue duty such as building breastworks or cooking at night, as well as the posting of pickets. During the daylight hours, only sharpshooters moved about as everyone else stayed in the works, whether it was hot or cold, wet or dry. According to Private James Daniel, 47th Alabama, life in the trenches or "ditches," as he called them, was "enough to kill a mule and it will kill us all if we stay here much longer."[54]

A resident of Spotsylvania County, Virginia, John McCalley frequently visited his son Bolivar, of Company I, at the camp of the 4th Alabama. He always brought plenty of good food, which made him very popular with Bolivar's friends and messmates. On his last visit the gentleman slept in Colonel Scruggs's tent to wait for Bolivar to complete his duty on the river. Scruggs warned him about the nightly shelling from the Federal batteries across the river, but McCalley assured him that, after dropping off to sleep, his rest would be unaffected. Soon a Federal barrage sent shell fragments through the camp, sending the frightened McCalley hurrying back to the safety of the cooking camps. In the morning, a servant bringing breakfast to the regiment also brought a message from McCalley that if his son wanted to see him, he was at the cooking camps out of range of the guns.[55]

Members of the 4th Alabama found the field works offered more than protection from enemy fire, the pine abatis in front often serving as soft bedding on the cool spring nights. When the Federal artillerists completed their nightly cannonade, shortly after taps, the Alabama soldiers, except those on picket duty, would climb over the breastworks and go to sleep. For added comfort, Scruggs one night slept on bundles of hay that he had obtained for his horse. A stray horse from a nearby artillery battery came over and began to eat the bed from under the lieutenant colonel. The hungry animal persisted even when Scruggs drove him away several times. To rid himself of the horse and get some sleep, Scruggs tied some of the fodder to the horse's tail and set fire to it. The horse bolted through the ranks of sleeping men, causing a commotion and alerting the Federal artillerymen on the right bank. They opened fire upon the Alabamians, driving them into the works. When the Alabamians learned no one was injured by the cannon fire, they enjoyed a good laugh over the incident.[56]

When confronted by Longstreet, the Federal commander at Suffolk asked the U.S. Navy to help defend the town. Major General John Peck, West Point graduate of the storied class of 1843, was an early Lincoln appointee. He wanted gunboats sent up the Nansemond, or at least to the Western Branch, because he feared Longstreet could get between his garrison at Suffolk and Norfolk if the Confederates controlled the river. As long as Peck held the river, Longstreet could not establish a true siege.[57]

Admiral Samuel P. Lee, commanding the North Atlantic Blockading Squadron, telegraphed within hours that three gunboats were already on the scene with Peck's two army boats, but if the army command expected these vessels to prevent a crossing by the Confederates, they would be disappointed. Although Admiral Lee ordered navy Lieutenant William B. Cushing to move his vessel to the confluence of the Nansemond and the Western Branch as additional help. April 11 began an uneasy relationship between the army and navy commands which continued even after the siege.[58]

The next day, April 12, the navy found itself playing a greater role than Admiral Lee desired. Peck transferred his artillery from the right bank of the Upper Nansemond to his southern defense line in order to oppose an advance up the Somerton and Whitemarsh roads by Pickett. The defense of the right flank was entrusted to the navy gunboats and three companies of the 13th New Hampshire.[59]

For this defense, the navy had four vessels that could operate above the sandbar at the juncture of the Nansemond and its western branch. These were: the 500-ton side wheel *Mount Washington,* commanded by Lieutenant Roswell H. Lamson; the *Stepping Stones* a stern-wheel ferryboat and, with a draft of four feet, the only navy vessel which could cross the bar at low tide, commanded by Acting Captain T. A. Harris; and two armed tugs, the *Alert* and the *Cohasset.* The army patrolled the same stretch of water with two armed steamers, the *West End* and the *Smith Briggs.* Admiral Lee was not pleased with the responsibility of defending the river against a Confederate crossing, and wrote Lieutenants Cushing and Lamson on April 13 that if the Southerners wanted to cross over, Peck would "find these little improvised gunboats a very insufficient defense for his rear."[60]

On the evening of April 13, Lamson transported Major General Erasmus Darwin Keyes down river from Suffolk on the *Mount Washington,* escorted by the *Alert* and the *Stepping Stones* sustaining casualties of one killed and one wounded from Hood's rifle fire. At daylight the next day, Lamson attempted to return with the *Mount Washington,* the *Stepping Stones* and the army's *West End* commanded by Lieutenant Frederick A. Rowe of the 99th New York.[61]

Hood's Confederates surprised Lamson at Norfleet's Point when they rolled out of the woods seven pieces of artillery and opened a very accurate fire upon his flotilla. The first shot from a 20-pounder rifle went through the boiler of the *Mount Washington,* putting her adrift and then aground. The *West End* was soon aground also, leaving the *Stepping Stones* to tow the disabled vessels to safety. Moving down river, the *Mount Washington,* harassed by Confederate fire, again ran aground on the sand bar at the confluence of the Nansemond and its western branch. Here it was engaged by more Confederate cannon, totaling, by Lamson's count, ten guns, with "six planted in a strong earthwork on Hill's Point, and four in the woods to the right, throwing a cross fire into our vessels."[62] The heavy Southern fire shot away the flagstaff mounted on the stern of the vessel. Lamson, Master Mate James Birtwistle and Seaman Henry Thielberg sprinted through the heavy fire, pulled the flag from the river and secured the pole so the flag was again flying in the wind. This heroic act produced three cheers from the Confederates on the left bank, who then ceased their fire and allowed Lamson to tow the stranded vessel unmolested.[63] The engagement lasted five and a half hours, and the *Mount Washington* would probably have been destroyed if the *Commodore Barney* had not brought her guns to bear upon the land batteries.[64]

In his report to Admiral Lee, Lamson declared the *Mount Washington,* "so completely riddled in hull and machinery" that he could not accurately assess the damage. Naval casualties on April 14 were four killed, thirteen wounded, and one missing.[65] Lamson's flotilla found the Confederate guns to be an effective deterrent to gunboats. The Confederate batteries cut communications on the Upper Nansemond, caused severe damage to the *Mount Washington,* and inflicted numerous casualties on the small naval presence on the river. The U.S. Navy found that it either had to reestablish its communications, or leave the upper reaches of the Nansemond between Suffolk and the Western Branch in Confederate control.

Contentious Confederates

The same day Longstreet assigned command of all the artillery "serving with his forces at Suffolk" to French.[66] Even though Longstreet did not bring his First Corps artillerymen with him to Suffolk, French believed the assignment was part of Longstreet's plan to give French's two brigade division to his protégé, Brigadier General Micah Jenkins. But, French, believing Longstreet had assigned the artillery to him with an ulterior motive, reassigned most of the batteries to Hood's and Pickett's artillery chiefs.[67] Whether French distributed his "Special Order No. 2" outside of his own command is not known, but Longstreet, Pickett, and Hood were unaware of French's presumptuous reassignment.[68]

French requested headquarters send three companies of infantry to him as support for a battery of 30-pounders, placed in pits approximately two-thirds of a mile west of Fort Huger and commanded by Captain David L. Smoot of the Alexandria Light Artillery, Virginia Artillery.[69] Major G. Moxley Sorrel, Longstreet's assistant adjutant general, sent French a note the evening of April 17 with word that Longstreet had given him the largest regiment in the army as infantry support, the unbrigaded 55th North Carolina Regiment, commanded by Colonel John K. Connally.[70] Thinking French might believe he was to take only three companies of the 55th North Carolina as his infantry support, Longstreet wrote a clarifying note later that night telling French he should have Connally's entire regiment to protect the artillery.[71] Longstreet understood French needed infantry to support several batteries of artillery. Longstreet never questioned why French requested only three companies of infantry to support at least nine batteries of artillery. French, in his turn, did not reveal to Longstreet that he intended to support only Smoot's battery of 30-pounders placed in their pits west of Fort Huger. It must have been obvious to French that Longstreet did not know he had taken upon himself the authority to dispose of the several batteries which had been assigned to him, yet he did not bring the misunderstanding to his commanding general's attention. French wrote in his autobiography that he was justified in reassigning the artillery to Hood's and Pickett's Divisions because Longstreet did not assign the guns to him in the proper military fashion.

On April 15, Law's Brigade moved to the left three or four miles to relieve Anderson's Brigade, taking position along the Upper Nansemond from the area of Norfleet's Landing to Fort Huger. One of the skirmishers of the 15th Alabama was killed by Federal shelling during the day's movement. Private Eugene B. Woodham of Company C threw himself to the ground to avoid the artillery barrage but died when a shell hit close in front of him and exploded under him, literally tearing him to pieces.[72]

Hood ordered the Alabama brigade to replace the Georgians because of his disapproval of the way Anderson's men had conducted operations on Tuesday, April 14. Anderson's Brigade was assigned fatigue duty constructing artillery positions, and the work details suffered constant shelling while they worked the night of April 13.[73] At daylight, the Georgians engaged the Federal gunboats before withdrawing from the river. A typical Confederate spat, this affair included a Georgia captain who demanded a court of inquiry into his conduct, while Hood threatened to arrest Anderson over the latter's remarks about the incident and Anderson attempted to move his command to another division. The Georgians were transferred from their place on the river amid the taunts of the Alabamians, who took their place.[74]

The U.S. Navy Engages the Alabamians

When Captain Robert M. Stribling replaced one of Hood's batteries at the redoubt with his "Fauquier Artillery" at 11 p.m. on April 16, the infantry occupying Fort Huger were Alabamians of Law's Brigade. Major Thomas Coleman of the 4th Alabama was in the old fort with a detachment of infantry when Stribling arrived.[75]

At the same hour that Stribling was placing his battery in Fort Huger, Lamson was taking 200 troops on board the USS *Stepping Stones,* to launch an attack against the earthen fort. That afternoon, Lamson had suggested the plan to Brigadier General George Washington Getty, division commander recently transferred to reinforce Peck at Suffolk. The plan was for the infantry to be landed above the fort, capture the garrison, and depart again on the *Stepping Stones* before reinforcements could reach the secessionists. Lamson believed the Confederate reserves were "several miles distant" from the fort.[76]

The landing went off without a hitch but the Federal infantry marched only a short distance before they met Coleman's 4th Alabama pickets, who immediately sounded the alarm. The landing party fired off two rockets to signal the *Stepping Stones* to pick them up and take them back to the right bank. Their departure was so rapid that skirmishers of the 4th Alabama could find no enemy when they advanced upriver a few minutes later.[77]

Coleman was under orders to report to Law any attempt by the Federals to cross the river but had no courier. Captain Stribling volunteered his sergeant because he had a horse. The sergeant reported the crossing and returned with word that a supporting regiment was in the nearby woods, three-quarters of a mile away, should it be needed.[78] This aborted assault against the fort did not excite the attention of the Southern command.

Adjutant Coles recalled the event from the Confederate point of view, repeating the report of Lieutenant Dan Turner of Company I, 4th Alabama, who commanded the pickets along the river. When the landing party moved toward the artillery battery, they encountered Turner and several pickets. Turner knew his small force could not stop the landing party, so he shouted orders to bring forward two more regiments, as if support was near. With the withdrawal of the Federal infantry, Turner believed his ploy had been successful.[79] Considering the rapid departure of the raiding party, it is difficult to argue otherwise.

On the morning tide of April 17, Cushing attempted to run past Fort Huger with the vessels *Teaser, Alert,* and *Coeur de Lion.* Both the *Teaser* and *Coeur de Lion* grounded. The *Teaser,* previously a tender to the CSS *Virginia* before being captured by the Federal navy, was gotten off easily, but the *Coeur de Lion* took some hours to move back down river.[80] During this time the guns in Fort Huger could not fire upon the *Coeur de Lion* because the embrasures, cut the night before, were too narrow.[81]

Lieutenants Cushing and Lamson blamed the failure to capture the redoubt the night of April 16 on the army's lack of effort, believing they had been driven away too easily.[82] On April 18 Lamson met with Getty again to propose another attempt that night to silence the battery at Hill's Point. The two then met with Peck for his approval of the plan which, after some discussion, was modified to include the landing of four howitzers with the infantry and the addition of covering fire from the other naval vessels. The Federal infantry was too slow arriving, and Lamson postponed the attack because he did not want to assault the fort in daylight.[83]

The Fall of Fort Huger

The disposition of Confederate troops on the left bank of the Nansemond on April 19 is only partially known. Inside Fort Huger with Stribling's artillery were Companies A and B of the 44th Alabama Regiment under command of Captain David L. Bozeman, leading a force of five officers and 67 men.[84] The Alabamians had used the fort as a platform for sharpshooting the gunboats and Federal soldiers on the opposite bank since their arrival at the river on April 15.

At Norfleet's Landing, upriver of the old fort, was Captain W. D. Bradford's battery of four 12-pounders.[85] Between Fort Huger and Norfleet's Landing, infantry was positioned to harass the enemy's vessels. Some of these men had been detailed to rifle pits by Captain John Cussons of Law's staff. Cussons claimed the soldiers were as secure in their holes "as prairie dogs."[86]

Sometimes called "Law's Wild Man" or "Hood's Indian," Cussons was an Englishman who had immigrated to the United States as a youth and lived with a western Indian tribe before becoming editor of the Selma *Reporter.*[87] A big man with long hair that he wore in the style of Buffalo Bill Cody, Cussons possessed a thorough disregard for danger. While a lieutenant in the 4th Alabama, he served as chief of scouts in Whiting's division in 1862 before joining Law's staff as captain and aide-de-camp. Law wrote after the war that Cussons was an "experienced frontiersman whose skill and nerve were equal to any emergency." He believed the Englishman was "one of the most daring and successful scouts in our army."[88] His deeds as a scout became legend among the Alabama troops.

At about 10 a.m. on Sunday, April 19, artillery fire was exchanged between Smoot's battery and Federal gunboats below Hill's Point.[89] The gunboats above the point, along with the Federal batteries on Cahoon's Point, opened against Fort Huger by 1 p.m. and a heavy cannonade continued until about 4 p.m.[90] Stribling's artillerymen waited patiently for their opportunity to return fire until a Federal gunboat ran into their line of fire as it attempted to steam past the fort.

The infantry kept their heads down during the cannonading from the Federal batteries and the constant sniper fire from the opposite bank. While the 4th Alabama was on duty at the fort on April 17, Sergeant James H. Hunter, Company B, was wounded by a shell fragment, and Private John F. Barker of Company A was shot by a sharpshooter. Vaughan commanded the two companies of the 4th Alabama before the relief of the 44th Alabama. While in the fort he and his men stayed under a bombproof made from a dirt-covered plank laid over a pit.[91] It was this danger that had prompted Stribling's order, upon his entry into the fort, to keep the men under cover as much as possible.[92]

Bozeman's small force had been at the earthen fort since relieving Companies A and B of the 4th Alabama at 8 p.m. on April 18. The men of the 44th Alabama at first took up positions as pickets around the fort. Had Lamson's aborted attack been launched on that night, the detachment of Alabama infantry would likely have given the Federal landing party a warm reception. On April 19, however, Companies A and B were moved into the fort.[93] Either from negligence or from a misunderstanding of responsibilities, Bozeman posted no pickets outside Fort Huger. Perhaps Bozeman, a twenty-nine-year-old citizen soldier, felt no need of pickets since the Federals had been driven into Suffolk and the lines were separated by the Nansemond River. Why risk injury to his men for no reason? After all, it was the Federals who were besieged, was it not?

The fierceness of the artillery barrage prompted Longstreet to write a note to French asking that he be told the "result of the furious cannonade now going on as soon as you learn." "Have you the regiment of infantry so placed," Longstreet continued, "as to support the batteries in time should the enemy attempt to land an infantry force against them?"[94] He was unaware that French at that moment considered the infantry support for the artillery in Fort Huger to be Hood's responsibility.

French's reaction to the note from his commanding general was immediate. He sent both a note and a courier to position the 55th North Carolina as Longstreet desired. In his note, French used almost the same words as Longstreet had used to him. "Let me know what the result of the heavy cannonade now going on." French then instructed his artillery chief, Major L. M. Shumaker, to show the message to Connally and order him to place his regiment to protect the batteries.[95] "They had better move down," French suggested of the North Carolinians, "near the battery of Stribling," belatedly ordering the placement of the infantry in the proper position. Incredibly, this note did not reach Shumaker until 8 p.m., well after the old fort had fallen.[96]

To ensure his instructions got through to Connally, French also sent Colonel George A. Cunningham of his staff to talk with the colonel of the North Carolina regiment. Although there is disagreement among the participants as to time, Cunningham did deliver French's message to Connally. Cunningham reported trying to give Connally French's message before noon but was unable to actually do so until 4 p.m. Connally reported receiving French's order to support Stribling, through Cunningham, some time between 4 and 6 p.m. Connally sent Lieutenant Colonel Maurice T. Smith and Major Alfred H. Belo to find the battery and determine the proper troop deployment. The fort was captured before they returned, loud cheering signaling the Federal success.[97]

Early in the morning of April 19, on the right side of the river, Federal officers studied Fort Huger from the vantage point of a tree and discussed ways to silence its guns. Getty, with his adjutant, Captain Hazard Stevens, met with Lamson to plan yet another attempt to open river communications past the old fort. Stevens and Lamson decided, while up in the tree observing the Confederate positions, to suggest to Getty a daylight attack against the fort on Hill's Point. Getty approved the plan, and decided to assault the fort that very evening.[98]

Lamson's plan, altered by Stevens' suggestion to attack during daylight hours, called for 500 men to board the *Stepping Stones* for the landing against Fort Huger, but only 130 soldiers of the 8th Connecticut and 140 men of the 89th New York actually went aboard the vessel at Doctor Council's Landing.[99] These were veteran regiments whose men had seen action at Sharpsburg and Fredericksburg.

Near 6 p.m. Lamson sounded his steam whistle as the signal to begin a covering fire from the gunboats on the river and the two Federal batteries on Cahoon Point. The *Stepping Stones* steamed downriver as if to run past the fort as before but just above the fort, she again sounded her whistle to halt the supporting fire and ran under the bluff 200 to 300 yards above the fort. With cheers from their audience aboard the boats and in the batteries, the landing party, led by Adjutant Stevens, who leaped first into the waist-deep water, rushed the Confederate battery. No time was wasted in forming the men into lines but orders were given to charge the works immediately upon landing.[100]

"The rebel works," Lamson reported to his admiral, "consisted of two lines with an impassable ravine between." The landing party quickly carried the first line which allowed the 89th New York to run protected through the ravine to gain the rear of the garrison and cut off a Confederate retreat.[101]

Lamson's howitzer battery fired directly into the unprotected rear of the redoubt from the ravine's edge.[102] In response, Stribling's artillerymen turned two guns against the assault party, and the Alabama infantry opened fire, stopping the Federals momentarily. Stribling reported that the Federals had flanked him on both sides and even climbed the parapets on the river front of Fort Huger.[103] The capture was quickly accomplished. Lamson accepted Stribling's sword, making good his boast to capture the battery which had disabled the *Mount Washington*.[104] Years later, Lamson returned his prized trophy to its original owner with a letter in which he praised Stribling's courage during his defense of the earthworks at Hill's Point.[105]

To their credit, the surprised soldiers of the 44th Alabama did inflict damage on the landing party. Getty's report noted the Alabamians "opened a hot fire of musketry" which resulted in four Federals killed and ten wounded.[106] Even though no pickets were posted, Lamson's report indicates some of the men of the 44th Alabama were outside the bombproofs by the time the Federals reached the rear of the redoubt. Perhaps they had emerged after the Federal barrage had lifted to allow the *Stepping Stones* to disembark the landing party, or they may have been alerted to the presence of the enemy by the Federal cheers. They quickly retreated into the fort but felled some of the charging Federals first, getting off at least one volley.[107] In spite of the howitzer fire directly into the rear of the fort and the rifle fire of the Federal infantry, no Confederates were injured.

After surrendering by squads, the captured Confederates, along with the Federal wounded, were loaded aboard the *Stepping Stones* by 9 p.m. and taken across the river to Doctor Council's Landing, where they were replaced with reinforcements and more artillery for the Federal occupation of Fort Huger.[108] Left in the bombproof was the body of a soldier of Company B, 44th Alabama. Private Reuben C. Harkey was killed in action on April 19, though not by members of the Federal landing party.[109] Stevens and a member of the *Stepping Stones* crew, both observed the body of the twenty-nine-year-old Trion, Alabama, farmer lying on the earthen floor of the dugout inside the fort. Stevens noted he had been dead for some time, though he did not know if the cause of death was from previous hostile action or, as was rumored among the Federals, at the hands of a Confederate officer.[110] No evidence can be found to substantiate Stevens's suggestion that Harkey died from any but honorable causes.

One hundred thirty captured Confederates were transported across the Nansemond

River. Stribling's command lost 59 to the raid while 71 members of the 44th Alabama were captured. Companies A and B lost five officers and 66 enlisted men to the Federal raid against Fort Huger.

Lieutenant Colonel John Jones, commander of the 44th Alabama, submitted a report which gave the total of 71.[111] A thorough examination of the Compiled Service Records in the National Archives and Historical Muster Rolls in the Alabama Department of Archives and History yields a total of 72, including Harkey. Jones did not count Harkey because his list was of the captured Alabamians removed from the redoubt.[112]

At the moment the Confederate earthwork fell to Getty's landing party, Cussons was the ranking officer along the river bank. He had supervised the placement of Law's infantry in rifle pits about half a mile upriver of Fort Huger to "make it disagreeable for passing gunboats."[113] With the capture of the fort he rode for Law's headquarters, two miles away.[114] About halfway there, Cussons found a Confederate regiment and decided to use it to recover the fort. Leigh Richmond Terrell, also on Law's staff, joined Cussons at this point, having ridden ahead of the two companies of the 48th Alabama he was taking to the redoubt as relief. Terrell found Connally near the Riddick house, but Cussons did not wait on protocol before ordering a regiment unknown to him to charge the captured fort. He did not get the response he wanted. "I then learned," Cussons wrote after the war, "that the colonel and major of the regiment were absent, and that the company officers were asking each other who Terrell and myself were, and by what authority we were acting." The captains of the 55th North Carolina decided the Alabamians did not possess sufficient authority and refused their orders. Cussons then returned to the river to withdraw his flanked riflemen from their holes.[115]

Connally and Terrell discussed the situation. According to Connally, the young Alabamian, familiar with the ground, told him it was impossible for the seven companies of the 55th North Carolina on the scene to retake the fort because the Federal batteries and gunboats played upon the open ground before the redoubt.[116]

In an interview with the Petersburg *Daily Express*, Stribling's sergeant, Daniel Murray Mason, a native of Fauquier County, Virginia, detailed the itinerary of the captured enlisted men after they were floated across the river Sunday night. Marching on the edge of the Dismal Swamp, they took a "circuitous route" from Doctor Council's Landing to Suffolk, where they were locked in the city jail until their parole on the night of April 20. In the Suffolk square, the captives and their guards were met by a crowd of young women "who waved their handkerchiefs and flats most enthusiastically." This elicited a rousing cheer from the captured secessionists. The women persisted with their waving even after a Federal officer ordered the ladies to stop "their rebel demonstrations," and the soldiers from Virginia and Alabama let loose another cheer. Inspired by this Southern patriotism, the author of the piece declared Suffolk women were "overpowered but not subdued."[117]

On Monday night, April 20, the prisoners were loaded onto a transport and sent to Hampton Roads. By nine in the morning on April 22 they reached City Point and off–loaded under a flag of truce. Mason reported the food the captive Confederates received while in enemy hands was "the best their commissary could afford," and good food was certainly something a Confederate could appreciate.[118] The whole affair turned out to be a lark for the defenders of Fort Huger. Meanwhile, captured officers of the 44th Alabama and Stribling's battery were sent to Fort Delaware, paroled on April 25, and exchanged at City Point on May 5.[119]

The situation at Hill's Point remained quiet through the night of April 19. The Federals reinforced and entrenched, anticipating an attack the next morning while the Confederates defended their line against further intrusion.

At 1 a.m., Law arrived on the scene, and reported the landing to Hood, who sent the news to Longstreet.[120] After learning of the fort's capture, Law probably feared, at least for a time during the night of April 19, a general attack. Law decided against trying to retake the fort immediately, feeling that it was his responsibility to hold the line along the river against a crossing. He sent a courier to French's headquarters with word that none of his brigade could be taken off the line to retake the fort.[121] Whether he thought it a good idea to make the attempt at all is not known. He may have believed, as French did, that the Federal position, isolated on the point, was untenable.[122] Law's prudence, approved by both Hood and French, proved to be the right course, for the Federal force evacuated the fort in less than twenty-four hours.

Just before retiring for the night on April 19, the rest of the Alabama brigade was ordered to assemble and told of the capture of the fort. They took up positions behind the earthworks in anticipation of a Federal advance. Hood's Texas brigade commanded by Brigadier General Jerome Bonaparte Robertson was moved over from their position on the Western Branch as well.[123]

Vaughan was chagrined at the capture of his fellow Alabamians but noted his respect for the enemy in his diary entry of the 20th, declaring "it was a brilliant affair."[124] Perhaps Vaughan was impressed because, had he remained in the redoubt at Hill's Point, he would have been a prisoner himself. After the casualties in his company, Vaughan and his men had also moved into the bombproof.

As brilliant as it seemed to Vaughan, the assault against Fort Huger should not have succeeded. Stevens, the first member of the Federal landing party to jump from the *Stepping Stones,* believed the landing was successful because there was no supporting infantry near the earthen fort. "If a regiment had been posted near the fort in support," Stevens declared, "the attack would probably have failed, and in that event few of the assailants could have escaped."[125] With pickets placed and infantry in support of the battery, the capture of Fort Huger would probably have been a failure, known not as the capture of Stribling's battery but as the capture of the USS *Stepping Stones.*

After evaluating his isolated position on the left bank, Peck decided to evacuate his troops from the isolated fort. By silencing the guns and reopening the navy's communications, the general felt the army had accomplished its mission. To hold the old fort against any serious effort by the Confederates to retake it would have been costly, if not impossible.[126] But the abandonment of Hill's Point and the loss of their river communications a second time was too much for the naval authorities to accept, and as a result, all the navy's gunboats were ordered out of the upper reaches of the Nansemond River. The army and navy exchanged several angry notes on the subject. The navy stayed out of the upper reaches of the river until ordered back by the assistant secretary of the navy after he had received complaints from the army.[127]

The Confederate command had ample opportunity to thwart the Federal plan to capture Stribling's battery. Four to five hours before the assault against the earthworks, Law and Shumaker discussed enemy movements that suggested the landing of troops against the Confederate lines. But no warnings were issued, nor were troop deployments made to counter a Federal landing.

About one o'clock in the afternoon of April 19, Shumaker was at Morel's house on the Reed's Ferry Road. He had just been relieved by Colonel George A. Cunningham after supervising the installation of Smoot's two 30-pounder Parrott guns in their pits about two-thirds of a mile west of Fort Huger. At Moore's house, Shumaker received reports from Major Francis J. Boggs and Captain Martin. Martin's battery of the 12th Virginia Battalion had just been relieved at Norfleet's Landing. Martin told French's artillery chief that he had seen a Federal regiment, if not more, moving downriver the previous afternoon. Boggs reported the Federal gunboats above Fort Huger had moved farther upriver earlier in the day and their decks were crowded with infantry. These reports seemed to Shumaker to have some importance, so when Law arrived at Moore's, Shumaker repeated the reports to the general.[128]

What Law thought of this message is unknown, as are any actions he took in response to it. After the Federal attempt to capture the fort on the night of April 16, this later intelligence should have increased the vigilance of the Confederates but did not. Ironically, the report of an attempted assault against the fort on April 16 may have caused Law to discount the reports of the afternoon of April 19 because the report of the earlier landing was not believed in the Confederate camp. Like the story of the boy who cried wolf, the first report discredited the second. Adjutant Coles joked with Turner that he had been hallucinating when he thought he saw Yankees on the left bank.[129] Henry Stokes Figures, of the 48th Alabama, wrote home on April 17 that the regiment had been awakened early in the morning because of a report from the 4th Alabama that Federals had landed but that it was a mistake.[130]

Longstreet put the blame for the capture of Fort Huger on the infantry in the fort. Upon hearing of the fall of the fort, he wrote French with instructions to learn the facts of the matter and "apply a remedy" to prevent its happening again. Longstreet made clear who he faulted for the loss, when he wrote "I fear that our infantry has not been doing its duty properly."[131]

Longstreet wrote to French because he thought the infantry in the fort was under French's command, namely, the 55th North Carolina. On April 22, Sorrel chastised French in a note with the remark that Longstreet had assigned him the "artillery, and particularly the river defenses" because Longstreet believed French was able "to select positions for batteries and to assign proper infantry supports for their protection." Sorrel added that Longstreet had not worried about the protection of the artillery since he had given French the entire 55th North Carolina instead of only three regiments as French had requested. Sorrel then clearly stated that French had led Longstreet to believe he had placed three companies of the 55th North Carolina in the fort prior to the attack by the Federal amphibious operation.[132] French answered the criticism by claiming he was not responsible for the support of Stribling's battery and raised the question of how the infantry in the fort, who were placed there by generals Hood and Law, was caught unprepared.[133]

After the facts in the case became clear, Longstreet expanded his criticism to include Connally, claiming the North Carolinians could have recaptured the fort and battery with moderate losses.[134] His strongest censure was reserved for Bozeman's command, noting it was totally surprised "and is probably less excusable than other parties in the affair."[135] He did not cease his condemnation of French's insubordination, however. He believed the fort would not have been lost if French had obeyed his orders to support the artillery batteries. Sorrel's letter to French on the morning of April 22 expressed Longstreet's great disappointment in French.[136] Longstreet decided not to bring formal charges against anyone over the fall of Fort Huger, hoping the incident would serve as a lesson to all concerned.[137]

The fall of Fort Huger and capture of Stribling's battery were the result of a failure of command. However, it could have been worse. Although Stribling's guns and men, along with two companies of the 44th Alabama, were captured, this was perhaps the only occasion during the war when muddled command did not result in Confederate casualties.

An Affair of Honor

A notorious result of the capture of Stribling's battery was the duel fought between officers of the 55th North Carolina and officers of Law's staff. After the capture of the redoubt, an unquestioned embarrassment to the Confederates, gossip reached the camp of the 55th North Carolina that Law's aide-de-camp, Leigh Terrell, laid the blame for the capture on the Tar Heels, claiming they had retreated instead of supporting the battery as ordered. Terrell's remarks about the 55th North Carolina were undoubtedly aimed at that regiment's behavior before the two officers conferred near Riddick's farmhouse, not its refusal to attack the fallen fort. The Alabamians were embarrassed at the loss of two companies of infantry. They were ridiculed by the Georgians in Anderson's Brigade, who were delighted to return the taunts they had received from the Alabamians only a few days before. One Georgia officer described Law's men as "chagrined" and "sore" at the capture of Fort Huger and suffering under a heavy "scrapping" from the Georgians.[138] Under these circumstances, if Terrell believed the 55th North Carolina had been ordered to support the fort and had not done so, he likely would have made a comment.[139] Cussons, in Belo's words, was "implicated with Terrell in his aspersions on the regiment."[140] Clearly, honor was at stake. Connally believed Terrell so impugned his honor and that of his regiment that he demanded satisfaction.

Oates was an eyewitness to the confrontation between the irate Connally, defending his and his regiment's honor, and Law and his staff officers. Connally rode to Law's headquarters to determine the source of the rumor. Still on horseback, he asked Law if he had reported the North Carolinians to have acted in a cowardly manner. Understanding the cause of the junior officer's rudeness, Law replied that he had received such a report from Terrell and Cussons. Law and Oates followed as Connally went to see the two staff officers about the accusation. Terrell would not retract his accusation. When Connally asked Cussons if he also accused the 55th North Carolina of cowardice, the Englishman replied, "No, Colonel, I did not; but I tell you what I now say: That if you gave your men orders to retire when the enemy appeared in their front, they obeyed orders d——d promptly last night."[141]

It was impossible, at this point, for either Connally, Terrell or Cussons to change his position without losing face. When Connally decided his regiment was accused of cowardice, he sought to have his honor satisfied. Connally rode back to his headquarters and met with the field officers and captains of his regiment. He proposed that Terrell and Cussons be challenged by himself and Lieutenant Colonel Smith, and, should they be killed, each officer of the regiment, in turn, should challenge the Alabamians until honor was satisfied. Smith declined to fight a duel on religious grounds. Belo assumed his place.[142]

Belo rode to Law's headquarters the next day and issued the challenges to Terrell and Cussons. According to Oates, the North Carolinian then courteously informed Cussons that he, not Smith, would be his opponent in the duel. This change, wrote Oates, "seemed perfectly satisfactory to Cussons, or, in other words, he manifested a reckless indifference whom he was to shoot or who was to shoot him."[143] Terrell chose double-barreled shotguns "loaded with balls," while Cussons selected the more common Mississippi Rifle, both at forty paces.[144] As an officer usually armed with sword and handgun, Belo did not own a Mississippi Rifle and had to borrow one for the duel from a member of the "Coahoma Invincibles," 11th Mississippi Regiment.[145] Captain E. Fletcher Satterfield and Lieutenant W. H. Townes served as seconds for Connally and Belo, respectively.[146] Terrell's and Cussons's seconds are unknown.

On the damp and cloudy morning of April 28, four Confederate officers took to the field of honor, intent on killing or dying to preserve their good names, putting aside the cause for which they daily risked their lives as less important than the personal challenges.[147] Belo and Cussons met in a clearing cut from a stand of pines, out of view of Connally and Terrell, who were in another field just beyond a point of high ground. According to Belo's medical attendant, they went directly to the purpose of their meeting while the seconds to Connally and Terrell entered into discussions.[148]

A postwar account written by the doctor provides details of the arrangements. Cussons took his place near the trees, the muzzle of his rifle held down but ready. His attitude was "cold and calm and unrestrained as though the presence of danger was a pleasant anticipation." As was his custom, Cussons wore his black hair to the shoulders. He was dressed in a civilian gray shirt and black trousers. Belo stood in the clearing, holding his Mississippi Rifle muzzle up, wearing full-dress uniform, buttoned to the throat. To his surgeon he "looked the picture of a warrior and a cavalier, representing the highest type of the Southern soldier."[149]

Forty paces separated the two officers. The seconds placed themselves halfway between the duelists, twenty paces off the line of fire. The two medical attendants stood near the seconds, each facing his prospective patient. Cussons's second opened the proceedings with "Gentlemen, are you ready?" The duelists answered in the affirmative. The second counted to three and shouted "fire." The shots were nearly simultaneous. Cussons fired as he raised his weapon and Belo fired by lowering the muzzle of his rifle toward his target. Neither man fell. They returned their rifles back in their original positions and stood motionless. Cussons's second asked if they were satisfied. Belo answered that he was not satisfied. The process was repeated.[150]

The only result of the two exchanges was the passage of a ball through Belo's coat, drawing blood according to the Alabamians, not drawing blood according to the North Carolinians.[151] After the turn of the century, Cussons, with no apparent interest in the argument about who drew blood, would claim Belo was treated for a scratch on the shoulder at an ambulance brought to the field for that purpose.[152] The minor wound was confirmed by Belo's medical attendant, Doctor Benjamin F. Ward, surgeon of the 11th Mississippi, who believed it was the insulting "sting" of Cussons's second ball which caused Belo to ask for a third shot.[153] Ward recalled Cussons bowed toward Belo and remarked to his opponent on their poor marksmanship: "Bad shooting, Major." Belo answered the Englishman with the suggestion that "we must do better than that when we meet the enemy again."[154]

Before shots were fired between Connally and Terrell, their seconds made a settlement acceptable to both parties. Oates noted that Connally's second "unconditionally withdrew the challenge," while a history of the North Carolina regiments reported Terrell "became satisfied that he had been mistaken in the report which he had made."[155]

As Belo and Cussons prepared for their third shot at each other, the surgeon of the 4th Alabama, Doctor William O. Hudson, in attendance at the second duel, rushed into the field, waving his hat over his head and shouting for the combatants to delay their next shots: "Don't fight so d——d fast; we are about to settle this matter over yonder."[156] Ward remembered that the participants then met at the ambulance for the gallon of medicinal whiskey that it held.

Belo and Cussons had never met before the duel and, as Belo noted in his memoirs, had no personal feelings. Belo practiced before the duel with cartridges of one-third loads that he thought about right for the duel. The seconds, he learned, had loaded to one-half for the duel. Cussons, noting a difference from the firing, asked about the loads after the duel was settled, wondering if the ball which passed near his head was a full load.[157]

Cussons believed Belo "was acting clearly within his right," when he issued the challenge. Cussons clarified his beliefs about the affair at Suffolk and dueling in general in response to questions from a newsman: "I accepted the major's invitation partly because he had an unquestioned right to extend it, and partly because it offered a satisfactory solution to an awkward situation, but chiefly because it has been my life habit never to send a challenge and never to decline one."[158] The two duelists exchanged letters after the war but did not meet again. Cussons sent flowers to Belo's funeral.[159]

It was an affair of honor and, though a violation of army regulations, most acceptable in polite society.[160] Law made no effort to stop it. If the participants had followed the formal procedure of the code duello, however, shots would probably never have been fired. Under the accepted practice, not only well known to Southerners but one formalized into a written code, once a principal felt aggrieved, he was to select a second to speak for him, not entering into discussions with his antagonist again until the matter was settled. Seconds were responsible for obtaining an honorable settlement to the dispute without bloodshed and, when possible, even before a challenge was issued.[161] Once the seconds began talking in the dispute between the Alabamians and the officers of the 55th North Carolina, even after they had reached the dueling field, the affair reached an honorable agreement.

A word from General French or a member of his staff might have averted the duel altogether for if, as Oates later wrote, the action of April 19 was the talk of the army, surely the duel on April 28 generated equal interest. All French needed have done to stop the duel was explain the orders issued to the 55th North Carolina and the timing of those orders.

Stalemate on the River

Cussons led a small party into the fort as the Federals crossed back to the right bank of the Nansemond under cover of the dark night of April 20.[162] Confederate soldiers reoccupied Fort Huger early on the April 21.[163]

Except for the normal sharpshooting and artillery fire which had become routine during the siege, the opposing lines along the Nansemond River were quiet for more than a week. During the lull, the army complained to Washington that the navy's presence was needed in the upper reaches of the river. The assistant secretary of the navy telegraphed Admiral Lee that the president expected the navy to give the army its complete cooperation.[164]

Admiral Lee still believed the upper Nansemond was unsafe for his vessels unless Federal forces occupied Hill's Point.[165] To that end, the army decided to reoccupy Hill's Point with a picket from the 117th New York. Plans were drawn for the 117th New York to cross on the night of April 27 and again on the night of April 29, but the men from the Empire State failed to move against Fort Huger either night.[166] Lamson, irritated with the army for what he believed was needless delay, retook the redoubt with a squad of his sailors on the morning of April 30, easily driving out a small picket of Confederates.[167]

This time, Hood moved his Texans to support Law and called for Anderson's Georgians to also reinforce the left of his line in case the landing was the prelude to a general advance by the Federals. With most of his division massed on the small front offered by the point of land where the fort was built, Hood could have struck a strong blow against any crossing force.[168] That night, the first clear night after three days of heavy rain, the Butternuts of Hood's Division drove the Federals across the river yet again.[169]

With the loss of Stribling's battery from Fort Huger, the Confederate command did not want to risk the capture of more artillery. And the isolated position of the earthwork at Hill's Point apparently kept them from placing more than a picket in the fort. Captain

Henry McDaniel of Anderson's Brigade and future governor of Georgia declared Hood was mortified by the fall of Fort Huger. Whether mortified or not, Hood prepared to meet another incursion with all the force at his command.[170] Ironically, the Federal command also utilized only a small picket of sailors to occupy the redoubt, and they were easily driven into the water.

New Field Officers for the 15th Alabama

Colonel Treutlen resigned his commission, effective April 28, 1863, citing health. Treutlen had been absent most of 1862. His certificate of disability stated that Treutlen suffered diseased and unsound lungs. After the war, Treutlen was a planter in South Carolina, but in 1878 moved to Washington, D.C., and worked for the U.S. Congress. Treutlen died February 27, 1908, and is buried at Eufaula, Alabama.

Lowther was entitled to be colonel by right of seniority, but he had been absent since early December 1862. During the absence of Treutlen and Lowther, Oates commanded the 15th Alabama. After the 15th Alabama transferred to Law's Brigade a warm friendship developed between Law and Oates. Law observed with satisfaction Oates's handling of the regiment and the discipline he was able to instill in it. The two had several similarities in battle. Both knew no personal fear under fire; both believed in leading by example and invariably both could be found at the front where the fighting was the most severe.

During the winter and spring of 1863, Lowther sent several statements of disability to brigade headquarters. When the first statement was rejected and returned because it was from his attending physician and not from a physician associated with an examining board, Lowther sent in subsequent statements signed by physicians from an examining board in Columbus, Georgia, which Law simply ignored. In February 1863 the War Department issued an order which permitted officers absent without leave to be terminated from the service, and sometime in March 1863 the order was amended to stipulate that absent officers be summoned before a military court before dismissal from the service. Law declared Lowther absent without leave and issued a summons to report before his examining board. When Lowther failed to appear, Special Order Number 15 of 1863 was issued removing Lowther from the rolls. In the process Law ignored one provision in the War Department orders which required the examining board to investigate the case before the officer was dropped.[171] Once Law decided to unilaterally drop Lowther from the rolls, Feagin, as next senior in rank, could have claimed his right to be colonel of the 15th Alabama. Instead Feagin elected to wave his claim in favor of Oates. Both were summoned before an examining board. Oates was examined for colonel and Feagin for lieutenant colonel. Both were found competent to perform the duties. Law then submitted an application for Oates's and Feagin's appointments to the War Department for processing.

Return to Lee's Army

At this time the stalemate along the Nansemond became secondary to events along the Rappahannock River as Major General Joseph E. Hooker initiated the turning movement against the Army of Northern Virginia that began the Battle of Chancellorsville. Hooker's chances of success were enhanced if he could turn Lee's left before the Confederates could be reinforced by Longstreet's detached force at Suffolk. Hooker received assurance from Peck on April 26 that Longstreet was still along the Nansemond.[172] On April 29 and 30, Peck suggested Hooker need only concern himself with that part of Lee's army based along the Rappahannock, confidently declaring that he could keep Longstreet at his front for some time.[173]

Lee anticipated the next Federal strike would be against him and delivered by Hooker. As early as April 27 he had asked Longstreet when he could send back to the Rappahannock some of the troops detached with him. He did not indicate any urgency, however, suggesting any attack Longstreet was considering against Suffolk was left to the discretion of the detached officer.[174]

Hooker's offensive stirred the Army of Northern Virginia into action. Longstreet received two messages from Adjutant General Samuel Cooper on April 29 to begin preparations to move back to Lee and, on April 30, the order for him to "move without delay," to rejoin Lee on the Rappahannock.[175] Longstreet felt constrained to move his whole command at once. He began to gather his forces, scattered over portions of Virginia and North Carolina, issuing urgent orders to hurry the trains across the Blackwater as quickly as possible, hopefully by the evening of May 3, when the infantry would follow. In an effort to hold Longstreet at Suffolk or at least to know when he moved to reinforce Lee, the Federal army watched Longstreet closely the night of May 2 and made a reconnaissance in force on the morning of May 3. Getty personally led the operation on May 3.[176]

The main Federal force marched out of Suffolk along the Providence Church Road while two other groups crossed the Lower Nansemond, planning to link up and capture the Reed's Ferry Road. The middle column, consisting of 250 members of the 4th Rhode Island Infantry, commanded by Lieutenant Colonel Martin P. Buffum, crossed over at Hill's Point before daybreak, under the protection of naval guns, once again flushing a small detachment of Confederates from Fort Huger.[177]

Hood immediately made Longstreet aware of the landing by the 4th Rhode Island. Longstreet, however, was determined to carry out his evacuation plan even if Peck intended to give battle on May 3. He wrote to French that the Confederates must not be detained from the scheduled operation. Later, he again wrote to French that Hood reported the Bluecoats were "displaying force in front of General Law," and French must ready a portion of his command to support on the left if they were needed.[178]

The 4th Rhode Island, now under the leadership of its brigade commander, Colonel Arthur H. Dutton, advanced across the same open ground which Federal guns in Fort Huger played upon the night of April 19, intent on reaching the woods beyond. Dutton had followed the 4th Rhode Island across and, after becoming angry at Buffum's handling of the regiment, took charge of the reconnaissance.[179]

To stop the Rhode Islanders, the 15th Alabama and four companies of the 4th Alabama skirmished through the trees which bordered the field to the west of Hill's Point and took position behind a fence near the tree line.[180] The Alabamians fired several volleys at the Rhode Islanders, and Dutton, estimating the Confederate strength at 200 to 400, withdrew from his exposed position. The 4th Rhode Island received reinforcements of 100 men from the 117th New York Regiment and a detachment from the USS *Barney*. A howitzer from the boat encouraged Dutton to move forward again, but, after pushing Law's soldiers back into the timber, he halted. Dutton felt an assault across the last quarter to half mile of open ground would result in too many casualties.[181]

As Law's men withdrew from the fence line to the timber, they left behind forty-three-year-old James Willis, of Company B, 15th Alabama, mortally wounded by a minie ball through the abdomen. The last Confederate to speak with Willis was William C. "Billy" Jordan, who could do nothing for his friend and reluctantly made for the safety of the woods.[182]

Hood engaged some of his artillery against Dutton's troops and Dutton answered by exhausting all of the available ammunition for his howitzer. The engagement lasted several hours until the Federal broke off and withdrew to Fort Huger.[183]

With nightfall, Hood commenced the movement of his division to the Blackwater River. Those companies of the 4th Alabama engaged with Dutton's landing party were called in to join the regiment's withdrawal. The Alabamians were exposed to the fierce shelling by the Federal batteries in Suffolk, compelling them to run to the breastworks under fire. They reached safety by leaping into the trenches, then waist deep in water.[184] A detail from the 15th Alabama was selected as rear guard for Hood's retreating division and under command of Cussons, stayed on picket until the early morning hours of May 4, when they quietly withdrew after the rest of the division had been gone for several hours.[185]

Although only a skirmish, the action on May 3 became hot for some members of Law's Brigade. There were nine killed and 35 wounded in the brigade. Lieutenant Noah B. Feagin of the 15th Alabama received the second of four wounds he suffered during the war. Two officers of the 44th Alabama were wounded. Captain Joseph S. Johnson, a Bibb County physician in Company H, was severely wounded in the leg. Lieutenant Joshua Johnson of the same company was struck in the thigh.[186]

Hood's Division moved toward the Blackwater, clogging the road to Franklin on the morning of May 4. Crossing the river before noon on the 4th, Hood's men removed the pontoon bridge and destroyed the other bridges "as only to allow persons on foot to pass," a concession by Longstreet to the comfort of the mostly "Secesh" inhabitants in the region.[187]

After crossing the Blackwater River, Law's command cooked rations at Franklin and rested until the cool evening hours before resuming the march to Ivor Station to catch the cars to Petersburg. Riding the Norfolk and Petersburg and Richmond and Petersburg railroads, the Alabamians reached the city by nightfall of May 6. Billy Jordan caught up with the command as the trains began leaving Ivor Station. When he discovered the car Company B had boarded had pulled out, Jordan made a dash for his comrades and managed to board the car amid the cheers of his comrades.[188]

The troop train made a short stop at Petersburg, where a large contingent of the 4th Alabama rushed to the dining room of a hotel near the depot. There was just enough time to order food before the regimental officers came to take them back to the train. The soldiers gathered up everything they could carry and hurried back to the cars, leaving the dining room tables bare.[189] A short time later, Law's Brigade was on its way back to the Army of Northern Virginia.

Chapter 4

The Route to Gettysburg

Longstreet's two divisions returned to northern Virginia by way of Richmond, Law's Brigade passing through the Confederate capital on May 8. From there the Alabamians went by train to Culpeper and then to camps near Raccoon Ford on the Rapidan River, arriving there May 14. Their route was by way of Frederick Hall on May 10, Louisa Court House, Orange Court House and finally Culpeper, arriving there on May 12.[1] The brigade remained at Raccoon Ford from May 15 until June 3. During the brigade's absence from the Army of Northern Virginia, Lee had led his men in the Battle of Chancellorsville on May 1–4 in a battle that is generally recognized as Lee's greatest victory, though marred by the loss of Stonewall Jackson who was mortally wounded on the second day of fighting. After Jackson's death the army was organized into three corps of infantry and the cavalry, Longstreet retaining the First Corps, Ewell succeeding Jackson as commander of the Second Corps and Lieutenant General A. P Hill taking command of the newly created Third Corps. The cavalry remained under command of Major General James Ewell Brown (Jeb) Stuart. Longstreet's First Corps consisted of three divisions under Hood, Pickett, and McLaws. Hood's Division was four brigades strong. The two Georgia brigades were commanded by Brigadier Generals Henry Lewis Benning and Tige Anderson. Hood's old brigade was under the able leadership of Jerome Bonaparte Robertson. The fourth brigade was Law's Alabama brigade.[2]

Lee was concerned about the dwindling size of his army and the need for provisions. Losses were not being replaced and supplies were increasingly hard to obtain.[3] Lee's instincts told him little could be gained by remaining on the defensive. He believed the Confederacy's best chance to survive was to draw Hooker's army from its secure positions around Fredericksburg and strike it a decisive blow.[4] Lee reasoned a decisive victory on northern soil would reinforce a growing peace movement in the North and perhaps obtain foreign recognition of the Confederacy.

On June 3 Longstreet put Hood's and Pickett's divisions in motion for Culpeper, arriving there June 5. McLaws's Division marched from Chancellorsville and joined the First Corps at Culpeper. As the First Corps divisions converged on Culpeper, Hooker crossed the Rappahannock River with a small force. Hood's Division was sent to Ellis Ford on June 6 to check Hooker. But Hooker quietly withdrew before shots were fired.[5] Except for that brief excursion, Law's Brigade remained in camps around Culpeper from June 5–15.

Stuart put his cavalry on review June 8, the lines of horsemen stretching three miles in a magnificently impressive show. Hood brought his entire division out for the affair.[6] Because a large Yankee force was just five miles away, Hood positioned his men on the north side of the field in case the Yankees put in an unexpected appearance.[7]

The Brigade Attends to Administrative Details

During the five weeks between the brigade's departure from Suffolk and its departure from Culpeper, numerous changes had taken place in the brigade officer ranks. Thirty-eight commissions were issued, and eight resignations were received. One resignation was submitted, but not acted on and one officer died. John G. Grice, second lieutenant of Company E, 4th Alabama, and Jesse Alldredge, lieutenant colonel 48th Alabama, resigned because of wounds received at the Battle of Second Manassas. Before the war Grice was a twenty-six-year-old merchant at Evergreen, Alabama. His right leg was amputated as a result of his wound, and he was succeeded by Archibald D. McInnis. After being shot through both legs, Alldredge was disabled from further service. At the time of his resignation he had not recovered the use of one leg. He was succeeded by William Hardwick. Spenser C. Tyler, Company E, 48th Alabama, resigned while on furlough in Alabama, and no action was taken to replace him. He did not return to the regiment and died June 24, 1864, but was not dropped from the regimental rolls until December 7, 1864.[8] John McKee, captain of Company G, 47th Alabama, died at Richmond.[9] First Lieutenant William D. Oakley, Company F, resigned his commission in the 44th Alabama because he was elected sheriff and returned to Oakleyville, Alabama.[10] Francis V. Ross, Company E, 48th Alabama, resigned because of conduct unbecoming an officer, in connection with an order issued by Sheffield on May 10 prohibiting loaded guns in camp. That evening one of Captain Ross's men killed another private while attempting to cap his gun. The private who was capping his gun had just returned from the hospital and was told the gun was not loaded. Sheffield placed Ross under arrest and charged him with disobedience. Ross submitted his resignation May 19 and was allowed to go home.[11]

Major Lowther returned to the 15th Alabama about the first of June 1863, and much to his surprise and displeasure, Oates was the new colonel and Isaac Feagin the lieutenant colonel. Two captains he considered his junior in rank had been promoted over him. In Lowther's mind Law had ignored military procedure governing seniority. Lowther had not waived his right to the office and therefore, in Lowther's opinion, Law had denied him the office of colonel of the 15th Alabama. This was an obvious miscarriage of justice which he immediately set out to correct. Old acquaintances of influence and former superior officers were enlisted to intercede on his behalf and petition the War Department. Lowther lodged a protest, though outside the normal military channels.[12] Shortly afterwards Lowther submitted a copy of the protest to Law with a request to forward it to the department. Lowther's action caused a year long investigation by the Richmond authorities into the circumstances surrounding Oates's appointment. In the meantime Lowther declined to serve under Oates until the Wilderness Campaign of 1864.

While Lowther pursued justice for himself, Oates selected Henry Brainard as his replacement in Company G. Oates's brother, John, became the company's first lieutenant and Barnett H. Cody the second lieutenant. Cody, the son of a Methodist minister, entered the service at age 16. He was just barely 18 years of age when he became the company's second lieutenant.

Thomas James Eubanks, co-owner and co-editor of the *Marshall News* before the war, became the captain of Company D, 48th Alabama. He enlisted with Sheffield in the 9th Alabama and was given the honor to receive his company's flag from the local ladies. Once in Virginia he fell into disfavor with John Rayburn, who asked his influential father to use his leverage with Sheffield to remove him from the regiment. It was suggested that Eubanks could be adjutant to Sheffield. He became the 48th Alabama's second adjutant and was serving in that capacity when promoted to captain.[13]

Eubanks was replaced as adjutant of the 48th by Henry Figures, formerly an orderly sergeant in the 4th Alabama. Figures came from a prominent Huntsville, Alabama family where his father, an influential politician in the North Alabama area, was publisher of the Huntsville *Democrat*. When the Confederacy was formed, Figures had secured his only son a clerkship in the War Department, but the youthful Figures wanted to go to war and began a campaign to acquire his parents' permission to enlist in the 4th Alabama. Figures wrote his father while Secretary of War William Randolph wrote his mother. His parents eventually consented and eighteen-year-old Henry began his military career at Winchester, Virginia, in July 1861.[14] The youngster immediately became accustomed to the soldier's life, acquiring friends easily, enjoying the camaraderie with young men his own age and enjoying the experience of being a soldier. Older officers became his role models, and he very much desired an officer's commission. He spent considerable time following that pursuit, an endeavor supported by his father. Figures and his father each sent several letters to the State House in Montgomery and to the War Department in Richmond. When the adjutant's vacancy occurred Figures jumped at the opportunity. In the highly political environment of the day, it is probable that Sheffield and the elder Figures were acquainted. Figures's rank dated from May 1, 1863.[15]

Marching to Pennsylvania

While the Confederate hierarchy considered its options, the army grapevine was extremely active. About the first of June rumors making the rounds throughout the camps had it that the army was about to move north. After much correspondence and discussion between Lee and the seat of government, the decision was made to do just that.

Lee's plan called for the First and Second Corps to concentrate around Culpeper, while the Third Corps remained in position near Chancellorsville to watch Hooker's army in its defenses around Fredericksburg. The move would be initiated by sending Ewell's Second Corps through the Shenandoah Valley, driving off or capturing Federal forces located there and then continuing into Pennsylvania to gather supplies. Longstreet's First Corps was to march near the eastern base of the Blue Ridge Mountains to threaten the rear of Hooker's army and occupy strategic passes through the Blue Ridge. Stuart's cavalry was assigned the task of staying between Hooker's army and the First Corps.[16] Simultaneous with Longstreet's movement, the army's trains and the Third Corps were to travel north on the western side of the Blue Ridge.

About 5 a.m. on June 15 the army took up the line of march for the Shenandoah Valley.[17] Law's Brigade made an extended march the first day, crossing the Hazel River about 3 p.m., and then on to Woodville and Sperryville. Thornton's River was forded at 5 p.m. Camp that night was in the vicinity of Washington, Virginia.[18] June 16 found the line of march along the road to Salem. The brigade crossed the Rappahannock at Rock Ford and moved on to Piedmont before going into bivouac the night of June 16 near Markham Station on the Manassas Gap. Turner Vaughan looked at the station, recalling vividly the day 23 months earlier when the 4th Alabama boarded the cars in July 1861 en route to the Battle of First Manassas.[19]

Early on the morning of June 17, Hood's Division marched to Upperville and turned onto the road to Paris, the division later crossing the Blue Ridge Mountains through Ashby's Gap. As the sun rose higher in the morning sky the air became oppressively hot, and passage through the gap was made worse by narrow winding roads.[20] Men began falling out from heat exhaustion. The brigade passed through Paris about 11 a.m. and about 2 p.m. in the afternoon forded the Shenandoah River at Berry's Ford. Despite the extreme heat, there

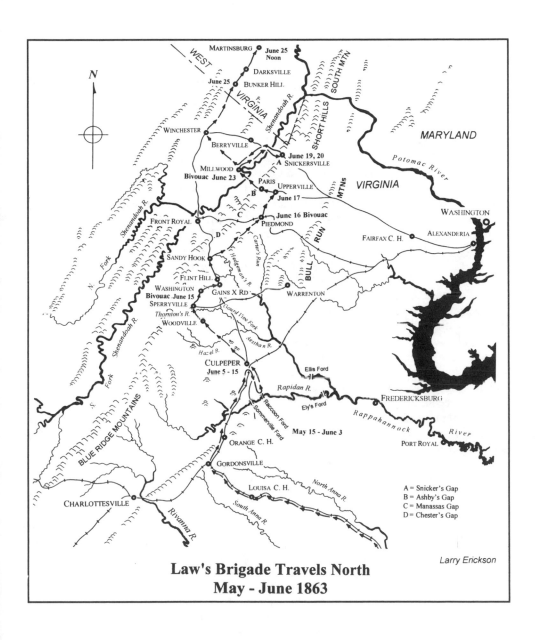

WEST VIRGINIA

MARTINSBURG June 25 Noon
DARKSVILLE
June 25 BUNKER HILL
SOUTH MTN
SHORT HILLS
MARYLAND
Potomac River
VIRGINIA
WINCHESTER
BERRYVILLE
Shenandoah R.
June 19, 20
A SNICKERSVILLE
MILLWOOD
Bivouac June 23
PARIS
B UPPERVILLE
June 17
WASHINGTON
FRONT ROYAL
C
June 16 Bivouac
PIEDMOND
D
FAIRFAX C. H.
ALEXANDERIA
Carter's Run
Shenandoah R.
N. Fork
SANDY HOOK
Hedgeman's R.
BULL RUN
MTNs
FLINT HILL
WASHINGTON
Bivouac June 15
SPERRYVILLE
GAINS X RD
WARRENTON
Thornton's R.
WOODVILLE
Thoroughfare Fork
Hazel R.
Aestha'n R.
CULPEPER
June 5 - 15
Ellis Ford
Rapidan R.
FREDERICKSBURG
Ely's Ford
Rappahannock River
S. Fork
Shenandoah R.
Raccoon Ford
Sommerville Ford
May 15 - June 3
PORT ROYAL
BLUE RIDGE MOUNTAINS
ORANGE C. H.
GORDONSVILLE
North Anna R.
LOUISA C. H.
A = Snicker's Gap
B = Ashby's Gap
C = Manassas Gap
D = Chester's Gap
CHARLOTTESVILLE
Rivanna R.
South Anna R.

N

Larry Erickson

Law's Brigade Travels North
May - June 1863

were those who objected to the idea getting their clothes wet.

Private William Youngblood, Company I, 15th Alabama, saw Hood sitting on his horse watching his division splash into the water. Youngblood boldly approached Hood, seeking permission to remove his clothes before entering the water. He was told to wade into the river as there was no time for dressing and undressing. Although the day was quite warm Youngblood recalled the Shenandoah's "water was biting cold." About halfway across Youngblood decided to climb upon a rock and warm himself. Youngblood's time in the sun was all too short. An officer soon rode by and ordered the private to hasten his way across the river.[21] From Berry's Ford the line of march was then downriver to Snicker's Ferry in a rainstorm. The men bivouacked the night of June 17 on the west side of the Shenandoah River.[22]

Longstreet's column resumed its march June 18 and halted for a midday rest. No sooner than rations were distributed to the regimental messes and fires started, orders came to recross the river and occupy Snicker's Gap, about 12 miles downstream. Hood sent Law with his own and Anderson's Brigade and a detachment of cavalry to the gap. Reports had the Federals approaching in force. Law hurried his detachment over narrow winding, often hilly, roads. The intensely hot weather and physical exertion caused men to fall out by the score. Fortunately a heavy afternoon thunderstorm cooled the air and brought relief to the struggling column. Law's command endured a damp bivouac that night. Both brigades recrossed the river the next morning, moved up the mountain and deployed across Snicker's Gap. Just before darkness settled over the mountain another late afternoon thunderstorm drenched the soldiers. To protect against a surprise advance against his line, Law ordered his men to sleep with their weapons at the ready. But the only thing that descended on the Snicker's Gap that night was a mixture of dense fog and heavy mist. Weary men slept in damp blankets and clothing. Next morning the line of battle was literally in the clouds, although there was sunshine at the foot of the mountain.[23]

The Federal threat failed to materialize, and in the afternoon the brigade retraced its steps to the Shenandoah and waded the river for the third time. Heavy rains from the past few days had caused the river to rise, producing a fairly strong current. The water was waist deep, presenting some peril to the men during the crossing. As a precaution, a detachment of cavalry was stationed below the ford to catch any unfortunate soldier that might lose his footing and be swept downstream. Law divided his brigades into several columns which splashed into the Shenandoah at the same time. Privates attached cartridge boxes to their bayonets to keep the ammunition dry, as others yelled encouragement to companions encountering difficulty. Horsemen loudly cursed their fidgety mounts. Some found the soldiers' plight amusing, and laughter intermingled with cursing and encouragement.[24]

Adjutant Coles of the 4th Alabama was following his regiment on a small mare and thought he would be able to get across in a relatively dry condition. Several men even handed him their valuables for safe transport across the river, but just before reaching the west bank the little mare dropped down so that only her head was above water. Much to his dismay, Coles was thoroughly soaked as he and the mare left the water to the hoots and laughter of those near enough to see the incident.[25] Because the crossing was not completed until late in the afternoon, the brigade bivouacked the night of June 20 a short distance from the river. Most of the next two days were spent in marching and countermarching along the river's west bank. The men bivouacked the night of June 22 a mile beyond Millwood, only ten miles on a straight line from the camps of the night of the 20th.[26]

Law's Brigade remained in camp June 23 resting in a quiet little valley on the estate of a wealthy gentleman. Coles observed that the owner maintained a large reserve for a herd of English fallow deer. However, there is no report of any deer finding their way into Confederate kettles.[27] William Youngblood took advantage of the rest to approach Longstreet and request assignment as a courier. Interestingly enough, Longstreet accepted his request and sent Youngblood on a leave of absence to obtain a mount. He rejoined Longstreet at Chambersburg.[28]

The camp rumor mill was active again. One story going around was that Hooker had left Fredericksburg with the Federal army and was moving in great haste for Washington, his mission, the Confederates believed, to guard that city against Lee's army. Henry Figures got his information directly from the brigade surgeon. The Army of Northern Virginia would be moving into Maryland and Pennsylvania where Lee intended to subsist his army in greener pastures, at least during the summer months. A day later the camp rumor proved accurate once more. At daylight on the morning of June 24 the brigade resumed its march.[29] Again the direction was north, for the Army of Northern Virginia's destination was Pennsylvania.

By 7:00 a.m. the brigade reached Berryville, and bivouacked that night two miles beyond the hamlet of Midway. The First Corps had been leading the army, but A. P. Hill's Third Corps overtook Longstreet at the Shenandoah River. Daylight of the 25th found the brigade marching toward Bunker Hill and passing Martinsburg about noon. Camp that night was near the Potomac, not far from Falling Waters.[30]

During the night another heavy rainstorm moved in, drenching the camps. There was no need to worry about clothing that was already soaked. This time the privates simply waded into the river, which like the Shenandoah, was more than waist deep. A short distance from Williamsport the rain subsided and eventually stopped.

Hood then halted to let the men rest and dry out a bit, as Longstreet ordered a large store of confiscated whiskey brought out for the weary troops.[31] Private Henry H. Sturgis, Company G, 44th Alabama, later recalled "boys help yourself was the order of the day." Hood's men received their portions by passing before barrels from which the tops had been removed.[32] Each soldier dipped his own portion with whatever was available. Some portions were larger than others and when quickly consumed, caused more than one Confederate to become quite intoxicated. Some most likely gulped their portions down and went out in search of an additional portion.

Wet clothes were hung to dry by roaring campfires while Hood's men warmed their insides with Longstreet's "medicine." Sergeant William C. Ward, Company G, 4th Alabama, considered his portion too precious a delicacy to down in one setting and filled his canteen with the whiskey. His resolve was to make the portion last as long as possible and, if necessary, use the whiskey for future medicinal purposes. An hour later the column stopped to rest and most of the men, including Ward, lay down on the wet ground to rest. When he rose to resume marching Ward sadly found the canteen's contents had been spilled. He later remembered that all the good things that came his way never compensated for the loss of that portion of whiskey.[33] Corporal Joseph B. Polley of the Texas brigade recalled many years later the "road's width that afternoon was more of a problem than its length."[34] Private Henry Sturgis, 44th Alabama, was less diplomatic in his description of the affair when he remembered that men were scattered from the Potomac to the night's bivouac, "lying along the roadside dead drunk." The night was well along before most of the drunk "came staggering in."[35]

Law's Brigade crossed the border into Pennsylvania the evening of June 26.[36] The Alabamians boasted they breakfasted in Virginia, dined and wined in Maryland, and ate supper in Pennsylvania. Coles jokingly recalled they "marched in four states that day, the fourth in a state of intoxication."[37] Law's Brigade spent the night a short distance south of Greencastle, Pennsylvania.[38]

While the brigade was at Greencastle, Lee issued orders which strictly forbade disturbing personal property and burning rails, even for the purpose of cooking.[39] More than one soldier ignored the order and took the opportunity to leave camp in search of fresh meat, butter, eggs, and chickens. The soldiers of Law's Brigade helped themselves to anything edible they came across and each night burned fence rails in their campfires. They had, according to Lieutenant Reuben Kidd of the 4th Alabama, "killed, captured or destroyed everything that came in our way."[40] Men from the 47th Alabama wasted little time in foraging among the local farms, boldly going to houses and demanding what they wanted. Few resisted because they were terribly afraid of the Rebel hordes and gave with the fervent hope the unwelcomed visitors would go away.[41] Willful acts of thievery disturbed the youthful Henry Figures. He sadly recalled the Federal occupation of Huntsville in 1862 and the stories his mother wrote describing the Federal soldiers' behavior. Figures wrote home that he did not kill the local farm animals, but, indicated there was much to eat. He assured his mother that everything he ate was bought. His mess enjoyed short mutton, light bread, butter, and fresh apples, milk and plenty of vegetables.[42] If the rest of the Alabama brigade fared as well as Figures, there was ample food for all.

A large spring near camp became the brigade's source of water. The night of June 26 a private from Company K, 48th Alabama, went to the spring for water. He carried a large kettle which he attempted to lift directly from the spring. A somewhat weakened conditioned caused by a meager diet in Virginia and the weight of the full kettle caused him to lose his balance. He staggered about the spring's perimeter trying to lift the kettle to his shoulder. In the process his hat was knocked from his head. Losing his hat was a serious matter and the Alabamian searched for it unsuccessfully in the darkness. The hat's resting place was in the spring, and because it was saturated with dirt, oil, and perspiration from long service on the road, it quickly disappeared beneath the spring's surface. Sometime later Sergeant John (Jack) Stewart, Company G, 4th Alabama, appeared out of the darkness with his kettle. He quickly dipped it in the pool and returned to camp. Stewart then cut up a ration of beef, threw it in the kettle and set it over a low fire to cook all night. When Stewart's mess rose early the next morning the broth in the kettle was dingy. Traces of oil floated on the broth's surface and surrounded chunks of beef. Someone stirred the dirty looking broth and discovered the cause of the vile looking liquid was a very soiled hat. Stewart's messmates were thoroughly disgusted and hurled loud expressions of displeasure at the unlucky cook. His mess was forced to leave without eating.[43]

Law's Brigade entered Greencastle the morning of June 27, the march through town becoming a festive occasion for the Alabamians.[44] Outside of town, Sheffield ordered his regiment's drum and fife to the front to belt out a lively tune through town. The 48th Alabama's musicians followed with their rendition of "Bonnie Blue Flag." Sergeant Ward passed by an open window and saw in the shadows a young woman singing along. She was obviously caught up in the mood of the moment, and Ward remembered many years later she sang with much gusto and kept time with the drum and fife by a swaying motion of her hips. Local citizens lined the streets for a look at the Confederate visitors. Somewhere on the line of march a well-dressed man leaned over a picket fence for a better view. He and two lady companions were completely absorbed in watching the ragged gray line when a tall, rangy Alabamian drifted toward the trio. His head was hatless, leaving bare a shock of thick hair. The Alabamian carefully timed his gait so that when he drew abreast the Greencastle citizen he was just at arm's length. In the blink of an eye the observer's hat

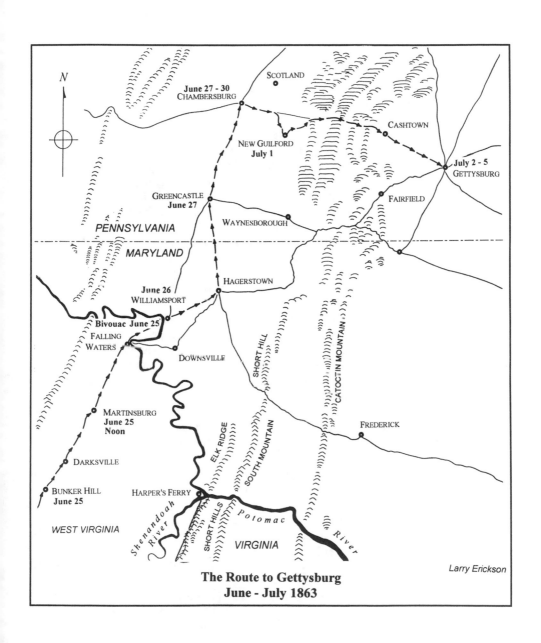

N

June 27 - 30
CHAMBERSBURG

SCOTLAND

CASHTOWN

NEW GUILFORD
July 1

July 2 - 5
GETTYSBURG

GREENCASTLE
June 27

FAIRFIELD

WAYNESBOROUGH

PENNSYLVANIA

MARYLAND

HAGERSTOWN

June 26
WILLIAMSPORT

Bivouac June 25

FALLING
WATERS

DOWNSVILLE

SHORT HILL

CATOCTIN MOUNTAIN

MARTINSBURG
June 25
Noon

ELK RIDGE

SOUTH MOUNTAIN

FREDERICK

DARKSVILLE

BUNKER HILL
June 25

HARPER'S FERRY

SHORT HILLS

Potomac

River

WEST VIRGINIA

Shenandoah River

VIRGINIA

Larry Erickson

The Route to Gettysburg
June - July 1863

was cleanly picked from his head and the Alabamian disappeared into the marching column. A bewildered man, less one hat, and two very amused women were soon left behind.[45]

As John W. Young, a private in Company I, 4th Alabama, passed through the village he remembered the Federal occupation of Huntsville, Alabama, the year before. His folks were forced to endure pillage and humiliation. Unlike Henry Figures he decided a little retribution was in order, simply walking up to an elderly gentleman standing in a doorway and removing his beautiful felt hat. It wasn't much in the way of revenge, but the deed was done. Young apparently experienced some satisfaction from the act and quickly continued on his way.[46]

The brigade left Greencastle by the northeast pike, and a short distance outside the town a beautiful house stood on a hill overlooking the turnpike. Several well-dressed women stood in the front yard, defiantly waving Federal flags at the passing Confederates. A rather buxom young lady was somewhat more conspicuous than her friends, vigorously waving her flag while shouting taunts at the passing troops. Not to be outdone a Texan left the line of march, ambled up to the trio and in his best Texas drawl, addressed the young lady: "Madam, you are doing a dangerous thing waving that flag at Confederate soldiers." "How sir?" came the tart reply. The Texan blandly retorted, "We rebels never see that flag flying over breastworks without charging them." The young lady was speechless, her companions enjoying a rather good laugh at her expense. The Texan, satisfied he had scored another victory for the cause, shouldered his Springfield and went on his way.[47] Law's Brigade reached Chambersburg in the evening, and bivouacked that night two miles beyond town.[48]

Two days' rest followed while the brigade made a sizable dent in the local supply of apple butter and light bread.[49] Men lounged around camp or engaged in a variety of activities to pass the time. Some engaged in card games, while others passed away the time in idle conversation or explored the surrounding countryside. Still others wrote letters home. Even though Lee had issued orders against taking private property there were those who chose to relieve the local populace of foodstuffs.

Circumventing Lee's orders required some ingenuity. As in all armies, some individuals are always up to the task. A servant named Ned accompanied a soldier from the 4th Alabama north to Pennsylvania. It was decided to send Ned out to mingle with the locals. The idea was that some unsuspecting farmer would take pity on him, a humble servant, and decide to do something for him. So Ned went trudging off in search of pity. Just in case he found some he was loaded down with canteens and other means of conveying charity back to camp. It worked. Ned returned with every canteen filled with milk.[50]

Private Henry B. Love, Company F, 4th Alabama, noticed a number of fine looking large barns. The barns were not unlike the one his grandfather once owned in Madison County, Alabama. His grandfather had the misfortune of living near where an ambush of Federal troops took place the previous year which led to punitive action against the local populace. The Federals burned his grandfather's house and surrounding buildings. As he sat in camp Love thought about the events in Madison County and decided it was time for justice on Yankee soil. He ventured from camp with the intention of burning several big barns, but when he selected the first barn Love found he was unable to deliberately set fire to the structure. After some deliberation, he decided he would have to be very angry to burn a barn. With the aim of provoking the owner into an action that would warrant retaliation, Love proceeded to tell the man how mean the Yankees were and adding a few other choice statements. The callous burning of his grandfather's property and insulting behavior of the Federal soldiers were carefully recounted. Love placed great emphasis on the wanton destruction of private property. The only problem was that the Pennsylvania farmer was totally sympathetic with Love. The farmer went so far as to say the Yankee soldiers were certainly a sorry lot. In the end Love did not have the heart to set fire to the farmer's barn. He killed a chicken instead and returned to camp.[51]

Private James Daniel, Company H, 47th Alabama, looked over the countryside and noted its vast difference from Virginia and Alabama. Wheat grew as high as his head, corn was plentiful and the pasture land plush. Writing to his wife from Chambersburg, Daniel noted that the buildings, which were generally constructed of brick and rocks, were the finest he had ever saw. He astutely observed that the people of southern Pennsylvania had never felt the war but that would change if the Confederate army continued foraging.[52]

During the night of June 28, one of Longstreet's couriers galloped into the First Corps headquarters and reported the Federal army across the Potomac and in pursuit. He also brought news that reported the head of the Federal column was at South Mountain and thus threatened communications through Hagerstown and Williamsport. Another bit of surprising news was that Major General George G. Meade was the new commander of the Federal army.[53]

While Law's Brigade was camped at Chambersburg, the 4th and 48th Alabama were sent to guard commissary stores near Scotland, a hamlet about two miles from the brigade camp.[54] Camp was opposite a large house occupied by a family with two young daughters. The gentleman of the house proved friendly to the Confederates, and spent considerable time with the Alabamians. In short time a warm relationship developed, though the young ladies of the house drew most of the attention. They were frequent visitors, charming, and a delight to the young Alabamians so far from home. Henry Figures was captivated by their charms, and in a letter to his sister Figures claimed they were almost as pretty as the women in Huntsville, Alabama.[55]

While at Scotland, the 48th Alabama roll for May–June 1863 was prepared and their fighting condition assessed. Their clothes and military appearance were judged as "bad." However, on the plus side their discipline, instruction, arms and accouterments were recorded as "good."[56] The Alabamians did not exhibit a good military appearance, their clothes appearing shabby at best, but in June 1863 their esprit de corps was high. They were part of an army that felt itself invincible.

When orders arrived to rejoin the brigade, the soldiers of the 4th and 48th Alabama were saddened by the departure. The return route on the morning of June 30 took the 4th Alabama through Chambersburg, but this time the locals were not amused by the Confederates' march through town. Women stood on porches or looked out from open windows and shouted insults at the Alabamians. The situation could very easily have gotten out of hand because the Alabamians themselves were not in the same festive spirit as the first time they passed through town. Fortunately the 4th chose only to exchange insults with the local populace. Henry Figures recounted the incident by letter to his mother, assuring her he never said a word.[57]

After the 4th Alabama returned to camp, Law's Brigade and Captain William K. Bachman's South Carolina battery (German Artillery) were detached for outpost duty, on July 1 at New Guilford, traveling by way of Fayetteville.[58] Turner Vaughan described the small hamlet about three miles south of Fayetteville as an insignificant place. Camp was in a large oak grove located in a picturesque little valley. Fortunately there was an ample supply of apple butter, pigs and light bread, and the men continued to eat well.[59] A large herd of pigs browsing near the 15th Alabama camp caused many mouths to water in anticipation of fresh pork. Near the end of the day word came that the 15th Alabama would be without a supply of meat. Even though Lee had issued orders forbidding the slaughter of poultry and livestock, Oates gave his permission to slaughter a hog for the evening mess. Oates ordered a detail formed to look for forage, with Captain William A. Edwards drawing the assignment and sending a squad out with instructions to kill the largest hog they could find.[60] Three hogs were slaughtered before Edwards discovered the extent of his men's foraging, and a fourth was so near death that he let the men finish the job. Two soldiers from Company E in the detail were Silas B. Peters and Sergeant Samuel Hogg. Peters, a small one-eyed man with a dry sense of humor, loved to play jokes on his fellow soldiers.[61] During the episode Hogg, a large man, became the object of his sport. Peters threw rocks at the hogs instead of using his musket and accidentally struck Hogg a sharp blow on the leg. Hogg was furious and though in considerable pain went after his antagonist. Peters ran for his life with Hogg in hot pursuit. Hogg was fast for a large man, and was about to catch Peters when Edwards saw the two. Peters was yelling and called out for Edwards to save him. Questioned on the circumstances leading to the chase, Peters blandly replied that they had been detailed to find the largest hog, and Hogg was the largest one he saw. Hogg suddenly realized how ludicrous the whole thing was and burst into laughter. With a noticeable limp he turned and made his way back to quarters. Boiled hog's head, spareribs and baked bread were the day's fare.[62]

We Must Go Quickly Because General Lee Needs Us

The first day of July was a warm cloudy day and quite humid. Occasional showers made the roads muddy and very slippery. In the afternoon the distant boom of cannon rolled in from the east, and during the night a courier rode into camp and asked for the brigade commander.[63] Longstreet's orders were to join the First Corps at Gettysburg. Regimental commanders prepared to move at a moment's notice. Law brought his pickets in and ordered three days' rations cooked.

Haversacks were barely packed when a second courier arrived with urgent instructions to join Hood's Division. Departure was set for 3 a.m. but Law was unable to get the brigade in motion until almost 4:00 a.m.[64] Eighteen miles separated the Alabamians from Gettysburg, Pennsylvania. In between lay South Mountain and rolling Pennsylvania countryside.

At this critical moment Bowles was under arrest on Law's orders, though the specific charges against Bowles are not known. It is known that Law had him court-martialed and a four month sentence imposed. Bowles petitioned Longstreet to investigate the matter, but Longstreet either declined or ignored the request.[65] The facts of the case are obscure, and Bowles was angry over his arrest for many years, but by 1909 his anger had subsided sufficiently for him to serve as a witness when Law applied for a pension.[66]

Lawrence Scruggs commanded the 337 men of the 4th Alabama as it approached Gettysburg. Oates led the 15th Alabama, the largest regiment in the brigade with 487 men. The 4th, 44th, 47th and 48th numbered 319, 290 and 275 men, respectively. Brigade strength was 1,714 officers and men.[67]

Daylight found Law's column descending into the valley at Cashtown. Behind them lay the summit of South Mountain and the fertile land that provided such marvelous food the past few days. Later in the morning the brigade passed the smoking ruins of Thaddeus Stevens's ironworks, and moved onto the level ground west of Gettysburg.[68] The morning of July 2 brought a boiling sun, but, because of the urgency Law set a blistering pace with no rest stops.[69] As the morning wore on, canteens began to run dry, the heat and exhaustion causing stragglers to appear behind the column. Two or three miles from town, field hospitals provided the first evidence of the previous day's fighting.[70]

Eight hours after he led his brigade from its bivouac, Law joined the Texas brigade on Hood's right near Herr's Tavern on the Chambersburg Road. Longstreet would write many years later that no other brigade in either army did as good a day's marching to reach the battlefield.[71] Accounts as to the time and miles covered differed, but most of the eyewitnesses appear to include the distance from Herr's Tavern to their position in front of Round Top in the total miles covered.[72] Law's march from New Guilford to Herr's Tavern covered approximately 20 miles nonstop. Because they made a significant detour on the march to Round Top that portion of the march covered about five miles. When Law's Brigade went into position before Round Top, it had covered about 25 miles. They still had another mile to charge before engaging the Federal infantry. By any measure this was an incredible feat in the heat of July and with little water.

Chapter 5

Attack on the Federal Left

The Battlefield – Afternoon of July 2

In July 1863 Gettysburg, Pennsylvania, was a thriving little town, nestled in a shallow valley and surrounded by rich farmland. The most prominent landmarks near Gettysburg were two ridge lines. Seminary Ridge ran north and south about one-half mile west of town. Cemetery Ridge lay south of Gettysburg, its north end curving like the eye of a fish hook and capped by an elevation known as Culp's Hill. Cemetery Ridge was firmly anchored at the south end by two steep hills. The smaller one would forever be known as Little Round Top. The larger, more southerly hill is known as Round Top.

Farther west of Seminary Ridge are two other ridges known as McPherson and Herr's. Willoughby Run flows south between these ridges to empty into Marsh Creek south of the battlefield. Seminary Ridge terminated near the Snyder and Warfield houses and rose again south of the Warfield house. The new elevation is referred to as the Warfield Ridge and crossed the Emmitsburg Road west of Round Top.

From Warfield Ridge the ground sloped down to a valley through which ran a small stream known locally as Plum Run. Devil's Den lay several hundred yards to the east of Round Top's northern base. Its huge boulders range in size from six to fifteen feet in height.[1] Spaces between the boulders were just wide enough for men to pass through and provided winding passageways carpeted with moss.[2] Perry later remembered that some of the passages were so dark that it seemed doubtful the light of day had ever made its way to their location. Devil's Den was at the terminus of a low ridge known as Houck Ridge, named for John Houck who owned 47 acres on the ridge's eastern slope.[3] The ridge, its crest rising approximately 60 feet above the valley, sloped gradually downward to the north before merging into Cemetery Ridge.

Round Top rises 300 feet above the valley floor south of Devil's Den. Its western face and the crest were thickly covered with trees which hid huge boulders scattered over its surface. Little Round Top's crest is 200 feet above the valley floor. Its western face was sparsely covered with trees and bushes. Large boulders and rocks covered the western slope. About three-quarters up the eastern slope the rocks and boulders formed natural fortifications. Plum Run flowed south through a valley formed by Little Round Top and Houck Ridge, through a rocky wooded ravine known as Plum Run Gorge which lay between the foot of Devil's Den and the northern end of Round Top, and emptied into a valley below Devil's Den which was bounded on either side by Round Top and Warfield Ridge. A tributary, known as Rose Run, flowed into Plum Run south of Devil's Den, creating a "Y." Plum Run Valley encompasses the area from its source to the south end of Round Top.

The terrain between Warfield Ridge and Round Top was covered with numerous fields. At least two were freshly plowed, some were cultivated, others were grassy hayfields and meadows. Many of the fields were enclosed by wooden worm fences and several low stone fences dotted the landscape. Two farmhouses and associated dwellings the Alabamians would long remember were situated south of Devil's Den. The Bushman farm buildings were situated a short distance east of the Emmitsburg Road. The Slyder dwellings were just west of Plum Run.

A Brief Rest and Then We're Off

After joining Hood's Division the Alabamians quickly fell out, sought relief from the noonday sun under nearby shade trees, and listened to the sounds of skirmishing and the thunder of artillery coming from their front and right. Law's Brigade rested on Herr's Ridge. The 4th Alabama sent out a detail to find water. Each man carried a dozen canteens. A quick search of the surrounding area uncovered a small pond filled with standing rain water. The water was greenish in color, but it was the only water in the immediate vicinity. Canteens were quickly filled and the detail started back for the regiment.[4] The 4th Alabama's water detail was still making its way back when the brigade took up the line of march. Catching up required considerable effort on the part of the water detail. The breathless group finally joined their comrades after the march was well under way.[5]

Henry Figures took the opportunity to set out on his own search for water. He found a house about one hundred yards from the road occupied by women with small children. Figures's presence visibly upset the occupants. A shell bursting overhead agitated the women even more. The civilians began crying and running about. An elderly woman thought the shells were meant for Figures and cried out in anguish for the young soldier to move on. The elderly woman's plea was sufficient to dispel Figures's ideas of finding fresh water at that house. Figures decided he had found an absolutely terrible situation and was better off with the brigade.[6]

Lee's Plan of Attack

On the morning of July 2 Lee was determined to maintain the initiative exhibited by his army July 1. It was acertained very early in the morning that Meade was well entrenched on the north end of Cemetery Ridge. But his left, which extended south along the Emmitsburg Road as far as the terminus of the ridge, was in the air. Sometime around mid morning the commanding general decided that an attack against the Federal left offered the greatest opportunity for success.[7] The First Corps was to capture the Peach Orchard and the high ground west of Little Round Top. Colonel E. Porter Alexander would use this elevated ground to give artillery support for the oblique assault against Cemetery Ridge by the infantry.[8] Ewell was to attack the Federal right while A. P. Hill was to threaten the center to prevent Meade from sending reinforcements to either wing.[9] Two divisions of Longstreet's First Corps would open a general advance.[10] Hood and McLaws were near army headquarters while the plan was being finalized. Lee called McLaws to his side and pointed to the exact location on a map of the area where the Georgian was to place his division. McLaws was instructed to get there without being discovered by the Federals, place his line across the Emmitsburg Road, and lead the assault.[11] It is not known if Lee gave personal instructions to Hood, but he was to follow en echelon on the right of McLaws.

Longstreet opposed Lee's plan. He wanted, instead, to place the army between Meade and Washington. He proposed turning the enemy's left to put the Army of Northern Virginia between Meade and Washington. Lee's mind was made up. The Army of Northern Virginia would attack Meade's army where it lay.[12] Lee believed a turning movement was impractical. Withdrawing through the mountains with his long train would be very difficult. In addition, the commanding general knew supply for his army would be nearly impossible if he held his position for any length of time. Lee explained to the president that a battle on July 2 was unavoidable.[13] Lee ordered Longstreet to send his troops to the attack at 11 a.m. but on Longstreet's request agreed the First Corps could wait until Law's Brigade was up. At that time the Alabamians were expected at any moment.[14] The First Corps's artillery was sent on to the Confederate right to deploy. Colonel E. Porter Alexander, commanding Longstreet's artillery, was also cautioned to remain concealed from the signal station on Little Round Top. After a careful reconnaissance, consuming the better part of three hours, Alexander sufficiently understood the ground over which he was to travel to move southward. By traveling through fields and hollows three battalions of artillery managed to navigate the route undetected.[15] In the meantime McLaws returned to the his division near Herr's Tavern and at the head of his column, sat on his horse and observed in the distance the Federal infantry filing onto the battlefield.[16] The Confederates' opportunity to deliver a decisive blow to the Federal left was slipping away.

A Circuitous March to Battle

The brigade's rest was brief. Orders to move out came about 1 p.m. Law's Brigade led Hood's Division over a road that ran along the west side of Herr's Ridge. Law followed McLaws's Division. Longstreet rode in the center of the column. McLaws rode at the head of the column with Lee's staff officer who was acting as a guide.

From the start the march was slow with frequent halts.[17] Colonel W. W. White, 7th Georgia, reported the march "was made under a boiling sun."[18] This only served to make the lack of water more of a problem. As the head of the column topped a rise the signal station on Little Round Top was visible. After conferring with Lee's staff officer McLaws thought the only way to avoid detection was to countermarch.[19] The column subsequently took a circuitous route south. Why the column did not follow the path followed by the corps's artillery has never been explained. Certainly the tracks were visible.

The head of the column was some distance south of the Black Horse Tavern when it halted, retraced its route almost to the starting point, marched east to Willoughby Run, turned south again, and then marched toward the Emmitsburg Road.[20] In spite of all the efforts to remain undetected, the Federals did discover Longstreet's column. Federal batteries played on the column much of the way.[21] Longstreet became impatient with the delay. He knew his column had been discovered by the enemy. The First Corps was approaching the Emmitsburg Road when Longstreet began issuing orders for the impending attack. He reminded McLaws that he would deploy on the enemy flank.[22] Brigadier General Joseph Brevard Kershaw, leading McLaws's Division, was just opposite the Peach Orchard when Longstreet informed the South Carolinian his brigade was to turn the Federal left flank and extend his line along the road adjacent to the orchard with his left resting near the Emmitsburg Road.[23] Hood's Division was approaching Pitzer School when Longstreet ordered Hood to push ahead of McLaws.[24]

Kershaw emerged from the woods along Warfield Ridge expecting to see the Federal flank to his left. Much to the Confederate's surprise the Federals were not where they were supposed to be. Federal infantry, supported by artillery, lay in strength on his front. The Federal line stretched southeast, extending almost to Little Round Top. Kershaw quickly surmised that carrying out his orders would present his right and rear to a destructive fire and communicated the situation to McLaws. McLaws was also astonished at the strength of the Federals massed on his front.[25] The plan of battle, as formulated in the morning, was unworkable in the afternoon.

Lee's battle plan underwent an eleventh hour change. His objective remained the high ground on the lower end of Cemetery Ridge and to achieve that goal his right would attack up the Emmitsburg Road. Lee ordered Longstreet to open the attack with his right division, Hood's, instead of McLaws as originally planned. Hood was given the order to attack up the Emmitsburg Road, holding his left as close as possible to that road. McLaws would follow Hood en echelon.[26] Kershaw reported that Hood was still filing past his position when orders were received directing him to commence his assault as soon as Hood was engaged. It was his understanding that Hood "was to sweep down on the enemy's line in a direction perpendicular to his own line of battle."[27]

Before the Round Tops

A quick look at the terrain over which his division would fight was all Hood needed to realize that his men were in for a rough afternoon. The enemy line, extending from the base of Round Top toward the Peach Orchard, was generally concave and well entrenched. As a result his line would come under fire from the flank, rear and front. To make matters worse, his line would be broken by the rocks around Devil's Den. Even if the seemingly impossible feat of carrying the heights were accomplished, Hood concluded it would be at a fearful sacrifice of his brave and gallant men.[28]

Before he arrived at the Emmitsburg Road, Hood sent out a squad of scouts from Robertson's Texas brigade with instructions to locate the Federal left and report back. His division was filing into line when the scouts returned with good news. The Texans found that the Federal left lay near the Round Tops. Surprisingly the Round Tops were not occupied though Federal trains were observed parked in the rear of the hills. The Federal left was in the air and vulnerable from artillery placed on the Round Tops. Hood's men could easily get in the Federal rear through open woods and pasture land about Round Top.[29] Hood sent a messenger to Longstreet with an urgent request to modify the plan and permit him to turn the mountain at its southern base. The First Corps commander quickly replied: "General Lee's orders are to attack up the Emmitsburg Road." Hood did not lack courage on the battlefield, which he had amply demonstrated at Gaines's Mill, Manassas, and Sharpsburg. But the intended attack, as he saw it, would bear little fruit and result in the destruction of his division. A second request was sent to Longstreet. Again the reply came back: "General Lee's orders are to attack up the Emmitsburg Road."

Hood was very busy during the short time available to prepare for the attack. Messengers scurried back and forth between division and corps headquarters. Brigade commanders were briefed on the assault. But Hood remained highly disturbed over the assignment his division had drawn. Preparations for the attack were barely under way when he concluded the Federal position, was as he termed it, "...impregnable and that independently of their flank fire, they could easily repel our attack by merely throwing and rolling stones down the mountain side, as we approached." In a desperate move Hood went to Moxley Sorrel, chief of staff for Longstreet, and begged him to examine the situation and convince the First Corps commander to modify the plans. Sorrel did go to Longstreet on his behalf, but the answer came back the same as before.[30] In the meantime Hood superintended the placement of his brigades.

It is not known if Longstreet gave his division commander the specifics of his formation and the order of attack by brigade, or if Hood was permitted the latitude to arrange his brigades. In any event, Hood formed his division in two lines. Law's Alabamians and Robertson's Texans were on the front line. Law's Brigade became the extreme right of the Confederate line, deploying in a wooded area under cover of Warfield Ridge. His brigade was east of the road. Law was designated the brigade of direction and would lead the assault with succeeding brigades taking up the attack en echelon from the left.[31]

Law's objective was the Federal left flank, which when the orders were issued, Hood believed either rested on the terminus of Houck Ridge above Devil's Den or extended to the base of Round Top.[32] Robertson reported his orders were to keep well closed on Law's left while his left hugged the Emmitsburg Road. His brigade of four regiments crossed the road at an angle. The 3rd Arkansas, on the extreme left, lay about 200 yards west of the road. Because of the wooded terrain, the road was not visible to those regiments on the left of the Texas brigade.[33] Benning's and Anderson's Georgia brigades went into position about two hundred yards in rear of the Alabama brigade.[34] Hood told Benning only that the division was to attack the Federal left and that he was to follow Law's Brigade at a distance of about 400 yards.[35] Hood's division artillery was to the front. Captain James Reilly's North Carolina (Rowan Artillery) battery was on Law's right. A battery was in position on Robertson's right and slightly forward of the 5th Texas.[36]

The First Corps artillery had been in place sometime when Hood's Division began filing into position.[37] Alexander's gunners had already seen action, though the shelling had by now ceased. Results of the previous action were clearly evident to Law's men. A three inch gun had burst and was lying by a gun carriage. Reilly's gunners welcomed Law's men with "surpressed cheers."[38] Coles implied the cheers were expressions of joy at having infantry support. More likely, the cheers were a good-natured rebuke directed at the infantry for taking so long to march south.

From left to right Law's order of battle was the 4th, 47th, 15th, 44th and 48th Alabama Regiments.[39] The 47th Alabama led Law's Brigade across the Emmitsburg Road, but was not on Law's right when his line was formed.[40] Law placed his senior ranking colonel, Jim Sheffield, in that position. Sheffield's right was just about opposite the center of Round Top.[41] His junior regimental commander, Oates, was in the center. The 4th Alabama's left was practically touching elbows with the 5th Texas.[42] Law completed deploying between 3 and 3:30 p.m.[43]

The Federal Left

The Federal left, anchored by a battery and its infantry support, lay along the terminus of Houck's Ridge. The only Federal presence on the Round Tops was the signal station and a picket line on the lower slopes of Round Top. Meade sent his chief engineer, Brigadier General Gouverneur K. Warren, to observe the situation on the Federal left. Warren reached Little Round Top about 3:30 p.m.[44]

When Warren reached the crest of Little Round Top, Hood's men were already hidden in the woods along the Emmitsburg Road.[45] A signalman thought he had seen Confederate troops between Plum Run and the Emmitsburg Road. Warren decided to identify their position. A short time later a shell from the Federal battery above Devil's Den whistled over Hood's men, its ominous sound causing the hidden troops to instinctively move or look in the direction of the shell's flight. The glint of sunlight from the Confederate musket barrels revealed to the Federals their presence in force and in position to overlap the Federal left. Warren knew the Federal left was in danger of being turned, and immediately sent an aide to Meade requesting a division.[46]

The shell came from Captain James E. Smith's 4th New York Battery of the III Corps

Artillery Brigade. Smith arrived on the field at 9:30 a.m. and parked in a wheatfield until 1 p.m., at which time Captain G. E. Randolph, III Corps chief of artillery, personally led the battery south to the terminus of Houck's Ridge. Smith's 4th New York Battery became the anchor of the Federal left. There was only room for two sections on the crest and none for the limbers, which were placed at its base. Once on the ridge Smith found his gun elevation could not be lowered to cover an advance through Plum Run Gorge. The remaining section was then placed one hundred to one hundred fifty yards to the right and rear in Plum Run Valley, facing south to cover Plum Run Gorge.[47]

Brigadier General John Henry Hobart Ward's Second Brigade, First Division, III Corps, deployed in a "L" shape, provided Smith's support. The base of the "L" was on Smith's left and at the time became the extreme Federal left. The 124th New York and 4th Maine provided direct support for Smith's battery. The 4th Maine, commanded by Colonel Elijah Walker, lay to the rear and left of Smith's guns and formed the base of the "L" shaped Federal left. Walker's objective was to cover Plum Run Gorge and the approach to Devil's Den. Walker was unhappy about his position, because his left was in the air and the woods on his front concealed the approach of Confederates moving north through the woods. The 124th New York lay behind and to the right of Smith's guns, its right extending into Rose's woods immediately north of Devil's Den. Eight companies of the 2nd U.S. Sharpshooters, under command of Major Homer R. Stoughton, covered Walker's front.[48] Smith's supporting infantry went into line around noon and spent the early part of the July afternoon in relative leisure.

The U.S. Sharpshooters were an elite unit. In 1861 the War Department had authorized Colonel Hiram Berdan to organize the 1st Regiment U.S. Sharpshooters. Its ranks were filled from companies recruited from all the states. Selection was by an exacting test of shooting ability. Each recruit was required to place ten consecutive shots within five inches of the center of a circle two hundred yards distant.[49] Berdan's recruiting effort was so successful that two regiments were ultimately formed. Members wore deep green uniforms instead of the regulation blue, and each man wore leather leggings a cap with a black plume.[50]

Stoughton spent the morning of July 2 picketing the north end of Plum Run Valley. One company was posted on Houck's Ridge, four lay in line perpendicular to Emmitsburg Road, and three were held in reserve. About 3 p.m. Stoughton was sent forward to cover the terrain south of the Devil's Den area. His men deployed behind stone fences on the Slyder and neighboring farms and in the edge of woods along Plum Run. Stoughton spent the afternoon personally adjusting his companies.[51]

Law Evaluates the Right

The Federal line was clearly visible in the Peach Orchard and around Devil's Den. Law concluded that if the Federals occupied the Round Tops the task confronting his brigade was formidable, if not impossible.[52] The absence of cavalry on his right and no visible evidence of infantry, either in the form of skirmishers or a line of battle, led Law to believe the Round Tops were not defended. But Smith's guns and his supporting infantry caused Law much concern, so Law decided on a reconnaissance of Round Top. Law personally selected six scouts to reconnoiter as far as the summit of Round Top. From this vantage point they were to look for the Federal left and send back a runner to report their findings.

A few minutes after the scouts left, several men were seen crossing the fields south of Round Top, moving in the general direction of the Emmitsburg Road. The unlucky fellows were quickly captured and proved to be Federals with surgeons' certificates headed for what they hoped to be the Federal rear at Emmitsburg, Maryland. These captives reported the Federal ordnance and medical trains were parked on the other side of Little Round Top, both lightly guarded. They told Law of a good farm road around the mountain which offered easy access to the trains, confirming what Hood's scouts had reported earlier. Even better was the news that the Federals did not expect an attack to come from the left. Law was convinced that Round Top was the key to victory. It should be secured and the Confederate line extended toward the Taneytown and Baltimore Roads to envelope the Federal left and rear.[53]

Law wanted to change the plan of attack outlined by Longstreet, and set out to find Hood. Along the way one of his scouts arrived from Round Top with the report that there were no Federal troops on Round Top, confirming the report of the captured Federals. Law found his division commander near the left of the Texas brigade, and quickly explained his findings and outlined a proposed modification of orders. Hood agreed with Law but reminded his subordinate that the orders were explicit. Longstreet's Corps was to attack en echelon up the Emmitsburg Road. Law persisted, lodged a formal protest, and outlined four reasons why the Round Tops should be occupied and the Confederate line extended around the Federal left. The points of his protest are repeated in his own words:

"1. That the great natural strength of the enemy's position in our front rendered the result of a direct assault extremely uncertain.
2. That, even if successful, the victory would be purchased at too great a sacrifice of life, and our troops would be in no condition to improve it.
3. That a front attack was unnecessary – the occupation of Round Top during the night by moving upon it from the south, and the extension of our right wing from that point across the enemy's left and rear, being not only practicable, but easy.
4. That such a movement would compel a change of front on the part of the enemy, the abandonment of his strong position on the heights, and force him to attack us in position."[54]

Of course, Hood had previously made two unsuccessful attempts to change Lee's plan.[55] Hood decided on one more appeal to Longstreet, his third direct appeal to the First Corps commander. Captain James Hamilton, of his staff, was brought forward and Hood asked Law to repeat his protest and plan in the officer's presence. Hamilton was then sent to Longstreet's headquarters with Hood's endorsement of the protest.[56] Ten minutes later Hamilton returned with Longstreet's adjutant, Colonel John Walter Fairfax, who repeated Longstreet's orders while Law was still present to hear the message.[57] The attack would follow the orders as issued.

Off to the right of the group, Law's Alabamians saw the colonel gesturing and pointing in what appeared to be the direction of the Round Tops. The tall colonel in his dress uniform was easily recognized by the men. He had gained the reputation of appearing in the location where the fighting was expected to be the severest.[58] Hood turned to Law and inquired if his brigadier understood the order. There was no need to reply.[59] Law immediately returned to his brigade.

Send the Troops Forward

After his position had been exposed by Warren, Hood's artillery began a duel with Smith's battery. Fifteen minutes later the general attack on the Federal left was under way.[60] Adjutant Leigh Terrell started the brigade forward by riding to the front of the 4th Alabama and shouting commands which were passed down the line. Somewhere in the ranks Private W. C. Ward, Company G, 4th Alabama, prayed silently for just thirty minutes more to rest, but his wish was not to be granted.[61] Next came the call to arms, as all down the line rang out the commands: "Shoulder arms! Right shoulder! Shift arms! Forward, guide center, march!" In the rear of the 47th Alabama Colonel Jackson struggled to his feet and called his regiment to arms, ordering a quick time march at trail arms.[62] Along the line ranks were hastily dressed and tired bodies suddenly filled with renewed energy. According to Ward "...the men sprang forward as if at a game of ball."[63] It was a little after 4 p.m. when Law's Alabama brigade moved forward at the quick step.[64] Reilly's gunners temporarily paused from their work when the 4th Alabama passed through the battery.[65]

Although Colonel Jackson began the charge, he soon collapsed, the first of four regimental commanders in Law's Brigade to be lost. Bulger was on the regiment's right and unaware that Jackson was down. Before Bulger would assume command, the 47th Alabama descended into Plum Run Valley.

Longstreet rode up as Hood started forward, the latter still complained about the plan of battle and expressed his regret that he could not turn the Federal left. Longstreet responded, in effect with, "We must obey the orders of General Lee."[66] Hood rode ahead of the Texans and started down the slope toward the wheatfield west of the Slyder house. Twenty minutes later a Federal shell fragment tore into his left arm.[67] Law, as senior brigadier on the field, ascended to divisional command. However, Law was to the right with the Alabama brigade, and it is uncertain when he became aware that he was the new division commander. More importantly, Hood's Division was without a commander during this period of time.

Confusion in the Attack

Hood's Division had barely begun its charge when the plan of attack began to fall apart. Law quickly experienced trouble maintaining formation within the brigade. Men clamored over numerous fences as best they could. None of the participants describe the obstacles in their path, but some of the men probably paused to tear down sections of worm fences. There was no time to redress the lines as Law pressed on. On the right of the line Sheffield marched through the rocks and trees on the north end of the Bushman woods.

During the descent into Plum Run Valley, officers from the 4th Alabama sprinted past the front ranks urging the men to move faster. Private Rufus B. Franks, Company I, sporting a new uniform recently brought from home, was yelling that the 4th Texas would be there before the 4th Alabama. As if on queue, the brigade, with a shout, went to the double quick step.[68] A few minutes later the Alabamians, the indescribable Rebel Yell filling the air, were running.[69] Terrell rode through the line of the 4th and attempted to restrain the men. But, they were now in open ground, crossing a plowed field south of the Bushman farmhouse, and in full view of Smith's guns posted above Devil's Den.[70] Stoughton's sharpshooters began to pepper the line with bullets from long range as shells exploded within the ranks. Law's Alabamians ran for the wooded slopes of Round Top.

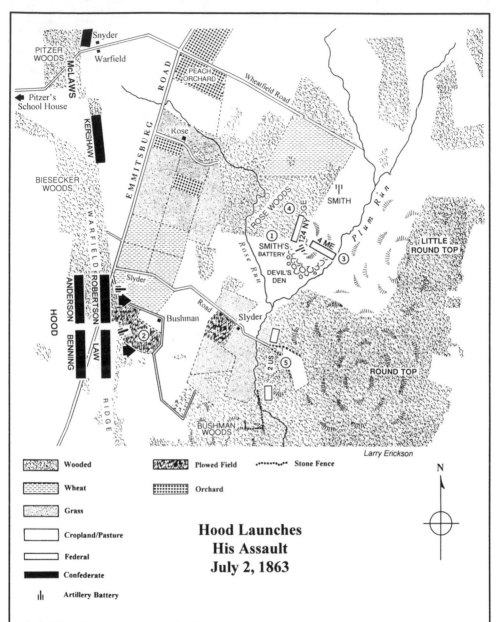

Larry Erickson

Wooded	Plowed Field	········ Stone Fence
Wheat	Orchard	
Grass		
Cropland/Pasture		
Federal		
Confederate		
⅛ Artillery Battery		

**Hood Launches
His Assault
July 2, 1863**

N

1. Smith's battery, stationed above Devil's Den, fires into Hood's Division before it moves forward and continues to play on Hood's men with telling effect as they move into Plum Run Valley.
2. Hood's Division begins its assault at approximately 4 p. m. Robertson's and Law's men race forward. Benning and Anderson move forward after the front brigades are in the valley.
3. The 4th Maine is deployed in rear of Smith's battery. Smith has requested that Walker move forward and to the left into the ravine through which Plum Run flowed.
4. The 124th New York supports Smith's right.
5. Stoughton's 2nd U.S. Sharpshooters are deployed as skirmishers east of the Slyder house. The Federal marksmen open, at long range, on Law and Robertson.

On Law's left Robertson was also experiencing difficulty. He was having trouble staying closed on Law and it became necessary to move forward at a run to keep up with the 4th Alabama. Almost immediately Robertson discovered the road fell away to the west much more rapidly than either he or Hood had believed when the assault was planned. Law's line of attack was also presenting a problem because, to make matters worst, Law was moving too far right. With the two events working against him Robertson found it impossible to hug the Emmitsburg Road and at the same time maintain contact with Law's left. A gap developed in the brigade when the 3rd Arkansas and 1st Texas attempted to follow the Emmitsburg Road while the 4th and 5th Texas remained connected with Law. Robertson concluded that Smith and his infantry support held the key to overrunning the Federal left. He decided, as he later reported, "to abandon the pike and close on General Law's left." The 3rd Arkansas and 1st Texas were ordered to close to the right, but did not establish contact with Law's line before arriving at the Federal defenses around Devil's Den.[71] The gap was then partially filled by the 44th and 48th Alabama.

Above Devil's Den, Smith made the most of his opportunity by pouring shot after shot into the charging Confederates. His voice rang out in concise commands above the roar of battle which left a lasting impression on men of the 124th New York.[72] Officers and available men from the 124th became ammunition bearers and labored furiously to carry shells up the ridge from the limbers below. Smith used case shot, with fuses set at five or six seconds as the Texans and Alabamians advanced across the fields.[73] Shells exploded over their heads or fell into the charging ranks. Ward later recalled he "...could hear the shot passing over us with the noise of partridges in flight."[74]

In the meantime Stoughton's Sharpshooters continued to fire on Law's line, inflicting a number of casualties. A spent bullet struck Sergeant Ward's left thigh a painful blow, but he managed to keep pace with his charging comrades.[75] His friend Sergeant John Taylor Darwin, Company I, 4th Alabama, was not so lucky. He suddenly stopped, quivered in agony, then sank to the ground with a bullet lodged in his brain.

William O. "Bill" Marshall, Company G, 4th Alabama, challenged Ward for the honor of reaching a stone fence first. Billy paused at Plum Run for a drink of water and was never seen again. His only legacy for services rendered was a muster roll inscription which declared he "...was noble and gallant."[76]

Private John M. Anderson, Company K, 48th Alabama, suffered from shrapnel wounds to a leg, arm and his forehead. He wrote his wife in Alabama that "the shot and shell fell like hail while the miney [*sic*] balls were whistling around on every side."[77] Second Lieutenant John M. Turnbow, Company G, 4th Alabama, fell dead near the Slyder dwellings.[78]

Isaac Feagin, 15th Alabama, went down with a leg wound which led to amputation. Within the 15th Alabama ranks Privates Alsop Kennedy, Company B, and William Trimmer, Company G, fell dead. Private G. E. Spenser of Company D took a severe wound from a shell fragment. He was permanently disabled and honorably discharged from service.[79]

Plum Run Valley

The line was just reaching the Plum Run Valley floor when skirmishers were thrown out to cover the right flank. These were Companies, A, D, and F from the 47th Alabama and Companies A and H from the 48th. During the remainder of the afternoon the five companies acted as two uncoordinated units. Captain Henry C. Lindsay, Company D, commanded the 47th Alabama's skirmishers, while Captain Randolph Graves, Company A, commanded those from the 48th Alabama. Both battalions moved quickly to the right and toward the Federal sharpshooters posted across Plum Run.[80]

The 4th Alabama, 1st Texas and 5th Texas made a dash through a grass hayfield, yelling for all they were worth. Coles recalled they were "...firing and running like demons."[81] As the three regiments advanced across the field south of the Slyder house, Stoughton's Sharpshooters waited behind a stone fence east of the house and just across Plum Run. A few scattered shots greeted the Alabamians and Texans as they approached, Scruggs took the precaution to order the 4th Alabama to fix bayonets. Men tumbled over the wall to find the Federals gone. The sharpshooters had disappeared into the adjacent woods.[82]

These elite marksmen were more comfortable firing at long range than fighting at close quarters. With the fighting fast developing at close range Stoughton's men began falling back. His left wing sought cover in the woods. Five companies fell back toward Walker's line at Devil's Den. The remaining three moved onto the slopes of Round Top.[83]

It now became necessary to halt and realign the ranks. Scruggs collapsed from heat exhaustion, the second regimental commander to fall out since the charge began.[84] Major Coleman assumed command, his first time to actually command troops in battle, but the young officer managed to gather his men and move off in a northerly direction over Round Top's lower slopes.

Coleman sent Adjutant Coles to the rear in search of stragglers. Coles found several men struggling forward and gave them encouragement, then passed on to the rear where he found others simply too exhausted to go farther and lay where they had fallen. Near the edge of the wheatfield, Coles thought he saw a familiar form lying face down. Prodding with his sword failed to convince a comrade he thought to be Private Charles T. Halsey, Company F, 4th Alabama, to get up. Coles thought his friend's conduct was strange "...because," according to Coles, "he knew Halsey was one of the best fighting men in the regiment and could always be found on the firing line." Coles left in some disgust and started back toward the 4th Alabama. The men were about to advance over the northwestern slope of Round Top as Coles rejoined the regiment in edge of the woods.[85]

The 4th Alabama's progress was greatly hampered by fallen timbers and large boulders scattered about. Each man freely issued commands to his neighbor as the line made its way through the obstacles. Men assisted each other over the boulders while others passed between them. By chance, Coles saw Halsey to his front, very much surprised at his friend's quick recovery and exclaimed: "How in the world did you get here?" "Get here?" Halsey asked, "I've been here all the time." Coles later mused that happily it was a case of mistaken identity. In spite of all the interchange, alignment soon fell apart. Many men simply fell down, victims of heat exhaustion and lack of water. The 25-mile march to the battlefield was taking its toll. Officers attempted to put the line in motion, but the soldiers needed more rest before making the climb to the crest of Little Round Top.[86]

The 47th Alabama's charge also became disorganized while the men were running and crossing fences. There was no commander to dress its ranks. Bulger was puzzled when it appeared that Jackson was not attempting to control the regiment but as he looked to the left, Jackson's familiar form was missing from its usual place. Bulger did not know the colonel had collapsed shortly after the regiment began its charge. However, he ran out in front of the 47th to get its attention. He managed to halt the regiment, but not before it crowded the 15th Alabama, mingled with Oates's left and disrupted the progress of both lines.[87] After closing the ranks, Bulger sent it forward again, this time the 47th moved smartly at the double quick. Bulger was guiding it toward the cover of the boulders and thick woods on Round Top's lower slopes. A few minutes later Terrell rode up and informed Bulger that Jackson was down and that he was in command of the 47th Alabama.[88]

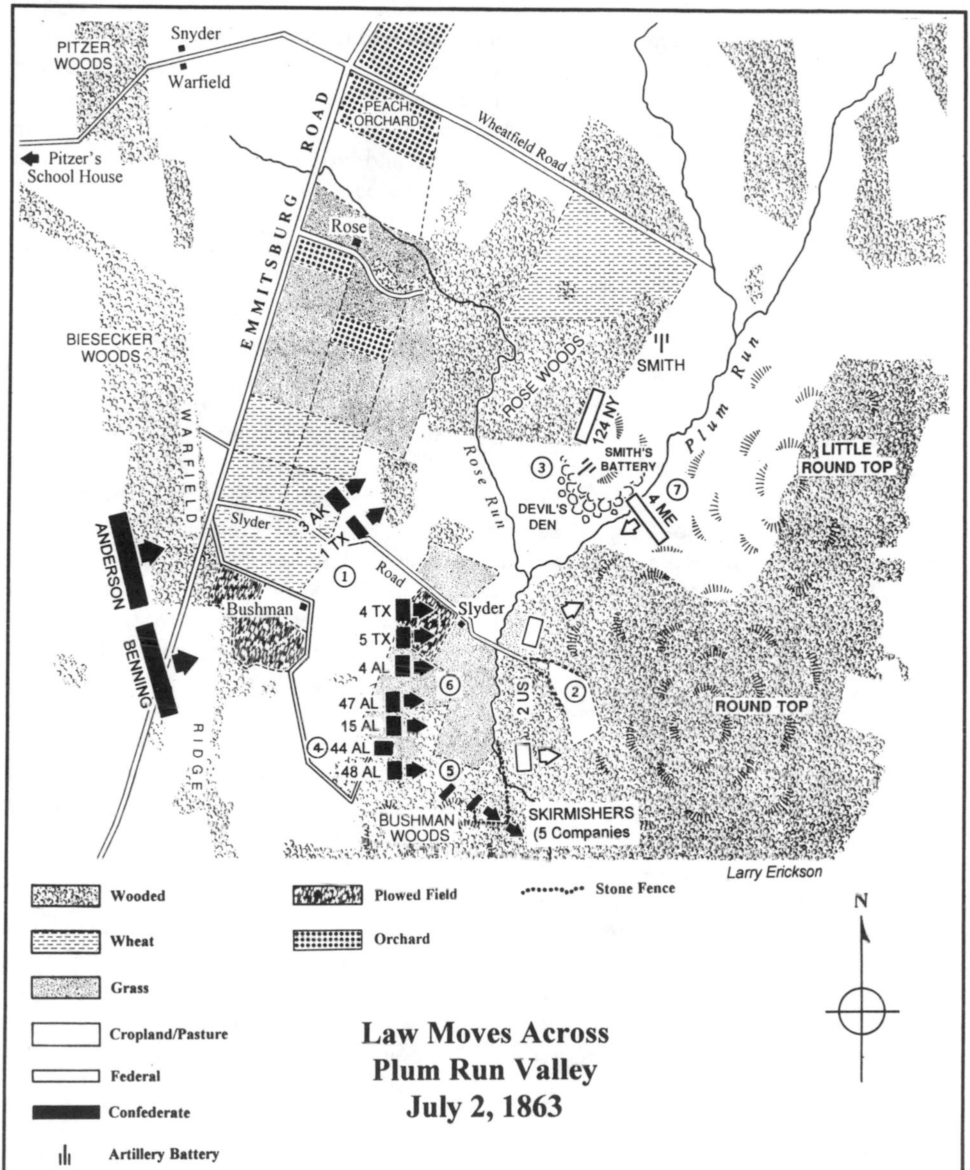

PITZER WOODS
Snyder
Warfield
Pitzer's School House
PEACH ORCHARD
Wheatfield Road
EMMITSBURG ROAD
Rose
BIESECKER WOODS
WARFIELD
RIDGE
ROSE WOODS
SMITH
124 NY
Plum Run
Rose Run
SMITH'S BATTERY
DEVIL'S DEN
4 ME
LITTLE ROUND TOP
3 AK
1 TX
Slyder
Road
ANDERSON
BENNING
Bushman
Slyder
4 TX
5 TX
4 AL
47 AL
15 AL
44 AL
48 AL
2 US
ROUND TOP
BUSHMAN WOODS
SKIRMISHERS (5 Companies
Larry Erickson
Wooded
Plowed Field
Stone Fence
Wheat
Orchard
Grass
Cropland/Pasture
Federal
Confederate
Artillery Battery
N

Law Moves Across Plum Run Valley July 2, 1863

1. A large gap appears in Robertson's Brigade as he tries to hug the Emmitsburg Road.
2. Stoughton's Sharpshooters continue to fire on Law's line as it crosses Plum Run Valley. As Law's men approach Plum Run Stoughton's force divides and falls back. The right moves north and joins the 4th Maine around Devil's Den. The left falls back on Round Top to menace the 15th and 47th Alabama.
3. Smith's battery continues to play on Law's line, inflicting a number of casualties.
4. Law has withdrawn the 44th Alabama from the brigade's right and sent it against Smith's battery.
5. Law orders the 48th Alabama from the extreme right to support the 44th Alabama in its attack on Devil's Den. Skirmishers from the 47th and 48th Alabama are moving south and advance to the eastern side of Round Top.
6. The 47th and 15th Alabama continue toward Round Top. The 4th, 5th Texas and the 4th Alabama cross Plum Run, move into the woods and prepare to assault Little Round Top.
7. The 4th Maine is moving forward to cover an attack from the woods.

Stoughton recorded that he saw one regiment thrown into confusion and rally before continuing forward.[89] It is likely that he witnessed the confusion of the intermingling of the 15th and 47th and Bulger halting the 47th to regain control.

Smith's cannonading was so effective that Law decided the Federal battery had to be eliminated. Law's line was west of the Slyder house and crossing a grassy fenced in area when he ordered in succession the 44th and 48th Alabama regiments out of line to oblique sharply left.[90] Prior to the advance Law had not communicated the plan of battle to his regimental commanders.[91] This was probably the first indication that any of them had that the intended objective was the Federal left.

Sheffield was senior to Perry and normally would have acted as commander of both regiments. However, Perry reported the 44th Alabama "was detached from its place in line, by order of General Law." His regiment was expected to capture the battery that had been playing on the line from the moment the charge began.[92] Sheffield only acknowledged command of the 48th and then brigade command in his battlefield report. Because the two regiments operated independently it has to be assumed Law communicated separately with Perry and Sheffield. Both regiments crossed behind the brigade and entered the woods east of the Slyder buildings. A short time later Perry discovered he was too far east and executed a left wheel maneuver toward the sounds of the battery.

Law next informed Oates that the 15th Alabama held the Confederate extreme right. It is believed that Oates, at the time, was just east of Plum Run and fronting the southern slope of Round Top. He was instructed to execute a left wheel and move in the direction of the heights on his left.[93] However, Oates did not identify which heights, Devil's Den or Little Round Top. When the Alabamians were in that part of Plum Run Valley the only information available to Law on Federal positions was gathered by his scouts before the charge began. There would be no reason for him to believe that Little Round Top was occupied, nor could he have known that plans were under way to fortify the hill. While still in Plum Run Valley Bulger believed his objective was Smith's guns and the infantry defending it.[94] It is reasonable to expect that Bulger acted under the same orders. Law probably directed Oates to advance in the direction of Devil's Den.[95]

Law also told Oates that Bulger would be instructed to keep the 47th Alabama closed on the 15th Alabama. Oates later claimed he understood Bulger was to act under his command in the event the 47th and 15th Alabama regiments became separated from the remainder of the brigade.[96] Oates did not see Law again until the following day.

There is no indication from Bulger's description of the charge that he at any time considered himself acting under Oates's orders.[97] His actions after assuming command of the 47th support this observation. However, the 47th more or less stayed on the left of the 15th Alabama, though it did arrive before Little Round Top ahead of the 15th.

Law's skirmishers did not engage Stoughton's men. Instead they crossed Plum Run near a bridge and continued around the southern base of Round Top to the eastern side. Because they were thrown forward prior to the 47th and 48th receiving orders to turn north there is no reason to believe that the officers in charge knew the brigade would change direction. Skirmishers from the 47th and 48th Alabama went as far as the northern base of Round Top without encountering Federal troops. The skirmishers remained on the eastern side until nightfall when they rejoined their regiments.[98] The five companies represented the loss of half a regiment from the fighting strength of Law's Brigade.

At this point in the charge, Law's advance divided into four separate thrusts. The 4th Alabama and the 4th and 5th Texas were on a course to take the three regiments over the lower slopes of Round Top. The 15th and seven companies of the 47th Alabama would eventually sweep north over the crest of Round Top. Perry with the 44th and Sheffield with eight companies were about to launch an attack on Smith's guns above Devil's Den. Five companies, acting as skirmishers, were making their way around the southern end of Round Top.

The Federal Position – Devil's Den Area

Walker and his 4th Maine waited in the valley beside, and in the gorge in front of, Devil's Den. He was in the gorge against his better judgment and at the moment experienced much anxiety. His mission was to cover Smith's guns and he was convinced that mission could best be accomplished from his former position. Earlier in the afternoon, when Smith discovered his guns could not cover an attack from below Devil's Den, he requested the 4th Maine move into the ravine in his front. Walker declined, so Smith then went directly to Ward and requested Walker be ordered into the ravine. Ward agreed and sent his adjutant to Walker with orders to move forward. Walker protested once again, but grudgingly moved his men into position as Hood's Division began its advance.[99]

After posting skirmishers among the rocks of Devil's Den, Walker moved the rest of his regiment into the ravine. Walker had lost sight of the Confederates in the field, but the sounds of skirmishing in the woods to the south indicated the advance was nearing his position. To cover his left flank, Walker extended his line by sending skirmishers into the woods on the lower slopes of Round Top.

While Walker and the 4th Maine waited in Devil's Den, the surrounding fields and woods were teeming with activity. The Alabama brigade and the Texas regiments pressed their advance on Devil's Den and the Round Tops, while a Federal brigade moved over the crest of Little Round Top and began deploying on its southern slopes. Walker felt a little better about the situation when a line of skirmishers from the unknown brigade was thrown out on his left. At first he thought the troops intended to connect with his left, but a short time later Law's men appeared on his left and drove the new arrivals back on the main line.[100] Elements of the 2nd U.S. Sharpshooters fell back through Walker's skirmishers and joined the 4th Maine among the boulders of Devil's Den. Next, a body of troops Walker described as a strong skirmish line appeared on his front and left flank. These were followed a few minutes later by a second line in greater strength.[101] Walker's brief moment of relief passed, for his impending fear that he would encounter disaster in the ravine below Devil's Den was about to be realized.

The Federal brigade on Little Round Top was Colonel Strong Vincent's Third Brigade, First Division, V Corps.[102] The skirmishers that Walker thought would connect with his line had been thrown out by Vincent to cover his front. The large body of troops off to his left were the 4th Alabama and 4th and 5th Texas. After executing a wheel left west of Round Top they were advancing on a line to attack Little Round Top. The troops about to engage Walker's 4th Maine were the 44th and 48th Alabama. Benning's Brigade was advancing some distance to the rear of Perry and Sheffield. Walker waited for the Alabamians to attack.[103]

Attack on Devil's Den

Neither Perry nor the rest of his regiment suspected imminent danger. Walker's men lay hidden among the boulders of Devil's Den, and as the 44th Alabama emerged from the woods a few scattered shots from the boulders gave the only hint that a Federal line lay nearby. Perry was barely able to yell "down" before a sheet of flame erupted from the boulders, as the 4th Maine's first volley tore into the ranks of the 44th. When the entire

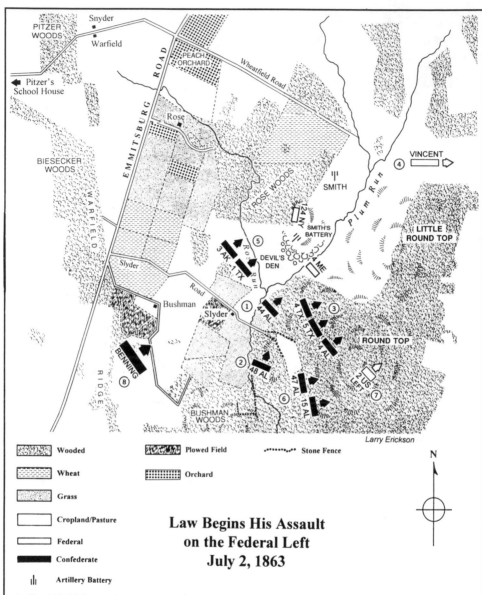

Larry Erickson

Legend

Wooded		Plowed Field	
Wheat		Orchard	
Grass		Stone Fence	
Cropland/Pasture			
Federal			
Confederate			
Artillery Battery			

N

Law Begins His Assault
on the Federal Left
July 2, 1863

1. The 44th Alabama advances on Devil's Den to engage the 4th Maine.
2. The 48th Alabama has withdrawn from the main line and is moving to support the 44th Alabama.
3. The 4th Texas, 5th Texas and 4th Alabama enter the woods and advance over Round Top's lower slopes toward Little Round Top.
4. Vincent's brigade moves around the northern end of Little Round Top to ascend the eastern side.
5. The 3rd Arkansas and 1st Texas prepare to assault Devil's Den from the western side.
6. The 15th and 47th Alabama enter the woods on Round Top's southern end. The 47th and 15th Alabama are ordered to advance north toward Little Round Top, but Oates is unsure of the Federal strength on his front and decides to move up Round Top's southern slope.
7. Stoughton's men fall back and fire on the 15th Alabama as both clamor up the mountain.
8. Benning emerges from the woods along the Emmitsburg Road and mistakes the 3rd Arkansas and 5th Texas for Law's Brigade, which he is supposed to follow, and instead follows them toward Devil's Den.

line went down, Walker thought he had achieved a complete surprise and had wiped out the entire regiment. Perry later reported his casualties from the first volley were relatively light.[104] In fact over one quarter of the line fell dead or wounded.[105] The 44th lay where it fell while Walker managed to get off five to eight volleys. When the 44th Alabama did return the 4th Maine's fire, a close quarter fight developed that lasted 20 to 30 minutes.[106] Casualties in the 4th Maine mounted rapidly and the men sought cover among the boulders of Devil's Den. Despite a painful wound, Walker continued to command his regiment.[107]

In the meantime the 48th Alabama emerged from the woods into open ground in front of Little Round Top. Sheffield began deploying in line of battle on Perry's right and engaged the 4th Maine's left from a distance of 20 paces.[108] Casualties mounted rapidly on the left of the line. The right was partially protected by the woods and it fared a little better. The Federal line on Little Round Top joined in the attack on the 48th Alabama which brought fire from the front and right flank. His left was forced back to the cover of the woods on Round Top's lower slopes, while his right tenaciously maintained its position in the edge of the woods. Sheffield rallied the men and brought the left forward, once more, into line of battle.[109] The 48th prepared to resume its fight when Benning arrived on the scene.

Devil's Den Is Secured

Benning emerged from the woods along the Emmitsburg Road and was immediately awed by the scene before him. Devil's Den and Little Round Top were alive with Federal activity. Smith's battery and his supporting infantry were clearly visible. Vincent's line was in place below the crest of Little Round Top. Skirmishers extended Vincent's line to the floor of Plum Run Valley. Five guns on a ledge above Vincent commanded all approaches to Little Round Top. In all, Benning counted 11 guns. About 400 yards ahead he saw a Confederate line he thought was Law and followed. Actually Law's Brigade was farther right, hidden from Benning's view in the woods. Benning mistakenly followed Robertson's left regiments to the fight for Devil's Den.[110]

By this time Law knew he was division commander and had joined the fight around Devil's Den. Very little is known about his activities that hot afternoon in southern Pennsylvania for, unfortunately, he failed to prepare a report of the action. None of his post-war articles speak in any detail of his direct involvement. It is known that after assuming division command his time was spent around Devil's Den. However, it appears that communications with his subordinates suffered. The fighting around Devil's Den was almost over before Sheffield knew he was brigade commander.[111] Robertson did not learn for sometime that Law was division commander and communicated directly with Longstreet when Hood was reported wounded.[112] Apparently Law did not communicate directly with Robertson so he must, therefore, have limited his attention to Benning, Anderson and Perry. As Benning and Anderson came up, Law threw their regiments into the fray, and after that Law disappeared into the smoke and haze around Devil's Den.[113]

Benning's right wing, composed of the 2nd and 17th Georgia regiments moved up on the left of the 44th.[114] As the two Georgia regiments moved through the woods, they picked up Federal stragglers and sent them to the rear. Walker was concerned about his exposed flanks when he discovered Smith in the process of abandoning his guns. A short time later he realized his line was in danger of being overrun and gave the order to fall back. Perry seized the opportunity to hasten Walker's retreat as Perry ran through his line yelling "forward." [115] The entire line rose as one and followed its colonel.

Perry's right wing scrambled over the boulders while his left, led by Major George Walton Cary, scaled the south end of Houck's Ridge and made for Smith's abandoned guns.[116] The colors of the 44th went down and were picked up by sixteen-year-old Private James L. Forte. Perry reached the base of Devil's Den, but that was as far as he was able to go. Exhaustion from the heat, lack of water and the final burst of energy required to make the charge forced him to fall out and seek cover among the boulders. Perry became the third regimental commander of the brigade to collapse. He was forced to seek cover among the boulders while his men swarmed over Smith's guns. Forte mounted a gun carriage and began waving the regimental colors. A Federal gunner grabbed a gun swab and knocked the young flag bearer senseless.[117] About one hour after the charge began, Devil's Den belonged to the Confederates.[118]

Cary seized the regimental flag and led the charge farther up Houck's Ridge. He soon returned and joyfully displayed swords captured from officers of the 4th Maine.[119] Case shot suddenly began to rain down on Devil's Den from the direction of Little Round Top.[120] Perry saw that the missiles of destruction came from a section of battery that had been placed on a shelf above the Federal infantry. Cary once again disappeared into the smoke but quickly returned with news that caused Perry great concern. A Federal force in sufficient strength to overlap their position was advancing down Plum Run Valley. Perry struggled to his feet and attempted to scale the rocks for a view of the advancing troops, but the colonel's legs refused to support him and he sank back to the ground.[121] Cary and the survivors of the charge were left to confront the new threat.

Walker rallied the 4th Maine some distance behind Devil's Den and ordered bayonets fixed, the click of steel against steel as the bayonets snapped into place becoming permanently etched in his mind. He then moved the 4th Maine slowly forward until the regiment was about even with Smith's original position and once again became engaged.[122] To his rear the 6th New Jersey and 40th New York regiments were moving up in support. Smith opened with his two remaining guns and fired down Plum Run Valley toward the gorge entrance. The combined onslaught dealt Sheffield's line severe punishment, particularly his left wing. The regimental flag went down three times.[123] He was forced back to the cover of the woods, a second time, on Round Top's lower slopes. After rallying the men, Sheffield brought the line forward, once more, only to have the regiment driven back a third time.[124]

Sheffield's young adjutant, Henry Figures, assumed a number of roles that afternoon. At one point he saw the flag lying on the ground and became the regimental color bearer. During the hottest part of the engagement he retrieved a musket and fired a few rounds at the opposing line. That accomplished, he turned to the task of assisting his fellow officers in keeping the men in line. But the thing that made the most vivid impression on the young soldier that afternoon was Little Round Top. Its height grew as the afternoon wore on, and a few days later he wrote home that it was the steepest hill he had ever seen.[125]

When the 48th Alabama was driven back a third time, Sheffield decided to pull back some distance and regroup. His regiment had been engaged at least a hour and a half and was pretty well fought out. Ignoring their fatigue and thirst, Sheffield was in the process of bringing his men back into rank when he was notified to take command of the brigade. The 48th was turned over to Captain Thomas Eubanks, Company D, who completed the task of reforming the north Alabamians, and a short time later the 48th Alabama made its fourth appearance on the front line.[126]

Warren Finds a Brigade

The Federal V Corps was just making its way onto the field when Warren set out to find troops to man the Round Tops. Vincent's Third Brigade of the Third Division was in the lead with Colonel Joshua L. Chamberlain's 20th Maine, accompanied by Vincent, at the head of the brigade.[127] The young Federal commander was not yet a brigadier, but the similarities to Law are worth noting. Like Law, Vincent was 26 years of age, the youngest brigade commander in Meade's army, and a strict disciplinarian and was gaining a reputation as being fearless in battle. Vincent was about the same height as Law, if not a bit taller, and a splendid horseman. Just after the start of hostilities he had enlisted in the 83rd Pennsylvania, becoming its first lieutenant-colonel and later colonel.[128]

The Third Brigade had just reached the Rose Woods and began preparing to go into line when someone spotted an officer galloping toward them. Vincent rode out to meet the rider, as his standard bearer and a staff officer followed a short distance to the rear. Men watching from the ranks saw a great deal of pointing toward Little Round Top. The horseman was the staff officer sent from Warren seeking troops for Little Round Top. Vincent immediately took responsibility for occupying the eminence.

Vincent directed his senior colonel to bring up the brigade while he and his standard bearer rode ahead to search for a position. After two attempts to climb the northwestern slope failed, the two galloped around to the eastern side. A few minutes later the brigade flag was visible through the trees on the crest of Little Round Top.

To the southwest, Vincent spotted part of Hood's battle line making its way across the fields east of the Emmitsburg Road. He saw men dropping from the ranks as shells burst around them.[129] He couldn't see Law's Alabamians in the woods on Round Top's western slopes. Unaware of the impending danger, Vincent began surveying the ground his brigade was to defend.[130]

Vincent's brigade made its way past Little Round Top's northern slopes, with the 44th New York in the lead. Next in line came the 16th Michigan, 83rd Pennsylvania, and finally the 20th Maine.[131] The brigade, 1,141 muskets strong with each man carrying 60 rounds of ammunition, moved completely around to the eastern side, turned right and climbed through the wooded slopes toward the summit.[132] Shells from Hood's artillery were still exploding among the trees and rocks as they scrambled up Little Round Top's slopes. The air was filled with slashing and humming sounds as shell fragments ripped branches from trees and rock fragments flew about. Officers dismounted and sent their horses to safety.[133]

Vincent personally supervised each regiment's deployment. The 44th New York should have gone into line on the right of the 16th Michigan. However, its commander, Colonel James C. Rice, wanted to go into line with the 83rd Pennsylvania because his regiment had stood side by side with the 83rd in previous engagements. Rice may have been superstitious, or he may have been acting on a whim, but he saw no reason to change. He requested Vincent place the two regiments in line together. Vincent agreed and sent the 16th Michigan into line on the brigade's extreme right.[134] The 44th New York took up position on the 16th Michigan's left. The 83rd Pennsylvania was next in line and threw out skirmishers onto the lower slopes. The 20th Maine became the anchor of the Federal army's left.[135]

Chamberlain was an unlikely hero, which he was to become that day. Though he came from a long line of volunteer soldiers, his education and profession did little to prepare him for his place in history. Born in Brewer, Maine, he had received his grade school education at a military academy. He was a graduate of Bowdoin College, class of 1852, and the Theological Seminary at Bangor, Maine, in 1855. Chamberlain returned to Bowdoin College as a lecturer the same year. Refused a leave to volunteer for military service at the outbreak of hostilities, Chamberlain, in 1862, requested and was granted leave to study in Europe. Instead, he became the lieutenant colonel of the 20th Maine.[136]

Chamberlain, Rice and Vincent watched the right regiments as each went into line. The trio apparently stood near the 16th Michigan's center and had a good view of the fighting raging below in the Devil's Den area. Vincent accompanied Chamberlain to the left as shells exploded among the rocks and trees. As Vincent left to make his way back to the brigade's center his parting words to Chamberlain were: "Hold at all hazards."[137] Those few words were the last communications between the two men.[138] Chamberlain's line faced slightly west of south.[139] Vincent's brigade formed a huge quarter circle which wrapped southward around Little Round Top and terminated near the northern end of a valley between the Round Tops.

The valley which was relatively flat and covered with brush and trees lay between the men from Maine and Round Top.[140] Because of the vicious fighting which occurred there later in the afternoon, the historian of the 83rd Pennsylvania referred to the valley between the Round Tops as the "Valley of the Shadow of Death."[141] Across the valley lay the northern slopes of Round Top. Chamberlain conducted a quick reconnaissance and found his left uncovered. Captain Walter G. Morrill's Company B was ordered to extend the 20th Maine's line farther south by moving to the woods across the valley.[142] Instead of extending the 20th Maine line, Morrill led his company across the valley and entered the woods on the far side.[143] Chamberlain later explained that although Morrill's instructions were to act as the situation dictated, his primary objective was to prevent a surprise assault on the 20th Maine's left flank.[144] Morrill's trip into the woods would prove very fortuitous as the events of the afternoon unfolded.

A company from the 83rd Pennsylvania and 44th New York went forward to the lower slopes of Little Round Top as skirmishers. These were the men that Walker thought were about to connect with his left. The right of Vincent's line had directed the fire on Sheffield and contributed to forcing his left back.

Vincent's commanders mustered every man available, including the drummers from the 83rd Pennsylvania who tossed away their drums and took a place in line. Every pioneer and musician who could carry a musket went into the ranks of the 20th Maine. Footsore soldiers and the sick made their way into the lines. Chamberlain even relieved some men under arrest and put them into line.[145]

To see what was on his left Vincent sent his acting assistant inspector general, Captain Eugene A. Nash, to climb Round Top and observe the Confederate movements. As he left Little Round Top, Nash saw two or three lines advancing without skirmishers in Plum Run Valley. Since the fight in Devil's Den was in progress at the time and Oates and Bulger were in the woods on Round Top's lower slopes, these were probably Benning's and Anderson's Brigades. Nash was on Round Top when he discovered a large boulder from which to get a good view of the western side. The Texans and Alabamians were in plain view and just beginning their assault on Little Round Top. The line of the 47th Alabama was visible through the trees on Round Top's lower slopes. As he observed the Confederate movements, random shots began to zip in and crash among the rocks scattered about, so Nash hastened down Round Top to join the fight for Little Round Top.[146]

Attack on Vincent's Center

Vincent's brigade had been in place less than fifteen minutes when the Alabama and Texas lines emerged from the woods. The 83rd Pennsylvania's color bearer's flag staff was

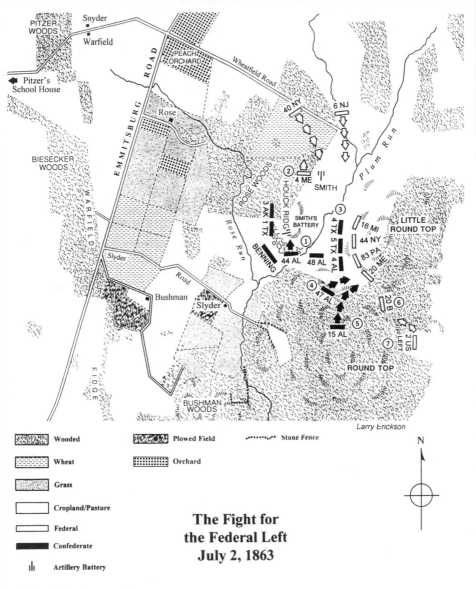

Larry Erickson

Wooded		Plowed Field	········ Stone Fence
Wheat		Orchard	
Grass			
Cropland/Pasture			
Federal			
Confederate			
ılı Artillery Battery			

N

The Fight for
the Federal Left
July 2, 1863

1. The 44th Alabama participates in overrunning Smith's battery. Its men are the first among the New Yorkers' guns.
2. The 4th Maine has retreated north in Plum Run Valley where it will reform to counterattack. The 40th New York and 6th New Jersey are moving to support the defense of Devil's Den.
3. The 4th Texas, 5th Texas and 4th Alabama continue their attack on Vincent's center and right.
4. The 47th Alabama advances over Round Top's northern slopes to attack the 20th Maine's right and center.
5. The 15th Alabama descends Round Top, enters the valley between the Round Tops, and advances to attack the 20th Maine's left.
6. Captain Morrill, commanding Company B, extends the 20th Maine's left across the valley between the Round Tops.
7. A small detachment of Stoughton's Sharpshooters descend Round Top's eastern slopes to join Morrill.

firmly planted in the crevice of a rock. He gripped a musket and awaited the order to fire. In the meantime Vincent's skirmishers retreated up Little Round Top.[147]

Musket fire erupted from the mountain's crest as soon as the Confederates emerged from the woods. The first volley took a heavy toll on the front rank of the 4th Alabama. Sergeant Ward and two companions on either side went down together. Ward's wound was in the lower part of his body. He experienced a sharp pain, falling to the ground unconscious.[148]

Men from the second rank rushed over their comrades and struggled around and over boulders scattered over the slope. The brunt of the assault fell on the 83rd Pennsylvania and 44th New York. According to Captain William Robbins it was difficult to determine during the initial assault which Confederate regiments fought a given regiment in Vincent's line, as all regiments on both sides were connected. He later concluded the 4th Alabama's initial attack was against the 83rd Pennsylvania and the 4th and 5th Texas fought the 44th New York and 16th Michigan.[149] The Confederate lined staggered under a galling fire from Vincent's men. Alabamians and Texans paused to fire into the Federal ranks above them. Some were able to fire from the protection of boulders. But the line was soon forced to fall back in confusion.[150]

Ward regained consciousness and immediately knew from the sound of musket fire above that the main Federal line had been found. His legs were useless, but Ward managed to drag himself to the cover of a large boulder which was four or five feet high. A private from Company A passed by, stopped and offered assistance, but was told to go on. The private did as he was told and received a severe chest wound. A second private, without a weapon, stopped to help and was sent on with Ward's rifle. Sergeant John W. Mosely, Company G, 4th Alabama, came up and took shelter behind the same boulder with Ward. The sixteen-year-old Mosely had become too exhausted to keep up with comrades and was probably one of the stragglers that Coles had seen on his trip to the rear. Ward chastised the young man for not moving on to join his regiment. Mosely mustered sufficient strength to struggle forward and eventually took his place in line. The young Alabamian was within 50 yards of Vincent's line when he was struck down.[151] His fate would lie in the hands of the Federals.

A second charge came within several yards of Vincent's line before a terrific fire caused it to halt. The Texans and Alabamians were so close to the line of the defenders it became quite hazardous to retreat. After wavering a few moments the Confederate line broke in confusion. Some of the men chanced a hasty retreat. A few held up handkerchiefs or hats to signal surrender, while others chose to take cover behind boulders and a slight elevation not far from the Federal line and fire on the defenders.[152]

Private Rufus Franks suddenly stood up from his place in line and started for the rear, still holding his rifle. As he passed Adjutant Coles the young soldier quietly pleaded with Coles to seek out Major Coleman and convince him to order a retreat. Franks felt that a few Confederates would be unable to beat the entire Federal army. Coles thought that Franks had suffered a minor wound and subsequently lost his courage. It was then that Coles noticed Franks's face was deathly white. Without looking back, Franks told Coles he was wounded and continued on. He was able to make his way back to the base of the mountain where he was placed in an ambulance wagon. Franks was wounded in the abdomen. He suffered greatly with spasms and severe nausea as the wagon bounced its way toward the division field hospital where he died a painful death.[153]

From the crest of Little Round Top, a Federal battery opened fire on the Alabamians, Texans and Georgians fighting around Devil's Den. The battery, commanded by Lieutenant Charles Hazlett, went into position shortly after the 4th Alabama began its assault.

When Hazlett fired his first round Vincent's men paused momentarily. The 44th New York's historian wrote that "No military music ever sounded sweeter." A loud cheer erupted along the line as the first shell exploded near Devil's Den.[154] This was the fire brought to bear on Perry after the 44th Alabama overran Smith's guns.

The 4th and 5th Texas fell back to an open space to regroup.[155] The 4th Alabama retired to a position farther to the right of the Texans and covered some companies of the 20th Maine's right.[156] Major Coleman rallied the survivors for a third attempt to break Vincent's line. Men fired, sought cover behind a boulder, and then ran up the mountain to the next boulder. Captain Robbins stood at the 4th Alabama's right flank while a leaden hailstorm rained down on his position. Private Decimus Barziza, 4th Texas, recalled "The trees were barked and thousands of bullets blew to atoms against the hard rocks."[157] Grit and gravel chipped from surrounding boulders felt like needles jabbing the skin. Dust particles filled the eyes bringing a flow of tears. After the third attempt was repulsed the 4th Alabama was totally exhausted. There was no fight left in the 4th, its men drifting back to the cover of the woods and lying prostrate among the rocks and boulders.

Coleman attempted to reform the 4th Alabama at the base of Little Round Top. Nearly 25 percent of the regiment were casualties. Many others were scattered around the battlefield, victims of the morning's sustained march. Coleman was in the process of rallying the 4th Alabama when one of Longstreet's staff officers rode up and in a loud voice inquired for the person in command. No one within sound of his voice responded. Someone eventually pointed in the direction of Coleman. The staff officer mistook Coles for the 4th's commanding officer, rode over to the adjutant and pressed his foot hard on Coles's shoulder. At the same time he loudly ordered the regiment to charge Little Round Top. Coles politely informed the staff officer of his mistake and directed the man to Coleman. Apparently the staff officer decided the task of finding the commander was impossible and rode into the woods.[158] Coleman reformed the 4th Alabama and the regiment retired to the woods covering the western slopes of Round Top, as his men maintained a brisk fire from the cover of rocks and trees.[159]

Oates Occupies Round Top

After crossing a fence beyond Plum Run, Oates noticed a few stragglers from Stoughton's Sharpshooters making their way up Round Top. The main body of sharpshooters disappeared into the woods, and Oates was trying to decide the next course of action. He was under orders to turn left. However, Oates was more concerned about the force he perceived to be somewhere in the woods on Round Top and felt he had to deal with this enemy. He decided to disobey the order. Oates later tried to justify his disobedience by complaining that the 47th Alabama was pressing his left too closely and causing confusion in his ranks. He further explained that in order to obey he would have had to turn into the 47th Alabama. In addition the 15th Alabama's right flank would have been exposed to an enfilading fire from the enemy on his right.[160] The 15th Alabama continued to press forward in search of the sharpshooters and began climbing the rugged slopes of Round Top.

Stoughton's men scrambled up the mountainside with Oates in pursuit. It was not an easy climb for either force. Men were forced to climb by clinging to rocks, bushes and tree limbs or by crawling over boulders. Stoughton's men moved up a short distance, fired at the 15th Alabama and then took shelter. Most of the shots whizzed harmlessly overhead. The 15th Alabama's return fire also failed to find its mark. Shots striking the rocks around Nash as he observed the fighting below were probably from the 15th Alabama. About halfway up the mountainside Stoughton divided his command into two squads. One squad was sent to the eastern side of the mountain, while the other fell back and moved westward and around the 47th Alabama's left. Departing shots from the men in green uniforms as they moved off to the right of the 15th Alabama caused Oates to detach Company A to protect his right flank. Oates then scrambled onto the crest of Round Top.[161]

Bulger Encourages His Men

On the lower slopes Bulger halted to realign the 47th Alabama. Now that his men were protected by the boulders and thick woods, Bulger took the opportunity to explain the task ahead. He intended to drive the enemy as ordered, but he was also concerned for the safety of his men, particularly because of the fire from the battery posted above Devil's Den. Bulger instructed his men to advance, using the boulders for protection from the Federal infantry fire, and at the same time use the Federal troops as a shield against the Federal battery. At the appropriate moment Bulger intended to turn on the battery and overrun it. His plan was simple: move cautiously, get behind a boulder, carefully select a target and fire, then advance again. As Bulger turned his attention to finding the Federal left somewhere above, the 47th Alabama renewed its advance.

Oates Proposes a New Plan

During the brief time the 15th was permitted to rest before the charge, the men discovered a well several hundred yards to the rear. Oates knew the men would need water before the afternoon was over, and sent out two men from each company as a water detail. The charge began before the detail could get back to the regiment. They followed the charging line across Plum Run Valley and entered the woods on Round Top's slopes in search of the 15th Alabama. Unfortunately the squad stumbled onto a detachment of Stoughton's Sharpshooters and were captured along with the water.[162]

Exertion from the climb and heat exhaustion coupled with lack of water caused many of Oates's men to fall out, so Oates decided to rest a few minutes on the crest. Below and slightly to his right, Oates caught a glimpse, through the veil of smoke and haze, of the battle raging about Devil's Den. From the rattle of musket fire farther to his right he guessed the Federal left had been located. Oates understood the military importance of Round Top, for in his words, "It was higher than the other mountain and would command the entire field." Artillery placed on Round Top would wreak havoc on the Federal left. Oates decided then that Round Top should be fortified.

Terrell found Oates observing the battle unfolding below and inquired why the regiment had halted. Oates told him the 15th Alabama could fight better after some rest. Terrell then informed Oates that Hood was wounded and Law was in command of the division. Oates recalled that Terrell said: "General Law's order was for me and Colonel Bulger to lose no time, but to press forward and drive the enemy before us as far as possible."

It was then that Oates presented his new idea. "Within half an hour," Oates informed Terrell, "I could convert it into a Gibraltar that I could hold against ten times the number that I had." Oates became the fourth commander to propose a change in the original battle plan. Terrell was merely a messenger, with no authority to act on his own. Oates persisted and inquired as to where Law was at that particular time. Oates probably asked Terrell to find Law and present this new idea. Terrell knew only that Law was somewhere to the left and was in no mood to trouble himself with the change. As far as Terrell was concerned Oates's orders were clear, which he reiterated: "Lose no time, but press forward and drive the enemy as far as possible." This time Oates obeyed and put his regiment in motion. The tired Alabamians obliqued to the left and clamored down Round Top's rugged northern slope in search of the Federals.[163]

The 47th Alabama Attacks the 20th Maine's Center

The 4th Alabama's final assault against the 83rd Pennsylvania and 20th Maine was still in progress when the 47th emerged from the woods onto the valley floor between the Round Tops. Turning right, the 47th began filing east to extend the Confederate right. Its line was in fairly good order and roughly parallel to the 20th Maine's center. Bulger ordered his men to move forward firing, and off they went at a quick step. A hundred feet or so above, the 20th Maine waited behind a low rock ledge.

The 47th Alabama crossed the valley floor without incident and began the climb up the southwest slope to move into line on the right of the 4th Alabama. Halfway up the slope Lieutenant Thomas L. Christian, adjutant and inspector general for the brigade, rode up with an order from Law. It was simply "Charge." At that moment Bulger was not really interested in exchanging pleasantries nor adhering to military protocol. He quickly retorted, "Tell Law I am charging to the best of my ability. Put the 15th Alabama on my right and we will drive them when we come to them." Bulger continued climbing Little Round Top.[164]

The 47th attacked the center of the 20th Maine. Bulger and his men stormed up the hill to the ledge protecting the Federal defenders. Chamberlain recalled the Alabamians "...burst upon us in a great fury."[165] The fight turned into hand to hand combat among the rocks. Muskets were used for clubs, and for a few moments it looked as though the Alabamians might break the Federal line.[166]

Bulger was shot through the chest but by force of will was able to stay on his feet. Though severely wounded he struggled down the hill some distance where he sought cover behind a large boulder. It was only then that he eased to the ground and rested his back against a tree.[167]

Campbell assumed command of the 47th. The regiment fought until its left was uncovered when the 4th Alabama retired after its third and last charge.[168] With the 4th Alabama gone the 83rd Pennsylvania and the right companies of the 20th Maine directed a destructive fire into the left of the 47th. Oates recalled its "...men were mowed down like grain before the scythe." A few minutes later it was forced to fall back. All the fight was gone from the men of the 47th Alabama and the regiment drifted rearward to the woods on the southern edge of the valley.[169] From there the men, from the cover of rocks and trees, exchanged fire with the 83rd Pennsylvania and 20th Maine.

The 15th Alabama Joins the Fight

While the 47th engaged Chamberlain's center, Oates reached the valley floor and moved quickly by the right flank. His heartbeat probably jumped when, two hundred yards ahead, he saw a Federal wagon train. The 15th Alabama was close to the Federal rear and in position to turn the Federal left. To do this Oates decided to go around the mountain. Shaaff, commanding Company A, was detached with instructions to capture the ordnance trains and bring them to the cover of a spur of Round Top. When he saw Federal troops east of the wagons he became afraid of being captured should he attempt to bring the wagons off and withdrew to the woods on the northeast side of Round Top.[170] Unfortunately for Oates and the rest of the 15th Alabama he remained there while the fighting raged around him.

The 83rd Pennsylvania and 20th Maine saw the 15th Alabama emerge from the woods and file by the right flank. Both gave the 15th Alabama a volley.[171] From his position on the

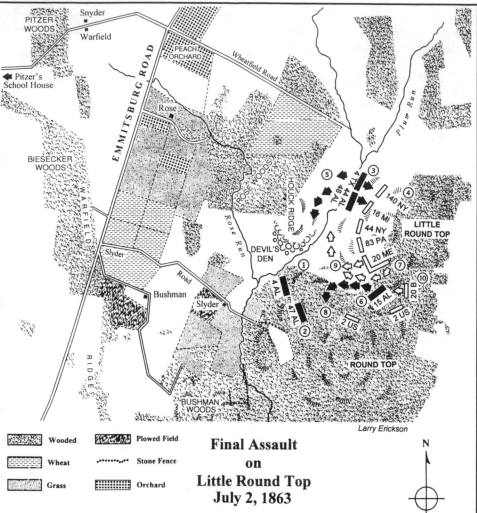

Larry Erickson

Final Assault
on
Little Round Top
July 2, 1863

Legend:
- Wooded
- Wheat
- Grass
- Plowed Field
- Stone Fence
- Orchard

N

1. After its last assault against the 83rd Pennsylvania and 20th Maine failed, the 4th Alabama retired to the woods on Round Top's northern slope.
2. The 47th Alabama retired from Little Round Top when the 4th Alabama left and uncovered its left.
3. With Devil's Den secured, the 4th Texas, 44th Alabama and 48th Alabama move north in Plum Run Valley and assault Vincent's right.
4. The 140th New York moves into line on Vincent's right and aids in repelling the attack by the Texans and Alabamians.
5. The 4th Texas, 44th Alabama and 48th Alabama retire to the cover of Houck's Ridge and eventually join their brigades south of Devil's Den.
6. After repeated assaults against the 20th Maine, Oates discovers that both of the 15th Alabama's flanks are threatened and considers withdrawing.
7. Chamberlain, fearing that the 20th Maine cannot withstand another assault by the 15th Alabama, orders a charge.
8. The 15th Alabama makes a disorderly retreat before the 20th Maine's charge and retraces its route up Round Top.
9. The 20th Maine sweeps the valley between the Round Tops and returns to its original position on Little Round Top.
10. Morrill follows the 15th Alabama up Round Top until he is stopped by fire from Oates's men.

20th Maine's extreme left Major Ellis Spear realized that the 15th Alabama's flanking maneuver would overlap the 20th Maine or at least strike the left flank. A suggestion was immediately sent to Chamberlain, who was farther up the hill near the regiment's center, to refuse a couple of companies on the left.[172] Chamberlain mounted a large boulder behind the line to survey the situation for himself.[173] What he saw made his blood run cold.

The 15th Alabama was moving by the right flank at the quick step. From his position in rear of the 83rd Pennsylvania Captain Orpheus S. Woodward, commanding the regiment, also saw the danger to Chamberlain's left and sent a courier to inquire about the condition of Chamberlain's line. When the courier returned with a request for a company, Woodward declined since his front was also under attack. Instead, he suggested Chamberlain extend to his left and Woodward would fill the gap.[174]

Because the regiments to the right were already engaged, Chamberlain decided to extend his line to the left and refuse the extreme left of the 20th Maine, which he accomplished while the 15th Alabama filed to the right. The left was extended down the hill by going into single rank with the right. Two companies on the extreme left swung back to follow the natural contour of the lower slope. Company K was on the left of Company F, the color company, and so that its line was parallel to the direction which the 15th Alabama would attack. When Chamberlain completed extending his line it roughly resembled a horseshoe with the color company at the apex.[175] His left now lay concealed behind a rocky ledge. Chamberlain's men waited for the fury of the fighting to burst upon them.

Oates was unaware of the impending danger until his line drew within 40 or 50 paces of Chamberlain's left. The men from Maine suddenly rose up and poured a deadly volley into the 15th Alabama, sending a shock wave through its ranks. The Alabamians halted but did not break ranks. The 20th Maine kept up the fire, and although Alabamians went down, the ranks were quickly closed.[176] Oates's men stood their ground, opened fire at close range and quickly took the measure of Chamberlain's left.[177] Chamberlain's two left companies began giving way after two volleys from the 15th Alabama.[178] Oates ordered a charge.

Halfway to the 20th Maine's line the fire become so intense the advance of the 15th Alabama stalled. By Oates's account his line "...wavered like a man trying to walk against a strong wind." Company G took the brunt of the fire, losing three officers within a few minutes. Lieutenant Barnett Cody went down, mortally wounded. Captain Henry C. Brainard fell, his last words were of his mother in Alabama and his desire to see her one more time. Oates's younger brother, Lieutenant John Oates, was shot eight times during one volley.[179]

A short distance away Captain James H. Ellison cupped his hand around his ear to better hear a command from Oates. Through the smoke and haze Oates saw the gesture and repeated the order to go forward. Ellison never heard the words, as a bullet pierced his skull, killing him instantly.

Chamberlain's line held. The 15th Alabama fell back among the rocks and trees of the valley.[180]

Oates then discovered the 47th Alabama falling back and quickly ordered a change of front to his left, partly for the purpose of relieving the pressure on the 47th Alabama and partly to deliver an enfilade fire into the 20th Maine.[181] Oates saw he was now alone in the attack on Chamberlain's left. The Maine men were fighting with the benefit of cover. He recalled that to "...stand there and die was sheer folly; either retreat or advance became a necessity."[182] Oates decided to charge. Waving his sword and yelling for his men to follow Oates rushed through the line. According to Chamberlain the 15th Alabama came "...with a shout, firing as they came."[183]

Oates mounted a rock and discharged the contents of his pistol at Chamberlain's line. The Alabamians managed to reach the ledge and slowly pushed the defenders toward a second ledge farther up the slope. The Maine men soon had their backs against this second ledge.[184]

A short distance above the combatants Hazlett's guns blasted away at targets in the Devil's Den area. Bullets flew into Hazlett's left and rear. It was very trying for his gunners, but they ignored the close quarter fighting between the men from Maine and Alabama. Lieutenant Benjamin Rittenhouse later recalled the gunners' "duty was to take care of our front, and trust to our people at other points to take care of theirs, as they are trusting us."[185]

Four times the Maine men rallied and charged and were driven back four times. Twice their advance came within arm's reach of the Alabamians, who used bayonets to repel the charge.[186] During one assault by the 20th Maine, Oates stood near a large boulder and steadied his men. His regimental colors were held by John G. Archibald. A Maine man reached for the flag staff. Archibald deftly stepped out of reach while Sergeant Patrick "Pat" O'Connor promptly drove his bayonet through the man's head. Chamberlain reported the fighting was "...literally hand to hand. The fight rolled backward and forward like a wave. Dead and wounded were now in the front and then in the rear."[187] Assaults were made and repelled with great carnage, he said.[188] The fifth charge by the 20th Maine finally dislodged the 15th Alabama, then pushed it down the hill.[189]

Every regiment had its share of stragglers, and there were many on this afternoon. Though most had legitimate reasons, there were a few who sought to slip away. One example was a private in the 15th Alabama. John Nelson, Company K, was an Irishman by birth and seemed to take great delight in a good fight. He would personally fight any man, but when bullets flew in battle he quickly lost his desire to fight. Nelson would go into line when the shooting started, then at the first opportunity nearly always managed to slip to the rear and safety. His company commander, Captain William J. Bethune, was a stern disciplinarian. At the beginning of the charge Bethune ordered Sergeant O'Connor to keep a close eye on Nelson and use whatever means necessary to hold the man in line. Sure enough, somewhere on the slopes of Little Round Top Nelson slipped out of line and started for the rear. O'Connor grabbed Nelson and held him in line until a bullet snuffed out the Irishman's life. The sergeant let the lifeless form down with words: "I guess you'll stay in line now."[190] Sometime in the fight Bethune also fell, severely wounded by a shot in the face.[191]

While Oates regrouped, Chamberlain took advantage of the lull in fighting to pick up wounded and gather ammunition from his fallen men. He also ordered arms collected from the wounded to replace those that were no longer serviceable. Chamberlain had loose stones piled up in the more exposed areas of the defense line. Even then, the works were no more than 18 inches high and barely covered a man lying prone on the ground.[192]

Adjutant DeBernie B. Waddell approached Oates requesting permission to take 40 or 50 men and advance to the cover of rocks on the 15th Alabama's right for the purpose of delivering an enfilade fire into the Federals. Oates consented and soon Waddell's men were doing splendid work. Bullets flying into the 83rd Pennsylvania's rear caused Captain Woodward to send his adjutant to see if the left was being turned. Woodward was concerned because his only avenue of escape was a small space between the 83rd Pennsylvania's line and a large rock in his rear. He moved his center back 10 or 12 spaces which shortened his line. Satisfied that he could better command his line of retreat, Woodward returned to the business of directing his regiment's fire.[193]

Attack on Vincent's Right

After Devil's Den was secured and while Oates engaged in his private war with the 20th Maine, fighting spread north through Plum Run Valley. The 44th and 48th Alabama joined the Texans in an assault on Vincent's right. Their advance was directed toward the right flank of the 16th Michigan. This was accomplished by advancing north from Devil's Den using the rocks between Plum Run and the western face of Little Round Top for cover.

The Texans and Alabamians were able to achieve some initial successes due to a breakdown in communications, the right companies of the 16th Michigan gave way. While rallying the 16th, Vincent was mortally wounded by a shot to the groin. The young Pennsylvanian had been a favorite target of sharpshooters as he moved about the line. As he was carried from the field Vincent remarked: "This is the fourth or fifth time they have shot at me, and they have hit me at last."[194] Vincent died July 7, 1863.[195]

Before the advantage gained could be exploited, however, Federal reinforcements arrived. Warren had continued to look for infantry to place on Little Round Top and found the 140th New York, command by Colonel Patrick H. O'Rorke, preparing to move into line further to the right. O'Rorke was, at first, reluctant to respond to Warren's request to move onto the mountain, but acquiesced at Warren's insistence. A few minutes later the 140th New York, apparently accompanied by Warren, was scrambling over and around the rocks toward Little Round Top's crest. When O'Rorke paused to dress his lines Warren urged the Irishman forward who once again responded and led his men in a scramble down the western slope. O'Rorke's line slightly overlapped the 16th Michigan's right, but the Federal line was extended sufficiently right to hold against the Confederate assault.[196] After a short vicious fight in which O'Rorke was mortally wounded, the Alabamians and Texans were driven back into Plum Run Valley.[197] The fight for Vincent's right was over. The 44th and 48th Alabama Regiments were engaged over one and one-half hours, both losing slightly over one-quarter of their compliment. Perry lost most of his men from the initial volley by the 4th Maine.[198] The 44th and 48th withdrew southward to positions on the lower slopes of Round Top.[199]

Neither Perry nor Sheffield mentioned an attack by their regiments on Little Round Top. Coles said the Texans were the only regiments that advanced up Little Round Top with the 4th Alabama. However, Major John P. Bane commanded the 4th Texas during its last charge against Vincent and reported the 44th and 48th Alabama accompanied his regiment. The apparent discrepancy in the accounts as to whether the 44th and 48th participated in the charge deserves an examination.

Neither Perry nor Sheffield were in command of their regiments when the 4th Texas made its last charge, which explains the absence of comment on their part. However, the 44th and 48th Alabama saw fighting after Perry and Sheffield relinquished command. The 48th Alabama made four charges. Sheffield only accounts for three, none against Little Round Top. It is clear from Sheffield's description that the 48th Alabama was on a line perpendicular to Little Round Top. Sheffield moved up to command Law's Brigade after the third charge and reported that Captain Thomas Eubanks took command of the 48th Alabama and brought it to the front. Private John Anderson of Company K wrote on July 17, 1863, that the 48th Alabama "...charged on top of a mountain to the enemy's breastworks," obviously referring to Little Round Top.[200] There were no breastworks, as such, around Devil's Den, but the charge was firmly etched in Anderson's mind when he wrote home. Anderson could only be referring to Little Round Top. Therefore, two eyewitnesses place the 48th Alabama on Little Round Top.

The most likely scenario is the 44th and 48th Alabama fought around Devil's Den until it was overrun and secured. Both then participated in the last charge made by the 4th Texas. This does not discredit Coles because the 4th Alabama became separated from the Texans. Coles would not have known the 44th and 48th Alabama joined the 4th Texas.

Should We Stay or Retreat

Oates sent Sergeant Major Robert Cicero Norris to find the 4th Alabama. He returned a few minutes later and reported the 4th Alabama was nowhere in sight and that Federals were moving up the mountainside. Captains Park and Hill reported the presence of Federals to the rear, both thinking two regiments were in position. Oates went to the rear and saw two battle flags and units with two different uniform colors.[201]

The supposed two Federal regiments were actually Morrill's Company and Stoughton's U.S. Sharpshooters who had menaced Oates's right during his ascent of Round Top. Morrill later wrote that the detachment of sharpshooters was under the command of a non-commissioned officer. Both moved up within sight of the 15th Alabama and opened fire on Oates's flank.[202] Under the circumstances Oates concluded Park was correct.

Both Hill and Park suggested the time had come to fall back. Oates declined and told the two captains: "Return to your companies; we will sell out as dearly as possible." There was no reply from Hill, but Park, smiling, saluted Oates and replied: "All right, sir." Oates thought there was some chance of reinforcements, but that was a hopeless thought. Men were being shot from the front, rear, and flank, some falling with multiple wounds caused by bullets from different directions. Oates knew the fighting spirit was rapidly leaving his men, and he began to consider the merits of retreat and went so far as to advise his men to run at his signal.[203] Norris was sent to the company commanders and informed each the regiment would retreat on Oates's signal. Their orders were simple: "Run in the direction from whence they came and halt on the top of Round Top." Norris either did not know that Oates had sent Waddell to the right with a squad, or in the excitement of the moment simply forgot to tell Waddell. In either case, Waddell remained ignorant of Oates's plan.

On the Federal side, Chamberlain was not sure of his regiment's fighting condition either. Members of his color guard were either dead or wounded, and the same was true for most of his color company.[204] Many of the regiment's muskets were unusable. Men were forced to scavenge ammunition from fallen comrades. His anxiety was increased by bullets flying into his rear from the opposite side of Little Round Top. These were probably from the attack on the 16th Michigan by the Texans and Alabamians. Chamberlain's immediate fear was that the Confederates may have surrounded Little Round Top. Men were firing their last round and "...getting ready to use their muskets as clubs."[205]

Chamberlain looked across the valley and believed he saw two lines, en echelon on the far side of the valley and felt sure his adversary was preparing for one final assault. Actually, Oates was probably preparing to cover his withdrawal from the field. Waddell's detachment was forward of and off to the right of the 15th Alabama's main line. Therefore, it's easy to see how Chamberlain concluded Oates was forming his regiment en echelon for his next assault. Chamberlain's men opened on the Alabamians with their remaining rounds, but he knew it would be impossible to fight off another assault.[206]

This scholarly man from Maine decided on a bold move. He gave the order to fix bayonets and charge. He recalled: "The word was enough. It ran like fire along the line."[207] At the word "charge" a shout rose from the center and right of the regiment. Spear had not received the word when his men saw the colors move out and heard the shout, but he immediately knew a charge was under way. Without a moment's hesitation he joined in the charge as he and the left companies made a mad rush down the hillside until they came in line with the center.[208]

Oates faced a critical decision. His exhausted men had suffered a great number of casualties on the slopes of Little Round Top, and he was unsupported. The Alabamians were receiving fire from the rear and right flank as well as from Chamberlain's entrenched soldiers. The young colonel believed "...the entire command was doomed to destruction."[209] When the New Englanders rose up with a shout and began to charge down the hill, Oates concluded it was time to give the signal to withdraw.

The 15th Alabama Leaves the Field

The 15th Alabama's withdrawal was not accomplished in an orderly fashion. At Oates's signal the men bolted and ran like "...a herd of stampeding cattle." On Oates's right flank, Morrill yelled loud commands to deceive the Alabamians into thinking his body of troops was larger than it really was. Some of the sharpshooters on Oates's left made the mistake of getting in the way of the retreating Alabamians. They were rewarded for their trouble with a trip to the Confederate rear as prisoners.[210]

John Keils, Company H, ran past Oates as blood spurted from a severe throat wound which cut through his windpipe. A hissing noise came from his throat as the wounded private attempted to breathe. He actually made it to the rear and a field hospital where he died two days later.[211]

Waddell saw the retreat begin and correctly surmised the order to withdraw had been given. However, Spear and his men overran Waddell and his detachment before they could move. Waddell escaped, but most of his men became prisoners.[212] Toward the center of the charge Chamberlain rushed up to Captain Robert H. Wicker demanding his surrender. Wicker calmly aimed his pistol at Chamberlain's head, fired, and missed. That bit of business over with, the Alabamian surrendered his sword and pistol.[213]

As Waddell reached the valley floor he met Shaaff and Company A emerging from the woods on the east side of the valley. Waddell took command of Shaaff's company and went to find the rest of the regiment.[214]

When Spear came abreast of the main line, Chamberlain executed a maneuver he termed "...an extended right wheel." His right company acted as a pivot while the remainder of his line "...swung like a gate upon a post." A heavy skirmish line from the 83rd Pennsylvania dashed forward and participated in the charge.[215] The 15th Alabama's main line retraced its approach route through the valley. Those in the rear were forced to fall back, fighting from tree to tree.[216]

A squad from the 15th Alabama found Bulger's familiar form slumped against a tree and attempted to rally around the wounded officer. They were no match for the 20th Maine. Bulger was left choking in his own blood. When a Federal soldier passed by Bulger called for water. The soldier cut his canteen strap and tossed it to the old man. To his surprise Bulger found the liquid was not water. The Federal's canteen was filled with whiskey, which the Federal volunteered was "...a great deal better for you." His good deed done for the day, the Federal returned to fighting. He positioned himself behind a boulder and commenced firing at the retreating Alabamians.[217]

After clearing the valley the men from Maine were so charged with excitement that Chamberlain found it difficult to bring them under control. From the ranks men declared "...they were on the road to Richmond." Chamberlain found himself in a rather exposed position and became concerned about his ability to fight off an attempt to retake the ground just lost by the Confederates. Despite his men's enthusiasm to continue the charge, he regained control over the regiment and returned it to his original position.[218]

In the meantime Morrill followed the 15th Alabama as it climbed Round Top. Oates was not able to reform his regiment until it reached the crest of the mountain, since most of his men were scattered, some helping the wounded. The few available joined Waddell and Company A, and fired several shots at Morrill's men. Two of his men were quickly wounded. Since Morrill was unsupported, caution seemed a wise course of action. He sought cover and waited for the Alabamians' next move.[219] It would be 9 p.m. before relief came.

In the charge, an officer of the 20th Maine and two of his men became separated from the main line. As the men made their way around the brow of Round Top they encountered Lieutenant Joseph R. Breare, Company E, 15th Alabama, with 15 men. The three Federals surprised the Rebels and demanded their surrender. With Breare and his men under guard the Federal officer began making his way toward the 20th Maine's last known position. Breare quickly surmised the Federal force was only three strong and that he surrendered too easily. Before the group entered the Federal lines he confirmed his suspicion with the enemy officer and was so impressed with the Federal's exploit that he retrieved a silver cup from his haversack and presented it to his captor.[220]

Somewhere on the crest of Round Top, Oates fainted from exhaustion. He became the fourth regimental commander of Law's Brigade to fall out. Command of the 15th Alabama was turned over to Captain Blanton Hill, while a stretcher was found for Oates. Four hours after it began its charge, Hill led the 15th Alabama into position along the southwestern base of Round Top.

Oates remained convinced that had Shaaff returned from his reconnaissance and joined the 15th Alabama, he could have turned the Federal left, but the premise is doubtful. Even with Shaaff's company of 28 men, the 22 men lost of the abortive water detail and the addition of the estimated 100 men who fell out from exhaustion, it is unlikely that Oates could have turned the Federal left. Had Oates managed to get in Chamberlain's rear, Federal reinforcements would probably have driven them off Little Round Top. Both regiments were almost evenly matched. The 20th Maine went into line with 358 rifles. When Oates engaged Chamberlain his strength was about 380. Chamberlain enjoyed the advantage of fighting behind fortifications. Even with that advantage, the 15th Alabama inflicted about as many casualties as it sustained. Chamberlain suffered 136 killed and wounded, while inflicting 172 casualties on the 15th Alabama.[221] The 47th Alabama caused some of Chamberlain's casualties, but it is impossible to know the exact number.

It is with justified pride that Oates later wrote of the fighting prowess shown by the Alabamians that afternoon in July 1863. They were terribly fatigued when the assault began and worse still, they were forced to fight without water. When the 15th fell back the last time its men were exhausted. In the final analysis, the Federal left was fairly secure once Little Round Top was occupied.

Night Finally Ends the Fighting

As daylight turned to dusk, fighting was limited to sharpshooting. Hood's Division settled down behind boulders, logs or trees to exchange fire with Vincent's line.[222] Anyone exposing himself for too long became a target. The Federals above enjoyed the advantage of looking down on the Confederate line and all too often the Southerners became easy marks. Ignoring the danger, John Cussons ventured out to inspect the forward positions. Law's scout was oblivious to the fire as he moved from boulder to boulder. A private from the 4th Texas observed the Englishman's calm demeanor and marveled at his bravery.

Arriving at the Texan's position Cussons advised those around him to aim well. Suddenly realizing that Cussons was drawing fire dangerously close, the Texan yelled for him to move on.[223] As on other battlefields Cussons led a charmed life and escaped unharmed. A private from the 5th Texas recalled that he only saw two men standing in the open that late in the afternoon. One was the major of the 5th Texas atop a boulder delivering a speech to anyone who would listen. The other was Cussons.[224]

Occasionally men from Vincent's brigade ventured out to bring in wounded Confederates. Joseph Nellis, 83rd Pennsylvania, went out twice before becoming too fatigued to go out alone. One or two men volunteered to accompany him, but quickly retreated when shots whizzed their way. Nellis moved on only to be shot dead in the act of assisting a wounded Confederate to his feet. Both were found the next day lying side by side.[225]

Night brought a merciful end to the slaughter of the late afternoon. Hood's Division held Devil's Den, the southern end of Houck's Ridge and the northwestern slopes of Round Top. Law extended his line farther south to encompass most of Round Top and put his men to work constructing fortifications. His Alabamians occupied the extreme right. From right to left the Alabama brigade's order was the 15th, 47th, 4th, 48th and 44th Alabama regiments.[226]

The 20th Maine, barely 200 strong, made its way up the northern slopes of Round Top about 9 p.m. Chamberlain's men were still without ammunition and climbed with bayonets fixed. Here and there squads of Law's men contested the advance, but there was little resistance and Chamberlain soon occupied the crest of Round Top. Captain Thomas Christian was making his way up Round Top with a squad of twenty men he intended to post as pickets. The group stumbled into the 20th Maine's line and was captured.[227] Chamberlain immediately began positioning his men behind boulders and sent for ammunition.[228] About midnight the 83rd Pennsylvania went into position on the 20th Maine's right. Both sides constructed breastworks throughout the night in anticipation of renewed fighting at daylight.[229]

After the fighting ceased Rice ordered detachments from the 44th New York and 83rd Pennsylvania forward to "...secure all fruits of the hard earned victory."[230] The scene on Little Round Top's lower slopes was appalling. The dead and wounded lay about in great numbers, while the wounded called for water.[231] A line of dead and wounded marked the location where Vincent's first volley ripped into the Alabama and Texas line. It was difficult to cross the area without stepping on a lifeless or wounded body.

As the Federals moved over the field a sergeant from the 44th New York discovered a severely wounded Confederate who begged to have the strap attached to his cartridge box be cut because it lay on his wound. After responding to the man's request the sergeant moved on and found another man asking not to be stepped on.[232] Among the wounded Alabamians were Bulger and Mosely.

Bulger lay motionless and waited for either death or assistance. His wound looked fatal, and his men certainly thought so. Campbell reported Bulger's death.[233] The elderly Alabamian drifted in and out of consciousness and eventually pulled his hat over his face. A private from the 44th New York walked by and noticed Bulger's motionless form propped against the tree. He too thought Bulger was dead and on inspection discovered the lieutenant colonel's sword and belt, both prized trophies. So the Federal bent down over the motionless form and proceeded to remove the dead officer's hat, sword and belt. Bulger suddenly revived and reacted by slapping the offending hand away. A very surprised Federal jumped back, raised his musket and demanded Bulger to surrender.

The old gentleman might have been seriously wounded, but he still managed to retain a strict sense of military protocol. An interesting exchange followed, going something like this:

Bulger: " My good fellow it seems strange to me that a U.S. soldier doesn't know he has no right to disarm an officer. You should direct me to an officer as near as possible to my rank."

The Federal private responded: "But you are unable to go."

Bulger quickly retorted: "Then you should find an officer."

Apparently Bulger made a convincing argument. The private went to find an officer suitable to take the old gentleman's surrender. A short time later the private returned with an officer who introduced himself as Colonel Rice of the 44th New York. A short exchange of pleasantries took place after which Rice informed Bulger that it was his duty as an officer of the U.S. Army to demand the Confederate's arms. Since Rice was a colonel, the old gentleman's sense of military protocol was satisfied. His sword and pistol were handed over to Rice. Bulger remarked he "...had a short loan of the sword, which had been taken from the lieutenant colonel of the 22nd Maine a short time ago and presented me yesterday."[234]

Rice personally procured a litter and escorted Bulger to a makeshift field hospital somewhere in the rear. Rice also made sure a doctor examined Bulger's wound and then led the litter bearers to a barn where a bed of hay was prepared for him. A number of Federal soldiers were curious about their captives and came to visit. A man from the 83rd Pennsylvania remembered Bulger as "...courteous and pleasant in manners." At midnight the elderly officer lay shivering from the chill in the night air.[235] Rice returned the next morning with a Dr. Clark of New York. Bulger later received special attention from the Federal physician. He was convinced Rice was personally responsible for saving his life.[236]

In later years Oates described Bulger's capture in his history of the 15th Alabama. Oates and Chamberlain were at the time embroiled in a heated debate over how far Oates had advanced up Little Round Top. Chamberlain immediately took issue with Oates's account. In 1903 Chamberlain wrote Colonel John P. Nicholson, Gettysburg Military Park Commissioner, that Bulger had surrendered his sword to him and that he, Chamberlain, ordered Bulger sent to a Federal hospital.[237] Chamberlain's report of the battle, dated July 6, 1863, does mention that two field officers and several line officers were sent to the rear.[238] Rice prepared the brigade report of the battle, dated July 31, 1863. He obviously utilized information from his regimental commanders and identified the two field officers as colonels and the line officers as 15 commissioned officers. He did not identify either colonel by name.[239] Oliver W. Norton, who was on Vincent's staff, said the incidents of the fight were much discussed around brigade headquarters. He claimed that if the capture had been as Oates described in his history it would have been the subject of conversations and he thus would have heard about it. Norton further stated that had Chamberlain not taken Bulger's surrender, Rice would have required Chamberlain correct his report. Norton, therefore, accepted Chamberlain's version.[240] Since Chamberlain did not mention Bulger by name there would been no reason for Rice to correct Chamberlain's report. It is possible that Chamberlain saw Bulger and ordered him taken to the rear. But, in the excitement of the charge which carried well past the fallen Bulger, it does not appear that Chamberlain stopped to formally accept his surrender. Bulger's description corresponds to the events described by the Federal participants and identifies his captors as being from the 44th New York. The more probable explanation is that Bulger surrendered his sword to Rice.

John Mosely was another hapless Confederate since he and his captors knew his wound to be fatal. Somewhere in the Federal rear the dying boy requested a note be sent home to his mother in Alabama. The next day a short letter found its way through the lines. It read:

Battlefield G'burg Penn
July 4, 1863

Dear Mother:
I am a prisoner of war and mortally wounded. I can live but a few hours
more, at best; was shot within 50 yards of the enemy's line. They have
been exceedingly kind to me. I have no doubt of the final result of the
battle and hope I may live long enough to hear the shouts of victory yet
before I die. I am very weak. Do not morn my loss, I had hoped to have
been spared, but a righteous God had ordered it otherwise and I feel
prepared to trust my case in his hands. Farewell to you all. Pray that
God may receive my soul.

Your Unfortunate Son
John[241]

A wounded soldier from the 4th Alabama called for a friend named John. Others prayed and groaned in agony. Some begged for death.[242] Private William N. Johns, Company B, 15th Alabama, lay on his back all night and the next day, unable to turn himself over. That night he nearly died of thirst, but the heavy rain from a severe thunderstorm the next day almost caused him to drown. John managed to survive by placing his hat over his face until the rain subsided.[243]

The wounded from Hood's Division were carried to a makeshift hospital on the John E. Planck farm. Litter bearers brought in Captains William W. Leftwich, Company F, 4th Alabama, and Joseph S. Johnston, Jr., Company B, 47th Alabama. Wounded from Law's Brigade totaled 14 officers and 287 privates and non-commissioned officers. They were sorted out as they came in. Surgeons tried to look after the more seriously wounded first, but the number was so large many were forced to wait hours or days before receiving medical attention. Sergeant Ward lay in agony until well after midnight when a surgeon administered a sleep-inducing drug. He woke to the thunder of the cannonading which preceded Pickett's charge. Hunger caused him to reach for his haversack, only to find that it and the rations prepared at New Guilford were gone. Some rascal, he sadly concluded, thought he was dead or would die, and walked away with his food.[244]

Several men from Company H, 15th Alabama went out in search of Oates's brother and Lieutenant Cody. They managed to pass through the Federal line on Round Top, but were discovered near Little Round Top and driven back before the wounded could be located. Unfortunately very few of the wounded were retrieved. Most of the severely injured lay where they fell. One picket from the 44th New York spent his entire time on duty attending to them, giving water, cutting off shoes and otherwise helping the wounded in whatever way he could. He remembered the night "...was terrible, some were crying, some praying and some swearing. All wanted help."[245]

The opposing lines were so close that each side could hear the other. Law's Alabamians listened to the distinctive sounds of rocks dropping into place as the Federals constructed fortifications. In the Federal lines, Chamberlain's men listened to Confederate officers giving commands.[246] Men on both sides rested as best they could and waited for the dawn.

Chapter 6

Farnsworth's Charge

Confederate Right – July 3

The dawn of July 3 did not bring an immediate renewal of the fighting, and John Cussons ventured forth at first light to scout between the lines. This was not unusual for Law's scout and trusted aide, for he was often seen on similar missions on other battlefields. This time, as he walked into the Federal lines, the Englishman's luck ran out and he was captured. Later in the day, Cussons sat on the crest of Round Top, watching the splendor of Pickett's Charge.[1] During the early morning hours Law's men were content to stay concealed behind breastworks and the rocks and boulders. Those who did expose themselves became targets for sharpshooters stationed among the rocks farther up Round Top. One was Lieutenant Henry D. Simmons, Company B, 47th Alabama, who fell victim to a sharpshooter early in the morning.[2] Another, John Young, Company I, 4th Alabama, was out on a scouting detail and paused to rest near a boulder. Young only partially concealed himself, while leaning against the boulder and resting his hand on the gun barrel. A ball struck his right hand, severing a finger. This could have posed a major problem for Young because he was a printer and the ability to set type was a necessity. He was greatly relieved to discover that his thumb and forefinger remained intact. A little while later he returned to the company and happily remarked to his comrades that when the war was over he would be able to set type as well as ever.[3]

Law's line extended north from the southern base of Round Top to the north side of Devil's Den. Law's Brigade, commanded by Sheffield, occupied the extreme right. Scruggs was sufficiently recovered from the exhaustion he suffered the previous afternoon to resume command of the 4th Alabama.[4] Robertson's Texans were next in line, connecting with Sheffield's left, with Anderson next, then Benning on the extreme left.[5]

Earlier in the morning, two of Law's batteries were placed under the command of Colonel Porter Alexander to help shell the Federal position south of Cemetery Hill.[6] He still retained 12 guns under Reilly and Bachman, and strategically placed these on his right flank to cover the threat of Federal cavalry, commanded by Brigadier General Hugh Judson Kilpatrick, Third Division, Cavalry Corps, Army of the Potomac, which were massing there.[7] About mid-morning Longstreet visited the right and instructed Law to ready his men to renew the attack. Law considered the renewal of fighting on his front to be madness.[8]

Early in the afternoon a tremendous booming erupted farther north, signaling the beginning of the great cannonade as Pickett's Charge began. Law looked in that direction and saw that the hills on either side of Plum Run Valley were "...capped with crowns of flame and smoke." Great clouds of smoke soon enveloped the infantry positions and settled in the valley separating the opposing lines. Law recalled that the shells which exploded over the lines "...lit up the clouds with their snakelike flashes." He would remember the cannonading as "...one of the most magnificent battle scenes witnessed during the war."[9]

While the cannonading was in progress, Federal Brigadier General Elon J. Farnsworth's cavalry brigade (First Brigade), of four regiments began forming in the timber which extended from the Currens house near the Emmitsburg Road to the base of Round Top.[10] Law initially countered this threat by changing Reilly's and Bachman's batteries to the right and opening fire on the cavalry position, causing Farnsworth to withdraw beyond the timber.[11] Law pulled the 1st Texas from its position in the main line and placed it midway between the Currens house and Round Top. Kilpatrick extended his line by sending Brigadier General Wesley Merritt's cavalry, Reserve Brigade, First Division, in on Farnsworth's left. In the meantime, a squadron from the 1st Vermont Cavalry of Farnsworth's brigade broke through the 1st Texas skirmish line and rode north as far as the Bushman house before turning back. Although the Federal horsemen were under fire from Law's skirmishers and artillery, only two troopers were lost.[12]

Law sent a courier to Anderson's Brigade for a regiment, and received the 9th Georgia which he placed near the Currens house. About this time Colonel John L. Black of the 1st South Carolina Cavalry reported with about 100 hundred men collected from the medical trains along with three guns of Captain J. F. Hart's South Carolina Battery which were positioned on the Emmitsburg Road.[13] Black and his men were placed on the flank which extended the right beyond the road. A short time later two more regiments were requested, and in response the 7th and 8th Georgia were sent to the right to support Black and the 9th Georgia.[14]

Merritt next extended his Federal line across the Emmitsburg Road, which Law countered by placing the 7th and 8th Georgia on his right flank. The Georgians and Black engaged in heavy skirmishing until about 3 p.m.[15] Merritt made occasional attempts to break Law's line and continually moved to his left. At one time Law personally led the Georgians forward to stop an advance by Merritt.[16]

Law was aware that his defensive line was stretched dangerously thin, and he knew cavalry had the advantage of mobility over infantry in open ground and over an extended line. However, Merritt elected to dismount and fight as infantry. In Law's estimation, Merritt's advantage was now gone and he "...lost no time in taking advantage of this temporary equality." Law detached the 11th and 59th Georgia from the main line and sent them to the right where he personally guided the 11th Georgia into position. With his right now extended west of the Currens house, Law then seized the initiative and sent the Georgians into action with orders to hit the Federal line "...on its end and double it up." Merritt's left flank, under Law's pressure, rolled up as far as the Emmitsburg Road which shortened Law's front and gave him greater concentration of force.[17]

Farnsworth Prepares for Battle

Law was near his artillery batteries when Farnsworth launched his cavalry attack against the 1st Texas. Farnsworth had received his promotion to brigadier on the eve of the battle but was unable to procure a proper uniform for his new rank. His mentor and former commander, Major General Alfred Pleasonton, had willingly shared his own wardrobe. On the afternoon of July 3, Farnsworth wore Pleasonton's blue coat with a single star.[18]

Farnsworth's orders were to drive the 1st Texas and break the Confederate line. This would give Meade's infantry, positioned opposite Law, the opportunity to drive the Confederates into the open, defeat them and break the line of Lee's army. Farnsworth thought the plan of attack, formulated by Judson Kilpatrick, was senseless and would most likely result in a useless waste of men. A heated argument ensued between the two generals when Farnsworth questioned the order of his commanding officer.[19] Kilpatrick challenged the new brigadier's courage and offered to lead the charge himself. At this point, Farnsworth was not about to be intimidated and reluctantly consented to lead the charge. The 1st West Virginia Cavalry and two battalions from the 1st Vermont Cavalry from Farnsworth's brigade were selected to make the attack. Captain H. C. Parsons led the First Battalion and Major William Wells led the Third. Farnsworth rode with Wells and the Third Battalion.[20]

Law Lays a Trap

The West Virginians made the initial charge against the 1st Texas, but were repulsed. Farnsworth, with two battalions of Vermont cavalry, then charged to the right of the 1st Texas and easily broke through the skirmish line. Continuing in column of fours with sabers drawn, the Federals galloped forward in near perfect formation. From his vantage point above the valley floor Law marveled at their bravery and wished he could descend into the valley under a flag of truce to explain the futility of their mission. Law knew the horsemen were no match for his infantry, but his responsibility as commander was to defeat them.[22] From experience, he knew the fate of the Federal cavalry, remembering that after he and Hood had broken the enemy lines with their shock assault at Gaines's Mill, members of the U.S. 5th Cavalry made a futile charge upon the Confederate infantry. Even though the Texans and Alabamians were scattered by their charge, they broke the cavalry attack with little effort. The episode, Law wrote, "...consumed scarcely more time than it takes to write it."[23]

After ascertaining the cavalry's general direction, Law sent Lieutenant E. B. Wade of his staff across the valley to direct the first infantry regiment he found to engage the Federal horsemen. Wade was also instructed to order Oates to close up on the 1st Texas which, in effect, meant Law was closing the door on Farnsworth and his cavalry.

Farnsworth's Charge

Wade found the 4th Alabama and sent it scrambling through the woods toward the west. Men of the 4th Alabama broke into a sprint with the most fleet of foot leading the way. They emerged from the woods east of the Slyder buildings to find Parson's First Battalion bearing down on them. Lieutenant Vaughan, Company C, loudly exclaimed, "Cavalry boys, cavalry! This is no fight, only a frolic, give it to them!" The Vermonters were only 30 or 40 paces away when the 4th fired its first volley, enveloping the cavalry in smoke. When the smoke cleared Captain James Taylor Jones, on the right of the 4th, was disappointed to see only one horse down. A private down the line turned and pointed proudly to the horse, explaining: "Captain, I shot that black." Jones chastised the private for not shooting the horse's rider, and received a quick reply that they would get the rider anyway, but he hadn't seen a deer for three years and he was not about to miss the opportunity to bring down some game. Most of the first volley zipped harmlessly over the Vermonters' heads. There was not a second volley as such, since each man in the 4th loaded and fired as fast as he could. A Federal near Coles went down with his horse. Instead of surrendering, the trooper jumped over his horse, fired a shot at the 4th Alabama, and attempted to get away, but a well-aimed shot brought him down.[24]

Parsons guided the front companies of his battalion away from the 4th Alabama and regrouped southeast of the Slyder house under cover of a slight wooded elevation. The rear companies reformed south of the house and fought their way through the 1st Texas skir-

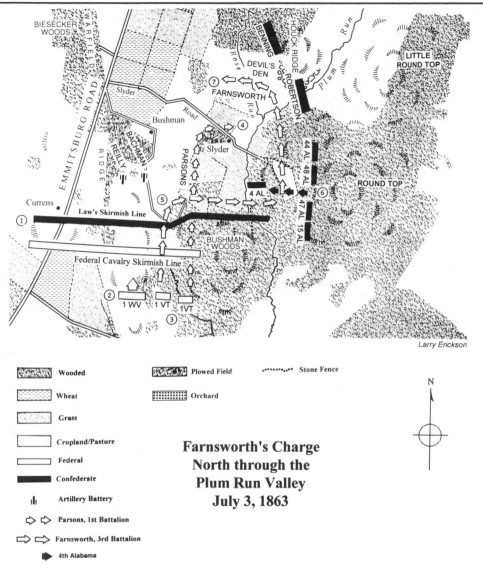

Larry Erickson

Farnsworth's Charge
North through the
Plum Run Valley
July 3, 1863

N

1. At 3 p.m. Law's skirmish line extends west from the main line to just past the Currens house. Law has his headquarters flag near Riley's and Bachman's batteries.
2. A charge against Law's skirmish line by the 1st West Virginia Cavalry fails.
3. Two battalions of the 1st Vermont Cavalry, Farnsworth and Parsons commanding, break through near the 1st Texas and ride north into Plum Run Valley.
4. Parsons rides as far as the Slyder house before turning east.
5. Farnsworth initially rides parallel to and west of Parsons. After passing Law's skirmish line Farnsworth turns sharply to the east, riding almost parallel to Law's skirmish line, then turns and races north behind the Confederate line.
6. Law sends a staff officer to order a regiment from the main line. The 4th Alabama withdraws and advances toward the Slyder house to confront Parsons.
7. Farnsworth turns west as he nears Devil's Den and comes under fire from Benning's Brigade. Farnsworth's horse is killed but a trooper gives his horse to the young general.

mish line. Parsons started south riding adjacent to the woods on Round Top.[25]

While Parsons rode toward his encounter with the 4th Alabama, Farnsworth and Wells rode to Parson's left before coming under fire from Bachman's battery. After turning sharply right and crossing Parson's track, Farnsworth, with his saber drawn, raced north along the base of Round Top in rear of Law's Brigade. As he approached Plum Run Gorge, Farnsworth turned abruptly left and came under fire from Benning's right. Farnsworth's horse was killed, and a trooper gave his horse to the general, whose battalion now divided into three groups. One group rode south through Plum Run Valley, charged through Law's skirmish line and reentered the Union lines. Farnsworth and a few others retraced their route through the valley. The third group swept west toward Bachman's and Reilly's batteries.[26]

Bachman quickly changed his front to face Farnsworth's horsemen and was preparing to open fire when the 9th Georgia arrived. The Georgians immediately faced right and advanced between the guns to confront the oncoming Federal cavalry. One volley emptied several saddles, but some horsemen were able to get among Reilly's guns.[27] Two were unhorsed by gunners wielding rammers for weapons while the remaining troopers escaped.[28]

Parsons and Farnsworth were in sight of each other as they raced toward the Confederate skirmish line at the south end of the valley. Law's Alabamians appeared in the rocks above the Federal cavalry and opened fire as the troopers rode past. A sergeant riding ahead of Parsons was shot and fell from the saddle. Parsons's horse stumbled as it ran over the dead trooper and stopped, leaving Parsons afoot. A squad from the 47th Alabama ran up and attempted to make Parsons a prisoner. Instead, the cavalry officer raised his saber over his head and was rewarded for his defiance by bullet in his chest, fired at close range. Parsons's horse was wounded and bolted frantically to safety through the ranks of the 47th Alabama. The wounded Parsons was carried to safety by a Federal corporal.[29]

Meanwhile Farnsworth and one of his officers rode at the head of their small squadron, sabers raised. The officer's silk handkerchief waved in the wind. As the 4th Alabama watched the squadron approach the skirmish line at long range, they thought the silk handkerchief fluttering in the breeze was a flag of truce.[30] Actually Farnsworth harbored no intention of surrendering. He boldly charged the 15th Alabama skirmish line which was moving west at the double quick across the southern end of Plum Run Valley. A canister round fired at Farnsworth as his group passed, overshot the horsemen and fortunately the 15th Alabama, too. Oates later recalled the shot made a sound like a covey of partridges in flight as passed overhead.[31]

Oates's skirmishers were under the command of Lieutenant John D. Adrian of the 44th Alabama. Adrian needed a horse and thought the skirmish line might be a good place to acquire one. The skirmishers were just ascending a slight rise when Farnsworth charged, waving his pistol and demanding the surrender of those nearest to him. Adrian carried a repeating rifle he had recovered from the battlefield, and he and his skirmishers immediately replied with a volley. Farnsworth was knocked from his saddle and, although not killed outright, suffered from multiple wounds, any one of which would probably have proved fatal. Farnsworth still grasped his pistol when Adrian approached and demanded surrender. Private Craig, 9th Georgia, had followed the horsemen into the woods and witnessed the scene. He recalled that Farnsworth retorted, "...he would die before he would surrender and turned the pistol and shot himself."[32] Oates saw the encounter but did not pay much attention to the group gathered around Farnsworth until someone brought him a shoulder strap. It was supposed, at first, that Farnsworth was a major because he wore a star on each shoulder strap. Oates concluded that Farnsworth was a brigadier and went at

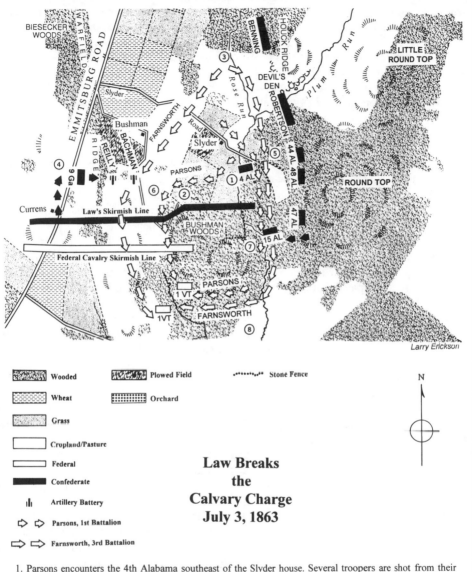

Larry Erickson

	Wooded		Plowed Field	⚫⚫⚫⚫⚫⚫⚫⚫ Stone Fence	N
Wheat		Orchard	
Grass			
Cropland/Pasture			
Federal			
Confederate			
ılı Artillery Battery			
⇨ ⇨ Parsons, 1st Battalion			
⇨ ⇨ Farnsworth, 3rd Battalion			

Law Breaks
the
Calvary Charge
July 3, 1863

1. Parsons encounters the 4th Alabama southeast of the Slyder house. Several troopers are shot from their saddles. Parsons's battalion splits into two groups.
2. One group turns southwest, reforms under cover of some woods and eventually fights its way through Law's skirmish line to safety.
3. Farnsworth's battalion also splits into two groups. Farnsworth leads one group south along the original route north. The second group gallops southwest toward Bachman and Reilly.
4. The 9th Georgia arrives to support the artillery as Farnsworth's troops approach.
5. Parsons initially rides east, then turns south and rides parallel with Farnsworth.
6. Farnsworth's men are easily repulsed by the 9th Georgia and Law's artillerymen. The Federals continue south and pass through Law's skirmish line.
7. The 15th Alabama blocks Farnsworth's escape route. Parsons and several troopers are severely wounded. Farnsworth is mortally wounded.
8. Survivors from the encounter with the 4th and 15th Alabama return to their original position.

once to the body. Several letters were found in Farnsworth's pockets, at least one being from his wife. Oates subsequently destroyed all the letters to keep Farnsworth's personal correspondence from falling into the hands of souvenir hunters.[33]

Several versions of Farnsworth's death circulated throughout the brigade that night. Oates said at one time that Farnsworth blew his own brains out. In later years he recalled that Farnsworth shot himself through the heart. Parsons claimed that when Farnsworth's body was taken from the field five wounds were discovered none of which were in the head. However, Adrian and Craig steadfastly maintained that Farnsworth took his own life by turning his pistol on himself.[34]

After the fighting ended a squad from the 4th Alabama went over to Reilly's battery where some of the gunners laughingly told the Alabamians they had "...a hot time defending their guns." They recounted how the two Federal cavalrymen had been knocked from their horses with rammers. As the Alabamians roamed the field, dead Federal troopers were found lying in a number of places. Private Reuben Nix spotted one and climbed over a fence to investigate. He returned with a roll of greenbacks.[35]

In the end Farnsworth's ill-fated charge contributed nothing to the Federal cause. Meade's infantry had been content to watch the cavalry's adventure from the sidelines. Law cleverly boxed Farnsworth in by moving the 15th Alabama toward the 1st Texas and then correctly anticipated Farnsworth's moves. He agreed with others at the scene that Farnsworth's charge was foolhardy. Felix H. Robertson, a captain of Texas artillery, was more blunt in his assessment of the charge. He termed it an "...inexcusable military blunder."[36] Longstreet was pleased with his brigadier and in Law's words "...warmly congratulated me on the manner in which the situation had been handled."[37]

A Case of Poor Communications

From his vantage point near the Emmitsburg Road, Major General Lafayette McLaws watched the destruction of Pickett's line as his men stormed the Federal center. As he prepared to cover Pickett's withdrawal, McLaws saw the Federals made no move to follow. Because his division was well protected from the Federal artillery by wooded terrain McLaws felt sufficiently secure to stay in position and observe the Federal line. A short time later one of Law's staff officers requested a brigade to replace Anderson in his main line. McLaws told the man to inform Law that "...Picket had been thoroughly routed" and advised Law to close left because they might be called upon to meet a Federal advance. Fifteen minutes later Colonel G. Moxley Sorrel, of Longstreet's Staff, rode up, and before Sorrel could deliver his order McLaws proceeded to inform him of Law's request and his reply. "Never mind that now," Sorrel interrupted, "General Longstreet directs that you retire to your position of yesterday." When McLaws asked who would tell Law his division was to withdraw, Sorrel indicated he would. McLaws then launched into a lecture on the ill-advised nature of the order, the importance of the position, and the fact it had only been won after a hard struggle, Sorrel felt compelled to interrupt again: "General, there is no discretion allowed, the order is for you to retire at once."[38]

As McLaws withdrew, his men came under artillery fire which did little damage. Sorrel reappeared after McLaws reached his new position and countermanded the previous order to retire. McLaws immediately asked, "Why?" "Because," replied Sorrel, "General Longstreet had forgotten that he had ordered it, and now disapproved the withdrawal."[39] McLaws declined to move, and later recalled that Sorrel "gave no orders to try and retake the position, and I did not attempt it."[40] Law saw the danger in McLaws's withdrawal and sent a courier to inform Benning that he wished a regiment moved to the left to an elevation to replace McLaws. Benning did not know which hill, and neither did the courier, because when Law gave the order he had simply waved his hand in the general direction he wished the regiment moved. Unfortunately the courier left without a clear understanding of where Benning was to go. Benning assumed Law meant for him to occupy the ground vacated by McLaws, and ordered the 15th Georgia to move farther left.[41]

Law then sent for McLaws to join him in a discussion of the situation near his position. Benning also joined the two and as the trio conversed, Federal infantry was seen advancing toward McLaws's old position. Law's flanks were now in the air and the generals decided that Law's position was untenable. However, Law had not received an order to retire.[42] Any doubts about the merit of withdrawing were soon removed from their minds. Colonel William McCandless's Federal brigade attacked the 15th Georgia on the front and both flanks, driving it back with considerable loss.[43] After the 15th Georgia rejoined Benning's main line, Law quietly withdrew his division to the Emmitsburg Road.[44]

Law's Brigade left its position without the 15th Alabama which held the Confederate extreme right opposite the enemy cavalry. Sheffield had sent a courier to order the 15th Alabama to rejoin the brigade but he was captured before reaching Oates. As darkness fell, Oates became concerned for the regiment's safety and started toward the brigade's last known location. On the way, he discovered another Federal skirmish line. Although Oates had no orders to leave his position, the presence of Federals on both his front and rear caused him much concern and he immediately decided to move. Marching in single file by the right flank, Oates led the 15th Alabama toward the Emmitsburg Road. As he walked through the dark, Oates heard the sounds of breastwork construction and moved in that direction. When he discovered the sounds were made by members of Hood's Division, he happily placed the 15th Alabama in the Confederate works. Just over 24 hours after it left, Hood's Division was back where it entered the fight at Gettysburg.[45]

Aftermath of Battle

Law's Brigade did its best to turn the Federal left and almost succeeded. Even though the Devil's Den was successfully assaulted and wrested from Federal hands, it was abandoned the next day. Most of the officers and men did their duty and courageously faced the foe. Scruggs said all his officers and men behaved with coolness and gallantry, while Perry applauded the efforts of Lieutenant Colonel John Jones, Major George Cary, and Adjutant Winns Becker.[46] He refrained from mentioning others because the list would be too long. Campbell stated all the officers, with the exception of Jackson and Adjutant W. H. Keller, acted well.[47] Campbell did not elaborate, nor has a record of any action against either individual been found. It can be assumed the negative remarks directed at Jackson resulted from the colonel falling out soon after the charge began. The charge against Jackson was unwarranted because his health was broken, and after Gettysburg he resigned from the service on July 16, returning to his father's farm in Georgia. He never regained his health and died near the end of the war. Any doubt about Sheffield's ability to instill discipline was gone, since he proved himself an able regimental commander at Gettysburg. He spoke highly of Lieutenants Reuben Ewing and Francis Burk while Captains Thomas Eubanks and Jeremiah Edwards also were specifically cited for their gallantry during the hottest part of the conflict. He closed by saying that, before being wounded, Lieutenant Colonel William Hardwick and Major Columbus St. John performed their duties very efficiently.[48]

Oates was uncharacteristically quiet in praise of his men but did take punitive action against Lieutenant William D. Wood of Company H, by charging him with conduct unbecoming an officer and placing him under arrest. Wood's resignation was tendered July 16, 1863, which Oates accepted as the most expedient means to rid the army of an unworthy officer.[49] Many years later, Oates wrote a short biography about his former lieutenant, and either did not, or chose not to remember that day at Gettysburg. Wood, according to Oates, had been a fair soldier.[50]

In the aftermath of Gettysburg, perhaps more than any other battle of the Civil War, the focus has been to determine who most directly caused the Confederate reverse. Even as the Confederate army prepared to leave the Gettysburg battlefield, the seeds of discord over the defeat were already sown. Longstreet and Law would soon be engrossed in a bitter dispute which one of Law's aides traced to the battle on the Federal left. After the war Longstreet's enemies sought to place the blame for the Confederate reverse on him, alleging negligence for not promptly carrying out Lee's order on July 2. It is true that Longstreet could have deployed the First Corps before noon. He could have captured the Peach Orchard and the high ground west of Little Round Top before it was occupied by the Federals.[51] Longstreet did not have to wait for the arrival of Law to do this. Law could have found Longstreet on the Emmitsburg Road. That premise has been studied in considerable depth by Freeman, Coddington, and Pfanz. None of the commanders charged with attacking the Federal left wanted to deliver the assault as it was envisioned by Lee. Law and Hood were well within their right, as division and brigade commanders, to offer protests when the Federal position was found to be significantly different from what they anticipated. If there is any fault to be found with either, it is that Hood continued the discussions about the turning movement too long. While the generals talked, Federal preparations were under way to occupy the Little Round Top, which did not occur until the charge had commenced. Had they attacked even a half hour earlier, the Confederates would have reached the summit of the famous hill before Vincent.

As Hood began deploying he was ordered to attack up the Emmitsburg Road and strike the Federal left. The original plan was changed to conform to the reality on the battlefield. It seems probable therefore that Hood's instructions to use the Emmitsburg Road as his axis of attack were also changed. Hood would have been under enfilade fire and fire from the rear if he had held his left to the road during the attack. The alignment of Hood's Division nearly parallel to the Emmitsburg Road gave him the best opportunity to strike the Federal left. Unexplained is why Robertson attempted to hold his left on the Emmitsburg Road. When it became impossible to both hold his left to the road and hold his right close upon Law, Robertson made the decision to stay with Law. A gap appeared in the middle of the Texas brigade, nonetheless. Law probably gave no thought to the Emmitsburg Road after he deployed his men in battle line, as it lay some distance to his rear. The Federal left was Law's target. To get to that objective, which Hood and Law believed to be at Devil's Den, it was necessary to pass across the Federal line under heavy and effective fire. Law then attempted to front his brigade to the north and the Federal left. Perhaps the terrain, the long slope down into Plum Run Valley and the enemy fire from the base of Round Top all combined to force Law's Brigade to the east. Much of the enemy musketry was from Stoughton's eight companies of Sharpshooters. They did effective work against Law's men. In addition, they probably appeared to Law to be a skirmish line for a stronger force which he could not ignore. Law strove to obey his order to roll up the Federal left. He moved the 44th and 48th regiments from the right of his line to the left. He ordered Oates to turn his regiment to the north and inflict as much damage as possible on the enemy's flank. Scruggs turned the 4th Alabama to the north, probably under the same order. All these maneuvers served to put his brigade in line opposite the enemy's left. As events unfolded, Law's Brigade did attack the Federal left with considerable striking power.

Once the charge got under way, Law displayed the same boldness and aggressiveness that caught Lee's eye at Gaines's Mill. While his lines were being swept by artillery and musketry, he moved two Alabama regiments, in a flawless execution under fire, from the right of the line to the left by an oblique left, which put more men at the point of the heaviest fighting at the moment. He was forced to move the 44th and 48th to the left to attack Smith. Since Benning filled the gap, had Law left the Alabama regiments on the right, he would have found a greater opportunity for success there because the fight for Little Round Top was a near thing. With two more regiments, even two as small as these, the Confederates may have wrested the hill from Union hands. Unfortunately the five regiments which did assault Little Round Top did so without benefit of unified command, attacking the hill piecemeal. To make matters worse the most junior regimental commander in the Alabama brigade was entrusted to turn the Federal left. It is certainly a tribute to the fighting ability of the Alabamians and Texans that the Federals were almost thrown off Little Round Top. On July 3, with only a day's experience in division command, Law performed with the competence of a veteran division commander as he skillfully maneuvered his regiments to defeat Farnsworth's cavalry attack.

It has not been the subject of discussion by historians, but the absence of Benning's Georgians on the right was critical to the Confederate failure to roll up the Federal left. In the fog of battle, Benning mistakenly followed two regiments of the Texas brigade to Devil's Den. Had he followed Law as planned, the Confederate strength on the right would have been vastly superior. In addition, the Confederates would have had another general officer in that sector. As it was Law tried to control the nine regiments of Hood's front line virtually alone. Of course, lack of adequate staff was not new to Confederate commanders. Law experienced an almost identical situation at Chickamauga. Discussing Confederate staff problems, Alexander wrote after the war, "Scarcely any of our generals had half of what they needed to keep a constant and close supervision on the execution of important orders."[52]

Sometime during the day of July 4, the 118th Pennsylvania moved forward to develop the Confederate positions near the Devil's Den. They were greeted by a pitiful and horrifying sight. Hood's dead lay in plain view. Squads of dead lay shielded by the rocks, probably killed by shell bursts. Some were still kneeling behind rocks and boulders, their sightless eyes turned toward the Federal positions. Others managed to crawl behind boulders before succumbing to their wounds. Many, unable to move after being shot, had dug shallow trenches for some protection. Several were killed instantly in the act of firing and fell clutching their muskets. For many their last hours on earth were agonizing as death came slowly. Bits of grass and twigs held between clenched teeth attested to the agony they must have suffered. Most of the dead perished with lavish chews of tobacco in their mouths. Just south of Devil's Den, a neat row of dead marked Perry's line where the 4th Maine's first volley sent it to the ground. Among the dead were Captain William Dunklin. Even in death, it was obvious the Alabamian was a fine specimen of southern manhood, being of large proportions and handsome features.[53]

Brigade casualties from the Battle of Gettysburg totaled 526 killed, wounded and missing. The 4th Alabama lost four officers killed, four wounded and three missing. There were 14 men killed, 45 wounded and 20 missing for a total of 90. The 15th Alabama incurred the largest number of casualties, sustaining 172 killed, wounded and missing. Four of its officers lay dead on the field, one was wounded, and three were missing. Eighteen of its men were killed, 66 wounded and 81 were missing. The 44th Alabama lost three officers killed and two wounded. Twenty-two of its men lay dead in front of Devil's Den, 62 were wounded and five missing. The 47th Alabama lost four officers killed, one wounded and two missing. Six of its men died on the slopes of Little Round Top, 39 were wounded and 15 were reported missing. The 48th Alabama counted seven officers wounded and two missing. Ten of its men were killed, 61 wounded and 22 were missing.

Law's brigade left 154 of its officers and men behind, either wounded or captured. Four of the officers left in field hospitals died before they could be removed to prison camps and are included in the count of officers killed. Five of the missing officers were wounded and eventually recovered. Of the eleven officers captured, eight would be exchanged but only one, Thomas Christian, would return to duty. Seven of the 14 wounded officers would eventually return to duty. Therefore, when the number of captured and wounded that would not be returned to duty are considered, the brigade effectively lost 38 officers or 21 percent of its officer strength.

A few days after the armies departed the field, captured Confederates began arriving at Westminister, Maryland, under heavy guard. From there the prisoners were transported to Baltimore by train and temporarily housed in Fort McHenry until sent to prison camps. On August 8 the Richmond *Dispatch* reported 120 prisoners arrived at Baltimore for transfer to Johnson's Island. Most of the prisoners from Law's Brigade were sent to Fort Delaware. For them the next leg of their journey to prison was by steamer down the Chesapeake via Fort Monroe and then to Fort Delaware. Some thought the trip down the Chesapeake meant they were going to be exchanged at City Point, Virginia, but that proved to be only a false hope. In late August the officers were sent to Johnson's Island on the shores of Lake Erie. The camp was three miles from Sandusky, Ohio, and covered five or six acres of land.[54] Cussons did much to enliven the camp and provide entertainment for his fellow prisoners. A theatrical company was organized and a number of productions given throughout the winter months of 1863–64. Cussons managed to solicit sufficient contributions from his audiences to procure needed goods for the camp's sick and wounded. The audiences were not only Confederate prisoners, but Federal soldiers and the local populace as well.[55]

Several of the brigade officers were exchanged in the spring of 1864, including Cussons and Christian on March 17, 1864. Christian returned to the brigade and assumed his duties as adjutant and inspector general, but Cussons never seriously considered returning to active service.[56] He was still a British subject and immediately applied for leave to return to England. When he returned, Law was on wounded leave and Cussons applied for additional leave, using Law's absence as his reason. The leave was granted and Cussons elected not to return to Confederate service.[57] Instead, he married and settled in Glen Allen, Virginia.

For some time after the battle it was thought that Bulger was dead, but he miraculously survived his wound. By late July he was able to travel and was transferred to a hospital in Baltimore. After spending the winter in a Federal prison he was selected, in February 1864, to be exchanged and transferred to Point Lookout, Maryland.

It was by sheer luck that First Lieutenant John P. Breedlove, Company B, 4th Alabama, survived his wound. A bullet entered the left side of his lower abdomen, near the groin, tearing a hole in the lower intestine.[58] He lay in a field hospital six weeks before receiving any attention.[59] An examination on August 29, 1863, revealed the wound was discharging heavily. A special diet was prescribed and by November 9 Breedlove was transported to West Building Hospital in Baltimore.[60] He was then sent to Fort Delaware, Maryland, remaining there until August 1864. Breedlove was one of 600 Confederate prisoners sent to Morris Island in the Charleston, South Carolina, harbor and placed under fire of Confederate guns from Fort Sumter.[61] The prisoners were placed in open camps next to the Federal batteries in retaliation for Federal prisoners being placed in private homes shelled by the Federal batteries. From there he was sent to Fort Pulaski, Georgia, and finally exchanged in January 1865.[62] After the war Breedlove farmed a few years near Tuskegee, Alabama, then entered the mercantile business. He later served as tax assessor for Macon County.[63]

Captain Jeremiah Edwards, 48th Alabama, and Lieutenant Robert H. Wicker, 15th Alabama, spent the remainder of the war in Federal prison camps. Edwards was sent to Johnson's Island and not paroled until July 3, 1865. Wicker was imprisoned at Fort Delaware.[64] Lieutenant Joseph Breare, 15th Alabama, was exchanged March 17, 1864, obtained leave for 30 days and returned to Alabama. When he did not return to the 15th an order was issued for his arrest.[65] He managed to avoid that unpleasant experience when, as Oates later reported, Breare, an Englishman by birth and lawyer by profession, raised a company of cavalry in the conscript service.[66]

Several of those left behind did not survive the Gettysburg field hospitals. Cody died July 22 and John Oates on July 25. Junior Second Lieutenant Andrew Ray, Company E, 47th Alabama, died July 4. Captain Joseph S. Johnston of the 47th Alabama died July 18.[67] Captain William Leftwich, twenty-one-year-old bachelor druggist from Huntsville, Alabama, was dead of his wounds.[68] He was disliked by the men in his company because he was a strict disciplinarian.

Private William Penny, Company E, 47th Alabama, was an ordinary private. He could also be described as the son of a typical Confederate family with a deep rooted southern heritage. His family traced its origins to the 1680s in southern Virginia. The Penny family migrated through North Carolina into Alabama as the lands were opened. William and three brothers joined the Confederate armies. An older brother, Riley, was killed at the 47th Alabama's first battle at Cedar Run, Virginia. William was just 18 years old when he marched into Pennsylvania where in his first battle at Gettysburg he was seriously wounded in the assault on Little Round Top. Because his wounds were severe, he was left behind when the ambulance train departed. William languished in a makeshift field hospital until he succumbed to his wounds.[69]

Retreat to Virginia

Hood's Division occupied Warfield Ridge during the morning of July 4. Word came that the army would be leaving the field late in the evening. The plan was to send the wounded through Greencastle under guard of Brigadier General John D. Imboden's cavalry brigade. The infantry would travel by way of Fairfield and act as a screen between Meade's army and the ambulance train. A severe thunderstorm rolled over the battlefield near noon, the rain continuing all afternoon and most of the night. Men began loading the wounded about the time the rain began, but some of the injured refused to go, preferring a Federal prison to the trip back to Virginia, lying on a floor of wet straw, in a springless wagon. By necessity the badly wounded were left behind. For those who did go, the ride was torturous. The wagon train, consisting of ambulances and supply wagons, was 17 miles long and moved out around 4 p.m. Rain fell in torrents, transforming the roads into bogs. As darkness settled over the countryside occasional lightning flashes and accompanying loud thunderclaps startled the horses. When a team bolted, the wagon's wounded occupants were either jolted or sent tumbling into the mud. At Fairfield the train followed a short cut to Greencastle. The head of the column arrived there near dawn July 5. Groups of local civilians gathered and attacked several wagons. A few wagons were disabled by having the spokes cut.[70] The 1st New York Cavalry charged a portion of the train, capturing 134 wagons, 600 horses, two guns and 645 prisoners.[71] First Lieutenant James S. Ridgeway, Company D, 48th Alabama, was among those captured. He was exchanged October 31, 1864, but did not return to service.[72]

The infantry began its withdrawal from the battlefield late in the evening of July 5.[73] The order of march was Hill's Third Corps, Longstreet's First Corps and Ewell's Second Corps. Longstreet, being the center of the column, was given the task of guarding the

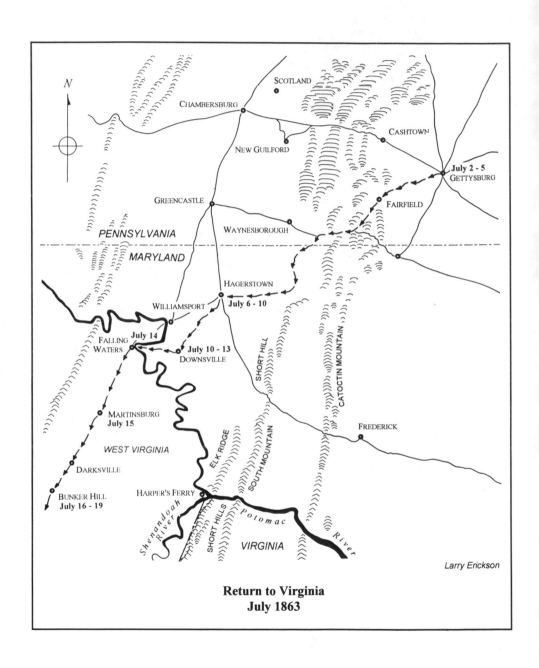

Return to Virginia
July 1863

Larry Erickson

prisoners. Those in the ranks knew the army had fought well and did what was asked of them, but they also knew the army had suffered a great defeat. Some would return many years later as old men to relive memories of the fight at Gettysburg and to once more charge the Federal positions. A battlefield commission would be established to preserve the field of conflict and sort out the various positions of the combatants. Captain William M. Robbins would be the second Confederate representative on the commission.

Many, like Sergeant George Thomas, Company D, 4th Alabama, would have harrowing stories of near brushes with death to tell their children and grandchildren. Thomas came to Gettysburg with a Bible, picked up from a distant battlefield, tucked safely in his haversack. Inside the Bible an inscription read:

> *"Presented to Harrison Preston Reid on April 27, 1849, by his affection-*
> *ate mother. May it be a lamp to his path and may he live that at last he*
> *be gathered among the saints in heaven."*

Somewhere on the battlefield a bullet struck the haversack and ripped into the Bible. Part of the Bible was destroyed, but fortunately Thomas was spared a potentially serious wound.[74]

Before departing, several members of the 4th Alabama made one last visit to the wounded at the field hospital on the Planck farm. Someone removed John Breedlove's cap because the gold braid indicated his rank. An older, well-worn hat was placed over Breedlove's face. Scruggs removed the braid from Henry Roper's hat, which was better than his, and replaced it with his own. Some of the more seriously wounded would stay in the hospital several months. Every day there was someone to bury, usually in a shallow grave in the nearby peach orchard. When the wounded finally left, all the yard and garden fences were gone, as were all the poultry and livestock. Wood had been torn from the dwelling and surrounding buildings and burned in campfires.[75]

Law's Brigade did not march until 2 a.m. on July 5. The rainfall was still quite heavy.[76] The march took the infantry across the mountains to Hagerstown by way of Fairfield. Camp the night of July 5 was on a damp and chilly road at Monterey Springs. Law's Brigade reached Hagerstown about midnight July 6 and took up position a few miles from town. Rations were distributed and cooked July 7. Rain fell in a steady downpour throughout the day of July 7 and most of the night. Major Coleman participated in an engagement with cavalry near Funkstown. A courier, chased by Federal cavalry, arrived July 8 with the division's mail. On July 10, Law's Brigade left its camp at 7 a.m. and marched toward Williamsport. At 9 a.m. the brigade went into line of battle fronting the Antietam. After several hours it marched toward Dam Number 4 and made camp near Downsville. Next day the brigade moved a mile nearer to the Potomac where rifle pits were constructed.[77]

Law's Brigade remained in the fortifications near Downsville until the night of July 13 when orders were received to recross the Potomac. They took up the line of march about 10 p.m., slogging along all night in a heavy rainstorm. The route, over small farm roads that were rough, narrow and hilly in good weather, had turned to mud, five or six inches deep in most places. It was the dark period of the moon and the clouds shut out the starlight. An artilleryman remembered the night was so dark that his hand, placed a short distance from his face, was not visible.[78] Artillery carriages and wagons dug muddy trenches in the already bad roads. All too often, shoes sank up to their tops. Ten hours after it started for the Potomac, Law's Brigade struggled across the pontoon bridge at Falling Waters.[79] The 4th Alabama was the last regiment in Law's Brigade at the crossing. They were met by Lee with instructions to remove the bridge as soon as a squadron of cavalry behind them had crossed. Part of the 4th entered rifle pits, receiving an ineffective artillery and rifle fire.

The remainder began to dismantle the bridge. Lieutenant Colonel Thomas H. Carter's Artillery Battalion of Major General Robert E. Rodes's Division, Second Corps, supported the 4th. Federals appeared in the distance a short time after the bridge was cut loose and caused a few anxious moments. A detachment of skirmishers appeared on the opposite banks. For a few moments it appeared the Confederates might be stranded and face certain capture but, fortunately, a few shots from the artillery forced the Federals to keep their distance while some boats were sent across to retrieve the stranded soldiers.[80] The Alabamians' second excursion onto Northern soil was ended.

Chapter 7

On the Rappahannock

After crossing into Virginia, Law's Brigade marched toward Martinsburg, and camped the night of July 14 along the road. About 1 p.m. on July 15 they resumed the march, passing through Martinsburg and making camp below Darksville where they cooked their first rations in five days.[1] At daylight on the 16th, Longstreet's corps marched for Bunker Hill. Law's Brigade encamped a mile north of the village. The brigade remained in camp four days and enjoyed a much needed rest.

Law's men had returned from Gettysburg exhausted, their clothes reduced to tattered rags.[2] Many had walked miles over the pike roads without shoes and their feet were in terrible condition.[3] The men of Law's Brigade were veterans, however, who expected this late in the war to march fast and far through ankle deep mud, or on dry roads which covered them with dust, with few or no rations and scarcely any water. They had signed on for "three years or the war" and expected to fight for the duration. Lieutenant Isaac M. Newell of the 47th Alabama Regiment, a veteran who had enrolled on May 2, 1862, at Loachapoka, Alabama, was one such soldier. He wrote his sister, the widow of his former captain, John V. McKee, that "I don't expect to get to come home myself till the war closes without I get wounded."[4] Hardened veterans or not, the Alabamians realized the significance of the retreat from Pennsylvania and the fall of Vicksburg. Newell expressed concern about morale in a letter home. "If there ever has been a dark and gloomy time since the war commenced, I think it is just at this time. "The fall of Vicksburg and the Gettysburg affair," he added, "has greatly discouraged the soldiers."[5] Reuben Kidd, 4th Alabama, also felt, "things in our little Confederacy begin to look blue," after Gettysburg.[6] James Daniel, Company H, 47th Alabama, wrote home that "our boys is [sic] in mighty low spirits."[7]

Securing the Mountain Passes

Lee suspected that Meade planned to cut him off from his railroad link to Richmond, and on the morning of the July 20 he sent the First Corps to gain possession of Ashby's Gap. With Longstreet in control of the pass through the Blue Ridge Mountains, future movements of the Army of Northern Virginia could be guaranteed.[8]

The First Corps marched up the Shenandoah Valley at dawn, through Winchester, taking the turnpike which passed through Ashby's Gap en route to Culpeper. Law's command camped the night of July 20 about four miles below Berryville. Arriving at Millwood the next morning, Longstreet's troops found the Shenandoah River too high to ford. The Federal army had crossed the Potomac River east of the Blue Ridge Mountains, advancing along the eastern slope toward the mountain gaps through which the Confederates must pass to reach safety. Brigadier General George A. Custer's cavalry reached Ashby's Gap ahead of Longstreet's infantry. Ashby's Gap was occupied down to the river by the 5th and 6th Michigan Cavalry regiments of Custer's command.[9]

Longstreet turned his column up the Shenandoah Valley toward Manassas and Chester Gaps, the next two passes through the Blue Ridge. The First Corps, with Pickett in the van, hurried along the western slope of the Blue Ridge while the Union cavalry on the east side of the range raced them for possession of the mountain passes.[10]

At Front Royal, opposite Manassas Gap, Brigadier General Montgomery D. Corse, of Pickett's Division, crossed his brigade over the two forks of the Shenandoah River.[11] Corse detached the 17th Virginia to hold a position at the west end of the narrow mountain gap against the Federal horsemen who had already entered it from the east, and sent the rest of his Virginians to Chester Gap, still farther south in the Blue Ridge.[12] Corse's Brigade secured Chester Gap before the Union cavalry could reach it. The Federal horsemen had reached Gettysburg ahead of the lead elements of Lee's army, holding the town until infantry could arrive, but on this occasion the Confederates were faster.[13]

Hood's Division, under Law's command, crossed the Shenandoah at Berry's Ford near Front Royal on July 22 and relieved the 17th Virginia at the west end of Manassas Gap, its job being to protect the Confederates from the Federal cavalry and artillery occupying the pass.[14] Law deployed his infantry to drive the Union cavalry back into Manassas Gap, away from the Confederate column.[15] Two roads passed through Manassas Gap, one next to the tracks of the Manassas Gap Railroad, the other over the mountain through the village of Wappen.[16] Benning's Georgia brigade was positioned on the road through the gap with Robertson's Texans on his left, the 4th Alabama on his right and Anderson's Brigade on the extreme right. The rest of Law's Brigade, commanded by Sheffield, was held in reserve. Enemy cavalry was visible in the pass and on the heights above. The division moved eastward into the pass, turning the flank of the Union horsemen and pushing them about a mile into the gap which provoked, according to a member of the 4th, "a dozen or more shells" from Federal artillery.[17] As Longstreet reported to Lee, the enemy "gave but little trouble" to Law's veterans.[18]

That evening, Law marched the other brigades of the division to Chester Gap, already in Pickett's possession, leaving Benning's Brigade and the 4th Alabama, commanded by Lieutenant Colonel Scruggs, to block Manassas Gap until relieved by the Third Corps.[19] During the night, the vanguard of the Federal III Corps relieved the Union cavalry. The Union infantry launched several attacks during the daylight hours of July 23 in the action known as the Battle of Wapping Heights, which began only an hour after Brigadier General A. R. Wright's Brigade relieved Benning at 9 a.m.[20]

Benning's Georgians and the detached Alabamians hastened to rejoin their division. It was necessary to pass A. P. Hill's column on the narrow mountain road through Chester Gap, which delayed Benning.[21] Benning and the 4th Alabama bivouacked the night of July 23 two miles south of Flint Hill, perhaps 15 miles from Front Royal, well behind the rest of Law's command.[22]

An Ambush Badly Sprung

Law marched through Chester Gap, and detached the 15th Alabama to picket the Warrenton Road near Gaines's Cross Roads. The 15th was ordered to get astride the road to prevent a surprise attack on the column. About noon, on July 23, after his soldiers had eaten their last rations, Oates marched his regiment down the Warrenton Road about a mile and a half before stopping at a defensible position near a clear stream. As the situation was calm, Oates allowed his men to bathe in the mountain creek, half the regiment at a time, but this pleasurable experience was interrupted by firing on the road toward Warrenton. The shooting, explained a Confederate cavalryman who rode into Oates's line, was by a Federal cavalry brigade pushing up the road, and his squadron was retreating before it.[23]

Oates quickly laid an ambush, using the Confederate cavalry to lead their pursuers into the concealed line of the 15th Alabama. Most of the regiment was near a fence on the crest of an elevation which bisected the road. Between this small hill and a bridge over the stream in which the Alabamians had bathed was an open field. When the Union riders entered the field the trap would be sprung.[24] Oates planned to bag the entire lot.

Company A was concealed near the open ground, lying on an elevation below the bridge with instructions to rush to the bridge to cut off the Federals retreat after the head of the enemy column had been stopped at the fence. Contrary to orders, however, the men of Shaaff's company opened fire when only the head of the cavalry column was on the bridge. This was too soon to spring the ambush, and most of the Federals escaped. Oates captured one prisoner whose horse had been shot from under him, and the Alabamians were able to identify their opponents as members of a West Virginia regiment, not a brigade as had been reported by the Confederate trooper.[25]

The 15th Alabama marched back to the Culpeper Road on the morning of July 24 to join Benning's Brigade and the 4th Alabama. Oates allowed his hungry men to stop for breakfast at a blackberry patch. At least one soldier, Orderly Sergeant Billy Jordan, credited the combination of short rations and berries with curing his chronic diarrhea, which he thought was caused by the lingering effects of typhoid.[26]

Benning had halted within two miles of Gaines's Cross Roads to allow time for the 15th Alabama to catch up.[27] He was not pressing his brigade, for the entire column was moving slowly to prevent its stretching out and giving the enemy cavalry the opportunity to cut off isolated Confederate wagons.[28] When the 15th Alabama arrived, the march was resumed, with the Third Corps close behind. As his column neared Newby's Cross Roads, Benning met two cavalrymen who reported advance riders of Custer's Second Brigade, Third Division, on the road between Newby's Cross Roads and Amissville. The two Confederates were going to Amissville to have their horses shod, and were unaware the town had been occupied by Custer the previous night.[29]

Fight for Battle Mountain

The 15th Alabama was the vanguard of Benning's command, and Oates was quick to volunteer his regiment to make a reconnaissance toward Battle Mountain, an elevation about half a mile from the crossroads. Benning accepted his offer. Oates led the 15th Alabama to the foot of Battle Mountain, where he found the Union cavalry arrayed on the mountain with its artillery covering the road. Oates's skirmishers began exchanging fire with Custer's Michiganders. Benning waited but was unimpressed with the volume of fire. Word arrived from A. P. Hill that he would relieve Oates, so Benning gave the order for his brigade and the 4th Alabama to resume the march to Culpeper.[30]

Custer, commanding the Third Division while Kilpatrick was on leave, ordered his brigade to attack up the Amissville Road, intending to halt the Confederate column moving toward Culpeper.[31] He sent forward to Battle Mountain the 1st, 5th and 6th Michigan Cavalry regiments and Battery M of the 2nd U.S. Artillery to engage the Confederates. The 5th Michigan had the advance of the Federal column, fighting the 15th Alabama on the right of the road as dismounted skirmishers while the 1st Michigan supported the artillery positioned on the crest of the hill to the left of the Amissville Road. The 6th Michigan reinforced the 5th Regiment on the right.[32]

Four companies of the Alabama regiment moved against the Federals deployed on the mountain. Lieutenant Edmond P. Head, of the "Ft. Browder Roughs," was killed and three men wounded while making the ascent of the mountain. All four were taken by ambulance to Culpeper Courthouse where Head, a favorite of his colonel, was buried with full military honors.[33]

Learning of the arrival of A. P. Hill, Oates halted the attack and rode to the general's headquarters for the loan of an artillery piece. Oates placed his borrowed cannon where it could enfilade the Federal battery.[34] Hill also placed artillery in position to fire upon the Federal cavalry. The situation remained in stalemate for an hour or more, the Federals holding the high ground and the Alabamians firing shells, case and canister that forced the Union cavalrymen to keep their heads down.[35] Oates was prepared to attack with his whole regiment when the Federals were driven off by Benning's surprise appearance at their rear.[36]

Benning had almost reached the Hazel River when a courier from A. P. Hill stopped him with the request that he wait for Hill's artillery. Before any artillery arrived, however, Hill sent another courier asking Benning to return to the area of Battle Mountain to block the retreat of the Union cavalry as Hill drove them from the mountain. Lieutenant Robert C. Stanard of Hill's staff and an elderly civilian led Benning through the Federal picket line. When the Confederates got possession of the road to Amissville, Benning believed he had bagged the entire enemy force. But Benning's guides had been mistaken when they told him there was no escape for the Union cavalry.

Benning had come up behind the artillery section and the 1st Michigan, but the artillery quickly retreated to the Amissville Road while the 5th Michigan withstood a volley before making a hasty retreat to the same road. When Benning executed his flank movement against the Union left, Oates saw an opportunity to attack and ordered the 15th Alabama, supported by at least two of Hill's artillery pieces, to advance against the Union right, splitting the force on the right of the road. But Oates and Benning had not moved in concert, and although surprised by the Confederate flanking movement, the Union horsemen eluded the trap.[37] The 15th gave only token pursuit as Custer's riders retreated from Battle Mountain.[38] Custer reported only 30 casualties in the engagement, though it was very nearly a disaster for his command.[39]

Since the route of their flanking movement put the Georgians and Alabamians between the Federal pickets and their main body, Adjutant Coles joined Lieutenant William F. Turner and another soldier of the 4th Alabama in a plan to capture the pickets. Expecting the pickets to attempt to rejoin their regiments as quickly as possible, the enterprising Confederates ran to the point where they believed they could intercept the Federal horsemen. The three captured one rider at a gate, although Coles admitted they succeeded due to negligence on the part of the Union cavalryman. Coles obtained the horse and saddle as spoils, the other two divided the contents of the saddle bags. In the bags was a toothbrush which Turner boiled and used for himself, declaring to Coles, ..."that he valued it more than any other trophy we had captured which fell to his lot."[40]

Southern Honor Tested

From Battle Mountain, the 4th and 15th Alabama marched with Benning's Georgians unmolested into Culpeper. Law's Brigade encamped at Culpeper on the same grounds they had occupied before the Pennsylvania campaign.[41] On July 31, Longstreet's First Corps left Culpeper for Fredericksburg, while Law's division in the van, crossed the Rapidan River at Morton's Ford, and took up position about five miles south of town on August 6, only hours before Union troops occupied the opposite bank of the Rappahannock River.[42]

On August 4, while en route to Fredericksburg, Law's Brigade was paraded to witness the punishment of a corporal of the 48th Alabama who had been convicted of desertion. Turner Vaughan noted in his diary that the soldier wore a barrel shirt with "deserter" printed on it. He was marched before the brigade for all to see, the regimental band marching behind him. To complete the punishment, the convicted man was fitted with a ball and chain which he had to wear for several months.[43]

Southern honor was tested along the way when Sheffield, commanding Law's Brigade while Law led Hood's Division, offered his resignation because his brigade had lost its lead position in the march. Sheffield believed he had to resign if Law thought him so slow in executing the order to march that Robertson's Brigade had to be moved in front of his own. Sheffield considered promptness in executing the order to march "...an important qualification for a commander of a brigade."[44] Law responded to Sheffield in a note dated August 8 with the careful explanation that he knew Sheffield always demonstrated promptness in executing orders but as Robertson's Brigade was already on the road while Sheffield was quite properly waiting for the order to march, he had ordered Robertson to move first to save time. Honor was satisfied and the Confederates arrived at Fredericksburg ready to do battle with the Union army.[45]

Law Seeks a Colonel

By mid July 1863 Colonel Jackson's health was completely broken, and he resigned from the 47th Alabama, effective July 16. He left the regiment on bad terms with one of his officers. Captains John V. McKee, Company G, and Joseph S. Johnston, Jr., Company B, had been appointed by the regiment to buy Jackson a horse as a gift. The rank and file donated $850 for the purchase. Unfortunately, the price of a quality mount was $1000. The two officers paid the difference from their own funds in the belief the regiment would reimburse the expense. Johnston was killed at Gettysburg. McKee died of disease, leaving a widow in need of money. Isaac Newell suggested the colonel pay the $75 due McKee to McKee's widow. Jackson refused, believing the regimental officers should make up the difference. The officers declined and the estates of Johnston and McKee were debited $75 each. In a letter to McKee's widow, Newell said, "I once thought him a fine man, but after acting in such a manner I have no more use for him."[46]

Jackson went directly to his father's plantation near Greenville, Georgia, where his wife had gone during his absence. In April 1865 Jackson was still bedridden when a Federal raid swept through Greenville and the surrounding area. Jackson's father hid his cattle in a wooded area about five miles from the plantation. When a group of Federal horsemen approached the plantation Jackson put on his uniform once more. On his way to the hidden livestock, Jackson rode to a hill about a mile from the house where he saw Federal soldiers. Jackson thought he was undetected, but unfortunately he was not. Some of the Federals went to the house, others went after Jackson. At the house the Federals threatened to kill Jackson, but his elderly blind mother told the officer in charge that Jackson had served his country just as the Federal had served his. With grief in her voice the elderly lady informed the Federal her son had come home to die. The group departed with the officer's word that Jackson's life would be spared. A short time later two servants arrived with news that Jackson was captured and probably dead. Jackson's mother and wife were grieving for their loved one when Jackson walked up. The Federal officer was a man of his word. Jackson was ordered released, but his horse was confiscated. His Federal captors permitted Jackson to ride part of the way home in a wagon, then forced him to walk. Jackson arrived completely exhausted and returned to bed, never to rise again. James W. Jackson died July 1, 1865. Before he died Jackson called his aged father to his bedside and asked the elder Jackson to look after his wife and two little children. Jackson was buried on Sunday July 2. His father collapsed and was buried the next Sunday.[47]

After Jackson's departure from the regiment Campbell was the only field officer present and assumed command of the 47th Alabama. At that time it was thought Bulger was dead. Campbell was entitled to the office by right of seniority. But Law openly opposed Campbell's promotion, making it known he had little confidence in Campbell's ability to discipline or lead the regiment.[48]

During the spring and summer months, Law observed operations at the 47th Alabama's headquarters and the conduct of its field officers. In Law's opinion Campbell was not very proficient at drill, did not perform his duties to Law's satisfaction and was entirely too lax with discipline in the 47th Alabama.[49] Campbell occasionally straggled on the march and was often seen grazing his horse for fifteen or twenty minutes while the brigade marched by. He was sometimes absent from the regiment overnight. As the summer of 1863 wore on Law observed nothing to change his opinion of Campbell.

By July 1863 it was routine practice to judge the qualifications of candidates for promotion through examining boards. Law knew an examining board was his only means to block Campbell's promotion. Law, as brigade commander, served as president of the three-man examining board. Henry Benning and Jerome Robertson served as the other two members. Campbell astutely surmised that with Law presiding over the board his chances of being judged competent were not very good. He complained to Lee, alleging that Law's presence on the board would deny him an impartial and unbiased examination.[50] Campbell won round one. Law was forced to remove himself from the board, but managed to have himself called as a witness.

The board heard evidence from July 29–31, 1863, calling as witnesses most of the company commanders from the 47th Alabama, Law and other regimental commanders from the brigade. Law believed lack of discipline in the 47th Alabama and Campbell's lack of efficiency were the primary issues. Campbell countered by raising the question as to whether he, as third ranking field officer, should be held accountable for the regiment's discipline, especially when one of the higher ranking field officers was present. Campbell won round two. The company commanders of the 47th Alabama deemed Campbell an efficient officer, all stating he was gallant under fire. Captains Isaac H. Vincent and Brandon said the regiment's discipline was not as good as it could be, but they made it clear the regiment's discipline was much better after Campbell assumed command. In contrast Major Coleman, Colonels Perry and Sheffield thought Campbell a very inefficient officer and implied that he either lacked the ability or the desire to discipline the regiment. Oates and Lieutenant Colonel Hardwick were indifferent in their views toward Campbell.[51] More important for Campbell's case, neither chose to say anything positive about Campbell as an officer. Law's testimony to the board left little doubt about his opinion of Campbell's qualifications:

> *"I regard Major Campbell, 47th Alabama Regiment, as a non efficient officer. He has been connected with my brigade since about the 23rd January 1863, a period of six months. During that time his regiment has been under miserable discipline. Major Campbell has several times been in command and at such times I have remarked no such improvement. I*

have observed Major Campbell closely and I have seen no field or line officer who straggles more. I have rebuked him on more than one occasion for indulging this propensity. When commanding his regiment Major Campbell exercises very little control over his officers and men. With regard to his qualifications as a drill officer I have very little."[52]

While Benning and Robertson considered the evidence, Law continued his efforts to block Campbell's promotion, appointing his adjutant, Leigh Terrell, colonel of the 47th Alabama. A campaign promoting Terrell's appointment as colonel of the 47th Alabama started at brigade headquarters. The 47th Alabama officers, however, strongly objected since none had waived their right to promotion. In a petition made directly to Lee, they requested Campbell's promotion and protested Law's action against him. Without specifically identifying Terrell, the officers further protested the effort to place Law's adjutant in command, and then pointedly informed Lee that when the regiment was organized there was a promise that vacancies would be filled by promotion from the regiment.[53] No immediate action was taken by the examining board. Lee did not respond to the officers' petition. For the present Law did not pursue Terrell's promotion. Summer passed into fall and Campbell remained the only field officer present in the 47th. Relations between Campbell and Law deteriorated until Law placed Campbell under arrest for incompetence.

By November 1863 it was known that Bulger survived his ordeal at Gettysburg and was a prisoner. By this time, however, the idea to appoint Terrell to colonel of the regiment had spread through the 47th. Its officers filed another petition which they sent directly to the War Department, this time requesting Terrell's appointment as their colonel.[54] Apparently no one considered that Bulger might be exchanged and might not waive his right to promotion to colonel of the 47th.

Campbell's examining board finally issued its opinion, which did little more than confuse the issue. Finding Campbell competent to discharge the duties of colonel, the board also judged him to be "a careless and negligent officer and therefore unworthy of promotion to that office."[55] The issue of Campbell's promotion remained unsettled. Law was justified in not appointing Campbell lieutenant colonel or submitting his name to the War Department for confirmation. Campbell could still claim his right to promotion by right of seniority. Undaunted by the board's opinion and the petition of his officers, Campbell went on extended leave a month later and took his case directly to Secretary of War Seddon.[56]

The War Department found the case a difficult one to resolve, but from the evidence presented, concluded that much of the discipline problems were the responsibility of Bulger. In addition, the Richmond authorities concluded Bulger should not be promoted to colonel while still a prisoner. The War Department concluded Terrell was probably the most qualified candidate for the position of either lieutenant colonel or colonel. But, there was the issue of Campbell's competency and his petition based on seniority. Nevertheless, in early January 1864 the department prepared a letter in which Terrell was endorsed for colonel. A short time later the Secretary of War reversed the decision and decided that a new board should be convened to reexamine Campbell.[57] The endorsement was released before the secretary made his decision and found its way to brigade headquarters and Terrell who was undoubtedly very pleased by the apparent promotion.[58] His pleasure turned to dismay when someone at the War Department realized Bulger was still alive and by right of seniority had claim to the office of colonel. A new application proposing Terrell for lieutenant colonel was submitted to the War Department, but the secretary was firm in his decision to convene another examining board for Campbell.[59] Longstreet ignored the secretary's order for nearly three months. Campbell was the only field officer present in the 47th Alabama when the regiment began the spring campaign at the Battle of the Wilderness.

Foraging Across the River

Law's Brigade, still commanded by Sheffield, was detached from the division on August 20 and sent to Port Royal, VA, to protect the army's foraging trains which were bringing potatoes, tomatoes, apples, corn, and beef from north of the Rappahannock.[60] Along the route, the Alabamians found peach and apple orchards that they happily picked bare. Turner Vaughan noted in his journal that when they began campaigning two years before most soldiers refused to enter an orchard without the permission of the owner, writing "Most of us thought it wrong."[61] Two years on a diet of "bread and bacon," however, had changed their attitude about living off the land.

The brigade camped outside Port Royal near the Rappahannock Academy, but only two regiments were deemed necessary there, so after reviews for Law and the people of Port Royal, the 4th, 15th, and 44th Regiments returned to Fredericksburg. Parades were staged in the morning and at 5 p.m. on Saturday, August 22, which required the whole brigade to decamp and move into the center of town for two nights.[62]

The 47th Alabama, commanded by Captain Eli Daniel Clower, crossed the river to guard the forage wagons, while the 48th, under the command of Lieutenant Colonel William "Mack" Hardwick, stayed south of the Rappahannock.[63] Private James P. Crowder, Company I, 47th Alabama Regiment, wrote home about the "...fine time down on the river" enjoyed by the men of his regiment. Crossing the enemy lines on August 22, the soldiers of the 47th foraged north of the river until their return on the morning of August 25. Crowder wrote his brother that while across the river the hungry southerners could "...get any thing to eat that we wanted and a plenty of it." Men of the 48th Alabama then took their turn on the north side of the Rappahannock on the morning of August 25. But Crowder reported that their stay was short, as the "Yankees run them back" the evening of the same day.[64]

Elements of Kilpatrick's cavalry had been reporting on the movement of Law's Brigade, though identifying it as Hood's, since its departure from Fredericksburg, including the foraging raids over the river. Kilpatrick's command skirmished with the 48th Alabama near King George Courthouse on Tuesday, August 25, resulting in the capture of an enlisted man and the wounding of Lieutenant James F. Adrian of Company H. The 48th was able, however, to get the wounded lieutenant across the river as well as all of the regiment's wagons. The Confederates believed they inflicted a dozen or more casualties on Kilpatrick's cavalry during the fight.[65]

For their foraging the Alabamians used boats that had been captured and sunk by Kilpatrick's command during the previous winter. Probably with the help of civilians, the Confederates found and refloated them. The local residents were "strong secesh," which explains the brigade reviews in the town of Port Royal itself.[66] On August 25, Sheffield hurried from brigade headquarters at Fredericksburg to view the situation at Port Royal first hand but decided it was unnecessary to order the other three regiments from Fredericksburg.[67]

Fight for the Gunboats

During the brigade's short stay at Port Royal, Lieutenant John Taylor Wood, Confederate States Navy, brought into town two Federal gunboats and two commercial vessels captured in a daring raid in Chesapeake Bay. The small flotilla was met by the 47th and 48th Alabama regiments, who, unsure of the armada's identity, first warned Wood not to land. When recognized, however, the Confederate sailors were welcomed with cheers from

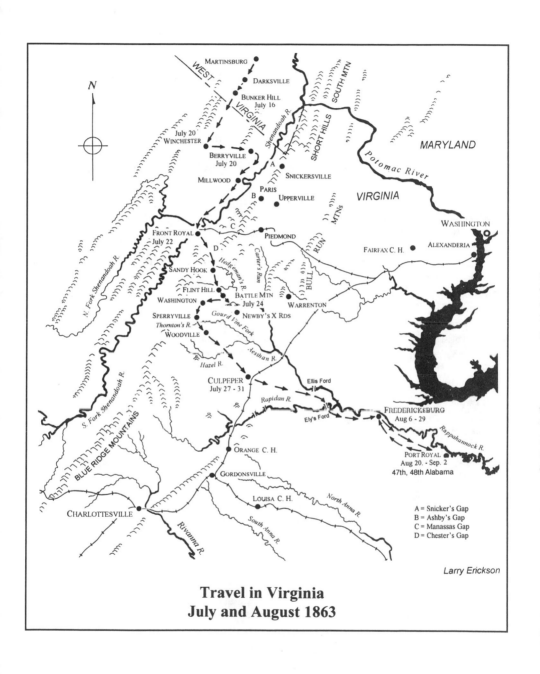

**Travel in Virginia
July and August 1863**

Larry Erickson

A = Snicker's Gap
B = Ashby's Gap
C = Manassas Gap
D = Chester's Gap

the Alabama soldiers.[67] They advised Wood of the presence of Federal troops at King George Courthouse, only 15 miles away.[68]

The captured gunboats, stripped by the Confederates of their machinery and guns, were a great embarrassment to the authorities in Washington, so much so that General-in-Chief Henry W. Halleck telegraphed Meade that he was to assist a Federal flotilla, including an ironclad, in an attempt to recapture the vessels. Halleck considered the operation a delicate one and suggested that "The most careful officer should be placed in charge." Judson Kilpatrick was selected, although Meade held out little hope for success even though the expedition exercised two brigades of cavalry, an artillery battery, and 5,000 infantry for several days.[69]

The 48th Alabama continued to forage across the river from late August into September. The 47th regiment returned to the brigade at Fredericksburg on August 29.[70] On August 27, Kilpatrick wrote Major General Alfred Pleasonton, commanding cavalry, for permission to move in force against the Alabamians and destroy their boats. Only the 48th Alabama was left at Port Royal on Tuesday morning, September 1, when the two regiments of Kilpatrick's cavalry struck. They moved by three roads against the forage train of the 48th Alabama, crashing into the Alabamians about half a mile from the King George Courthouse.[71]

Hardwick had about 100 soldiers of the 48th Alabama across the river to protect the wagons, and he immediately engaged the Union horsemen. "Bohemian," a reporter of the Richmond *Dispatch* who accompanied Wood on his mission, described the skirmish as a sharp one. The distance from King George Courthouse to Port Conway was about five miles by a narrow road through heavy woods. The adversaries fought along the country road as the Confederates slowly gave ground back to the river.[72] The Alabama infantrymen delayed the cavalry until the forage wagons could recross the Rappahannock by ferry at Port Royal. Hardwick's men then crossed by the ferry near dark, still under fire of the enemy cavalry. The fire poured upon the Alabamians as they crossed the Rappahannock in open boats impressed the Richmond reporter, who noted, "They received a volley from a squadron of cavalry but strange to say not a man was injured." Despite being armed with carbines, the cavalrymen were unable to inflict any casualties among the men on the ferry.[73] The newspaperman also reported the deaths of a captain and a private from a Michigan.[74] The dead officer was Lieutenant Pervical S. Leggett of Kilpatrick's staff. Besides Leggett, two privates of the Federal cavalry were killed and three wounded.[75]

On Wednesday an artillery duel ensued between the Union cavalry and the Confederate naval personnel operating guns removed from the captured vessels and placed in battery onshore near the town. Hardwick had evacuated Port Royal during the night as a precaution against civilian injuries, and the artillery action was confined to military targets. Kilpatrick wanted to recapture the Federal vessels but had to be content with making them his primary target. The Confederates had already stripped the boats, moving the machinery by a four-wagon shuttle between the vessels and Milford Station on the Richmond, Fredericksburg and Potomac Railroad and were satisfied with the enemy's help in destroying the boats. This action ended the Alabamians' stay at Port Royal.[76]

The 47th Alabama was assigned a new assistant surgeon while on duty along the river. Dr. J. P. Cooke replaced Dr. Michael A. Ridgeway, who resigned, and served as regimental surgeon for the rest of the war. Although he survived the war, Dr. Cooke was unable to survive the stab wound of a ruffian in his native Texas.[77]

The Great Revival

While encamped along the Rappahannock in August, the soldiers of Law's Brigade were caught up in the religious fervor that swept Lee's army from July through November 1863. Known as the "Great Revival," this renewed interest in religion was probably a continuation of the revival spirit which had begun in the spring but had been interrupted by the incursion into Pennsylvania. It was led by the chaplains and Christian officers and men of the regiments, with the assistance of pastors and missionaries from various denominations.[78]

Religious services in Law's Brigade had resumed after Gettysburg during the four day rest at Bunker Hill. On July 19 the Reverend W. H. Carroll conducted a service for the Alabamians, a prelude to the numerous meetings held during the brigade's rest at Culpeper and two week stay at Fredericksburg. Sponsored by the Domestic Missionary Board of the Southern Baptist Convention, Carroll came to Virginia as a missionary to Alabama soldiers, joining Lee's army as it returned from Pennsylvania. He was remembered by one Alabamian as "...the principal actor in these protracted meetings." After preaching at Bunker Hill and Culpeper, Carroll continued with the brigade to their camp near Fredericksburg.[79]

The brigade had enjoyed scant religious services of late. On the move since its rapid departure from Suffolk in May, the brigade also suffered casualties in its chaplain ranks at Gettysburg. The chaplain of the 4th Alabama was in the hospital. That of the 44th Regiment was captured, and chaplain of the 48th had been killed at Gettysburg. In Carroll's view, the Devil had the upper hand in Law's Brigade. "Christians, with but few exceptions," Carroll reported to the Missionary Board, "were in a cold backslidden condition, and some had become outbreaking."[80] Brother Carroll set to work.

Others helped in the revival. Samuel B. McJunkin, who had been discharged from the service with severe wounds to both arms at Second Manassas, joined Carroll in spreading the gospel. A schoolteacher and minister who served as a private in the 15th Regiment, McJunkin returned to his regiment on his own to preach.[81] Also arriving in Law's camp at this time was the Presbyterian minister A. W. Small of Selma who preached to Law's Alabamians for about ten days before leaving because of illness.[82] The chaplain of the 4th Alabama, Robert L. Frazier, returned to his unit from the hospital and joined in the preaching even though Carroll reported him still enfeebled. Campbell also took time out from his duties as commander of the 47th Regiment to minister to the troops.[83]

At Sunday services on August 23, the Reverends Frazier and Carroll both delivered outdoor services, Carroll afterwards baptized seven or eight in the Rappahannock River. Both preached again the next weekend, along with McJunkin. By this time the religious fervor had reached its peak; the three preachers were conducting services day and night for Law's Brigade. Frazier preached a sermon on Saturday, September 5, memorializing those of the 4th Alabama who had fallen at Gettysburg. It was the Alabamians' last weekend in Virginia until the spring of 1864.[84] The Reverend Carroll's Sunday meeting closed so late that baptism of the converted had to wait until Monday and then it was late on Monday night before the baptisms proceeded. The converts were anxious for the immersions as they did not know when it might be done, if not then. Billy Jordan of Company B, the 15th Alabama, held a lantern as Carroll baptized six soldiers of Law's Brigade.[85]

In his report to the Missionary Board, Carroll counted 39 soldiers baptized, 25 converts to the Methodist Church, and claimed more than 100 Alabama soldiers had found God during the weeks between Gettysburg and the brigade's departure for Georgia.[86]

Chapter 8

Fighting along the Chickamauga

Following setbacks at Vicksburg and Gettysburg, the Confederate government badly needed a victory. Generals Lee, Samuel Cooper, Braxton Bragg, Leonidas Polk and James Longstreet all had plans to reverse the Confederacy's sagging fortunes.[1] Longstreet proposed a classic concentration along interior lines to reinforce Bragg in north Georgia, his logic calling for the Army of Northern Virginia to remain in place and hold its position with two corps. They were to watch Meade's army, while Longstreet moved with the First Corps to north Georgia where Bragg was then retreating before the Army of the Cumberland under the command of Major General William S. Rosecrans. Once reinforced by Longstreet and divisions from Mississippi and Alabama, Bragg, commanding the Army of Tennessee would turn and defeat Rosecrans. In the end, a plan similar to Longstreet's was adopted which entailed the divisions of McLaws and Hood, then under the command of Law, with Alexander's artillery to be sent to Bragg.[2] Pickett's Division would remain in defensive positions around Richmond, and as a partial replacement for Pickett, Longstreet made application to have Micah Jenkins's Brigade of South Carolina troops added to the First Corps.[3]

Riding the Cars West

On September 6, 1863, Lee issued orders to move the bulk of the First Corps to reinforce Bragg. Seven days later, Lee informed Jefferson Davis that the New York *Herald* had printed the facts of the troop movement to Georgia. Lee pointed out that he had issued orders to move on the evening of September 6 and the *Herald* announced the movement on September 9.[4]

In reality, the secrecy of the troop movements, though not complete, was sufficient to surprise the Federals. It was first thought Lee's army would be reinforced by troops sent from Bragg's army in Tennessee. Then on September 8 Frank G. Chapman, a reporter for the *Herald,* wrote that Lee was not receiving reinforcements as had been rumored but was, in fact, dispatching part of Longstreet's corps to parts unknown. The next day the *Herald* published dispatches from Baltimore, dated August 21 and September 2, predicting a Confederate move against Meade and the city of Washington. To further confuse matters, the *Herald* asserted in its September 9 issue that Lee's army was in no condition to either attack or resist an "Onward to Richmond" move by Meade. The *Herald* concluded that it was probable that Lee "has been secretly sending off reinforcements to both Bragg and Beauregard," but none of this could be confirmed, and even as late as September 14, it was suspected that Lee was preparing to move again. The *Herald* wrote of a recent arrival from Richmond who had surprising news. A Mrs. F. J. Leech reported Confederate troops passing through Richmond on their way to reinforce Bragg and Beauregard. The *Herald* concluded that, "If correct, this information would seem to contradict previous statements that Lee's army was being reinforced from Bragg's."[5]

The military authorities in Washington fared no better than the New York *Herald* at sorting out the truth from rumors and false reports. The Federal high command initially thought troops might be dispatched from Bragg's army to reinforce Lee. In fact, Halleck wired Rosecrans that Bragg was probably doing just that. Then on September 13–14, Halleck received at least three reports that Longstreet was on the move. However, Halleck did not notify Rosecrans. On September 14, 16 and 17 the Federal War Department received telegrams from an agent in Georgia that reinforcements from Lee were traveling through the state. These reports were still treated as rumors, though a second cable on the 17th reported Lee's troops in Atlanta. Apparently, Rosecrans was still unaware of the Confederate move, and it was not until September 19 when Rosecrans discovered troops from the First Corps on the battlefield of Chickamauga, that Longstreet's move to the west was confirmed.[6]

The Confederate high command originally expected Longstreet's move to take two days, the shortest route to Bragg being from Gordonsville to Knoxville via the Tennessee and Virginia Railroad that connected Virginia and the major terminus at Chattanooga.[7] This route was suddenly closed when the Confederate force of 2300 inexperienced soldiers under Brigadier General John W. Frazer became trapped inside Cumberland Gap and were forced to surrender on September 9. All Confederate reinforcements for Bragg were then forced to travel south from Richmond through the Carolinas, into Georgia and then north to the vicinity of Chattanooga, Tennessee, stretching the planned two-day trip into eight. After leaving Richmond, Longstreet's divisions went first to Weldon, North Carolina, where they could choose from two available routes. One went through Wilmington, North Carolina, and Florence, South Carolina, and the other by way of Raleigh and Charlotte, North Carolina, and Columbia, South Carolina.[8] Law's Brigade traveled by the latter route.

Longstreet's troops, including the men of Law's Brigade, struck their tents on September 8.[9] In the meantime, Hood was still on convalescent leave in Richmond, leaving Law in command of the division. Sheffield commanded Law's Brigade. The Alabamians left their camps near Fredericksburg at daylight, marching along Telegraph Road, the historic route connecting Richmond with Washington, bivouacking the night of September 8 about ten miles north of Richmond. By 9 a.m. the next day, the brigade was in Hanover Junction ready to board the cars for the leg to Richmond, but was unable to board the train until 5 p.m. Unloading at Richmond, they crossed the James River and spent the night of September 9 in Manchester.[10]

Hood, his arm heavily bandaged and still suffering from the wound inflicted at Gettysburg, visited his men. The Texans gave him a rousing ovation and implored him to accompany them to Georgia. Pretty soon the entire division was clamoring for the general to lead them in their next fight. After an urgent appeal by most of his brigade and regimental officers Hood decided to make the trip and was on the train when it departed the next day.[11] Troop trains began leaving Richmond on September 9 and continued chugging southward, one after another for a week.[12] Law's Brigade did not depart Manchester until the evening of the September 10, making their first of several train changes at Petersburg late that night. The brigade reached Weldon, North Carolina, at 3 a.m. on September 11, and after waiting several hours for another train, the brigade left for Raleigh, North Carolina, late that afternoon.[13]

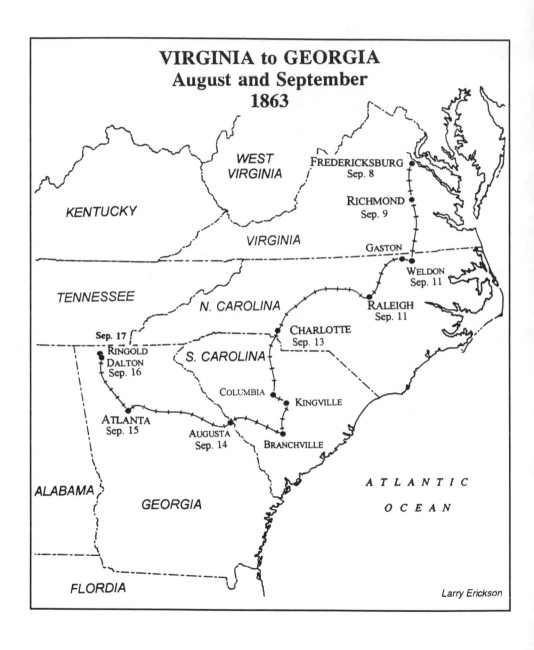

VIRGINIA to GEORGIA
August and September
1863

WEST VIRGINIA

FREDERICKSBURG
Sep. 8

RICHMOND
Sep. 9

KENTUCKY

VIRGINIA

GASTON

WELDON
Sep. 11

TENNESSEE

N. CAROLINA

RALEIGH
Sep. 11

Sep. 17

CHARLOTTE
Sep. 13

RINGOLD
DALTON
Sep. 16

S. CAROLINA

COLUMBIA

KINGVILLE

ATLANTA
Sep. 15

AUGUSTA
Sep. 14

BRANCHVILLE

ALABAMA

GEORGIA

ATLANTIC

OCEAN

FLORDIA

Larry Erickson

After arriving in Raleigh a regiment of Benning's Georgians decided to show its disfavor of one of the city's newspapers. The North Carolina *Standard*, published by William W. Holden, actively espoused peace policies, printing articles many citizens and soldiers believed to be pro-Union.[14] His editorials in the *Standard* were the topic of heated conversations around campfires in the field.[15] Benning's Georgians, who arrived in Raleigh a day ahead of Law's Alabamians on September 10, took it upon themselves to destroy the *Standard*. A single regiment marched to the *Standard's* office, and battered down the doors. The men flung cases of type into the street and poured kegs of ink into the street and over the equipment. During their rampage, they destroyed furniture and a large quantity of state printing. The printing press escaped destruction.[16] An irate Governor Zebulon B. Vance arrived and addressed the soldiers, imploring them to disperse.[17] It was 1 a.m. before Benning's men began returning to the depot. Vance immediately complained by telegraph to Davis that the people of North Carolina were considering burning bridges and blocking roads to keep Confederate troops out of their towns. The governor also informed Davis he was seriously considering the recall of North Carolina troops back to protect its citizens and property. Davis quickly wired the governor with assurances that the passing troops would no longer be allowed into North Carolina towns.[18]

At about 7 a.m., an angry crowd gathered at the rival *State Journal's* office and threw its contents into the street. Again Vance, this time accompanied by Raleigh's mayor, arrived on the scene and attempted to control the crowd. He made another impassioned speech, and it was clear from the shouts hurled at the governor that further demonstrations by soldiers passing through would cause another outbreak of violence.[19] An uneasy peace fell over the city as more trains carrying Confederate soldiers passed through.

Law's Brigade rolled into Raleigh at 4 p.m. on September 11 harboring the same intentions as Benning's Georgians. Several members of the 4th Alabama, unaware that Benning's men had already dismantled Holden's offices, left the train to find the newspaper's office.[20] Word quickly reached Vance that a group of Alabamians were headed toward the *Standard*. One day after receiving Davis's assurances of safety, Vance was once again wiring the president that "a large number of infuriated soldiers from an Alabama brigade were spreading terror by threatening murder and conflagration."[21] The locals refused to direct the irate transients to the newspaper office. After a fruitless search the Alabamians sheepishly started back to the depot. In the meantime the governor raced through the streets of Raleigh to the railroad depot. Once there he demanded the Alabamians be arrested. He sent Lieutenant Colonel Scruggs to arrest the offenders and bring them back. Scruggs found the subdued soldiers making their way back to the depot, where they were hustled aboard the cars until the trip to Georgia was resumed.[22]

Adjutant Coles remembered the trip was made on cramped and uncomfortable trains of every description of rolling stock, though most were boxcars. Cars were so crowded that many soldiers, like Private Billy Jordan, Company B, the 15th Alabama, rode atop a boxcar the entire trip.[23] A few were jostled from the train as a result of the overcrowded conditions on top of the cars, while others were toppled over the side by low hanging branches or other obstacles. Among the fatalities was Private Jesse E. Beatty, Company K, 48th Alabama, who fell to his death on September 14, 1863 between Charlotte and Columbia.[24] Inside the cars it was so crowded that soldiers were forced to stand virtually the entire trip to Georgia, leaving many of them totally exhausted when they arrived in Georgia.[25]

Citizens from the Carolinas and Georgia generously shared their food as Law's men passed through their towns. Along the route to north Georgia, crowds of cheering civilians offered food and drink.[26] At many stations, stops were arranged so the troops could enjoy lunches prepared in their honor.[27] Crowds lined the tracks and waved as each train passed by. Soldiers frequently sought to impress female observers by tossing *billets-doux* from the trains. Lieutenant Rufe Goodson, of the 44th Alabama, who was in his brother's estimation a "ladies' man," threw a letter to a young woman at Covington, Georgia and much to Captain Goodson's surprise, Rufe received an answer from the woman. Rufe, in turn, replied. Goodson did not record how long his brother and the Georgia woman corresponded.[28]

Law's Alabamians reached Atlanta at daybreak on September 15, where they were issued new clothing, including hats and shoes.[29] In August, Law's men had been issued new clothing while in Virginia but some of the men were better supplied than others.[30] Sheffield was diligent in his efforts to see that his brigade was as well clothed as any other, and with the uniforms issued in Virginia and the resupply in Atlanta, Law's Brigade was now as well dressed as at any time during the war.[31] When they arrived in north Georgia, many of the ill-clad Westerners were prompted to suggest a trade of a "Bragg jacket for a Lee jacket." Coles reported that his fellow soldiers of the west were not only deficient in clothing, but lacking in all equipment, including artillery.[32]

Confederate authorities scheduled Law's Brigade to depart Atlanta on the night of September 15. Again, the inadequate railroads of the Confederacy could not deal with the volume of traffic, and Law's men waited until morning for the roads to clear.[33] The closeness of Atlanta to their homes in east Alabama proved too great a temptation for some of Law's men, particularly the Fortykins. Several simply walked away from their brigade.[34] The sparsely populated, mountainous region of north Alabama was known to harbor many deserters and draft dodgers. In these counties, where slave owners were few, the soldier in the ranks had often been the breadwinners of the family. This area held the strongest pro-Union sentiment in the state in 1861. Many of the residents strongly resisted conscription. By 1863 a stronger motive yet was offered to the soldiers from north Alabama. When the cars brought Law's Brigade into Atlanta, fully a third of the families of the state of Alabama were indigent and receiving aid from the state.[35]

The day Law's Brigade marched from Fredericksburg en route to Bragg's army, the Richmond *Enquirer* printed a list of 27 deserters from the 15th Alabama.[36] Desertion depleted the ranks of the Alabama regiments no less than other units in the Confederacy, although most went home or to other regiments, not to the enemy.[37] The enlisted men in the Confederate army did not enjoy the privilege of resigning as did the officers, and since furloughs were exceedingly rare, desertion was the only available means to leave. By publishing the names and some few facts about the deserters, the army sought to return some of the absentees to the regiment. Several had left their company as late as July and August, while one had been gone since August 1861. The army offered a reward of $30 to anyone who would return a deserter to his company or confine him to a jail within the lines of the Confederate States army. The article, entitled "Desertions," ran a second time on September 11.

William A. Powell, a private in Company C, 44th Alabama, left his regiment in Atlanta. An Oak Level farmer, Powell was probably concerned about the welfare of his family. He was later arrested in Alabama, court-martialed and returned to duty on August 27, 1864, although with Company K, 44th Alabama. This thirty-two-year-old farmer was wounded at Darbytown Road on October 7, 1864, and died on November 10.[38] Two of the soldiers who deserted at Atlanta were later listed on the muster roll as "lying out in the woods."[39] One deserter, Allen Thompson, of the 47th Alabama, was a substitute who had served less than five months with his regiment. He probably left because he could not keep pace with his regiment. Thompson was 57 years old when he left Company H on September 15, 1863.[40]

The rest of the Alabamians continued on to north Georgia, arriving two miles below Ringgold, and from there marched on to Catoosa Station, a small platform farther up the line.[41] When Hood heard rumors of a Federal threat, he ordered Law's Brigade forward to check the anticipated advance, but the Federals were only reconnoitering and the fight failed to materialize. After the false alarm, the Alabamians went back to Catoosa to cook the rations they would need the next few days.[42]

Longstreet's men arrived in Georgia without tents, baggage, artillery, ambulances, or surgeons.[43] As they prepared to enter into battle they were equipped with their rifles and 40 cartridges per man. Some horses were brought by train, including Hood's, Sheffield's and Terrell's but, there were so few that Bragg's soldiers delighted in saying that Lee's brigade and field officers walked just like privates. Sheffield brought along the horse presented to him by the men of the 48th Alabama. The animal was an iron gray that the adjutant of the 4th Alabama remembered as having a long flowing mane and tail. While en route, the horse jumped from the moving train, forcing an unscheduled stop. The men recaptured the horse uninjured, and returned it to the car.[44]

Sheffield led Law's Brigade to a campsite just east of Chickamauga Creek where they spent the night September 17.[45] The following morning, the Texas brigade led the way toward Chickamauga Creek. Benning's men were detailed to guard the Ringgold depot, while Law's Brigade followed Robertson the same day, leaving Ringgold en route to what would be the Chickamauga battlefield.[46] Advancing toward battle on September 19, Company G, 15th Alabama, stopped their march long enough to elect, unanimously by proclamation, Captain DeBernie Waddell as company commander.[47] Oates felt Lieutenant Thomas M. "Tom" Renfroe, the only line officer of Company G to survive Gettysburg, was too young and inexperienced to hold the position and nominated Waddell, who was then the regiment's adjutant.[48] Waddell became very religious during the winter of 1863–64. He was highly respected and was sometimes asked by dying men to pray for them, and he frequently did so, even under fire. Incredibly, he was not wounded during the course of the war. Waddell's religious fervor did not cool after the war, and he was ordained an Episcopal minister.[49]

The Opposing Armies

The campaign that brought the armies to the Georgia woods began late the previous June when Rosecrans moved against Bragg, then defending the road between Murfreesboro and Chattanooga. Through a series of skillful maneuvers Rosecrans forced Bragg into Chattanooga, and early in September crossed the Tennessee River well below Chattanooga and then forced Bragg to the south. After concentrating his forces near the little town of La Fayette, Bragg moved north again and tried unsuccessfully to destroy isolated segments of Rosecrans's army.

On September 18, Bragg posted his army on the west bank of Chickamauga Creek along a line from Reed's Bridge to just opposite Lee and Gordon's Mill. Bragg organized his army into four corps commanded by Lieutenant Generals Leonidas Polk, D. H. Hill, James Longstreet and Major General Simon B. Buckner.[50] Since Longstreet was still en route when the leading brigades arrived, Hood assumed command of Longstreet's Corps. Rosecrans's army was organized into three corps. Major General George H. Thomas commanded the XIV Corps, Major General Alexander M. McCook commanded the XX Corps, and Major General Thomas Crittenden led the XXI Corps.[51]

The battle was fought over heavily wooded terrain, broken occasionally by cleared farm lands. Chickamauga Creek and La Fayette-Rossville Road ran parallel to each other from north to south. They were crossed by the Brotherton Road which ran east-west, while Snodgrass Hill, an elevation west of the La Fayette Road, would figure prominently in the fighting. Missionary Ridge loomed over the battlefield to the west. Chattanooga was nine miles to the north.[52]

Chickamauga, the First Day

Bragg placed Hood in command of his own and Brigadier General Bushrod R. Johnson's Division. Law, as senior brigadier present in Hood's Division, commanded the division. Sheffield moved up to command of the brigade, leaving the 48th Alabama in the hands of Hardwick. Scruggs led the 4th Alabama. Oates had command of the 15th Alabama, while the 44th Alabama was commanded by Perry who was next in seniority to Sheffield. Because no field officers were present with the 47th Alabama it was led by its senior captain, Daniel Clower. The thirty-three-year-old farmer from Youngville, known as Dan, entered the service with the use of only one eye and was the original and only captain to command Company F.[53]

Brigade strength was 1462 officers and men. There were 133 line officers present, and one company was led by a non-commissioned officer.[54] Law took his staff with him to division command, while Sheffield decided to leave his regimental staff with the 48th Alabama. This decision brought on the difficult, if not impossible, task of commanding the brigade without the benefit of staff officers. There were no officers to supervise the execution of orders or direct the movements of the regiments, an arrangement that led to confusion within the Alabama ranks. During both days of fighting at Chickamauga, the brigade would become split, fight piecemeal and lose much of its striking power.[55]

Law's division formed line of battle about 10 a.m. It deployed in thick woods 800 yards east of the La Fayette Road behind the junction of two other divisions on the first line.[56] Bushrod Johnson's Division lay to the front and left. Major General Alexander P. Stewart's Division, Buckner's Corps, lined up on Johnson's right. Most of Law's division formed in rear of Johnson's, the remainder overlapping Stewart's left.

The Ohio-born Johnson had come from Mississippi as part of the concentration of forces that brought Longstreet's veterans from Virginia.[57] His division was three brigades strong. Johnson's old brigade of Tennesseans was under command of Colonel John S. Fulton, while Brigadier General Evander McNair commanded a brigade of four Arkansas regiments and one North Carolina regiment. The third brigade, composed of Texans and Tennesseans, was commanded by Brigadier General John Gregg.[58]

A West Point graduate, Stewart also commanded a three-brigade division made up of Brigadier General William B. Bate's Brigade of Tennesseans and Georgians, Brigadier General John C. Brown's Brigade of Tennesseans, and an Alabama brigade commanded by Brigadier General Henry D. Clayton. Stewart's Division was part of the corps commanded by Buckner.

The order of battle for Sheffield's command placed the senior regimental commanders on the outside of the line and the least experienced commanders between them. Perry's 44th Alabama was on the right; Oates commanded the 15th Alabama on the left; the 47th Alabama was in the middle. Hardwick had the 48th Alabama between Oates and the 47th Alabama. The 4th Alabama was placed next to Perry.

Law's men were surprised when Hood rode past the Alabama regiments. They thought he was hospitalized in Richmond and were unaware he had joined the division. The Alabamians spontaneously cheered and waved their hats when they recognized him, although it was against military protocol to do so.[59] Hood was obviously in good spirits, and responded in kind to the Alabamians' salute. As he rode near the 15th Alabama, the Texas general encouraged Oates's men with the simple admonition, "Remember, boys, we are here to whip them."[60]

As Oates aligned his regiment for battle, he was approached by Robert W. "Bob" Brannon, first sergeant of Company K, who had been on light duty due to illness. Brannon told his colonel that he did not expect to regain his health and asked for a rifle so he could die in battle. Oates consented to his request and ordered the sick man into line. At the end of the day's fighting, Brannon lay mortally wounded.[61]

Hood opposed the Federal right, composed of elements from four Federal divisions, which lay along a line just east of the La Fayette Road.[62] These four elements had been rushed into position by Rosecrans to counter Bragg's plan to get between Chattanooga and the Federal army. The Federal line ran nearly parallel to the road with the most northerly brigades farther to the east than those on the south end of the line.

Fighting began in the morning to the north of the Alabamians' position as the Federals attacked the Confederate right. The battle was next joined by the Confederate center, with fighting gradually extending to the Confederate left as Bragg's various commands entered the fray. Law's troops were not engaged during the morning, but there was much strategic maneuvering in the thick woods. At first, Oates's 15th Alabama was on the front line of the division with Robertson's Brigade, the rest of Sheffield's command and Benning making up the second line. Oates was soon moved and again aligned with his own brigade behind Robertson. Finally, Sheffield was in line of battle with Robertson on the left and Benning in support behind Sheffield.[63] Coles later recalled that "as usual, the Texans and the 3rd Arkansas were on our left."[64]

About two o'clock Bushrod Johnson's skirmishers were driven back into their lines and the struggle commenced in earnest in front of Law's division.[65] The attack came generally from the southwest and three of Johnson's batteries and the brigades of Gregg and Fulton resisted for about half an hour. Then, Hood ordered Johnson's Division to move forward and drive back the Federal attackers.[66] Law's division followed Johnson's soldiers.

They Skedaddled in Fine Style

It was between 3 and 3:30 p.m. when Sheffield led Law's Brigade into the smoke-shrouded woods.[67] Robertson's Brigade advanced on his left, as Bate's Brigade from Stewart's command positioned itself on the right and slightly to the front. Sheffield encouraged his men to the attack with what Coles described as a "tremulous and quavering manner of voice peculiar to him." Hat raised above his head, the colonel rode in front of the 4th Alabama and shouted from atop his gray, "Forward, 4th Alabamians, forward! You have a name that will never, never die."[68]

After advancing about 200 yards, Robertson's Brigade met a strong infantry force accompanied by artillery on its left. Robertson was under orders to move in concert with Sheffield, and sent an officer to inform Law of his situation. Law ordered the Texas brigade to change front and meet the threat, a move requiring Robertson to break contact with Sheffield. A second courier was quickly dispatched to inform Sheffield of this movement. Benning was under orders to support Robertson and also inclined left. Their combined advance carried the two brigades southwest to the Viniard house where they fought hard until recalled for the night.[69] Law's Brigade advanced straight ahead without support on its left.

After advancing several hundred yards, Sheffield passed through two Confederate lines lying in the undergrowth. These were the remnants of Clayton's and Brown's brigades, exhausted and out of ammunition. They cheered and shouted encouragement to the Alabamians. Law's men invited them to join in the charge, but with empty cartridge boxes they had no choice but to decline. Perry, leading the 44th Alabama, recalled the trees were "barked" and the undergrowth riddled by bullets from the fighting which preceded the advance of Law's Brigade. These conditions caused Perry to fear for his horse, and he quickly put him in the charge of an orderly because he believed the animal would be lost once the fighting began.[70]

The Alabamians' advance was stopped by an unexpected volley from Federals concealed in grass and undergrowth in the timber east of the La Fayette Road. The hidden Federals suddenly rose not more than 60 yards in front of the advancing line and delivered a destructive fire.[71] Scruggs was knocked down. Several men rushed to his side, and upon examination thought a bullet had entered his abdomen near his sword buckle and exited through his belt on the other side of his body. Because soldiers seldom recovered from wounds to the mid-section, his men were certain the wound was fatal, and informed the fallen commander of his fate. But, in spite of the evidence Scruggs did not seem as badly injured as first believed. Someone examined the wound more closely and discovered the nearly spent ball had penetrated his belt but not the colonel. The bullet had followed the belt around his waist to its exit site, the resulting damage being a severely bruised hip. Scruggs went to the rear, and the command of the 4th Alabama passed to Major Thomas Coleman. Coleman commanded the rest of the day, and led the regiment into the fighting of September 20.[72]

Perry reacted to the Federal volley by ordering the 44th Alabama to charge the ambush. His idea was to cross the short distance between the lines before the Federals could reload. But the unexpected fire had disorganized the 44th regiment to such an extent that the men showed symptoms of breaking ranks. Upon further reflection Perry ordered his regiment to lie down and return fire, an order that was promptly obeyed. Perry initially watched the exchange from behind a small tree. After several minutes, the fire from the Federal line died out, and he again ordered the charge and started at the enemy on the run. The 44th Alabama gave the Rebel Yell and soon swarmed by the older Perry. The sudden attack caused the Federal line to retire to the northwest, the charge taking the 44th Alabama to the right oblique away from the brigade.[73]

Joab Goodson described the firing on September 19 as incessant. He saw ten members of Company B go down within a few minutes. When he ran out of ammunition he resupplied himself from the cartridge box of a wounded Federal. Goodson noted that the Federal soldiers fought them toe-to-toe while both sides were in position, but, when the 44th Alabama charged, Rosecrans's western soldiers "skedaddled in fine style."[74]

In Perry's words the 44th Alabama behaved as "a broken mass of howling demons," as it chased the Federals at breakneck speed.[75] The colonel soon realized his regiment was unsupported and probably in serious danger as it raced toward the enemy lines. Thinking the men might overextend themselves, he kept yelling for his men to halt. As the men continued to chase the Federals, the colonel kept falling farther behind. All Perry could do was repeatedly shout the order to halt.[76] Goodson was aware of the confusion within the battle line, but in the excitement of the chase he was apparently unconcerned at being separated from the brigade. He simply put it down to getting "scattered as we always do in the charge."[77]

The Federals accomplished what Perry was unable to do; a concealed artillery battery stopped the 44th Alabama in its tracks, turned it around, and sent it reeling backward. The scene was still vivid in Perry's mind many years after the war. He believed a single volley

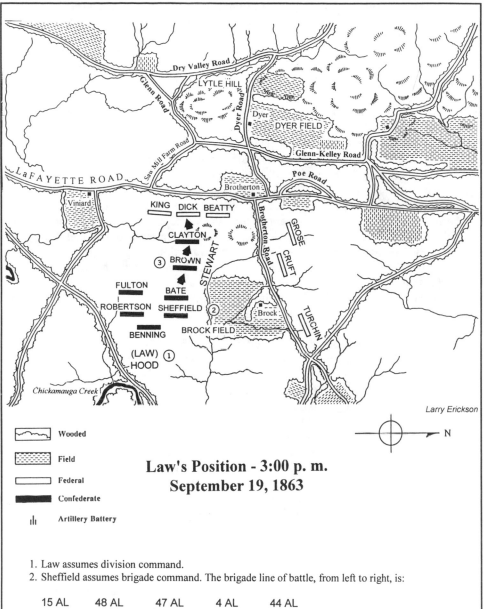

Larry Erickson

Wooded	
Field	
Federal	
Confederate	
Artillery Battery	

Law's Position - 3:00 p. m.
September 19, 1863

N

1. Law assumes division command.
2. Sheffield assumes brigade command. The brigade line of battle, from left to right, is:

15 AL	48 AL	47 AL	4 AL	44 AL
Oates	Hardwick	Clower	Scruggs	Perry

3. Stewart's Division attacks west in column of brigades (Clayton, Brown, Bate). Bate is in the lead by the time the division reaches the La Fayette Road.

could have easily silenced the battery. However, the 44th was not, at that moment, an organized fighting force and quickly turned from the cannon. "The suddenness with which the pursuit and those wild yells were stopped had in it a strong element of the ludicrous," was how Perry remembered the moment.[78]

The 44th Alabama, along with an unidentified battery, rapidly removed itself from the range of the Federal guns. Because he was on foot, Perry was temporarily unable to catch up with his regiment. He had already proven incapable of keeping up with the privates of the 44th, so in desperation he hopped onto a fast-moving limber as the artillery moved back to the east, and was soon ahead of his retreating men. Unfortunately for Perry, Law rode up as he reached the regiment's front. Law immediately thought he was witnessing the extraordinary scene of one of his regiments beating a hasty retreat with its colonel leading the debacle. He quickly intervened and stopped the retrograde movement. Then, ignoring Perry, an irate Law ordered Major George Cary to command the 44th and guard against any Federal counterattack.[79] The 44th Alabama was through fighting for the day.

In the confusion caused from the initial volley against Law's Brigade, a small body, numbering 40 or 50 men, became separated from the 4th Alabama. This detachment joined the 15th and 37th Tennessee Regiments, combined under command of Colonel R. C. Tyler. By Tyler's account, the men from the 4th Alabama joined his brigade after it moved forward 300 to 400 yards. While Tyler aligned the Alabamians with his own men, Bate resumed his advance without him. Not wishing to miss the fighting, Tyler quickly ordered his command forward. The detachment from the 4th Alabama advanced on his left. Their charge took the Tennesseans and Alabamians beyond the La Fayette Road before they retired for the night.[80]

While the 44th Alabama and the small detachment from the 4th Alabama fought their battles, the remainder of Law's Brigade was ordered forward. As the command was given, Sheffield's horse shied from an exploding artillery shell, throwing him unceremoniously to the ground, injuring his back. With Sheffield out of action, Perry was next in seniority, but was off with the 44th Alabama, thus brigade command fell to Oates of the 15th Alabama.[81] He did not learn that he was in command of the brigade until one of Law's staff found him and reported Sheffield's injury.[82]

Oates took command of the brigade, now consisting of the 15th, 47th, 48th and most of the 4th Alabama, and led it west through the trees and thick undergrowth of trumpet vine, blackberry briar and poison oak toward the La Fayette Road.[83] The Alabamians passed through the area where Fulton's brigade and elements of Stewart's Division had preceded them in the advance. In the heavy underbrush, Henry Figures, adjutant of the 48th Alabama, captured the wounded adjutant of the 9th Kentucky Regiment, First Brigade, Third Division, XXI Corps. Figures relieved Lieutenant J. H. Shepherd of his sword and belt and sent him to the rear as a prisoner.[84]

The brigade emerged from the woods just south of the Brotherton house, crossed the La Fayette Road, and moved into a field adjacent to the house. Oates halted the brigade after crossing the road because he was unable to see any Federal units to his front. On his left Fulton's men were receiving a pressing attack and began falling slowly back to the road, fighting as they went.[85] The attacking Federals were two regiments of Colonel Charles G. Harker's brigade from Brigadier General Thomas J. Wood's First Division, XXI Corps, who were sent from the south to reinforce the Federal line. Harker's men got astride the La Fayette Road, then marched by left flank until they were to the left rear of Fulton. When Harker poured a deadly flanking fire into their lines, Fulton's men moved quickly to their right and then retired back across the road with the Federals closely pursuing them.[86]

As the Federal regiments passed east of his own line, Oates ordered the brigade to about face, alerting the Federals to the Alabamians' presence. Before Oates's command could be executed the Federals delivered an enfilading fire into the ranks of the Alabamians, the 15th Alabama taking the brunt of the fire. Among the casualties were Private Jacob Pruett of Company B, killed on the field and Lieutenant Fred Porter of Company K, mortally wounded. Porter had served as first sergeant, the rank Oates called the most important in a company next to the captain. He had been present at every battle. As Porter lay dying, Private Pat McEntyre remained to care for him, resulting in McEntyre being captured and never exchanged. Oates rated McEntyre a fair soldier until this act at Chickamauga, believing McEntyre's effort to help Porter was foolish.[87]

Another casualty among the ranks of Alabama officers was Captain Reuben Kidd, Company A, 4th Alabama. He was killed near the La Fayette Road by a shot in the chest. An original member of the "Governor's Guards", Kidd had signed on as the orderly sergeant at the age of twenty-one and was promoted through the ranks to captain of Company A. The regimental historian recalled that Kidd had a resonant voice which could be heard clearly throughout the regiment even during battle.[88] Joe, his servant who had gone to war with Kidd, and J. B. Stone, also an original member of Company A, carried Kidd's body from the field in a tarpaulin as the brigade retired for the day. They buried Kidd that night under an oak tree which they marked for future identification. In 1866 the same two men returned to Chickamauga to disinter the body for burial in the cemetery of St. Andrew's Episcopal Church in Prairieville, AL. They located the original burial site under the oak but Kidd's body was never found.[89]

With a force of Federals between them and the rest of the Confederate army, under both rifle and artillery fire, Oates ordered his men to return to the road.[90] The men reacted in such disorder that Oates concluded panic had seized the command. He ordered his officers to shoot any man who crossed the road before his order.[91] The Alabamians may have been spooked by Lieutenant William O. "Buck" Newsome. Newsome shouted that the brigade was being flanked from its unprotected left. When his captain, William F. Karsner, saw the effect the lieutenant's warning had on the men, he gave the lieutenant a stern rebuke.[92] A sheriff before the war, Karsner would live to see the surrender at Appomattox. Newsome did not survive the war.[93]

Oates regained control and ordered the brigade to move east of the road. Only then did he send two companies from each regiment against the flank of the Federal soldiers pursuing Johnson's men. They successfully forced the Federals back to the west side of the road. Oates kept the Alabamians in the open near the road a few minutes longer before they slowly moved back to the east and the safety of the timber.[94]

Because Oates could not see Federals to his front he believed his brigade was far to the front of Hood's corps. That belief, coupled with Fulton's apparent defeat, caused him to retire east of the road. But he was mistaken, since the divisions of Johnson and Stewart had both preceded Law in the attack.[95] By the time Oates approached the La Fayette Road, some of Bushrod Johnson's men were returning to the rear, passing through the attacking forces of Robertson and Benning on Oates's left. But the men under Johnson's command had already effectively driven the enemy across the La Fayette Road, across the Brotherton field and beyond. It was the report of this Confederate success that reached Wood upon his arrival at the battle, prompting his order to Harker to move astride the La Fayette Road.[96] The Federal troops then rallied and forced Johnson back over the road while Oates's isolated band of Alabamians was still west of the road. Bushrod Johnson's brigades had crossed the La Fayette Road in an irregular fashion, giving Harker his opportunity to counterattack behind the regiments of John Fulton. When Fulton's brigade received fire from its left rear, Bushrod Johnson wrote that it "moved by one impulse to the right and

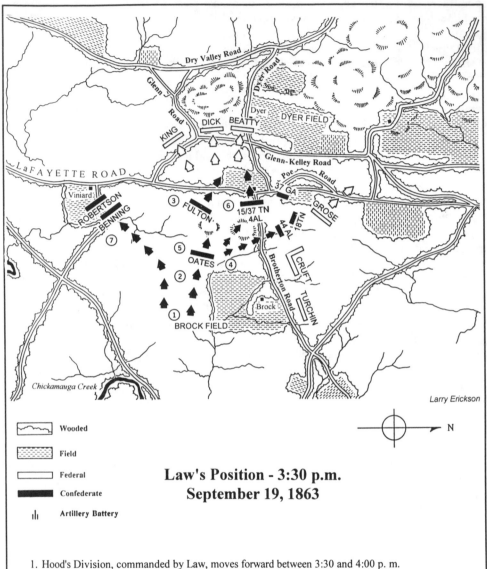

Law's Position - 3:30 p.m.
September 19, 1863

Larry Erickson

Wooded
Field
Federal
Confederate
Artillery Battery

1. Hood's Division, commanded by Law, moves forward between 3:30 and 4:00 p. m.
2. Robertson and Benning move across Stewart's rear and move to the left. Law's Brigade, commanded by Sheffield, inclines to the right.
3. Fulton moves northeast into the southern end of the Brotherton field and woods just south of the field.
4. The 44th Alabama separates from the brigade and charges to the northwest.
5. Sheffield is unhorsed. Oates assumes command and leads the brigade west toward the Brotherton field.
6. A portion of the 4th Alabama mixes with the 15th and 37th Tennessee. The Tennesseans and the segment of the 4th Alabama cross the La Fayette Road before retiring.
7. Robertson and Benning attack to the southwest, fighting near the Viniard house.

fell back to the east of the road."[97] To the men of Oates's command, on Fulton's right, it must have looked as though the Federals were pushing their comrades right onto their position.

Stewart's brigades of Clayton and Brown, followed by Bate, struck the Federal line against Brigadier General Horatio Phillips Van Cleve's brigades under Colonel George F. Dick and Brigadier General Samuel Beatty, driving these two Federal units from the field. Stewart's men made the farthest Confederate advance on September 19, reaching as far as the Glenn Kelly Road. They covered Oates's front and right, though he did not know it until, unsupported, they were pushed from their advanced position.[98]

The Errant 44th Alabama

The Federal units who Perry fought on September 19 are unknown. The meager evidence available has led most historians to believe Perry's opponent was the brigade of Russian-born Brigadier General John B. Turchin. He commanded a brigade in Major General Joseph J. Reynolds's Fourth Division of the XIV Corps. He wrote in his official report of the fighting on September 19 that he had driven back Law's Brigade and had prisoners from the 44th Alabama, mistakenly assuming the 44th was with its brigade.[99]

Years later, Federal General Ezra Ayers Carman attempted to sort out the puzzling events of that day for a history of the war. He concluded that Law's Brigade was indeed the unit Turchin engaged. Carman believed the Alabamians moved behind Bate's Brigade, striking the brigade of Brigadier General Charles Cruft, Second Division, XXI Corps, who had one battery of artillery in place, thus exposing Law's right flank to attack by Turchin. Both Cruft and Turchin, by Carman's account, then pursued the retreating Confederates. Carman also assumed the Alabamians in question were Law's entire brigade.[100] Perry's own account of the fighting on September 19, written at Carman's request, fails to identify the Federal units he encountered.[101]

Perry's location on September 19 is not known with certainty. If Turchin's report and Carman's analysis are accepted, the route of the 44th was almost due north and perpendicular to the rest of the Alabama brigade. Such an argument could be made based on the alignment of the two armies because the Rebel line traced an arc between the La Fayette and Brotherton roads. Holding the right of the brigade, Perry would tend toward the north to protect his exposed flank. This argument supposes his right was uncovered. In this scenario, Perry then joined Bate's right units and drove Cruft and Colonel William Grose until struck on the right by Turchin.

Among the reports of the day's fighting is that of Lieutenant Colonel Joseph T. Smith, who took command of the 37th Georgia prior to the charge. Smith reported an Alabama regiment mixed with his regiment, actually splitting it into parts. "About 50 men, several line officers and myself," wrote Smith, "became separated from the other portion of the regiment" by the intruding Alabamians. Undeterred by this turn of events, Smith simply moved to the right oblique, driving the Federals 400 to 500 yards until he was flanked right and rear by a Federal force. At that point, he ordered those members of the 37th Georgia still with him to fall back.[102] This is strikingly similar to the co-mingling which occurred between the 4th Alabama and the 15/37 Tennessee. Like the 37th Georgia, the 15/37 Tennessee was one of Bate's regiments.

The direction and distance the 37th Georgia charged agrees with Perry's recollection of the charge of the 44th Alabama. He recalled advancing 600 yards to the west and then charging 600 yards to the northwest.[103] Although he wrote about the charge a generation after it occurred, Perry also wrote accounts of Gettysburg and the Wilderness which proved to be accurate and detailed.

William Perry's Description of the Map Positions
(Opposite Page)

A. Position until 5 p.m. in the afternoon of September 19, 1863.
B. Passed through a Confederate line lying in reserve.
C. Second Confederate line.
D. Location of concealed Federal line.
E. Federal battery which opened at short range.
F. Sheltered position to which the 44th Alabama retreated.
G. Bivouac night of September 19–20, 1863.
H. Law's Brigade in third line, morning of September 20, 1863.
K. Federal position prior to the Confederate breakthrough.
L. Edge of open field.
M. Federal artillery line.
N. Confederate troops moving toward western boundary of the open field.
O. Confederate forces being driven back.
P. Location where Law's Brigade, less the 15th Alabama, reformed in the afternoon.
Q. Position in front of the Federal left wing, late afternoon.
R. Confederate artillery position.
S. Perry's line formed to attack Federal position.
T. Perry's skirmish line reported the Federals had retreated.

Note: Perry omitted (I) and (J) from his identification of the positions.

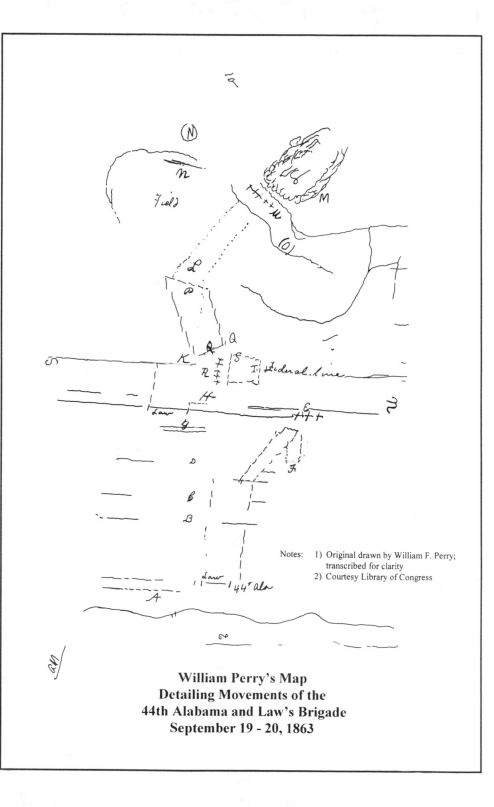

William Perry's Map
Detailing Movements of the
44th Alabama and Law's Brigade
September 19 - 20, 1863

Notes: 1) Original drawn by William F. Perry; transcribed for clarity
2) Courtesy Library of Congress

One of Brown's regiments provides a clue for the location of the 44th Alabama in the confused fighting of September 19. The historian for the 18th Tennessee claimed his regiment was supported by members of Longstreet's Corps in its assault against a Federal battery and support infantry. The 18th Tennessee mistook the Virginia transfers for the enemy and fired on them. Through the fog of battle, Longstreet's men may have looked like Federal soldiers in their new Confederate uniforms. Bragg's troops wore every variety of clothing, and, as one Federal later recalled, scarcely any two of them were dressed alike.[104] This friendly fire probably scattered the 44th Alabama and may have driven some of the regiment east and into Turchin's hands. The 18th Tennessee then charged and captured the battery.[105] The charge of the 18th took it north of Brotherton Road and near the main body of the 37th Georgia.

Turchin declared in his report that he drove Law's Brigade. However, in his memoirs, Turchin claimed it was Brown's Brigade of Stewart, not Law which was routed by his brigade.[106] He does not relate in either his report or his memoirs the circumstances in which he identified the Alabama captives. The 44th Alabama sustained casualties of 5 killed, 43 wounded and nine captured during the fight of September 19.[107]

Identification of the limber Perry rode is difficult, if not impossible, but would do much to verify Perry's position. There are several candidate batteries for it is known that Captain John T. Humphreys's 1st Arkansas Battery of Stewart's Division was rescued by troops belonging to Hood's Division after it was left near the La Fayette Road.[108] Also, three batteries supported Stewart and perhaps one or more of these moved when Cruft and Turchin launched their counterattack. Or, Perry may have leaped onto a captured limber of the 26th Pennsylvania Battery which had two guns removed from the field by the men of Captain T. H. Dawson's Georgia Battery. Additional evidence must come to light before ownership of the limber can be established with certainty.

Perry almost certainly took his ride on the limber while Oates was across the La Fayette Road. This is the likely scenario for two reasons. First, Perry charged before the 4th regiment moved west. Second, Perry's move to the northwest and back would take less time than Oates's round trip across the road.

When Perry rode the limber under Law's disapproving eye, he rode uphill toward his commanding officer. There are two possible knolls that Perry could have ascended. One is almost directly south of the Brock field, while the other is to the west, near the La Fayette Road. If Perry reached that part of the battlefield where the 37th Georgia and the 18th Tennessee found themselves, the second is the only candidate. In addition, Law's duties as division commander would require that he maintain a position which allowed him communications with Robertson and Benning to the southwest as well as Sheffield's brigade. The west knoll serves as a better observation point for Law, who was never far from the fighting.

The accounts of Perry and Goodson and the evidence provided by the 37th Georgia and the 18th Tennessee suggest that Perry's regiment crossed the Brotherton Road where it was struck by Grose's brigade and driven back. This scenario does not provide an answer to the question of where the 44th Alabama was for approximately six hours between the end of the fighting and midnight, when the regiment rejoined the Alabama brigade. Records do not show whether Law ordered the regiment to stay in position at the knoll or to take another position.

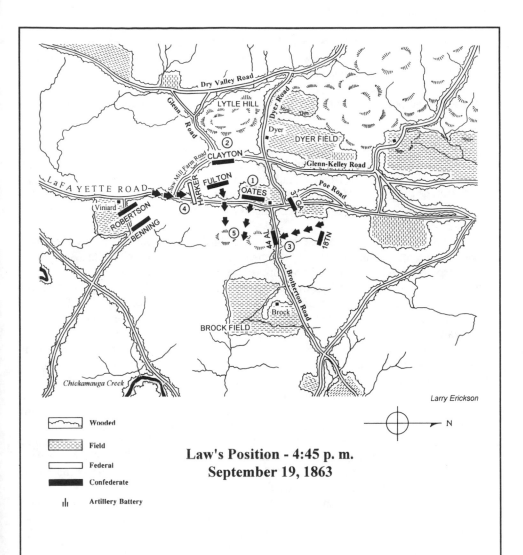

**Law's Position - 4:45 p. m.
September 19, 1863**

Larry Erickson

N

Wooded
Field
Federal
Confederate
Artillery Battery

1. Oates moves into the Brotherton field with the 15th, 47th, 48th and most of the 4th Alabama Regiment
2. Stewart's brigades have passed beyond Oates's position in the Brotherton field, clearing the field of Federals.
3. The 44th Alabama is driven back.
4. Two regiments of Harker's brigade strike Fulton in the left flank, driving him back across the road.
5. Oates is also forced out of the Brotherton field by Harker and recrosses the La Fayette Road.

Darkness Ends the Fighting

Among the wounded on September 19 was Second Lieutenant Ebernezer B. Coggin, Company H, 47th Regiment. Coggin was a prosperous thirty-one-year-old Chambers County farmer, who, even after receiving a mortal wound, continued to encourage his men to drive the Federals from the field before he was carried to the rear.[109] Coggin began his military career as third corporal of Company H and progressed steadily through the non-commissioned ranks before being promoted to second lieutenant in February 1863. He succumbed to his wounds on October 28, 1863.

Captain Joseph Nathaniel Hood, also from the 47th Alabama, lost an arm as a result of his wound and resigned from Confederate service in March 1864. After being promoted to captain earlier in September, Chickamauga was his first battle in command of Company E.[110] Unable to resume working his farm near Spring Garden, Alabama, Hood opened a hotel in Cross Plains. After Cross Plains changed its name to Piedmont, its citizens elected Hood its first mayor.[111]

Darkness ended hostilities for the day. Law's Brigade, still commanded by Oates, bivouacked in the woods about 400 yards east of the La Fayette Road and south of the Brotherton Road.[112] Hood ordered temporary timber breastworks built to secure the line.

Bragg's only orders to Hood for September 19 were to advance, but poor coordination of attack hampered units on the Confederate left.[113] The men of both Johnson's and Stewart's divisions made good gains on the battlefield, but lacked support and were unable to hold their advanced positions. Hood committed Law's division to the offensive too late to help either Johnson or Stewart. The attacks in this segment of the battlefield, the weakest point in the Federal line, were thus piecemeal, sapping the Southern strength, for no gain. As Coles wrote in his history of the 4th Alabama Regiment, it was a "most bungling affair."[114]

After the day's action, Oates sent a request to Law's headquarters for rations for the hungry Alabamians, most of whom had not eaten in 24 hours. The food arrived at 1 a.m. on September 20 and the soldiers were immediately awakened to eat.[115] The brigade was given a ration of rice flour, with which biscuits were prepared. The soldiers "managed to eat some of them while warm and fresh baked," remembered an officer of the 4th Alabama, "but when they became cold, [they] were as hard and equally durable as marble or bronze." Some were carried back to Virginia as souvenirs.[116]

Perry brought the 44th Alabama into camp about midnight in time to receive its share of rations. After Perry's return, Oates relinquished command to him, Perry being the ranking officer.[117] In the early morning hours of September 20, Oates and Perry discussed the day's fighting. During this discussion Perry told Oates of his ride as witnessed by Law, on the artillery limber. Perry explained his intention was to get ahead of his regiment to stop and turn it back against the Federals, but Law believed he was "fleeing disgracefully from the field." Oates advised Perry to speak with Law about the affair immediately because he understood the fighting would resume at daylight. Perry made his way to Law's headquarters intent on explaining the circumstances which led up to the event witnessed by Law. He returned to brigade headquarters convinced that Law did not accept his explanation. There was nothing he could do about it at that late hour, however. The two weary colonels shared Oates's blanket until daylight.[118]

Chapter 9

Charge through the Federal Center

Dawn, the Second Day

Law was at brigade headquarters early, probably before daylight. He soon learned that Sheffield was still incapacitated from his fall the previous day. Perry, as senior officer present, was entitled to command the brigade. Perry's earlier meeting with Law had not changed the general's perception of Perry's courage under fire, so Law sought out Oates and placed him in command. Oates knew military protocol as well as Law, and Law's action presented Oates with a dilemma. Perry was not under arrest, so Oates took Law aside to point out that fact, which Law, for the moment was ignoring. Law said he could solve that problem and arrest Perry. Oates was not convinced that Law's perception of Perry was correct and, to his credit, persisted in Perry's defense. He pointed out that Perry was extremely humiliated over the unfortunate incident and suggested he be given an opportunity to redeem himself. There was little question in Law's mind that his judgment of the incident was correct, but he reluctantly agreed to return Perry to command of the brigade. His parting comments to Oates, however, left little doubt about Perry's fate if he did not do his duty in the forthcoming fight. Oates's instructions were to "Watch him, and if he goes to flickering today, you assume command of the brigade at once."[1] In April 1864 Mims Walker received a letter from his fiancee in which she remarked that it was common knowledge in Alabama that Law and Perry were enemies. They never reconciled their differences.[2]

Longstreet reached the battlefield late the previous night, and after meeting with Bragg, spent the night near Bragg's headquarters. For the second day of fighting Bragg decided to reorganize his army by dividing it into two wings, placing Polk in command of the right wing and Longstreet in command of the left.[3] Longstreet probably arrived in the left wing's bivouac area shortly after Law's visit to brigade headquarters. Its right was about 600 yards south of the Brotherton Road and lay on a line about 800 yards east of, and roughly parallel to, the La Fayette Road. The front line, from right to left, was composed of the divisions of Stewart, Johnson, Major General Thomas Carmichael Hindman and Brigadier General William Preston.[4] Law's division made up a second line. Kershaw brought up two of McLaws's brigades before dawn, and both were in supporting distance behind Law's division.

Longstreet initially decided to leave his divisions in the order he found them. However, he discovered the wing's right flank was in the air. His right was supposed to connect with Polk's left, but Polk's line was hidden in the woods somewhere to the north. Between 6:00 and 6:30 a.m., Longstreet began shifting his lines northward in an attempt to close on Polk's left. An unseasonable cold snap had caused a heavy frost, and at dawn a dense fog settled over the battlefield.[5] Longstreet's search for Polk proved to be no easy task in the wooded terrain and dense fog. Stewart moved a half mile north before Polk's left was finally located. The problem was that Stewart's line lay a half mile in front of Polk. Because Longstreet's right flank was still in the air Stewart was ordered to incline his line rearward to cover the right flank.[6] Since Stewart's line was the only one shifted north, a sizable gap was subsequently created in the center of Longstreet's wing. This gap was filled by sending Johnson's Division forward into the front line between Stewart and Hindman. When the rearranging was finally finished, Law's division had moved a quarter mile north and Kershaw was still in supporting distance. Hood's command now formed a column of assault five lines deep. Johnson's and Law's division were in two lines each, while Kershaw's two brigades were deployed in a single line.

Bushrod Johnson's Division had completed its deployment by 7 a.m.[7] The 5th Texas was ordered into position in Johnson's rear at 7 a.m., and presumably, Hood's entire command was in place between 7:30 and 8 a.m.[8] Johnson's front was composed of two brigades and three regiments. From left to right, Evander McNair's and Fulton's brigades, the 50th Tennessee, First Tennessee (Consolidated) and the 7th Texas Regiment of Colonel Cyrus Sugg, commanding Gregg's Brigade lay on a line generally parallel to the La Fayette Road. The remainder of Sugg's brigade made up Johnson's second line and covered the rear of Fulton and McNair.[9]

Law's Brigade, with supporting artillery on either flank, lay approximately 400 yards in rear of Johnson's Division astride Brotherton Road. Hood's artillery was still on the rails somewhere in the Carolinas or Georgia. Dent's Alabama Battery, commanded by Captain Staunton H. Dent, had been temporarily detached from Brigadier General Zachariah Deas's Brigade and was on the 15th Alabama's left. The identity of the battery on the brigade's right flank is unknown. But Coles, Oates, and Goodson, participants in the fighting that morning, indicated their artillery support moved with the brigade.[10] Hood's fourth line was Robertson's Texans and Benning's Georgians. Robertson covered the left rear of Law's Brigade while Benning covered its right flank.[11]

The 44th Alabama was again on the brigade's extreme right, the 15th occupying the extreme left, the 47th the center with the 4th and 48th on the 47th Alabama's right and left, respectively. Four of the Alabama regiments were led by the same officers as on the previous day. Lieutenant Colonel John Jones assumed command of the 44th when Perry moved up to command the brigade. He was assuming regimental command for the first time. The brigade mustered 126 line officers for the second day's fighting. Eight companies were led by first lieutenants, five were led by senior second lieutenants and three companies went into the fight under the command of non-commissioned officers.[12]

Law's staff remained with him at division headquarters. After being given command of the brigade, Perry decided to leave his regimental staff with the 44th Alabama. Like Sheffield, Perry elected to exercise brigade command without benefit of staff support.[13] This, in effect, meant he planned to issue and convey orders and communicate to division headquarters himself. There was a very real danger in Perry's decision, for it meant he might be unable to maintain control over the five regiments. The situation confronting Perry was made even more difficult by the heavily wooded terrain in which the brigade would be fighting.

The Federals Leave a Gap

Unlike his counterpart on the Confederate side of the battle lines, Rosecrans personally supervised placement of his divisions. He was out and about early, surveying his lines and directing adjustments. The Federal right lay roughly parallel to the La Fayette Road and extended north past the Brotherton house before curving sharply east across the road and into the woods beyond. Eight divisions were in line when the day began, six under Thomas on the left and two under McCook on the extreme right. The Third Division, XIV Corps, led by Brigadier General John M. Brannan went into line before daybreak with two brigades. Colonel John T. Croxton's Second Brigade connected with Colonel Edward A. King's brigade of Joseph J. Reynolds's division. Colonel John M. Connell's First Brigade connected with Major General James S. Negley's division on Brannan's right.[14]

About 8 a.m., in an effort to reinforce Thomas, the entire Federal right began a general movement to its left.[15] In the early morning hours Brannan's left flank was south of Law's position. By 11 a.m. his division lay concealed in the woods just north of the Brotherton house, its front ranks located about one hundred yards west of the La Fayette Road. The relative positions of the divisions placed Law's right just about even with Brannan's right. During the interval of shifting divisions, Rosecrans replaced Negley's division with Wood's division.

Connell's First Brigade, only three regiments strong, was on the division's right, and Croxton's Second Brigade on the division's left.[16] Two of Connell's regiments, 17th Ohio and 31st Ohio, were on his front line; the third regiment, the 82nd Indiana, lay 60 yards to the rear on a line with the artillery limbers. Croxton had five regiments in line, two on the front and three at supporting distance on a line with the 82nd Indiana. Because Connell was short one regiment, Croxton's second line overlapped Connell's front line and supported Battery C, 1st Ohio Light Artillery, which was in position between the brigades and the 31st Ohio. Captain Josiah Church's 4th Michigan Battery of six guns was on the front line between the 17th and 31st Ohio regiments.[17] Brannan's line was completely hidden in the woods adjacent to the La Fayette Road. Wood's three brigade division was in line on Brannan's right. Colonel Sidney M. Barnes's brigade, temporarily assigned to Wood's division from Brigadier General Van Cleve's Third Division, XXI Corps, connected with the 17th Ohio Regiment. Colonel George P. Buell's brigade was on Wood's right, and Harker's brigade occupied the center.[18]

Between 10 a.m. and 10:30 a.m., one of Thomas's staff officers, passing in Brannan's rear on his way to Rosecrans's headquarters, failed to see Brannan's division deployed in the woods and concluded there was a gap in the Federal center.[19] Without stopping to investigate and verify the gap's existence, staff officer Captain Sanford C. Kellogg rushed to Rosecrans's headquarters and reported the observation. Rosecrans had personally inspected that part of the line earlier in the morning and had directed Wood to occupy the ground next to Brannan. However, he and Brigadier General James A. Garfield, his chief of staff, failed to remember that Brannan occupied the position in question or quite possibly thought Brannan had been ordered to the left.

Rosecrans detailed Crittenden's chief of staff to direct Wood to close left on Reynolds and support him. After receiving the order, Wood reported that Brannan was in position on his left and there was no vacancy between Wood and Reynolds.[20] The next communication Wood received from Rosecrans was a written order signed by Major Frank S. Bond, aide-de-camp to Rosecrans. It read: "The general commanding directs that you close up on Reynolds as fast as possible, and support him." Since Brannan's division lay between Wood and Reynolds there was only one way to accomplish the order, pull out of line and move to the left in rear of Reynolds.

Wood must have thought the order unusual because he took the precaution of showing it to McCook, who happened to be with him at the time. Wood suggested to McCook that support be moved to replace his division. The necessary orders were issued to pull his

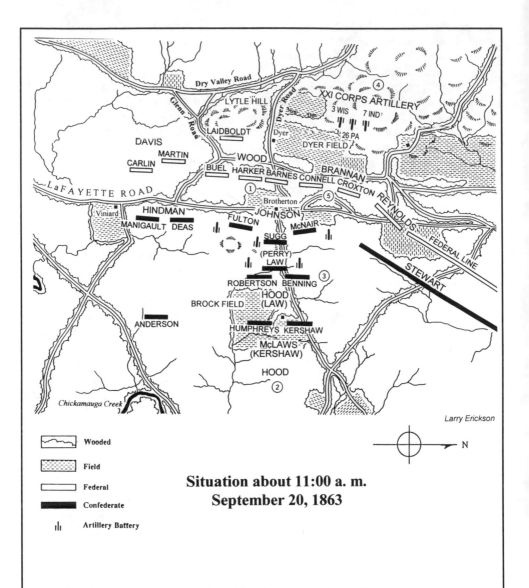

Larry Erickson

Wooded	
Field	
Federal	
Confederate	
Artillery Battery	

Situation about 11:00 a. m.
September 20, 1863

1. Wood receives orders to close on Reynolds and prepares to pull out of line.
2. Hood commands a column, five lines deep, that is poised to charge Wood's division.
3. Hood's Division, commanded by Law, forms the center of Hood's column. Perry commands Law's Brigade. Perry's order of battle is, from right to left: 44th Alabama, 4th Alabama, 47th Alabama, 48th Alabama, 15th Alabama.
4. XXI Corps batteries are arriving on a spur of Snodgrass Hill. Three batteries are already in line and facing east to cover the infantry.
5. Brannan's division lies hidden in the woods on Wood's left. Wood's departure will leave Brannan's right uncovered.

division out of line and Wood went in search of Reynolds. Wood did not find Reynolds but, ran into Thomas who ordered him farther left. Wood had his division completely out of line by 11:15 a.m. Barnes was north of the Dyer field, Harker was passing in Brannan's rear and Buell was in column along Glenn-Kelley Road south of the Dyer field. When Connell discovered that Wood's division was gone, he made an attempt to cover his right flank by sending skirmishers out. Connell also directed the right regiments to change front by the right flank should an attack come from that direction.[21] Except for Connell's skirmishers, a quarter mile wide gap lay directly in front of Hood's column of assault.

Let Every Captain Go Forward

Law's Alabamians spent the morning hours rather leisurely, and about 10 a.m. everyone was ordered to lie down, supposedly to let Polk's command pass through their lines, but that never occurred. Firing was heard off to the right, but for the most part all was quiet along Longstreet's line. The only thing to do was wait.

Bragg preferred a general attack on the Federal line at daylight, but the Confederates were slow to move. Unlike his Federal counterpart, who personally supervised the line adjustment, Bragg issued orders for the day and depended on his corps and division commanders to organize their lines. Longstreet was ready to go by the time the fog lifted. However, Polk's right wing was tardy, because some of the divisions were distributing rations when Bragg thought the attack was to begin.[22] As the morning wore on, Confederate attacks were piecemeal and not a general assault as Bragg wanted. Shortly before 11 a.m., Bragg became so frustrated with events that he sent a general order for his army to move forward. Longstreet later said the order was for an attack by divisions.[23] A contemporary source reported that Bragg, shouting expletives, cried out, "Order every captain to take his men instantly forward."[24] At that time Longstreet was considering the possibilities of a concentrated assault on his front. Concluding his column could probably achieve a breakthrough, Longstreet sent a courier to Bragg seeking permission to attack. The courier had not returned when Longstreet became aware of Bragg's general order. Stewart had already started forward, but Longstreet decided to hold his other divisions until his own order to advance was given.[25] At 11:15 a.m., Hood's column began its charge directly at the gap left by Wood.

Bushrod Johnson's Division crossed the La Fayette Road at the Brotherton house and quickly brushed aside Connell's skirmishers. His left passed south of the Brotherton house and struck the front and flank of Buell's column. Buell's troops had no indication of impending danger until Johnson's men came storming out of the woods straight at their right flank. Johnson's column sliced through Buell's near its front. Most of Buell's brigade retreated westward toward the Dry Valley Road. The remainder eventually joined Harker to the north.[26]

Hood's left met some resistance when Brigadier Generals Zachariah C. Deas and Arthur M. Manigault of Hindman's Division, encountered elements of Brigadier General Jefferson C. Davis's division.[27] After a brief fight, Deas and Manigault drove Davis's line back on its support causing both to fall back toward the Dry Valley Road. With Davis out of the way, Deas pushed on toward a low ridge a quarter of a mile west of the La Fayette Road. Two Federal brigades commanded by Colonel Bernard Laiboldt and Brigadier General William H. Lytle were deployed along the ridge's crest.[28] These brigades were not as easily dislodged, and Deas's advance ground to a halt.

The Federal Flank Crumbles

Johnson's right was not as lucky as his left. McNair's Brigade found Connell's line firmly entrenched behind log and rail fortifications. Heavy musketry and artillery fire caused McNair to halt and fall back in confusion, but McNair rallied his troops on Sugg's supporting line and moved forward again.[29] He was stopped a second time by musketry and canister. Losses in both lines mounted rapidly, and unless different tactics were employed there would be no alternative but to fall back. Sugg and McNair discussed the deteriorating situation and decided that Sugg's supporting line would pass through McNair's line and attack the Federal flank.[30] Sugg skillfully guided his brigade through McNair's left and assailed the 17th Ohio on Connell's right flank. The 17th Ohio's right wing broke and fled through the ranks of the 82nd Indiana located 60 yards to the rear.[31] The flight of the 17th Ohio produced a domino effect as Brannan's entire division began to fall back. The 17th Ohio's left wing followed the right and the 31st Ohio next on the left also gave way. Colonel Morton C. Hunter, commanding the 82nd Indiana, sent his regiment charging toward the abandoned front breastworks. His men managed to reach the original front line, but at a cost of 82 casualties. A few minutes later the 82nd Indiana was also retiring, though defiantly, from the woods. As the 82nd fell back, Hunter ordered the regiment to turn every 50 yards to face the charging Confederates and fire a volley.[32] With the 82nd gone the 4th Michigan Battery was left to its own defenses. Even though he had 35 horses shot down, Church managed to move four of his guns 50 yards to the rear. Three of these were limbered and subsequently moved to a reserve artillery line on a ridge in the rear of his position.[33] At some point in the fighting, Lieutenant Colonel Durbin Ward rallied part of the 17th Ohio and mounted a counterattack which reached the original breastworks before stalling. Church used the Ohioans' charge to cover an attempt to save his remaining pieces, but the 17th Ohio fell back before all his guns were run off the field. A few of his gunners defended their pieces until the position was overrun. Sergeant S. A. Allen fired his revolver until he was nearly run through by a Confederate bayonet. He managed to escape but left three of Church's guns to the Confederates.[34] Sugg and McNair had succeeded in dislodging Connell, though not without heavy losses themselves. McNair was among the wounded, leaving command of his brigade with Colonel David Coleman of the 39th North Carolina.[35] With Connell out of the way, both brigades continued toward the Dyer field.

Connell's exit left the second line of Croxton's right flank in the air and also uncovered Battery C of the 1st Ohio Light Artillery. Croxton attempted to cover his flank by swinging his second line to the right. It now faced to the south and nearly perpendicular to the original battle line.[36] The second line held until Sugg and Coleman threatened Croxton's rear, pushing it back until the entire line collapsed and eventually took up a position on Snodgrass Hill. With the second line gone, the front line, composed of the 10th and 74th Indiana, was forced to change front to the right. These regiments repulsed a charge, fired on a Confederate line moving north across Dyer field, and saved five guns belonging to the 1st Ohio Artillery.[37] Both regiments fought on until they drove the Confederates from Dyer field, then fell back on Reynolds to replenish their ammunition.[38]

Law's Brigade Is Left to Mop Up

The Alabamians began their forward movement in an orderly manner. When the command "Attention!" rang out along the line, men rose and took their places. At the command "Forward" the line moved out at a steady pace.[39] Just east of the La Fayette Road

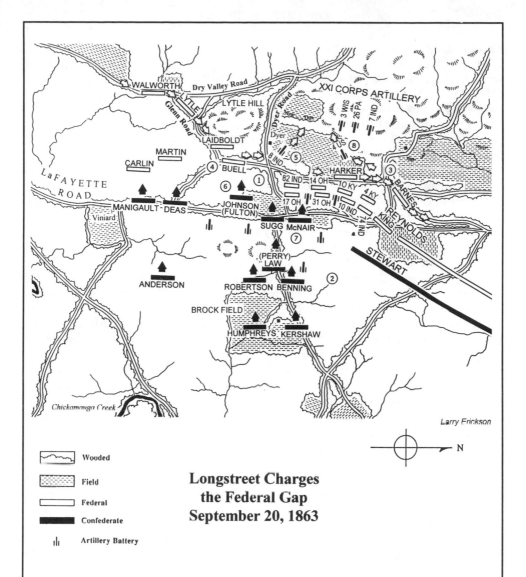

**Longstreet Charges
the Federal Gap
September 20, 1863**

Larry Frickson

Wooded

Field

Federal

Confederate

Artillery Battery

1. At 11:00 a. m. Buell, Barnes and Harker begin withdrawing from their position in the Federal line.
2. At approximately 11:15 a. m. Longstreet sends his wing forward.
3. Harker is to Brannan's rear, moving north. Barnes leads Harker and moves to Brannan's left.
4. Buell is in column on the Glenn-Kelley Road.
5. Estep, who has been supporting Buell, moves the 8th Indiana in line of battery across the Dryer field to join the XXI Corps artillery line.
6. Fulton's Brigade charges through the gap left by Wood's withdrawal and attacks Buell from the flank. Buell's column is driven from the field, carrying Laiboldt with it.
7. McNair attacks Connell's brigade on its right flank. McNair's advance stalls when Connell's line holds.
8. The 4th U. S. Battery has pulled out of line and is moving back to replenish its ammunition.

they advanced through virgin hardwood timber with little undergrowth. A thick canopy overhead allowed very little sunlight through, giving the Alabamians an impression of being in a large cathedral, their view of the fighting blocked by smoke drifting through the tall timber.[40] They were approaching the La Fayette Road as Brannan's division began giving way. An incessant roar of musketry and cannon fire indicated the fight ahead was a lively one. Excitement began to rise within the ranks, and the men instinctively went to the quick step. Anticipation of joining the fight was sufficient cause for the Rebel Yell to erupt from their ranks.[41] In fact, the exhilaration became so intense that captains found it difficult to control their companies. The line began to move at a double quick-step.[42] Perry's artillery accompanied the brigade and fired as it moved forward. The splendor of the scene unfolding before Joab Goodson made such a vivid impression that his next letter home described the charge as "the grandest sight of its kind that I ever witnessed."[43]

Perry experienced considerable difficulty in maintaining his battle line. The 15th Alabama became separated while the remainder of the brigade burst from the woods on the east side of the La Fayette Road, crossed the road and entered the woods north of the Brotherton house.[44] Debris lying in the wake of Sugg's and McNair's charge gave an indication of the intensity of the fighting a few moments before. Dead, dying, and wounded lay everywhere, as wreckage from Church's battery was scattered about. Injured horses whined piteously and wounded men groaned as the cracks of musket fire continued ahead.[45] Connell's troops had been in such a hurry to fire that more than one soldier had discharged his gun without removing the ramrod. A large number of these unlikely missiles were embedded in trees in front of the former Federal lines.[46] During the advance, Coleman went down with a serious leg wound. Command of the 4th Alabama devolved to a senior captain, William Karsner of Company H.[47]

Immediately after crossing the La Fayette Road, Perry detected a body of Federal troops forming to attack his right flank. Because the fighting along Brannan's line at this point was confused, Perry's would-be assailants can only be identified by the process of elimination. Church reported that none of his guns were removed until after the 82nd Indiana was driven from the breastworks. He also reported the 17th Ohio reformed and countercharged after this. It is reasonable to expect that in the confusion of the division's collapse that only a portion of the regiment was reformed. Connell reported that the 17th Ohio reached the breastworks with no Federal troops on its right or left. By this time it is also reasonable to expect that Sugg's and McNair's brigades had moved on and were either approaching or had reached the edge of Dyer field. The threat to Perry's flank can be presumed to be remnants of the 17th Ohio. Apparently Perry did not consider the threat serious because he sent the 4th, 47th and 48th Alabama regiments forward toward the Dyer field. The 44th and a section of artillery were detached to deal with the threat to his flank.

Benning's Georgians crossed the La Fayette Road north of where the Alabamians had passed a few minutes before. Benning could not see the Alabama regiments in the woods, but he saw the 17th Ohio forming to attack Perry's right flank and rear. He may have also seen Croxton's front line forming to the rear and flank of the 17th Ohio. Immediately after entering the woods near the Poe house, Benning ordered the Georgia brigade to change front to the right and attack the Federal line to the north.[48] A few volleys from the 44th Alabama, the supporting artillery and Benning was sufficient to send the 17th Ohio packing. Benning picked up Church's three artillery pieces and advanced on Croxton's right flank. This time he encountered stiff resistance. The 10th Indiana and 74th Ohio counterattacked and drove Benning back in some confusion, although he stubbornly exchanged fire with the Federals for some time.[49] There is no evidence that the 44th Alabama supported Benning or fought on its own after driving off the 17th Ohio. The number of casu-

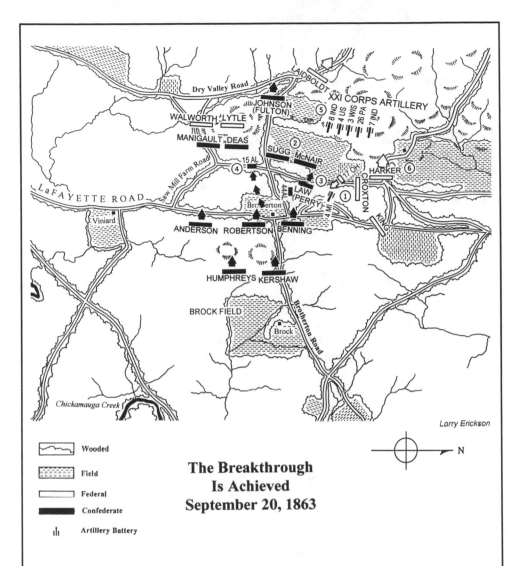

Larry Erickson

**The Breakthrough
Is Achieved
September 20, 1863**

Wooded
Field
Federal
Confederate
Artillery Battery

1. Sugg and McNair drive Connell's regiments from the woods. McNair is wounded and Coleman assumes command. Croxton's brigade changes direction by the right flank. The 17th Ohio regroups and counterattacks.
2. Coleman and Sugg emerge from the woods and come under fire from the XXI Corps artillery posted on the spur of Snodgrass Hill.
3. Perry's Alabamians cross the La Fayette Road north of the Brotherton house and enter the woods. Perry is advancing through the woods and detaches the 44th Alabama when his right flank is threatened. Perry continues west toward the Dyer field with the remainder of the brigade.
4. Oates becomes separated from the brigade east of the La Fayette Road and emerges from the woods south of the Brotherton house. He continues west toward Lytle Hill.
5. The 8th Indiana Battery had just deployed on the south end of the Federal artillery line.
6. Harker has turned back and is preparing to deploy in line of battle on the north end of the Dyer field.

alties on September 20 supports this thesis. The 44th had only six wounded the entire day, therefore, it has to be concluded the 44th simply deployed in the woods east of Dyer field while the battle raged around them.

There Is But One Last Obstacle

The brigades of Sugg and Coleman emerged from the woods on the southeastern end of a large expanse known today as Dyer field on which a ridge running the length of its western boundary sloped downward from north to south. The ridge's crest, free of timber, was actually an extension of a spur from Missionary Ridge that rose abruptly from the north end of the Dyer field. After the battle, the spur became known as Snodgrass Hill. When Sugg and Coleman emerged from the woods, the remnants of Connell's brigade were retreating across the field and up the slopes of Snodgrass Hill. Directly across Dyer field, five Federal batteries greeted the Confederates with shell and canister.

From the Confederates' left to right the 8th Indiana, Battery H, 4th U.S. Artillery, 3rd Wisconsin Battery, 26th Battery Pennsylvania Light Artillery, and the 7th Battery Indiana Light Artillery were deployed in battery with 26 guns. All belonged to Crittenden's XXI Corps.[50] The entire line was under the direct control of Major John Mendenhall, Crittenden's chief of artillery. Before arriving on the ridge, each battery had moved frequently and each time operated in brigade support. However, the heavily wooded terrain made it difficult to maneuver supporting artillery. Crittenden chose to deploy his guns on the ridge west of Dyer field, while Mendenhall probably began the task of withdrawing from the lines and deploying on the ridge about mid-morning, apparently following no particular order in posting the batteries.[51] The artillerists were in position to shell easy targets should the Confederates emerge from the woods. By the time Hood began his assault, three of the five batteries were on the ridge and in position. When Sugg and Coleman arrived at the Dyer field, all five were deployed.

Lieutenant Courtland Livingston's 3rd Wisconsin Battery arrived first. During the morning he had supported Barnes and finally came into position on the ridge after much maneuvering in which the battery was always moving to the left.[52] The 26th Pennsylvania, commanded by Captain Alanson Stevens, and Captain George Swallow's 7th Indiana Batteries arrived next.[53] Both batteries had spent the night quite some distance south of their present position, and before going into line on Livingston's left both batteries had remained close to each other, moving several times in support of the brigades of Barnes and Beatty.[54] Lieutenant Harry Cushing's Battery H, 4th U.S. Artillery had been in line near Thomas before ordered to fall back, find his caissons and refill his ammunition chests. Before Cushing could completely replenish his ammunition, Mendenhall ordered him to join the line of batteries on the ridge. Cushing was not yet in firing position when Johnson's column stormed through the gap in the Federal center.[55]

The 8th Indiana Battery, commanded by Captain George Estep, was the last to arrive, coming into position after the attack began on Buell's column. On September 19, Estep lost three of his guns, but recovered them when the Confederates were in turn overrun. He then spent most of the night repairing damage sustained in the fighting, and the following morning supported Buell and was moving in column with Buell when Johnson's leading brigades attacked. Estep headed north and just after crossing Dyer Road, changed direction to the left, crossing the south end of Dyer field and moving into battery position on the south end of the ridge.[56] He was on the extreme right of the battery line, probably 75 to 100 yards south of Cushing's battery.[57]

Crittenden came shortly after Estep, and much to his dismay, discovered his artillery had no infantry support. In fact, his batteries were close to being boxed in, for heavy woods lay to his rear, Snodgrass Hill rose abruptly above its lower slopes on his left, and Confederates were closing in on his front and right flank. Cushing expressed concern as he pondered available escape avenues to retire if the Confederates attempted to force the batteries from the field. Crittenden briefly entertained the hope that infantry support would arrive, and even though help might come in the form of infantry being driven back on him. But he soon acertained there was slim likelihood he would obtain infantry support, and quickly realized that the small infantry squad sent by Van Cleve behind the battery was insufficient. Crittenden left to find a general officer from whom he could obtain reinforcements.[58] Mendenhall and his battery commanders were left to their own devices.

The Guns Are Overrun

Sugg and Coleman were pinned down and exchanging fire with the Federal batteries when Perry's three Alabama regiments emerged from the woods along Glenn-Kelley Road.[59] There was no semblance of order within the Confederate ranks as the lines of Sugg, Coleman and Perry became one single mass of humanity. Their movement came to a standstill as the charge stalled and the troops scurried for cover.

An artillery section accompanying Perry unlimbered near the edge of the woods and immediately joined in the exchange of fire with the Federal batteries. Across the open field, Livingston's Wisconsin artillerists noted the new threat and directed fire into the woods to their immediate front.[60] As the Alabamians protected themselves as best they could, the situation quickly turned into a duel. Forty-four-year-old Stephen Quinley stood in the open to fire on the Federal batteries. Companions in the 4th Alabama, who called their friend "old man Quinley," earnestly beseeched him to seek cover. His reply was "A man born to be hung will never be shot."[61] Although he survived the day, he was wrong about being shot. Private Stephen Quinley was severely wounded at the Wilderness the following May.

Across Dyer field, Estep believed the Federal artillery could turn back the Confederate threat, but his optimism soon evaporated.[62] His infantry support failed, and Confederate fire was as much of a problem for the Federal artillerists as the Federal cannon was for the Confederates. Gunners of the 3rd Wisconsin Battery hugged the ground; one of them later wrote home that bullets were striking the gun carriages like a drummer beating his drum.[63] Other gunners, however, stood to their work and returned a devastating fire on the Confederates.

Captain Clower, 47th Alabama, observed the smoke belching from the Federal batteries and saw men falling from the case and canister showering their ranks. He knew the guns would have to be silenced if the Confederate advance was to succeed. In the rear of the Alabamians, Perry came to the same conclusion as Clower, but before they could act, Terrell galloped down the brigade line until he drew even with the 47th Alabama's color bearer. During a momentary pause, Terrell snatched the colors, wheeled his mount toward Dyer field, and yelling at the top of his voice, spurred his horse toward the Federal batteries.[64]

The 47th Alabama, seeing their colors advancing, moved out with a thunderous, sustained yell.[65] Perry drove his horse through the Alabamians, urging them forward. Coleman's brigade joined the Alabamians as the two ran en masse diagonally across the field. Canister rained down like hail from a summer thunderstorm as the Federal batteries managed to get off a few shots at the charging Confederates,[66] Perry's horse was wounded, but kept moving forward. A shell exploded overhead, knocking down Lieutenant William Ballard, Company C, 47th Alabama, and disabling him with a concussion.[67] As Private Theophilus F. Botsford, Company D, 47th Alabama, ran after the 47th Alabama's battle flag, his old straw hat, one of his more prized possessions, flew off his head. The hat was important but on this day the matter of his hat would have to wait. Botsford kept running.[68] Sugg's men surged forward to flank the battery line, attacking the guns from the right flank and rear.[69] On the right of the artillery line, Estep reluctantly abandoned his entire battery. This time his guns were in the Confederate's possession to stay.

On the left of the line of artillery, Swallow was too busy to count regimental flags. He looked at the mass of humanity bearing down on his battery and thought a single brigade was attacking his position.[70] At the same time Livingston saw that his position had also become untenable, many of his horses having been shot. Livingston ordered the bugler to signal limber up. In the battery's left section, driver William Plackett mounted his lead horse as the limber was being attached to the gun carriage. Looking to his right, Plackett saw the line melt away. Wounded horses thrashed about while the drivers attempted to unharness the wounded and at the same time limber up the guns. Just as he looked to the left, the adjacent gun completed limbering up and pulled rapidly out of line. The onrushing gun carriage came too close to Plackett's limber and the two became hopelessly entangled. A few minutes later the lieutenant commanding the section paused long enough to salute his battery with raised sword, told his men to save themselves and galloped off the field.[71] He barely made his exit before the Alabamians slammed into the batteries.

Those remaining with the guns put up a gallant but brief fight as possession of the guns evolved to hand-to-hand combat. Muskets and gun swabs were used for clubs.[72] Color bearer John Rogers, Company C, 48th Alabama, paused by a gun and firmly pressed the regiment's battle flag against the ground while his companions fought the guns' defenders. Rogers was new at the job, having been color bearer since the fight at Gettysburg. He was 32, an Alabama native, single, and before the war a farmer near Aurora, Alabama.[73] A few moments later a shot from a Federal defender ended his career.[74] On the Federal side, Alanson Stevens died defending his guns. Moments later Plackett and his fellow artillerymen were running through the woods while their pursuers yelled, "Halt, you damn Yankees!"[75] A few yards behind the line, several Federal gunners were found hiding in sink holes.[76] Livingston's men managed to escape with only one of its six guns.[77] In all, 15 of Mendenhall's 26 guns were either abandoned or captured.

Coleman left the mopping up to Sugg and Perry and moved forward into the woods beyond the battery line. Sugg took possession of nine abandoned guns and his men rushed them to the rear.[78] Some of the pieces were pulled by hand and some were drawn by horses with the Federal drivers mounted and under guard.[79] Perry was occupied with fire from the spur to the north. He decided to attack in that direction when a body of Confederate troops was discovered nearby. Perry approached the Confederate commander and proposed they both attack the Federal infantry on the spur. Perry suggested the officer attack from the western side while his own men attacked from the southern slopes. But Perry found his Alabamians were completely disorganized from the charge. In addition, the other Confederates were falling back which uncovered Perry's position.[80] The assault was not made. The Alabamians paused to give three cheers for Terrell, many expressing amazement that he was not hit. An eyewitness reported Terrell responded with an air of perfect nonchalance, saying "Oh, damn 'em! They can't hit me."[81]

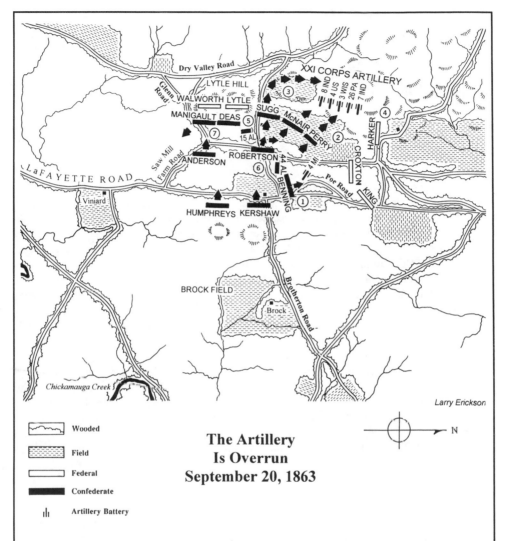

Larry Erickson

The Artillery
Is Overrun
September 20, 1863

Wooded

Field

Federal

Confederate

Artillery Battery

1. Benning has crossed the La Fayette Road, turned right and deployed to meet a threat from the right. His Georgians overrun the 4th Michigan guns and attack Croxton and King.
2. Perry arrives at the eastern edge of the Dyer field and finds McNair and Sugg engaged in a fight with the XXI Corps artillery posted on the spur of Snodgrass Hill. McNair's Brigade is now under Coleman's command. The three brigades charge the Federal batteries. Perry and Coleman charge diagonally across the Dyer field and overrun the artillery from the front.
3. Sugg moves forward and attacks the artillery from the flank.
4. Harker deploys in line of battle on the north end of the Dyer field.
5. Oates moves up on Deas's right flank with the 15th Alabama and participates in the attack on Lytle's brigade.
6. Robertson moves into the Dyer field, swings right and advances north.
7. Manigault withdraws under fire. Anderson takes the hill.

The Texans Meet Their Match

The Texas brigade exited the woods on the south end of Dyer field just as Coleman and Perry started across. Seeing a wide gap in the Confederate line to his right, Robertson moved in that direction. After executing a sharp right turn, he sent messengers to units on his right and left requesting support. The request went unanswered and Robertson began his advance northward through Dyer field, unsupported on either flank.[82] It is unclear which unit his messenger sought out on the left but the known Confederate units on his right at that time were the 44th Alabama and Benning's Georgia brigade. Kershaw was still advancing west of the La Fayette Road. Since Benning was heavily engaged in the woods near the Poe house, the unit Robertson referred to on his right had to be the 44th Alabama. As soon as he became aware of the Confederate breakthrough, Harker reversed his path and began deploying in line of battle on the extreme north end of Dyer field. Robertson's Texans were entering the field from its southern edge, and during this process were fired on from the front, flank and rear. Robertson was convinced his antagonists included the Confederate regiments that a few moments before declined to support him. Actually, Robertson's men were probably taking fire from the 10th and 74th Indiana regiments.[83] The 10th Indiana historian specifically described firing on a Confederate line advancing north in the open field, referring to Dyer field. Lieutenant Colonel Myron Baker of the 74th Indiana reported the 74th fought until the Confederates were driven back from the open field. The line referred to was Robertson's. Once Kershaw's Brigade entered Dyer field it drove the Federals back onto the crest of Snodgrass Hill. When he wrote his report, Robertson was probably still chafing over the event because for the first time in its illustrious career the Texas brigade had retired in the face of a foe.

When he saw the Texans falling back, Perry retraced his path across Dyer field and along the way encountered Hood trying to steady his old brigade which had retired into the edge of the woods at the south end of the field. Perry maneuvered his Alabamians in on the Texans' right flank, where he ordered the color bearers of each regiment to the front. He then reformed on the colors and restored order.[84] Shortly afterward, Hood received a serious leg wound. The last time Perry and the Alabamians saw their beloved general, he was passing through their ranks on a litter.

The Spoils of War Can Be As Simple As a Hat

Botsford rummaged through the battery wreckage and found a fine Carsnith hat to replace his lost straw hat. It was a fine hat indeed, complete with a feather, leading Botsford to conclude its previous owner was an officer. He proudly wore it as he went about the business of moving the captured guns to the rear. He and Anderson Glaze, also of Company D, 47th Alabama, were walking across Dyer field when a sniper's bullet hit Glaze in the left arm. Botsford accompanied his wounded comrade to a field hospital, arriving as the doctors amputated Hood's leg. Glaze's arm was so badly mangled from the bullet that he lost his arm to the surgeon's saw.[85]

The Honor of Capture Breeds Controversy

Apparently believing that possession was sufficient grounds to claim the honor of capture, Sugg later reported his brigade captured the nine guns, a claim Coleman vigorously disputed.[86] The discussion became sufficiently heated in the days following the battle to cause Sugg to ask Lieutenant Fletcher Beaumont, his aide-de-camp, to prepare a report addressing the issue.[87] Bushrod Johnson alluded to the dispute in his report but since he was not present he chose to remain neutral.[88] The controversy continued for the next 30 years until the North Carolinians thought the issue was settled in their favor. In fact, the argument has continued. The battlefield marker in the north end of Dyer field acknowledges the capture of only nine guns, apparently the nine disputed by Sugg and Coleman.[89] The 39th North Carolina's marker in the Glenn field mentions only nine guns, though the marker 300 feet east of Vittoe's indicates that both Coleman's and Sugg's brigades participated in capturing the 15 guns.[90]

Neither marker mentions Law's Brigade. Since the dispute was between Sugg and Coleman, the contribution made by the Alabamians has long since been forgotten. Coleman's and Sugg's reports written immediately after the battle, failed to mention Law's Brigade or the capture of 15 guns. Both men concentrated instead on the nine involved in the dispute. The question that should be addressed is: which units captured the 15 guns? The preponderance of the evidence indicates that Coleman and Perry charged en masse across Dyer field while Sugg flanked the artillery. Both Coleman and Perry have to be given credit for initially overrunning the Federal batteries. Beaumont, adjutant of the 50th Tennessee, confirms the nine guns in question were abandoned when Sugg's brigade took possession.[91] The incident illustrates the reason abandoned guns were quickly removed since possession was tantamount to claiming capture. In this case, however, credit should not be given to a single brigade. All three brigades charged the battery line, so it seems reasonable to conclude that the honor should go equally to the brigades commanded by Coleman, Sugg and Perry.

Oates Goes Exploring

While Perry and four of his regiments were capturing the guns, Oates had become separated from the brigade and was fighting alone. The 15th Alabama, accompanied by Captain S. H. Dent's Battery, crossed the La Fayette Road south of the Brotherton house and entered the woods well to the left of the brigade.[92] To its left lay a low ridge covered with timber, and a spirited fight for its possession was in progress. The antagonists were the brigades of Zachariah Deas and Federal Brigadier General William Lytle. Oates did not know the identity of the Confederate brigade but thought it was being beaten badly.[93] Deas later reported he was only stopped temporarily. Never one to miss a good fight, Oates quickly ordered his men to the assistance of the Confederate brigade. The 15th Alabama double-quicked by the left flank until it reached the rear of an old soap factory. After facing right and approaching a fence near the factory, the 15th Alabama came under fire of the Federal artillery on the ridge. Oates, with Dent's Battery maintaining a position just off his right, approached Deas's Brigade from the right rear.[94]

The Federal battery exhausted its supply of canister as Oates approached and began firing artillery shells.[95] A shell fragment struck Oates's leg, knocking him down. Fortunately, the only damage was a torn pant leg and a bad bruise. Lieutenant Thomas Renfroe, Company G, stopped to steady Oates until he was able to limp forward.[96] The 15th Alabama paused to fire on the Federal position off to their left and front. Fire passed over Deas's extreme right, and in the process a few scattering shots probably went into the Confederate ranks.

The unfortunate recipient of the stray fire was Colonel Samuel K. McSpadden's 19th Alabama. His first reaction was anger, but quickly concluded it was necessary to make the offending regiment aware the troops to their front were friendly. To get their attention, McSpadden sent his color bearer to the rear.[97] By this time Oates had rejoined the 15th

Alabama and ordered his men to hold their fire. He subsequently moved the 15th upon the right flank of the 19th Alabama.

McSpadden reported the incident and may have talked about it in later years because, in his memoirs, Oates found it necessary to write about his side of the occurrence. Oates adamantly disputed McSpadden's claim, admitting only to the left oblique march and joining McSpadden on his right. At the time the incident occurred, it is not likely there was organized Federal resistance on McSpadden's right and rear. Lytle's brigade was on the extreme left of the Federal line and on Deas's front. Bushrod Johnson's left brigade was somewhere to McSpadden's right and front because this brigade encountered less resistance moving through the gap left by Wood. That left the 15th Alabama as the most likely suspect. When Oates caught up with the regiment he called out, "Don't fire 15th until you are ordered!" He saw the men were about to volley a second time and called once again, "Don't fire until you are ordered, men!"[98] However, Oates, in later years, steadfastly refused to concede the 15th fired on a friendly regiment. Considering the excitement of the charge and with Federals firing on both regiments, it is likely that before Oates could get his men's attention some shots were accidentally fired into the 19th Alabama.

When the 15th Alabama came abreast of the 19th Alabama, Deas's battle line was extended sufficiently to the right to overlap Lytle's brigade. The Confederates then swept into the thick smoke that hung about head high over the ridge's crest and pushed the Federals from the ridge.[99] Oates spotted a richly adorned horse standing near the former Federal position. A few yards away lay the dying form of General Lytle. Oates discovered the horse was lame but only paused long enough to move the general to a shady place. Although hampered by his leg wound, he limped after the 15th Alabama, finding his men resting.[100] Deas rode up a short time later and they discussed their situation, both agreeing the advance had moved too far forward. Oates ordered the 15th Alabama to stack arms and sent the bareheaded to find suitable headgear. Noah Feagin's Company B was then ordered to take charge of two guns found in the wake of the Confederate charge and remove them from the field before another regiment claimed credit for their capture. Once the captured artillery was secured and the men rested, Oates marched the 15th Alabama back toward the soap factory.[101]

Oates encountered Bushrod Johnson and asked the location of Law's troops. Johnson knew nothing of the Alabamians, but indicated fighting was in progress in the woods north of their present position. That was all Oates needed to know as he boldly set out with his men at the double-quick north across the Dyer field, intent on joining the next fight. His bruised leg prevented him from keeping pace with the 15th, and he came upon a young boy also lagging to the rear. When Oates chastised him for being afraid, the young boy, about 15, replied defiantly: "Afraid, Hell, that ain't it! I'm so dammed tired I can't keep up with my company." Bryant Skipper had run away from home the previous March to join the regiment.[102] The youngster would remain with the regiment until the war's end.

Oates marched over the ground where Kershaw's South Carolinians had successfully charged and driven Harker before noon. He found Kershaw's Brigade at the north end of Dyer field on a plateau more than halfway up the slope of Snodgrass Hill. The 15th then moved into a gap between the 7th and 15th South Carolina regiments.[103] Still with plenty of fight in him, Oates determined to find the Federal line farther up the spur. He ordered Privates Billy Jordan and T. P. Thompson forward as scouts. Jordan spotted the enemy first and took cover behind a tree undetected. Jordan and Thompson had walked upon a Federal battle line being formed. They watched an unidentified regiment filing by its right flank and taking up position. Thompson found cover a short distance away and both began to fire into the Federal colors.[104]

In the meantime Oates attempted to persuade the South Carolinians to join his Alabamians in a charge against the Federal position. He failed to convince the South Carolina regimental commanders that the gains warranted the action. One captain from the 7th South Carolina agreed to follow Oates and went forward with his company, and surprisingly, the entire regiment followed. Oates then led his regiment and the 7th South Carolina up the spur.

A short time later the Carolinians and Alabamians opened a partial enfilading fire on the Federal battle line, but one well-aimed volley from the Federals sent both regiments scurrying for cover. Oates required the services of Lieutenant William Strickland of Company I to stop the headlong retreat of the Alabama troops. Oates was not as successful with the South Carolinians, but when they did reform, Oates led his Alabamians and a single company of Carolinians back up the spur. This time, it was the Federals' turn to break and run.[105]

The 15th Alabama next took up positions on the slope of Snodgrass Hill and exchanged fire with a Federal line, during which time Oates extended his line to the left to avoid being overlapped. His line had been reduced to a single rank with each man at least two paces apart. Oates moved from man to man giving each encouragement and adjusting positions where necessary. At one point he found seventeen-year-old Tommy Wright, one of four brothers to join the 15th Alabama, kneeling down and carefully taking aim at the Federal line. Oates was fond of the youngster and paused to exchange a few words before moving on. He felt a keen sense of responsibility for the boy, and when he returned a few minutes later Tommy Wright lay dead, a Federal bullet in his brain. Oates was momentarily overcome with emotion at the youth's death.[106]

When ammunition began running low, Oates sent Billy Jordan to search for cartridges on the battlefield. Jordan happened upon a wounded Federal, a youth of 18 years. They struck up a conservation and Jordan found out the young fellow was from Kentucky and had kin in the Confederate army. The Federal asked for a litter, which Jordan found before resuming his original task. While Jordan was searching for ammunition, Terrell found Oates and ordered him to withdraw from Snodgrass Hill and move back to the woods to join the brigade. When Jordan returned to where he had last seen the 15th Alabama, the regiment had withdrawn.[107] Jordan went in search of his regiment.

The rest of the Alabama brigade spent the afternoon in the woods next to Dyer field. Even though Reynolds's right flank and remnants of Croxton's brigade still posed a threat to the Confederate right, little fighting occurred along that front for most of the afternoon. Despite considerable maneuvering during the battle, all three brigades from Hood's Division were together by 5 p.m.

Law wasn't through fighting, however, and after a personal reconnaissance, he developed a plan to attack the Federals on his right. Law placed the division artillery in line and opened a lengthy barrage against Reynolds's division and Croxton's brigade.[108] The artillery was nearby because the Confederates attempted to use it as an offensive weapon at Chickamauga. The batteries advanced along with the infantry, but the terrain and see-saw fighting reduced its effectiveness.[109] Law sought to take advantage of the artillery, both as an offensive weapon and to cover his infantry in another advance. He ordered Perry to deploy for a charge against the Federal position.[110] Moments before the advance was ordered, the 15th Alabama rejoined the brigade. Oates soon learned the brigade was moving out. Billy Jordan had returned with cartridges, and the new ammunition was passed out as the 15th Alabama filed into line for the assault.[111] The advance was relatively easy as the brigade moved only 300 or 400 yards before the officer leading the skirmish line informed Perry there was no one to fight as the Federals were gone from his front.[112] That ended the day's fighting for Law's Brigade.

The Aftermath of Chickamauga

The brigade had begun each day of the Battle of Chickamauga in a reserve roll, but each day had been thrown into action where the firing seemed the most severe. Casualties were surprisingly large for a brigade in reserve, its percentage of losses comparable to those sustained at Gettysburg. Overall, the brigade casualties amounted to 30 percent with six officers and 53 enlisted men either killed or mortally wounded. The wounded totaled 27 officers and 333 men, one officer and 16 men were listed missing.[113]

Two officers, Reuben Kidd and Martin Billingsley, were dead on the field; four others, Fred Porter, Thomas Appleton, Ebernezer Coggin and Thomas Coleman, died later from their wounds. Five of the wounded officers, Joseph Hood, Joseph Swan, Robert E. Cary, John E. Jones, and John H. Brazile were unable to return to active duty, which brought their numbers to 11, or roughly 10 percent of the officers present for duty, the number permanently taken from the brigade as a result of the fighting at Chickamauga.[114]

Searching the Battlefield

When the 15th Alabama retired from the field, Oates ordered details of men to bring out the dead and wounded with the regiment, and the dead were buried that night. The 15th Alabama had gone into battle 450 strong, and sustained 132 casualties. Oates rejoiced that he survived the day, and that night he visited his men at every campfire in his regiment.[115]

On September 21 many Alabamians searched for friends among the wounded still on the field. Some visited the battlefield to view the destruction and search for the spoils of war. Thomas Batey, Company I, 47th Alabama, was found lying near a wounded Federal soldier. Both suffered from broken thighs and were in great pain. The Federal cried out for the Confederates to have pity on him and give him water, all the while lamenting over his broken thigh. Since there was a group of Confederates gathered around the wounded soldiers, Batey seized the opportunity to give three cheers for the Confederate army. With much enthusiasm he assured his comrades "...that though fallen, he was still unconquered and that we must triumph in the end."[116] Three days later he was dead.[117]

The battlefield was abundantly covered with the spoils of war. For the Alabamians this meant supplies, clothing and blankets. Joab Goodson and his company supplied themselves with blankets, and Goodson later wrote home on stationery picked up from the battlefield. Private James Crowder, Company I, 47th Alabama, found a splendid blanket he described as "the best I ever saw." Writing home September 23, he wrote his mother, "The boys had a fine time plundering the Yankee knapsack," and proudly declared to be "fixed up for the winter."[118]

Suffering of the Wounded

The large number of wounded presented a major logistical problem to the Confederates. The seriously wounded were transported south to makeshift hospitals in Georgia and Alabama. Some of Law's wounded were sent as far south as Augusta, Georgia. However, most were sent to Marietta and Atlanta. The wounded were crowded into cars at the railroad depot for the rough ride southward. After reaching their destination, they were forced to lie in the open by the depot for several days with little or no attention for their wounds. When they reached a hospital it nearly always turned out to be a crowded house or church.[119] Major Coleman, Lieutenants James Lusk, Fred Porter, Ebernezer Coggin and Private James

David King were among the Alabama wounded sent to the Atlanta area.[120]

Coleman was placed in the home of a Major Myers, where his leg wound proved more serious than believed, and his condition grew steadily worse. Within days he lapsed into unconsciousness. In his delirium the young major relived his command of the 4th Alabama, marshaling his comrades, forming his line of battle, and issuing commands to send the regiment against the foe. On October 3, 1863, Coleman fought his final battle, directing his last words to his servant and then to his men: "Frank, load my pistols for me." Then, "Charge boys and give it to them!"[121] Coleman died near the Georgia Military Institute where he had learned the rudiments of military science.

Even though a battlefield wound wasn't always fatal, many of the wounded, like Private James King, Company K, 48th Alabama, later died from causes directly related to their wounds. He suffered violent seizures that shook his body and prevented him from returning to duty. King returned to farming near Jacksonville, Alabama. On January 20, 1868, King and his ten–year–old son left Jacksonville for the family farm. They were traveling over a narrow mountain road in a farm wagon and had just crossed the mountain's crest, when King suddenly experienced an agonizing seizure. He screamed and pitched forward onto the wagon's double-tree where his feet became entangled in the harness. Startled by the screams and extra weight thrashing about, the mules bolted and raced down the mountain road. The young boy grabbed the reins, but was unable to control the runaway team and had to jump from the careening wagon. The mules dragged King over two miles before coming to a stop. Chickamauga had claimed another soldier.[122]

Chapter 10

Affair in Lookout Valley

By nightfall on September 20 hostilities ceased at Chickamauga with Bragg's Army of Tennessee in possession of the battlefield. Rosecrans's Federal army moved toward Chattanooga in disorganized retreat, discouraged by the knowledge that its right wing and its commanding general had fled the field. Virtually everyone on the scene that day expected orders from Bragg to pursue the retreating Federals. Oates, commanding the 15th Alabama, claimed every soldier in his command expected to be on the road behind the fleeing Federal army the night of September 20 or at the latest the morning of September 21. Oates's figured it was only common sense to follow up the victory achieved on Sunday. However, it was not to be. Bragg was content to let Rosecrans's army reach the safety of the fortifications around Chattanooga. "The victory of Chickamauga, won at a fearful cost," Oates later wrote, "was rendered barren by the inaction and lack of enterprise of the commanding general."[1]

When orders were issued to march on September 21, the soldiers of Law's command thought they were to pursue the escaping army. Longstreet delayed until September 22 to commence the march because Polk's wing blocked his route. McLaws was ordered to follow the Federals to Chattanooga while the rest of Longstreet's wing marched to Red House Ford, where the Rossville-Ringgold Road crossed Chickamauga Creek, with the apparent mission of crossing the Tennessee River to get to the rear of the Federal army. The move was aborted, and Longstreet was ordered to march his command to the investment of Chattanooga. Longstreet left early on the September 23, reaching the siege line south of Chattanooga in the early afternoon.[2]

Chattanooga sits on the south bank of the Tennessee River. Bragg's siege line faced north in a six-mile semicircle from the river on the right to Lookout Mountain on the left.[3] Bragg hoped to starve Rosecrans's army by denying it access to its supply base at Stevenson, Alabama.

Rosecrans could not supply his army by the Tennessee because the river was unusable a short distance below Chattanooga due to narrows and rough water known locally as "boiling pots." But, like the siege Longstreet laid against Suffolk in April, Bragg's siege was not complete. Although the Federal soldiers did, indeed, suffer for rations, the Federal army had open communications by two roads. The first was a mountain road over Walden Ridge, northwest of Chattanooga. The other route passed over a rough country road known as Haley's Trace and through Lookout Valley. The Confederates were never able to close the road over Walden Ridge because that route was entirely behind the Federal lines.[4] Further, they waited more than two weeks before closing the Haley Trace/Lookout Valley supply route and blocked its use only temporarily.

Law Is Denied Division Command

After Gettysburg, Law actively sought a commission as major general. On August 18, 1863, Jerome Robertson wrote to Confederate Attorney General Thomas H. Watts on Law's behalf. In a glowing account of Law's qualifications, the Texas doctor wrote, in part:

> "*I have served in the same division with Genl Law for near two years and formed an intimate acquaintance with him. I believe him one of the best officers we have. His long and faithful services entitle him to the promotion and he would give general satisfaction. His capacity will not be doubted by any who know him and under him as our Major Genl we would not feel the change. He has been in command of the division since Genl Hood was wounded and proven his ability by his efficiency in the position. If it will be consistent with your sense of right to render any aid in the promotion of Genl Law you will in my opinion promote the efficiency of the service and do me and the division a great favor.*"[5]

Governor John Gill Shorter sent a letter to the secretary of war on September 2. He added praise of Law's leadership abilities by saying, "There is no more gallant and efficient officer in the service."[6]

Law next obtained the recommendations of two more Alabama politicians, Representatives David Clopton and William P. Chilton. Writing to Davis in early October in a letter co-signed by Shorter, they recommended Law for promotion. They reminded the president that Law commanded Hood's Division with distinction half of the second day and all of the third day at Gettysburg, again at Chickamauga and the nearly three months between. The trio told Davis their wishes represented those of the people of Alabama:

> "*Alabama looks with pride upon her gallant son and therefore take great pleasure in recommending General law for the promotion he desires, and simply desire to say, in conclusion, that it would be particularly gratifying to the people of Alabama, if this event should occur.*"[7]

On the battlefield at Gettysburg, Longstreet praised Law's handling of troops in the repulse of Farnsworth's charge in the evening of July 3.[8] After Chickamauga, Longstreet wrote Law a note of commendation for his work there in command of Hood's Division:

> "*Permit me to express my entire satisfaction and admiration of your distinguished conduct in command of General Hood's Division, in the battle of the 20th inst. I trust you will soon receive the promotion which you so well merit.*"[9]

Law had every reason to believe his own promotion to command Hood's Division was imminent. Longstreet, however, had another idea for his new division commander. Pickett's Division remained in the defenses around Richmond after Longstreet went west, so he had asked for the large South Carolina brigade commanded by Micah Jenkins to augment his First Corps.[10] Jenkins had long been a favorite of Longstreet, who had recommended him for promotion as early as 1861 and made an effort to have him in his command in December 1862.[11] In the words of his aide-de-camp, Longstreet thought Jenkins, "...the best officer he ever saw."[12] According to a newsman, who shared Jenkins's tent while he served under Longstreet, he "...enjoyed the confidence of General Longstreet to a marked degree."[13] When he had the opportunity to utilize Jenkins's services at Suffolk, Longstreet favored him so openly that French believed Longstreet wanted Jenkins to have French's command. A handsome aristocrat from South Carolina, Jenkins had been a schoolmate of Law's at the Citadel, though graduating two classes ahead of Law. He was highly regarded in the army.[14]

Jenkins ranked Law as brigadier by two and a half months.[15] By right of seniority, Jenkins was entitled to command Hood's Division in the absence of the commanding general and could advance to permanent command should Hood be disabled. Until Jenkins arrived in Georgia, Law believed he was in line to succeed to command of Hood's Division. The stage was set for a confrontation between Law and Jenkins.

Colonel Asbury Coward accompanied Jenkins to Georgia as commander of the 5th South Carolina. He graduated from the Citadel in the same class as Jenkins and together they established the King's Mountain Military Institute at Yorkville, South Carolina. The classmates and comrades in arms met at Chester, South Carolina, on September 17 while en route to reinforce Bragg. In the course of their conversation, they discussed Law. Jenkins expressed concern that if Hood was unable to serve, there would be trouble between himself and Law over the command. Jenkins said he could not forget that he outranked Law. Coward suggested nothing more would happen to Hood.[16]

This exchange suggests Jenkins expected to assume command, and perhaps Longstreet told Jenkins that Hood's health would not allow him to continue on active duty. Transfer to Hood's Division gave Jenkins a better chance for higher command. It was not luck alone which brought him to Hood's Division but a conscious effort by Jenkins to change divisions. "I have succeeded in my efforts," he wrote his wife in December, 1863, "and am now in Hood's Division. Here I am senior brigadier and in Hood's absence command the division." Reminding Mrs. Jenkins of his objective, he added, "...where I was before, I was ranked by three brigadiers. It is painful to break up old ties but I feel satisfied that I have decided to my advantage and that of my brigade." In closing, Jenkins suggested his wife report to the Latta family that Law was in good health when Jenkins saw him two days before.[17]

It may be that rumors of Jenkins's efforts to join Hood's Division had reached some of the officers of the division. One historian has suggested these officers asked Hood to return to duty to prevent an outsider taking over the division.[18] The suggestion has credence. Upon his arrival, Jenkins took command of the division and immediately the brigade commanders of Hood's Division petitioned Longstreet to keep Law in command. Claiming to speak for the regimental officers as well, Robertson, Benning and Sheffield assured Longstreet that Law had the "...confidence of all the officers and men of the division." The petition was dated September 22, 1863.[19]

A member and historian of the Texas brigade, Joseph Polley, wrote of Law that the men of Texas had come to "...place a high estimate on his courage and ability and to regard him as the logical successor to General Hood."[20] John Dykes Taylor of the 48th Alabama asserted Jenkins's appointment was "...against the wish of a large majority of the division, both officers and men."[21]

Though the officers and men of Hood's Division respected Law's ability, Longstreet probably gave little thought to the merits of the petition on Law's behalf. Longstreet wanted Jenkins.[22] His note of commendation after Chickamauga was probably offered to placate Law for the loss of division command. Longstreet hoped Law would accept the commendation and go away, leaving Longstreet with his personal choice in command of Hood's Division.

Law was bitterly disappointed. He believed he had earned the command by virtue of his past performance at Gettysburg, Chickamauga and the time between those battles. Beyond his credentials for command, Law claimed Longstreet had promised him the post.[23] He bristled at the injustice. Longstreet's choice particularly galled him. Because both were South Carolinians and former schoolmates at the Citadel, Law and Jenkins had a natural rivalry. In addition, Law had served as an instructor at Jenkins's military school for two years before he relocated to Alabama. It was while they were at military school that and Law and Jenkins clashed. Both he and Jenkins appealed to Hood for help in obtaining command of his division, even though Hood had undergone a battlefield amputation only days before. Although he later gave Law great support in Richmond, in early October Hood supported the appointment of Jenkins, probably because of the difficulty inherent in overlooking Jenkins's seniority. After Law talked with Hood, the wounded general sent Jenkins his wish for his success. Unable to write himself, Hood dictated a note to Jenkins explaining his efforts to convince Law to accept the appointment of Jenkins as a fact. Hood wrote to Jenkins that he "explained explicitly to General Law your position and the circumstances by which you joined the division."[24] Apparently, Hood told Law that Jenkins was transferred to replace Pickett and just happened to be Law's senior in rank. Law was inconsolable, however, and never accepted the appointment of Jenkins to division command.

By the middle of the month, Hood had changed his mind about his successor. On October 14, he responded to a letter from Brigadier General George Washington Custis Lee, serving as advisor to the president, regarding the qualifications of both Jenkins and Law. Hood offered his opinion that both officers were well qualified to hold the rank of major general. Jenkins was too well respected to promote Law, a "junior brigadier," over him. Law, however, had a history with the division and his appointment to command would meet with the approval of the other general officers. Hood suggested Law's promotion would lead to better harmony within the division. The problem could be resolved, Hood believed, if Jenkins were promoted to major general and given command of a division composed of his brigade and the three brigades under Bushrod Johnson. Law, too, would receive the rank of major general under Hood's plan. His command would be the remaining four brigades of Hood's Division. To Hood, the solution to this problem was to promote both men which he believed the president was empowered to do. The tone of the letter suggests Custis Lee had asked Hood's opinion of the consequences of promoting Law over Jenkins.[25]

Perhaps Hood had learned of the petition of the other brigade commanders favoring Law's appointment to lead the division. Custis Lee's letter may have led Hood to believe the president favored the appointment of Law over Jenkins. Law may have been lobbying Hood to support him in his efforts to achieve command of the division. It is not possible, without more information, to know why Hood supported Law for the position on October 14 but did not on October 5. Whatever his reasoning, Hood's plan was not adopted.

In a private meeting on October 10, Longstreet discussed with President Davis the need for a major general for Hood's Division. Longstreet offered Jenkins's name for the post, noting Jenkins already held the command. Davis favored Law for the position on the basis of service with the division. Davis did not order Law's appointment, however, leaving Longstreet free to keep Jenkins in place.[26] Longstreet's position was strong. He could argue that the First Corps operations would be more harmonious if its commander had division commanders of his choice. Neither Law nor the president could oppose the assignment without bringing into question the Confederate seniority system. But the president was unsatisfied. Less than two weeks later, when Hood was promoted to lieutenant general, he again postponed the decision to appoint a commander for Hood's Division. "I have not received the reply which was desired," he wrote to Bragg from Atlanta, "before selecting a commander for General Hood's late division." His letter to Bragg hints that he was troubled by the overt ambition of the brigadiers. But Davis was more annoyed by Longstreet's insistence at having Jenkins command the division when the president believed the appointment would lead to dissatisfaction among its officers and men. He confided to Bragg that experience had taught him that friendship was not necessary for cooperation between officers and that the successful independence of the fledgling Confederacy required men to look beyond personal considerations.[27] The president seemed to wait for Longstreet to change his mind. By the time it was obvious that Longstreet was not going to budge from his position, Davis had waited too long.

Duty on the Siege Line

By September 24 Law's Brigade had taken position on the left of the Confederate line besieging Rosecrans's army as part of Jenkins's division. They deployed between Chattanooga Creek and Lookout Mountain.[28] The men of Law's Brigade were sanguine about their chance to starve out the Federals in Chattanooga when they observed enemy foraging parties hauling dry October cornstalks into camp for use as feed for horses.[29]

Shots were at first exchanged between the Federal soldiers behind their fortifications and the Confederate pickets.[30] During the first day opposite the enemy breastworks, Turner Vaughan's sword belt was shot off and a chess piece shot from his pocket while on picket duty.[31] Private Crowder, 47th Alabama, wrote his mother that while on picket September 28 he was kept awake all night by the constant firing between the lines. Crowder added Company I had sustained eight wounded and one killed in the first five days besieging Chattanooga.[32]

But as each side settled into their routines the familiar and forbidden fraternizing resumed. Some of the Alabamians, like Private Mitchell B. Houghton of the "Glennville Guards," 15th Alabama, traded newspapers and tobacco with the Federal soldiers.[33] Only a week into the siege, after the 4th Alabama had one night advanced their rifle pits to within shouting distance, the enemies were trading quips. At daylight, when the Federal soldiers could see the new picket line, one of them asked the Confederates why they had dug pits. A Southern soldier answered with an invitation to "Come over and see." The Confederate inquired why the Federals had thrown up dirt and logs in front of their own position. "Oh," responded the Federal, "we did that for the shade."[34]

It became so comfortable between the two armies that an agreement to reduce casualties was reached between Jenkins and the Federals opposing him. It was agreed between the commanders on the scene that Chattanooga Creek would serve as the boundary between the two lines. When the 74th Illinois sent men south of the creek, Jenkins warned its commander to honor the agreement or he would drive the Federal soldiers back.[35]

The Alabamians' rifle pits extended into a cornfield in the no-man's-land between the armies. Rations were short for the Confederates as well as the besieged Federals because the surrounding mountain region was ill-suited for extensive agriculture. The corn represented much needed sustenance to both sides. The commander of the 15th Alabama reported heated skirmishes occurred between men of his regiment and their "Yankee neighbors" over ownership of the corn until it was consumed. Oates believed his soldiers got most of the highly prized commodity.[36]

The duty was dull and the weather hot and dry. Perhaps to justify what seemed like wasted time, James Daniel, Company H, 47th Alabama, wrote home that the Federals would have marched right on to Atlanta if Longstreet had not been sent to the Army of Tennessee to reinforce Bragg. Daniel continued with the remark that the Federals were driven back by the Virginia transfers and are only safe behind works because Bragg had previously built the fortifications. Daniel added a veiled warning that they do picket duty every third day where the Federals "shoot at me occasionally but never has hit me yet but its ain't too late yet."[37]

Blocking the Federal Supply Line

On October 4 Law's Brigade was relieved from the battle line and sent to the rear for a short rest.[38] On October 9, Bowles was ordered to take the 4th Alabama west of Lookout Mountain into Lookout Valley. The valley lay between Lookout Mountain and Raccoon Mountain and ran north to the Tennessee River. His orders were to move to the point where Raccoon Mountain overlooked the Tennessee River and blockade the wagon road on the opposite bank.[39]

At this point the road, known as Haley's Trace, followed a narrow shelf between the river and the almost vertical wall at the base of Walden's Ridge. Federal supply trains from occupied Alabama had to pass along this narrow path to get to Chattanooga. As it was impossible to turn wagons on this narrow ledge, eight or ten sharpshooters detailed to the 4th Alabama followed the simple expedient of shooting the mules pulling the Federal supply wagons bound for Chattanooga. Hood's Division had a six-man squad of sharpshooters, comprised of Texans, Georgians and one Alabamian, who carried the English made Whitworth rifle. Using the sniper rifles brought from Virginia, sharpshooters, or scouts, as they were also known, made the road impassable.[40]

The first targeted train came onto the narrow trail at sunrise, its teamsters "whistling and cracking their whips in a merry mood, intirely (sic) unsuspecting of the impending danger." The lead wagon was allowed to reach almost to the end of the bottleneck before the first Whitworth was fired, exposing perhaps two miles of wagons. Once the lead mules were knocked down, all of the 4th Alabama opened fire on the train's mules with their Enfield rifles. The teamsters scrambled to safety while the Alabamians concentrated on the animals. Under orders to kill all the mules, they fired their Enfields nearly all day. At four hundred yards' distance, the soldiers were hard pressed to hit the flouncing, terrified beasts. At day's end, one charmed mule still stood, "in sleepy composure," untouched by the many bullets directed at it. About mid-day, the Federals opened fire at the 4th Alabama. Their fire was ineffective and did not hinder the bloody work of the Alabamians. Some of the men disliked shooting the mules but upon reflection, decided it was better than shooting men.[41] Adjutant Coles wrote of one occasion when two mules were killed with one shot. A single bullet passed through the neck of both animals as they stood next to each other in harness.[42]

The 15th Alabama followed the next day, bringing a section of Captain Overton W. Barrett's Missouri Battery which the men had to manhandle over the rugged mountain road.[43] Infantry was detailed to transfer the artillery in an effort to prevent the Federals across the river from knowing of the move. Since the route over Lookout Mountain was under the enemy guns on Moccasin Point, the Alabamians moved into the valley under cover of darkness.[44] The 15th deployed along the river's edge from Raccoon Mountain to Brown's Ferry to protect the sharpshooters of the 4th Alabama from a surprise enemy movement across the river.[45] The line occupied by Law's two regiments was about five miles long.[46]

Longstreet asked Law to study the ground in the valley and ascertain the force necessary to prevent a Federal crossing between Raccoon Mountain and Lookout Mountain.

Law spent a day doing so and reported that a strong division was required to secure the valley.[47] But when Longstreet asked Law if he would defend the valley with his brigade, Law accepted the job without argument.[48] Despite his later claim that it was a great risk to defend Lookout Valley with one brigade, Law's only caveat was that his brigade be assigned exclusively to that duty. Law's plan to defend the valley was to blockade Haley's Trace and picket the river with two regiments, keeping the other three regiments of his brigade and Barrett's section of 12–pound howitzers in reserve to throw at any enemy assault force before a lodgment could be effected.[49]

The 9th Kentucky Cavalry Regiment and some Tennessee cavalrymen were assigned to report to Law any movement of the Federal army from Bridgeport, Alabama, at his rear.[50] Law also sent scouting parties across the river at Williams Island to report any sign that the Federals might attempt a crossing.[51]

For two weeks the situation was quiet. The Federal army could not use the Nashville and Chattanooga Railroad, which the Confederates controlled at the foot of Lookout Mountain, nor Haley's Trace near the river. Federal supplies had to go over Walden's Ridge by mule train, a trip requiring up to eight days, and rations for the Northern soldiers were soon greatly reduced.[52] Rains in early and mid-October turned the roads over Walden Ridge into quagmires, further reducing the rations for the besieged troops in Chattanooga.

The rain also made life miserable for the Alabamians in Lookout Valley. It rained almost without interruption from October 11 through October 15, swelling the creeks in the valley so the daily supply run, maintained by one old mule, could not reach the 4th Alabama on Raccoon Mountain.[53] For rations they relied on stray sheep and hogs that they were able to kill in the vicinity.[54] To add to the discomfort caused by irregular rations, one private in the 15th Alabama recalled the "constant downpour of rain made the bread an unsavory mush."[55]

Law left the valley on the morning of October 25 to visit Hood's bedside, some thirty miles distance in the Armuchee Valley of Georgia.[56] While Law was away, Jenkins ordered the 44th, 47th and 48th Alabama regiments returned to the east side of Lookout Mountain. Two of the regiments were ordered to encamp along the Chattanooga Valley Road, the third to relieve the pickets of Benning's Brigade opposite the Chattanooga fortifications.[57] The force in Lookout Valley was thus reduced to only two regiments and two cannon. In this troop movement, which Law said was made "without rhyme or reason," the Alabamians probably served as little more than pawns in the rivalry between Law and Jenkins.[58] Though not serious on its face, the troop movement is the sort of irritant one might inflict upon a subordinate in the hope of driving him away. As it turned out, the move resulted in serious consequences for the Confederate army.

Later, Law suggested the move had a more sinister character. "Why had those regiments been ordered away?" he asked. "Was it part of the game of "cross purposes" at which our commanders seemed so fond of playing?" Although he did not categorically state he believed Longstreet and Jenkins had hoped to see him fail in Lookout Valley, regardless of the cost to the Confederacy, that is what he meant. In Law's view, reopening the supply line to the Federals bottled up in Chattanooga was the first step toward the disaster which befell Bragg's army. The second was the detachment of Longstreet to oppose Burnside in east Tennessee.[59]

Upon his return Law reported to the east side of the mountain, where the Confederate siege line was located, instead of Lookout Valley, where his brigade had been deployed, because he was scheduled to be in command of the division while Jenkins was away for a few days.[60] Despite irritation at the transfer of part of his command, Law could not reassign his three regiments to the valley without military reason. To the Confederates' great surprise and regret, there would be good reason to move Law's troops back into the valley.

The Capture of Brown's Ferry

The importance of Lookout Valley to the Federal army besieged in Chattanooga seemed to have escaped the notice of the Confederate high command.[61] This narrow strip of land between Raccoon and Lookout Mountains was the only avenue by which the Federal forces could supply themselves with an adequate volume of rations. If they could control the valley, the Federals could receive supplies by two roads from the depot at Bridgeport, Alabama. The first was from Trenton, farther up the valley, the other by Running Water Gorge through Raccoon Mountain. Both converged at the railroad station in Wauhatchie, about three miles up the valley from Brown's Ferry. The Confederate artillery on Lookout Mountain did not have the range to reach the supply road through Lookout Valley.

At Bragg's order, Longstreet sent riflemen to the base of Raccoon Mountain to blockade Haley's Trace and temporarily acquiesced in Law's request that the rest of his Alabamians be sent into the valley, but did nothing else to secure Lookout Valley for the Confederacy. While many Confederate soldiers must have wondered, as Joab Goodson did, "what our generals are up to," the Federal command prepared to break the blockade of Chattanooga.[62]

The plan to end the Confederate blockade was a bold one, calling for secrecy and coordination. The left bank of the river between Raccoon Mountain and Lookout Creek, occupied by the Confederates, was high and steep, rising perhaps 100 feet above the water. Through this bank were two breaks, one where the road reached Brown's Ferry, the second where a creek emptied into the Tennessee River above the ferry. The action required a force of infantry to float down the swift-flowing river from Chattanooga, a distance of approximately nine miles, to land at the two breaks in the river bank, establish a bridgehead, and bring reinforcements in the same boats across the river at Moccasin Point. Another body of troops, men of the XI and XII Corps under command of Major General Joseph "Fighting Joe" Hooker, sent from Virginia, would join the first by marching down Lookout Valley from Bridgeport.[63] The troops selected to make the float trip were part of Brigadier General William B. Hazen's brigade.

Hazen's assault force placed about 1,600 troops aboard fifty pontoon boats and two flat-bottom boats. The rest of Hazen's brigade joined the brigade of John Turchin as reinforcements for the landing party, marching in secret to the woods opposite the landing site at the ferry. The flotilla left the Chattanooga wharves at 3:00 a.m. on October 27, crossed to the opposite bank of the Tennessee, and, hugging the trees, floated quietly downstream, using oars only to steer. Passing perhaps seven miles of Confederate picket lines, they attracted no attention, even when a soldier was knocked from his boat by a low-hanging branch.[64]

Deployed astride the severed Federal supply route through Lookout Valley was the Alabama infantry under the command of William C. Oates. Oates's mission was to prevent the 4th Alabama sharpshooters from being cut off and captured. To accomplish his mission, the colonel placed five companies on picket along the river with six companies in reserve, perhaps a mile distant.[65] The men were thinly stretched along the river bank, "three to five men at a post," recalled Sergeant Billy Jordan, "at intervals from two hundred to four hundred yards apart."[66]

In the early evening of October 26, Oates was warned of a large Federal force crossing the river at Bridgeport which would soon be to his rear in Lookout Valley. Oates immediately sent a courier to Longstreet with his warning that a Federal attack against his position was imminent. Oates later claimed Longstreet had the message by midnight.[67] Longstreet took no action in response to this warning.

Company B, the "Midway Guards", commanded by Captain Noah Feagin, was on picket at the ferry. Using a small cabin as their company headquarters, the captain and Orderly Sergeant Billy Jordan were awakened before daylight by the shouts of a sentry that "Yankees are coming."[68] Feagin soon found himself in the unenviable position of commanding a company in retreat. Jordan was detailed to go for Oates and the reserves. Riding a calico pony belonging to a cavalry private who had been assigned as a courier in case of trouble, Jordan was dispatched instead because the cavalryman did not know the way to Oates's headquarters.[69]

Alerted by the firing, the colonel was waiting for a report. After receiving the intelligence that a landing had been made, forcing Feagin back, Oates ordered the reserves forward. Captain Shaaff's Company A and Company G, under command of Captain Waddell, led at the double-quick.[70] In his report of the affair Law estimated this reserve force at 150 men.[71]

The Alabamians, according to Hazen, who accompanied the amphibious force from Chattanooga, "came boldly up, along nearly our entire front," but the Federals' audacious enterprise was not to be stopped by a few Butternuts from Alabama.[72] Oates ordered Waddell and Shaaff to walk their men right into the enemy ranks, each man "to place the muzzle of his rifle against the body of a Yankee when he fired." Even this extraordinary action only delayed the Federal troops momentarily, though it might have succeeded had Federal troops not kept coming ashore. The new arrivals fired on Oates's right. He put in Company K, then another and another, until all six were in action but Oates could not cover the Federal line with his small force. Oates put in all the reserves he had but could not drive the landing party into the river.[73]

There was little the men of the 15th Alabama could do. They were surprised by a superior force and driven back. They abandoned their camp, leaving cooking equipment, tents, and clothes to the enemy.[74] Feagin got away with his horse but not his saddle. Oates sent Jordan to relieve the other companies along the river. Captain Leigh Terrell, Law's adjutant, went to get the 4th Alabama from Raccoon Mountain.

Casualties suffered by the 15th Alabama were six killed and fourteen wounded, including Oates, severely wounded in the hip. The colonel escaped capture only with the aid of two soldiers of his regiment who assisted him from the field. Oates was helped onto his horse and started for Lookout Mountain. Just before reaching the bridge over Lookout Creek, the colonel met the brigade surgeon, Doctor William O. Hudson, who put Oates in a nearby house for immediate treatment, over the objections of the mistress of the house, who did not want a "nasty rebel" in her home.[75]

The men of the 4th Alabama were aware of the fight taking place at the ferry landing, growing apprehensive about the prospects of being cut off by a crossing of enemy troops into Lookout Valley. Soon after the firing stopped, pickets rushed into camp with word that Federals had driven the 15th Alabama from the river's edge and wounded Oates. By Adjutant Coles's account, Companies D and I, on picket duty, were called in and the other members of the 4th Alabama were told "to get out the best they could."[76] The regiment's mule was loaded with the camp equipment but became excited and broke away, "braying and kicking down the mountain trail, the boys laughing and yelling and picking up scattered utensils." When recaptured the mule had one skillet handle on its back.[77]

To escape capture the 4th Alabama had to cross the valley, past the front of the Federal force just landed. They anticipated an attack from the enemy at any moment. Led by Bowles, the 4th met remnants of the 15th and the two Napoleons of Barrett's Battery engaged with Federal skirmishers. Bowles deployed flankers on his left and moved the entire force across the valley, across the bridge over Lookout Creek, to the security of Lookout Mountain.[78]

Law came over the mountain with his three other regiments and Robertson's Brigade during the morning. After meeting with Oates and looking at the Federal position himself, Law decided nothing could be done with the forces at hand except align his troops to protect the withdrawal of the 4th and 15th Alabama and the artillery. He then reported to Longstreet that the Federal lodgment had been made at Brown's Ferry.[79] News of the landing reached division headquarters by 7 a.m. Longstreet ordered Law to move the 44th, 47th and 48th Alabama regiments back into the valley. When he arrived, Law found the Federals, now about 6,000 strong, fortified on the elevations near Brown's Ferry.[80]

Axes had been issued to the Federal landing party, which immediately set to work building abatis on the captured ridge. After the boats discharged their first passengers, they crossed to the right bank to take on more men. The remaining soldiers of the assaulting party were loaded and rowed across without delay. Colonel Timothy R. Stanley, 18th Ohio, in charge of the boats, recalled "the whole force were ferried, 5,000 men, in less than one hour." By 4:30 in the afternoon, a pontoon bridge spanned the Tennessee adjacent to Brown's Ferry, the product of the efficient Federal engineers.[81]

Law reported to Longstreet on Lookout Mountain during the morning. Longstreet wanted to know about the Federal position and manpower at the ferry and whether it was feasible to attack. Law believed the Federal lodgment was too strong and cautioned against attacking. He suggested instead the column coming from Bridgeport should be destroyed before it could link up with the landing party already in the valley. "But with a fatality which seemed to follow every movement of the Confederates around Chattanooga," Law later wrote, "this bold and promising course was not adopted."[82] Major John P. Austin's 9th Kentucky Cavalry had encountered the Federal detachment under Hooker at Shellmound, and word of its movement toward Brown's Ferry was hurried back to Law, reaching him on the evening of the October 27.[83]

But Longstreet believed the Federal army planned to move troops across the valley near Trenton and flank the Confederates by moving down the crest of Lookout Mountain to his rear. In four extant notes to headquarters, written on October 26 and 27, Longstreet offered his opinion that Hooker's command was moving against his rear by Johnson's Crook and presented his plan to counter the action. "I have no doubt," Longstreet emphasized, "but the enemy will cross below and move against our rear. It is his easiest and safest move." He believed the landing at Brown's Ferry was a diversion, designed to cover the enemy's real intention of striking at his rear via Johnson's Crook, thus breaking the investment of Chattanooga. Longstreet proposed sending a brigade to Johnson's Crook unless he received word to the contrary from Bragg.[84] At 8:45 p.m., he detailed Sorrel to order Jenkins to prepare his division, except Law's Brigade, for a move toward Trenton at daylight, October 28.[85] By that evening, however, Hooker's column was approaching Law's Brigade, which was now deployed along the east bank of Lookout Creek. The Federal force in Lookout Valley was now a formidable one.

The link-up of the troops from Bridgeport and those landed at Brown's Ferry was accomplished on the afternoon of October 28, prompting an 8 p.m. wire from Major General U. S. Grant to Halleck: "The question of supplies may now be regarded as settled." The siege of Chattanooga had been broken.[86]

From atop Lookout Mountain, Bragg and Longstreet watched the XI Corps divisions of Brigadier General Adolph von Steinwehr and Major General Carl Schurz and Brigadier General John W. Geary's division of the XII Corps march down the Valley Road toward

Brown's Ferry.[87] At the railroad platform at Wauhatchie the Federals dropped off about 1,500 infantry and four guns of Knapp's battery, under the direction of Captain James A. Atwell. Geary remained at Wauhatchie to command the rear guard.

When Bragg learned of the landing at Brown's Ferry, he ordered Longstreet to make the necessary arrangements to immediately dislodge the Federal landing party from the left bank. In a letter to Davis, Bragg complained that no attack was offered so he renewed the order, this time giving Longstreet the use of a third division. It was to witness this fight that Bragg was atop Lookout Mountain at 10 a.m. on October 28. But the commanding general learned that Longstreet had still made no plans for an attack against the Federal landing party. As the two generals talked, Hooker's column came into view. Although Bragg at first refused to credit the report that Federals were marching through Lookout Valley, after observing the enemy column himself had no choice but to accept the news as fact.[88]

Night Fight at Wauhatchie

Bragg's siege of Chattanooga was finished if Lookout Valley was not again closed to the Federals. For the third time he demanded action from Longstreet, who responded with a night attack against the Federal detachment at Wauhatchie.[89] The attack was executed in two parts. Jenkins's Brigade of South Carolinians, commanded by Colonel John Bratton, was ordered to attack the Federal detachment at Wauhatchie while Law, supported by Robertson, was to block the Federal forces at Brown's Ferry should they attempt to reinforce Geary's command.[90] Benning, positioned between Bratton and Law, was to protect Bratton's withdrawal if the enemy force "proved too strong for him."[91]

The Federal detachment under Geary's command at Wauhatchie was about three miles from the main force at Brown's Ferry. The Valley Road, running north and south through Lookout Valley, connected Wauhatchie with the ferry. Between the road and Lookout Mountain was Lookout Creek, flowing through the valley to the Tennessee River and a series of hills, called "hogbacks" by the Confederate soldiers, both parallel to the road.[92] The road was out of the range of Alexander's cannons and the area covered by the hogbacks was not visible to observers on the mountain. Lookout Creek was spanned by two bridges, both without planking by this time. One was near where the Chattanooga and Nashville Railroad and the Chattanooga Road pass between the mountain and the river. The other was up the valley toward Wauhatchie. Jenkins's soldiers controlled both bridges.[93]

Late in the afternoon, Longstreet sent Law a note directing him to cross the lower bridge over Lookout Creek and gain possession of the intersection of the Valley Road and the Chattanooga Road "and capture any trains that might attempt to pass." Jenkins noted in his report of the night fight that Law was chosen to command the two blocking brigades because he knew the ground.[94] A short time later, Law met with Jenkins and learned the particulars of the plan for the night attack. The idea, as Law understood it, was to cross Lookout Creek "to cut off the enemy's trains and capture the rear guard and stragglers." Law considered the proposal unworkable and criticized it as dangerous. But Jenkins told Law he had positive orders to proceed on the expedition.[95]

Law received a report from a courier that Bratton's command was in motion, the signal to move his own.[96] Law's Brigade moved cautiously forward. Captain Thomas Eubanks led the advance with skirmishers, crossing the lower bridge between 7:30 and 8 p.m., to a clearing bounded by the "hogbacks" to the west, the Chattanooga Road to the south, the Tennessee River to the north and Lookout Creek. Here the men formed in line of battle of one rank per regiment and moved to the ridge, climbed to its narrow crest, and hastily built

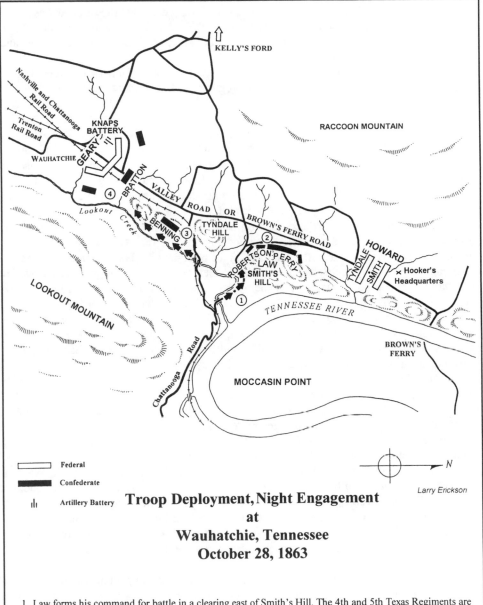

KELLY'S FORD

Nashville and Chattanooga Rail Road

Trenton Rail Road

KNAPS BATTERY

WAUHATCHIE

GEARY

BRATTON

VALLEY ROAD OR BROWN'S FERRY ROAD

Lookout Creek

BENNING

TYNDALE HILL

RACCOON MOUNTAIN

LOOKOUT MOUNTAIN

Chattanooga Road

ROBERTSON PERRY

LAW

SMITH'S HILL

TYNDALE

HOWARD

SMITH

× Hooker's Headquarters

TENNESSEE RIVER

MOCCASIN POINT

BROWN'S FERRY

Federal

Confederate

Artillery Battery

Larry Erickson

N

Troop Deployment, Night Engagement
at
Wauhatchie, Tennessee
October 28, 1863

1. Law forms his command for battle in a clearing east of Smith's Hill. The 4th and 5th Texas Regiments are ordered to remain in the clearing in reserve.
2. Law moves forward to Smith's Hill and places his own and Robertson's Brigade in ambush along the Brown's Ferry Road. The 1st Texas Regiment pickets the Chattanooga Road. The 3rd Arkansas is posted on the extreme left of Law's line. The order of battle of Law's Brigade is, left to right, 48th Alabama, 47th Alabama, 4th Alabama, 44th Alabama, and the 15th Alabama. Company G, 15th Alabama, is refused perpendicular to the road.
3. Benning is in position to Law's left.
4. Bratton advances toward Wauhatchie and attacks Geary.

breastworks from available material.[97] It was soon discovered that the brigade was not in its assigned position, that another hill lay between the occupied hill and the Valley Road. Skirmishers were sent to the hogback which overlooked the road between Wauhatchie and Brown's Ferry and found it unoccupied.[98]

Robertson's Texas brigade now joined Law. As senior brigadier, Law assumed command of both brigades. Two of Robertson's regiments, the 3rd Arkansas and 1st Texas, were placed in line with the Alabama troops, on the left. The 4th and 5th Texas regiments remained as reserve in the clearing where Law's command had formed for battle.[99]

Law's Brigade and Robertson's two regiments, led by the 4th and the 48th Alabama regiments, moved onto the elevation directly overlooking the road, climbed to its narrow summit, and threw up fortifications of logs.[100] Only loose timber could be used because the sound of axes would have alerted the Federals to Law's position.[101] This hill would become known as Smith's Hill, named for the commanding officer of the Federal brigade that would assault it before the night had passed.

Federal skirmishers were discovered on both sides of the Chattanooga Road as the brigade moved onto the ridge. Sheffield turned Captain Norman H. McDuffie's company left to meet the danger. McDuffie captured eight prisoners.[102] The Federals remained in the area, however. Captain Eubanks and several men of the 48th Alabama exchanged fire with those on the left of the ridge. The enemy troops were a 180 man patrol from the 141st New York Infantry, commanded by Major Charles W. Clanharty.[103] Three privates were severely wounded and Eubanks mortally wounded. Eubanks and the others were shot by Federal soldiers who had surrendered to them, then fired when the Confederates had relaxed their guard. Sergeant Taylor recalled with some bitterness that Eubanks "was the victim of the treachery of men whose lives he had saved."[104]

The attacking force, led by Bratton, crossed the upper bridge, and followed the road to its intersection with the Valley Road. This was the first time the South Carolinians had been west of Lookout Mountain and Bratton was led to his position by scouts supplied by the 4th Alabama.[105] Just past the bridge, the road passes between two hills. The one to the north would become known as Tyndale's Hill, after Brigadier General Hector Tyndale, leader of the attacking force which climbed the hill.[106]

The Federal rear guard at Wauhatchie under command of Geary, a Mexican War veteran, was not to be taken by surprise. Geary was aware that the signal station on Lookout Mountain had observed his movements since entering the valley and he, in turn, had seen its signaling. With a thoroughness that must have served him well in successful political campaigns as the first mayor of San Francisco and the governor of Pennsylvania, Geary prepared for an attack, even one at night. The men were directed to bivouac under arms, wearing their cartridge boxes.[107]

Colonel William Rickards, Jr., in command of the 29th Pennsylvania, learned the Confederates were just on the other side of Lookout Creek, no more than a mile and a quarter away. He also located the upper bridge over the creek. This intelligence was passed on to his commanding officer, who accordingly placed the 29th Pennsylvania on picket duty around the command with two companies on the road to the north of his camp, leading to the bridge over Lookout Creek.[108] Alert to danger, they waited.

About 10:30 p. m. Geary heard firing to the north and put his command under arms. This was the action on the south side of Smith's Hill involving the 48th Alabama and the stubborn Federal skirmishers that had resulted in Eubanks's death. When they learned the action would not involve them, Geary's men relaxed again. It remained quiet until 12:30 in the morning of October 29, when Bratton assaulted Geary's command.[109]

Wauhatchie was a small battle in the war, but it was an intense fight. Geary's nearly 1,500 men were not surprised and were in good defensive positions when the action began. In addition, the Federals had the added firepower of an artillery battery, while Bratton's troops had no artillery. Bratton's command outnumbered the Federal force by only a few hundred, not enough of an advantage for a night offensive against a well-positioned foe and without surprise.[110] The Confederates attacked the center and both flanks of the Federals' box formation. The exchange resulted in more than 200 casualties for Geary's command and over 350 casualties for the Confederates. It is a credit to the fighting spirit of the South Carolinians that they inflicted so great a percentage of casualties upon the Federal rear guard at Wauhatchie. Among the Federal dead was Lieutenant Edward R. Geary, the general's son.[111]

The rattle of musketry and the booming of artillery awakened the Federal troops camped in the vicinity of Brown's Ferry shortly before one o'clock in the morning of October 29.[112] Elements of Schurz's and Steinwehr's commands were moving to the relief of the detachment at Wauhatchie within half an hour. The relief column took the Valley Road which passed directly under the guns of the Alabamians, Arkansans and Texans on Smith's Hill.

The rough contours of Smith's Hill forced the road to curve away from the northern base of the hogback about two hundred yards. Law's line thus ran from as close as 30 paces from the Valley Road at its junction with the Chattanooga Road to as far as 200 yards away from the road on the line's extreme right. Law's Brigade spread out along the summit with the 48th Alabama on the left, the 47th Alabama on its right, the 4th Alabama in the middle, the 44th Alabama next, and the 15th Alabama on the right. The right company, Company G, of the 15th Alabama, was refused perpendicular to the brigade line across the top of the hill to protect against a surprise from the right flank. Each regiment threw out a picket line to its front. The 1st Texas, picketing the Chattanooga Road, and the 3rd Arkansas were on the left of Law's line but these two regiments were only lightly used.[113]

Although Law was sent to blockade the Valley Road, he did not place his troops astride the road. Instead he deployed his troops in the safer position of an ambush parallel to the road. Indeed, when Law considered the numbers he commanded against those of the opposing forces and the topography of the valley, he could only believe it foolhardy to put his force astride the road. Such a position would have been untenable. Law sought to minimize casualties in his command. He believed Longstreet's order was ill-advised and contrary to orders deployed his force as an ambush, probably with the rationale that he was only acting with the latitude normally granted the commander on the scene. Alexander, Longstreet's artillery chief, suggested Law chose the deployment on Smith's Hill instead of blocking the road "because he was too conscious of his weakness. His retreat was more assured and easier from the position which he took." Alexander supported Law's decision as "the more prudent course." He believed Law's command had little chance to stop the Federal column.[114]

Whether Longstreet cared if Law positioned his brigades across the road is not known. Jenkins, the commander of the operation, knew Law planned to occupy the hogbacks overlooking the Valley Road.[115] As the Federal reinforcements marched toward Wauhatchie, Law's command could fire into their left flank from Smith's Hill, but the Federal soldiers could—and did—move from the road in the direction of Raccoon Mountain to avoid the fire and continue on to Wauhatchie, leaving the immobile ambush behind the logs on Smith's Hill.

Listening to the battle at Wauhatchie, the Alabamians anxiously awaited their turn, their fighting blood roused by what they knew was to come.[116] Sheffield notified Law of the approaching Federal column, led by Tyndale's brigade of Schurz's Third Division, XI Corps. Law ordered the skirmishers back to the line and waited for the head of the column to reach the left of his position before firing. The Confederate fire scattered the Federals, sending the leading elements into the field west of the road. Tyndale's men attempted to reform in the south end of the field, but fire from the 48th Alabama and 3rd Arkansas again threw the Federal troops into confusion. Tyndale's New Yorkers and Midwesterners moved some distance through a bog and back onto the road, reforming near Tyndale's Hill.[117]

When the head of the column came under fire, the brigade following Tyndale, commanded by Colonel Orland Smith, Steinwehr's division, formed to attack Law. Sometime after 2:00 a.m., the 73rd Ohio and 33rd Massachusetts formed their line of battle in preparation for their assault against Law's barricaded brigade on Smith's Hill.[118] The attacking force climbing Smith's Hill had the disadvantage of attacking an enemy behind cover. Smith's men had one advantage, however. Because they were hidden by thick underbrush, they advanced halfway to the summit before they began to take casualties.[119] Nevertheless, during the assault against Smith's Hill, a third of the 33rd Massachusetts were killed or wounded, and half the line officers and a third of the rank and file of the 73rd Ohio were struck down.[120]

As the Federal line moved up the hill from the road, the two regiments lost alignment with each other and the 33rd Massachusetts was slowed by a deep ravine across its path. The 73rd Ohio emerged from the woods in front of the 47th and 4th Alabama regiments, who poured a destructive fire into the Ohioans. Adding to the discomfort of the men of the 73rd Ohio was the enfilading fire of the 48th Alabama upon its right flank. The angle between the road and the crest of the hill gave the Alabamians on the left the opportunity to fire at the right flank of the 73rd Ohio as it closed with the 47th and 4th Alabama. The 73rd Ohio withdrew into the cover of the tree line.

The 44th and 15th Alabama received the attack of the 33rd Massachusetts as the New Englanders burst from the trees only twenty yards from the Alabamians' breastworks. The first volley felled sixty members of the Massachusetts regiment.[121] They pressed so close against the Confederate line that their faces were blackened by powder from the guns of the Alabamians. Wadding from the guns of the New England soldiers fell in the Confederate breastworks.[122] Gun flashes revealed Federal flags were within five steps of the Southerners' fortifications.[123] The 33rd received an enfilading fire from the 44th Alabama on its right just as the Ohioans had from the 48th Alabama because the warring lines were not parallel. The men from the Bay State moved out of harm's way to reorganize near the bottom of the hill. When the Federals fell back, the Alabama soldiers could hear the officers rallying their men to reform. On the hill the Alabamians reloaded and fixed bayonets to meet the next assault.[124]

During the quiet following the first charge, Law realized the firing at Wauhatchie had stopped. A message was dispatched to Jenkins, warning him that the Federals could send reinforcements to Geary by moving behind those forces then engaging Law's command. A few moments later, Captain D. R. Jamison, of Jenkins's staff, arrived to inform Law that the Carolinians had encountered a large force at Wauhatchie and Jenkins wished Law to hold his position as Jenkins withdrew to Lookout Creek. Messages were now flying between the Confederate officers. Law received a second courier from Jenkins, bearing, as Law termed it, "substantially the same message delivered by Captain Jamison, and informed me further that Colonel Bratton's command was at the creek."[125]

Before the action resumed on Smith's Hill, Robertson notified Law of the presence of the enemy on the river road and in the woods north of the field where the Confederates had formed for battle. Robertson's report was substantiated by Alabama pickets on the right flank.[126] The force on the right was the 136th New York of Smith's brigade. Two companies of the 136th New York had been detached to skirmish up the smaller hill about 200 yards north of Smith's Hill while the rest of the regiment remained at the foot of the hill in line of battle perpendicular to the Valley Road.[127]

Robertson did not know the size of this Federal detachment coming over the hill but realized it would be in position to flank Law's men if it continued into the field where the Confederate blocking force had formed earlier. If such a flanking move succeeded, Robertson knew, it would block the only avenue of retreat open to Law's command and leave it virtually surrounded.

To counter this flanking movement, Law ordered Robertson to send forward the 4th Texas which was placed on the extreme right by Leigh Terrell. The 5th Texas was ordered to secure the bridge spanning Lookout Creek and picket the Chattanooga Road.[128]

Robertson, observing the troop movements around Smith's Hill from his excellent vantage point, feared too much uncovered ground lay between Law and the river, space where Federal soldiers could be concealed. He sent two men into that area to learn what they could of the enemy. In their haste to obey his order, they left before he learned their names and, to Robertson's regret, never returned.[129]

The determined soldiers of the 33rd Massachusetts launched another attack, this time directly against the fronts of the 44th and 15th regiments. Sheffield reported "the 44th Alabama, having given way," the Federals succeeded in breaking the juncture between the 44th and 15th regiments, pushing back parts of both of these units. The break was the result of moving two companies, one each from the 15th and the 44th Alabama, to support the single company on picket on the right just prior to the second Federal assault.[130] The right companies of the 44th and 15th regiments were moved to support the refused company of the 15th Alabama which served to protect the right flank of the brigade. The 44th did not extend its line to the right nor did the 15th extend its line to the left, probably because the troops were entrenched. The detachment left a gap of at least 30 yards between the 44th and 15th Alabama regiments.[131] The movement of the two companies of the 136th New York on his right made Sheffield apprehensive of an attack from that direction. He moved the two additional companies there to secure a supposed weak spot. Law had moved the 4th Texas to the right flank for the same reason. The 33rd Massachusetts was quick to exploit the gap left in the Alabama line by the shift of these two companies.

After breaking the connection between the 15th and 44th Alabama regiments, the 33rd Massachusetts turned to the right and pushed the 44th out of its entrenchments. On the right of the 44th Alabama, Waddell, commanding the left company of the 15th Alabama, began to receive fire from the rear. Waddell ordered his company to attack the 33rd Massachusetts within the Confederate breastworks but, even as he drove these Federals, more attacked him from the gap he left in the original line.[132]

It was a critical moment for Law's Brigade. Sheffield immediately directed Lieutenant Colonel Scruggs to wheel the 4th Alabama, which had driven the enemy from its own front, over to fill the gap. The 44th Alabama then rallied, and the Alabamians drove the attackers off the crest in hand-to-hand combat. It was an unforgettable moment for Major Mack Robbins. As minie balls whizzed along the line from enfilading fire from both sides, the shouting, cursing lines co-mingled. He recalled the night fight in Lookout Valley as a thrilling experience.[133]

Waddell saw the 44th Alabama, or at least those companies he could make out, falling back. He was taking fire from the front and rear. Waddell gave the order for his company to retire which caused the whole of the 15th Alabama to retreat.[134] Waddell did not realize

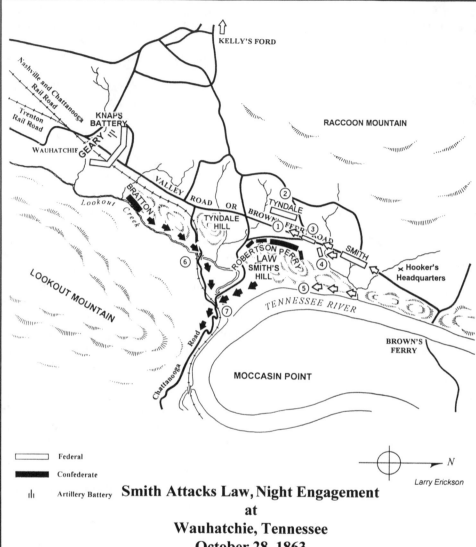

Federal

Confidential

ılı Artillery Battery

Smith Attacks Law, Night Engagement
at
Wauhatchie, Tennessee
October 28, 1863

Larry Erickson

1. Tyndale moves along the Brown's Ferry's Road toward the sound of fighting at Wauhatchie. When the head of the column passes Law's left, Law orders his command to open fire.
2. Tyndale's brigade moves into the field west of the road.
3. The 73rd Ohio and 33rd Massachusetts, of Smith's brigade, form into battle lines at the foot of Smith's Hill. The 73rd Ohio is on the right of the 33rd Massachusetts.
4. The 136th New York attacks up the north face of Smith's Hill against Law's right flank.
5. Federal troops are observed advancing between the river and Smith's Hill.
6. Bratton crosses Lookout Creek by the upper bridge.
7. Law's command crosses Lookout Creek by the lower bridge.

the 44th Alabama had reestablished its line. In the night, it appeared to the companies to the right of the 44th Alabama that the brigade was in retreat. Only the 15th Alabama retreated, however. Lowther left the 15th Alabama to help rally the 44th Alabama. After the 44th was again in line, he ran back to the 15th, but arrived just in time to see the regiment give way. He claimed the retreat was done in "pretty good order."[135]

Law issued the order to withdraw past the first hill to the field where the command had initially formed. He considered this the time to give up an enterprise he had thought ill-advised from the beginning. His brigade had withstood two assaults by a strong and determined enemy, he had reports of a Federal flanking movement to cut off his line of retreat, and Jenkins's command had withdrawn to the creek, ending the need for his presence. The 1st Texas covered the field as the rest of the command withdrew. While they moved toward the bridge, Sheffield could see Federal troops on the left flank and received a report of more enemy soldiers moving in his direction from the river.[136]

Law's command withdrew across the Lookout Creek bridge in a leisurely and orderly fashion. For some of the blocking force, however, the departure from Smith's Hill was not accomplished in an orderly fashion. The manner in which a part of Law's and Robertson's Brigades withdrew rather than their conduct while in place probably led to Longstreet's accusation that they abandoned their position. From their position on the right flank, members of the 4th Texas became aware that part of the 15th Alabama was falling back. If the Alabamians left Smith's Hill, the Texans were in danger of being surrounded. Some of the veterans of the 4th Texas believed themselves abandoned by the Alabamians and flanked. They withdrew toward Lookout Creek in spectacular fashion. The men of the 4th Texas had to endure a great deal of good-natured ribbing over the incident from the other Texas regiments during the next few days.[137] Billy Jordan of the 15th Alabama claimed "the Texans came out before being properly formed, hallooing "routed, routed.""[138]

The panic in the dark was contagious. In his reminiscences of the war, Jordan frankly stated his own company, while leaving the crest of Smith's Hill, "retreated in great confusion, some of the officers lost their swords, some lost their hats, etc."[139] Mitchell B. Houghton, also of the 15th Alabama, wrote in his memoirs that a portion of the regiment "stampeded to the rear." When Houghton recalled the incident, he noted the shooting was light and he could see no enemy soldiers. He and several others followed the panicked troops at a leisurely pace. A dozen or more members of the regiment, including Houghton, reformed on the hillside and returned to the crest of Smith's Hill. By then Law had issued his order to withdraw to the lower bridge over Lookout Creek. In the darkness, they did not realize the 33rd Massachusetts had entered the works in the meantime. They were all captured.[140]

Among the captured Alabamians was Captain William A. Richardson, a wealthy planter before the war who still had his servant with him in late 1863. Richardson remarked to a group of soldiers atop Smith's Hill, "Well, boys, that was a devil of a fright we got a while ago." He quickly discovered the men he spoke to were members of the 73rd Ohio. When told he was a prisoner of war, the aristocrat argued, "Look here, gentlemen, I am most egregiously mistaken. I thought this was the 15th Alabama. By heavens, this ought not to count."[141]

Law may not have known the 15th Alabama had been pushed off Smith's Hill. The other four regiments waited in the dark for sometime before he issued the order for their march by the left flank around the crest of the hill to the Chattanooga Road and the bridge over Lookout Creek. According to Bowles, commanding the 4th Alabama, they marched from Smith's Hill in good order. He thought the Federals had given up the attack.[142] A member of the 47th Alabama wrote home that Federals "was about to flank us" and the

Alabamians then retreated. His letter does not make clear whether they were actually flanked. Nor does this letter clarify whether the Alabamians were forced from the hill.[143]

The 136th New York Regiment did not fire a shot during its ascent of Smith's Hill. The soldiers from the western New York counties of Wyoming, Livingston, and Allegheny fired one volley from the hilltop at the retreating Confederates after reaching the summit.[144] The 73rd Ohio entered the breastworks after they had been abandoned by the Alabamians, not making its last charge until the 33rd Massachusetts was in the works.[145] The fighting was spirited and at close quarters. Ohioans and the soldiers from the Bay State would alternately curse the Alabamians and claim to be friendly troops. The Confederates would shout back that they knew they were friends "and send a shower of lead into them."[146] Fighting at such close range humanized the combat and left lasting memories of the enemy soldiers for one member of the 44th Alabama. Henry Sturgis of Company H came face to face with a Federal, their rifles discharging within feet of each other. The Federal soldier fired a minie ball through Sturgis's hat. Sturgis did not miss with his shot, however. Long after their close encounter, he held on to the terrible memory of his adversary falling back down Smith's Hill.[147]

After the war, Waddell had high praise for the gallantry of the men of the 33rd Massachusetts during their climb up Smith's Hill. Although "repeatedly repulsed," the captain recollected, "they immediately renewed the attack." Waddell believed the 15th Alabama did severe damage to the ranks of the regiment from Massachusetts because his men held their fire until the attackers were close enough for him to see them as individuals. Also, he "was always certain that [his] guns were depressed sufficiently to do execution."[148]

Recriminations

When the night attack at Wauhatchie proved a failure, Bragg blamed his subordinate general, writing to Davis within 48 hours of the attack that Longstreet had disobeyed orders. Bragg reported to the chief executive that Longstreet had attempted to capture the rear guard at Wauhatchie with a brigade after being instructed to attack with a division.[149] He was undoubtedly angry that his left was turned with so little effort, perhaps regretting his faith in Longstreet.

Longstreet initially assigned blame for the failed mission to the officers of the attacking division, complaining that "the officers do not seem to have appreciated a night attack." But by the time he wrote his report of the Battle of Wauhatchie, in March 1864, Longstreet blamed the failure on Law's "abandoning his position." Later, Longstreet would expand his criticism to include Robertson, commander of the Texas brigade at Wauhatchie.[150]

The plan for the night attack at Wauhatchie was Longstreet's. In his report of operations, Longstreet acknowledged that "about 8 o'clock at night on the 28th, I received notice that the commanding general had approved my plan." Further, in his endorsement of Jenkins's report of the night battle, Longstreet said, "The dispositions and movements of the forces, as mentioned by General Jenkins, were ordered by me."[151]

The object of Longstreet's night attack at Wauhatchie is unclear, however. In his official report his stated purpose was "merely to inflict such damage upon the enemy as might be accomplished by a surprise." If so, that was certainly not what Bragg, whose investment of Chattanooga had ended with the valley's reopening, desired of the night venture.[152] Bragg ordered Longstreet to recapture the valley from the Federal army.

Even with the destruction or capture of Geary's detached command, Longstreet could not have held the valley with Jenkins's division. Hooker's force at Brown's Ferry was formidable, and the Federals had an open road from Bridgeport to Lookout Valley to move reinforcements. Longstreet knew this. Explaining why he could not support a Confederate force in the valley, Longstreet noted in his report that he could not put artillery in the valley nor reinforce troops there. He backed up this contention by claiming the endorsements of Lieutenant General William J. Hardee and Major General John C. Breckenridge, who examined the terrain with him.[153] Longstreet ordered the attack against Wauhatchie because Bragg had ordered him three times to do something to rid the valley of the Federals. He had to act even though he knew the action he was taking would not result in the expulsion of the Federal army from Lookout Valley.

Whether or not Bragg and Longstreet disagreed on the objective of the night attack, most Confederates believed the fight at Wauhatchie was made for a very practical reason. In a letter penned within hours of the battle, a grateful Bratton, commander of the attacking South Carolinians, wrote his wife "I have been spaired [sic] through another battle. Last night I was ordered over Lookout Mountain to attack and cápture, if possible, a wagon train. We tried honestly," he continued, "and fought hard but did not succeed. Our first onslaught drove them from their train but we could not take possession of it."[154] In his report, Jenkins wrote that Longstreet instructed him to "endeavor to capture the accompanying trains," although he also asserted in the same document that his orders for the night were to attempt "the destruction or capture of the rear-guard of the Federal column."[155]

Lieutenant James A. Hoyt of Company C, the Palmetto Sharpshooters, believed long after the war that the object of the night attack was to capture the Federal wagons. At a reunion in 1885, his address to the attendees explained the expedition into Lookout Valley was "planned for the capture of a large wagon train in the valley." He recalled the men expected to grab the train without much difficulty but the affair turned out to be surprisingly costly for the South Carolinians.[156] Turner Vaughan noted in his diary that the Confederates had "attacked the Yankees with hopes of capturing their wagon train reported to be loaded with blankets and overcoats."[157] Sergeant William Augustus McClendon of the 15th Alabama remembered after the war that Longstreet was "anxious" to capture the wagons.[158] Like Bratton, McClendon believed the South Carolinians got among the wagons but were too few to hold them.

Captain James L. Coker, acting assistant adjutant general on Bratton's staff, substantiated this view in an article in the *Confederate Veteran*. Coker was sent by Jenkins on the morning of October 28 to gain intelligence about the Federals deployed in the valley. He spent most of the day scouting the enemy. Arriving at the Confederate camp at sunset, Coker found the men under arms and Jenkins prepared "to cross with the division over Lookout Creek and with one brigade pass behind a hill up the valley to capture a large wagon train said to be there." Coker told Jenkins a brigade was not sufficient to capture the train, which was defended by a formidable force of infantry supported by artillery. Jenkins, according to Coker's written account, then went to Longstreet with the report but returned with orders to proceed with the attack as originally planned.[159] Coker's services to the Confederacy ended when he was severely wounded near Wauhatchie.

Additional contemporary support for the belief that the capture of the Federal wagons was the object of the night attack is provided by the war correspondent of the *Charleston Daily Courier*. Felix Gregory de Fontaine was one of several war correspondents in camp with Bragg's army. De Fontaine filed his stories under the pseudonym "Personne." His had been a familiar face around Longstreet's First Corps since Second Manassas. De Fontaine thought the night attack in Lookout Valley was made to capture the wagons, not to free the valley of Federals. He reported "General Longstreet, however, who had carefully watched the march of the XI Corps determined to make an attack for another purpose —namely, to capture, if possible, a large park of wagons and its escort, numbering, as was supposed, from 1,500 to 2,000 men, who still remained in the rear." De Fontaine also reported Bratton took his South Carolinians to "capture the much envied wagon train" but the Federals were not surprised and fought so vigorously that it was claimed a division was in place at Wauhatchie. His newspaper account reported the Federal attempt to turn Law's right and praised Generals Law, Robertson, and Benning for holding against the "over-whelming demonstration made upon" them by 9,000 to 12,000 Federal soldiers.[160]

At least one senior member of the Federal army also believed Geary's wagons were the target of the night battle at Wauhatchie. Major General O. O. Howard, commanding the XI Corps, believed leaving Geary at Wauhatchie, three miles from the rest of the Federal forces, was foolish because Geary "had in charge a long train of wagons" with too few troops to defend it. In his autobiography, Howard claimed "it was like throwing bait with-out hook and line before a hungry fish" to leave those wagons parked before Longstreet's men.[161]

In a letter written to his wife within twenty-four hours of the night fight, Jenkins wrote that "12,000 men on the other side pressed against the brigades of General Law, who failing to prevent their passing his left, they reached the third supporting brigade, a very small one, and threatened to get between my brigade and us, thus compelling me to recall my brigade in the midst of success." [162] It is unclear from this ambiguous letter whether Jenkins blamed Law for the defeat at this early date. Jenkins surely blamed Law soon after he wrote to his wife, however. Most historians have accepted this document as a condem-nation of Law.

With daylight on October 29 it was obvious the South Carolinians had suffered serious casualties with no tangible results. Worse yet it was rumored Law's command had made an embarrassing retrograde movement in the face of the enemy. Following a common prac-tice in military organizations when plans go unrealized, Bragg blamed Longstreet, who placed the responsibility first on all the officers in his command, and then on Law, where the responsibility for the failure became firmly attached. No criticism was directed at Bratton's force. This indicates that neither Longstreet nor Jenkins investigated fully the failed attack. John Bratton asserted after the war that the attack was unsuccessful because the Palmetto Sharpshooters did not join in the fight. Bratton complained that, "But for the failure of this regiment to perform the part assigned it, it was my opinion that we should have carried the entire position of the enemy before the pressure on Law and Benning in our rear necessitated my withdrawal."[163]

On October 31, Sorrel wrote Jenkins requesting an explanation why the brigades of Law and Robertson abandoned their positions on the night of October 28. Robertson's response was in a curt note on November 2, 1863. Robertson denied that his brigade "abandoned its position" but instead left under orders after completing its mission.[164] Longstreet ordered that Robertson "be relieved from command of his brigade pending the proceedings of the board now examining the case."[165] This action was thwarted by Bragg. In January, Jenkins accused Robertson of pessimism which weakened the resolve of his men. He was found guilty and left the Army of Tennessee.[166]

Law also responded on November 2. Like Robertson, he said his brigade did not "aban-don its position" but left its blocking position after it had completed its assigned task. Law asserted he and Jenkins had discussed the situation at the time the Confederates recrossed Lookout Creek and Jenkins agreed that Law had done his duty. But the tone of Sorrel's note rankled Law and his response included an implicit threat "As I am led to believe from the tenor of your notes, that the onus of having failed in the discharge of our duty has been placed upon myself and my command, I shall request of the proper authority, a "Court of Enquiry" to investigate the implied charges."[167] No extant evidence has been found which indicates Law carried through with his threat to call for an inquiry. But notes between Jenkins and Osmun Latrobe in early January 1864 indicate that either Law's threat was being taken seriously or his conduct during the night engagement was to be the subject of an investigation.[168]

Jenkins's report had apparently been misplaced by the end of December 1863. Latrobe questioned him about the fact that his and Law's reports were at odds. On January 4, Jenkins claimed he had a copy of his official report to send to Latrobe "which will give (moderately and studiously stated) my views upon the matter alluded to." Jenkins added that he knew the two reports disagreed because he had the report of the subordinate officer in his hands when he wrote his own. "I regret that I can not explain the discrepancy, and will merely say that I am fully prepared to substantiate the correctness of my report upon the point at issue."[169]

This note to Latrobe shows Jenkins was by then prepared to accuse Law of disobedience even though he had not done so in October. Jenkins prefaced his second letter with an explanation about this delay. "I should perhaps have taken official notice of the disobedience of General Law, had it not been for my knowledge of his dissatisfied feelings in reference to my having command of this division as his senior, and my belief that the contrary course on my part might tend to harmonize this division and to advance the best interests of the service."[170]

Jenkins's case against Law included a sworn statement from Jamison regarding the orders he delivered to Law during the night fight in Lookout Valley. In his statement, Jamison asserted he took two messages from Jenkins to Law's command. The first was for Law to hold his position until further orders. This order he delivered to Law personally. The second was for Law to hold until he received notice from Jenkins to retire. The last message Jamison said was given to Captain Hamilton of Law's staff.[171]

By the time Law wrote his report of the night battle, the question of who should be blamed for the failure was on the mind of everyone in the command structure. Law defended his actions in Lookout Valley with his report of the engagement dated November 3. The report included Law's assertion that the firing at Wauhatchie had ceased while his brigades were still heavily engaged. He carefully pointed to the fact that he had sent a courier to Jenkins before he learned of Jenkins's withdrawal, with word that while the Federals were attacking Smith's Hill, "it was possible for him to pass troops in rear of those engaged in this attack to the point at which I supposed Colonel Bratton to be."[172] Law repeated this point a second time in his report. But the South Carolinians had suffered heavy casualties in the night attack to no purpose and they were angry. If Law had held off the Federal reserves, they reasoned, they would have bagged Geary and his wagons.

Law and Jenkins were already bitter rivals over the leadership of Hood's Division before the night fight in Lookout Valley. Oates, a defender of Law, suggested in his memoirs that Law and Longstreet were at odds over the decision to place Jenkins in command of Hood's Division to such a degree that Law "did not care whether he aided Longstreet or Jenkins in anything."[173] In the highly charged atmosphere of the Confederate camp, it is not surprising that Law responded to any criticism with a caustic remark. Immediately after the night attack, word spread—the rumor attributed to one of Longstreet's staff officers—that Law had made the comment that he "could not be expected to furnish silver spurs for Jenkins's new uniform as major general."[174] Law apparently believed Jenkins, having already received command of the division, expected him to sacrifice his command, reputation and possibly his life as well.

Although Longstreet stated in his endorsement of Jenkins's report of the affair that Law and Jenkins blamed each other for the failure in the valley, Law did not assign any blame to Jenkins in his report of the engagement. The commanding general became caught up in the storm of accusations by the South Carolinians and resulting defense by those supporting Law. Longstreet became a party to the fracas between the two brigadiers under his command.

The report written by Jenkins is at odds with Law's report on several important points. He agrees that Law notified him that the Federals were passing to Law's left and toward Wauhatchie. Jenkins, however, reported sending Law a sharp response telling the junior brigadier he was ordered to prevent the passage of the Federal reinforcements. He ordered Law to stop the Federal soldiers and, if necessary, to attack. Law made no mention of this message in his report. Indeed, Jenkins asserted in his report that he three times ordered Law to hold his position until he received positive orders to withdraw. Law made mention of one such message but said he received it after he had already started to withdraw.[175]

Jenkins reported that Bratton was withdrawn from Wauhatchie because of Law's message that the Federals were passing Smith's Hill and the report that Federal reinforcements were pressing against the right of Benning, whose force was inadequate to protect Bratton. These enemy troops were feeling out the Confederate position and preparing to attack. Jenkins offered no reason why the Federals gathered on the right of Benning did not attack. He did remark that Benning was "not actively engaged" in the fighting the night of October 28. Jenkins stated that he had to order Bratton's withdrawal, even though the attack "would have been completely successful, in my judgment, despite the disparity in numbers had the troops from Brown's Ferry been kept from interfering."[176]

Jenkins went to see Law the next morning at Law's headquarters. He reported asking Law why he had withdrawn before Jenkins had ordered him. Jenkins found Law's answer entirely unsatisfactory. Law did not deny pulling out too soon, Jenkins asserted. Law claimed he was hard pressed on his right flank and that a portion of his blocking force had failed to do their duty. "I mention this," wrote Jenkins, "as in his report he takes as the grounds of his withdrawing from his position that it was in accordance with the plan."[177] Although Jenkins accused Law of withdrawing from his blocking position before ordered and of writing a false report, he took no action against his subordinate.

Longstreet sustained Jenkins's contention that Law withdrew too soon, going so far as to claim that "had Law pressed his advantage after the first or second repulse of the enemy, we should have had a great success at a very light cost and trouble."[178] If Law had ordered an attack down Smith's Hill against the force sent to support Geary, the result could only have been a disaster. Law's men would have given up the advantage of the high ground and been in the midst of a superior enemy force without the means to extricate themselves. This statement was part of Longstreet's report of the night adventure in Lookout Valley, written in March of 1864, after he had preferred charges against Law.

Lost in the squabble was the word of probably the best Confederate witness to the affair in the valley on the night of October 28. Henry Benning was in place between Bratton's attacking brigade at Wauhatchie and Law's blocking force along the road to the ferry. Jenkins first ordered Benning to position his Georgians along the Valley Road, connecting with Law's blocking force to prevent the reinforcing of Geary's command. In a short time, however, Jenkins directed Benning to cross the railroad and take up a covering position for Bratton, who was ordered to break off his attack and withdraw across Lookout Creek. It is clear from Benning's report that Bratton's men were withdrawn before the main body of Federal troops reached the Georgian's position, although Federal skirmishers made contact.[179]

Soon after erecting breastworks at this new location, pickets brought Benning word that Federal troops were near and in a position that threatened to cut off the Confederate route to the bridge over Lookout Creek. Two South Carolina regiments returned by the same road they had taken to begin the assault against Geary. The rest of Bratton's men approached the bridge by a route nearer the creek. Benning took pains to protect them, but no Federal attempt was made to prevent their re-crossing Lookout Creek. Suffering casualties of three wounded and two missing, Benning regretted his report of the affair required "so many words for so little matter." Benning's report sustains Law's claim that the attacking force at Wauhatchie had been recalled before the Federals had reached the scene.[180] Longstreet's artillery chief also lends support to Law. Alexander believed Jenkins broke off the attack as Benning described because Jenkins received Law's message alerting him to the danger that Schurz's relief column could reach his rear.[181]

Confederate claims are obviously at odds regarding the affair in Lookout Valley. But the Federal reports of the night fight offer non-partisan views of the Confederate actions. Due to confused orders, Schurz's command did not reach Wauhatchie until after Bratton had withdrawn his troops. Schurz was at the head of the column when Tyndale's brigade scattered into the field between the Valley Road and Raccoon Mountain after Law's Alabamians sprang their ambush. After criticism from Hooker, both Schurz and Colonel Frederick Hecker, commander of Schurz's Third Brigade, requested an inquiry.

Reports filed by officers of Geary's regiments show the fighting ended at Wauhatchie about 3:00 a.m.[182] Testimony of witnesses at the court of inquiry prove fighting at Smith's Hill continued after the cessation of hostilities at Wauhatchie.[183] Indeed, the fighting stopped at Wauhatchie just as Tyndale's brigade reached the hill that bears his name. Even the report of the capture of Tyndale's Hill by Federal troops reached Hooker before fighting was halted at Smith's Hill.[184]

Before Schurz consolidated his position on Tyndale's Hill, a junior officer reported seeing a column passing to the right of the hill.[185] This column was two of Bratton's regiments returning from Wauhatchie by the Valley Road as described by Benning. The Federal relief column was at the foot of Tyndale's Hill, but not yet in motion toward Geary's position, at 4:30 a.m. It did not reach Wauhatchie until 5:00 a.m., a full two hours after Bratton had broken off his attack.[186]

Schurz confirmed both the timing of the action as reported by Law and Law's conclusions as to the danger that Schurz's column presented to Bratton. Schurz placed his position between Law and Wauhatchie, at the foot of Tyndale's Hill, as Law had suspected and, because of the delays, after Bratton had withdrawn. In Schurz's words "The firing at Wauhatchie had for a while slackened and then died out altogether. It was evident that Geary, after a fierce fight, had succeeded in repulsing the rebel attack. But there was still more firing going on in my rear near the hill from which the volley had been thrown upon us."[187]

It is clear that Jenkins believed Bratton's command was in danger of being overwhelmed. He probably concluded that Law had put Bratton in jeopardy when he failed to stop the Federal reinforcements sent from Brown's Ferry. When he learned of the great difference in casualties sustained by his South Carolinians and those sustained by Law's Alabamians and heard the rumor that some of the blocking force had abandoned their position, it was not difficult for Jenkins to conclude that Law had withdrawn prematurely. When the rivalry between Law and Jenkins is considered, the brouhaha in the division is not surprising.

As it was, the Battle of Wauhatchie was a draw because the Federals did not press their advantage. They could have reached Wauhatchie with sufficient force to crush Bratton but were too slow. A Federal force could have moved behind Law and cut off his retreat but did not. Indeed, after the splendid service rendered by Smith's men against Law's command, they made no attempt to pursue the Confederates from Smith's Hill. The Federal forces stopped atop Smith's Hill, and Law's men retreated across Lookout Creek "in a quiet and leisurely manner."[188]

Robertson's Texans occupied the timbered western slope of Lookout Mountain the next day while Law, Benning, and Bratton were in position along Lookout Creek to prevent a crossing by the Federal forces in the valley. Jenkins's division remained in the valley only one more day, marching around Lookout Mountain on the afternoon of October 31, conceding the valley to the Federals.[189]

Chapter 11

Campaigning in East Tennessee

A few days after the Battle of Chickamauga, Bragg's generals were in a mood border-ing on revolt. They believed his failure to follow and destroy Rosecrans's army had wasted the sacrifices of September 19–20. Longstreet forwarded his complaints of Bragg to the secretary of war, and others wrote to Davis asking that Bragg be relieved of command. Instead, D. H. Hill and Leonidas Polk, two of the signers of the letter to Davis, were relieved, and the president gave Bragg the means to rid himself of Longstreet.[1]

Writing from Atlanta, Davis suggested that Bragg send Longstreet's two divisions to East Tennessee to defeat Major General Ambrose E. Burnside, then based at Knoxville with the Army of the Ohio. He could achieve two results from this detachment. First he could separate the quarreling Bragg and Longstreet and secondly, the separation would place Longstreet in position to return more quickly to the Army of Northern Virginia should Lee need him. Apparently, Bragg so desired Longstreet's removal from his com-mand that he was willing to accept this suggestion even though it meant dividing his army in the face of a stronger adversary.[2] Major General Joseph Wheeler accompanied Longstreet with three brigades of Bragg's cavalry. The total of Longstreet's detached command was approximately 12,000 men.[3]

Law's Brigade was relieved from picket duty on the east side of Lookout Mountain on November 5. The Alabamians marched through deep mud for Tyner's Station, Tennessee, on the East Tennessee and Georgia Railway, arriving the night of November 6.[4]

The feeble Confederate rail system could not move Longstreet's entire command, so when Law learned no cars were available for his troops, he marched his brigade to Cleve-land, Tennessee, on November 9 to board cars for Sweetwater.[5] Arriving there on Novem-ber 12, the men learned the rest of their division was already at Loudon, a railroad station on the Tennessee River, northeast of Sweetwater.[6] They set off for Loudon on November 13 and, by the next day, Law's Brigade was reunited with Jenkins. The sixty mile trip from Tyner's Station to Loudon had taken a week.[7]

Although no cars were available to carry Law's infantry to Loudon, his horses were sent ahead by rail which forced the brigade officers to march with their commands. The rank and file were delighted and according to Law, the officers received many jeers for "having to foot it." The enlisted ranks were more than delighted when many officers fell out before the march was over.[8]

By the time they reached Sweetwater, some of the command had been without rations for two days, and time was lost foraging in the vicinity.[9] To defeat Burnside or drive him from East Tennessee, Longstreet had to extend his line of communications nearly 65 miles through inhospitable country. He moved his headquarters to Tyner's Station to supervise the movement of his command. Because his force had no supplies, and rail transport was insufficient, the move was necessarily slow. Opposing the Confederate detachment was a Federal force of 12,000 under Burnside.[10] The waiting Federals knew the terrain and were ready with a plan for opposing Longstreet.

Pontoons were laid across the Tennessee River by Bratton's South Carolinians who were in the van of Jenkins's command. Soldiers guarding the bridge when the Alabamians marched across on November 14 told them there had been no Federal resistance to the crossing. Instead, the enemy said they looked forward to seeing the Confederates the next day.[11] Law's men threw up entrenchments at the bridgehead to wait out the night. No fires were allowed since the lines of the two armies were close together. The night of November 14 was cold and rainy, the discomfort being heightened because the men were tired and on short rations. By the early hours of the frosty morning of November 15 the Alabamians were anxious to engage the enemy so they could replenish their supply of food and equipment, especially blankets.[12]

Burnside did not oppose Longstreet's crossing of the Tennessee River, for it was the Federal plan to draw the detached Confederates toward Knoxville and away from Bragg. U. S. Grant ordered Burnside to hold Kingston and Lenoir's Station as long as possible, but, in the event that line became untenable, his instructions were to use his own judgment.[13] Grant told Burnside to tie Longstreet down long enough for Major General William T. Sherman to reach Chattanooga with the reinforcements needed to drive Bragg from Missionary Ridge. This would leave Longstreet trapped between Grant and Burnside with his lines of communications cut. Grant wanted Burnside to gain time by skirmishing with Longstreet while falling back to Knoxville, where he was to hold Longstreet in place.[14]

If Longstreet expected to meet the Burnside he had known at Fredericksburg, he was mistaken. On November 14 Burnside ordered part of the IX Corps to reconnoiter Longstreet's crossing. This reconnaissance, conducted in heavy rain, was not a serious attempt to drive the Confederates into the river. Lieutenant Turner Vaughan of the 4th Alabama referred to it in his diary as simply a demonstration.[15] This demonstration provided Burnside with intelligence of the strength and disposition of the Confederate forces and gave him room in which he could maneuver unmolested. Longstreet, however, did not know the strength of Burnside's forces immediately to his front nor the intentions of his old adversary.

With sunrise on November 15, Longstreet was at the front, inspecting the lines on foot. Passing through the camp of the 15th Alabama, the commanding general walked near Orderly Sergeant Billy Jordan, warming by a fire allowed the pickets now that the sun had risen. The general said nothing to the Alabama soldier, and Jordan neither spoke nor rose.[16]

That morning, the 4th Alabama was ordered forward to determine the strength and position of the Federals opposite them. The regiment's skirmish line caught the 111th Ohio Regiment by surprise, putting the Ohioans to flight and capturing their camp equipment.[17]

Lenoir's Station

On November 15, Burnside retreated east along the rail line to Lenoir's Station, a distance of nine miles from Loudon, while Longstreet crossed the Tennessee at Huff's Ferry and followed the Hotchkiss Valley Road eastward.[18] Jenkins led and McLaws followed on the crossing. By four in the afternoon the column had reached a fork in the road.[19] The route to the left led to the road between Kingston and Knoxville, by way of Campbell's Station; the right went to Lenoir's Station, which was little more than a platform on the rail line. Longstreet ordered Jenkins to the right, in pursuit of Burnside. He

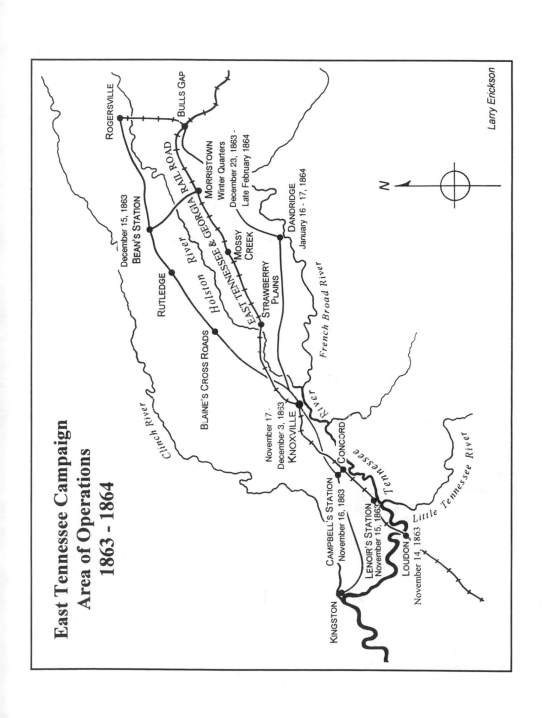

**East Tennessee Campaign
Area of Operations
1863 - 1864**

Clinch River

ROGERSVILLE

BULLS GAP

BEAN'S STATION
December 15, 1863

Holston River

RUTLEDGE

EAST TENNESSEE & GEORGIA RAIL ROAD

MORRISTOWN
Winter Quarters
December 23, 1863 -
Late February 1864

MOSSY
CREEK

BLAINE'S CROSS ROADS

STRAWBERRY
PLAINS

DANDRIDGE
January 16 - 17, 1864

French Broad River

KNOXVILLE
November 17 -
December 3, 1863

River

CONCORD

Tennessee

CAMPBELL'S STATION
November 16, 1863

LENOIR'S STATION
November 15, 1863

LOUDON
November 14, 1863

KINGSTON

Little Tennessee River

N

Larry Erickson

gave orders for McLaws to hold at the fork and be ready to move at daylight on November 16. From a hill above Lenoir's Station, Longstreet used an eyeglass to observe Burnside's trains and artillery batteries moving toward Knoxville.[20]

It was raining and cold, and the mud from two days of heavy rain made marching difficult for both armies. Jenkins put forward a strong skirmish line that was closely engaged from the river to Lenoir's Station. Law's Brigade was not in action on this march. The Alabamians instead followed the skirmishers to the railroad depot.[21] Jenkins's men took up positions on the elevations overlooking Lenoir's Station.

The Federals had left unmanned the gaps through the hills overlooking Lenoir's Station, and from the heights Law had a good view of the Federal trains and artillery rapidly retreating. There was not time enough to deploy before darkness. He later claimed "two more hours of daylight would have settled the East Tennessee campaign at Lenoir on the 15th of November." Law blamed the lack of time on the slow movement of Longstreet's command which, though virtually unopposed, moved only seven miles during the day.[22]

In Law's view, there was no reason to hesitate, for it was obvious that Burnside did not plan to make a fight at Lenoir's Station. "If such had been his intention the range of hills which commanded the position would have been held by his whole force and the fight would have been made for their possession instead of the valley below." Not only was Lenoir's Station intrinsically weak, Law noted it could be easily turned from the hills to the west, in the direction of Campbell's Station, Burnside's only line of retreat.[23]

The weather was cold and wet again during the night of November 15 as both armies lay in line of battle, too close together to allow for warming fires. For Jordan, that night stood out among many bad nights in a long war as one of such awfulness and unpleasantness that he could never forget it.[24] Burnside's soldiers also lay in line of battle, suffering equally in the cold rain without fires, though members of the IX Corps may have suffered more with the knowledge that they lay only a mile from the snug winter quarters which they had left the day before.[25]

After dark, Longstreet employed guides to lead a portion of his troops around the enemy lines to cut off the Federal escape route and Jenkins advanced his brigade forward to occupy the hill nearest the railroad in preparation for an attack on the 16th.[26] However, the guides put the troops on the wrong road.[27] Worse yet, the soldiers of the XXIII Corps decamped from Lenoir's Station during the night without alerting Jenkins's men.[28] This was accomplished even though Burnside ordered his men to destroy close to one hundred wagons along with supplies, equipment, and ordnance that his command could not move because the mules from that portion of his train were needed to haul his artillery through the thick mud. Up to two dozen mules were required to pull an artillery piece over the muddy roads.[29] Confederate troops also struggled with their artillery, in some cases moving the pieces by hand. They burned the fences along the road to provide light for their work.[30]

During the night of November 15, Burnside ordered four companies of cavalry to capture the junction of the Kingston and Concord Roads southeast of Campbell's Station. He then instructed Colonel John F. Hartranft to push his Third Division, IX Corps, along the Concord Road to Campbell's Station and secure the crossroads with infantry. Burnside believed Longstreet would attempt to seize that intersection to cut off the Federal line of march into Knoxville.[31] His train had been moving nearly all night, and by daylight of November 16, his entire command was on the road.

Campbell's Station

Longstreet ordered pursuit, sending McLaws's men, who left some time after 8 a.m., marching toward Campbell's Station by the Kingston Road.[32] Jenkins followed Burnside's column from Lenoir's Station along the Concord Road parallel to the railroad. Jenkins tried to force the retreating Federal column to turn and make a stand, but could not, except momentarily at Turkey Creek, close to Campbell's Station, where he engaged only the rear guard of three Michigan regiments.[33]

When the Federal rear guard reached Campbell's Station, with Jenkins in close pursuit, Hartranft was blocking the Kingston Road south of the intersection, Brigadier General Julius White had his Second Division, XXIII Corps, across the same road north of the junction, and Brigadier General Edward Ferrero, commanding the First Division, IX Corps, was deployed northeast of the crossroads.[34] South of the Concord Road was a wood, and north of the road was an open area, half a mile wide and stretching west one mile from the Kingston Road. This field was bordered to the north and south with wooded hills.[35]

After Burnside's train had passed through the intersection, Hartranft moved to the left (east) of White.[36] The Federal line was established east to west on an elevation running through the open field.[37] The Confederates were in the woods south of the Concord Road, with McLaws astride the Kingston Road, and Jenkins to his right.

Law's Brigade followed Bratton's South Carolinians and Anderson's Georgians to Campbell's Station. When the Alabama soldiers arrived, Jenkins placed them to the right of Anderson.[38] Longstreet considered the Federal position a strong one and the Confederates waited in position three to four hours before attacking, though contact was maintained and firing was nearly constant.[39] He ordered Jenkins to move around the Federal left to attack the flank. McLaws was to assault the Federal front after Jenkins had moved against Burnside's left flank.[40] In their reports, the two division commanders each stated that he waited for the other to attack. Jenkins grew impatient and went to see Longstreet about 3 p.m. Longstreet issued the command to start Anderson and Law, supported by Benning, around the left of the Federal line, swinging far enough to bring Anderson's left regiments even with the enemy line and Law's Brigade to the Federal left rear. As senior brigadier, Law commanded the flanking movement.[41]

While Law led his detachment around the Federal left, the enemy saw the Alabamians as they passed over a hill in the woods east of the open ground. Burnside himself, as well as hundreds of Federals along the Federal line, saw the flanking movement. Burnside believed the high ground, commanding his left, was the object of the Confederate move. As he had too few men to extend his line farther to the left, Burnside ordered his entire line to break contact and move to a second position. This second line, perhaps a quarter of a mile north and higher still than the elevation of the first line, had already been selected as the next position.[42] His intent, plainly stated in his report of the action, was to delay Longstreet's pursuing column and withdraw to his second line.[43] The Confederate generals involved in the fighting at Campbell's Station disagreed on what happened next. Law remembered that he had reached his flanking position and formed his command to attack when he was ordered by Jenkins to wait for the rest of the division before commencing the assault. "As the Federal troops were moving back from one position to another," Law explained, "this order was fatal to the success of the movement." Law believed it was a mistake by Longstreet to hold McLaws's attack until the flanking movement was developed. A frontal attack by McLaws, he reasoned, would have held Burnside in position for the flanking movement to succeed.[44] Law was simply describing the tactical turning movement as it was generally employed during the war. Most officers used an attack on the enemy's front to hold him in place while a part of his force assaulted the enemy's flank or rear. If the enemy attempted to escape while under attack, his retreat usually became a rout. Longstreet, however, may have actually intended for his flanking force to attack first before he launched his frontal attack, a tactic he used at the Wilderness.

Jenkins recalled the events differently, claiming that Law had reported he was in place to attack. Jenkins, however, found Law was too far in advance of the Federal line, putting Anderson in front of the Federal line and Law's own brigade only on the enemy's flank. Law explained to Jenkins that the Alabama brigade had obliqued too far to the left because his regiment of direction had closed up on Anderson. Jenkins stopped Anderson, whom he had already started, and ordered Law to attack alone. Obtaining assurance that Jenkins would protect his flanks, Law moved to the attack, but this second attempt was halted by darkness.[45] In his report of Campbell's Station, Jenkins wrote a scathing indictment of Law, stressing that Law knew the plan of attack, and as commander on the field was responsible for the proper handling of his troops.[46]

Longstreet's report of the fighting at Campbell's Station noted Law's flanking move (and artillery fire) caused Burnside to "retreat in some haste." Longstreet believed a victory at Campbell's Station would have captured East Tennessee for the Confederacy. That would have freed Longstreet to return to Bragg, perhaps changing the outcome of the battle between Bragg and Grant later that month. Once again, as at the Battle of Wauhatchie, Longstreet and Jenkins blamed Law for lack of success. Jenkins claimed the Confederates had only a short time in which they could have gained a victory at Campbell's Station but Law's "...causeless and inexcusable movement lost us the few moments in which success from this point could be attained."[47]

In his memoirs, Longstreet attributed the failure at Campbell's Station to something more sinister than Law's mismanagement. Quoting an unnamed staff officer, he accused Law of deliberately delaying his attack until Burnside got clear because Jenkins would receive credit for any success achieved by Hood's Division.[48] Alexander, commanding Longstreet's artillery at Campbell's Station, recalled the same camp rumor in his recollections of the war. Although he wrote he was unable to sort out the truth and expressed admiration for both brigadiers, Alexander nevertheless noted that Law led the flanking column where it was seen by the Federal line. Again, the reason ascribed to Law's action was to prevent credit for a successful assault from going to Jenkins. The artillery chief even claimed some of the company officers in the Alabama brigade wrote letters making that charge against Law, although no such correspondence has been found.[49]

Law and Longstreet agreed that Campbell's Station was only a skirmish. They agreed as well that failure at the obscure Tennessee crossroads had far-reaching results. Law, however, believed Longstreet committed an inexcusable error by not sending McLaws's Division ahead to occupy the intersection near Campbell's Station before Burnside reached it. McLaws was on the Kingston to Knoxville road at 4 p.m. on November 15. He was under arms at daylight on November 16, but did not march until 8 a.m. Law believed McLaws should have been at the crossroads ahead of Hartranft's column. By failing to have him there, Longstreet provided Burnside with a secure line of retreat into Knoxville.[50]

Longstreet's command was in crisis, morale suffering badly from the factions in headquarters, where Longstreet quarreled with Bragg, McLaws, Robertson, and Law, who also quarreled with Jenkins. The rivalries divided the command into various camps, adding to the serious problems facing the men who suffered from the lack of ample rations, winter clothing, and equipment. Moreover, Burnside outmaneuvered Longstreet, further lowering the esprit de corps of the Confederates. Blaming Law for the failure at Campbell's Station only demonstrates the depth of the crisis within Longstreet's command.

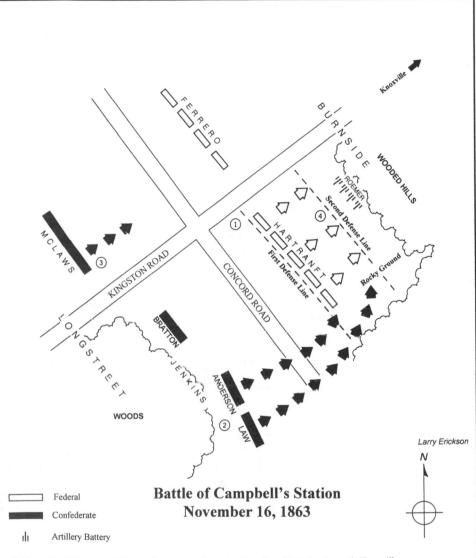

Battle of Campbell's Station
November 16, 1863

Larry Erickson

N

Federal
Confederate

ılı Artillery Battery

1. Burnside initiates a holding action against Longstreet to allow his trains to reach Knoxville.
2. Longstreet orders Jenkins to flank Burnside. Jenkins orders Law to lead his and Anderson's Brigade against the Federal left. Anderson is to strike the Federal line while Law gets in its rear.
3. McLaws is ordered to attack the Federal front after Law's assault.
4. Burnside sees the flanking movement and orders a withdrawal to a pre-determined second line about a quarter of a mile behind his first.

The division was torn by the strife. Longstreet earlier asked Bragg to relieve Jerome Robertson from command of the Texas brigade for incompetence and an uncooperative attitude. The commanding general claimed Robertson's attitude caused his Texans to abandon their position in Lookout Valley on October 28.[51] The division was a shell of the fighting force that had left the Army of Northern Virginia on the banks of the Rappahannock.[52] Attention was on disputes within the command rather than the campaign against Burnside. Added to the problems of insufficient supplies and inadequate transportation already plaguing the Confederate soldiers was the additional burden of a command acting at cross purposes.

Both Jenkins and Longstreet wrote their reports of Campbell's Station after Law had left Longstreet's command under the worst possible circumstances. By the time Longstreet wrote his memoirs, he and Law were bitter enemies. And, finally, Alexander's comments about Campbell's Station were not meant for publication and therefore he made no effort to determine the truth. No inquiry or court-martial was held to establish the facts in the case. Law's only defense against the rumor was his emphatic denial of the charge.[53]

Within the ranks of Law's Brigade, there was more concern with obtaining a meal than conducting a post-mortem of the attempt to flank Burnside at Campbell's Station. The men had made a rapid march over the rough ground of rocks, briars and scrub oak in the flanking move only to be disappointed when they discovered the Federals were moving to their second line. They were ordered to try again, but darkness forced them to abandon the attempt. Tired and hungry, the Alabamians went into bivouac.[54] Lieutenants Coles and William Turner divided a supply of potatoes among the officers and men of the 4th Alabama, an allotment of two potatoes each. Turner convinced Coles to draw straws for their portion, four potatoes. Coles later claimed it broke his heart when Turner won the lot. Coles did not have to go hungry, however, as he bargained for a slice of bacon and shared Major Robbins's dinner of two potatoes and a handful of peas, which they boiled in an oyster can.[55]

The Siege of Knoxville

Burnside started his command into Knoxville after dark on November 16. He had escaped serious damage to either his train or his infantry both at Lenoir's Station and at Campbell's Station by deftly engaging the Confederates long enough for his train to move to safety but not long enough for Longstreet's superior numbers to overwhelm him. A few hours later Burnside was safely behind the Knoxville fortifications. Longstreet was under orders to destroy Burnside or drive him from East Tennessee but was now faced with the prospect of a protracted siege.[56]

Knoxville is on the right side of the Tennessee River. A small town in 1863, it was situated on a plateau more than a 100 feet above the river. On the western approaches Burnside enclosed his defensive line on the river and laid out a fortified line which ran north of town until it reached the East Tennessee and Virginia Railroad, where it then bent around the north of Knoxville. Fort Sanders, an earthwork fronted by abatis and a deep ditch, was the strongest fort on the Federal line. It faced west on the line between the river and the railroad and was garrisoned with infantry and artillery.

South of the river lay three elevations which were occupied and fortified by Federal troops. On these elevations opposite Knoxville were built the Federal strongholds of Fort Stanley, Fort Dickerson and Fort Higley. Also across the river was a brigade of Federal infantry, two batteries and a cavalry detachment of unknown strength.

Arriving in front of Knoxville on November 17, the troops of the 4th Alabama received a share of the rations captured since the Confederates had crossed the Tennessee River. The Confederate commissary issued flour, bacon, mutton, and large quantities of sugar and coffee. Enough was available for the issue of two days' back rations, which the Alabamians began to eat immediately. As a result, most of them became ill. This was typical of the Confederate soldier who throughout the war preferred to eat his rations rather than carry them. The regimental surgeons declared the sickness to be the result of eating "sick flour." However, Coles diagnosed the malady as the simple result of hungry men eating too much, too fast.[57]

Dinner on November 17 proved more difficult for the soldiers of the 15th Alabama, however, as Jenkins's division was ordered to the left of the Southern line, skirmishing and slowly advancing into the corporate limits of Knoxville. Jenkins advanced to the front of Fort Sanders where rifle pits were dug and breastworks were rapidly thrown up. Orderly Sergeant Billy Jordan and another man were detailed to cook their company's rations, about two miles behind the front line, but the rations were not issued until 10 p.m. By sunrise about half the food was ready and Jordan delivered it to soldiers on line as they exchanged fire with the besieged Federals. Jordan then rejoined the other soldier to cook and deliver the remainder of his company's food.[58]

The Confederate picket line was pushed closer to Fort Sanders and its adjoining earthworks whenever possible. During the night of November 22, Major Robbins, commanding the 4th Alabama, ordered his men to advance the picket line nearer to Fort Sanders.[59] Their new position took them within 300 yards of the fort, so close that one veteran recalled the position was under the guns of the fort.[60] By daylight, the energetic Alabamians had a line of waist deep rifle pits running parallel to the fort, manned by one battalion of the regiment, the other held in reserve.[61] They occupied a portion of a new line extending from the woods north of the East Tennessee and Virginia Railroad line, southwest into the open field before Fort Sanders. Their new line placed them in the field of fire from the battery of 20-pounder Parrots of the 2nd U.S. Artillery and a section of Captain Jacob Roemer's 2nd New York Light Artillery.[62] To the left of the 4th Alabama, and in advance of the Alabamians, were pickets of the 3rd Georgia Battalion of Sharpshooters.[63] Opposing the Alabama picket line were three Michigan regiments deployed behind the Federal works north of Fort Sanders. These were the 2nd, 17th and 20th Michigan of the Third Brigade, First Division, IX Corps. Inside the fort were two companies of the 79th New York regiments from the First Brigade in support of the artillery.

During daylight hours, musket fire from the 4th Alabama made daily activities in Fort Sanders a hazardous undertaking. Private David Lane, a schoolteacher and father of four serving in the 17th Michigan, usually climbed the embankment of Fort Sanders each morning to see what moves the Confederates had made the night before. On the morning of November 24, he was greeted by a minie ball whizzing over his head and another in the dirt at his feet. At breakfast, a round from the Alabama trenches knocked over a camp kettle next to Lane just before another went through the cheeks of another Michigander, taking most his tongue with it. Lane's mess moved over a small hill to eat their morning meal in peace.[64]

The Federal IX Corps commander ordered his Second Division to retake ground lost the evening before. He sent a note to Ferrero, in command of the First Division, ordering him to seize any opportunity afforded by the attack to capture the advanced rifle pits occupied by the annoying 4th Alabama. Ferrero passed along the order to Colonel William Humphrey, commanding the Third Brigade of three Michigan regiments and one Pennsylvania regiment. Humphrey, in turn, detailed Major Cornelius Byington's 2nd Michigan to drive the Alabamians from their advanced position.[65]

Just after daylight on the foggy morning of November 24, the 2nd Michigan moved out of their rifle pits, formed for the charge, and marched to the picket line of the 20th Michigan.[66] Byington, sword drawn, placed himself at the head of his regiment. At the word "charge" the Michiganders ran down the slope at the left oblique, through the debris in front of the fort, under the covering fire of Federal batteries, and across the 300 yards separating the lines.[67] Members of the 2nd Michigan began to fall as the regiment cleared their own picket line.[68] During the charge, their right flank was almost perpendicular to the picket line of the 3rd Georgia Battalion, whose fire enfiladed the attackers as they rushed toward the guns of the 4th Alabama. Byington fell at the edge of the Alabama rifle pits with a broken leg and a mortal wound in the side.[69]

Robbins hurried the reserve battalion the short distance to the line of rifle pits as soon as he saw the 2nd Michigan attacking. The 4th Alabama unleashed a deadly volley against the charging Federals when they were only steps away.[70] The rest of the 3rd Georgia Battalion then advanced to support the 4th Alabama. The firing lasted only minutes before the attack of the 2nd Michigan was broken.[71] Adjutant William Noble, along with most of the 2nd Michigan who had advanced with him, fell dead in front of Company G of the 4th Alabama. Captain Henry Moseley, commanding Company G, vividly remembered Noble after the war, because, Noble "was such a nice looking young man." Also, Moseley took Noble's sword for his own, since it was a better sword than the one he carried, giving away his sword and using Noble's for the remainder of the war. In 1879, Moseley sent the sword to Noble's sister in Michigan.[72]

The remnants of the Michigan regiment started back to the protection of the fort, some carrying wounded. Officers of the 4th Alabama issued orders not to fire on those who helped their comrades from the field. They also tried to communicate to the Federals to cease their fire so they could remove their wounded from the field. They were unable to get their message across the smoky battlefield, however. Federals posted near the fort opened fire on any Confederate who stepped out into the open. The men of the 4th Alabama forgot any intention of helping the wounded and leaped back to cover, some firing on the fort.[73]

The charge on the Confederates was an ill-conceived plan with dire results, like many of the charges in this bloody war. John S. Maltman, a sergeant in the 17th Michigan, in a letter to his brother, characterized sending only the 2nd Michigan to dislodge the Confederates from their new trenches as the "...blundering idea of some general."[74] The toll of killed and wounded in the charge of the 2nd Michigan was high. Losses totaled 83 of the 160 who made the attack, including Noble, Byington, Lieutenants Frank Zoellner and Charles R. Galpin killed, six sergeants who each lost a leg, and the color bearer who was mortally wounded.[75] Eleven of the sixteen men of Company C who made the charge were killed or wounded.[76]

Robbins ordered Byington made as comfortable as possible in a wood behind the Confederate line. As the two officers talked the Federal major learned his opponent was an Alabamian. It was then that he explained to Robbins that his brother had moved south several years before and had become "a secesh." He was then serving as an orderly sergeant in the 44th Alabama. Did Robbins know his brother? Robbins told Byington the sad news of his brother's death only three weeks previous. He related how Samuel S. Byington "fell with a bayonet in his breast, having transfixed his salient in a like manner," during the fight for Smith's Hill in Lookout Valley. Unfortunately for the dying colonel, Robbins's report was a mistake. Sam Byington was captured at Lookout Valley but was not killed.[77]

South of the River

The same day, November 24, Law's Brigade was detached and sent across the Tennessee River to join Robertson's Brigade.[78] They occupied elevations south of the river and to the right of the Rebel lines. Although these hills offered a scenic view of the city, they did not overlook the Federal positions. The hill that looked into the fortifications of Knoxville were entrenched and held in force by the Federals.[79] South of the river, Law's detached command immediately began an exchange with sharpshooters of Colonel Daniel Cameron's brigade of the XXIII Corps.[80]

Longstreet ordered Law to make a demonstration against the Federal breastworks "to ascertain the nature and location of its defenses as well as the force with which it was held."[81] Because the ground nearest the river was nearly impassable, Law moved his force around to the Federal left, away from the river. In addition, Law sent two flanking regiments farther to the right, across the Maryville Road, to overlap the enemy's most advanced line of trenches.[82]

Following an artillery barrage that started early on November 25, Law attacked Cameron.[83] With orders to drive the Federals out of their trenches, skirmishers of the 1st Texas, 4th, 15th, and 48th Alabama regiments moved from their hill into the field below and up the opposite ridge, against the position of Cameron's sharpshooters.[84] The ridge, covered with a growth of cedar, was left unoccupied, and Law's Confederates pushed on into the hollow beyond.[85] At this point Cameron's troops fired down from the next hill into the ranks of the Confederates and counterattacked.[86]

Law's men halted and then fell back. Company G of the 15th Alabama, the left regiment of the Alabamians, took cover where available. The Texas skirmishers moved up on their left, drawing some the Federal fire away from the Alabamians. Waddell ordered Company G, which was unsupported and nearly surrounded, to fall back farther. Sergeant John McLeod fell at this point, killed instantly by a ball through the head.[87]

The Alabamians retreated to the foot of the cedar hill, seeking shelter in the woods at its base. From the cover of the cedar break, they commenced firing at the onrushing Federals. Private James O. Dell of Company G, 15th Alabama, was mortally wounded there.[88] Several members of Company B took up position behind a fence at the wood's edge. The fence did not afford Private Theo P. Thompson protection from the Federal fire, however, as a minie ball whizzed through a crack in the fence, hitting him in the heart. Sergeant Billy Jordan, next to Thompson along the fence line, remembered his friend did not take another breath after being struck. Captain Frank Park, the physician from Orion who served in the 1861 Alabama legislature, was carried from the field mortally wounded.[89]

First Lieutenant William L. Wilson of Company H, 15th Alabama, received a severe gunshot wound to the leg during the day's fighting. He suffered the amputation of the leg below the knee on November 26.[90] Wilson was unable to travel when Longstreet's army left Knoxville and was captured December 4 when surgeons of the 79th New York took charge of the Confederate hospitals.[91] He convalesced in Chattanooga, at the residence of a Mrs. Crawford, until strong enough to be moved to the U.S. Army Military Hospital in Knoxville. After a short stay at the Federal prison camp on Johnson's Island, Wilson was sent to the military prison camp at Hampton, Virginia, in September 1864. He was exchanged later that month at City Point. He retired to Troy, Alabama in February 1865.[92] Wilson had enlisted in the 15th Alabama at the outbreak of hostilities while in Alabama as a member of a traveling theatrical group.[93]

Major Osmun Latrobe, aide to Longstreet, was south of the river and witnessed the attack by the Alabamians and Texans. In his diary, Latrobe wrote that Law's skirmishers were "heavily engaged." He believed their failure to take the Federal trenches was due to a lack of prompt support for these troops. It is unclear from this cryptic remark whether Latrobe thought anyone was at fault or the fortunes of war had intervened against the Confederate attack.[94]

A Diversion

After the reconnaissance in force on the 25th, Law simply held his place south of the cold river, awaiting Longstreet's orders. Law claimed the commanding general ordered him to return to the north side for a dawn attack against Mabry's Hill on November 28. McLaws was to make a diversion against Fort Sanders at the same time, but Longstreet changed the plan before preparations could be completed.[95]

Longstreet sent Law a note on November 27 with instructions to prepare his and Robertson's Brigades for an attack the next morning. Longstreet wrote that he would come to the south side with two brigades of infantry and two brigades of cavalry. Law was not to attack until his arrival, but this plan, too, was changed.[96] Longstreet did not come south with reinforcements.

The plan was changed so the assault against Fort Sanders would be the main point of attack. In a note dated November 28, Longstreet ordered Law to launch a diversion south of the river before daybreak on November 29, before McLaws's Georgians made the assault against Fort Sanders.[97] Longstreet also wanted Law to take part in an effort to isolate and destroy the Federal forces south of the river. After the fall of Fort Sanders, Longstreet intended to push on and capture the Federal pontoon bridge spanning the Tennessee River. He expected Law to drive the Federals south of the river and link up with the Confederates north of the bridge.

McLaws advanced his skirmishers in front of Fort Sanders during the night of November 28. Law went to the artillery position on the south side to watch the fighting north of the river. Years after the war, Law remembered, "The opposing lines of skirmishers were distinctly defined by the flashes of musketry, and I could easily trace the progress made by the Confederates." Law believed the night fight north of the river would draw Federal forces away from his front.[98]

Before daylight, Law gave the order for an artillery barrage against the Federal fortifications on the south side of the Tennessee River. The artillery fire was directed at the breastworks south of the river until McLaws began his assault on Fort Sanders, then it was turned on the Federal fort and lines on the north side.[99] Unfortunately McLaws's attack against Fort Sanders was repulsed with great loss to his command and virtually no loss to the Federal defenders.

Law formed his infantry and one dismounted cavalry brigade in column of attack to move against the enemy position. Only a portion of the 4th Alabama was used in the diversion on November 29. Companies C and F, about 65 soldiers, pushed back the Federal skirmish line and then held against Federal reinforcements while the other eight companies of the 4th remained in reserve. Though not as grand as the charge at Gaines's Mill or Gettysburg, Law recalled the advance of his veteran soldiers with pride: "No advance of skirmishers had been made during the night, and as the column moved swiftly and silently, the first line of works was carried with small loss, the Federals retreating rapidly to the inner line, where their batteries had been established."[100]

This second line was stronger than the first, because of artillery support and a narrow front. The Federals had the advantage in firepower and terrain. Law went forward to make a personal reconnaissance. He believed the enemy works could be taken. But his orders were clear. Any further movement was dependent on success north of the river. Law went to the signal station to contact Longstreet. Even though he could see clearly that the Federals in Fort Sanders had repulsed the Georgians, Law signaled Longstreet, "I can take everything on this side of the river. Shall I go on?" Longstreet signaled back, "Retire to your original position."[101] There could only have been relief among the Alabamians when no order was issued to attack the strong enemy fortification.

Law may have been reluctant to assault the Federals south of the river as vigorously on the 29th as he had on the November 25 because his and Robertson's Brigades together suffered total losses of 116 on the 25th with no tangible results. Acting with more caution on the 29th, perhaps waiting to see positive results north of the river before committing all his forces, Law only lost two killed, six wounded, and one missing.[102]

Pushing the Federals back into their trenches on November 29 gave members of the 15th Alabama the opportunity to remove the dead left on the field when they hastened back to their trenches on November 25.[103] The cold weather had prevented serious decomposition. Billy Jordan found the body of Theo Thompson and removed it for burial. According to Jordan, the thirty-six-year-old Thompson was an excellent shot and a brave soldier who left a widow and eight children when he fell in Tennessee. Jordan was particularly impressed with Thompson, whom he described as "a strictly first class soldier," because Thompson was a substitute.[104]

In an addendum to his report of the East Tennessee campaign, Longstreet mentioned the work of the Texas and Alabama brigades across the Tennessee River. He gave them credit for holding Federal troops south of the river who were designated as reserves for the garrison in Fort Sanders. However, this addendum to his report, penned in January 1864, was not written to compliment Law and Robertson but rather to substantiate further the case Longstreet was building against McLaws.[105]

Shortly after the repulse of the Georgians from the front of Fort Sanders and probably before the Alabamians returned to their breastworks south of the river, Longstreet received a message from Davis that Grant had driven Bragg from Chattanooga to Ringgold, Georgia. During the afternoon of November 29, Longstreet received three more dispatches regarding Bragg, who had moved to Dalton, Georgia, leaving Longstreet to his own devices. Longstreet called a meeting for the evening of November 29 with McLaws, Jenkins, Bushrod Johnson, Kershaw and Alexander to decide whether to move toward Bragg or Virginia. The decision was to remain before Knoxville, occupying Burnside and subsisting on the supplies obtained from enemy territory.

A captured dispatch from Grant to Burnside gave notice to Longstreet that Sherman was en route to relieve the besieged troops at Knoxville.[106] To avoid the Federal trap, Longstreet decided to move into East Tennessee. On December 3, he ordered his trains to follow the route of the East Tennessee and Virginia Railroad, under escort of the brigades of Law and Robertson and one battery of Alexander's artillery. Law's escort command crossed the Holston River at Strawberry Plains by the railroad bridge, while the rest of Longstreet's army moved the night of December 4.[107] Law's Brigade rejoined Jenkins's division December 9 at Rogersville, Tennessee, after a sixty-five mile march from Knoxville.[108]

A couple of days after Longstreet lifted his siege and moved east Burnside was reinforced. He sent a detachment of cavalry to follow Longstreet. But, apparently thinking Longstreet was evacuating East Tennessee, Burnside sent his reinforcement back to Grant's army. He soon found himself with too small a force to defeat Longstreet or push him out of the state.

East Tennessee: "Footprints stained with blood"

Some in Law's Brigade predicted hard service guarding the long train over bad winter roads but were surprised to find the duty without incident. Although unhindered by Federal forces, conditions on the march were deplorable. The weather continued bitterly cold, the roads were frozen and many of the Confederate soldiers traveled barefoot. Sergeant John Taylor, of the 48th Alabama, believed the suffering of Longstreet's men in Tennessee compared with that of George Washington's soldiers in the Revolutionary War. He remembered "thousands of them left their footprints stained with blood" as they marched away from Knoxville.[109]

Porter Alexander recalled "bloody stains" left by shoeless Confederates in November, even before the army reached Knoxville. When Longstreet marched his army to meet the Federal cavalry at Dandridge in January, Sorrel of Longstreet's staff could not forget the incident after the war. "It was bitter winter weather," Sorrel noted, "the ground hard and sharp with ice, and not less than 2,000 of our little army were without shoes. Their bleeding feet left marks at every step."[110] Longstreet, too, remembered his soldiers left blood on the icy ground, their feet cut by frozen mud as sharp as "freshly-quarried rocks," while marching toward Dandridge, Tennessee.[111]

Shoes were often made by the simple expedient of wrapping rawhide around the feet. Longstreet found tanners and cobblers among the ranks of the army and established a shoe factory, which did much to alleviate the shortage.[112] By late January, two hundred soldiers were employed making footwear.[113] Railroad connections were reopened to Virginia in February, and, later that month three thousand pairs of shoes were received from the Confederate quartermaster general.[114]

The campaign in East Tennessee would always be remembered as the time of greatest hardship for the soldiers of Law's Brigade. Throughout the winter of 1863–64, a harshly cold winter with heavy snowfall, the Alabamians suffered critical shortages in rations and clothing.[115] Adjutant Coles of the 4th Alabama was unequivocal in his description of his experience in Tennessee: "This was the coldest winter the regiment experienced, and in which we suffered more hardships than during any other winter campaign of the four years of incessant marching and fighting."[116] For most of their time in East Tennessee, the Virginia transfers would suffer from inadequate supplies. They had come to Georgia in September without any of their winter clothes or equipment.[117]

As early as late December, Longstreet's detached army was suffering badly for want of shoes and clothes. He wrote Adjutant General Cooper on January 2 that his army was so reduced by the problem that he could not remain at military readiness near the enemy, perform work details (thirteen companies were building bridges) and "...live by foraging," which required large numbers of infantry for guard duty.[118]

Those Alabamians with threadbare clothing and no shoes often sat near a fire, wrapped in a blanket while others marched from camp.[119] For example, when the 47th Alabama left camp the morning of January 15 en route to their skirmish with Federal cavalry at Dandridge, three men of Company I were left behind. Henry Figures stayed in camp because of the bad condition of his feet, frostbitten in Virginia the year before, while other soldiers remained behind with various ailments.[120]

Longstreet was worried that the Confederate camps, defended by the sick and barefoot, might be attacked by Federal cavalry while the bulk of the troops were away. He issued orders to organize the sick and lame left behind.[121] Joab Goodson of the 44th Alabama believed the Federal cavalry that followed the Southern army from Knoxville to Morristown did so "with the avowed purpose of driving us out of our winter quarters; they thought that we were nearly all barefooted, I suppose." After the fight at Dandridge, Goodson wrote home that his regiment was enjoying what they had fought the Yankees for, their snug winter quarters.[122]

Bean's Station

On December 13, Longstreet ordered Law to march his Alabamians and Robertson's Brigade to Bean's Station, where the rest of Jenkins's division was poised for an attack on the Federal column that had followed the Confederates from Knoxville.[123] It was late on the 15th of December, after the fighting had ended, before Law arrived at Bean's Station.[124] By Longstreet's reckoning, Law was at least a day late and had marched only eight miles in eight hours on that day. The enemy had escaped him, Longstreet claimed, because of Law's slothful marching.[125] At sunrise the next morning, the 4th Alabama was in line of battle next to Brigadier General Benjamin G. Humphreys's Brigade of Mississippians, waiting for Confederate cavalry to drive the Federal force into their guns. Unknown to the Alabamians lying in ambush in underbrush and briars, the enemy had withdrawn during the night. By noon, several soldiers of the 4th Alabama had become engrossed in chasing a hapless rabbit through the briars, all thoughts of battle forgotten.[126]

In his report of the action at Bean's Station Longstreet said he ordered Law to aid Jenkins in an attack. Instead Law made a case of hardship on behalf of his troops, and Jenkins did not attack when he was not reinforced. Longstreet claimed Law's force would have made the difference in the fight. Law's complaint of hardship followed by one day McLaws's refusal to fight unless his men were fed.[127] Longstreet complained bitterly about Law, but the truth of the matter cannot be determined. Again, Longstreet took no action against Law. His charge that Law could have moved and did not, thus freeing Federal cavalry from the trap, would seem to warrant charges, but none were made. Longstreet tallied another mark against Law to go along with those recorded at the Battle of Wauhatchie and Campbell's Station.

Winter Quarters

After a week north of the river, the Confederates exhausted the resources of the area between Rogersville and Blain's Cross Roads. Longstreet ordered his army to cross the Holston to Morristown to establish winter quarters along the railroad. Law's Brigade arrived at Morristown, on December 23. The brigade made Morristown its home until late February, 1864.[128] Huts were started on Christmas Eve and completed in less than a week.[129] Forage trains shuttled back and forth from camp to the fertile valley between the Tennessee and French Broad Rivers. The region held an abundance of supplies for Longstreet's army, including cattle, sheep, swine, vegetables, and honey, which soon filled his commissary wagons. But supplies, which at first seemed ample, were consumed all too fast.[130] During the month of January, Law's Brigade was generally occupied in the pursuit of food and warmth, and there was the usual picket duty. Law's men were also called upon several times to chase away Federal cavalry which came too close to the camps.[131] The Federal cavalry constantly probed Longstreet's defenses with hit-and-run raids.

Law's Brigade received orders on January 11, 1864, to march to Panther Springs, Tennessee, for picket duty.[132] Leaving the sick and barefoot in Morristown, the brigade endured severe weather for four days.[133] Most of the 4th Alabama pickets and Colonel John Jones, commanding the 44th Alabama, used a church overlooking the village for protection against the harsh conditions. While at Panther Springs, the Alabamians became acquainted with a family with Southern sentiments whose colonial-style home was within the picket line. When outposts of the 4th Alabama exchanged fire with Federal cavalry, the rest of the regiment immediately ran to the action. As they passed the house, they saw the two young girls of the local "secesh" family atop their fence. The young girls were oblivious to minie balls striking their house as they pointed out the cavalry positions.[134]

Immediately after picket duty at Panther Springs, Law's Brigade was ordered to Dandridge, where they found Confederate and Federal cavalry dismounted and exchanging fire. Law's men charged the Federal horsemen and drove them off. Private McClendon of the 15th Alabama believed the constant probing by the Federal cavalry did them no good other than to learn what manner of men the Alabamians were. At Dandridge, McClendon said, they found out for he believed many Federal riders were killed that day.[135]

The 44th Alabama got into the battle line too late to give the Federals anything but farewell shots. They followed the retreating cavalry and became engaged again on the 17th of January. The Federal cavalry retreated toward Knoxville, leaving their killed, wounded, and about 200 prisoners. The Confederates had about 75 casualties.[136]

Winter Foraging

The Confederate column marched from Knoxville to Blain's Cross Roads and then to Rutledge, where Longstreet learned Federal cavalry were in pursuit. Bragg's cavalry had been sent back to his army, so without sufficient cavalry to secure his forage details and screen his army from enemy horsemen, Longstreet decided to put more distance between his army and Burnside's army.[137] When Longstreet reached Rogersville, Tennessee, on December 9 he found abundant supplies in the area. Wagon trains were immediately sent out. However, the mills around Rogersville could only grind one day's ration of flour. To build up a supply of flour, Longstreet reduced the ration to half.[138]

As the supplies nearest the camps were consumed and winter deepened, foraging became more difficult. The wagons ranged farther from camp on each expedition. Some of the trips took the foragers as far as North Carolina to find supplies.[139] The Federal cavalry was always nearby, and the local populace, with strong Union sentiments, made it necessary for details of infantry to accompany the supply wagons.[140]

On the first day of March, the division quartermaster detailed Company B, 44th Alabama, as the escort to a train of fifteen wagons. Led by Captain Goodson, the expedition left camp near Bull's Gap in a rainstorm, following the East Tennessee and Virginia Railroad for two days. The foragers passed through Greeneville on the first day and the village of Jonesboro on the second where they left the rail line in favor of a mountain road to the east. The train passed through narrow mountain valleys, where Goodson was sure bushwhackers lurked on both sides of the road. He believed his command was spared from an attack because Confederate cavalry had killed several bushwhackers in recent days, making the bandits timid.[141]

Goodson tired of sleeping on the ground after two nights and sought shelter at the residence of the Stimpse family. Mr. Stimpse was away from home. Goodson assumed the man of the house was in the Federal army or a bushwhacker in the nearby hills, where he believed all the men from that region could be found. He learned Mrs. Stimpse was in a bad humor because members of the Texas brigade had taken three of her ducks in a raid. Goodson could not convince her that he had nothing to do with her ducks. When he declined her offered food, she said he was not hungry because he had been eating duck.[142]

There was real danger for the forage guards who risked capture by opposing forces. In January 1864 the Federals captured Private James Young Adams, Company D, 4th Alabama, near Mossy Creek, Tennessee, while he was on guard detail. By October 1864,

Adams had had enough of the Federal prison at Rock Island, Illinois and enlisted in the 3rd U.S. Volunteers for frontier service. He was a good soldier, reaching the rank of first sergeant before he was mustered out of the army at Fort Leavenworth on November 29, 1865.[143]

Picket duty in January 1864 required the 4th Alabama to camp without tents in a snow-covered sugar maple grove near the Nolichucky River. Their bivouac provided them with some food when they harvested the sap from the maple trees. They boiled the sap and strained it into their canteens through the few handkerchiefs found among the troops. More food was obtained when the men ignored the deep snow to catch rabbits. Sergeant Tom Matthews of Company K and his detail of twelve men of Company K stole a pig while on the same outpost duty and Coles was one of the lucky ones who got a share. His portion went into the headquarters mess where Bowles and the rest of the staff of the 4th Alabama ate stolen pork with no questions asked.[144]

Davis kept Longstreet in East Tennessee to protect Virginia from a Federal advance. The president told Longstreet he might maneuver in Tennessee as he wished but he had to keep the Federals from passing through Cumberland Gap to invade the Confederacy.[145] Longstreet's presence in East Tennessee also restricted any plans Grant might have entertained to advance south into Georgia. Law's Brigade suffered great hardships and privation in East Tennessee for these strategic reasons. But the soldiers of Longstreet's command saw the campaign in Tennessee as a needless hardship for no gain. The skirmish with Federal cavalry at Dandridge in mid-January was their only military action in Tennessee in 1864. They had become an ill-clad, hungry, lousy band foraging off the land. They were dispirited, and wanted to rejoin the Army of Northern Virginia.[146]

Quarreling Generals

By mid-December 1863, relations between Longstreet and Law had become intolerable. In addition to laying the blame for Confederate failures at Wauhatchie and Campbell's Station on Law, Longstreet had found Law's conduct at Bean's Station worthy of censure.[147] Law, for his part, having lost any chance to command Hood's Division, also lost any affection for Longstreet and his former classmate Micah Jenkins. He was bitter and cooperated as little as possible with his superior officers.[148]

On December 17, Law resigned his position as brigadier general in the Provisional Army on grounds that he had been passed over unjustly. He outlined for Longstreet his recent duty as commander of Hood's Division from Gettysburg through Chickamauga, a time he described as the "most eventful period in the history of the division." Law challenged his commanding officer to dispute his claim of competent leadership, knowing Longstreet had already acknowledged his good work with a note of congratulations following Chickamauga. Law also reminded Longstreet that officers under his command had expressed their confidence in him to the president.[149]

Law clearly stated his belief that Longstreet had treated him unfairly. Although he admitted Jenkins ranked him, Law nevertheless asserted rank alone was not enough to promote Jenkins over him. Law had a history with the men of the division while Jenkins was "not identified with it by association or service on a single battlefield of the war." In addition, Law pointed out Longstreet nominated his protégé for permanent command in opposition to the wishes of the division's officers. Besides the injustice Law felt was done him, he warned Longstreet that if promotion due for faithful service was not forthcoming, the enthusiasm required for effective military service would disappear from the officer ranks of the army.[150]

Law added that he had submitted to this injustice since Chickamauga out of duty. He believed the end of the campaign freed him to seek a new, though more humble, position in the army. "This resignation is not tendered in a spirit of resentment or pique," Law assured Longstreet, "but under the deliberate conviction that in the unsatisfactory and unpleasant circumstances that have been stated, I cannot serve the country with that intense enthusiasm which she has a right to demand from all of her sons."[151] Though hostility existed between the two generals by the end of 1863, the tone of the letter was conciliatory. He accepted the inevitable. He was unable to serve in the division after Jenkins had gotten the position which he felt was rightfully his and which he believed Longstreet had promised would be his.[152]

Longstreet granted Law a leave of absence and allowed him the unusual latitude of taking the resignation to Richmond himself, probably relieved to be rid of him.[153] In Richmond, Law visited with his friend Hood who was convalescing at the home of Gustavus W. Smith.[154] Hood knew Law's resignation would be costly to the Confederacy because he knew Law to be a brave and capable officer, respected by the Alabamians and his own Texans. He persuaded Law to allow him to take along the resignation letter during an unofficial visit to the secretary of war. The paper never went through the regular channels at the Adjutant and Inspector General's Office.[155] It was decided not to present the resignation to the Richmond authorities, apparently on the assumption that if it was never officially offered, Law was not resigned, only on leave of absence and still in command of his troops.[156]

While in Richmond, Law lobbied at the War Department for promotion to major general and command of Hood's Division. A fellow South Carolinian, Samuel W. Melton, worked in the adjutant and inspector general's office at that time. The quarrel between Law and Jenkins generated enough heat within the offices of the department to warrant its mention by Melton in a letter to his wife. He did not approve of the way the two brigadiers from his state conducted themselves. He wrote his wife that Law was in Richmond, then added "He and Jenkins have quarreled terribly— both are fighting for the same place—to command Hood's Division. I like to see a house divided against itself. Hope they'll have a merry time."[157]

Meanwhile, on December 20, 1863, at Bean's Station, Tennessee, the regimental officers of Law's Brigade submitted a petition for transfer from Longstreet's Corps. The document was given to Perry, commanding the brigade in Law's absence, who approved it and forwarded it to Jenkins. The petition asked for a transfer to Alabama or Georgia so the brigade might recruit its ranks, "so greatly reduced by the hardships of active service and the casualties of war," before the beginning of the spring campaign. The document made no mention of dissatisfaction.[158]

Longstreet was furious. His endorsement of the petition was a virtual accusation of mutiny, for to him, the presentation of the petition immediately after Law's resignation involved an obvious conspiracy among the Alabamians aimed at their transfer to, as he put it, "less arduous service." It was Longstreet's view that if Law had nothing to do with this petition, the regimental officers should offer a statement which proved it. Otherwise, these officers owed their country an explanation.[159]

The Alabama officers, with one exception, furnished Longstreet with an explanation on December 26, simply stating that a transfer had been desired by the regimental officers for several months and none of them had "the slightest inclination of the recommendation of another officer for promotion over General Jenkins. We could state in conclusion that Genl Law was ignorant of the movement and that we had no reason to believe it coincided with his wishes."[160]

Lowther, commanding the 15th Alabama, did not sign the letter of explanation. Instead, he wrote a separate note explaining his motive for signing the petition of December 19. Lowther disavowed any desire for a transfer from Longstreet's Corps, claiming he signed only "in deference to the wishes of his brother officers." His concluding sentence must have given pause to Longstreet. Lowther said he signed the petition because "He was informed that Genl Law wishes this petition forwarded."[161]

Longstreet made much of the petition for transfer to support his case against Law and the regimental officers of Law's Brigade. It was, however, much ado about little. He had already received a request from Benning to transfer his brigade to Augusta, Georgia, to recruit its ranks and Longstreet approved Benning's request. The Texas brigade made a similar request in January, which prompted a letter from Longstreet to Cooper on January 5, rescinding his approval for Benning's move to Georgia. He wrote Cooper that he had to deny Benning in the name of fairness because he had received other requests for transfer to recruit. Longstreet said he had to deny all such requests if he denied any.[162]

With Law gone to Richmond, it looked as though the way was clear for Jenkins's promotion to major general and command of Hood's Division. But, in a move that seemed to put the welfare of the division ahead of Jenkins's personal ambition, Longstreet offered the name of Major General Robert Ransom, Jr., to lead Hood's Division. He explained that the jealousy between Jenkins and Law had destroyed the effectiveness of the division and he believed the assignment of another major general instead of a promotion would best restore the division to fighting trim. If Ransom was not acceptable, Longstreet suggested yet another candidate, Major General William H. C. Whiting.[163]

Authorities in Richmond did not consider either Ransom or Whiting as suitable replacements for Hood. When he saw Longstreet's nomination of Ransom or Whiting, however, President Davis ordered a response to the general which included a suggestion: "If General Jenkins were assigned to another command, the difficulty, long since anticipated, might be overcome."[164] This comment from Davis indicates more disagreement between him and Longstreet than was previously thought. It suggests Davis had warned Longstreet that a rivalry would arise between the two brigadiers if Jenkins was given command of the division. Their discussions about command of Hood's Division may explain why Longstreet did not recommend Jenkins. He knew Davis would oppose the nomination. Unfortunately, Adjutant General Cooper took the extraordinary step of ordering the sentence deleted from the official response before it was sent to Longstreet.[165] Why Cooper edited the president's remarks is not known. Longstreet did not see Davis's remark and any response he might have made is lost to history.

By January 7, 1864, Longstreet had decided he had been tricked by Law. He endorsed and forwarded the Alabamians' petition, complaining that Law deceived him with the pretense of offering his resignation to get to Richmond. Once at Richmond, Longstreet believed Law intended instead to use political influence to remove his brigade from the First Corps. Additionally, Longstreet claimed Law maintained his influence over the officers of his brigade with the implied promise of a transfer to a safer location, an accusation which would have no doubt inflamed the Alabamians. As far as Longstreet was concerned, Law's resignation had been offered and accepted, even though it had not yet reached Cooper.[166] Longstreet requested that he be informed if Law had not submitted it to the War Department.[167]

The officers of Law's Brigade, unable to obtain a transfer out of Longstreet's Corps, next tried to secure the brigade commander of their choice. Writing directly to Cooper on January 28, 1864, from camp near New Market, Tennessee, the officers, believing Law's resignation had been submitted and accepted, nominated Perry to command the brigade. Their letter reminded Cooper that Perry commanded the brigade on September 20, and the last two months, and suggested Perry's promotion would please the entire command.[168]

Both Jenkins and Longstreet approved the letter, Jenkins adding the remark that he had observed Perry as an efficient commander in the field and in camp. Citing Perry's good work in leading the brigade in the charge against Federal cavalry at Dandridge, Longstreet observed that Law had left the brigade "in bad condition," but that "it seems now in good discipline and fine morale." Whether he believed Perry an able officer worthy of promotion or simply the vehicle to permanently remove Law from his corps is put to question by the concluding lines of his endorsement: "Gen Law's resignation should be accepted at once."[169] Perry was also recommended for brigade command by Alabama congressmen who wrote to Davis on February 9, 1864.[170] Seven of the nine Alabama representatives signed the letter, probably motivated as much by the desire to have a native son command the Alabama brigade as by Perry's good work.

On the same day Longstreet tried to clarify for the adjutant general his remarks regarding the effectiveness of Hood's Division while under Jenkins's control. In endorsements and letters Longstreet had mentioned the division's loss of efficiency while both Law and Jenkins served as brigadiers. Explaining his recommendation of Ransom to command Hood's Division, for example, Longstreet wrote Cooper that he was unable to use the division effectively because of jealousy between Law and Jenkins. The efficiency of the division, Longstreet added, was greatly reduced by the rivalry.[171]

In a letter now lost, Cooper asked Longstreet to explain the inefficiency of Hood's Division while under Jenkins. From Morristown, Tennessee, Longstreet wrote Cooper that his written comments on various documents had been misunderstood and had led to a false impression of Jenkins's ability. Longstreet noted his displeasure with the division during part of the five months Jenkins commanded but assured the adjutant general that no fault lay with Jenkins. The blame lay entirely with generals Law and Robertson, both "disaffected and discontented officers." Longstreet offered his opinion that since the departure of these two officers the division was as good as ever.[172]

On February 12, 1864, the officers of Law's Brigade sent a second petition, this time to Adjutant General Cooper. They disavowed any "efforts . . . to produce the impression with the War Department that the promotion of Brig Genl M. Jenkins to the command of Hood's Division would cause discontent with command, and prove injurious to the service, beg leave, most respectfully to state, that, in our opinion, no such result would fallout." The Alabamians offered this petition as an act of justice to Jenkins, whom they claimed to esteem. This was probably the case, for the Alabama officers did not know Jenkins before his assignment to temporary command of the division. But they wanted to serve under Law. In addition, they wanted out of Longstreet's Corps. The petition no doubt reflected their acceptance of the inevitable and they hoped it would make service under Longstreet and Jenkins more harmonious.[173] Longstreet's influence, however, was not enough to win the division for Jenkins. Richmond authorities settled the quarrel with the appointment of Charles W. Field as major general and assigned him to command Hood's old division.[174] Like Hood, Field was Kentucky born and a West Point graduate. He had led a brigade at Seven Pines, Cedar Mountain, and Second Manassas, where he had been severely wounded.[175] He was still crippled by his injury when he took command of Hood's Division.[176] Field would lead the division with distinction for the rest of the war. Longstreet was not happy with Field's appointment and he fought against the order, further alienating himself from Richmond.[177]

Longstreet Prefers Charges Against Law

By the middle of February, the authorities in Richmond had resolved the problem of command for Hood's Division but were unable to reach a decision regarding command of Law's Brigade. Law was on leave of absence until March 1, while the authorities in Richmond tried to sort out the equities of his case.[178] No resignation had been officially offered by Law, and Perry led the brigade while Law was absent on leave. Longstreet continued to fume.

In early March, he acted against Law. After his leave of absence, Law returned to the First Corps and was placed under arrest, charged with "conduct highly prejudicial to good order and military discipline."[179] This charge stemmed from Longstreet's belief that Law obtained a leave of absence under the pretext that he was resigning from his command when he did not really intend to resign. Further, Longstreet still claimed Law had encouraged the officers of the brigade to petition for a transfer. Longstreet asserted this was a misuse of "...the influence of his high official position to create discontent amongst his troops." Law retained Oates and Benning, both attorneys before joining the army, to represent him in the expected court-martial.[180] Benning was another brigadier in Longstreet's disfavor at the time and was happy to oblige.[181]

Longstreet was slow in preparing the necessary documents to officially charge Law but rumors of Law's arrest soon reached Richmond.[182] Cooper telegraphed Longstreet, on March 12, asking if he had placed Law under arrest and, if so, to send the charges to Richmond immediately.[183] Longstreet happened to be in Richmond, conferring with Davis and Lee, so Major General Simon B. Buckner, in temporary command of the First Corps, wired Cooper that his dispatch would be waiting for Longstreet when he returned.[184]

By March 18, Longstreet was back in Tennessee, and his answer to Cooper's question was short but confident: "General Law is in arrest by my order. The charges will be forwarded as early as possible."[185] Cooper received Longstreet's charges against Law on March 22.[186] Law wrote Longstreet on the same day requesting a copy of the charges against him. Although he had been under arrest for almost three weeks, Longstreet had not written out the charges and specifications for Law or the War Department. Sorrel responded to Law with a curt note that the charges were not yet prepared but would be sent to the brigadier "within a few days or at the earliest practical moment."[187] On April 8, Longstreet added a second charge against Law, that of "conduct unbecoming an officer and a gentleman." This additional complaint accused Law of destroying his resignation, which Longstreet considered the property of the Confederate War Department.[188]

Longstreet found no support in Richmond for his efforts to court-martial Law. First, the adjutant and inspector general countermanded Longstreet's order separating Law's Brigade from the First Corps. Longstreet had planned to leave the brigade, regardless who commanded it, in Tennessee with Buckner when the First Corps returned to the Army of Northern Virginia. This was a way for Longstreet to vent his anger at Law and the Alabama officers who petitioned to leave his command.[189] He would be rid of them and the Alabamians would be posted where they least wanted to serve.

Instead, on April 18 Cooper ordered Buckner to send the brigade to Charlottesville, Virginia to report to Field. In addition, the adjutant general ordered Law restored to command. Next, Cooper telegraphed Longstreet on April 27 that none of the charges he had preferred against Law would be entertained and, further, Law was to rejoin his brigade in Field's Division. Cooper's message was a response to Longstreet's telegram the day before asking if the adjutant general had received the additional charge preferred against Law.[190]

It was Lee who informed Longstreet on April 26 that charges against Law would not be pursued and that Law and his brigade were to again serve in his corps.[191] Lee learned of Cooper's order to Buckner to send the Alabamians back to Virginia before Longstreet was aware of it because the War Department considered Longstreet under Lee's command and forwarded the orders through the chain of command. Though more than a week had passed since Cooper had ordered the charges against Law dropped and Law restored to command, Longstreet was ignorant of this order until Lee told him.

Lee had, in fact, initiated the order to reunite Law's Brigade with the First Corps. In a letter of April 16 to Bragg, Lee asked to release the Alabama brigade for service with the Army of Northern Virginia, citing the War Department's order to Longstreet to report back to Lee. Interpreting the order literally, Lee insisted it should include Law's Alabamians. Lee said Longstreet had explained the detachment of Law's Brigade from the First Corps as a temporary measure designed to equalize the strength of the units within his command in Tennessee.[192] Coincidentally, Lee's desire to keep all his available manpower served the wishes of the Alabamians and thwarted Longstreet's plan to rid his command of Law and his brigade.

Bragg, serving Davis in roughly the capacity of chief of staff, quickly passed on Lee's request to Cooper.[193] "As the charges against General Law are not sustained by the Department," offered Bragg, "he should be restored to his command." Bragg suggested Cooper notify Longstreet by telegraph to expedite the matter, but Cooper chose instead to tell Lee that Law's Brigade, with Law in command, would be returned to his corps.[194]

Longstreet, determined that Law would never again serve in his command, wrote Lee for support against Law.[195] He told Lee that he blamed Law for the failures at Wauhatchie and Campbell's Station and pointed out the gravity of the charges preferred against Law. Longstreet declared he could not remain in command of the First Corps if his efforts to maintain discipline were to be overturned by the authorities in Richmond. It was a choice, therefore, of Law's court-martial or Longstreet's resignation. Finally, Longstreet informed Lee of his intention to rearrest Law when Law returned to Virginia.[196] Indeed, Law was again arrested when he rejoined Longstreet's Corps in Virginia, probably on April 28, 1864.[197]

Lee believed Longstreet was issuing an ultimatum and wrote Cooper on April 30, declaring the charges against Law were "of a very grave character," and suggesting that a court should determine Law's guilt or innocence. If there was no time at present to convene a court-martial, Lee felt Law should be relieved from duty until one could be assembled.[198] In effect, it was Lee's opinion that the Confederacy needed Longstreet more than it needed Law.[199]

Cooper forwarded Lee's letter to Davis on May 5, 1864.[200] It was not well received. In a note to Secretary of War Seddon, Davis made it clear that both he and the secretary were fully informed regarding Law's conduct. He ordered Seddon to make the facts of the case clear to Lee.[201]

The president rebuked Longstreet for making "injurious statements" about Law in his letter to Lee. Davis declared Longstreet had "seriously offended against good order and military discipline" when he again arrested Law upon the latter's return to Virginia. "If General Law has misbehaved at Lookout Mountain or elsewhere in the face of the enemy," Davis continued, "charges should have been preferred."[202]

Law Retaliates

From the start of his quarrel with Longstreet, Law fought his commanding officer with every resource at his disposal. He had the support of members of the Confederate Congress for promotion to Hood's command. Hood helped at the War Department. Cooper and Davis, perhaps because of Longstreet's impolitic behavior, gave Law the benefit of the doubt throughout. The fact that Davis had recommended Law to lead Hood's Division in October and had been rebuffed by Longstreet's insistence on appointing Jenkins very likely influenced the president in Law's favor in the spring of 1864. In addition, Law tried to gather enough evidence of neglect of duty to file charges against Longstreet, hoping to drive him from the service.

Before his return to duty on March 1, Law visited with Bragg to secure an ally and gather evidence against Longstreet. Law talked with Bragg about regaining his command, while Bragg, for his part, believed he already had evidence of Longstreet's "disobedience, neglect of duty and want of cordial cooperation and support, which resulted in all the disasters after Chickamauga."[203] Of course, Bragg and Longstreet had been enemies since Chickamauga and the crisis in Bragg's command which followed that battle. Further, if Bragg could deflect some of the blame for his disastrous campaign, he would do so. Law made a judicious choice when he enlisted Bragg as an ally.

In addition to garnering Bragg's support, Law forged an alliance with McLaws which was based on their mutual hatred of Longstreet. The two disaffected generals may have begun plotting against Longstreet even before they left his command in Tennessee. They shared information received from a spy in Longstreet's headquarters, Major John F. Edwards, formerly commissary chief for McLaws's Division. Assigned to Longstreet's headquarters by the time both Law and McLaws were under arrest, he passed on news to McLaws through an intermediary. He also met with Bragg and Law.[204]

McLaws began his own campaign against Longstreet with a letter circulated among his supporters in Richmond while his court-martial was in session. In this open letter, McLaws accused Longstreet of pursuing a vendetta against him for his refusal to join with Longstreet and others in their attempt to oust Bragg after Chickamauga. Further, McLaws alleged that Longstreet had preferred charges against him to divert attention from his own responsibility for the failed Tennessee campaign. Citing specifics, McLaws indicted Longstreet for not attacking Burnside before the Federals reached Knoxville. He claimed Longstreet's negligence led to the siege of Knoxville and, in turn, was the cause of Bragg's defeat at Chattanooga.[205]

Writing to McLaws while under arrest at Gordonsville, Virginia, Law was nonetheless jubilant at the prospect of winning his struggle with Longstreet. He related the decision of the Richmond authorities not to hold a court in his case. Law was now ready to take the offensive in his struggle with Longstreet, suggesting that he and McLaws both file charges against Longstreet. He planned to collect evidence proving Longstreet guilty of neglect of duty at Lookout Valley and "conduct unworthy of an officer and a gentleman" for writing a false report of the fight of October 28. "If you will cover the Knoxville campaign in your charges," Law added, "I believe we can oust him."[206]

Law suggested McLaws charge Longstreet with not bringing the enemy to battle before Knoxville, citing two specifications to the charge. First, the Confederates arrived at Lenoir's Station with at least two hours of daylight, plenty of time for an attack. Law believed the testimony of Benning, John Bratton, in command of Jenkins's old South Carolina brigade, and Major James M. Goggin, adjutant to McLaws, would sustain that specification. Second, McLaws could point out Longstreet's failure to send "one division, at least, to Campbell's Station to cut off the enemy from his only way of retreat." For more evidence against Longstreet, Law suggested McLaws could call Colonel Francis H. Little, commanding the 11th Georgia, to testify that he discovered Burnside's retreat from Lenoir's Station at 2 a.m. on November 16, but was denied permission to attack. If

McLaws wanted, he could also point to Longstreet's slowness of pursuit from Lenoir's Station on November 16. To this slowness Law could testify, as well as the fact that when Law's Brigade passed the captured Federal wagons at the late hour of nearly 10 a.m., Longstreet was "dismounted and among the captured wagons."[207] The two disgruntled generals did not actually file charges against Longstreet. Perhaps they did not wish to pursue the issue once they had been reinstated to command. More likely, the death of Jenkins and the wounding of Longstreet in the Wilderness only a week after Law's letter made filing charges inappropriate.

Lee feared a repeat of trouble between Longstreet and McLaws and requested the Georgian be assigned to duty in another theater.[208] Law proved a more difficult problem. It was a combination of good politics by Law, Longstreet's mistakes, and Lee's desire to hold on to all the veteran troops of his army which kept Law in command of his brigade.

Davis delayed making the decision whether Law or Jenkins or someone else should be given permanent command of Hood's Division. The jealousies and disputes were left to Longstreet to settle. But Longstreet was a participant in the quarrels and was unable to stop the dissension tearing at his command. By the end of his second independent command, Longstreet had brought charges against McLaws and Brigadier Generals Law and Robertson. He also thoroughly alienated himself from the Confederacy's high command in Richmond.[209]

Brigadier General William Flake Perry

Reproduced from William A. Baugh,
Confederate Faces, *69*

**Colonel William Calvin Oates,
15th Alabama**

Reproduced from William C. Oates, The War

**Lieutenant Colonel William Houston
Scruggs, 4th Alabama**

Courtesy ADAH

**Adjutant Henry Stokes Figures,
48th Alabama**

*Courtesy Huntsville–Madison County
Public Library*

**Lieutenant Colonel Isaac Ball Feagin,
15th Alabama**

Courtesy ADAH

227

Captain James H. Young, Company K, 4th Alabama

Courtesy Annewhite T. Fuller
Huntsville, Alabama

Private John M. Anderson, Company K, 48th Alabama

Courtesy William Simpson
Holly Pond, Alabama

Captain Reuben Vaughan Kidd, Company A, 4th Alabama

Courtesy ADAH

First Lieutenant Erwin Foster Rice, Company K, 48th Alabama

Courtesy J. C. Rice
Scotsboro, Alabama

228

**Captain Major Dowell Sterrett,
Company C, 4th Alabama**
Courtesy ADAH

**Captain John W. Purifoy,
Company C, 44th Alabama**
Courtesy ADAH

**First Lieutenant Alvin O. Dickson,
Company A, 48th Alabama**
Courtesy ADAH

**Captain John B. Fondren,
Company F, 44th Alabama**
Courtesy ADAH

**Second Lieutenant William A. Beaty,
Company K, 48th Alabama**
Courtesy Don D. Beaty
Kress, Texas

**Captain David L. Bozeman,
Company B, 44th Alabama**
Courtesy George Jones
Princeton, New Jersey

**Private Anderson Walker,
Company B, 4th Alabama**
Courtesy Gregg D. Gibbs
Austin Texas

**Private James David King,
Company K, 48th Alabama**
Courtesy Jesse Henson
Terre Haute, Indiana

Chapter 12

Fighting Alone in the Wilderness

The order returning Longstreet to Virginia brought joy to the camps of Law's Alabamians. They left East Tennessee for the Army of Northern Virginia without regrets. The corps broke camp near Bull's Gap, Tennessee on March 20, 1864, crossed the Holston River and camped at Zollicoffer a few days. From there the brigade marched on to Bristol, Tennessee near the Virginia state line.[1]

Chaplain W. G. Starr offered up a prayer for the men's safety and well-being in the upcoming campaign, as the 47th Alabama received a new battle flag on the morning of March 21. Before the formal flag presentation, Major James Campbell delivered a lengthy speech which many in the rear ranks could not hear. But that made little difference, because Law's Alabamians were in good spirits and needed little encouragement from the regiment's commanding officer. They were headed for Virginia and "Marse" Lee's army. Private James Daniel, Company H, mused that there had been considerable talk of having the Alabamians remain in Tennessee on guard duty, but then he thought the authorities had wisely concluded that the army "could not go to a good fight without our brigade." A short time after the ceremony ended, orders came down from headquarters to cook rations for departure the next day.[2]

Law's Brigade boarded trains for Charlottesville, Virginia, 260 miles to the northeast. Though the "trains were dilapidated," Adjutant Coles of the 4th Alabama recalled the trip was made in easy stages.[3] The 47th and 48th Alabama left April 22 and arrived at Lynchburg the next day. After another short train ride aboard the Orange & Alexandria Railroad on Sunday the 24th, the regiments camped at Charlottesville.[4] The 44th Alabama left two days behind the twin regiments and, making better time, arrived at Lynchburg on April 25 and bivouacked that night at Charlottesville.[5] The Alabama brigade marched about fifteen miles the next morning and established camp at Cobham Station near Gordonsville.[6] The Alabamians were in excellent spirits and eager to get at the Federal army.[7]

With the return of the First Corps, the organization of the Army of Northern Virginia looked much as it did the previous summer. Lee commanded three corps of infantry and the cavalry, while Longstreet retained command of the First Corps. In April 1864, however, he had only two divisions under his immediate command, Field's and Kershaw's. Pickett's Division was on duty in North Carolina and would not rejoin the First Corps until late in May. Ewell commanded the Second Corps and A. P. Hill the Third Corps.

Lee's army occupied a line about 45 miles long, roughly parallel with and south of the Rapidan River. Ewell was near Mine Run, a few miles to the south.[8] Hill was at Orange

Court House. Longstreet's forces guarded against the chance of a Federal flanking maneuver from the southern end of the Shenandoah Valley.[9] Lee's headquarters was two miles northeast of Orange Court House. From an observation post on nearby Clark's Mountain, signalmen kept a steady watch on the Army of the Potomac.

Meade remained in command of the Army of the Potomac, but there was one difference now, one that would prove a significant factor in future battles fought by this army. The Federal armies had a new commander, a man named U. S. Grant who came onto the scene with good credentials, having already bested four Confederate generals.[10] Grant chose to make his headquarters in the field with the Army of the Potomac. Law believed Grant had been out-generaled at Shiloh, but was saved by reinforcements. Rumor attributed his other victories to weak opponents. Law knew Grant was aggressive but suspected his boldness came from an advantage in numbers. The fighting between the Union and Confederacy clearly entered a new phase after Grant took command because, before his arrival, the Federal army fought and retreated after being bloodied. For the duration of the conflict, the Army of the Potomac and the Army of Northern Virginia remained locked in fierce combat. After Law participated in the fight against Grant's army in the spring of 1864, he remarked, "We were not prepared for the unparalleled stubbornness and tenacity with which he persisted in his attacks under fearful losses which his army sustained."[11]

The Confederate Quartermaster Corps busied itself during the winter gathering a supply of clothing, the Alabamians receiving new uniforms at Gordonsville.[12] The 47th Alabama's attire was plain, but sufficient. Pants were gray, and jackets were either black or gray, and better yet, new Enfield rifles were issued. In Company H, 47th Alabama, Private James Crowder's spirits were exceedingly high that April of 1864. He proudly caressed his Enfield with its new coat of black paint on the barrel, considering it one of the best guns in use.[13] Private James Daniel, Company H, 47th Alabama, reported the regiment was not only well clothed but also in excellent spirits.[14] Also, food was actually sufficient for the first time in many months compared to the meager fare in East Tennessee. Each meal was a sumptuous affair. The men especially liked the rations commandeered from the Federal commissary.[15] Each mess included a pound and a quarter of meal daily for each man. They were also issued a pound of bacon, sugar, coffee, rice, salted vegetables and beans.[16] Those in the ranks were not sure how long the rations would be this plentiful, but each intended to enjoy every morsel.

Lee Reviews the First Corps

As the days grew warmer the men devoted themselves to drilling. A rumor made the rounds in camp that Lee planned to review the First Corps. When word arrived that his visit was to be on April 29, Field reviewed his division on the 28th.[17] On the big day Longstreet honored his commander with a full dress parade, which Joab Goodson of the 44th Alabama described as a grand affair.[18] It was a very festive occasion, taking place a few miles south of Mechanicsville in a valley with large pastures and old fields. Guns were burnished and rubbed down while cartridge boxes and belts received a good buff. Brass buttons and buckles were polished until they looked like new, and shoes and boots were greased to perfection. One of Jenkins's South Carolinians said that after everything was considered, Longstreet's troops were rather decent looking soldiers. Longstreet formed his two divisions in two columns with the artillery on the flank. Lee appeared old to Goodson. The commanding general was honored with a 13-gun salute as he rode onto the parade ground.[19] He sat elegantly astride Traveler and passed along the long line of troops. In fact, he rode so close that the men were able to get a good view of his facial features.[20]

The Rebel Yell was loud and continuous, as soldiers flung their hats high into the air.[21] Color bearers dipped and waved their flags while the drummers and fifers struck up "Hail to the Chief." In recognition of the salute, the commander of the Army of Northern Virginia lifted his hat and rode to the center of the column.[22] Alabama soldiers, Goodson wrote to his niece, had the utmost confidence in Lee. The general expressed his hope that the troops would all do their duty in the hard fighting he expected in the coming campaign. Goodson predicted a great battle within two weeks.[23] A formal grand parade, which in column of companies required several hours, followed. Each company gave a salute as it passed the commanding general and his party. Few if any knew it at the time, but this was to be the last review for their general.[24] When the last company passed in review the corps was again assembled once more for Longstreet and Lee to conduct an inspection of the splendid ranks.[25] The men's spirits remaining high as more regimental and brigade drill followed the review.[26]

Law, still under arrest, did not participate in the event. Longstreet ordered him to move his tent away from the brigade, which Perry now commanded.[27] On the morning of May 2, Perry moved the brigade to a new campsite near Gordonsville. They marched by Law's tent as he stood outside with his aides and each regiment gave him a hearty cheer.[28] Oates took the opportunity to stop and exchange pleasantries, and they discussed Law's arrest. Law asked the colonel's advice on the matter. When Oates discovered Law did not have a copy of the charges against him, he suggested Law demand a copy. The general immediately sent an aide to First Corps headquarters. Sorrel, Longstreet's chief of staff, told the aide that Law had been supplied with the charges. This was not the case. Oates then suggested to Law that he send his aide-de-camp, Mims Walker, to Richmond with a note to the secretary of war requesting a copy of them.[29] Walker went to Richmond that night.

The Spring Campaign Commences

May 4 began innocently enough. The brigade drilled early that morning, and since the day was unusually warm, the men lounged in the shade after returning to camp. Early in the afternoon, officers issued orders to prepare a three-day supply of rations and to be ready to march within the hour.[30] The men rushed to get ready, but before half of the bread was baked they were forced to stuff raw or half-baked dough or cornbread into their haversacks. They tossed away accumulated plunder and began rolling blankets. When the command to fall in was given a half hour later, they were ready to march. Law's Brigade left Gordonsville by Lawler's Road about 4 p.m. The spring campaign had began.

Two days earlier Lee met with his corps and division commanders at Clark's Mountain where he predicted Grant would cross the Rapidan and attempt to turn the Confederate right. Grant did just that with his cavalry, crossing the Rapidan at Germanna and Ely fords just between 2 and 4 a.m. on the morning of May 4, 1864.[31] The Army of the Potomac plunged directly into the area known as the Wilderness. Grant's objective was the Confederate capital at Richmond.

In May 1864 the Wilderness was a tract of low ridges and swampy hollows covered with a dense growth of timber, its boundaries encompassing about 15 square miles. Geographically it was about equidistant between Orange Court House and Fredericksburg. Spotsylvania Court House lay about ten miles to the southeast. The Chancellorsville battlefield was about ten miles to the east. Timber in the Wilderness was primarily second growth consisting of stunted scrub pine, sweet gum, dwarfed oak, ash, walnut saplings and cedar, the original growth having long been cut to fuel nearby iron furnaces. Over the

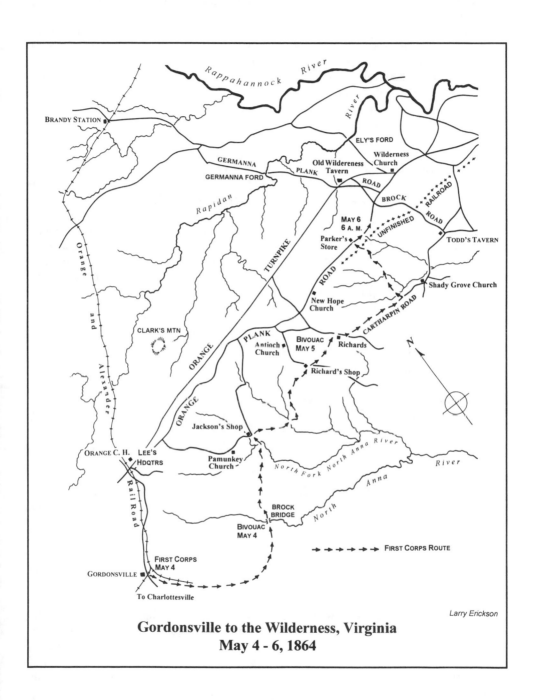

Gordonsville to the Wilderness, Virginia
May 4 - 6, 1864

Larry Erickson

intervening years, the additional sunlight had encouraged a thick growth of matted under-brush, including hazel, laurel and chincopin, other bushes and briers. In some places, it was almost impossible to penetrate. Shallow marshy depressions and small sluggish streams laced the terrain, draining into Wilderness Run which emptied into the Rapidan. An occa-sional small farm or abandoned clearing accounted for the limited agriculture within its boundaries. Once inside the Wilderness, it was difficult in some places to see more than 50 feet in any direction. From Orange Court House, two roads ran easterly across the Wilderness toward Fredericksburg. The Orange Turnpike was the closer of the two to the Rapidan. This turnpike intersected the Germanna Plank Road at the Wilderness Tavern, an abandoned stagecoach stop. The second was the Orange Plank Road which intersected the Brock Road about four miles south of Wilderness Tavern. Both roads, in general, ran parallel and followed the general direction of the river.[32]

After fording the Rapidan, the Army of the Potomac followed the Germanna Plank Road which joins the Brock Road near Wilderness Tavern.[33] Lee moved to attack the Army of the Potomac from the flank, ordering Ewell to march by the Turnpike. A. P. Hill, with the divisions of Major Generals Henry Heth and Cadmus M. Wilcox, marched on the Plank Road. Lee directed Longstreet to march with Hill. This order caused considerable congestion and delay, so Longstreet asked and received permission to take an alternate route.[34] The First Corps subsequently marched over backroads that would bring the troops into the Wilderness along the Catharpin Road.

The strength of the Alabama brigade going into the spring campaign is estimated at 1176, including field, company and staff officers.[35] Three companies in the brigade were without commissioned officers, and altogether there were 113 officers present. Only the 4th Alabama had the luxury of a full compliment of field officers; the 44th Alabama had two; the 47th Alabama had one, and the 48th Alabama was commanded by its senior captain, John W. Wiggenton.[36]

When the brigade left Gordonsville, each man carried 60 cartridges, a bedroll and whatever could be stuffed into his haversack. The brigade marched 12 miles and halted to rest near Brock's Bridge on the North Anna River.[37] Soon afterward, Longstreet and his staff crossed the plain and rode toward the northeast. To those in the ranks it quickly became apparent that the entire First Corps was in motion. Except for brief rest stops, the column marched throughout the night. Law's Brigade did not bivouac until nearly sun-down on the evening of May 5 near Richard's Shop in the vicinity of the Antioch Church.[38] The line of march was now along the Catharpin Road which converged with the Orange Plank Road near Chancellorsville. Bivouac that night was at a point where the two roads were nearly parallel and about six miles apart.[39]

At an early hour on the morning of May 6, a staff officer arrived from Lee with urgent orders to march. When the men were roused from their sleep, the Palmetto Sharpshooters' band struck a lively tune to serenade Jenkins.[40] It was a fortuitous decision, because the early serenade was to be their last chance to play for the general. During preparations to move out, each man was alone with his thoughts. Most contemplated the expected battle and what the day might bring. Some chose to share their thoughts with a comrade. More than one soldier had premonitions that the day would end in death. David H. B. Abernathy, his nephew William F. Abernathy, and their friend Andrew J. Wilson, all of Company I, 47th Alabama, talked as they prepared to march. Wilson sensed his death was near, while William felt he would escape unhurt. David predicted he would receive a wound in the arm. He carried a thick notebook in his left breast pocket and hoped the notebook might offer some protection from a direct shot to the heart. As the trio talked, David carefully folded a large cloth he used to polish the barrel of his musket. He placed it in front of the notebook and carefully positioned this protection over his heart.[41] Satisfied he had taken all safety precautions available to him, David Abernathy marched off to battle.

Dawn, May 6 – The March into Battle

Longstreet's column changed direction for the Plank Road and moved out briskly in the predawn darkness.[42] Kershaw's Division led the way as the men marched over old roads deeply furrowed and pocked from lack of maintenance.[43] The men tramped through thick woods and across fields wet with dew. Somewhere ahead, guides searched for an old road that connected with the Plank Road.[44] The good mood of the previous day was gone, the only sound from the column being the monotonous tramp of feet and the sharp bark of officers urging the men to quicken the pace.[45] When the column had trouble following the road, Longstreet became concerned with the irksome delays. While the guides searched for the road, Longstreet ordered the First Corps into columns by division. When the march resumed, Field's and Kershaw's Divisions were side by side in double lines.[46] Anderson's Georgia brigade led Field's Division, followed in turn by the Texas brigade, commanded by Brigadier General John Gregg, Benning's Georgia brigade, Law, and Jenkins's South Carolina brigade.

Light was beginning to appear in the eastern sky when Longstreet's column came to a fork in the road just before it intersected the Plank Road. Kershaw's Division took the right fork. Field took the left and turned onto the Plank Road near New Hope Church.[47] Once on the road the gait became easier, and the men soon moved into a quick step. Four miles later the brigade passed Parker's Store. Field came up on the left and pulled within a hundred yards of the front of Kershaw's column, both divisions, once again, marching parallel with each other, Kershaw on the right side of the road and Field on the left. The column presented a front of eight men, or four lines per division.[48] It was the first and only time in the war that Coles remembered "two divisions marching into battle side by side."[49]

Soon musket fire crackled in the distance, the first indication of fighting ahead. From the continuous roll of musketry it was apparent that the battle had resumed in earnest.[50] As the column marched toward the firing, the sun appeared over the Wilderness, taking on a blood-red hue through the dust and smoke. The Alabamians saw the sun's red face as a bad omen, and within the ranks the prediction was, "There will be a hot time in the wilderness today, for there is blood in the sun."[51]

Crisis on the Plank Road

Wilcox occupied Heth's former position along the Wilderness Run and Poplar Run. Heth's Division had fought itself out the previous evening. His weary men simply slept in place where the fighting ceased at dark. A. P. Hill and Lee both anticipated that Longstreet would relieve Wilcox's men during the night. Unfortunately, the First Corps was still making its way to the battlefield when the Federal left, commanded by Major General Winfield S. Hancock, II Corps, resumed fighting. Major General David B. Birney, commanding the Third Division, exercised command on Hancock's right with brigades from his own and three other divisions. After Birney's line advanced some distance Brigadier General James S. Wadsworth's Fourth Division of the V Corps joined on the right and crowded Birney across the Plank Road.[52] Hancock's blue column slammed into Wilcox's line shortly after 5 a.m.[53] Wilcox's Division had little fight left, melting away in front of the Federal onslaught, taking Heth's Division with it. The first elements of Longstreet's column arrived at the battlefield around 6 a.m.

Rush into Battle

The Alabamians saw the first evidence of battle when the brigade marched near the Third Corps field hospital. They were greeted by hideous sights such as piles of amputated arms and legs outside of makeshift operating tents and clusters of wounded men on blankets or on the bare ground, most of them unattended. Beyond the field hospital a continuous stream of wounded trudged and limped to the rear seeking medical attention. Some were carried on stretchers; others staggered along with the help of friends. Those able to walk by themselves shuffled along as best as they could.[54]

Accounts of the fighting differed, depending on the rank of the soldier questioned. Typically privates responded with: "They are sorter driving us back." Officers expressed a slightly different and somewhat more optimistic view. Most replied that the fighting was "about a stand on both sides."[55] The plain truth was that the fate of the Army of Northern Virginia hung in the balance. Grant's forces had gouged a bloody path through Lee's line. A gaping hole lay exposed, waiting to be exploited, a situation that appeared to be similar in several ways to the Confederate route of the Federals at Chickamauga. This time, however, the Confederate and Federal roles were reversed.[56]

In the rear of Field's Division the Alabamians witnessed the confusion resulting from the rout. The scene was daunting. Heth's men swarmed through the woods near the roadside, as officers dashed madly about, urging the men to halt, usually to no avail. Members of the First Corps taunted the fleeing Confederates of Heth's Division. "Do you belong to Lee's army?" seems to be one remark which best expressed their disgust at the routed corps.[57] Coles later wrote that the confusion that morning was the most appalling he ever saw.[58]

The thought of what was to come made more than one man examine his conscience. This was especially true of those prone to playing cards and other games of chance. It was one thing to play an occasional game of cards around the campfire. It was quite another matter to die with such tools of iniquity tucked into one's pocket. Some thought of lying lifeless on the battlefield while their pockets were searched. Others pictured a stranger removing and reading private letters from home. As a result, the roadside was littered with bits of paper that a short time before were playing cards and letters.[59]

Field's and Kershaw's Divisions arrived just in time. Hancock's advance was thwarted by Gregg's Texans and Benning's Georgians and the leading elements of Kershaw's Division. It was a terrible clash as the Texans slammed into the advancing blue column. Gregg's soldiers broke the enemy's advance, but over half of the Texans lay dead and wounded.[60] Benning suffered a like percentage, as Wadsworth's and Birney's regiments were thrown into confusion. All organization was pretty much lost when the Federal regiments and brigades became intermingled.[61] Some commands waited for orders, others drifted to the rear but for the moment, the Federal thrust was stymied.

While the Federals regrouped, Perry brought his Alabamians on the field. He immediately ordered them to form on the left side of the Plank Road where the Texans and Georgians had gone into battle. Gregg's Brigade passed through Perry's lines as his Alabamians filed by. Going into line, the Alabamians passed within a few paces of a large group of horsemen watching the progress of the battle. The riders were Lee and his staff. Their attention was directed to the south side of the Plank Road where Kershaw's troops were engaged. An artillery battery to their right blasted away at targets on both sides of the road.[62] The sight of Lee burned a vivid impression in the memories of those who saw him. He sat erect on Traveler, his black cape casually draped over his shoulders. Those passing nearest to him clearly recalled a face with dark penetrating eyes and a gray beard.

Oates later remembered that at that particular moment he thought the commanding general was the "...grandest specimen of manhood I ever beheld. He looked as though he ought to have been and was the monarch of the world."[63] As Perry passed Lee he thought "his countenance, usually so placid and benign, was blazing with martial ardor." Perry found it impossible to believe any man in the general's presence that morning would not firmly believe him to be the greatest of heroes.[64]

Lee asked a passing man the identity of these troops. Someone in the ranks proudly replied, "Law's Alabama brigade, sir." Lee exuberantly responded, "God bless the Alabamians!"[65] Only minutes before, the famous Lee-to-the-rear incident had occurred when the general attempted to lead the Texans into battle.[66] Lee was once again caught up in the excitement of the moment, his face reflecting anxiety while he wheeled Traveler back and forth along the column as Law's Alabamians filed into the field. Lee saw thirty-one-year old Captain James J. Hatcher, Company L, 15th Alabama, struggling to keep up with his company. He rode alongside the obese captain, encouraging him forward. He called out, "Go on my brave Alabama captain and drive them back!"[67]

Staff officers hurried about yelling orders and prodding the line forward. From his position at the head of the 4th Alabama, Bowles could see the army staff officers scurrying about and Lee imploring the Alabamians to move quickly forward. Before entering previous battles, Bowles had witnessed commanding officers deliver speeches intended to arouse inspiration and patriotism. But this was different. There was a sense of panic in the air and confusion everywhere. Bowles concluded the situation was "a little squally" and moved on.[68]

Wounded Texans were straggling from the woods, their bloody task complete. The battle on the Plank Road had swayed back and forth most of the morning in desperate combat. Now it was the Alabamians' turn. They knew they fought under the eye of General Lee. Thus encouraged they stood against great odds and gathered for themselves much glory. The fight they were about to enter is best summarized by Law:

> *"The tide was flowing the other way. It ebbed and flowed many times that day, strewing the wilderness with human wrecks. Law's brigade captured a line of breastworks in its front, but had held them only a few moments when their former owners came back to claim them. The Federals were driven back to second line several hundred yards beyond, which was also taken. This advanced position was attacked in front and on the right from across the Orange Plank Road, and Law Alabamians' advanced backward without standing on the order of their going, until they reached the first line of logs, now in the rear. As their friends in blue still insisted on claiming their property and were advancing to take it, they were met by a counter-charge and again driven beyond the second line. This was held against a determined attack. The position again becoming untenable by reason of the movements of Federal troops on their right, Law's men retired a second time to the works they first captured. And so, for more than two hours, the storm of battle swept to and fro, in some places several times over the same ground, and settling down at length almost where it had begun the day before."*[69]

Perry Deploys for Battle

Perry and his Alabamians formed their line of battle facing east in an old field on the Widow Tapp's farm. The Plank Road, on their right, ran generally east and west. The Tapp farmhouse was to their rear, or west. The field was bounded on the north and east by dense woods and undergrowth. One or two hundred yards to the east of their line a small slug gish tributary of Wilderness Run flowed north several hundred yards and disappeared into the woods. The open field where Perry formed his line of battle sloped gradually down-ward for two or three hundred yards before dropping off sharply to the stream bottom which Perry described as a morass.[70] East of the stream the ground rose to a higher eleva-tion than the location where the Alabama line formed. A dense stand of scrub trees and undergrowth, much of it hazel brush, stretched from the opposite side of the tributary to the Brock Road a mile to the east.[71]

A crude breastworks constructed of decaying logs and brush lay several yards inside the wood line. The right of the works rested on the Plank Road. These works will be identified as the first line of works. Perry formed inside a line of breastworks that were shaped like a horseshoe. The northern side of the shoe lay on his left and extended on an east-west line into the woods. The Widow Tapp farmhouse lay at the base of the shoe. The works which formed the toe lay on either side of the Plank Road a hundred yards east of the wood line. That portion of the works north of the road will be identified as the McGowan works after Brigadier General Samuel McGowan, Wilcox's Division, whose brigade oc-cupied the works the previous night.

From left to right Perry's line of battle was the 15th, 48th, 44th, 47th, and 4th Ala-bama. Their line, formed in two ranks, lay west of the Wilderness tributary and perpen-dicular to the Plank Road.[72] The right of the 4th Alabama rested on the Plank Road. In their haste to bring the troops into line Perry and Field each issued orders to the Alabam-ians. While Perry attended to his left and center, Field communicated directly with Bowles. Because Bowles was the senior commander on the right, Field ordered Major Campbell, commanding the 47th, to act under his command should the two regiments become sepa-rated from the remainder of the brigade. Field also directed Bowles throw out a skirmish line, "place his right on the Plank Road, and keep it there." The division commander's parting words were that the 4th Alabama was the regiment of direction for the brigade.[73]

Federals were clearly visible at the edge of the woods on Perry's center and to his left when Perry completing forming his line of battle. Later describing the Federal force as a "blue mass of humanity," he gave the command to move forward as soon as Oates came into line. As the Alabamians moved forward, a few Federal squads were attempting to cross the swampy bottom land of the tributary. Some of the Federals were already across and firing into the Alabamians' left and center.

Enemy fire from the left intensified as the Alabamians descended the slope toward the stream. A body of Federals had crossed the morass where the tributary entered the woods and occupied the treeline at the north end of the field. Perry's left was uncovered and he sent Terrell with a message for Oates to detach the 15th Alabama and advance in the direction of the fire.[74] Perry then started the remainder of the line forward, his first rank firing a volley and charging into the stream bed. The suddenness and ferocity of the charge surprised the Federals on Perry's front, causing them to deliver a scattering fire before retiring into the woods.[75] The 48th and 44th Alabama crossed the stream bottom and moved toward the high ground, firing as they advanced. In doing so the regiments obliqued left, creating a gap between the 44th and the 47th Alabama. Perry did not know the size of the force on his front, except that the Federal line extended beyond both flanks.[76]

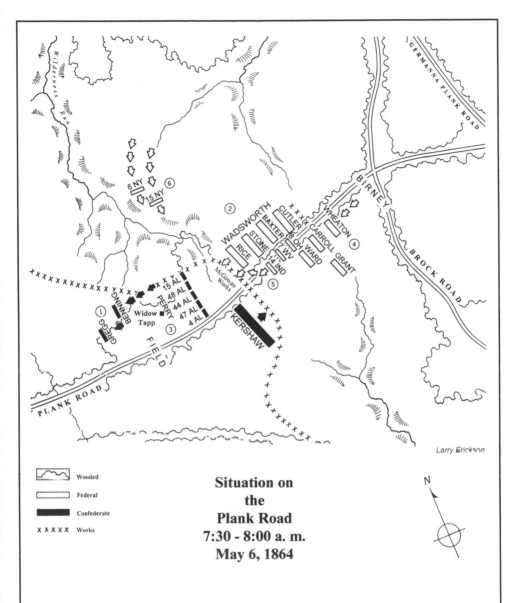

Situation on
the
Plank Road
7:30 - 8:00 a. m.
May 6, 1864

Larry Erickson

Wooded
Federal
Confederate
X X X X X Works

N

1. Gregg and Benning thwart the Federal advance, incurring frightful losses. Both brigades are retiring as Perry's Alabamians form their line of battle.
2. Wadsworth's and Webb's regiments are intermingled after engaging Benning and the Texans. The Federal formation north of the Plank Road is roughly four lines.
3. Perry forms line of battle.
4. Birney's rear brigades (Wheaton, Carroll, Grant, Ward) advance slowly along the Plank Road as Perry goes into line.
5. Carroll orders the 14th Indiana, 7th West Virginia and 8th Ohio forward. The three regiments turn right, enter the woods north of the road, and advance toward the Alabama line.
6. The 15th New York Heavy Artillery and the 6th New York Heavy Artillery are advancing on the Federal right and move into position to threaten Perry's left flank.

Because the largest force appeared to be covering his left and center Perry turned his attention to that sector, leaving Bowles to operate on his own.

The Alabama line divided into three parts. Bowles, commanding the 4th and 47th, entered into a fight which flowed back and forth along the Plank Road. Because of a Federal threat from the left Oates fought a separate action near the entrance of the Wilderness Run tributary into the woods. He later rejoined the main line and acted under Perry's command. Perry initially exercised command over the center of the brigade. That portion of the line containing the 44th and 48th and later the 15th will be referred to as Perry's. The line of the 4th and 47th will be referred to as Bowles's.

The Alabamians' Foes

Federal units on both sides of the Plank Road figured heavily in the fight waged by the Alabama brigade. Though Perry and the Alabamians did not realize it, they were about to tangle with elements of four Federal divisions and Kitching's Independent Artillery Brigade which was serving as infantry.

As the Alabamians prepared to enter the fray, a three brigade division commanded by Wadsworth, on the north side of the road, lay in three lines on the Alabamians' immediate front. Brigadier General James C. Rice's Second Brigade held the front. The 76th New York deployed in front of Rice's main line. The Federals that Perry saw on his center were skirmishers from Rice's brigade. Colonel Roy Stone's Third Brigade of Pennsylvanians, commanded by Lieutenant Colonel John Irvin and Brigadier General Henry Baxter's Second Brigade from Brigadier General John C. Robinson's division, (Second Division, V Corps), made up the second and third lines. Wadsworth's First Brigade, also known as the Iron Brigade, under Brigadier General Lysander Cutler marched in rear of the column.[77]

Immediately south of the Plank Road Brigadier General J. H. Hobart Ward's First Brigade, and Colonel Samuel S. Carroll's Third Brigade, from Gibbon's Second Division, II Corps, and Colonel Lewis A. Grant's Second Brigade, Second Division, VI Corps, were engaged with Kershaw's Division. Six of Carroll's regiments lay in two lines behind an irregular breastworks abandoned by the Confederates earlier that morning. The remaining three were on the north side of the Plank Road in front of the 76th New York, slowly advancing toward the clearing of the Tapp field. Ward occupied a line in front of Carroll, the right of both brigades resting on the Plank Road. Grant was in line behind Carroll, while Brigadier General Frank Wheaton's brigade of Getty's division was slowly advancing from the Brock Road toward Grant.[78]

Oates's adversary was Colonel J. Howard Kitching's Independent Brigade consisting of the 6th and 15th New York Heavy Artillery.[79] Originally organized as the 3rd Battalion Heavy Artillery at New York City, the 15th New York Heavy Artillery had been performing light duty in the defenses around Washington until April 1864. When the regiment arrived at the Wilderness it was commanded by Lieutenant Colonel Michael Wiedrich.[80] The 15th New York, armed with old Remington rifles equipped with sword bayonets, entered the Wilderness Campaign 1,525 strong. Like its sister regiment, the 6th New York Artillery pulled easy duty until the Wilderness. Equally large as the 15th, it had manned the defense line around Washington, D.C. Before the fighting in the Wilderness neither regiment had fired a shot in combat. Kitching managed to get his brigade in place by 5:30 a.m. and after a short rest, received new orders to move forward and take up a position on the left of the II Corps. When the 15th New York began forming a line of battle, Wiedrich found the task very difficult because of the dense undergrowth.[81] He had barely completed his dispositions when his men began firing on Perry's left flank.

Bowles Struggles on the Right

The 4th and 47th Alabama followed their skirmishers across marshy ground between the source of the tributary and the Plank Road. After moving a few feet into the dense woods, the skirmish line disappeared from view. They soon ran into skirmishers from the 14th Indiana of Carroll's brigade and stopped to wait for the main line to come up.[82] Carroll's brigade of nine regiments began the morning in support of Birney's main line.[83] After moving slowly forward south of the Plank Road, Carroll was ordered to send three regiments across the road.[84] This assignment fell to the 14th Indiana, 8th Ohio and 7th West Virginia. The 14th Indiana led the regiments to the north side and entered the timber in front of the main Federal line.

When Bowles arrived with the main line, he found his skirmishers engaged in a lively exchange with the opposing skirmishers. Both regiments went forward at the double quick, the Rebel Yell erupting from the Alabamians as the sounds of a volley echoed from their muskets.[85] After advancing several yards, the first line of breastworks materialized from the smoke and undergrowth. The 14th Indiana skirmishers were just disappearing from view when the Alabamians arrived. From the condition of the works Bowles surmised its former occupants arrived only a short time before his regiment. Logs were stacked up, some dirt had hastily been piled on the logs, and other logs were still lying in disarray on the ground.[86] It was obvious to Bowles that the ferocious charge of the 4th and 47th Alabama had surprised its occupants who quickly vacated the works and disappeared into the woods.

Though Bowles could not see his antagonists, both sides exchanged fire for several minutes. The 14th Indiana, the 8th Ohio and 7th West Virginia were west of the McGowan works. From the sound of heavy firing off his right flank south of the Plank Road, Bowles concluded the Confederates there were encountering stiff resistance. The Federals were present in force on both sides of the road. A few minutes later the Federals to the front of Bowles struck back. The 14th Indiana bore in, firing low and determinedly pressed Bowles's Alabamians. Bowles ordered a charge. Bowles was very aggressive the morning of May 6, leading his opponents to believe his force was much larger than his two regiments. Rumors in the Federal ranks claimed a Confederate division was crashing through the woods.

Bowles's Alabamians boldly rushed forward screaming at the top of their lungs. They let loose a volley at the first glimpse of the 14th Indiana, throwing the ranks of the Hoosiers into confusion as they fell back. To their left and rear, men of the 8th Ohio saw the Alabamians streaming past at almost a run. The Ohioans made a futile attempt to change front to the left, but "stiff and crooked hazel brush" prevented any kind of an orderly formation. Word raced through the ranks that they were flanked.[87] A few moments later the 8th Ohio also fell back, carrying the West Virginians with it.[88] A member of the 14th Indiana mistook Bowles's command for a much larger force when he wrote they were "no match for the Reb corps."[89]

While Bowles exchanged fire with Carroll's regiments, the 44th and 48th Alabama on the left of the 47th Alabama slogged across the marshy stream bottom, and after gaining the opposite side, reformed line of battle. A short time later Perry's men began pushing the forward elements of Rice's brigade back on their main line. Men of the 76th New York nervously waited under orders not to fire because of the Federal infantry on their front.[90] Because of the dense woods and thick underbrush around them they were unaware that Carroll's three regiments lay on their right front and carried on a fight with Bowles. But the sound of musketry from that quarter indicated a lively fight was being waged.

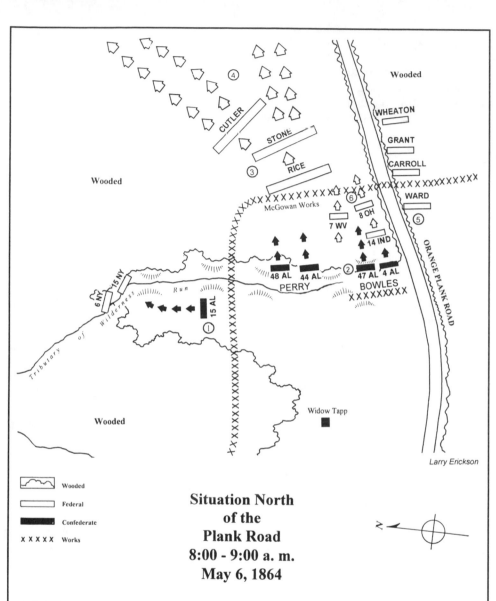

Larry Erickson

**Situation North
of the
Plank Road
8:00 - 9:00 a. m.
May 6, 1864**

1. Perry detaches the 15th Alabama from his line and sends it left to engage the 15th New York. The 6th New York joins the 15th New York in its fight with the 15th Alabama.
2. Bowles makes a vigorous attack on the 14th Indiana. After a brief but sharp exchange of fire, the 14th Indiana gives way. The regiment falls back in disorder. The 8th Ohio retreats when its left is uncovered and Bowles's Alabamians begin streaming past. The 7th West Virginia follows suit.
3. Wadsworth's division brigade is thrown into confusion by Carroll's regiments retreating through their ranks and fall back toward the Brock Road.
4. Cutler's brigade retreats toward the Wilderness Tavern carrying part of Stone's brigade with it. Rice and the remainder of Stone's brigade retire toward the Brock Road.
5 Bowles fires into Ward's right, causing it to fall back.
6. Bowles continues on to the second line of works where he engages in a fierce fight with Carroll, Grant and Wheaton.

The New Yorkers were unable to see Carroll's line breaking or Perry's two regiments entering the woods. Their first indication of danger came when someone rushed up yelling, "The Rebs were in four lines!" and rushed for the rear. A moment later Carroll's three regiments fell back through the 76th New York, throwing it into confusion. Suddenly the air vibrated with the sound of whizzing bullets as the 44th and 48th let loose a volley. Now and then a jittery soldier from the 76th fired in the direction of the Confederates. A Federal private had just squeezed off a round when he noticed the line of the 76th dissolving around him.[91] A moment later the entire line was breaking for the rear.

Most of Wadsworth's division was caught up in the confusion. A portion of Rice's brigade ran through Stone's brigade of Pennsylvanians which in turn fell back in confusion on Baxter in the third line which was partially swept away. Baxter's men quit the field and retreated north toward the Wilderness Tavern, carrying a portion of Cutler's brigade with them. Rice and the remainder of Stone's brigade drifted toward the Brock Road.[92] Three regiments from Stone's brigade, the 143rd, 149th and 150th Pennsylvania, reformed northeast of the McGowan works.

The 4th and 47th, led by Bowles, fought their way to the McGowan works where they discovered Ward and Carroll on their immediate right. Carroll and Ward were each in two lines. Before Bowles arrived two regiments from Ward's front line withdrew to replenish their cartridge boxes. Two regiments from the second line moved forward to fill the vacancy created by the departing troops. Neither Ward nor Carroll sent reserves to fill the void in Ward's second line which left the right of the 3rd Maine exposed.[93]

Unaware of the Confederates on their right flank, the Federals were occupied with the fighting on their front. Bowles arrived on the flank of the 3rd Maine and wasted little time in making his presence felt. His soldiers opened a devastating fire on the Federals' right flank. Over half of its men were quickly hit and the right flank was thrown into confusion. The destructive fire was more than the men from Maine could endure and its line began melting away, leaving only Carroll's brigade to deal with the Alabamians.[94] For the moment Bowles and his men felt relatively secure behind the substantial works, which were about three feet high. Incredibly Bowles and his two regiments had pierced a hole in Birney's center.[95] He was, in fact, surrounded by Federals.

The 4th Alabama began receiving fire from the right front which came from Carroll's brigade south of the Plank Road. The plucky Alabamians launched their third charge of the morning, moving forward from the security of the McGowan works. They fought tenaciously, and surprised the right flank of the 10th New York Zouaves. Two companies of the Zouaves were ordered to swing right to protect Carroll's flank. A few minutes later a volley rattled from left to right, which was immediately answered by return fire. On the left of the regiment a company made up largely of French immigrant recruits fell a few steps to the rear to reload, as was the European custom. Following suite the entire regiment stepped out of line. Rushing forward of the main line, the color bearer waved the regimental standard for the men to reform on. The regiment moved to the front of Carroll's main line. Sixty men quickly toppled from the ranks, victims of shot from the front and flank. Though only a few yards separated the combatants, the Confederates were seldom visible, which the historian of the 10th New York attributed to the density of the woods and the colors of the rebel uniforms blending into the trees and underbrush.[96] Carroll's line, except for the 14th Connecticut, eventually gave way.[97] The 14th Connecticut's historian related the regiment "stuck out like the toe of a horseshoe." The New Englanders and Alabamians lashed into each other with vengeance. Both suffered greatly, but after a 20-30 minute duel, the 4th was able to get the upper hand. The 14th Connecticut was forced to grudgingly fall back and regroup a short distance to the rear where it continued its fight with the 4th Alabama.[98]

Grant was uncovered by Carroll's withdrawal. Bowles moved forward and fired into Grant's right flank. The 4th Vermont executed a change of face to the right and engaged the Alabamians. Grant became concerned for the safety of his right flank and requested support from his division commander. Wheaton was sent forward and went into line parallel to the road and connecting to the 4th Vermont on Grant's right. His men immediately added the weight of their firing into Bowles's right flank.[99] By this time Bowles charge was spent and the 4th Alabama retired into the cover of the works. It settled into exchanging fire with Wheaton and Grant.

Perry's Drive Grinds to a Halt

While Oates and Bowles fought on either flank, Perry drove forward in search of Wadsworth's retreating division. Several yards east of the McGowan works Wadsworth desperately sought any units that were not running to the rear. He was very active that morning, always at the hottest part of the fighting, and frequently leading regiments forward. A man of wealth and a politician, Wadsworth had made his mark in the army. Though he had no formal military training he had exhibited the knack of leading troops and served with distinction at Gettysburg.[100] As the morning progressed the Alabamians would become very familiar with the fighting spirit of Wadsworth.

By chance he came upon three of Stone's Pennsylvania regiments. The 143, 149th, and 150th were holding steady while squads of Blue Coats bolted around their flanks and through their ranks. Yelling "Give it to them Bucktails," Wadsworth sent the Pennsylvanians forward. One volley ripping into the ranks of the 44th and 48th Alabama was sufficient to halt Perry's advance. A second sent the Alabamians scurrying west toward the Widow Tapp field. The three Pennsylvania regiments began pushing forward.

Bowles Engages a New Opponent

From left to right, the Pennsylvania alignment was the 150th, 149th and 143rd. The left of the 150th rested on the Plank Road. Its right was not connected with the 149th.[101] The 149th Pennsylvania was feeling its way through dense smoke when its left ran into the 47th which began peppering away at the intruders. On hearing the firing on his left Bowles sent Coles to investigate. When he arrived Coles made an unnerving discovery. The 44th and 48th Alabama were nowhere in sight. As Coles hurried back to Bowles with the disturbing news, he imagined a Federal lurked behind every tree waiting to take him prisoner. Coles knew that U. S. Grant had just issued an edict that Confederate prisoners would no longer be exchanged.[102] The thought of spending the remainder of the war in a Federal prison was very unappealing. He did not know the Alabamians' exploits had thrown the Federal line into disarray. All Coles knew at the moment was that the Alabamians' flanks were in the air. He was thankful for a safe journey back to the 4th where the men, ignorant of the critical situation they were in, were busily loading and firing. The story of their plight had just been relayed to Bowles when bullets began to zip in from across the Plank Road. It was only then that Coles realized that they were beyond the main Confederate line and suggested his commander order a retreat to the first works just inside the treeline. But Bowles was not quite ready to give up dearly won ground.[103]

In the meantime the 150th Pennsylvania, on discovering the line of the 4th Alabama, prepared for battle, and from very close range delivered a deadly volley.[104] The 149th Pennsylvania continued to pound the 47th Alabama and began to turn its left flank. When his left began to give way Major Campbell sent word to Bowles that he was falling back.

Lieutenant Colonel Scruggs brought the news of the exit of the 47th and reported a force closing on their left.[105] Shot was flying in from the front and right flank, and with his left in danger Bowles finally decided to retreat and ordered his small command back to the first line of works near the edge of the woods on the east side of the Tapp field. Across the Plank Road Wheaton saw the plight of the Alabamians and watched as they vacated the McGowan works. He mistakenly thought the two Confederate regiments were a weak reconnoitering force in the van of the main line and later reported that "on account of the dense woods the Confederates could not exploit the advantage gained."[106] The Alabamians retraced their steps through the tangle of brush and scrub trees to the first works with the 150th Pennsylvania hot on their heels.[107] Bowles and his men tumbled over the works to safety amid a shower of bullets.

Oates Secures the Brigade's Left

While Bowles fought his private war along the Plank Road, Oates prepared to meet the threat on Perry's left. He saw his left flank was in danger of being overlapped and was forced to extend his line 200 yards to the left. This he accomplished by filing into a single line. Oates next pulled off a minor miracle. While fire poured into his line from the front and left flank, he ordered a wheel left. The 15th then executed a perfect counterclockwise motion by pivoting about its left until the line squarely faced the woods where the tributary entered the woods. Perry later recounted he "never saw anything comparable." As soon as his regiment was positioned, Oates ordered a charge into the enemy. The 15th Alabama sprang forward yelling for all they were worth.[108] Wiedrich's New Yorkers had not experienced this type of warfare before, because a few well-directed volleys were sufficient to send the 15th New York scurrying for cover. Most were dropping their haversacks as they stooped over to avoid fire from the 15th. Billy Jordan, Company B, 15th Alabama, recalled the Wilderness was the "richest battlefield that I ever beheld."[109] That said much about the booty of this battlefield because Law's Brigade had gleamed many winter supplies from the Chickamauga battlefield.

Oates pushed forward to the opposite side of the stream bed and settled into a lengthy skirmish with the 15th New York which made a stand on the high ground. The 6th New York came up and formed a second line. Kitching's men were able to inflict several casualties upon the 15th Alabama, forcing the Alabamians to seek whatever cover was available. Loose limbs were quickly piled up and men lay prone to fire into the 15th New York's ranks.[110]

Jordan saw a new blanket lying on the ground and discarded his old one for the Federal issue. Later in the morning he discovered more booty rolled up in the blanket. There was a "fancy laundered shirt" and two new linen tents. Jordan was generous with his spoils of war. The shirt was given to a friend in Company B. Jordan and his messmate, William Callaway, shared the blanket and tent for the remainder of the war. Once again Kitching's men were unable to withstand the heat of battle and began withdrawing. Oates mistakenly thought he was being flanked and withdrew to the west side of the tributary.[111] The opposing regiments quickly placed considerable distance between each other. Kitching's New Yorkers withdrew northward toward Wilderness Tavern. Oates regrouped on the edge of the field bordering the stream.

The lack of fighting spirit in the Federal force opposing the 15th Alabama puzzled Oates. Its numbers were considerably larger than his own regiment and the Alabamian obviously expected a better showing from his opponents. It was not until after the war that he learned the New Yorkers were a regiment trained to support heavy artillery. Oates correctly attributed his regiment's success over superior numbers to lack of experience on their part.

Perry Hangs on in the Center

While the 150th Pennsylvania tangled with Bowles, the 143rd encountered the 44th and 48th Alabama. On hearing the renewed firing to his right Oates put his regiment in motion and moved to join Perry. Fortunately for Perry the Federals did not discover the gap between the 44th and 47th. For the present the 44th Alabama's right did not appear threatened, but until the 15th arrived the 48th's left flank was uncovered and in danger of being overlapped by the 143rd Pennsylvania. Perry rode back and forth behind the line attempting to steady both regiments. Lieutenant Colonel John Jones went down with a painful wound. Major Cary seized the 44th's colors and rushed to the front waving the flag with his left hand and his sword with the right. While passing behind the 44th on his way to the 48th, Perry's horse was shot from under him. Undaunted, he continued on foot, finding the 48th's left still hard pressed and slowly giving way. The Federal line was deployed in two ranks and was firing by rank. Several men from the 48th left the firing line and sought shelter behind nearby trees.[113] From his vantage point in rear of the 48th, Captain Thomas Christian, Perry's adjutant and inspector general, saw the left of the 48th wavering, and without hesitation he seized the colors and dashed through the line to the front of the regiment. Waving the flag above his head, Christian shouted for the men to rally on their standard. His bold action instilled new confidence in the 48th, and the men steadied in the face of the Federal volleys.[114] Momentarily, at least, the regiment stayed intact. Fortunately for Perry and the 48th Alabama, Oates arrived just in time to see the 48th start to give way. Once again Oates formed his line of battle under fire, maneuvering from a marching column into line of battle which placed his regiment at right angles with the Federal flank. A single volley was sufficient to send the 143rd Pennsylvania reeling backward, rendering Perry's center secure.[115]

Bowles Secures the Right Flank

While Perry fought the 143rd Pennsylvania, Bowles, with the 47th back on his left, continued his fight with the 150th Pennsylvania at the first line of works. The Pennsylvanians drove within 30 yards of the works. The antagonists were so close to each other that the muzzle flashes were clearly visible through the smoke that hung over the battlefield. Bowles decided on the same course of action that worked against Carroll's men. He ordered a charge, his fifth of the morning, and the Alabamians surged forward with the fierce Rebel Yell erupting down the line. Wadsworth watched as the 150th Pennsylvania, taken by surprise at the ferocity of the Alabamians' charge, grudgingly fell back across the McGowan works.[116] At this time reinforcements in the form of the 20th Georgia came up and formed on Bowles right, its line parallel to and facing the Plank Road. The 47th Alabama was still on the 4th Alabama's left. The Federal line was so close that the Georgians and Alabamians could hear the Federal officers shout their orders above the din of battle.

Wadsworth went in search of fresh troops to throw into the fray. Finding the brigade of Brigadier General Frank Eustis, Fourth Brigade, Getty's division, VI Corps, the general rode to the head of the column yelling for a regiment to follow him. Colonel Oliver

Edwards led his 37th Massachusetts from its place on the right of the column and formed line of battle with his left resting on the Plank Road. After struggling through dense scrub tress and underbrush while the ever present briers tore at the men's clothing and flesh. Edwards ran head long into Bowles's command. Out of the smoke a well-directed volley stopped the New Englanders in their tracks. Two color bearers were shot down in rapid succession. Men toppled from the ranks. Wadsworth, seeing the dilemma that had befallen the 37th rode up and exclaimed: "You have made a splendid charge!" Praise was heaped on Edwards. "Your regiment alone has done all that I wished and more than I asked," he said. The gray haired general concluded by saying, "I must go and reform my lines and you must fight your way as best you can." To say the least the regiment was in a tight spot. Its right was in the air. All too often the Alabamians were finding their mark. Edwards and his lieutenant colonel were considering a charge against Bowles when it was reported Confederates were closing in from the right. Deciding to extricate himself from the tenuous situation, Edwards ordered the regiment to retreat. This was accomplished by the front rank firing, then moving 25 paces to the rear to load while the rear rank fired. The process was repeated until the 37th was safely out of sight.[117]

After leaving the 37th Massachusetts, Wadsworth's fighting spirit was still aroused and he was determined to break the line held by the stubborn Alabamians. The 150th Pennsylvania was brought forward to take on the Alabamians again. Five times the Pennsylvanians threw themselves against Bowles, charging into the face of a destructive fire, and five times the survivors were sent reeling back.[118] To the Pennsylvanians the Federal general was the very picture of a warrior as he sat erect in the saddle, superintending the execution of each charge. When the men recoiled from the leaden storm of hail sent by the Alabamians, Wadsworth, showing no concern for himself, rode through their ranks, speaking kindly to calm jittery nerves and breathing new life into weak hearts.

When the Pennsylvanians fought themselves out, Wadsworth rode in search of fresh troops and came upon Brigadier General Alexander S. Webb's brigade of Brigadier General John Gibbon's Second Division, II Corps. Because he was senior in rank Wadsworth assumed command over Webb. Just at that time a Federal brigade ambled by, making its way to the rear. None of its officers were attempting to rally the men. A much surprised and angry Webb was relieved of command and sent after four regiments to herd the retreating brigade to the front.[119] With Webb gone Wadsworth turned to the 20th Massachusetts and attempted to lead it forward. At that time the New Englanders lay behind log breastworks on the north side of the Plank Road and anchored Webb's line. When he was told the regiment was under orders not to move, Wadsworth became irate. He ridiculed their manhood, shouting that they were afraid. He spurred his horse through the ranks of the 20th. Yelling for the men to follow, forced his horse to jump over the works and rode out onto the Plank Road.[120] A volley from the 4th Alabama wounded his horse, causing it to thrash about and stumble. Wadsworth pitched forward and fell to the ground with a thud. He was lying on the ground, stunned by the fall. The 4th Alabama soldiers on the right flank saw the prostrate form lying in the rode and that it was an officer. A few ran into the road and discovered a Federal general officer had been unhorsed. They assumed he was either dead or severely wounded.[121] Word of their accomplishment quickly spread through the line.

A few minutes later the 20th Georgia, on receiving fire from across the road, retired toward the first line of works. Suddenly the firing around Bowles died down. Taking advantage of a lull in the fighting, Bowles sent details to gather the wounded and get them to the rear. Once again he grew concerned about his support and concluding that his position was untenable ordered his men to retrace their steps to the first line of works. The

4th moved out first, followed a short time later by the 47th. Several volleys were fired at the departing Confederates, but this time the Federals were content to let the Alabamians go in peace. Two hours after his fight began Bowles led the 4th Alabama into the first line of works near the edge of the woods. A few minutes later the 47th Alabama resumed its position on his left. The 20th Georgia settled in farther to the Alabamians' rear. This time the Federals did not follow.[122]

The Brigade Takes a Rest

It was around 10 a.m. when the Alabamians settled in behind the first line of works and began taking stock of their condition. Up until that time Field's Division had been engaged three hours and Perry's men had been fighting steadily for almost two hours. In that time the Alabamians had virtually destroyed the brigades of Ward, Carroll, Stone, Baxter, Rice and Cutler. Kitching's two regiments had retired from the field rather than take on the 15th Alabama, and for a time there was a lull in the fighting. During the course of the fighting Bowles had initiated five charges, was twice driven from his position by Federal charges, and finally ended the morning virtually where he started. Incredibly eight charges were directed at the 4th and 47th. Six were repulsed, and on two occasions Bowles, in turn, drove the attackers with countercharges. Oates had initiated two charges and Perry at least one if not more. Many of the wounded from both sides had watched the flow of battle ebb back and forth. Survivors later reported that as many as six lines of battle passed over them as they lay on the ground.[123]

Bowles welcomed the break and sought out the wounded of the 4th Alabama. William Mack Robbins had been severely wounded. The young major was in front of his men waving his sword when he was struck in the head. The impact of the ball spun him around and sent his sword flying as he fell face down on the ground. At first he was thought to be mortally wounded but then it was discovered the bullet did not penetrate his skull. The wound resulted in a severe scalp wound which paralyzed his left side for several weeks.[124]

Adjutant Coles had found his friend Private Quinley wounded. The adjutant was reminded of that second day at Chickamauga nearly eight months earlier. Quinley stood in the open and defied Federal bullets, predicting that a man born to be hanged would not be shot to death. The private's wound proved to be serious but not fatal. Quinley would live to be hanged if that was to be his fate in life.[125] Private Francis M. Smith, Company B, was one of those lucky to escape unhurt that day. During the heaviest part of the fighting he had sought refuge behind a large oak tree. When the fighting died down Smith counted 17 bullets lodged in the tree. All were low enough to have killed or severely wounded him had they not struck the tree first. He escaped with minor wounds.[126] Two of the 4th Alabama officers were down for good: Captain Baylis Brown was dead on the field. Captain John Kunzie's wounds proved fatal, though he lingered until June 9.[127]

The Confederate Line North of the Plank Road

When the fighting died down, Field found the time favorable to search for his brigades, which were scattered over the field. He found Bowles resting behind his works and lamented, "This is all of my command that I can find."[128] He moved toward the right in search of the Texans and Georgians.

At that time the Alabama brigade was the only brigade in line immediately north of the Plank Road. Both flanks were in the air. However, Perry's immediate concern was his left which had been threatened earlier in the morning, and he decided to seek support.

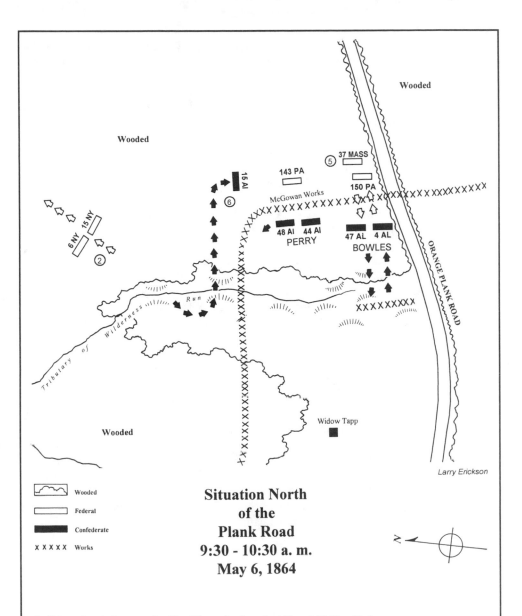

**Situation North
of the
Plank Road
9:30 - 10:30 a. m.
May 6, 1864**

Larry Erickson

Legend:
- Wooded
- Federal
- Confederate
- X X X X X Works

1. Oates retires to the opposite side of the ravine from the 15th and 6th New York.
2. The 15th and 6th New York retire from the field.
3. After engaging Federal brigades south of the Plank Road Bowles's command retreats under pressure from the 150th Pennsylvania's advance. The 150th Pennsylvania cautiously follows Bowles to the first line of works.
4. Bowles regroups and drives the 150th Pennsylvania beyond the second works and retakes the ground just lost.
5. The 37th Massachusetts charges Bowles's position and suffers a bloody repulse. The 150th Pennsylvania fails, in several attempts, to drive Bowles from his forward position.
6. The 15th Alabama reinforces Perry's left just as the 48th Alabama gives way to an attack on its left. The 143rd Pennsylvania is then driven back.

Unable to find Field, Perry sent a request for support directly to Lee. Word came back that he would be relieved. This was not what Perry had intended, and Adjutant Terrell was then sent to Lee to clarify his request.

Brigadier General Abner Perrin, Anderson's Division, came on the field with his brigade. A staff officer approached Perry and requested advice for placing the brigade in line. At Perry's suggestion, Perrin went into line with his right resting on the Plank Road. To make room for Perrin, Perry ordered Bowles to rejoin the brigade.[129] Brigadier General Edward A. Perry, also from Anderson's Division, arrived with his Floridians and went into line on Perrin's left. Colonel Perry withdrew his Alabamians to supporting distance. The three brigades were then the only Confederate units in line north of the Plank Road.[130]

About 10 a.m. the Confederate high command determined that Hancock's left rested a short distance south of the Plank Road. A general plan was quickly devised to roll up the Federal left and then drive it east toward the Brock Road.[131] Longstreet detailed Sorrel to collect some inactive brigades and "hit hard." An hour later Sorrel was in position with three brigades.[132] Longstreet informed Field that he wanted his division to attack (east) up on the Plank Road. Colonel Perry understood the three brigades north of the Plank Road were to conform to the movement of the brigades south of the road.

It was around 11 a.m. when Longstreet informed Field that troops had been sent to the right to attack the Federal left.[133] At first it seemed like another Chancellorsville was in the making as the din of battle rolled north as the three brigades successfully turned the Federal left and drove toward the Plank Road.[134] Longstreet sent Field east to press the advantage gained. The three brigades north of the Plank Road moved out slowly, encountering little resistance. South of the road Federal regiments, at first fell back slowly, then broke in confusion and fled toward the Brock Road.[135]

Longstreet, his face flush with excitement, rode up to Field. "Seizing my hand," Field remembered, "Longstreet congratulated me in warm terms on the fighting of my troops."[136] Longstreet left and joined Jenkins and Kershaw at the head of Jenkins's Brigade, then advancing east on the Plank Road. The group was no more than 30 yards from Field when a few scattering shots rang out from north of the road. These were quickly followed by a volley from south of the road. Unfortunately, as at Chancellorsville, the chief architect of the assault was struck down. Longstreet was seriously wounded and Jenkins killed.[137] The advance along the Plank Road ground to a halt.

Attack from the Left

Fighting around the Alabamians was over by noon and relative quiet prevailed in the early afternoon immediately north of the road.[138] Law's Alabamians lay down and enjoyed the lull, but unknown to Perry, Federals from Burnside's IX Corps were about to threaten their left flank.

Burnside had received orders from U. S. Grant to move left and support Hancock.[139] At the time Burnside had two divisions in line along the turnpike near Wilderness Tavern. After some discussion it was decided that Burnside should send his troops through the woods and attack the Confederates wherever they were found. In the end only the division of Brigadier General Robert Potter, commanding the Second Division, was withdrawn and sent to the left. He followed the Brock Road toward its intersection with the Plank Road.[140] A mile later Potter turned to his right and plunged into dense woods and undergrowth. Colonel Simon G. Griffin's Second Brigade led the advance with Colonel Zenas R. Bliss's First Brigade in supporting distance to his left and rear. The advance immediately slowed to a crawl. Visibility had improved little, if any, during the day, preventing officers from seeing their lines more than a few feet away. The general line of advance was toward Perry's left flank. Lieutenant Washington P. Bass, Company A, 15th Alabama, was to the left of the Alabama brigade with an ambulance detail. He was looking for wounded Alabamians in the area where the 15th fought Kitching's New Yorkers. Bass and his men were found by forward elements of Potter's advance and captured.

Colonel Perry was not yet aware of Potter's movement through the woods on the opposite side of the swampy stream to his left. He was, however, apprehensive about an attack from that direction and sent out a squad as skirmishers. When word came back that Federals were moving on the left, Perry sent for Oates and went to confer with General Perry.[141] Oates found the two discussing the situation. They decided to move to their left en echelon by battalion. General Perry would lead with the 15th and 48th following in supporting distance under Oates's command.[142] The movement was meant to be a probe, and should a sizable force be located the 47th, 44th and 4th Alabama regiments were to follow in support.[143] Oates was given discretion to act as required should an attack be launched against the 15th Alabama. He was not in favor of the plan and so stated, convinced a strong Federal force lay hidden in the woods. He further anticipated an attack on the 15th Alabama's front as soon as the advance uncovered his regiment. Oates cited as evidence the capture of Bass and their ambulance detail.[144] Colonel Perry was determined to protect his flank and felt the way to do that was to find the Federal force and drive it back. He ordered Oates forward. Although the maneuver was against his better judgment, Oates trudged off after the Florida brigade.

The 4th Alabama was resting when Colonel Perry rode by on his way to the brigade's left to look after the 15th and 48th Alabama. Coles was lying down with his back against a tree. At the time the 4th knew nothing of Perry's planned probe on the left. Perry paused in front of Coles and remarked, in what Coles described as a "very self satisfied manner": "Well, Bob, I propose this evening to make a spoon or spoil a horn." To Coles this was double talk. He had been a soldier too long to worry about a commander's greater strategy. Coles was still unaware of Perry's intentions, so he simply wished Perry success in whatever the endeavor was.[145]

Oates took the precaution of throwing out skirmishers under Captain Shaaff. The Florida brigade had barely cleared a small rise near the tributary when Potter's Second Brigade sent a volley into its left flank. Oates immediately executed a maneuver to face the threat. He moved his men into position behind a line of abandoned log breastworks.[146] Colonel Perry heard the firing, but was not in position to see the cause, but suspected an attack was developing. For the second time that day, Perry decided to communicate directly with Lee. This time he sent a note detailing his observations and started preparation to move the remainder of his brigade to aid Oates. Before he could get the three remaining regiments under way a staff officer approached with instructions. The officer told Perry a Confederate general advance was planned. Perry was ordered to close up on the brigades on his front. Though it meant Oates would be left to his own devices, Perry temporarily delayed sending his other regiments to support Oates.[147] When the firing intensified on his left he decided to act on his own responsibility and go to the assistance of Oates and the Floridians. Colonel Perry found the 15th Alabama behind the log works exchanging fire with the enemy. A large gap existed between the right of the 15th Alabama and the left of the Florida brigade. Colonel Perry decided to plug the hole with the 4th Alabama while sending the 44th and 47th Alabama regiments to the left of the 15th Alabama. From right to left the Alabama line deployed as the 4th, 15th, 48th, 44th and 47th Alabama regiments. Colonel Perry was concerned about the length of his line, sending Terrell to seek reinforcements. He also sent a runner to General Perry requesting the Florida brigade to change front by the left and align on his Alabama regiments.[148] General Perry consented, and was changing his line when Potter moved forward to the attack.

Potter's assault surprised the Floridians which broke and quickly dissolved. Oates's combative spirit was aroused, and he wasted little time in taking the offensive. The 15th Alabama mounted a countercharge. The 44th Alabama followed but both regiments were quickly outflanked.[149] Federal fire into its rear threw the 47th Alabama into confusion, precipitating a rapid retreat. This uncovered the left of the 44th Alabama, forcing it to fall back. Colonel Perry saw his left regiments falling back and started in that direction with the intent of rallying the Alabamians.[150] His horse was shot from under him, the second of the day. Perry sustained a flesh wound but arrived on foot in time to see the 44th, 47th and 48th Alabama start a headlong retreat to the rear.[151] Oates saw his right flank was also enveloped. For the second time in his military career, he thought it appropriate to order a retreat.[152] The 4th Alabama was amazed to suddenly see the regiments on their left running from the field with Yankees "right at their heels yelling like devils and cursing the Rebels." Coles recalled, "It only required a moment to convince the regiment that this was no place for them."[153] Bowles yelled for the 4th Alabama to follow the 15th Alabama just as a charge was launched against his flank. Federal officers and noncommissioned officers loudly urged their privates on. Bowles later wrote that he believed each Federal who captured a Confederate prisoner was given a promotion.[154]

When the fighting started Major Campbell, 47th Alabama, sent Captain John Ham to the left to find the Federal flank. Unfortunately, Ham and his men were cut off from the main line when it broke and Ham surrendered all but one of his squad. Private Sanders Avery, Company G, 47th Alabama, decided a bullet in the back was better than a stay in a Federal prison. He swiftly zigzagged through the thicket and escaped amid a hail of bullets.[155] Bowles's last glimpse of the fight that afternoon was a group of Federals chasing a lone Alabamian.[156]

The retreat was very disorderly. After some distance the Alabamians met Brigadier General William T. Wofford's Brigade, the reinforcements Colonel Perry had requested. Law's Alabamians were through fighting for the day, and Wofford was left to stop the Federal advance. The Alabamians did not halt until they reached the field where they had first formed for battle that morning. Reinforcements had arrived just in time to avert a disaster, but not in time to avoid the embarrassment of a rout. This was the only time Law's Brigade was driven from the field of battle.[157]

Perry's wound proved to be more severe than he had thought and he had to be assisted from his horse, the third he had ridden during the day.[158] His Alabamians were winded after their hasty exit from the battle line. Men dropped to the ground for a much needed rest as they arrived. In tribute to Perry's statement to Coles earlier in the afternoon about "making a spoon or spoiling a horn" the men later called his little venture the "spoon movement." After the Alabamians realized the spectacle they presented, Perry's men laughed heartily at the situation and gave him full credit for causing the rout.[159] As the Alabamians collected their thoughts and mused over their embarrassment, Heth's Division filed by on their way to support Wofford.[160] Oates caught Bowles's attention and the two watched an Alabama private sitting by a wounded Federal. He was obviously waiting for the unfortunate fellow to die. Oates surmised the Alabama lad's intention was to acquire the man's shoes. Toward night fall the Alabama brigade was ordered to the right side of the Plank Road where it bivouacked.[161]

Perry Counts His Blessings

Law's Alabama brigade could be proud of their accomplishments of May 6. Even though it was in the third wave that morning, the brigade played a prominent part in stemming the tide of the Federal attack. The Alabamians fought tenaciously against a vastly superior foe. It was no small feat to hold off four Federal divisions and an artillery brigade serving as infantry over two hours and firmly anchor the north side of the Plank Road. Law's Brigade tangled with at least 13 Federal brigades, those of Carroll and Webb of Gibbon's division; Ward of Birney's division; Cutler, Rice and Stone of Wadsworth's division; Baxter of Robinson's division; Wheaton, Grant and Eustis of Getty's division; Kitching of Burton's Artillery Reserve and Potter's division of Burnside's IX Corps. Perry considered himself fortunate, attributing his success in large part to the terrain which, in his words, "was such that we burst like a thunderclap upon the enemy and turned them into flight, before they had time to inflict any injury, or see that there were no supporting lines behind us.[162] It was also a battle of good timing. Oates twice arrived just in time and covered Perry's left flank. Bowles hit the Federals along the Plank Road at just the right moment to send an entire Federal line into confusion.

Perry was proud of his men and justifiably so. The words he wrote after the war to describe the fine work of the First Corps apply equally to his own brigade:

> *"They had arrived in the midst of confusion and apparent disaster. Their lines had been formed under fire and in the presence of the enemy moving forward in dense array and perfect order. Such had been the urgency of the crisis that single brigades and sometimes regiments, as their formation was completed in succession, assailed the foe with almost resistless fury. Less than two hours from the time that the head of their column had reached the field, two small divisions, numbering in all nine thousand men, had met and rolled back in confusion eight full divisions of the enemy."[163]*

Law's Brigade experienced its finest hour at the Wilderness and unfortunately its worst. The Texans received much of the glory for stalling Hancock's assault in the morning. Little credit has been given to the five Alabama regiments who fought unsupported, repulsed repeated Federal assaults and fought Hancock's right to a standstill. On the other hand, they unceremoniously quit the field in the afternoon. Consolation can be found in the fact that an entire Federal division was required to accomplish the feat. The price of glory had been high, with total casualties of 268, or 22 percent of the strength carried into the fight. Five officers were dead on the field, and two more were mortally wounded.[164]

Adjutant Henry Figures, 48th Alabama, died as he thought an officer should, at the front of his regiment, encouraging his men onward. In late afternoon he rode at the front of his regiment when it broke under pressure from the Federal attack. As Figures was rallying the men, a Federal bullet struck the young officer in the head, killing him instantly. Henry was buried in a shallow grave beneath a peach tree, his blanket roll serving as a makeshift coffin. A crude wooden cross marked the burial spot. Two years after the war the senior Figures traveled to the Wilderness and brought the body of his only son home to Huntsville, Alabama. The young soldier's final resting place is Maple Hill Cemetery.[165]

Forty-nine-year-old Ensign John Archibald, native of North Carolina, had carried the regiment's flag the previous year.[166] He was described as one of the bravest men in the regiment. If placed in the second ranks when a line of battle was formed, Archibald would trade places with someone in front. His stated reasons were that he did not want to be shot with a dirty bullet. Archibald suffered his second wound, which inflicted terrible damage to his face. The bullet entered below his left cheek bone and exited the right side of his neck. Everyone who saw the flag bearer carried from the field believed the wound to be mortal. Archibald's recovery was nothing short of miraculous. Six weeks later he was back in the front ranks carrying the regimental flag.[167]

Andrew Wilson's premonition was correct, as he was shot dead shortly after the 47th Alabama made its initial charge against Wadsworth. Just as he predicted early that morning, William Abernathy came through unhurt. David Abernathy's sixth sense also proved correct. During the late afternoon engagement David saw a Federal take aim in his direction. David aimed his gun to fire when he saw the Federal's gun belch a puff of smoke. The bullet struck his arm between the wrist and elbow. The bullet glanced off his arm, penetrated the book over his heart before deflecting into his upper arm near the shoulder. David's arm was later amputated near the shoulder.[168]

Private Robert Eugene Hentz, Company F, 4th Alabama, lay dead on the field. He was 25 years of age, single. A Pennsylvanian by birth, before the war he was a printer residing in Huntsville, Alabama. Of French ancestry, he was born into a family with a strong military tradition. His father was an officer under Napoleon. His grandfather, who was later exiled for his political activities, served as a member of the National Convention during the French Revolution. Hentz came to Huntsville as a young man and served an apprenticeship under the publisher of the *Democrat*. He followed the family tradition at the first call for volunteers and met the soldier's fate May 6, 1864.[169]

Early the next morning Bowles visited the battlefield where the fighting had been the heaviest. Ten dead Federals for every dead Confederate lay where Kershaw's Division had fought. He counted six Federal dead for every dead Confederate where Law's Brigade fought Wadsworth's and Birney's commands. Before the fighting began it had been difficult to see 20 yards. On May 7 one could easily see several hundred yards.[170] A Federal soldier recalled, "Trees were riddled with bullets from their roots to the tops, and the brush was cut away as if mowed with a scythe."[171] Where Bowles walked the battlefield it was ominously quiet. Details removed the dead and wounded from the battlefield all day.

Longstreet's wound would keep him from service until late fall. Lee selected as Longstreet's replacement Major General Richard H. Anderson, a veteran division commander from the Third Corps. He was the second most senior major general in the army, and his credentials were solid.[172] He had been a brigadier under Longstreet and a division commander. After Chancellorsville he was given command of a division in the Third Corps.[173] Anderson was a man with whom the rank and file felt comfortable. When the commanding general sought his opinion about a new commander for the First Corps Sorrel told Lee, "We know him and shall be satisfied with him."[174] On May 7 Anderson was officially assigned command of the First Corps.

By nightfall it was obvious that Grant was a worthy opponent. Instead of scurrying toward Washington after being bloodied, this new general stood his ground. In fact, with nightfall the Federal army began sliding around the Confederate right flank.[175] Grant was determined to gain ground toward Richmond.

Chapter 13

On the Confederate Right at Spotsylvania

The Race for Spotsylvania Court House

As soon as he ascertained Grant's intention, Lee hastily put the Army of Northern Virginia in motion, his objective being to keep his forces between the Federal army and Richmond. On May 7, Lee ordered a reconnaissance to his right to find a suitable path for his army to overtake Grant. When a suitable road was not located, the pioneers cut a rough road south through the woods until it intersected the Catharpin Road. About 10 p.m. on May 7 the First Corps began leaving its breastworks for Spotsylvania Court House.[1] As the leading elements moved out, somewhere in the First Corps a private yelled "Three Cheers for General Lee!" He was heartily rewarded with the Rebel Yell which swept in turn from each brigade northward toward the Rapidan.[2] The entire army was caught up in the moment. Twice more the Rebel Yell rose from the leading elements of the First Corps. Twice more the spine-tingling sounds of the unique war cry raced through each brigade toward the Rapidan. Weary bodies gained new life after the rousing cheer. The Confederates needed the new-found energy to deny the Federals a clear road to Richmond. At Spotsylvania Court House the Confederate army had its first opportunity to block Grant's thrust against the rebel capital.

Kershaw's Division led the way. Law's Brigade led Field's Division, marching immediately behind Kershaw. The Confederate and Federal armies traveled essentially parallel routes. Burning trees lit up the night. Fires that were started during the previous fighting still burned furiously. Progress through the woods was slow, the road narrow and marching was greatly hampered by tree stumps in the road. Occasionally a tree, laying where it fell, created one more obstacle to slow the march.[3] Except for a 30-minute rest Anderson's corps marched all night. The column intersected the Catharpin Road east of Todd's Tavern, and from there, turned slightly southwest until it reached the Shady Grove Church. It then turned onto the Shady Grove Church Road and marched toward the Block House Bridge at the Po River.[4] Seven hours after it left its entrenchment, Law's Brigade halted for a quick meal.[5] They were somewhere between Shady Grove Church and the Block House Bridge.

Law's Brigade approached the Block House Bridge about mid-morning,[6] and sounds of musket fire greeted the brigade as it neared the Brock Road.[7] The Army of Northern Virginia barely won the race to Spotsylvania. Jeb Stuart's cavalry encountered the leading Federal regiments and fought a holding action near the intersection of the Brock and Old Court House Roads until Kershaw's Division arrived. Anderson then ordered Kershaw to

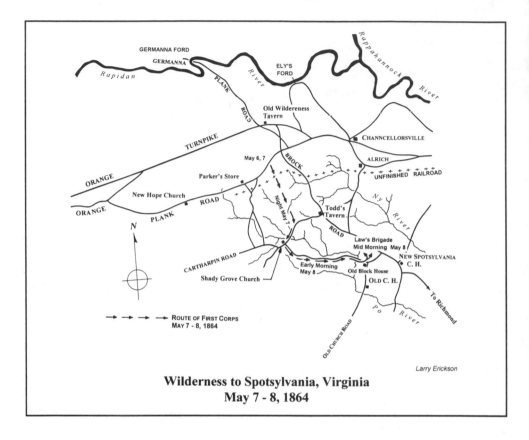

GERMANNA FORD
GERMANNA
Rapidan
River
ELY'S FORD
Rappahannock River
River
Old Wildereness Tavern
CHANNCELLORSVILLE
TURNPIKE
May 6, 7
BROCK
ALRICH
ORANGE
Parker's Store
UNFINISHED RAILROAD
New Hope Church
ORANGE
ROAD
Night May 7
Todd's Tavern
Ny River
PLANK
N
ROAD
Law's Brigade Mid Morning May 8
CARTHARPIN ROAD
Early Morning May 8
Old Block House
NEW SPOTSYLVANIA C. H.
Shady Grove Church
OLD C. H.
To Richmond
Po River
→ → → → ROUTE OF FIRST CORPS
MAY 7 - 8, 1864
OLD CHURCH ROAD

Larry Erickson

Wilderness to Spotsylvania, Virginia
May 7 - 8, 1864

send two brigades north toward the Brock Road, directing that Kershaw and his remaining two brigades move to the court house. The final leg of the race turned into a sprint for possession of an old rail fence which stretched along a slight rise running southwest from the Brock Road.[8] A growth of cedar and scrub pine partially covered the ground, and to the northwest lay a dense wood through which the Brock Road passed. Confederate Colonel John W. Henagan's and Brigadier General Humphreys's Brigades arrived at Laurel Hill just as Federal Major General Gouverneur K. Warren's V Corps began deploying for possession of the Old Court House Road.[9] At the time, Henagan's brigade lay on both sides of the Old Court House Road and extended west toward the Po River. Humphreys's Brigade entrenched on Henagan's right. After repulsing the initial charge, Henagan's South Carolinians began constructing breastworks from rail fences and logs lying about. The Federal line extended to the right so that Henagan's left was in danger of being turned. Stuart met Law's Brigade at about 10 a.m. as it approached the intersection and asked assistance for the beleaguered brigades facing Warren's troops.[10] Field immediately ordered Perry forward to their support, then proceeded toward the court house with the rest of his division to support Kershaw.[11]

Perry and Oates rode some distance ahead of the brigade, and as they approached the Confederate line, firing erupted beyond a wooded area on their front. Perry sent the 15th and 44th Alabama regiments forward to confront the threat. Oates, who had been given command of both regiments, ordered an advance under the cover of skirmishers, led by Captain Shaaff from Company A of the 15th. Oates decided his horse was of little use in the woods, so he dismounted and ran after his men.[12] The Alabamians emerged from the woods and found the Federals advancing in force, their musket fire forcing Shaaff's skirmishers back on the main line. Private Jep Brown, a member of the 15th Alabama, fell, shot through the heart, dying with his hand clutching his chest and a curse on his lips. Oates believed the curse was understandable and probably forgiven by a Supreme Being.[13]

Oates saw the Federal battle line overlapping his flanks and ordered the Alabama regiments to retire 200 yards.[14] Their assailants were Colonel Edward Bragg's Pennsylvania brigade, reinforced by the 6th Wisconsin.[15] When Bragg continued to press the Alabamians, Oates fell back toward the brigade. During the confusion, Confederate regiments in the rear, anxious to stem the advance, fired on the Federals. Unfortunately, several in the 15th and 44th Alabama regiments were wounded by the friendly fire. Among them were Captain David L. Bozeman, Company A, 44th, who was carried from the field and First Lieutenant Frank L. Boothly, Company H, 15th Alabama. It was believed that fire which felled Bozeman and mortally wounded a private standing near the captain came from the 47th Alabama.[16]

The confusion that led to the unfortunate incident may have been caused by Field bringing up the 4th, 47th and 48th from their supporting positions in the rear of Humphreys. Before Field reached the court house, word arrived that the Federal threat had disappeared. Field then turned northward toward the Brock Road and joined the fight.[17] Upon their arrival the three regiments were placed in line, Perry ordering Oates to fall back on the rest of the brigade where a line of battle was being formed. Oates extended his line right and left to prevent the Federal line from overlapping the 15th Alabama, then ordered the men to tear down a fence in the rear and construct a crude breastwork of rail, logs and dirt. In short order only the men's heads were exposed.[18] Pine poles were later hoisted on top of the works. Soldiers placed a piece of wood under each end, raising the pole sufficiently to provide a slit to fire at the enemy.[19]

Anderson's Georgia brigade came up and formed on Perry's left. Gregg's Texans arrived after the Georgians and went into line on Anderson's left. The 4th Alabama occupied the brigade's right with the 15th Alabama on the left, and the 48th Alabama was on the 15th's left.[20] Next in line were the 47th and 44th. They found that fighting behind breastworks brought on a marvelous sense of security and self-confidence. Adjutant Coles, 4th Alabama, later admitted that firing from the breastworks was a significant factor in making one's aim steady.[21]

Confederate skirmishers went out and exchanged shots with the Federal line the remainder of the day. Sergeant Henry B. Love, Company F, 4th Alabama, sustained a severe wound to his right foot by a minie ball. It was his third wound of the war. He entered the hospital May 17 and never returned to service with the 4th Alabama.[22]

Soon after he was hit, Bozeman's friend, Quartermaster Sergeant Thomas B. Somerville, telegraphed Mrs. Bozeman that her husband was wounded. Somerville did not, at first, believe the wound was serious but two days later, on May 11, he had to write Mrs. Bozeman that he could not offer hope for her husband's recovery.[23] Bozeman also realized he could not recover from his injury. A minie ball had struck him in the left hip, traveled through his lower abdomen and exited his right groin. His digestive tract was destroyed and, as Somerville wrote, "His urinating function refuses to operate." Bozeman told his friends he knew death was imminent but that it was God's will and he must not complain. He regretted that he had to die without seeing his wife and children. He lingered for eight days, alert to the last.[24] Private Leonidas Whatley of Bozeman's company stayed at his captain's bedside throughout, nursing him and making him as comfortable as possible. He and Bozeman had enlisted together at Pleasant Hill, Alabama, on March 17, 1862. Bozeman was the original second lieutenant of Company A, 44th Alabama. He commanded the company during most of 1862 because its captain and first lieutenant were seldom present. Both were dropped from the rolls in March 1863 and Bozeman was appointed captain. He commanded the company during all its battles until being wounded at Spotsylvania. Whatley remained a private, detailed as a regimental teamster.[25]

During her correspondence with Somerville, Mrs. Bozeman asked what her husband said about receiving a wound from his own men. Somerville wrote her that Bozeman knew he was hit by the 47th, but carefully avoided telling Mrs. Bozeman what her husband said of the incident. He explained that death by friendly fire occurred all too frequently and is greatly deplored, "but a man in the line is not only exposed to the enemy but sometimes to the danger of being shot by his friends." He offered the opinion that she should not spend time on "what ifs" but accept Providence.[26]

Bozeman, dressed in his military coat, was buried on the Andrews farm near Spotsylvania Court House. His only pants were torn and blood stained and therefore unusable. A blanket served to cover him. His sword was lost on the battlefield but his watch was recovered for his family.[27] The assistant surgeon of the 44th Alabama wrote to Mrs. Bozeman as did Lieutenant Colonel John A. Jones, commanding the regiment. Jones told Bozeman's widow that the officers and men of the regiment "all loved Captain Bozeman."[28]

First Lieutenant Frank L. Boothly sustained his second wound in the Wilderness. He returned to active service for the Battle of Cold Harbor, but remained only a few days before sickness caused him to return to the hospital. He did not die from battle wounds, however. He died at Richmond, Virginia December 15, 1864 of acute dysentery.[29]

Fighting on the Confederate Left

The limited skirmishing of May 9 on the army's left escalated early on the morning of May 10. Confederate sharpshooters were particularly active and dangerously accurate. A brief exposure brought immediate gunfire. More than one Federal paid the ultimate price for carelessness. The vicious firing tapered off before noon.[30]

Law's brigade rested behind its newly constructed breastworks of logs and fence rails packed with dirt.[31] Confidence in their ability to withstand a Federal assault grew steadily. As the sniping died, the Federal ordered a demonstration on Field's front to determine his strength. Cutler's men swarmed out of the woods in front of Perry, as artillery fire and musketry from the Confederate works opened with telling effect. On Cutler's left, the 84th New York, also known as the 14th New York State Militia, was forced into the woods fronting Perry, while the rest of Cutler's division retired from the terrible Confederate fire. The troops from Brooklyn hugged the ground as solid shot and shells ripped limbs from the trees and plowed furrows in the ground. Except for the casualties sustained by the 84th New York, Cutler's division received little damage. Perry's Alabamians mistook Cutler's feint for a concerted assault that was easily repulsed.

Between 4 and 4:30 p.m., Warren launched an attack against Law's Brigade and the brigades on either side.[32] Three brigades of Cutler's division attacked the Alabamians. Confederate artillery pounded the assaulting column with canister while it was still in the woods on Law's front.[33] The Federals were disorganized when they emerged from the woods, and a few well-directed volleys sent Cutler's brigades reeling back to regroup. Law's Alabamians now felt so secure behind their breastworks they taunted the retreating Federals. They cheered loudly and begged the Federals to attack one more time.[34] Perry sent several details to collect discarded Federal weapons from the dead and wounded.

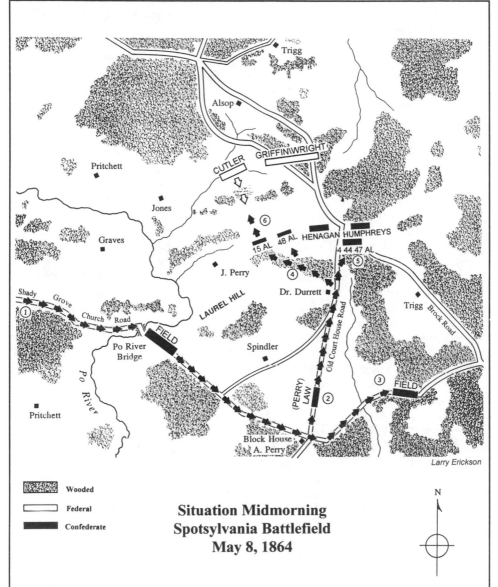

Situation Midmorning
Spotsylvania Battlefield
May 8, 1864

N

1. After leaving the Wilderness battlefield around 10 p. m., Law's Brigade, at the head of Field's Division, takes breakfast on the Shady Grove Road near daybreak.
2. When Law's Brigade arrives at the Old Block House, Stuart detaches Perry, commanding Law's Brigade, and sends him to support Kershaw, then fighting Federal units on the Old Court House Road.
3. The remainder of Field's Division continues toward Spotsylvania Court House.
4. As the Alabamians approach the rear of Henagan and Humphreys, Perry sends the 15th and 48th Alabama into line on Henagan's left where they immediately engage Cutler.
5. The 4th, 44th and 47th Alabama move to support Humphreys.
6. The 15th Alabama advances on Bragg's brigade of Cutler's division and is repulsed.

When all the captured weapons were brought in, the supply amounted to four or five rifles per man.[35] Field deployed a line of skirmishers to his front.

Brigadier General James C. Rice, the Alabamians' old nemesis from Gettysburg, fell before the Alabamians with a serious wound and was carried to the rear where surgeons amputated his leg. Before he could be removed from the field hospital, his condition deteriorated to the point that it was obvious his wound was fatal. Rice grew restless, but was unable to move himself. An aide asked which way to turn the dying man over. His voice barely above a whisper, Rice replied, "Toward the enemy. Let me die with my face to the foe." A few minutes later he was dead.[36]

The Federals launched the final attack of the day near sunset, a Federal staff officer stupidly riding along Cutler's line, yelling that the men would charge the Confederate works.[37] The signal to move out would be a cheer from the right, but the men of the 84th New York silently waited for the signal which meant certain death. Finally, the signal raced along the line from the right. The 84th New York raised a hearty cheer in response and sprang forward with the rest of Cutler's division.[38]

The Confederates on Field's right saw the assaulting column first. Word was quickly passed down the line, "Look out on the left; massing on your front!"[39] The Federals entered the woods in front of the Confederate line and drove Field's skirmishers back toward their entrenchments. Once in the woods failing light made it difficult for the Federals to maintain order and Confederate artillery pounded them, adding to the confusion. All at once the Confederates ceased fire. The historian of the 14th New York Militia recalled, "There was surprise at first, then the horrible truth, the Confederates were reserving their fire until the Federals were near the works."[40] Cutler's ranks emerged from the woods, pushed down the ravine on Perry's front and began scrambling up the opposite bank.[41] Long blue lines, appearing dark in the fading sunlight, came on at the quick time, then a trot. Finally, the Federal line broke into a run as it rushed for Field's works.[42]

Cutler sent two brigades against Law's men, who responded with a deafening roar of musketry. To the Federal attackers a sheet of fire seemed to run along the Confederate position. Suddenly "an awful leaden hail of solid shot and grape and canister" ripped into the Federal ranks.[43] The Alabamians poured a withering fire into Cutler's front rank, privates firing and tossing empty guns to the rear for reloading. Officers assisted in loading for the front line; Coles recounted how the officers, in their haste to load, often removed the cartridge flap by biting the flap and pulling, then inserting it in the muzzle and slamming the butt against the ground to ram the cartridge home.[44] The withering fire was so intense that Cutler's charge died almost as soon as his brigades emerged from the woods.

A heavy rainstorm rolled over the battlefield May 11, the first rain since the fighting began on May 5. The downpour brought a welcome relief from the heat and dust. After the initial fury of the storm subsided, a steady rainfall set in and continued most of the day.[45] As a result, fighting was limiting to sharpshooting. Marksmen from opposing lines concealed themselves in trees or in some other favorable vantage point. They kept a careful lookout for careless or unsuspecting individuals. All too frequently a sharpshooter's bullet wounded or killed the soldier who grew careless or unnecessarily exposed himself.[46]

Since the lines were so close, a major concern on both sides was a surprise night attack. To guard against this, Perry posted pickets between the lines and left a thin rank in the breastworks while the remainder of the brigade rested. Watches were two hours long. Since leaving Gordonsville on May 4, the men had slept for only short periods. By May 11, they were very fatigued and edgy. For the third watch of the night of May 11, Oates sent the 15th Alabama's pickets forward under Sergeant John White, Company I. After the pickets were in place, Oates lay down behind the breastworks, intending to rest a short period and did not remove his sword and spurs. To ward off the chill of the night, he wrapped himself in a blanket and quickly dozed off.[47]

Pickets became drowsy, and some even slept standing up. Since the bushes and brush lying on the ground were wet from the rainstorm it was easy to move about without making noise. Privates Billy Jordan, John W. Hughes and Jack McDonald, all of Company B, 15th Alabama, got very close to the Federal pickets without being detected. Jordan was so near to one that he could hear the man's footsteps as he paced his watch. Hughes and McDonald moved even closer and decided to fire. Guessing at the pickets' location, each squeezed off a round. Hughes's gun failed to go off but McDonald's fired cleanly. Jordan saw a ball of fire as big as his fist dart from the barrel as the discharge erupted in the darkness. It seemed the shot could be heard for miles as it reverberated throughout the surrounding woods.[48] Reaction from both sides was immediate, as musket fire erupted and extended quickly to the right and left.[49] Oates struggled to get up, but in his haste discovered his spurs and sword were entangled in the blanket. After thrashing about, he finally freed himself and dashed forward to investigate the cause of the firing. It took a few minutes to discover that an assault was not in progress. Several more minutes were required to calm down the privates in the entrenchment. When the firing died out, Oates remembered White and the pickets.

They were caught between the lines with bullets flying in all directions. White knew the Federals were not attacking, so he hurried toward his own line to stop the shooting. A Georgian mistook him for a Federal attempting to scale the works and shot him down. He was brought into the lines mortally wounded. During the short time remaining White reminisced about his life. He regretted being shot down by friends, and his last request was for Captain Waddell to pray for his soul. A few minutes later he departed this life.[50]

When the firing started, Private Bryant Wilson, Company I, 15th Alabama, was one of those asleep on his feet. Wilson was a deeply religious man and believed in the concept of predestination. If he was destined to die that night Wilson was quite willing to accept his fate, but after more reflection, he decided it might be prudent to aid his Lord in preserving his earthly body a little longer. To do that he took cover behind a tree. Then he discovered it was difficult to determine which side of the tree offered the best protection because bullets were flying from all directions. So he decided to hug the ground until the firing died down. Jordan, Hughes and McDonald remained where they were and came back in the lines at sunrise.[51]

Mysteriously, the nightly disturbance continued about the same time each night. Firing would erupt and last until the officers were able to calm the troops. Both sides then remained awake, worrying about a surprise attack. Orders came down for the regimental commanders to be on the lookout for the cause of the disturbance. On the fourth night Oates, at about midnight, saw Private James M. "Jim" Rhodes, Company K, 15th Alabama, who was not on duty, approach the line. Rhodes was a fun-loving individual who thoroughly enjoyed the life of a soldier, loved to plunder after a battle and took great delight in playing jokes on his fellow companions. After a battle he would invariably slip away and later return with so many watches that the ticking reminded those who heard it of a jewelry store. Rhodes told the men on guard to get behind trees, then moved forward and positioned himself behind a tree. Holding a pistol in each hand, Rhodes barked a crisp command: "Forward, guide, center!" He then began firing. As expected the Federals thought a surprise attack was under way and returned fire. When the firing ceased Rhodes came shuffling back, laughing and remarking to anyone in general, "It was a good one." Oates immediately accosted the private and sternly inquired what he was trying to accomplish. Rhodes blandly replied, "Why, colonel, that is the best way to whip them. Break them of their rest, and we can wear them out and whip them in a short time." Apparently he had not considered that his comrades suffered as much from lack of sleep as the Federals did.[52]

Fighting was renewed May 12 when the Federal II Corps attacked Lee's right on that portion of the line known as the "mule shoe." The thrust came before daylight in a heavy rainstorm, the initial assault almost spelling disaster for Lee's army.[53] It broke over Lee's works and took much desperate fighting to restore and hold the line.

The battle was still raging on Lee's right when the Federals, late in the afternoon, launched a weak attack on Lee's left. In this attack Cutler's division made its third and last assault against Law's Brigade.[54] Progress through the woods on Law's front proved just as difficult as during the previous charges. Terrific shelling from a Confederate battery on Cutler's left flank greatly impeded his progress.[55] Cutler's brigades exchanged a few volleys with the Alabamians, but for all practical purposes his charge stalled. After a brief meeting between Cutler and Warren, the Federals decided to withdraw.[56] For the second time in a week Perry's men fought a much larger force, but Cutler's numerical superiority was not enough to overrun Perry's well-placed Alabamians.

Rain continued throughout the night of May 12 and all day on May 13 before letting up late on the morning of May 14.[57] Little fighting occurred during those three days, as Law's Brigade remained in position from May 13–15. Sharpshooting from both lines intensified. The Confederates sought to locate as many of the Federal sharpshooters as possible in an effort to silence them. Late in the afternoon, a Federal marksman concealed behind a tree became very annoying to the men of the 4th Alabama. The man took care not to expose himself long enough for the Confederates to draw a bead on him. Lieutenant Colonel Scruggs decided to try a new tactic—to treat him like a treed squirrel. Scruggs sent two men to the left of the Federal while Scruggs went to the right where he could see the opposite side of the tree. On a signal from Scruggs, the men on the left fired at the sharpshooter. The sniper instinctively moved to the opposite side of the tree for protection. Scruggs only required one shot to bring him down. That night an Alabamian crawled out and brought in the dead man's blue cap with a hole in it.[58]

Skirmishing and unusually heavy sharpshooting continued through most of the morning of May 14 then ebbed as the noon hour approached.[59] Those behind Law's breastworks thought it had stopped. Major Campbell took advantage of the lull to seek a moment's rest, moving to the rear of the breastworks recently occupied by his men. Major Cary joined Campbell and the two sat down to rest and were soon relaxed and engaged in idle conversation.[60] Campbell sat with his back resting against a tree.[61] Oates was standing behind his lines about sixty yards from Campbell. By chance, he was looking at the major when he heard the report from a musket some distance way. Campbell toppled over unconscious, shot through his hat band.[62] From the look of Campbell's lifeless form, Oates knew the wound was serious. Campbell was still breathing, but Oates suspected the wound was fatal. Stretcher bearers quickly carried the unconscious major to the field hospital.

Major Cary noted the general area from where the shot was fired. Private Henry H. Sturgis, Company G, 44th Alabama, was shown the suspected location and ordered to find the sniper. After a cautious search, Sturgis located him in the top of a tall pine tree about three quarters of a mile away. Sturgis lay down behind a log, took aim and fired, but missed his mark. The Federal fired back. Two more shots were exchanged with no effect by either man. On Sturgis's third try, he was rewarded with a return shot so close that his face was stung by bits of bark and wood kicked up by the Federal's bullet. A lot of luck would be required to bring the Federal down. Sturgis went over to a battery and pointed out the tree in which the sharpshooter hid. He asked the artilleryman to shoot off its top, and a few minutes later Sturgis had the pleasure of watching Campbell's assailant, still clinging to the tree top, fall 60 feet to the ground.[63]

Campbell's friend, Private Robert A. McCaghren, Company E, 47th Alabama, happened to be in the doctors' quarters when Campbell was brought in. A few minutes later the Reverend Major James McDonald Campbell of Cherokee County, Alabama, answered the last roll call.[64] The Confederate War Department had still not resolved the dispute over who should hold the rank of lieutenant colonel in the 47th Alabama. It took a Federal sniper's bullet to settle the issue.

Before nightfall, Field's Division was ordered out to occupy the deserted works on their front.[65] Fighting on the Confederate left was over.

Grant Moves Again

By May 15, Grant's army was resuming his relentless thrust toward Richmond, his aim to slip around Lee's right. Law's Brigade left its position between midnight and by 1 a.m. on the morning of May 16, moved southward. At dawn they were in position on Lee's flank near the Crutchfield Farm.[66] Field's Division now anchored the Confederate right. Law's Brigade was near the bridge over the Po River where a strong line of works was constructed. The position, located just east of the barn and dwelling, was on the crest of a slight hill, facing to the east.[67] The Alabamians confidently settled in behind breastworks and looked forward to an assault by Grant's army.

To the delight of his men, Law rejoined the brigade at the Crutchfield farm and resumed command. He wasted little time before nominating Terrell for lieutenant colonel of the 47th Alabama. Congressman David Lyon and Terrell's old friend, Captain James T. Jones, Company D, 4th Alabama, were already working on Terrell's behalf. On April 21, 1864, Jones wrote Lyon, "Our service does not possess a more dashing and gallant officer than Captain Terrell or more entitled for promotion."[68] Terrell, also actively sought the lieutenant colonelcy of the 47th Alabama, seeking Lyon's influence in obtaining his immediate appointment. He reasoned that a board appointed to reexamine Campbell's competency would not meet for months. Since he had been appointed the 47th's lieutenant colonel once before and in light of the need for a field commander, he thought it prudent to seek immediate appointment to the office.[69] After Campbell's death, eleven officers from the 47th Alabama finally made it possible for the War Department to consider Terrell's appointment by waiving their right to claim promotion by seniority.[70] Perry approved the request and forwarded it with the following endorsement: "He (Terrell) is remarkable for his coolness and gallantry in battle and great power of controlling others combined with military judgment."[71] However, all the officers of the 47th did not waive their right to the office of colonel, which should have been a problem. The War Department reasoned that since the regiment was badly in need of a commander, this might be a case where it was prudent to appoint an outsider.[72] Bulger was exchanged March 10, 1864, and temporarily reentered the picture. Since Bulger was now exchanged, the department acted quickly, appointing Bulger colonel of the 47th Alabama June 15, 1864. Terrell received his appointment as lieutenant colonel the same day.[73] The 47th Alabama had a dashing young field officer to lead its men.

After spending a few days with his regiment the fifty-seven-year-old Bulger found his health still seriously impaired from his wound and was admitted to the Howard's Grove Hospital on June 2, 1864. Little could be done for the elderly gentleman. His lung was infected and he was transferred to the Ladies Hospital in Montgomery, Alabama. In August he was declared unfit for duty and sent to De Soto, Alabama, on 60 days furlough. On

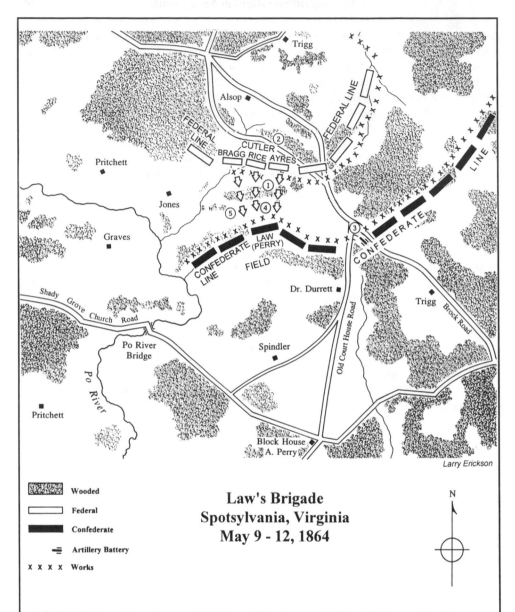

**Law's Brigade
Spotsylvania, Virginia
May 9 - 12, 1864**

Larry Erickson

Wooded

Federal

Confederate

⇥ Artillery Battery

x x x x Works

N

1. Cutler's division makes a demonstration in front of Perry between 10:00 and 10:30 a. m. May 10.
2. A general Federal assault is launched against Field's line about 4:00 p. m. May 10. Cutler's division advances through the woods toward Perry.
3. Artillery in line between Field and Kershaw pound Cutler while he is still in the woods.
4. Cutler's ranks emerge from the woods in considerable disarray. Cutler's charge is easily repulsed by Perry's Alabamians firing from behind fortifications.
5. Cutler moves forward in another general assault near sunset May 10. This charge meets the same fate as the previous assault.
6. Cutler makes his last assault against Perry on May 12. After coming under heavy fire from Perry's Alabamians and the Confederate battery, Cutler's charge dies in the open ground after emerging from the wooded area.

December 27, 1864, a medical board recommended he be retired and forwarded the appropriate papers to the War Department. His discharge from the service came on February 8, 1865, by Special Order 32/7. After the war Bulger returned to farming and later resided at Jackson's Gap, Alabama.[74]

While the Alabamians lay behind breastworks near Crutchfield farm, Bowles planned a reconnaissance to his right. He asked Adjutant Coles to accompany him, and since the day was warm, Bowles walked with his hat in his hands. The pair moved at a leisurely pace and were crossing a road when a shot rang out. A sharpshooter firing from the cover of a pine thicket knocked Bowles's cap from his hand. It fell in the road as Bowles dove for the cover of the woods. Coles became convinced the Federal was out for some fun because he kept cutting down scrub pine near the cap to prevent its retrieval. One of the two finally obtained a pole and fished it from the road.[75]

Chapter 14

A Bloody Day at Cold Harbor

Race for the North Anna

The previous two weeks were perhaps the most difficult period for Law's Alabamians. When the Federal infantry was not charging the Confederate works, incessant sharpshooting kept the men's nerves on edge. Private James Daniel recalled that during one stretch of eight days and nights smoke hung constantly over the battlefield. U. S. Grant's army also surprised the Alabamians with its new found courage and tenacity. Daniel wrote his wife that the Federals would charge right up to the breastworks. Human targets were so plentiful that he told her he had killed more in one fight than in all previous engagements in which he had participated. Brutal though Grant's tactics may have seemed at the time, Confederate losses incurred in the fighting could not be replaced. On May 21, 1864, Daniel sadly noted that the 47th Alabama looked no larger that one of its companies from earlier days.[1]

Grant was on the move again by May 21, relocating to the east side of the Mattapony, after the roads had dried out following recent heavy rains. A cloud of dust rising in the distance indicated the Federal army was in motion. Lee suspected Grant was placing the Mattapony between the Army of the Potomac and the Army of Northern Virginia. From available intelligence, he concluded Grant would once again try to turn the Confederate right.[2]

Lee sent a message to Field to have scouts verify the cause of the dust. Since Law's Brigade was on the extreme right of the army, Field ordered Law to furnish the scouts. Two men from the 44th Alabama were dispatched down the Po River toward the Mattapony.[3] They waded a quarter-mile downstream without being detected, then found a ford with a path leading to a main road. A mile later, the pair discovered a large body of Federals and watched several units pass before concluding that the entire Federal army was in motion. Back at headquarters, Field quickly relayed the information to Lee. The return message simply read "Thanks to the scouts."[4] Lee sent word to the Confederate War Department that he was extending his line with the intention of keeping his forces between Grant's army and Richmond.[5]

That afternoon Lee ordered Field to march toward the North Anna River. The division left at dusk, marched by Dickerson's farm to Mud Tavern and down the Telegraph Road. Lee pushed his army hard, permitting little if any rest, in a desperate attempt to stay between Grant and Richmond. The gray column marched throughout the night of May 21, all the next day and well into the night.[6] Law's Alabamians were permitted their first rest in a day-and-a-half about 3 a.m. on the morning of May 23 when Field halted for two hours.[7] After reaching the North Anna, the 4th Alabama picketed the river in the vicinity of the bridge while the First Corps passed.[8] Meanwhile, the remainder of Law's Brigade marched downriver and went into position astride the Richmond and Fredericksburg Railroad. Earthen works were quickly erected on both sides of the railroad embankment, with the 15th Alabama straddling the railroad.[9] A 12-pounder Napoleon sat on the tracks, ready to fire down the rail line. During the rest of the afternoon, both lines kept up a lively exchange of fire.[10]

Early the next morning, both sides resumed firing, and continued until late afternoon. On May 26, the Federals advanced on Law's position, and Field ordered Law to counterattack.[11] Law sent forward two companies from each regiment with the Napoleon, a move which stopped the Federal advance in short order.[12]

Very little fighting took place during the brigade's stay on the North Anna, with action limited to an occasional demonstration by the Federals and periodic sharpshooting. After one demonstration, a group of Federals halted in a thicket and fired on Law's line. Oates, ordered to send forward a company to drive the Federals back, chose Waddell's company, but the task proved more difficult than anticipated. The men in blue put up a stiff fight and Waddell was unable to dislodge the Federals from their position. Both sides settled in and exchanged fire. Privates William A. McClendon and Barney McArdle, Company G, 15th Alabama, came under fire from a sniper hidden behind a large tree. Fortunately, the Federal's shots only stripped off bark above their heads. McClendon located the Federal sharpshooter by the smoke from his rifle. McArdle was in a better position to fire on the Federal, but missed. McClendon then moved farther to the side where he could get a better view, yet remain hidden from the sniper. Soon McClendon saw the Federal slowly moving around the tree for a shot. When the Federal's head was exposed sufficiently to present a good target McClendon yelled: "Fire!" McArdle dropped him with one shot. The two remained hidden until they spotted a lone Federal moving cautiously through the brush on their front. They waited patiently until the man, who turned out to be an officer, was near enough to reach out and touch. McArdle trained his gun on him while McClendon relieved him of his sword, and the Federal was soon on his way to Richmond.[13]

The 15th Alabama's position across the railroad exposed its men to constant fire from the Federal entrenchment. For protection the men loaded their muskets, then leaned the weapons against the embankment and moved to cover behind earthworks on either side of the railroad. On one occasion, Law passed the exposed position and was warned to fall down just as a bullet whizzed by his head. He grabbed a musket and fired, but missed. The Federal was unaware of the 15th's practice of keeping a supply of loaded weapons handy and calmly went about the task of reloading without seeking cover. Law took a second musket and fired. Both men were surprised by the results, the Federal at the speed with which his adversary reloaded and Law at hitting his mark.[14]

Other members of the brigade were not as lucky as Law. Sharpshooters on both sides maintained a constant lookout for men who were exposed too long. From May 24 through May 26, the brigade lost four officers to sharpshooters. Lieutenant James W. Hornbuckle, Company G, 4th Alabama, became the first casualty on May 24; Captain Jason M. West, Company A, 4th Alabama, was the second on May 25; Lieutenant Eli A. Baker, Company B, 4th Alabama, was the third on May 26; and Captain John B. Hubbard, Company K, 48th Alabama, became the fourth, also on May 26. Baker was killed while the other three suffered wounds from which they later recovered.

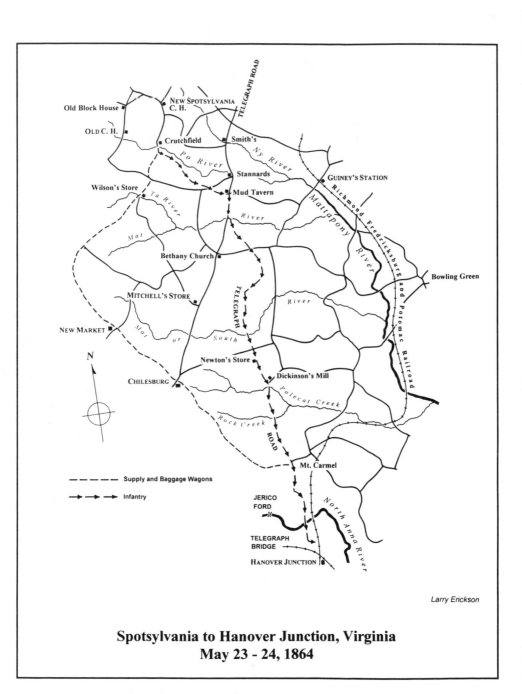

Spotsylvania to Hanover Junction, Virginia
May 23 - 24, 1864

Entrenching at Cold Harbor

Grant recrossed the North Anna on May 27, continuing his attempt to get around Lee's right. Once again, Lee quickly moved his army between Grant and Richmond. The First Corps left the North Anna, marched through Ashland and camped between Half Sink and Hughes's Cross Roads. From there it moved on to Atlee's Station on May 28 and bivouacked between Hundley's Corner and Walnut Grove Church.[15] On May 31, Lee entrenched near Gaines's Mill. This area was not tactically significant to Lee but he wanted to deny Grant direct access to Richmond. The Battle of Second Cold Harbor began in earnest on June 1, 1864. Law's Brigade was not engaged the first day. The Alabamians waited as reserves in the left rear of the First Corps.

Early on the morning of June 2, Law was ordered to take his brigade and Anderson's Georgians to the Confederate right to reinforce the line. His orders were to exercise his own discretion as to where reinforcements were most needed.[16] Law left his brigades in place and set out on a personal inspection. Pickett's Division was first in line, then Kershaw's and Hoke's. Law found the line in satisfactory condition until he stopped at Kershaw's headquarters. Kershaw had not repaired his line from a near breakthrough late the previous afternoon. His right inclined to the rear at nearly a 45-degree angle before connecting with Hoke's left.[17] The line ran down an incline, across a sluggish little stream and up another incline. A large stand of trees covered the works where it crossed the stream.[18] A salient had been formed with the point resting near the thicket. The salient's base was in open ground and was vulnerable, if attacked. Its right face ran along a slope with a small marshy stream in front, and slightly elevated ground rose in front of the marsh where a rough works, now occupied by Brigadier General William T. Wofford's Georgia brigade, had been constructed when the fighting ceased the previous day.[19] Law quickly concluded the salient was indefensible and proposed to construct new works across its base.[20] Kershaw accepted Law's proposal, but since lively skirmishing was going on, Law decided to wait until darkness to begin work.[21] Late in the afternoon, a heavy rainstorm pelted the area.[22] Unknown to Law and the defenders of the salient, a Federal assault scheduled at 5 p.m. was postponed. It is unlikely the salient could have been successfully defended.[23]

While Law surveyed the works, the Federals disappeared from the brigade's front. The Alabamians took this opportunity to move behind the lines and lounge in the shade of nearby trees. During the rest period mail arrived from Richmond. The more fortunate in the brigade received letters from home. Soldiers read aloud from newspapers for the benefit of the illiterate. They were interested in the latest news of the war and editorial opinions about its progress.[24]

Later in the morning, rapid firing erupted on the Alabamians' right. Orders came to support the threatened line, but by the time they arrived the Federal advance had been repulsed. Then Perry, in Law's absence, marched the brigade some distance to the rear to await further orders. As it crossed a road in the rear of the breastworks a recently slain Confederate lay by the roadside, the victim of a sharpshooter. Despite that ominous warning, Private Ephraim Powell, Company E, 4th Alabama, unwisely ventured from cover. He was just turning to call to a companion when a sharpshooter's bullet inflicted a mortal wound. Powell died June 23, 1864.[25]

Finding no more Confederate targets, the sharpshooter began popping away at battle flags. A few minutes later, a bullet shattered the 4th Alabama's flag staff. Someone quickly cut down a sapling and fashioned a makeshift staff. The color bearer defiantly placed the 4th Alabama's battle flag in full view. The sharpshooter again demonstrated his shooting skill.[26] This was repeated several times before the Alabamians decided to put a stop to the sharpshooter's mischief. They discovered his hiding place in the top of a tree about five hundred yards away. Several members of the 4th Alabama tried in vain to bring him down. The long range shot required better accuracy than their Enfield rifles provided. Tired of the Federal nuisance, a Whitworth rifle was requested. One shot felled him, the last sight the 4th had of their antagonist was his headlong fall from the treetop to the ground below.[27] All was quiet until a courier arrived with orders to report to Law.

Law went out after dark and personally marked off the new line connecting Kershaw and Hoke.[28] He laid out the new line to put the marshy ground in front of the Confederate breastworks and provide a clear field of fire across it. Law not only strengthened the position but also shortened his lines.[29] His and Anderson's Brigade toiled throughout the night with whatever tools were available. The Pioneer corps came up with a few picks and spades, while some of the Alabamians and Georgians used bayonets to loosen the soil, and others used their hands to pile the dirt onto a parapet.[30] First Lieutenant Turner Vaughan, Company C, 4th Alabama, grabbed a spade and worked hard to set a good example for his men. Most were not used to officers working alongside the privates, and he was the subject of considerable jesting. Orderly Sergeant Steve Murphy, Company I, took time out to admire the lieutenant's work. He complimented Vaughan on "his deftness and graceful manipulation" of the spade. Murphy, who spoke in an effeminate voice, jokingly remarked: "My goodness, Lieutenant, you certainly beat any of us at it." Vaughan was in no mood for fun this night and sternly replied: "Yes, and if you realized what is going to happen in the morning you would beat it yourself."[31] While Law's and Anderson's Brigades constructed their earthen works, the Wofford's men worked to destroy the old works to the front. Apparently the works were not completely torn down because Federal reports identified the old line as rifle pits. Wofford finished before daylight and withdrew to the rear of Law's new line.[32]

The breastworks followed the line of the base of the old salient. The Confederates were remarkably efficient and the breastworks were ready by 4 a.m. on June 3. A parapet about five feet high covered the distance between Kershaw's right and Hoke's left. On its front, a four-foot deep ditch guarded the approach to the works. A wide shallow ditch ran along the rear of the works. Immediately behind the parapet, the men fashioned a small ledge to stand on while firing.[33] A shower fell shortly after the works were completed, turning the freshly worked dirt into mud as Law's and Anderson's Brigades went into line. Law was between Kershaw's Division and Anderson's Georgia brigade. Earlier in the night Oates had requested artillery support, and two Parrott guns arrived just as the works were completed.[34] One gun was placed between Oates and the 13th Mississippi on Oates left. The second was deployed between Law and Anderson.[35] The artillerymen placed the guns so that each could easily be wheeled around to deliver an enfilade fire over the ground previously occupied by the old works and to cover the front of Law's Brigade.[36] Law was particular about the placement of his artillery support, believing the Federal success at the "Mule Shoe" on May 12 was due to the lack of Confederate artillery.[37] From right to left, the Alabama regiments in line were the 15th, 4th, 44th, 47th and 48th.[38] The Alabamians stood in three ranks, the front rank exposed from the waist up.[39] Oates ordered his officers to arm themselves with axes in the event the expected Federal assault succeeded in breaking through the line.[40]

A company from each of the five regiments was selected for picket duty, with Cary in command. He and his pickets moved forward across the marshy land toward the woods fronting Law's position.[41] Defensive preparations prevented anyone from sleeping during the night. As the men settled into the new entrenchment, several of Law's officers drifted to the rear for coffee and smoking. Bowles sat some distance away from a fire where coffee was brewing and watched low clouds move overhead. After drinking a cup of coffee he lit his pipe for a leisurely smoke. A predawn rain shower had passed, and the air was still damp. Great dark clouds hung low over the woods into which Cary and his men had recently entered. Bowles looked up and imagined "the clouds were chasing each other in rapid succession like great balloons."[42] Law was farther to the rear resting on a slight incline, and from his position the entire line was in full view.[43] A short distance behind Law, Brigadier General Goode Bryan's Brigade stirred about, preparing an early morning meal. Day was just breaking.

"We Really Mowed Them Down"[44]

Firing suddenly broke out from the woods on the Alabamians' front, and just as Bowles looked in that direction an officer in the line called out, "Look! Look! Look at our pickets!"[45] Bowles and the men saw the pickets making a mad dash for the new works. Cary and his men reached the parapet just as a mass of Federals emerged from the woods. To Law's Alabamians it seemed the advancing Federals were on dress review. On they came at the double quick, five lines deep in front of Law and Anderson.[46] All along the Alabama line came the warning, "Look out! They're coming!"[47]

Grant had ordered a general assault for 4:30 a.m. The XVIII Corps, commanded by Major General William F. Smith and fresh from service in the vicinity of Bermuda Hundred, fronted Field's position. Brigadier General James H. Martindale's Second Division assaulted Law's and Anderson's positions. Smith was under general instructions to attack in conjunction with the VI Corps under Major General Horatio G. Wright who was on Smith's left. When Smith asked Wright for his plan of attack, Wright simply replied that he was "...going to pitch in."[48] Smith decided to attack with Martindale's division of two brigades. This division was composed of Colonel Griffin Stedman's Second Brigade and Brigadier General George Stannard's First Brigade.[49] Stedman's brigade led the assault, supported by Stannard. Martindale formed his line of battle along a slight elevation under cover of the woods to Law's front. From his vantage point on the slight rise a private in Stannard's brigade looked to his right and saw the entire V Corps arrayed in line of battle. Off to his left, the VI Corps was also visible. Ahead, a column of blue gave him some comfort in the thought that there was safety in numbers. Optimistically, he commented to a comrade, "We'll be all right today. Look ahead. There are enough men up there to drive clear through to the Gulf of Mexico."[50] Precisely at 4:30 a.m. Martindale sent his brigades forward, progressing slowly until they cleared the woods. Between 4:30 and 5 a.m. Martindale's men charged out of the woods toward the old works. The Federals first glimpse of Law's and Anderson's Brigades was a line of men standing shoulder to shoulder exposed from the waist up.[51] Nine battle flags were counted fluttering over the works occupied by the Confederates. Martindale's initial thrust was directed against Anderson's Georgians.[52] Stedman's and Stannard's brigades marched at trail arms with bayonets fixed and in perfect order.[53] Shells from a six gun battery in the Federal rear burst over the heads of the Confederate defenders. As they waited fragments rained downed on the line of Alabamians and Georgians and into their rear.

The Federal right flank presented an excellent enfilade target for Law's Brigade and its supporting Parrott guns. Law's line held its fire, but Martindale's left was subjected to a flanking fire almost from the time his lines came out of the woods. There was little damage from the initial volleys, and Martindale managed to reach the line of the old works relatively unscathed. When Cary's pickets scurried back to the main works, Martindale's front ranks were encouraged because they mistakenly believed that Cary's pickets were defenders being driven from the front line of works. They probably thought they were about to overrun the Confederate's works with little opposition. Stedman's brigade swept over the line of the old works with a loud cheer and entered the marshy depression in front of the new works.[54]

Law observed that the Federal column covered a front of little more than his "own brigade of less than a thousand men; but line followed line until the space enclosed by the old salient became a mass of withering humanity, upon which our artillery and musketry played with cruel effect."[55] Anderson and Law held their fire until Stedman's front rank came to within 70 yards of their breastworks. Suddenly, a solid sheet of flame signaled the opening volley from the Georgians and Alabamians.[56] Law's second rank loaded while the first rank fired several quick volleys. Blasts from the Parrotts, loaded with canister, tore gaping holes in Stedman's flank.[57] The effect of the artillery on the densely packed ranks of Stedman's New Yorkers and New Englanders was simply to cut men down by the dozens. Bowles later recalled that "heads, arms, legs and body parts, and muskets were seen flying in the air at every discharge." The front line halted under the impact of shot and shell, wavered and fell back on the second. Each volley from Anderson and Law drove Stedman's lines farther back. Both lines were soon mingled with the third and fourth. Two or three more volleys sent Martindale's men retreating toward the woods.[58] Martindale reformed his line just inside the wooded area on Law's front.[59] Because his front ranks were visible to the Confederates a number of casualties were inflicted by musket fire.

Pinckney Bowles immediately began preparing for the next assault. He decided to employ the rapid fire technique that had worked so well at Spotsylvania. The 4th Alabama was arranged so the men were four deep. Three men would sit and load while the fourth, standing in the firing line, aimed and fired. After firing, the gun was to be quickly exchanged for a loaded one.[60]

From a position to the rear, Law observed his men with growing concern. Would the frequency of volleys deplete his ammunition before a fresh supply could be brought up? Was the size of his defending line large enough? Even though the initial Federal charge was easily repulsed, Law suspected the enemy would regroup and launch a second wave. Would the next assault, by its overwhelming numbers, overrun his works? Law sent for a fresh supply of ammunition, then went forward to regulate the firing.

On the Federal side, Smith personally inspected Martindale's front and superintended reforming his broken lines. To counter the heavy enfilade fire from the right, Smith ordered Martindale to face a line to the right so that it fronted Law's Brigade. Martindale threw out three regiments from Stedman's brigade to protect his right flank during the next attack. Stannard's brigade moved up on Stedman's left.[61] Before launching the second charge, Smith went to his left to ascertain conditions there, instructing Martindale to advance only when he saw the line on his left move out. However, Martindale was sustaining considerable casualties in its exposed position, and feeling it necessary to move, ordered his command forward.[62] Smith heard the firing on his right and immediately knew that Martindale had launched his assault.[63] Before Smith could return, the second charge was repulsed and a third was in the process of suffering the same fate.

Bryan's Georgians came up and loaded for Law's men to fire. Smoke hovered low over the entire field in front of the Alabama and Georgia brigades. Stannard's line came on swaying, first to the right, then to the left, "like great waves in the sea." Men were frequently struck by two or three balls before falling to the ground. Bowles described the Federal charge as being "like a flock of sheep against a stone wall."[64] Private William Griffin, Company K, 44th Alabama, was awed by what he saw, comparing the slaughter to cutting hay in his field back home. He wrote his wife, "We really mowed them down."[65]

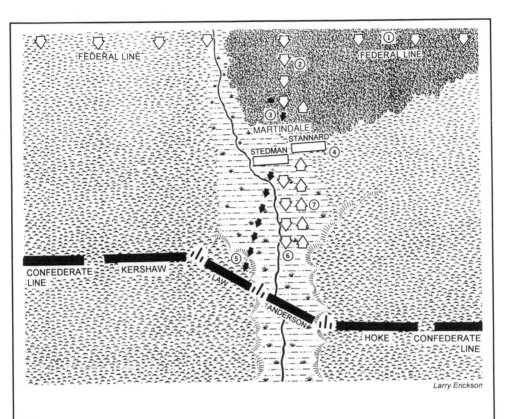

Larry Erickson

 Wooded

 Marsh

Grass/Brush

Federal

Confederate

ıʰ Artillery Battery

N

Initial Attack on Law's Brigade
Battle of Second Cold Harbor, Virginia
June 3, 1864

1. A general Federal assault against the Confederates begins at 4:30 a.m.
2. Martindale pushes forward through the woods in front of Law and Anderson.
3. Law's skirmishers, posted in the woods, retire in the face of the Federal advance.
4. Stedman and Stannard emerge from the woods fronting Law and Anderson. Their advance takes them toward Anderson.
5. Law's skirmishers reach the safety of the works as Martindale charges into the marshy area.
6. Law and Anderson hold their fire until the Federal advance is within 70 yards of the Confederate works. A devastating fire is delivered into the Federal ranks.
7. Martindale's charge stalls. Stedman and Stannard fall back in confusion to regroup under cover of the woods.

Fighting superior numbers was by now routine for the Alabama soldiers but their success against Martindale created extra excitement. Law's men talked excitedly and laughed as they fired. Officers gleefully took off their hats, and running up and down the line, slapped the men with joy. The excitement spread to the rear. The surgeon of the 4th Alabama, caught up in the fervor of the moment, rushed to the works, grabbed a gun and was standing in the firing line when he was discovered by Bowles.[66] Law was appalled by the sight. He had seen the horrible butchery at Fredericksburg and Manassas, but in three years of war he had seen nothing to match the carnage before his lines. Federal dead and wounded piled on each other five or six deep. Blood mingled in the stream until it flowed red past the Alabamians' line.[67] Even Sharpsburg seemed mild compared to this, the ground in front turning horribly blue with fallen Federals. Law concluded this was not war but murder.[68] Like Law, privates in the ranks were astounded by the numbers involved and the ease by which the charging column was decimated. Private James Daniel, 47th Alabama, called it slaughter. He fired 60 rounds, aiming and firing at targets with the same ease that he had once picked off squirrels in Alabama. When the battle was over Daniel's shoulder was badly bruised from the constant recoil of his musket.[69]

The assaulting lines suddenly stopped and became nothing more than a mass of humanity surging backward. During the Federal retreat, the colors of the 23rd Massachusetts fell to the ground, lying on the Confederate side of the old works and were trampled. Forgetting his own safety, Sergeant David Wallis jumped over the works, sprinted toward his regimental flag, scooped it from the ground and rushed back to the works, tumbling over them amid a hail of musket fire. The only evidence of his brush with death were two bullet holes in his blouse.[70]

Bowles took advantage of a brief lull in the fighting to replenish his ammunition. A few minutes later the familiar "huzzah" rose from the woods on his front. Incredibly, the Federals were preparing for another charge—the fourth—against Law's Alabamians.[71] But Bowles noticed that the Federal cheer was noticeably feeble. Then a single blue-clad regiment materialized from the woods. From the front line, Law's men called out, "They are coming again!"[72]

Lieutenant Colonel Orson Moulton, 25th Massachusetts, led the last assault. With one hand he waved his sword over his head, and with the other, waved his men onward, leading them in a mad dash directly at the 4th Alabama. Bowles and his Alabamians watched with admiration at the heroic courage of the men in blue, most of whom faced certain death. Coles wrote that it appeared to be downright murder to kill men in the "performance of an act as courageous" as that of the 25th Massachusetts.[73] But this was war and at 60 yards from its objective a deadly volley ripped into the New Englanders. When the 25th began to falter, Corporal John Lewis ran to the front with the regimental colors. A handful of men following him either fell dead or wounded, leaving Lewis standing alone and an easy target. Several bullets quickly found their mark. The wounded corporal attempted to move forward, but found himself staggering and wobbling on his feet. His last act before sinking to the ground was to look skyward, holding his flag defiantly over his head, as if asking for guidance from above. The colors gently settled over his lifeless body.[74]

Moulton and several of the 25th became separated from the main body and found themselves stranded in the open about 50 or 60 yards in front of Law's Brigade. They had no choice but to lie down to keep from being shot.[75] Suddenly no man was standing on Law's front. One man raised his head and briefly looked around. Oates saw the man and called for him to come in. The fellow decided that was better than spending the day between the lines and started for the 15th Alabama, but was rewarded for his efforts with shots from his own people. Oates learned from him that many more live Federals were out there among the dead and dying.[76] These men would have to wait until dark to be captured.

Fighting ceased along Law's front by 7:30 a.m., the brigade escaping with only four officers wounded, none killed, and relatively few casualties.[77] Law sustained the most serious wound when an artillery shell exploded above him, inflicting a wound to the left eye that could easily have blinded him or killed him. The wound was to the left eye socket just at the eyebrow line.[78] The injury paralyzed the scalp, affecting the vision in his eye and making it very sensitive to light.[79] He obtained a medical leave and went home to Darlington, South Carolina, to recuperate. Despite the seriousness of the wound Law did not go to the hospital, feeling perhaps as many did, that hospitals were deadly. After medical treatment he went on his way, although he did stop by the War Department on June 4. What he did in Richmond is not known.[80] Colonel Perry assumed command of the brigade. Major Lowther of the 15th incurred a slight wound and used that excuse to leave the field, making his way to Richmond. Lowther had personal business that needed his attention, specifically acquiring his rightful promotion to colonel.

Lieutenant Thomas L. Samuels, Company A, 4th Alabama, sustained a bullet wound to the head and was in and out of hospitals throughout the summer and fall of 1864.[81] His final stay was in the General Hospital at Charlottesville, Virginia. When it was obvious that he would not be able to return to field duty, he was retired to the invalid corps and assigned to special duty on January 10, 1865. His last assignment was as an officer in the reserves in Alabama.[82]

Captain Henry Lindsay, Company D, 47th Alabama, lost his index and middle fingers from his right hand. This was his second wound. The first was an injury to his left ankle at Sharpsburg. Loss of his fingers caused him to be absent only through June. Lindsay returned to service and surrendered with the brigade at Appomattox.[83]

Cold Harbor was the only battle in which Sergeant Thomas V. Warren, Company K, 4th Alabama, had taken part, because since his enlistment in 1861 he had been detailed the regimental wagonmaster. He was severely wounded in his face, which resulted in a broken jaw. He was absent until October 1864 when he resumed his duties as wagonmaster.[84]

All Federal attacks ceased by 1 p.m. The Confederate wounded were then moved out of harm's way and the lines repaired.[85] Both sides settled into the now usual routine of sharpshooting. The ground in front of Law's Brigade seemed to undulate as the wounded thrashed grotesquely about in agony. Crippled Federals cried pitifully for water. Men moving behind both lines became targets for sharpshooters from the opposing side. Federals caught in the open between the lines became ready prey. When darkness fell over the field, Perry sent Cary out with a detail to bring in the wounded Federals.

Cary found two Federal officers, Moulton and Second Lieutenant Thomas Sauls, trying to make their way back to their entrenchments. Moulton intended to deny the Confederates the pleasure of acquiring his sword as a trophy by covering it with dirt during the day. Cary suspected the 25th Massachusetts's flag was nearby, showing more interest in it than Moulton's sword. To Moulton, Cary declared, "Your flag is out here somewhere and I'm going to get it." Cary searched the area where he had last seen the flag, but his efforts were in vain. Actually, the 25th Massachusetts's flag was safely within its line. The color guard had risked his life to retrieve it and carry it off the field.[86] Moulton and Sauls were ushered into Law's works, and both were soon on their way to Richmond for stints in Confederate prisons.

A private from the 4th Alabama sent forward on picket duty ran into the muzzle of a Federal musket and received a serious chest wound. The man lay where he fell until Bowles sent out a detail to bring him in. Three weeks later the private had recuperated sufficiently to earn a "wounded leave of absence" and was on his way home.[87]

Sometime during the night, a Federal artillery captain wandered too far from his own lines while searching for a place to locate his battery. He blundered into Law's line. When he realized his mistake he attempted to reach the Federal lines. He was unhorsed for his efforts and brought back within the lines, limping badly from a gunshot wound to the leg. The man spent his short time in the Alabama lines complaining about the stupidity of his aborted mission.[88]

A heavy fog settled over the field during the predawn hours of June 4. Law's Alabamians enlarged the ditch in front of the parapet to ten feet wide and eight feet deep. As soon as the fog burned off, sniping resumed in earnest. Three men from 4th Alabama were hit in rapid succession. Sergeant George H. Newbill and Private Joseph A. Zahn, both of Company K, were hit by the same bullet. Newbill survived to be promoted junior second lieutenant of his company. Zahn, an Indiana-born resident of Huntsville, Alabama was killed instantly. Private Melville Harris, Company A, was killed a short time later. He was just 17 years of age when he enlisted in February 1864.[89]

No truce was called to remove the severely wounded. Those who were unable to leave the field by their own means were forced to lie in the hot sun and suffer for two days. Most of them died. By June 5 the stench of decaying flesh had become very strong. The only relief from the pungent odor for the Confederates confined to the trenches came when the wind occasionally blew the stench toward the Federal lines. On the afternoon of June 7, Federal details went out under a flag of truce to bury their dead. Law's men sat atop their works and watched the men going about their gruesome work. Numerous Federal soldiers ventured forth to look for fallen comrades or to barter with the Confederates for tobacco, the latter always needing coffee. After four days of lying in the boiling Virginia sun, it was difficult to identify deceased comrades, and in most cases their identity could be surmised only by remembering where a person had fallen. The surgeon from the 27th Massachusetts struck up a conversation with Cary. When talk turned to the carnage and destruction inflicted on the Federals, Cary told the surgeon their charge was the bravest and most useless he had ever witnessed.[90]

Getting food, water, and ammunition to the men in the Confederate works proved a difficult and often terrifying task. A spring with a fresh supply of cold water lay only a few yards behind the 4th Alabama. However, it was impossible to go directly to it without being seen by a sharpshooter. After dark on June 3, Coles staked out a zigzag trench between the spring and the center of the 4th Alabama. The trench provided some safety for the water details, but only if a person kept moving and did not expose himself too long. Coles nearly became a casualty by ignoring this precaution. While he sat atop the dirt thrown up from the ditch eating a cold piece of cornbread a beautiful bird dog wandered up seeking a bite to eat. When he handed the dog a morsel, a sharpshooter's spent bullet struck the animal a glancing blow on the side of the head, sending it scurrying. Coles was sure the poor animal thought he was the culprit when, in fact, the dog may well have saved Coles's life.[91]

All was quiet on Law's front until June 13, when Grant's army attempted another flanking maneuver, this time heading for Petersburg. The entire First Corps was put in motion toward the south, crossing the Chickahominy at McClellan's Bridge. The march continued past Seven Pines to Charles, then followed the Charles City Road to Williams. There, the corps bivouacked the nights of June 13–14.

Oates Loses His Commission

In mid-June Lowther returned from Richmond. To Oates's dismay he presented his commission as colonel of the 15th Alabama. Lowther also brought with him commissions for lieutenant colonel and major, all confirmed by Congress. Isaac Feagin was now lieutenant colonel and Oates major of the 15th Alabama. Oates's appointment as colonel had been issued by the War Department, which he accepted on October 21, 1863.[92] Until that day in June 1864, he had no reason to suspect that his commission was subject to being revoked.

After sorting through all the data, the Richmond authorities decided that Law had illegally promoted Oates in April 1863. In a statement issued June 24, 1864, the War Department upheld the seniority established at the regiment's organization. Cooper went into considerable detail to establish Lowther's credentials for the rank of colonel. Law was cited for presenting a biased consideration of his appointment. Richmond concluded that Law improperly dropped Lowther from the rolls without due consideration.[93] Oates's commission as colonel was revoked, and he was now Major William C. Oates.

Lowther's appointment brought on a new flurry of activity, this time on Oates's behalf. Oates was held in high regard by his superiors and was very popular with his men. Field, Hood, and Perry quickly submitted letters protesting Lowther's appointment. Invariably each stated outright or strongly implied that Oates was more competent than Lowther in every way. Perry continued to address Oates as colonel. Congressman J. L. Pugh began a tireless effort to obtain justice for Oates. On June 13 he wrote Davis "I have just learned that a great wrong has been done a constituent of mine and I appeal to you most earnestly for his relief."[94] Field and Perry submitted applications to request Oates's transfer to a command with a vacancy for colonel. In his application for Oates's reassignment, Perry informed Cooper "Oates has proved himself to be an officer of the finest order of merit. He is cool and collected in action and has again and again showed that infallible test of a good commander, the ability to maintain perfect control over his men amidst the excitement and dangers of battle."[95] Field was more blunt in his petition to the War Department. He wrote in part:

> *"Nearly one year ago he (Oates) received the letter of appointment of Colonel of the Regiment and subscribed the oath involved. Were he and Colonel Lowther equal in merit it certainly would not be a hardship to displace him and elevate Colonel Lowther above him. But I think it rightly to say whilst I can not speak my own knowledge officers of the brigade in whose judgment and honesty I have confidence, tell me that imprint of merit – in all the qualities which go to make a solider –that Colonel Oates is measurably his superior. For the good of the service and the regiment especially I respectfully request the department reconsider the question of rank between the gentlemen."*[96]

Hood wrote Cooper that "I always regarded him (Oates) as one of my best colonel's in my division and I know of no officer more worthy of promotion."[97]

Unfortunately for Oates, no vacancy existed, and apparently he never entertained the idea of resigning the service. He also never considered the idea of serving under Lowther. He informed Cooper:

> *"Having ever performed my duties as an officer faithfully and to the best of my humble ability I have but to request Genl that I be relieved from*

my present unpleasant position. I have the very best reasons of a private character for not desiring to serve in a subordinate position in the regiment I have so long commanded."[98]

Oates eventually visited Davis to present his case. Davis listened patiently and expressed his sympathy for Oates's dilemma. The fact was that congress had confirmed the appointment, there was nothing the president could do.

The only possibility for Oates to retain a command seemed to be with the 48th Alabama. At the time it had no field officers present. It was apparent that Sheffield would not return, and Lieutenant Colonel Hardwick was a Federal prisoner with little likelihood of being exchanged. Perry needed a seasoned commander to restore the 48th Alabama to fighting shape. The obvious solution was to transfer Oates to the 48th Alabama. Sheffield partially solved the problem by resigning his commission. However, Hardwick stood in the way of restoring Oates to the rank of colonel as long as the possibility of Hardwick's return existed.[99] Perry applied for Oates's appointment to the rank of colonel in the Provisional Army of the Confederate States and assignment to temporary command of the 48th Alabama. His application read, in part:

> *"I respectively ask that W. C. Oates recently displaced from the command of 15th Alabama Regiment by the promotion to the colonelcy of Major A. A. Lowther receive the appointment of colonel in the provisional army of the Confederate States on account of special skill and gallantry and that I be authorized to assign him temporarily to the command of the 48th Alabama Regiment in their brigade."*[100]

But the law had no provision to grant Perry's request. The only solution was to transfer Oates as major and place him in temporary command. Lee offered his opinion that if an examining board determined no officer in the regiment competent to fill the position of colonel, Oates could then be appointed.[101] Oates was hesitant to accept the temporary command. For the record he made it known that he did not want to keep any qualified officer in the 48th Alabama from his rightful promotion, but in the end his only alternative was to accept temporary command of the 48th Alabama.[102] On July 1, 1864 Oates terminated his long association with the 15th Alabama and assumed command of the 48th Alabama.[103]

Casualties from the Wilderness to Cold Harbor

Law's men had been under fire almost every day from May 6 until June 14. The brigade began the Wilderness Campaign with 114 officers. Forty-nine became casualties, 32 were wounded, three were captured and 12 killed. Nine of the wounded officers would not return.

Two of the casualties from the officers' ranks were physicians. Both were severely wounded May 6 in the Wilderness and neither returned to active service. Captain Joseph Johnson, Company H, 44th Alabama, was twice wounded before the Wilderness and as a consequence was on wounded furlough much of the time. Lieutenant Pulaski Brown, Company H, 15th Alabama, on the other hand, spent most of his prior service on detached duty as a hospital steward. He was unable to fully recover from his wound and toward the end of 1864 was placed on detached duty at a hospital in Opelika, Alabama. He resigned January 1865.[104]

The men in the ranks now knew they were facing a determined Federal commander. Instead of retreating after a hard fight to regroup, Grant doggedly pressed on. Men began to suspect the Confederacy's days were numbered, but most were not yet ready to quit. The siege of Petersburg, fighting along the James, and the harsh winter of 1864–65 were yet to come. In the immediate future, however, loomed the summer of 1864.

Chapter 15

Richmond and Petersburg Besieged

Law's Alabamians left the trenches of Cold Harbor on June 13, 1864, with the rest of the First Corps infantry. The number of officers present in the brigade was reduced to 80. When the Wilderness to Cold Harbor campaign began, three companies were without officers. At the end of this costly campaign, that number had grown to 12.[1] The corps's trains crossed the river by New Bridge, their march taking them through Seven Pines and down the Charles City Road to bivouac near the battlefield at Frayser's Farm.[2]

Grant had abandoned the breastworks opposite the Confederates at Cold Harbor, and his whereabouts was unknown. Law's Brigade was part of Lee's blocking force between White Oak Swamp and Malvern Hill, protecting Richmond until the Federal army could be found. Perry shifted position to Three Mile Creek on June 14 where, between the Chickahominy and James Rivers, he awaited orders.[3]

Near midnight, on June 15, Major General Pierre Beauregard notified Lee that he had abandoned his line at Bermuda Hundred to concentrate his small force at Petersburg.[4] This freed the Federal forces under Major General Benjamin F. Butler, commanding the Army of the James, to take both the Richmond and Petersburg Railroad and the Osborne Turnpike, cutting communications between Petersburg and the capital. The Federal army had cut Confederate communications between Richmond and points to the north and east by the summer of 1864. Richmond was therefore dependent on Petersburg for supplies. Richmond depended on the roads and rail lines converging on Petersburg for war material and even the necessities of life.[5] For this reason Grant gave up the bloody effort to capture Richmond by direct assault and invested Petersburg. He knew Lee's army could not continue to fight without the supplies pouring through Petersburg. If communications between the two cities were not reopened, Grant had an excellent chance to capture Petersburg quickly, perhaps within days. Grant besieged Petersburg, beginning in mid-June 1864. Petersburg under siege meant Richmond under siege, and from June until the war's end in April 1865, this siege represented the slow strangulation of the Confederacy.[6]

Richmond was separated from Petersburg by approximately 20 miles, but connected by an excellent road and the Richmond and Petersburg Railroad. It was defended by strong fortifications, some begun in 1862, which faced eastward in a long arch. The main lines of protection were a line of forts and trenches called the interior line, a line just outside the first, known as the intermediate line, and the exterior line which carved a path from Chaffin's Bluff on the James River to north of the capital.

Petersburg, too, was protected by earthworks facing east. Together these fortifications protected the two cities with an almost continuous barrier of nearly 35 miles. Behind it,

Lee could usually depend on good communications between Richmond and the rail center to the south.

Most of the major roads in the area fanned out from Richmond in a generally easterly direction. Running nearly due east was the Williamsburg Road. Two important roads branching from this road to the southeast were the Charles City Road and the Darbytown Road. New Market Road ran southeast below the Darbytown, near New Market Heights and past Deep Bottom. These fortifications and roads became very familiar to the men of Law's Brigade.

Beauregard suggested the Bermuda Hundred Line be reoccupied by a division from Lee's army. Lee instructed Anderson to personally lead the First Corps to Bermuda Hundred to plug the hole. He also requested Beauregard hold his skirmishers in place until Anderson arrived.[7] At 5 a.m., two hours behind Pickett's Division, Field started his division across the pontoon bridge at Drewry's Bluff.[8] Moving two divisions across a large river was a slow process, however. It was 9 a.m. before Pickett's entire command was over the pontoon bridge and perhaps another hour before Field had crossed.[9] Anderson, at the head of the First Corps column, found the Federals opposite Chester about mid-day. He informed Lee that communications with Petersburg were broken. And he reported Butler's progress. "It is presumed," wrote the South Carolinian, "that he has possession of our breastworks opposite Bermuda Hundred."[10]

Pickett's men were soon engaged with Federal soldiers, driving them east from the Petersburg Road toward the Ware Bottom Church, while Field's Division continued down the turnpike. Law's and the Texas brigade encountered Federal regiments cutting down telegraph poles and immediately drove them from the road.[11] By day's end, Field had pushed south to Port Walthall Junction, on the Richmond and Petersburg Railroad.[12]

Except for a portion of the Howlett Line near the Clay farm, fighting from mid-afternoon until 11 p.m. on June 16 had restored the Confederate works abandoned by Beauregard and occupied by Butler in the morning.[13] If the Federals could be driven back to their old entrenchments, Lee's line of communications would again be secure. When they halted their advance at that late hour, Law's Alabamians were within 200 yards of the trenches still held by the Federals.[14] From morning until early afternoon of June 17, Pickett waited in front of the Clay farm while Field's Division waited in line of battle on his right just to the south of the farm. Their veterans were poised to attack the Federals still occupying the old Confederate first line.[15]

As skirmishers of the 15th Alabama lay in an open field between the two lines at about 2 p.m., a rumor spread along the skirmish line that they would soon charge the breastworks. There would be no protection if they had to assault the trenches, and some of the veteran Alabamians declared they would refuse to obey such a foolish order. Opposite the Alabama skirmishers, Federals defending the captured works were just as concerned. Butler manned the trenches with only a strong picket, instead of a force adequate to hold them against an attack.

While Law's Alabamians waited for the anticipated order to deliver an assault, the Confederate high command examined the ground in question. By direct order of Lee the First Corps commander assessed the strength of the lines and determined that an assault to retake the old fortification was not necessary.[16] According to Anderson, the newly established line was as good as the old one. Anderson quickly countermanded the assault order, sending separate orders to Field and Pickett. Field received his order and immediately abandoned plans to drive forward, but Pickett's Division was already on the move when word reached his headquarters.[17] Then occurred an assault—known to Law's Brigade as the Battle of Chester Station—that should not have been launched.

Pickett informed Gregg, who was immediately on his right, that he would need cover on his right flank. Even though the assault had been called off, Gregg readily moved to Pickett's support. Law's, the next brigade in line, saw that Gregg's right needed support and it, too, moved to the ready. Incredibly an instantaneous reaction occurred along Field's line. His entire division, without orders, leaped forward and swept toward the Federal works.[18]

Lowther's skirmishers raced ahead of the rest of the 15th Alabama and entered the old trench line. However, some of them, as they had threatened to do earlier, wavered and held back some 30 yards.[19] Writing after the war, Orderly Sergeant Billy Jordan recalled how he and Private John McIntosh were the first of the skirmishers to reach the breastworks. Luckily the Alabamians suffered little in the way of casualties, as the Federals had little desire to fight, offering no resistance to the charge of the 15th Alabama. Jordan attributed their passivity to the Texans who flanked the Federals before the skirmishers reached them.[20]

The skirmish line continued beyond the works to rifle pits. The Alabamians expected to find rifle pits where they better could position themselves to shoot at retreating Federals. The rifle pits had been filled in by the Federals, however, and the 15th Alabama skirmishers found themselves under artillery fire in a wheatfield. They moved quickly back to the protection of the breastworks. The shelling stopped after about half an hour, allowing members of the 15th Alabama to collect the guns, cartridges and haversacks that littered the battlefield.[21] During this scavenging for booty in the open, Private John W. Posey, of Company B, was severely wounded in the thigh by a sharpshooter, ending his military experience.[22]

Afterwards, Anderson sent a dispatch to Lee that word did not reach Pickett in time to stop his impetuous attack against the breastworks.[23] Lee, in turn, congratulated the men of Pickett's Division for the capture of the entrenchment.[24] Accounts of the affair in Richmond newspapers reported the works were carried by Pickett alone. No mention was made of Field's Division in reports of the action, which created an uproar within the Alabama camps.

Oates, commanding the 15th Alabama, credits the Texas brigade with carrying the breastworks. "To the Texans solely belonged the honor of capturing that line," wrote Oates in his history of the 15th Alabama, "although the Richmond newspapers of the next day gave all the credit to Pickett's Division." He remembered the men of Hood's old brigade started the attack without benefit of officers, covering the distance on the run, and followed by units on both their left and right.[25]

Adjutant Robert Coles, 4th Alabama, was angry that Pickett received all the credit for recapturing the Confederate line. In his 4th Alabama history, he remembered the Alabamians' irritation with reports of Pickett's success when they believed the two front brigades of Field's Division, the Texans and Law's, initiated the attack together.[26] Coles changed his mind after the war because of the published report of another eyewitness to the attack, Colonel Charles S. Venable, who claimed Pickett's men led off and Field's troops then took up the charge.[27] He felt Venable gave Law's Brigade credit for their part in the unauthorized charge. Coles insisted that throughout the remainder of the war, the men of Law's Brigade believed they—with the Texans—led the assault of June 17, 1864. Billy Jordan's account indicates the Texans arrived at the breastworks ahead of the Alabamians by a slim margin, lending credibility to Oates's recollection that the Texans jumped off before Law's men.

The charge against the Federals occupying the Howlett Line near the Clay farm followed in the manner described by Venable and Anderson: Pickett's men rushed from their trenches and charged first, followed by the Texans and then the Alabamians. The extraordinary sight of men running ahead of their regimental flags and officers, attacking without orders, made a deep impression on both Oates and Coles, but their view of the field was probably limited to the area in their line of sight.

Duty on the Siege Line

Law's Brigade spent most of the night of June 17 reversing the breastworks of the recaptured Howlett Line.[28] The next day, Lee became convinced that Grant's army was south of the James, and he ordered Kershaw and Field to Petersburg. Kershaw led, relieving Bushrod Johnson's Division, while Field followed him and took up position on his right.[29] After breakfast, the morning of June 18, Law's Brigade left for Petersburg, arriving at the trenches outside the city at 9:30, although it was nearly noon before they actually reached their place on the line.[30] They were in the breastworks only a short time before enemy sharpshooters began their deadly work.

When Company K, 4th Alabama, entered the breastworks it was captained by Alexander C. Murray. A native of Pennsylvania, "Alex" was a merchant in Alabama at the onset of hostilities. He was killed while going to the rear through the zigzag trench behind the 4th Alabama position, when he exposed his head while passing another soldier in the narrow confines of the trench. Although acting captain of the company since April 24, 1864, Murray had only received his commission the day before his death.[31]

During the course of the war, Company K had, by one contemporary account, "been very unfortunate in Captains."[32] Its first captain, Lewis Ervin Lindsay, mustered into service in April 1861, was killed in action during the fierce fighting at First Manassas. Lindsay was succeeded by a Kentucky-born saddler, James H. Young, who resigned at the end of his one-year enlistment in April 1862. Company K's third captain was an attorney from Belle Fonte, Alabama. William H. Robinson tendered his resignation on August 10, 1862, after losing a leg at Doctor Gaines's Virginia farm. Bad luck continued to plague the office of captain of Company K with the death of James H. Sullivan on the battlefield of Sharpsburg. This Irish grocer was the third captain the company lost to enemy fire in its first eighteen months. Bad luck stayed with Company K, when only three months after Sullivan was killed in action, his successor, thirty-five-year-old James H. Keith, was killed in action at Fredericksburg.[33] Captain John D. Ogilvie, a teacher before the war, held the ill–fated post the longest, from December 13, 1862, until he succumbed on March 17, 1864, to one of the myriad diseases found in Civil War camps. Alex Murray succeeded Ogilvie to the captaincy.[34]

Law Recuperates in South Carolina

By June 23, Law was sufficiently recovered from the wound he received at Cold Harbor to begin his trip home to Yorkville, South Carolina. He complained that both of his eyes were weak and could not tolerate much activity and but little light. Writing to his aide, Mims Walker, on furlough at his family plantation, Cedar Grove, Alabama, Law offered his opinion that Walker had enough time to be married. The brigadier wrote his lieutenant of his hope that when they returned to the field they would share "matrimonial fellowship."[35]

In closing, Law asked Walker to carry a message to his uncle (Walker's), Senator Robert Jemison, to "keep matters stirred up in Richmond," an obvious reference to Law's feud with Longstreet. He thought a letter from Jemison to the president might be useful to his cause, but he would leave that up to the senator. "Thank him most warmly for his kindness heretofore. I trust it will not be long," Law concluded, "before I will know him and be able to thank him in person."[36]

When Law wrote his aide-de-camp again on July 4, his wound was nearly healed and he believed he could return to active duty by July 15. Law was not in a good frame of mind, however. Bored by inaction and apparently miffed by the lack of letters from his brigade, Law complained that Walker had treated his commanding officer "villainously" by not writing. "Why don't you write? Are you alive? Are you married? or what is the matter," he asked.[37]

Law knew Longstreet had passed through South Carolina ten days before—probably on his way to Georgia—and wondered if Walker had news of him. His hatred of Longstreet clearly had not abated nor had Law's own wound caused him to empathize with his wounded commander. "Can't you bury him down there?" he asked Walker. Continuing in the same blunt language, Law offered his opinion that, "The Army of Northern Virginia has no need of him. An abominable puppy!"[38]

He wrote Walker that he heard from Leigh Terrell that Longstreet's staff had asked after Law but, in a way which he interpreted as insincere. Law was positive their inquiries were made with the hope that the reply would be the report of his death. Dismissing both Longstreet and his staff with a paraphrase of a Biblical quote, he wrote to Walker, "They stink in my nostrils as well as their illustrious chief."[39] Law suggested that Walker and Terrell meet him so the three of them might return to active duty together, but Law did not return to command of the Alabama brigade as he planned. He was granted another leave on his surgeon's certificate of disability for thirty days, dating from August 25, 1864.[40]

Trench Warfare

The Alabamians stayed in the same line of Petersburg trenches until almost the end of July.[41] The lines of the opposing armies facing each other east of Petersburg were as close as two hundred yards as they ran parallel north and south from the Appomattox River to the Jerusalem Plank Road. The armies were close enough that the Confederates enjoyed the music of the Federal bands and often plainly heard the commands of Federal officers.[42] The lines diverged south of the Plank Road. Field's Division first occupied the breastworks from Pegram's battery, 200 yards north of the Baxter Road on his left, to near the Jerusalem Plank Road.[43] The distance between the lines near the battery in the area known as Elliot's Salient was approximately 500 feet, making that sector a dangerous place, indeed.[44] The closeness of the lines invited the Federals to take up the ancient practice of mining which resulted in the Battle of the Crater.

Two deserters from the 44th Alabama forced the cancellation of the First Corps plan to assault the Federal V Corps in the early hours of July 18. Anderson made a personal reconnaissance on July 17 in preparation for the attack. On July 18, he continued his study of the enemy positions and ordered other preparations be made. The First Corps diarist noted in his itinerary that Anderson canceled the attack because of the two deserters. It was well that Anderson stopped the charge because the Alabama deserters outlined the plan for V Corps Headquarters, including the location of the ravine where fatigue parties had cleared a place for the attacking force to form and the time of the assault. Because of information from a deserter from the 64th Georgia and the Alabama deserters, Law's Brigade was located on the right of Field's Division, manning the Confederate line from the Jerusalem Plank Road to the Chimneys.[45]

Law's Brigade remained in the trenches until the division was recalled to the north side of the James on July 29. This was not war as the Alabamians had come to know it. The

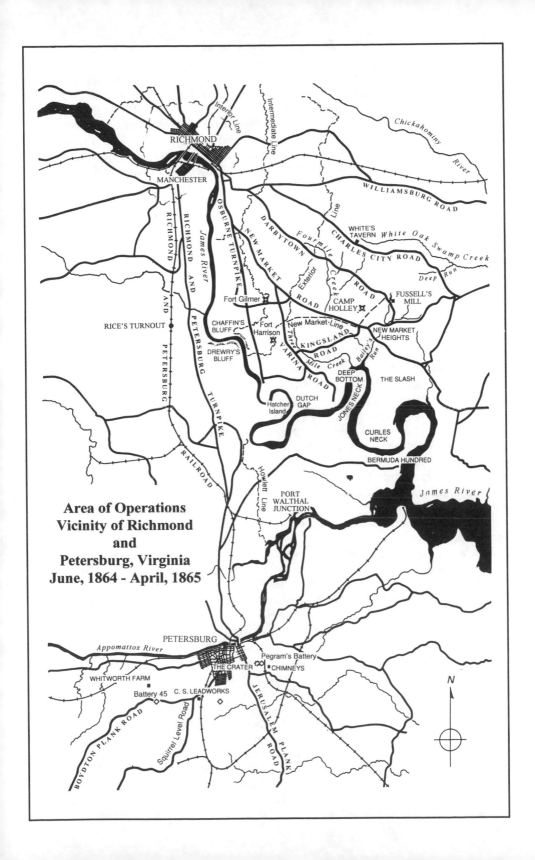

**Area of Operations
Vicinity of Richmond
and
Petersburg, Virginia
June, 1864 - April, 1865**

RICHMOND

MANCHESTER

Chickahominy River

WILLIAMSBURG ROAD

Interior Line

Intermediate Line

Line

DARBYTOWN ROAD

Fourmile Creek

Exterior ROAD

WHITE'S TAVERN

CHARLES CITY ROAD

White Oak Swamp Creek

Deep Run

NEW MARKET

James River

RICHMOND

RICHMOND AND

OSBURNE TURNPIKE

Fort Gilmer

CAMP HOLLEY

FUSSELL'S MILL

RICE'S TURNOUT

CHAFFIN'S BLUFF

Fort Harrison

New Market Line

KINGSLAND ROAD

NEW MARKET HEIGHTS

AND

PETERSBURG

DREWRY'S BLUFF

VARINA ROAD

Three Mile Creek

Bailey's Run

PETERSBURG

DEEP BOTTOM

THE SLASH

Hatcher Island

DUTCH GAP

JONES NECK

TURNPIKE

CURLES NECK

RAILROAD

BERMUDA HUNDRED

Howlett Line

PORT WALTHAL JUNCTION

James River

PETERSBURG

Appomattox River

Pegram's Battery

CHIMNEYS

THE CRATER

WHITWORTH FARM

Battery 45

C. S. LEADWORKS

BOYDTON PLANK ROAD

Squirrel Level Road

JERUSALEM PLANK ROAD

N

offensive strategy which had won glory for the Army of Northern Virginia was no longer possible. Now Law's Brigade, as part of Lee's army, was besieged by a larger, well supplied Federal army. Grant's siege of Petersburg would last nine and a half months, the longest campaign of the war. Lee often used Field's Division as a mobile reserve, to be quickly moved to any area the commanding general required it.[46] Between these rapid movements, however, Law's Brigade had to live by the dictates of trench warfare.

Law's Alabamians filed into the Petersburg trenches during a drought. Before it ended, "the earth," reported an Alabama soldier to the Montgomery (Alabama) *Daily Mail*, was "ground to a powdered dust. Consequently, the breeze when it blows, instead of bringing refreshing coolness on its wings, comes loaded with suffocating dust." Life in the parched landscape of Virginia that summer was to this reporter a "pismire life, this living like emments, in holes burrowed in hot, old fields."[47] Clouds of dust, previously a sign of enemy movements, came to signify nothing during the protracted drought. A Richmond paper noted, "Any movement whatever, any change of position or countermarching of a division, would be sufficient to raise clouds of dust." One weary reporter summarized the news of Petersburg on July 5, 1864, as "heat and dust, shells and minie balls, mangled and dying soldiers, fugitive women, decrepit old men, and children." When the drought broke, with a downpour on July 19, the dust was replaced with mud, with the degree of comfort in the trenches little changed.[48]

The soldiers of Law's command served in the trenches six days at a stretch and were relieved from duty for two days.[49] While in the trenches, it was vital to avoid the ever present Federal sharpshooters. Practically no place was safe. Even the most secure places along the line could be penetrated by glancing minie balls.[50] Sharpshooting was taken up by Confederate officers and enlisted men alike to relieve the monotony of trench warfare. It was a welcome break from what one Southern officer called the passive endurance which trench warfare required.[51] Earlier in the war this practice was generally believed to be bad form, but became acceptable practice by the summer of 1864. Life seemed to mean less than it did in 1861. Death became so common an event it was noticed only if the victim was a friend or mess mate.[52] Sharpshooting became so much a part of daily routine that the Confederate First Corps issued orders for its practice on division scale. On June 21, 1864, Sorrel issued an order for Field to increase the fire along his division front at the time of night when the enemy changed picket details. The declared purpose of this musketry was, "That some damage may in this way be inflicted upon the enemy's relieving parties and his skirmishers as they come out of their pits."[53]

While on duty, the soldiers of the Alabama brigade stayed in the trenches. Company officers were required to stay in the line with their men. Brigade staff had pits only a few feet behind the trench line.[54] When the weather was dry, wind blew dust onto the men in the line or enemy shells would knock dirt and dust into the ditches.[55] After it rained, they were bespattered with mud. There were places along the line where sleep was permitted outside the trench line but usually the men had to sleep in the line, constantly disturbed by inspecting officers or fatigue details or the almost incessant mortar fire.[56]

During the sultry afternoon hours of June 20, members of Company B, 44th Alabama, tried to find comfortable positions in the trenches while remaining safe from the constant buzz of minie balls. Company B occupied a portion of the line in a hollow. The Federal line opposite them was on an elevation about 500 yards distance. In an effort to reduce their exposure to the Federal sharpshooters, Joab Goodson ordered his men to stay down and not fire. Still, one soldier was severely wounded and Goodson and his brother, Rufe, were forced to move to a safer location.[57] The brothers stretched their tent across the ditch they occupied to get some relief from the sun, took off their coats and boots and relaxed. At

3 o'clock, Rufe got up for some sugar in a haversack hanging on the wall of the trench. He was immediately struck in the head by a bullet. Rufe died that night without speaking again.[58]

Joab Goodson dressed his brother in clean clothes, secured a coffin, and buried him near a cedar tree in the graveyard of the Fairgrounds Hospital. The Reverend William G. Perry, chaplain of the regiment, conducted services for Lieutenant Rufus Goodson.[59]

Mortar fire was a constant threat. The adjutant of the 4th Alabama recalled the mortars were detestable but seldom lethal missiles with great psychological impact. "Although these did only occasional damage, it was always doubtful in our minds for whom each one of those hurling, shrieking monsters, accompanied with whirling, lighted fuses, were intended and was imagined by everyone to be descending on his own devoted head."[60] The mortar shells were visible by day, making their parabolic trajectory into the Confederate trenches. At night, burning fuses traced their flight paths from the Federal lines to the Confederate side.

The trenches were filthy, a preview of the trench warfare in World War I. "Vermin abounded," recalled the brigade inspector of Hagood's brigade, "and diseases of various kinds showed themselves." The digestive organs of the men became impaired by the rations issued and the manner in which they were prepared. Diarrhea and dysentery were universal; the legs and feet of the men swelled until they could not wear their shoes; the filth of their persons from the scarcity of water was terrible; and they presented the appearance of inmates of a miserably conducted poorhouse rather than the soldiers of an army. Not the least of the evils encountered was the unavoidable stench from the latrines."[61] Clouds of flies hovered over the trenches, a constant nuisance to the men occupying those filthy ditches.[62]

Rations were prepared behind the trenches and brought up to the men once a day through a series of zigzag trenches which connected the front line to the rear areas. The food was mostly cornbread, supplemented by bacon, often rancid. The cornbread would quickly become unpalatable, so the whole twenty-four hour portion was usually eaten immediately. The bacon issue was sometimes cooked in the trenches.[63]

Field and his staff normally had the same issue of rations as the men in the trench line. Early in July, Field's volunteer aide, Richard W. Corbin, wrote to his family in England that he ate his ration of bacon and cabbage in a "perfectly wolfish" manner. On one occasion, however, the Alabama brigade furnished its headquarters' table with a treat. The provost guard caught several Alabamians butchering a calf. They explained that the animal had been wounded by enemy fire while grazing in a nearby field and they had only killed the beast to ease its suffering. Corbin and the rest of the division staff were royally feted when Field confiscated the carcass and the meat was consumed at headquarters.[64]

The Battle of Fussell's Mill or Second Deep Bottom

The Federal II Corps crossed the James River on July 27. There was little to stop a Federal move against the capital. Lee immediately directed that Heth's Division of the Third Corps, then the cavalry of Major General W. H. Fitzhugh Lee, to join Kershaw on the north side. On July 29, Field also crossed the river.[65]

Field's Division began leaving the trenches between the Jerusalem Plank Road and the Chimneys, just south of Pegram's battery, about 1 a.m. on July 29, marching through the quiet streets of Petersburg in the early morning hours.[66] Orders called for the move to be made without noise.[67] Soldiers of the 15th Alabama left the Petersburg works by the relief ditch behind the line, "half bent over, at a trail arms" to avoid detection.[68] Law's Brigade boarded cars of the Richmond and Petersburg Railroad at 8 a.m. for the short ride to Rice Station. From there, the soldiers crossed the James River at Drewry's Bluff and marched to New Market Heights.[69]

Before the Alabamians were in place on New Market Heights, about sundown, head-quarters' staff of the Army of the Potomac knew the brigade had left Petersburg for the north side. A deserter from the 4th Alabama had crossed over the lines even before his comrades left the trenches. He told Federal officers that Bushrod Johnson had relieved Field, baggage had been packed, blankets rolled and the disabled had been excused from marching before he left his post during the night of July 28. The prisoner added that his lieutenant told him they were to march to Drewry's Bluff.[70]

At 8 a.m., July 30, Field had his division in position to repel an expected Federal attack, but it was soon discovered the Federals had retired.[71] Lee's rapid deployment of force to the north side had blunted the Federal advance. Major General Winfield Scott Hancock abandoned his plan to destroy the Virginia Central Railroad and ultimately capture Richmond.[72]

Field established his line from Chaffin's Bluff to New Market Heights. Bratton held the right and Gregg, Benning, Law, and Anderson, in that order deployed to the left of the South Carolinians.[73] They occupied the breastworks left by Heth's Division. Field also had the use of the artillery north of the James, the Richmond City Battalion, John M. Hughs's brigade of Tennesseans and the cavalry of Brigadier General Martin W. Gary. These units served in the Department of Richmond, commanded by Lieutenant General Richard S. Ewell. Field nevertheless commanded these troops and, in his words, "made disposition to suit myself, without consultations with him, and received no orders from him."[74]

Anderson's Georgians conducted a reconnaissance of Deep Bottom on August 1 and found Federal soldiers at the lodgment at Deep Bottom.[75] The next day, Field sent out scouting details from all his brigades but did not feel threatened by the Federal forces north of the James.[76]

August 1, 1864 was election day in Tallapoosa, County, Alabama. Michael Bulger, 47th Alabama, was elected to the Alabama Senate by an overwhelming margin. A Montgomery newspaper declared the citizens of Tallapoosa County, "rewarded the noble patriotism of this battle scarred hero." The correspondent, "Conservative," reminded his readers that Bulger did not have to serve in the military at all. "It is well known," he wrote, "that Colonel Bulger earnestly opposed the disruption both of the old Democratic Party and the Union. Yet he did not skulk behind his age, though near sixty, when the war began, as many did who had been wide mouthed for secession, but buckled on his sword."[77]

Law's Brigade encamped at Camp Holly, on New Market Heights, which offered an excellent view of the James River and the Federal gunboats on patrol there. The Alabama troops learned they were camped where George Washington rested his army after the British surrender at Yorktown.[78]

For two weeks, duty north of the James was easy.[79] The sniper's bullet, the relentless sun, the dust and the stench of Petersburg's trenches were left behind. Field's Division, temporarily commanded by Brigadier General John Gregg, posted strong pickets between the heights and Deep Bottom to hold the Federals tightly against the river.[80]

On August 6, five members of the 4th Alabama left their picket detail and crossed over to the enemy lines at Deep Bottom, leaving a dangerous hole in the perimeter. All five were conscripts, enrolled in June and July of 1864. Four of the soldiers were 35 to 41 years old and were conscripted under the law of December 1863, which raised the age limit for field service to 45 years of age.[81] It is surprising that a picket detail would be made up of five conscripts when it was generally accepted that conscripts made poor soldiers.

On the morning of August 13, Law's Brigade moved from Camp Holly into the line of breastworks running along the heights between Deep Bottom Road and Fussell's Mill.[82] On the same day three ironclads and three wooden gunboats of the Confederate navy joined land batteries in a crossfire against Dutch Gap, where Federal fatigue parties worked to dig a canal with which the Federals hoped to bypass the Confederate obstructions in the James River.[83] In the afternoon, mortars at New Market Heights and howitzers between that elevation and the James River opened fire on the two pontoon bridges at Deep Bottom. The Confederate shells did no harm to the Federals at work on the canal. Nor could the Southern gunners hit the bridges spanning the James. The result was return fire from Federal land batteries and gunboats later in the day, some of the shells fell on the men from Alabama. The fire continued for three days.

On August 14–15, from the breastworks atop New Market Heights, Law's Alabamians could see clearly an enemy gunboat in the James River as it fired upon their position. This vessel was the USS *Agawam*, positioned off Four Mile Creek.[84] Its 100-pound projectiles would go through the breastworks or bury themselves deep into the ground before exploding. The result, according to an eyewitness, was the lifting of "barrels of dirt, rocks and pieces of the shell high into the air, to rain back on us." When the boat fired, the Confederates would first see smoke belch from the gun, then hear the shell as it passed over their line or hit nearby. Only then did they hear the report of the cannon. When smoke was seen puffing out of the cannon, the alert was sounded, "Look out!" and the enlisted men would seek the protection of the trenches, while company officers would lie down on the barren elevation.[85]

Oates denied his officers access to the trenches occupied by the enlisted men. Several officers of the 48th Alabama dug holes behind the line for protection from the naval shelling. When alerted to the gunboat's fire, the officers would leap into the holes. While Perry and Gregg examined the ground where it had been turned by the large shells, someone shouted the alert and the two tumbled into a nearby hole for safety. The cry of "Look out!" was a joke on this occasion but Perry came out of the hole with a sprained ankle which netted him a 30-day furlough.[86] Colonel Bowles took command of the brigade.

A few days after Field crossed the James, Lee sent Anderson to the Shenandoah Valley with Kershaw's Division and Fitzhugh Lee's Division of cavalry to reinforce Lieutenant General Jubal A. Early. Field believed he was intended to follow but he was held back when Grant sent Hancock back to the north side in a repetition of his July expedition.[87] Field's Division was needed to protect Richmond from Hancock.

Grant decided Lee had sent three divisions of infantry, artillery and one division of cavalry to the Valley in support of Early. He therefore directed Hancock to begin another offensive north of the James to force the recall of these divisions or defeat Lee in their absence.[88] In July, Grant had planned to draw Confederate forces from the Southside to north of the James with a threat against Richmond. This would allow him to launch an attack upon the strategic Weldon Railroad. The August plan was essentially the same. Two divisions of cavalry would make a dash at Richmond, their flank protected by the II Corps and two divisions of the X Corps. This time, Grant wanted to draw off enemy troops from the Southside and compel Lee to recall the recent reinforcements to the Valley. The cavalry raid on Richmond could only take place if Field's infantry was driven from its New Market Heights breastworks. Hancock determined to turn Field's left flank and, with superior numbers, roll the Confederate infantry back into the Richmond trenches, giving his cavalry an open road into the Confederate capital.[89]

During the hot night of August 13, the steady rumble of artillery wagons and the tramp of hundreds of horses alerted Field that the Federals were mounting an offensive against him. The signaling of dozens of boat whistles of Hancock's fleet of troop transports gave additional notice that it would be a major undertaking.[90]

The Case of John B. Hubbard

The 2nd U.S. Sharpshooters made contact with the pickets of Law's Brigade shortly after dawn on August 14. A four-man detail from the sharpshooters, including Sergeant Wyman S. White, of Company F, began firing at the Alabama pickets from the edge of a woodlot as soon as they discovered them. One member of the volunteer detail left the others momentarily and, upon his return reported seeing a man come from the trees, approach very near the other three Federals, then move stealthily back through the trees to the Confederate lines. The man was described as tall, wearing a gray hat and pants and a blue coat. He was unarmed, noted the observant Federal. The detail decided the man was a Confederate officer who would soon return with a squad in an attempt to capture them. They moved back some distance and waited. It was nearly dark and rain further darkened the sky, making it impossible for the detail of sharpshooters to see if the officer returned. Voices, however, were heard from the woodlot.

On the morning of August 15, White was again busy firing at the Confederate picket line. The Confederate officer reappeared and White was able to draw close upon the tall man in the blue coat before being discovered. When the Confederate became aware of White, he surrendered. White told his prisoner to walk toward the Federal lines. The Confederate looked back to his own lines, tempted, in White's view, to make a run for it but the closeness of White's rifle caused him to think better of it. The Confederate was unarmed, which saved his life.[91] The tall man in the blue coat was 6 foot 2 inch tall Captain John B. Hubbard, Company K, 48th Alabama, who was given over to the Provost Marshall of the Army of the Potomac on August 16.[92] The questions of why he was beyond his own picket lines and how he fell into enemy hands created a stir within the Confederate command.

It was Second Lieutenant Erwin Foster Rice who first raised the issue of Hubbard's intentions. He was in command of Company K in the absence of Hubbard and First Lieutenant H. L. Pettit, who was furloughed after receiving a wound on August 18, 1864. Rice believed Hubbard deserted and, on September 3, made application to have Hubbard dropped from the muster roll of the 48th Alabama. His application carried the endorsement of the regimental commander, Captain Thomas J. Lumpkin, who also believed Hubbard had walked away from the war.[93]

The Federals listed Hubbard as a prisoner of war and the soldier who captured him, Sergeant White, also considered him a prisoner. The officers in Hubbard's regiment branded him a deserter. Lumpkin was "confident that he went to the enemy for the purpose of getting out of the Army." As evidence, Lumpkin reported to Bowles that Hubbard told his company vedette that he was going to exchange papers with the Federal pickets. Bowles's statement to Field was, "Nothing has been heard of Captain Hubbard since he left; neither have any more facts developed themselves, save, that he refused to be shown the vedette posts by the officer whom he relieved and otherwise acted strangely. The general impression in the regiment is that he deserted."[94]

Lee became involved in the question of whether to drop Hubbard from the muster roll. The Office of the Inspector General made no distinction between officers captured and those who had deserted to the enemy. Lee wanted to drop from regimental rolls those officers who had gone to the enemy. He felt this case gave him the means to reverse the decision of the inspector general. Captured officers could remain on the rolls but Lee wanted those who had deserted and were in enemy hands dropped from muster rolls. "How are such cases to be dealt with," he asked. "How (sic) get rid of officers who will never return to their commands?" Lee did not believe Hubbard was accidentally captured. He believed Hubbard was an officer who walked beyond the Confederate lines to voluntarily give himself up to the Federal pickets. He recommended Hubbard's dismissal.[95] It looked as though the matter had been settled to everyone's satisfaction.

Hubbard was dropped from the rolls on November 2, 1864. Pettit was promoted to captain and Rice received the commission of a first lieutenant. This was Pettit's second time to serve as captain of Company K. He was first appointed captain in August 1862 to succeed Moses Lee. However, he was found unqualified by an examining board and Hubbard was selected instead. Pettit remained in command of Company K until Appomattox.[96]

Hubbard wrote to his brother in September from the Federal prison at Fort Delaware, Maryland, telling him, "I am a prisoner at this place." His brother sent Hubbard's letter to Pettit, who forwarded it through the chain of command. This was the first word anyone in the army had of Hubbard and it reopened the issue of whether Hubbard was captured or deserted.[97] Was Hubbard unjustly labeled a deserter? Discussion on the subject ended on December 11 when Lee held to his earlier decision. "I can recommend no change," wrote the general. "The officer, in my opinion, was properly dropped from the rolls." Lee's opinion was enough to end further discussion.[98]

The Battle of Fussell's Mill

Law's Brigade was to contest more than a detail of Federal sharpshooters on Sunday, August 14. The Third Division of the II Corps was ordered to drive the Confederates behind works along the New Market Road back toward the exterior line. The other two divisions of the II Corps were instructed to move to the right of the Third Division and attack near Fussell's Mill. Major General David B. Birney would send his X Corps against the Confederate works along Four Mile Creek and push up the Kingsland Road. The Federal cavalry was to cover the right of the infantry until it had pushed the Confederates back to the Richmond fortifications, then make the dash for Richmond.[99]

Elements of Birney's X Corps opposed Law's Brigade that hot August morning. At 5 a.m., Birney's First Division, commanded by Brigadier General Alfred H. Terry, moved first, its Third Brigade in the lead. Brigadier General Robert A. Foster deployed the Third Brigade across the Deep Bottom Road and slowly pushed the pickets of Bratton's brigade and Law's Alabamians to a line of works north of the Kingsland Road.[100]

The Alabamians and Bratton's South Carolinians had the advantage of position. From the Kingsland Road to Four Mile Creek was about 300 yards with a rise in elevation of perhaps 50 feet. Directly behind the Confederate works was a deep ravine cut by the creek, and their left was protected by a bog, with the right flank secured by heavy woods. The Federals could not move through the bog or the heavy woods and did not relish charging directly up the slope into the face of the Confederate guns.

For an hour, Foster's troops exchanged fire with the pickets on the hill. If any man, Federal or Confederate, showed himself, he was showered with bullets. Those officers who found it necessary to move along their line were the targets of scores of rifles.[101] Foster decided to break the stalemate with a frontal assault against the entrenchments. He ordered the 24th Massachusetts to attack the Confederate line, supported by the 10th Connecticut on its left and the 11th Maine on its right. Behind them was the rest of Foster's brigade, the 100th New York and 1st Maryland Cavalry (dismounted) and the 6th Connecticut of the Second Brigade. The First Brigade attacked on the left of the Third Brigade.[102]

The Confederate pickets gave way as the 24th Massachusetts, in double column of companies, gave a loud cheer and rushed up the incline at the double time.[103] Most of the pickets escaped because the Federal left was refused where the Third Brigade overlapped the supporting First Brigade. They escaped across Four Mile Creek through the woods to the west. That was their planned route of retreat but had the Federal line been dressed, more of the pickets from Alabama and the Palmetto State would have been captured. Bratton reported the "picket line was finally driven in, pretty badly mutilated."[104] The pickets moved rapidly from Four Mile Creek into their main line of works along New Market Road. This uncovered the right of the 8th and 59th Georgia regiments, supporting the skirmishers and Lieutenant Colonel John C. Pemberton's 8-inch howitzers between the creek and main works. Several Georgians were captured before they could withdraw, and the guns were abandoned.[105]

The pickets of Bratton's and Law's brigades did excellent work on August 14. The Federal X Corps did not reach the main line of works near the New Market Road. These pickets had been placed well out in front of the first line above the Kingsland Road.[106] The stubborn resistance of this small band consumed most of the morning. Terry's attack was not the main assault which was delayed by the slow pace of Hancock's expedition but it was a good effort by the outnumbered Confederates.

The captured picket line yielded an unexpected breakfast for the soldiers of the Third Brigade. During the hour before the charge, the veterans of Field's Division prepared breakfast. They had to leave their hot meal when they were overwhelmed by the Federal charge. The Federals helped themselves to the bacon and bread. One Federal soldier described the bread as "cooked in the peculiar Southern style, in Dutch ovens covered with coals."[107]

Oates and an officer on Field's staff give much credit for holding back the Federal X Corps on August 14 to the accurate fire of the Confederate artillery. Richard Corbin, an English volunteer on Field's staff, wrote his mother less than two weeks later that he could not help admiring the sight of the cheering Federal lines attacking with banners overhead and bands playing.[108]

On August 14, Field's line extended from Chaffin's Bluff to New Market Heights, but the entrenchments continued on another mile, though unmanned, to Fussell's Mill. His left was in the air and in danger of being turned at that point. From New Market Heights, Field could see a steady stream of troops moving to the left. During the remainder of the day, Field shifted troops to the left, extending his line to prevent the Federal flanking movement. His works were manned in single line in most places, unmanned in several places. Field telegraphed Lee the circumstances and the commanding general responded with reinforcements. Hancock obliged Lee by delaying his *coup de main* until they arrived. By then, Field had extended his line beyond the mill toward the Charles City Road.[109]

The remainder of Sunday and Monday, the Alabama brigade remained at New Market Heights. Lee came to the north side on August 15. He used the breastworks on the heights to survey the field with his glasses.[110]

Hancock shifted the X Corps on Monday night from the Federal left to the right. Watching the Federal moves from New Market Heights, the veteran Alabamians anticipated an attack in force by Hancock somewhere along the line on Tuesday. "We were all put on the qui vive," is how a newly appointed lieutenant of the 15th Alabama described the night of August 15.[111]

Field's infantry was stretched thin by Tuesday, August 16. Bratton manned the works from the James River to New Market Heights with his command, Colonel John M. Hughs's Tennessee regiments, and detachments from the Department of Richmond and Cadmus

Wilcox's Division. Field's own division, commanded by Gregg, occupied New Market Heights. The division was without the storied Texas brigade, detached Monday night to support Gary's brigade of cavalry on the Charles City Road. To Gregg's left, Brigadier General John C. C. Sanders led his brigade of Alabamians and Brigadier General Victor J. B. Girardey's Georgia brigade. Brigadier General James Conner held the extreme left with two brigades of infantry. Before the battle opened, the 9th and 11th Georgia regiments went to the left, falling in between Conner's two brigades. Field held a line four miles long,[112] which, by the accepted standards of the day, required 3,000 to 5,000 troops per mile of works. Field's command was only a third to a half of the size needed to protect a four-mile line. Field held his four-mile line with approximately 7,000 soldiers.[113]

Birney's X Corps attacked Field's left on August 16. The 11th Maine led the assault against Girardey's Georgians, and was repulsed. But that charge and the next were against what Field described as his weakest point of defense. About 600 yards above the mill, the ground was irregular and the thick growth of oak and pine screened the Federal infantry up to fifty yards of the works.[114] After the initial repulse of the Federals retreat from Girardey's front, Field and his staff, in the saddle since dawn, rested about 100 yards behind the Georgians.[115] Only half an hour after they had dismounted they heard the musketry and cheering signaling another attack. Field had only minutes before seeing Girardey turn back a Federal charge. He was confident the result of this attack would be the same and did not rise from the comfortable grass.[116]

His adjutant did rise, however, and suddenly exclaimed to Field, "General, they are breaking."

Field replied, "Well, I knew they would," thinking his aide was referring to the enemy.

To Field's surprise, the staff officer said, "But General, it's our men."

Field immediately got to his feet and saw the Georgians and Brigadier General James H. Lane's Brigade of North Carolinians breaking in the face of the Federal charge. "I saw at a glance the most appalling, disheartening sight of my life," he later wrote of the incident.[117]

Colonel Francis B. Pond led Terry's First Brigade in the breakthrough. Clearing the woods in front of Girardey, the mixed brigade of Illinois, Ohio and Pennsylvania soldiers met a withering fire from the Georgia troops.[118] Nearly their whole front line was knocked down. The rest quickly covered the 50 yards of cleared ground in front of the works and were on the Confederates, fighting hand to hand. Overwhelmed, the Georgians, then the Tarheels, broke.[119] Victor J. B. Girardey was mortally wounded while trying to rally the Georgia brigade. This young officer had received the extraordinary promotion from captain to the temporary rank of brigadier general only three weeks before for his valor at the Battle of the Crater.[120]

Field sent his volunteer aide, Richard Corbin, to bring Law's Brigade and Benning's Brigade, to the break while he tried to link up with Conner's two brigades.[121] Isolated and left to his own devices on the left, the aggressive Conner organized his forces and moved to the offensive. Leaving a small detachment to hold the Confederate extreme left, Conner moved McGowan's and Lane's brigades forward to attack the Federal troops in the captured works.[122]

Field found his path to the left blocked by the cheering Federals who had split his division. He knew nothing of Conner's actions. It appeared Hancock had a clear road into Richmond. "I felt that nothing but a miracle could save us," Field later remembered.[123]

The 15th and 48th Alabama regiments arrived first, having covered the mile from the heights to the break at the double time. Field later recalled the Alabamians had formed a battle line within minutes of the breakthrough. The Alabama men formed under heavy

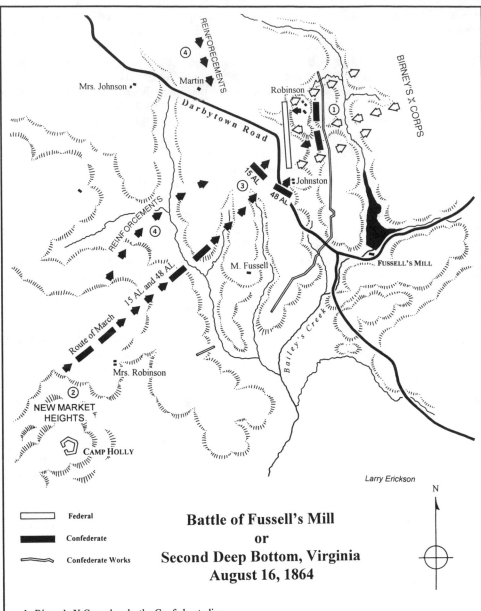

REINFORCEMENTS

④

Mrs. Johnson ·▪

Martin ▪

Darbytown Road

Robinson

①

BIRNEY'S X CORPS

▪Johnston

15 AL

48 AL

③

REINFORCEMENTS

④

M. Fussell ▪

FUSSELL'S MILL

15 AL and 48 AL

Route of March

Mrs. Robinson ▪

Bailey's Creek

②

NEW MARKET
HEIGHTS

CAMP HOLLY

Larry Erickson

N

▭	Federal
▬	Confederate
∿	Confederate Works

Battle of Fussell's Mill
or
Second Deep Bottom, Virginia
August 16, 1864

1. Birney's X Corps breaks the Confederate line.
2. Field sends his aide to New Market Heights for Law's and Benning's Brigades.
3. The 15th and 48th Alabama Regiments arrive first. They form up in woods under artillery fire and attack the Federal column, breaking the advance.
4. Reinforcements arrive and the Confederates take the initiative. The Federals are driven back and the works reoccupied by Field's troops.
5. The 15th and 48th Alabama Regiments sustain severe casualties, particularly among the officer ranks.

artillery fire. "The shelling was positively infernal," recalled an officer present while Law's men prepared for battle. "All the woods at the rear of the battlefield were torn and chopped to pieces by the enemy's artillery."[124]

Eight companies of the 15th Alabama and the 48th Alabama formed in the trees south of the open ground behind the breastworks.[125] This ground was cut by a ravine running to the southeast behind Girardey's sector of the breastworks and passing through the works, on Girardey's right.[126] The ravine was part of the water shed which filled Fussell's Mill pond, though not a water hazard this dry August.

Three companies of the 15th Alabama were on picket duty in Deep Bottom, leaving eight companies of this eleven-company regiment to fight at Fussell's Mill.[127] Captains Waddell and Lagrand L. Guerry led the companies on picket at Deep Bottom, probably Companies C, F and K.[128] Lowther commanded the 150 men of the 15th who answered Field's call for help.[129] As ranking officer, he commanded both regiments in the detachment, although Oates was soon the senior officer on the field. Eight officers of the 15th Alabama are known to have been present at the Battle of Fussell's Mill. So acute was the officer shortage in the regiment that Company E was commanded by Sergeant James R. Edwards on August 16.[130]

The 48th Alabama was on the right of the 15th Alabama, commanded by Oates. In his history of the 15th Alabama, Oates gave the strength of the 48th Alabama at Fussell's Mill as 300 enlisted men and fifteen officers[131] but he confused the combined strength of the 15th and 48th Alabama regiments with the number of the 48th alone. The 48th Alabama had 116 present on August 16, less Company K, for which numbers are unavailable.

Moving across the field behind the captured works toward the two Alabama regiments was a well-supported Federal line of battle. The right of the Federal line disappeared into the trees north of the open ground and its left was nearly opposite Lowther's detachment. The Alabamians marched by the right oblique to a rail fence at the edge of the field which put them on the Federal left, slightly overlapping the battle line.[132] "We were not fifty steps apart when both lines opened a terrific fire," Oates remembered in his memoirs. Lowther was hit in the side, leaving the 15th Alabama under command of Captain Blanton Hill who was mortally wounded within minutes of Lowther. The command then devolved onto Captain Shaaff, a professional soldier. Captain William Strickland, leading Company I of the 15th, suffered a painful wound when a minie ball went into his left hand between the little finger and the next, exited his wrist and cut off part of his left ear and most of his hat brim.[133] Lieutenant Dozier Thornton, leading both Company D and Company L, took gunshot wounds to the right ankle, right buttock and left leg, ending his military career.[134] At least three of the eight companies the 15th Alabama brought onto the field on August 16 were commanded by lieutenants and two of those fell, leaving them without commissioned officers.[135]

While the 15th Alabama held its place at the fence, the always aggressive Oates ordered the 48th Alabama to charge, overlapping and enfilading the Federal line and pushing it back about 200 yards to the ravine. The colonel noted the cost to the regiment in casualties was fearful as "some of my men fell dead or horribly wounded at every step."[136] The 48th pressed on until it reached a farmer's irrigation ditch. In desperate need of cover, Oates ordered his men to sit in the ditch and fire at the Federals across the ravine, about 100 yards distance. By this time, every officer in the regiment's five left companies was dead or disabled.[137]

A minie ball shattered Oates's right arm as he stood behind the irrigation ditch. He relinquished command, at the same time ordering the new commander to charge across the ravine. The 48th Alabama charged again, across the ravine and up the opposite slope. At the crest, it was stopped by heavy fire which felled Captain James W. Wiggenton, who led the charge in Oates's absence. The regiment then rolled back to the ditch again. In the charge, the 48th Alabama came upon dozens of Federals who had taken shelter in the tall grass in the ravine. These men surrendered as the Confederates ran through their position.[138]

Shortly after the 48th Alabama blocked the Federal breakthrough at the ravine, Asbury Coward arrived with the 5th South Carolina, forming on the left of the Alabamians. Colonel Dudley M. DuBose arrived immediately after Coward with the 15th, 17th and 20th Georgia regiments of Benning's Brigade, taking position between the 15th Alabama and the South Carolinians.[139] The Georgians passed the rear of the 15th Alabama and to its left. After the Georgians' right passed the left of the 15th, they fronted right to align with the Alabamians.[140] The 15th had moved past the fence at the edge of the field at this point, probably supporting the 48th in its charge. The 48th was at the ravine by this time. Two members of the regiment remembered the 15th Alabama receiving fire from both the left and front just before the Confederates drove the Federal troops from the works, unlikely if they had remained at the rail fence.[141] The 4th Alabama and 2nd South Carolina regiments came up in time to become engaged as support in the attack to retake the captured works.[142] As each new Confederate regiment arrived on the field during the afternoon, they were cheered by the units already in place, steadily increasing the enthusiasm of the Confederates.[143]

When the Federal left doubled up under the heroic charge of the 48th Alabama, their assault was broken and the Federals fell back into the breastworks, although some remained in the open. Oates was down, as were many officers in the 48th. The veteran Alabamians knew they could not recapture the works and withdrew to the woods where they originally formed to attack.

DuBose ordered a counterattack to retake the Confederate works with all available forces. The Confederates charged across the open ground between the woods and the ravine where Oates fell. The Federal artillery and musketry tore holes in their ranks and the attack faltered. Pausing in the ravine to redress their lines and settle their nerves, the Confederates renewed the attack and pushed the Federal line back. The Federals broke from left to right. Foster's brigade, on the extreme left of the Federal breakthrough, was pushed back, uncovering first one, then another Federal regiment, until they all had to retreat.[144] A correspondent of the *Richmond Enquirer* witnessed the 48th Alabama plug the leak in Field's lines and the charge ordered by DuBose. Field's men, with DuBose in overall command, "acting in concert with Colonel Coward and the Alabama regiments on the right and Colonel Little on the left, with a yell that only rebels know how to make, charged and carried the works under a galling fire."[145]

Shaaff, commanding the 15th Alabama during the charge, remembered the attack to regain the lost breastworks in a letter two weeks later. "Our boys moved with spirit and alacrity, and, upon reaching the front, showed Grant's chargers how to charge." In Shaaff's view, another attempt to capture Richmond had been repulsed by the desperate attack at Fussell's Mill.[146] Oates believed the assault of the 48th not only plugged the gap in Field's army but prevented Hancock from reaching the Richmond exterior line, thus saving Richmond. He did not mention in his memoirs whether he knew Lowther had been wounded, leaving him in command, or whether he acted without regard to Lowther's senior position. The *Richmond Enquirer* reported the Alabama mountaineers of the 48th Alabama made their charge against the Federal flank "with an impetuosity that was almost irresistible," holding the enemy advance until more Confederate reinforcements could arrive.[147] It is remarkable that so few could have such impact on so many. But the Civil War soldier feared nothing more than an attack on the flank or rear. When Oates and his small band struck the end of the Federal line, it rolled right up.

No more than two hours were needed from the time word reached New Market Heights that help was necessary to stop Hancock's advance on Richmond until the Confederates had regained their lost works near Fussell's Mill.[148] William J. Defnall carried the colors of the 15th Alabama at Fussell's Mill. Oates described Defnall as the best wrestler and most powerful man in the regiment. As the screaming gray lines neared the captured breastworks, an artillery round took off Defnall's left arm while he held the flag aloft. Captain Noah Feagin and Color Sergeant Billy Jordan were closest to Defnall when he was hit. Feagin steadied him and Jordan took up the colors. Even with immediate medical attention, Defnall died after arriving at a nearby hospital.[149] Lieutenant William McClendon led Company G, the 15th Alabama, in the absence of Waddell, who was commanding the three companies on picket at Deep Bottom. During the final charge against the captured works, McClendon received his only wound of the war when a spent minie ball stung his upper lip, loosening his two front teeth.[150]

About 2 p.m., Hancock ordered his Third Division to make a demonstration against Field's troops remaining at New Market Heights. Reports that reinforcements were moving from the heights to halt the Federal advance were received at his headquarters as late as 1:50 p.m. which gave Hancock hope that these works had been stripped of troops by Field's need at Fussell's Mill. Shortly after 3 p.m., Hancock was informed that the heights were still manned, a skirmish line was out and artillery was in place.[151]

The 44th Alabama sustained casualties, including Major George Cary and Captain Thomas C. Ferguson. This was Cary's only wound of the war. Both men returned to duty and were present at Appomattox.[152] Neither the 44th Alabama nor the 47th Alabama are mentioned in reports, official or unofficial, of the Battle of Fussell's Mill. It is thought they stayed in the works atop New Market Heights and opposed Mott's demonstration.[153] Two companies of the 44th Alabama were detached and sent to White's Tavern, on the Charles City Road. Historical memoranda for Companies F and H put them at White's Tavern on August 16, 1864. It was not previously known that any other troops of Field's Division were supporting Gary's cavalry with the Texans on the Charles City Road.

One enlisted man, Lorenzo W. Hocutt, of Company F, the 4th Alabama, was killed in action at Fussell's Mill. Four other men of the 4th are known wounded on August 16, one severely.[154] No officers were reported wounded in the 4th Alabama.

Hancock could not reach the Confederate capital. His incursion had failed. Nevertheless it prevented Lee from further reinforcing Jubal Early in the Valley. In addition, Lee noted that it caused him to reduce his troop strength on the Southside. Grant took advantage of the reduction and launched an attack against the Weldon Railroad.[155] The exhausted Alabamians were proud of their defeat of a portion of Hancock's II Corps, who they considered among the best of the Federal army.[156] Lee complimented Field on his handling of troops in what must have been a vicious, if short-lived fight.[157] Color Bearer Billy Jordan called the Battle of Fussell's Mill the worst he had participated in, considering its small numbers and short duration.[158] Fussell's Mill had been a near miss for the Federal forces north of the James River, who came very near to breaking through to Richmond. Field later noted the residents of Richmond were unaware of their danger. Few were even aware that a battle had been fought and won.[159]

Under flag of truce, Hancock requested a two hour cessation of fighting for the afternoon of August 17. Field said the request was to remove the Federal dead near the Confederate lines.[160] Hancock, on the other hand, had asked for the truce to remove the wounded and bury the dead between the lines. Hancock was, in his words, mortified to learn there were no Federal wounded. Field's men had removed all the wounded when they regained the lost ground. Hancock had not intended to admit defeat.[161]

Law rode out to New Market Heights from Richmond on August 17, surprising the Alabama troops. Only a month before, a rumor had reached the brigade that Law's wound was more serious than previously thought and he might lose the sight in his injured eye. One member of the brigade expressed his belief that Law, whom he called "our little chieftain," would never leave the Alabama unit as long as he could mount a horse. Indeed, he asserted that neither the brigade nor the country could afford to lose Law's services.[162] The Alabamians assumed Law would again take command, perhaps the next day.[163] But Law did not resume command because he was in Richmond lobbying to move his Alabamians to a new command. He still refused to serve under Longstreet.[164]

After a refreshing rain on August 17, Law's Brigade made the best of living at New Market Heights. The troops, always alert to the activities of general officers, noted Lee and Davis were in their immediate area, leading them to conclude another major engagement would soon take place. Fortunately, this rumor proved unfounded.[165] The Alabama brigade was in single rank atop New Market Heights on both sides of the New Market Road, its strength down to 700 rifles,[166] although seven or eight artillery pieces added additional firepower to the infantry in the trenches.[167] They waited from August 17 until August 24 at the entrenched elevation but no Federal attack came.

Grant ordered Hancock back across the James, and on August 21, Field's pickets found no Federal troops north of the river except those at Deep Bottom.[168] Lee immediately began returning troops to the Southside, including Law's Brigade.[169]

Chapter 16

Guarding the Roads
to Richmond

Lee again used Field's Division as his mobile reserve, sending it to the Southside to support the attack at Reams Station, but this time dividing Field's force. The brigades of Anderson and Bratton went south of the James on August 21, with Law's Brigade following on August 24 while Gregg and Benning remained on the Peninsula.[1] The Alabamians marched the nine miles from New Market Heights to Rice Station to take the cars to Petersburg.[2]

Arriving in the evening, the Alabama brigade went to the extreme right of the Confederate line before Petersburg.[3] The brigade was put on alert as reserve for Major General William Mahone's Division of the Third Corps. Though under arms several hours, no call came for Law's troops, and they stood down on August 25.[4]

Since returning to the Army of Northern Virginia in April, the only respite from fighting for the Alabamians had been trench duty. But life in the trenches was not conducive to good military routine and discipline. There was no suitable parade ground near the trenches and Field would not allow troops moved far enough away from the works to drill. Regimental and company books and records were not properly maintained because duty as a flying reserve meant baggage was left in the depot.[5] On the Southside, the Alabama brigade again returned to the drill and again received instructions in picket duty and guard duty. The men cleaned accumulated grime of New Market Heights and Deep Bottom from their Enfield rifles.[6]

Many rifles and nearly all the military equipment in the possession of the Alabamians came from the Federal army. One newspaper correspondent on duty in Virginia believed it would "astonish an outsider to see how great a portion" of the Confederate supplies came from capture. It was said the Confederates were so eager to grab anything of value from their enemy that "The Yankees are very shy of placing their best foot foremost when very near the ragged and perishing Rebels." He reported Federal blankets, rubber cloths, knapsacks, rifles, Navy pistols and cooking utensils in plentiful supply in Field's Division. The correspondent added, "Many privates sport captured sword belts to their bayonet scabbards and cap pouches."[7]

Little could be done to improve the appearance of the Alabamians whose uniforms resembled rags. According to the report of the brigade assistant inspector general, the Alabama troops were particularly short of shoes and pants with "many men entirely destitute of both."[8]

The five Alabama regiments mustered 736 enlisted men and 64 officers for inspection on August 29. After their costly charge at Fussell's Mill, the 48th counted only 106 rank and file and 11 officers. The 48th Alabama remained the smallest of the five regiments for the rest of the conflict. Bowles had only four staff officers with which to command the brigade.

More officers were absent than present, the record showing fifty-five absent with leave, ten were considered absent without leave, and 19 were listed as prisoners of war. As always, some officers and men were assigned to guard duty, scouting and cook detail. On August 29, probably six officers and 65 to 70 enlisted men were on such duty.[9]

First located in a ravine between the Jerusalem Plank Road and the Lead Works after they returned to the Southside, Bowles's troops moved their camp to the Whitworth farm on Cox Road, their base for most of September.[10] They were still at the Lead Works on the 4th but were in encamped on the farm by September 8.[11] Shortly after their move to the Whitworth farm, Field's men helped build a line of works from the city's fortifications, running southwest from Battery 45 and parallel to the Boydton Plank Road. After only a few days on this detail, they began fatigue duty fortifying the Squirrel Level line.[12] Work on the fortifications was done at night and the men relaxed in relatively secure camps during the daylight hours.[13]

Because of the condition of the brigade during inspection on August 29, Bowles held a second inspection nine days later. When he looked at the troops on September 8, he rated their personal cleanliness and military bearing as good.[14] He may have only seen the result of a few days rest, but he was also looking at men of great stamina and determination who looked fit in spite of the heavy work they had done. After so many months of campaigning, Law's Brigade had only hardened veterans among its ranks.

One of the First Corps brigadiers was pleased but surprised at their period of inactivity. "Even the sharpshooting and 'mortar shelling' has assumed a languor," he wrote his wife, "that threatens cessation," and would have stopped, he felt, had it not become habit. The easy duty was particularly appreciated by the men of Field's command because they felt the shelling of Petersburg—only four miles away—had increased.[15]

Lieutenant Mims Walker of the brigade staff was not comforted by the quiet, interrupted only by the occasional artillery exchange, in their sector. He was not sanguine about the prospects of the Confederacy for the winter. In a letter to his fiancee, Walker noted the Federals had built a rail connection between City Point and the Weldon Railroad to supply the army during the upcoming winter. By contrast, Walker feared, "The Army of Northern Virginia will have a harder time this winter than it has ever had yet." He predicted Grant would make an effort to capture the Southside Railroad, which he believed would lead to "a considerable fight."[16]

Although Walker believed "we Rebels" in the Eastern theater will have a difficult time finding food during the cold months to come, he worried more for the civilian population of the Confederacy who he felt would suffer during the winter of 1864–65. He was concerned by the condition of the civilians he saw around Petersburg. "Hardly a day passes but some little children come by our quarters and beg for something to eat, saying they haven't eaten anything that day." Walker could only predict the situation would worsen during the coming cold months.[17]

Like many Alabama families, both Walker's and the family of his fiancee, Mary Gray Pitts, suffered the loss of a son to combat. The brother of Mary Pitts, John Davidson Pitts, of Pitts Folly, Alabama, was killed at Gaines's Mill while a member of Company D, 4th Alabama. Walker's brother, John Marshall Walker, known as "Mack" was mortally wounded in 1864 at Resaca, Georgia while serving as a captain in the 36th Alabama.

Conditions in Alabama

By the time Walker expressed his concern for Confederate civilians, conditions on the home front had become nearly intolerable. For many Alabamians, the war had brought hardships from the start. Mobile was closed to normal commerce in 1861, and the Federal blockade proved very effective after 1862. Federal gunboats pushed up the Tennessee River to Florence in February 1862, initiating the Federal occupation of Alabama north of the river for the rest of the war, except for a short period in the winter of 1862–63.

Shortages of essentials soon became acute. In December 1862, about 20 women forced the railroad agent at Greenville, Alabama, to divide a shipment of salt among them with the threat of violence. At Talladega, Alabama, a group of women looted a store of shoes in September 1863.[18] Women whose husbands served in the army took to the streets of Mobile in April and September of 1863 in what came to be known as the Mobile bread riots. Some carried a banner along Spring Hill Avenue proclaiming "Bread or Blood." By the spring of 1864, barefoot women were begging for corn in Bibb and Shelby counties.[19]

Alabamians serving in the Army of Northern Virginia were aware of the hardships at home. A month after Gettysburg, the adjutant of the 4th Alabama warned his sister in Summerfield, Alabama, that there was a chance the Yankees would occupy her home. He recommended she escape but if she could not, he said, "Bear yourself like a true Rebel—the daughter of an old Rebel, and the sister of several who have evidently given abundant proof of their rebellious dispositions."[20] Sam K. Rayburn, retired from the 48th Alabama for being overage, complained to Governor Thomas Watts in July 1862 that women and children in Marshall County were without bread.[21] Colonel Sheffield, while on leave from the 48th Alabama in April 1864, wrote the governor that conditions in Marshall County caused soldiers to desert the Confederacy rather than leave their families in peril of starvation.[22]

Armed resistance to conscription occurred in Randolph County in September, 1862.[23] The deserters in Alabama were able to disrupt normal life to such an extent that it was not possible to collect taxes in 14 counties by June 1863.[24] Legal proceedings were interrupted for two years in Coffee and Dale counties when the circuit judge refused to hold court without military protection.[25] Normally law-abiding citizens hid their crops and livestock from impressment agents just to survive. The greatest suffering occurred in those counties with few slaves, the very counties which opposed secession in 1861. Law cited Gettysburg as the turning point of the war and Oates claimed the war was lost at Sharpsburg but for many Alabamians the war was lost when the breadwinners left home.[26]

Fort Gilmer

The calm was shattered on September 29 by a two-pronged Federal offensive in which Grant sent two corps north of the James with the intent of breaking the exterior line and capturing Richmond. This assault forced Lee to dispatch men from the Southside to prevent a breakthrough. Meade waited at Petersburg with more than three corps, planning to extend the Federal line westward and capture the Southside Railroad.

Early on the morning of the 29th, Lee received the news that the enemy occupied Fort Harrison and that "affairs look serious." He ordered out the local defense forces, asked the navy to help and sought reinforcements to halt the Federal advance.[27] Field's Division—Lee's mobile reserve—was at Petersburg with three of its brigades. The Texans and DuBose's Georgians were still on the north side under Gregg's command.

Lee summoned Field to army headquarters, showing him the telegram from Gregg which announced the capture of Fort Harrison. Lee ordered him to the north side to reinforce his two beleaguered brigades there. Field immediately set off with Law's Brigade, but the lack of rail transport prevented the Kentuckian from taking more than one brigade to the Peninsula.[28] The Alabamians were eating breakfast when they received the order to march. They quickly crowded on the train for the ride to Drewry's Bluff, carrying only a few biscuits in their haversacks, a canteen and forty rounds of ammunition.[29]

No orders awaited Field when he detrained, and he knew there was no time to waste. He asked a passing officer where the Federal attack was most pressing and was told Fort Gilmer.[30] Bowles quickly covered the five miles from the rail line to that earthwork with the Alabama brigade, moving at the double-quick until the men could not continue the pace. They alternately walked to regain their wind when they again moved to the double-quick.[31] The Alabamians, with Field and Bowles at their front, arrived at the fort shortly after 2 p.m.[32]

They got there as the Federal assault against the north face of the redoubt was repulsed. A few of the new arrivals rushed into the fort but most of them took a position behind the unoccupied intermediate line west and north of Fort Gilmer.[33] They were warmly welcomed by the exhausted troops who had held until more men could get to the north side. Their exuberant response was noted by Adjutant Coles who believed, "The old 4th Alabama never in all its existence received such a royal welcome. Cheer after cheer went up time and again from our hard pressed comrades."[34]

They were barely in place when the determined Federals launched an attack against the eastern face of Fort Gilmer. Law's Brigade was on the left of the Texans, while DuBose's Georgians held the right.[35] From their position along the intermediate line, Bowles's command had a spectacular view of the attack.[36] The Negro troops of the X Corps, the first United States Colored Troops (USCT) the Alabama soldiers had seen, made the assault. The Negro troops came under artillery fire as soon as they made their appearance, and when they came within range, the Fort Gilmer cannon fired case and canister at them. When the Negroes got within a hundred yards of the fort, the Alabamians watched as the men of the Texas brigade poured a withering fire into their ranks. Since there was nothing in their front, the 15th Alabama yelled as if they were on a charge.[37] The attack was of insufficient numbers and in detail and was easily repulsed by Field's Texans and Georgians. In spite of these errors, the Negro volunteers succeeded in reaching the moat outside Fort Gilmer. Field's volunteer aide, who was in Gilmer and used his Adams repeater to shoot into the ranks of the charging Negro troops, was impressed with their courage.[38]

Forts Harrison and Gilmer were part of the Richmond defenses. Harrison was a large work near the convergence of the exterior line and the fortifications around Chaffin's Bluff. Fort Gilmer was the first Confederate earthwork of the Chaffin's Bluff defenses in the interior line. The exterior line had been breached with the capture of Fort Harrison, uncovering the compound at Chaffin's Bluff. The intermediate line would be broken if Fort Gilmer fell.

The Alabama soldiers were angry and frightened by the prospect of fighting Negro soldiers. They knew that colored troops were in the Federal army but had not fought them. Rumors of Negro atrocities had reached their camp, however, which served as the focus of their anger.[39] But they also watched the soldiers of the USCT brave a destructive fire from artillery and rifle to reach the moat of Fort Gilmer. That added manpower for the North seemed too much to overcome. "It fairly made the hair rise upon my head," was how Rufus Hollis of the 4th Alabama felt when he thought about fighting the Yankees "and all the Negroes of the South thrown in; this was very discouraging indeed."[40] Only weeks later the unequal numbers caused the Alabamians to support the use of Negroes in the Confederate army.

Even though Grant's men had captured Fort Harrison, the New Market line and part of the exterior line, the threat to Richmond was relieved when they failed to exploit their opportunity. Field felt the time to retake Fort Harrison was immediately after the Federals had been driven from Fort Gilmer. In addition, the Unionists had not had time to close the open gorge of the fort. Field proposed the immediate assault to Lee, who had just arrived from Petersburg. The commanding general thought it better to wait. It was now sunset and Bratton and Anderson had also joined Field.[41]

Lee wanted to wait for the additional troops before attacking. Perhaps, too, he wanted to rest the men before attacking. Some had been on the move all day without rations. Certainly, the Alabamians were without food or water by nightfall of September 29, having arrived at the north side without supplies and would not be issued rations until the 30th, after the attack against Fort Harrison.[42]

Before long, John Gregg told Field that Lee wanted him to retake Fort Harrison that night as he had suggested. The major general gathered his three newly arrived brigades, already asleep on the ground near Fort Gilmer and marched two miles to a point opposite the open face of Fort Harrison. The men were deployed as near the fort as possible and by 1 a.m., they were ready for a moonlight assault.[43]

Field went to Anderson's tent to report all was ready for the attack. He was surprised to find the corps commander asleep. When awakened, Anderson told Field there was a mistake, and he did not intend Field to retake the lost works that night. The disappointed Kentuckian pulled back his brigades, who resumed their sleep. Field knew the Federals did not sleep, however, saying, "All night long we could distinctly hear the enemy in Fort Harrison hard at work strengthening it, and by next day it had become, in strength, a most formidable place." When he did assault the fort, it cost Field dearly in casualties.[44]

Fort Harrison

Under the personal supervision of the army commander, the Confederate force assembled to retake Fort Harrison.[45] Field marched the Alabamians and the brigades of "Tige" Anderson and Bratton back to the position they had taken during the night. Local Defense Forces, called out to meet the crisis, replaced Bowles near Fort Gilmer.[46] Field was to advance his brigades across the open ground northwest of the fort. Joining Field in the assault to recapture the fallen fort were the brigades of Major General Robert F. Hoke's Division. Hoke deployed in a ravine west of Fort Harrison which masked his force from Federal fire. His position was half the distance from the captured fort as Field's. He was to hold his men until Anderson and Bratton could cross half the open ground, then both divisions would strike the back of Fort Harrison simultaneously.[47] The attack would be preceded by a twenty to thirty minute artillery barrage, personally directed by Porter Alexander.[48]

The plan went awry immediately. It called for Anderson to advance only half way, nearly on a line with Hoke, and wait for Bratton's South Carolinians, then the Southern brigades would overwhelm the Federals and seal the breached line. Incredibly, Anderson did not explain the plan to his commanders, who went to the attack unsupported.[49] Hoke would not attack before the prearranged time. There was no concentration of Confederate force and they were disastrously repulsed. "Had General Anderson sufficiently instructed his men to wait for the proper moment," remembered Field, who had no difficulty in assigning blame, "or had Hoke attacked when I did, the result might have been very different."[50]

On the morning of September 30, Bowles marched his command from Fort Gilmer to a position behind a line of works west of Fort Harrison. There the men of the Alabama brigade left all their belongings except their canteen, forty rounds of ammunition and their Enfield rifles.[51]

Bowles held Field's left. Field ordered Bowles to advance when he sent Bratton hurrying after the Georgians.[52] The Alabamians were not in the attacking column, however, their mission being to clear the old Confederate works on Field's left of any Federals and capture a redoubt northwest of the fort. For the second time in as many days, the Alabama troops encountered Negro soldiers. This time they drove U.S. Colored Troop skirmishers from the small, isolated fort.[53] And when the 22nd USCT sallied out of their works to counterattack the repulsed Confederate column, they came under the muskets of Law's Brigade.[54] After they witnessed the mass slaughter of Lee's assaulting columns, it must have been little consolation to the Alabamians that they accomplished their own mission.[55] Under cover of darkness, they moved back to their jumping off point northwest of the fort.[56]

Some who witnessed the destruction of the columns on the 30th believed they saw a loss of the fighting enthusiasm which had characterized the Army of Northern Virginia. A Richmond newspaper simply reported Lee's men "did not attack with their usual impetuosity."[57] At army headquarters, a young staff officer acknowledged the lack of dash and determination in the attempt to recover Fort Harrison. Colonel Walter H. Taylor wrote his fiancée, "Matters were not executed as well as they were planned."[58] The failure was the result of loss of hope and weakened command, and the condition would only worsen with time.

While protecting the Confederate left, the brigade lost one killed among its officer ranks. James L. Gaskin, captain of Company E, 47th Alabama, was buried behind the wall where the brigade had left their haversacks and personal belongings before the assault.[59] Gaskin was an original officer of the victimized Company E. Of the ten men who held officer commissions in Company E, four died in battle. Gaskin was the fourth. Two others resigned after receiving serious wounds, and two others left the ranks for reasons of health. Although Lemuel Cobb succeeded Gaskin as captain, no officer represented Company E at Appomattox.[60]

Grant's operations on the Southside, under Meade, had failed and Grant concluded that, if the Confederate right was not weakened, Lee's left must be vulnerable.[61] The Federal commander, therefore, ordered Butler to reconnoiter up the Darbytown Road toward Richmond on October 1 and take advantage of any opportunity presented to him.[62] Grant kept the pressure on, and when Lee learned of the enemy reconnaissance up the Darbytown Road, he countered with the Alabamians and Pickett's Provisional brigade, commanded by Colonel Edgar B. Montague, both under Field. The diarist for Anderson's First Corps asserted Field was "hurried off" to meet the threat. When Field arrived near the capital, he found the intermediate line manned by Local Defense Forces and he held his force in reserve in case the Federals broke through. He posted Montague on the New Market Road and put Bowles astride the Darbytown Road. Bowles remained in place only one day, then he returned to Chaffin's farm.[63]

First Battle of Darbytown Road, October 7, 1864

Lee was determined to retake the exterior line above Fort Harrison. If he did not recover the lost works, the commanding general would have to retrench between the lost line and the intermediate line.[64]

He ordered Local Defense Forces to replace Hoke's and Field's Divisions in the trenches during the night of October 6.[65] Lee sent the Alabamians and Brigadier General Martin W. Gary's cavalry north of the Darbytown Road, beyond the Federal right flank. Lee's plan called for Gary's dismounted cavalry and Law's Brigade to attack the Federal right and push down in the rear of the Federal line. The rest of Field's men, along with Hoke, would then assault the front of the works occupied by the Federals.[66]

Moving about dawn, Gary's South Carolina cavalry and the Alabamians easily swept aside the Federal cavalry outposts. Gary sent some of his horsemen southeast along the Charles City Road, where they met and drove back elements of Brigadier General August V. Kautz's cavalry. He sent the bulk of his cavalry and Bowles's infantry almost due south behind the captured Confederate exterior line. At the same time, Bratton and Anderson pushed down the Darbytown Road where they overwhelmed the Federal defenders at that point and turned south.

Giving forth the rebel yell, Law's Alabamians ran, firing as they went, routing Kautz's troopers, driving rapidly into the enemy camps. Major Robbins, holding aloft a captured frying pan instead of his sword, joked with the men of the 4th Alabama that he had finally found a prize worthy of a fight. Before he could enjoy his trophy, however, a bullet from a Spencer repeater holed the frying pan.[67]

Leigh Terrell led the 47th Alabama. Though his commission dated from June 15, 1864, Terrell had accepted his rank of lieutenant colonel only four days before. He had jumped from captain to lieutenant colonel by the "constitutional authority" of President Davis. The delay was due to a gunshot wound to the left shoulder received on June 17, 1864.[68] The presidential appointment came after the petition from most of the regiment's officers which endorsed Terrell and cited his courage, particularly at Chickamauga.[69]

Led by Terrell, the 47th drove through the Federal camps and captured an artillery piece. The Federal gun crew fired some canister before they abandoned their piece. One of the grape shot hit Private Theophilus Botsford in the left ear, deafening him forever.[70] Lieutenant Nathan Crawford Kimball fell mortally wounded when a minie ball struck him in the chest. The twenty-four-year-old from Loachapoka, Alabama, was wounded earlier at Cedar Run, VA.[71]

Company G of the 15th was deployed as skirmishers for the regiment. While out in front on that duty, General Gary, the ranking officer on the Confederate left, ordered Lieutenant McClendon to hold a company of Federal cavalry in place while the South Carolinian moved to the flank and captured most of the enemy. Later, Company G lost two wounded and one killed in this action while capturing a cannon which had fired a few rounds of canister at the advancing Rebels before its crew fled.[72] From near the artillery piece, McClendon had a splendid view of his brigade advancing in line of battle against the disorganized Federal cavalry.

A short distance past the cannon, McClendon was startled when a Federal soldier, described by the lieutenant as large, stepped from behind a pine tree brandishing a revolver which McClendon remembered as being oversized. The Yankee demanded his surrender but before either man spoke again, Private Jim Rhodes of Company K, drew down on the big Federal with his rifle and ordered, "Surrender yourself, G——d d——n you." McClendon liberated the Yankee's sword belt which he wore home from the war. Rhodes wanted his ring but McClendon allowed the prisoner to keep it, accepting the story that his mother gave it to him as he departed for the war.[73]

The Federals fell back about two miles until they reached a strong line of fortifications near New Market Road.[74] The Federal right was refused to face the fast-moving Confederates crashing against their flank. Terry took shelter behind works which ran east to west

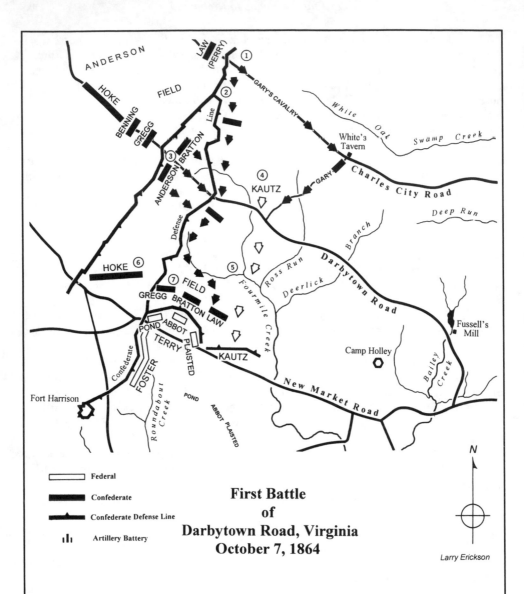

**First Battle
of
Darbytown Road, Virginia
October 7, 1864**

Larry Erickson

Federal

Confederate

Confederate Defense Line

Artillery Battery

1. Gary's cavalry advances at dawn on the Charles City Road, followed by Law's (Perry) infantry. Gary drives the Federal cavalry down the Charles City Road.
2. Law's Brigade and the bulk of Gary's cavalry turn behind the Federal breastworks, easily pushing the Federals through their camps.
3. At 3:00 a. m. Anderson and Bratton advance down the Darbytown Road, breaking the Federal line and turn south behind the works.
4. Kautz is routed and leaves several artillery pieces in Confederate hands.
5. The Federals retreat two miles to works on the New Market Road where they make a stand.
6. Hoke deploys to Field's right but does not advance.
7. Between 9:30 and 10:00 a. m. Field deploys the brigades of Gregg, Bratton, and Law for an assault against the new Federal position along the New Market Road. These attacks are repulsed with heavy loss. General Gregg is killed here.

near the New Market Road. Field deployed Gregg, Bratton and Bowles for an assault against Terry, as Hoke moved into place near the New Market Road, his right connecting with the road.

McClendon advanced until his company lay in a line of rifle pits while Federal artillery dueled with a Confederate battery which had limbered up directly behind his position. Soon a Georgia colonel ordered McClendon to advance toward the Federal position to develop their strength. They moved only a short distance before a volley pinned them to the ground. McClendon ordered the company to retire, momentarily giving the enemy a shot at their backs.[75]

Edward J. J. "Jackson" Ward, a childhood friend and schoolmate of McClendon, fell as the company made for safety. Ward fell in front of his lieutenant, who stepped over him. Ward reached for his friend, hoping he would help him to the rear but McClendon kept moving. After dark, the lieutenant and another soldier found Jack Ward and got him to Howard's Grove Hospital where he died on October 9.

Oates, original captain of Company G, had been admitted to the hospital after losing an arm at Fussell's Mill. Color Sergeant Billy Jordan had been in the hospital after being struck on the elbow by a pick ax while constructing fortifications. The next morning Jordan was called to the colonel's bedside. Jordan found Oates "lying there with his arm off reading a book." He told Jordan that he had promised Ward's father that he would take care of his boy. To that end, he wanted Jordan to go to Richmond to make funeral arrangements. Despite risking arrest for desertion, Jordan left the hospital twice to obtain a zinc–lined pine coffin, painted red, and to telegraph Ward's father to make his sad journey to Richmond.[76]

Field launched his frontal assault against Terry's position but Hoke did not attack.[77] In his report of the fighting on October 7, Bratton remarked, "The brigade on my left fell back and retired entirely from the contest," though he did not identify the unit. This brigade was almost certainly Bowles's command. The heavy fighting was on the Confederate right. Bratton's casualties came mostly on his right regiments where he, too, was wounded.[78] The Texas brigade was heavily engaged to the right of the South Carolinians, where Brigadier General John Gregg fell mortally wounded with a shot through the neck.[79]

The Alabamians were off to the left, attempting to flank the Federal works, although Bratton did not know it. Bowles may have taken this action on his own initiative as the attacks were not coordinated. Bowles attacked late, after the Texans and South Carolinians had been repulsed with great loss.[80]

When the Confederate assault got under way, Terry began preparations for a stand. He chose the breastworks along the New Market Road to stop the rout, which meant the Federals were pushed about two miles before they reached the works. This new line was south and nearly perpendicular to the original.

After the failed attack against Terry's left, Federal scouts reported Confederates were forming for an attack in a field 500 yards in front of the extreme Federal right. Terry's Third Brigade, who fought the Alabamians at Deep Bottom in August, shifted troops to defend its right.

Bowles men advanced in two lines, without skirmishers, against the Federal breastworks. Coming out of thick woods into a sparse stand of pines, they received a fierce fire from the 10th Connecticut and the 100th New York regiments. The Alabamians pressed forward with a determined assault, their rebel yell resounding through the Virginia woods, pushing the 100th New Yorkers from behind their works. As the 10th Connecticut stood firm, the 100th New York then rallied behind the adjutant of the 11th Maine.[81]

The attack was broken. Alabamians lay dead within steps of the breastworks, including Captain John D. Adrian, commanding Company K, 44th Alabama. Adrain transferred from the 4th Alabama in 1862 and was promoted captain on July 2, 1863. He suffered a minor arm wound at the Wilderness before he fell on the New Market Road. Five Alabama soldiers lay next to the twenty-one-year-old lawyer.[82]

The fight on October 7 did not regain the exterior line as Lee had hoped. Nine pieces of artillery, ten caissons, two battle flags, 100 horses and over 100 prisoners were the net gains.[83] Two horses were captured by privates of the 4th Alabama, one of which was kept by Lieutenant Colonel Scruggs and named in honor of John Gregg.[84] The Confederates moved back to align behind Cornelius Creek. Field took the left, near the Darbytown Road, while Hoke held the right.[85]

Four days after the fight on October 7, Turner Vaughan penned a letter to his cousin in Alabama. The Alabamians were weary of war, he said, as he told his kinswoman the attitude of many soldiers at this stage of the war. Vaughan wrote about the fight, describing how the Alabamians drove the Federals and captured 10 artillery pieces, with only three members of his company wounded. He reminded his reader that the First Battle of Manassas, "which made so many heroes," was only a skirmish compared to battles now fought which go unmentioned. Vaughan recalled how, for many months, soldiers would talk about Manassas. Now, battles are discussed around the campfire at night, perhaps an account of the fight is read from the papers and there the matter ends.

Second Battle of Darbytown Road, October 13, 1864

Unable to recapture the exterior line, Lee ordered a retrenchment between the lost line and the intermediate line to the west, cutting off Fort Harrison. This new line was planned to extend from Fort Gilmer to the exterior line near the Charles City Road but was laid out only as far as the Darbytown Road.[86] Lee had no choice in this matter, as he had to have fortifications for his outnumbered army. He believed Grant was massing a force large enough to extend his lines beyond the Confederates' flanks. Should Grant succeed, Lee knew the Army of Northern Virginia could not keep the Federals out of Richmond.[87]

Field and Hoke moved in front of Cornelius Creek on October 10 and laid out a line of rifle pits in front of the retrenchment line. Gary covered the left with two regiments of horsemen.[88] The Confederates worked on the new breastworks for two days before word of the retrenchment reached Grant at his headquarters at City Point. The Federal commander ordered a reconnaissance in force to drive the Confederates from their construction work. He selected the First and Third Divisions of the X Corps for the job.[89]

Field was concerned that his digging would invite an attack, and he guessed the Federals would march up the Darbytown Road and attempt to turn his left flank. Field asked that Hoke extend his left so he could throw a brigade across the Darbytown Road to protect his left. When his request was ignored, Field pulled the Texans from his right during the evening of October 12 and moved them north of the road on his own initiative.[90]

The Federal X Corps was ready to attack at 3:25 in the afternoon of October 12, well before Field had moved the Texas brigade north of the road. Fortunately for the Confederates, a flag of truce was in force between Butler's Army of the James and the line held by Ewell which postponed the Federal assault until October 13.[91]

The Federal battle plan instructed Brigadier General William Birney, commanding the Third Division, X Corps, to position his division to assault the Confederate works south of the Darbytown Road while Brigadier General Adelbert Ames's First Division would turn left from north of the road. Kautz would cover the Federal right with his cavalry division and support Ames.[92] The X Corps attack had a good chance of success on October 12, but by the 13th, Field had protected his left from surprise after his men had built a formidable defensive line south of the road.[93] The Federal assault force left its camps at 4 a.m. The weather was clear and cold with a layer of frost left by rain the previous day.[94] The infantry was in place at dawn but did not attack until about 7 a.m. because Kautz was slow getting into position.[95]

Lee, on the scene and aware of the danger to his flank, ordered Field to reinforce the left. Field moved three more brigades north of the road, including Law's Alabamians who took a position to the left of the Texans.[96] They immediately began constructing fortifications with the materials at hand. The Federals advanced at about 8 a.m., firing steadily at the men of Company K of the 15th who were on picket duty.[97] First Lieutenant Henry W. Glover of Company B, commanded Company K as he had since early in 1864. Oates considered Glover an excellent officer and thought the twenty-five-year-old lieutenant could command a company.[98] When the Federal skirmishers slowly reconnoitered toward the Confederate works, one of their shots struck Glover a mortal wound to the head. His men hurried him from the field but he died in General Hospital 9 on October 19.[99] The ranking officer of Company K, Captain William J. Bethune, had suffered a ghastly wound to the face in 1863 that was still unhealed, and accepted a recruiting job in Jacksonville, Alabama. On August 31, he told a medical board he wanted to return to his company because it was without officers. He returned to active duty late in the year, and was paroled at Appomattox.[100]

Terry's reconnaissance convinced the temporary commander of the X Corps that the enemy position was a formidable one. Brigade commanders in Ames's division north of the Darbytown Road reported the Confederate breastworks were protected by slashes 100 to 200 yards and rifle pits and artillery. At 10:30, Terry advised Butler of the situation: "As at present advised, I think we cannot pierce their works except by massing on some point and attacking in column. I hesitate to do this without further instructions from you after our conversation of last night. Please direct me in regard to it."[101]

Butler referred the matter to Grant and told Terry at 12:10 to wait for orders. Grant told Butler not to attack fortifications, advising him instead to locate the Confederates left for future reference and withdraw. Grant noted, "To attack now we would lose more than the enemy and only gain ground which we are not prepared to hold."[102] This was contrary to his original order to drive the Confederates from their new works, but was a sensible response from the man who had ordered the costly attacks at Cold Harbor.

At 1:30 Butler informed Terry of Grant's decision, ordering him to fall back at his leisure. By then, however, Kautz had provided Terry with intelligence that beyond Ames's right there was a place in the line without "works of consequence and that the enemy was still entrenching," where a breakthrough might be achieved. Terry ordered Ames to extend to his right and attack the weak point.[103] He received Butler's order to withdraw while Ames was assaulting.[104]

It was the lately arrived Alabama brigade which manned the perceived weak point. The men from Alabama were digging in about half a mile from the Charles City Road.[105] Bowles ordered his brigade to improve their hastily constructed field works and cut down the underbrush to their front while they waited for the attack.[106] His command numbered between 700 and 800 veterans with which he was to hold the left of Lee's army against an unknown force.

A Confederate cavalryman passed through the lines of the Alabama work parties, riding toward the Federal lines. Almost immediately, he returned to the safety of his own lines with a Federal horseman in pursuit and rapidly closing the gap between them. The Yankee was bent over his charging mount's neck, saber drawn, intent on his quarry when a fusillade of rifle fire killed both rider and horse. The Confederate cavalryman did not slow his speed, but galloped out of sight. A member of the 15th Alabama joked that he was going to tell Jeff Davis how close he had come to being run down by the Federal rider.[107]

Ames issued the order for his right brigade, the First, commanded by Colonel Francis B. Pond, to attack the weak point in the Confederate line. Ames sent a portion of the 10th Connecticut which was not on the skirmish line of the Third Brigade (about 70 strong) and the 3rd New Hampshire, which he suggested be held in reserve, to bolster Pond's strength.[108]

Pond deployed in a wood about 300 yards from the Confederate line, forming his attacking force in double columns at half distance. The 67th Ohio held the left, the 10th Connecticut was on the right with the 39th Illinois and 62nd Ohio between them. Pond kept the 85th Pennsylvania and 3rd New Hampshire in reserve.[109]

The men from Alabama could hear the Federals forming for the attack, the shouts of the officers echoing through the woods until the command to go forward was clearly heard. They knew the enemy was coming but they did not know their strength. Nevertheless, they "resolved to stand to the last and give them the bayonet in the event they came near enough," remembered Lieutenant McClendon of the 15th Alabama. As he looked at the men around him he knew "there was no thought of surrendering or retreating."[110]

At about 2:30 in the afternoon, Pond's column advanced with a cheer, struggling through the thick scrub oak which broke the impetus of their attack.[111] After moving nearly 300 yards, they ran into the slashing in front of Bowles's troops where they received a murderous fire from the front and left flank.[112] The first volley destroyed their formation even though the remaining officers continued to urge them forward. The Alabamians poured a galling fire into the mass of men crowded into the small area of slashings.[113]

Major Henry Camp, of the 10th Connecticut, waving his drawn sword, encouraged his men to follow him. He got close enough to the Alabamians for McClendon to fire two shots at him with his Remington revolver, one of which McClendon thought struck Camp in the face. Camp fell immediately, riddled with bullets. The major was left where he fell, while his men escaped from their trap as rapidly as possible.[114] The next day, a small delegation, including Chaplain Clay Trumbull of the 10th Connecticut, came to the Confederate line to retrieve Camp's body. Captain Robert M. Sims, a South Carolinian on Bratton's staff, helped the Federal men retrieve their friend's body. After the body had been exhumed, they learned Camp's sword, pistol, watch, papers and outer clothing had been taken. Chaplain Trumbull protested strongly about the loss of Camp's diary, which Sims was able to locate and return. Trumbull escorted the body to Hartford, Connecticut, where the Yale graduate was buried.[115]

Pond had 882 muskets in his four regiments, though he estimated his attacking column numbered only 570.[116] Of that number, his assaulting force sustained 217 casualties. Surprisingly, only 14 of them were killed.[117] Pond believed that figure was so small because the volleys from the Alabamians were fired extremely low.[118]

His division commander faulted Pond for his indifferent attitude and for using too few of his men in the attack. Ames claimed Pond's estimate of the opposition was exaggerated.[119] Homer A. Plimpton, a young officer in Company G, the 39th Illinois, viewed the failed assault from a different perspective than his division commander. He later wrote:

"The circumstances surrounding us at the time were very discouraging indeed. We were compelled to charge their works at a point where they had a heavy flank fire upon us, and through thick underbrush and small timber, and then over heavy slashing where their artillery could rake us. The men all knew before going in the difficulties ahead; all the officers

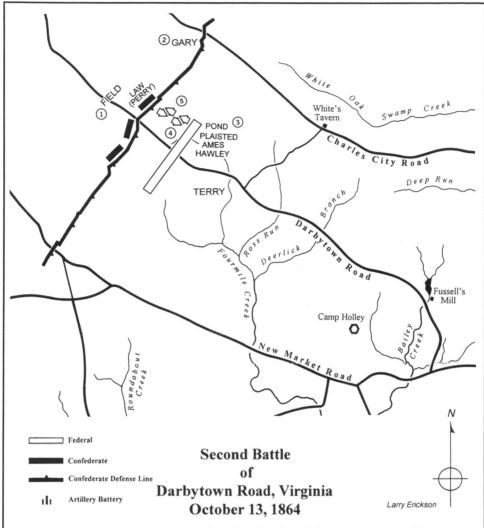

**Second Battle
of
Darbytown Road, Virginia
October 13, 1864**

Larry Erickson

Legend:
- Federal
- Confederate
- Confederate Defense Line
- Artillery Battery

1. Field begins work on retrenchments October 10th. Rifle pits and abatis are constructed. Slashings are made where possible.
2. Gary covers the left with two regiments of cavalry.
3. The Federals deploy about 7:00 a. m.
4. Federals drive in the Confederate skirmish line between 8:00 and 10:00 a. m.
5. Pond attacks at 2:30 p. m. and is repulsed with heavy loss. The Federals withdraw about 4:00 p. m.

of the brigade were opposed to the charge, and reported so to the general commanding the corps but it made no difference. Charge we must and charge we did and Death reaped a rich harvest as the result."[120]

In his report of the part taken by the 10th Connecticut in the attack, Colonel John L. Otis offered no apology for the failure of his men to drive Law's Brigade from its position. In a scathing indictment of Federal planning, Otis said, "I have not seen a more hopeless task undertaken since I entered the service than that attempted by the assaulting column today."[121]

The brave Leigh Terrell fell during the attack of October 13, pierced through the side by a gunshot which carried away one of his kidneys. The Uniontown lawyer was moved to General Hospital 4 where he lingered until October 22.[122] Terrell was buried with full military honors and Masonic honors from St. Paul's Church. As the funeral procession, complete with riderless horse, passed slowly through the Richmond streets, a newsman who watched was touched by the look of Terrell's horse. To the reporter, the riderless horse, following directly behind the hearse, looked as if he had lost his best friend.[123]

Beginning on October 14, Bowles's men began constructing permanent works which they finished in November. Directly behind this new line of fortifications, the Alabamians built their winter quarters, in full view of a Federal observation post. They remained in this area until the frantic days of April 1865.[124]

While the brigade dug new breastworks between the Darbytown and Charles City Roads, three of its men worked on the Federal effort to cut a canal across Dutch Gap. The project was started in the summer to allow Federal vessels to avoid Confederate batteries on the James River. Reports had been received the month before at headquarters of the Army of the James that captured Negro soldiers served in labor gangs or had been sent into slavery. The truce which delayed the assault against Field's left from October 12 until October 13 was declared to deliver an ultimatum on the subject from Butler to the Confederate authorities. Butler threatened to retaliate by using Confederate prisoners of war as laborers in his army if the practice was not curtailed.

Since then Negro soldiers captured at the Crater and earlier in October, including troops of the 5th, 7th and 30th USCT, were taken from prison and put to work on fortifications. Butler had reports that some of these prisoners were laboring under the fire of his guns. Carrying out his threat, Butler sent captured Confederates to dig the canal at Dutch Gap, under the fire of Alexander's artillery. Three of these were from Law's Brigade.

An exchange of letters between Lee and Grant resolved the matter but not before the Virginian had intensified the shelling of Dutch Gap to show he would not be intimidated. Fortunately, no prisoners were injured by this fire. John E. Lawrence, Company F, the 44th Alabama, took the oath to the Union after he was released from the canal digging. J. E. McGraw, Company G, the 44th, and William H. Tibbett, Company B, the 47th Alabama, both chose to go to Camp Lookout Prison.[125]

Longstreet relieved Anderson of command of the forces north of the James on October 19, although he was still without the use of his right arm. Under his command, Hoke occupied the recently dug trenches from New Market Road to Darbytown Road and Field manned the new works from there to the Charles City Road. Gary again picketed the left with his horsemen.[126]

The Third Battle of Darbytown Road, October 27, 1864

Grant ordered a general advance both north and south of the James River, to commence on October 27.[127] On the north side, Terry's X Corps began heavy skirmishing against Longstreet's line from New Market Road to Charles City Road. Longstreet was unconvinced by the performance of the X Corps and, expecting a turning movement, ordered both Field and Hoke to move to the left behind the works. Field held the left, just beyond the Williamsburg Road, and Gary was sent all the way to the Nine Mile Road. They arrived at the unoccupied works near the Williamsburg Road just in time to foil the flanking movement, resulting in the capture, mainly by Bratton's South Carolinians, of eleven stands of colors and hundreds of prisoners.[128] This was Grant's most ambitious effort to flank Lee's line in 1864 and his worst failure. Longstreet boldly thinned his works to throw most of his available forces to the left. His veterans did not disappoint him when they reached the empty trenches to the north. They quickly routed the XVIII Corps.

The Alabama brigade sustained casualties of one killed, five wounded and two missing during the engagement on the Williamsburg Road, none of them officers. The 4th Alabama was sent to Nine Mile Road with the cavalry, while the other Alabama regiments were positioned on the Williamsburg Road.[129] The brigade was in the thick of the fighting, but the victory was so complete that Field's entire division suffered only 45 casualties.[130]

A Cold December Reconnaissance

After October 27, the Alabamians were not involved in any large-scale action until they were urgently called from their winter quarters in early April. On December 10, in response to Grant's raid on the Weldon Railroad, Field's Division made a demonstration on the north side to hold the Federals there in place.[131]

Field received his orders for the demonstration on the night of December 9.[132] His English volunteer aide carried the word to the headquarters of Field's brigades. Riding in the darkness through the war-torn Virginia landscape, which he described as a vast morass, both Corbin and his horse fell into the slush after the beast tripped over a hidden snag. Arriving at brigade headquarters, Corbin was "savagely growled and scowled at by drowsy brigadiers" who made no effort to conceal their anger at the prospects of a movement in such conditions.[133]

Carrying three days' rations, the Alabamians left snug winter quarters and tramped down the Darbytown Road to New Market Heights. A two-inch snowfall the night before made the march very difficult and it was so cold that one Alabamian claimed the men could not load their rifles with their "benumbed" fingers.[134] Despite the conditions, Perry began preparations for an attack even though the enemy position was strongly entrenched and supported by artillery.[135] Much to the relief of the weary Alabamians, Longstreet ordered his corps back to winter quarters. Although there was no serious fighting during the reconnaissance, Lieutenant Thomas A. Nicoll, Company E, the 44th Alabama, was captured by Federal cavalry near Camp Holly. The Mobile resident was in Old Capital Prison in Washington, D.C. by December 16 and out of the war.[136]

Riding ahead of his division to reconnoiter, Field came under fire from Federal skirmishers. Field, his adjutant and English aide quickly turned their horses and, digging their spurs into their mounts, sped for the safety of their own lines. In spite of the minie balls which whistled near his head, aide-de-camp Corbin likened the day to the parody of the French king who marched up the hill and then marched down again.[137]

Death of a Deserter

The fall of 1864 marked an increase in desertions from Lee's army. This was the last wave of desertion of the war, a swell which continued until Appomattox.[138] The Alabama soldiers were under great pressure to go home by then. While the Alabama citizens who served in the ranks of the Army of Northern Virginia were acutely aware of the advantage their enemy possessed in numbers, resources and position, they regularly received reports of the suffering which their families had to endure back in their home state. Alabama counties north of the Tennessee River had been occupied by Federal forces since April of 1862. After being threatened for months, Mobile fell to a Federal fleet in August 1864.[139]

Shortages of every kind bedeviled the soldiers' families, while the Confederate tax-in-kind and impressment gangs impoverished them. Indigence in Alabama increased each year of the war despite the efforts of the State Legislature to provide money for needy families. During the twelve-month period ending in December 1864, Alabama appropriated eight million dollars for their support.[140] Sherman's grand raid through Georgia interrupted the flow of mail between the troops and their families in Alabama, increasing the soldiers' worry. To a great many Alabamians, desertion seemed less a criminal act than a moral duty. But to their credit, the vast majority stayed in the ranks until the end.

Lee believed the best deterrent to desertion was "a rigid execution of the law," meaning the execution of convicted deserters by firing squad.[141] One soldier of Law's Brigade paid that terrible price for desertion. Henry Howell, a nineteen-year-old farmer from Orion, Alabama was conscripted into Confederate service on June 23, 1864, and was already under arrest for leaving his command by July 20. On October 31, 1864, by order of Colonel Bowles, a firing squad of the 4th Alabama, shot Howell for desertion.[142]

Bowles ordered Sergeant Rufus Hollis, of Company K, to detail a firing squad to execute Howell but Hollis returned to headquarters with only one volunteer. Bowles sent Hollis back to his company with his edict that every soldier would stand to for the execution or suffer punishment. He also assembled a twelve-man detail to fire the fatal shots, though the men did not know who actually killed the condemned man because only half their rifles were loaded.[143]

Howell was delivered to the site of his execution by ambulance, riding atop his own coffin and under guard. He was escorted to a cross set in the ground and ordered to his knees where he was tied to the cross. He did not speak as he watched the officer of the detail load every other rifle with a minie ball while the twelve soldiers assigned to shoot Howell stood with their backs to their weapons. As the firing squad stood at order arms, the officer commanding the detail offered Howell his last chance to speak. Howell said his mother had written that she was wanting food and needed him to come home. "Now, when you get home," he told the assembled regiment, "tell her I tried to come home and lost my life." Howell began to pray. The deadly commands sounded loud and clear, "Attention! Shoulder Arms! Ready! Aim! Fire!" The detail fired its volley and Howell slumped to the side. He was buried in the Virginia piney woods west of the retrenchment and between the Darbytown and Charles City Roads.[144]

Many Alabama soldiers received the kind of letter Howell described and some went home, especially after the summer of 1864 when the cause of the Confederacy seemed a hopeless struggle. Though one historian described these damaging missives as ignorant letters to ignorant men, a note from home that impressment gangs had taken the livestock could have a profound influence on a soldier.[145] These were often men who had fought gallantly for years. Oates later wrote that many Alabamians were faced with the dilemma of conflicting duties that cost Howell his life. Oates added that if desertion was ever excusable, it was in the case of the Confederate soldier.[146] Howell was the only man shot for desertion among the estimated 6,260 who served in the all-Alabama brigade.[147]

The military courts rarely sentenced deserters to death. Often pardons or commutations were granted by army commanders or President Davis to those deserters sentenced to death. In the 4th Alabama two conscripts who had deserted in August 1864 were returned to their regiment under arrest in October, tried and sentenced to three months' hard labor. They had left the regiment after less than one month.[148]

The regiments of Law's Brigade had a history of leniency toward deserters. Muster rolls carried men as "absent without leave" for up to two and a half years without dropping them as deserters.[149] When Lieutenant Robert Crosswell left Company G, 44th Alabama, to care for his "helpless" mother and four sisters after his brother died, both Law and Perry believed he deserted. Although Law suggested Crosswell be brought back for trial no charges were brought against the officer. After moving his family to Mississippi, he returned to duty as a private in the 44th. He believed, and many agreed, that his resignation freed him from prosecution. He was later promoted and commanded Company G when Howell was arrested for desertion.[150]

By 1865 Lee seemed to have given up altogether the idea of punishing deserters. He offered an amnesty to deserters in January which utterly failed to stem the tide of desertion. It is not known whether Lee offered this amnesty from a change of heart or because the previous policy failed.[151] Lowther ordered a court-martial for a teamster of the 15th Alabama on a charge of desertion during Lee's amnesty period. Although the court ordered him shot, Lee reviewed his case and ordered him returned to the regiment. Private F. Pope Rucker may have decided to attempt desertion because of the amnesty. If he had succeeded he would have been safely at home, if not, his life would be saved by Lee's policy.[152] It is not possible to know if the court which heard these cases for Law's Brigade was particularly tough on deserters or whether Bowles made an example of Howell. Until more is learned, Howell's execution remains inexplicable.

Many of Field's deserters who went over to the enemy did so through a new growth of brush where the opposing picket lines were only about half a mile apart. On the Federal side, a cavalryman, armed with a carbine, waited to receive any Confederates who had had enough of the war. Lieutenant McClendon determined to capture the Federal rider. Lowther agreed to the attempt but lectured McClendon on the consequences of failure until the lieutenant almost canceled the plan. The young officer thought it over, finally decided his colonel was too cautious and enlisted three comrades of the 15th Alabama to go with him.

McClendon planned to lead his men in single file, concealing their rifles as much as possible, through the lines until they were close enough to grab the enemy officer. When challenged, McClendon intended to answer, "Don't shoot, we are deserters," so he could approach the cavalryman without drawing fire. As they neared the Federal officer, they received the expected challenge, "Halt and surrender." Just as McClendon replied that they were deserting, one of his companions shouted to the enemy officer, "Surrender yourself," which produced a round from the carbine. The Federal escaped capture and the Alabamians returned safely to their lines. McClendon reported the incident slowed desertion through that sector because the potential deserters feared they would draw fire.[153]

Law Departs the Alabama Brigade

On October 3 Adjutant General Cooper extended Law's leave 10 days.[154] Since this extension was issued by the adjutant general, it is probable that Law was now physically fit for duty, though not prepared to serve in Longstreet's Corps. Law was maneuvering for time while he sought another command. He obtained another twenty-day leave on October 8. This time the adjutant general's office questioned his reason for the request. After some discussion, the acting judge advocate offered a basis for leave acceptable to both the general and the War Department. Law telegraphed from Chester that he would "acquire twenty days on grounds (the Acting Judge Advocate) mentioned."[155]

On October 31 Davis wrote Lee, then at Petersburg, regarding Law, who had requested transfer to the division commanded by Hoke. Law believed Longstreet would treat him unjustly if he again served under the First Corps commander. Lee answered the president two days later with strong support for Longstreet. Lee did not anticipate Law would be treated unfairly by Longstreet and suggested "that Genl Law has nothing to do but his whole duty, & he need fear nothing." Lee was standing solidly behind Longstreet, just as he had when Longstreet wanted a court-martial convened against Law. Probably because he felt it would be good for the service to separate the two generals, Lee gave his approval for the transfer of Law's Brigade, but on condition of agreement of the other officers involved. Lee did not want the decision for a transfer to be Law's alone.[156] Nothing more is known of Law's idea to transfer to Hoke's command. In the meantime, Cooper ordered a ten-day extension of Law's leave while waiting for Davis and Lee to resolve the issue.[157]

Law was frustrated in his unofficial efforts to transfer from Longstreet's Corps. He decided to submit his request by more normal means, though not strictly through proper channels. Addressing his letter to Adjutant General Cooper, Law used two Alabama congressmen, David Clopton and F. S. Lyon, as his emissaries to deliver the letter to Davis.[158]

"I have the honor to ask of the War Department a transfer from my present, to some other command," was how Law opened his letter of November 8, 1864. Law explained his relationship with Longstreet was so bad "as to render it extremely unpleasant—and in my opinion, impossible without a sacrifice of self-respect—for me to serve again under his command." He included the almost obligatory statement that it was in the best interest of the Confederacy for the two of them to be separated. Law wanted an assignment in Wilmington, North Carolina, or in the cavalry in the Department of the Gulf.[159]

Representatives Clopton and Lyon conferred with Law after their meeting with Davis on the morning of November 10. The president suggested that a place could be found for Law if he were an "educated artillerist."[160] Law then wrote another letter, this one addressed to Clopton and Lyon for them to pass along to Davis, which he hoped would convince the president of his qualifications to command an artillery unit. "You will do me a favor by communicating to His Excellency the information that I was educated at the Military Academy of South Carolina," he wrote the Alabama representatives, "and have subsequently given much attention to the subject of artillery as professor in a military academy as well as during the war." Clopton forwarded the letter to Davis the next day, November 11.[161]

The same day Davis referred this second letter to Secretary of War James Seddon, who initiated a search for a position for Law as a brigadier general of artillery somewhere in the Confederacy. Seddon telegraphed Bragg and Major General D. H. Maury on November 17 and Lieutenant General William J. Hardee on November 18 to inquire of their need for such an officer. Bragg and Maury answered promptly that no artillery officer or any other officer of the grade of brigadier was needed in their commands. There is no record of Hardee's response, although he had not answered Seddon by December 2.[162]

Law anticipated a lengthy decision process from the Confederate authorities. He wrote to Cooper on November 11, asking an extension of his leave to await the answer to his request for transfer. He reminded the adjutant general that his "application is now in the hands of the president for consideration." The decision was indeed slow in the making. By November 21 Law had enough of the capital. Writing yet again to Cooper, Law asked permission to await the government's decision regarding his next appointment nearer home, at Columbia, South Carolina.[163] His request was granted.[164]

When Law left Richmond, he left his fate in the hands of others. While he was working with his political contacts in the Confederate government, he controlled events to some degree. He could exert far less influence from South Carolina. It was no coincidence that three days later, on November 24, the regimental commanders of Law's Brigade penned a letter to Cooper expressing their wish that Colonel William F. Perry receive permanent command of the brigade. The brigade officers wrote Seddon they had "been authoritatively informed that Brigadier General E. M. Law will not, in all probability, resume command."

They suggested, as they had in January, Perry's appointment would meet the needs of the brigade and, therefore, benefit the service.[165]

Field forwarded the petition with his approval on November 28, recommending Perry in the strongest terms. But Field realized the brigade already had a brigadier and he attempted to deal with that issue: "Brig Genl Law has been with his brigade only a few days during the present campaign. I heard unofficially that he expresses the determination never to return to it and that he is authorized by the War Dept to await orders at home."[166]

Word that Law had gone to South Carolina reached the brigade quickly, indeed. There was a faction within the brigade promoting Perry's appointment to brigade commander, though Law was probably unaware of it. It is not known whether the rank and file of the brigade believed that Law had forsaken them, as Field suggested. On December 1, Major Osmun Latrobe, Longstreet's adjutant general, forwarded the petition and Field's endorsement without comment. Two days later, Lee forwarded the documents with a strong condemnation of Law. Perhaps in answer to a question from Davis, Lee wrote one sentence: "I do not know the cause of Genl Law's absence & know no reason for its permanency."[167]

Lee did, of course, know of the feud between Law and Longstreet. He had known of it since the spring, and had exchanged letters with Cooper and Davis on the subject, the latest only a month earlier. With his remark to the chief executive, Lee was expressing his belief in "obedience to constituted authority."[168] Law's implacable refusal to serve under Longstreet did not impress the commander of the Army of Northern Virginia. Undoubtedly, it seemed arrogant individualism to Lee. Lee believed Law should accept the realities of the situation and do his duty and wrote as much to Davis in November. Lee gave the president his opinion that Law had nothing to fear from serving under Longstreet, probably because Lee had often proven he could control the rivalries between officers under his command. Had the alienation of Law occurred in Lee's camp, the Virginian may have found a way to reconcile points of view as he had on other occasions.

Whether it was Lee's influence, the petition of the brigade officers, Field's recommendation, or the combination of the three, Law's influence in Richmond was on the wane. It happened quickly. Only six weeks after Davis wrote to Lee on Law's behalf, Cooper directed his assistant adjutant general to send Law an ultimatum. In a letter dated December 15, 1864, Law learned Perry had been recommended for promotion and permanent command of the Alabama brigade. The short note read: "The Adjutant & Inspector General directs me to inform you of the fact, and to say, an officer will be permanently assigned to the brigade unless you return to it without delay."[169]

To return to the brigade meant Law would again serve under Longstreet, now recovered from his wound. This he could not do. His efforts to move his brigade to another command had been frustrated, so Law resigned from command of his Alabama brigade. Writing from Columbia, on December 20, 1864, and addressing his letter to Cooper, he wrote simply, "I have the honor respectfully to be relieved from the command of my brigade in Longstreet's Corps, Army of Northern Virginia." He signed it, "E. M. Law, Brigadier General."[170] Law was now officially separated from the Alabamians, though he had only served with them approximately three weeks since mid-December of the year before.

The War Department made some few inquiries in an effort to place Law in a command where his experience and leadership might be utilized. He, meanwhile, asked to serve in Wilmington, under Whiting. The Mississippian answered Law's letter inquiring of a position within his command with a strong endorsement of Law's ability and fighting prowess, and suggested Law show the letter to Davis.[171] When Whiting learned of the feud between Law and Longstreet earlier in the year, he recommended Law to Beauregard in glowing terms. "Try and get Law into your command. He was of the Fourth Alabama, and succeeded to command of my old Third Brigade; a most capital officer, and one of the best men in battle I ever saw. He is from South Carolina, and now with Longstreet, but in difficulty with him and wants to come to me."[172]

The president, never willing to lose an experienced combat officer, gave Lee another opportunity to keep Law in his army. In reply, Lee wrote that Law must have left the Army of Northern Virginia "upon his own application as it was not upon mine or through me." Lee dispensed with Law once and for all with a note to Davis: "I know of no objection to his being ordered to Wilmington."[173]

Special Orders, Number 5, from the Adjutant and Inspector General's Office, dated January 7, 1865, officially ended Law's affiliation with the Alabama brigade: "Brig. Gen. E. M. Law, Provisional Army, C.S., is hereby relieved from duty with the Army of Northern Virginia."[174] Mims Walker and John Cussons, his two aids and confidants, were also transferred. Law's exit paved the way for Perry's promotion to brigadier. That was accomplished February 21, 1865 with Perry's confirmation by Congress.[175] Law's Brigade officially became Perry's Brigade.

On January 13, 1865, Law accepted the position of commandant of prisons east of the Savannah River, although he did not serve in that capacity. Records indicate he may have accepted prematurely a post which was not actually available.[176] Or, it may be Law had the chance at a better appointment on January 17, when Lieutenant General Wade Hampton recommended him for promotion to major general and assignment to his cavalry.[177] The well-respected Hampton was a rarity in the Confederate service, being one of only a handful of officers without a military education who advanced beyond brigadier.

A proven infantry commander of unquestioned bravery was lost to Lee's army because of a purely personal conflict with his commanding officer. Law was an officer of good record and good reputation, never charged with any dishonorable conduct before the enemy, yet he served but a few days with his brigade from December 17, 1863, until his resignation on December 20, 1864.[178] True, Law was recuperating from the head wound received at Cold Harbor part of the time, but there can be no doubt that he was out of active service the greatest portion of that period because of his hatred of James Longstreet.

Who should bear the greatest blame for this unfortunate situation? Law clearly felt betrayed when command of Hood's Division was denied him in favor of Micah Jenkins. Longstreet just as clearly based his decision on his personal preference for Jenkins rather than on military reasons, although he was correct on technical grounds. The great failure in this affair was the inability of the Confederate high command to exert its authority in the case. President Davis refused to appoint either Law or Jenkins to permanent command of Hood's Division, permitting the bitter rivalry between the brigadiers to grow until it destroyed the fighting ability of that storied division. Nor did he insist that Longstreet transfer either or both of the quarreling generals, though he probably suggested that course to Longstreet. Had the War Department promptly issued orders for the appointment of either man, the bitter struggle for division command would have ended.

Richmond's failure to act left Longstreet to deal with the ambitious South Carolinians. His response was purely personal as he took an active role as participant in the conflict. Longstreet's actions toward Law were so obviously personal they earned him a strong rebuke from Richmond. Had the War Department instead promoted and assigned Law to the division, Longstreet would have had far less latitude for personal animosity without a frank display of insubordination. Alternatively, had the Richmond authorities favored Longstreet with his choice, Law would have been silenced.

Law had powerful friends in Richmond. But Lee's influence in the government was so great that the Richmond authorities, including Davis, usually acquiesced to his wishes.

When it came to a showdown between Law and Longstreet, Lee supported Longstreet. But Lee did not harbor a grudge against Law. He did not transfer Law from the Army of Northern Virginia as he often did when he found fault with an officer.[179] Lee ceased his criticism of Law after Seddon explained the facts in the argument between Law and Longstreet. In addition, Lee clearly stated to the president that Law left the army on his own hook and not from any word or deed by the commanding general.

With the clear vision of hindsight it is obvious that Law would have been better served using the good offices at army headquarters rather than those at Richmond. Had Law been in command of his brigade after recovering from his eye wound and serving in Lee's command, there was a good chance he would have been promoted to division command, though not necessarily Hood's Division. After three years of grim attrition among its general officers the Army of Northern Virginia suffered a severe shortage of proven leaders. Lee would not have wasted an officer of Law's proven ability had Law been available to him. If not in command of a division, Law would have been no worse off in the late summer and fall than he was while leading his brigade at Cold Harbor. Law respected Lee and could have continued to serve in his command. In post-war writings Law praised Lee and even defended his assault of Malvern Hill.[180] Had Law stayed on duty in Lee's army, Longstreet would have then been criticizing an officer who had served Lee well, something Lee would not tolerate. But Law no doubt felt Lee had taken Longstreet's side in the affair and chose to argue his case before the Richmond authorities.

Law was a proud man. He believed it was an insult to his personal bravery and, more importantly, an insult to his reputation in the army when Longstreet brought in an outsider to command Hood's Division. He could not forget that. He obviously believed Lee would support Longstreet against him after the corps commander returned to duty. Law knew what was due an honorable man and he felt he had not received his due.

A Question of Arming Slaves

During the last months of the war, as misfortune after misfortune befell the Confederacy, many in the South feared for the cause. As a means to refill the dwindling ranks of the army and perhaps gain recognition from European powers, the question of whether to follow the Union lead of arming Negroes was much discussed among the leadership, including Davis, Lee and his officers and men.[181]

Before it was a national issue, putting slaves in the field was discussed in Alabama. Perhaps because their state had suffered partial occupation, Alabamians came early to this debate. On September 2, 1863, the Montgomery *Weekly Mail* endorsed arming slaves, though its editor did not suggest emancipation for the Negroes who fought for the Confederacy. The paper made its recommendation while reporting the Alabama House debate on the matter. Opponents of the proposition feared such an act would result in "practical equalization of the races." The editor of the Montgomery newspaper countered that the South faced an emergency and if the Confederacy did not use Negroes, the Federal army would use them to subdue her.

The Alabama legislature sent the president, the secretary of war and the Alabama representatives to the Confederate Congress each a copy of a joint resolution on modifying the exemption law. This resolution also recommended drafting Negroes for service in the Confederate army.[182]

A generation after the war, Oates recounted his trip to Richmond in February 1863, to convince members of Congress of the efficacy of using slaves as soldiers. He was convinced that Confederate troops would soon be fighting Negroes in Federal blue. Oates remembered freedom for the slave was the point of contention. Members of the Confederate Congress, whom he referred to as the incapables, argued that slaves would desert to the Union at the first opportunity. Oates agreed and declared the slave must be given his freedom and 80 acres of public land. He was sure no slave would fight to continue in bondage.[183]

The issue of arming slaves was also debated among the rank and file of the Confederate army. The proposition had been argued in Field's Division since the summer of 1864. Among its officers the idea seemed a disagreeable but unavoidable last resort if national independence was to be achieved. Writing to his mother in England, Corbin insisted that independence was the sole reason for the conflict. "If we could maintain it with the maintenance of our servile institution," he wrote in December, "t'would be better for the whites as well as for the blacks, but if not, let us sacrifice even that on the altar of our country." To the Englishman, even immediate independence for the South would not alter the fact that "the life of our peculiar institution would be a very precarious one."[184]

To defuse arguments that the Confederate rank and file would quit the army if armed slaves entered the conflict, Secretary of State Judah P. Benjamin asked Lee to poll his troops for their opinion.[185] The division commanders of the First Corps received a note from Longstreet's headquarters asking their views on putting Negroes in the ranks. The request noted the slaves would be given their freedom.[186] One response received at Lee's headquarters, also printed in the Richmond *Enquirer* on February 21, 1865, was written by Lowther of the 15th Alabama. Lowther suggested Congress was "tender-footed" but his regiment favored political independence at any price. Of 200 men present for duty in the 15th Regiment, 143 supported the plan. By Lowther's count, 88 of these soldiers were willing to take Negroes into the ranks with them. Lowther added that the 4th and 44th regiments also shared the sentiments of the 15th. He did not speak for the 47th and 48th Alabama regiments. The petition suggested the government arm 200,000 Negroes to counter the "determination of the Federal government to finally subjugate us, confiscate our lands and property, (and) free our slaves." The editor of the *Enquirer* declared the 15th Alabama was a regiment in earnest about independence. By the time the Confederate Congress acted on the matter, however, it was too late to get slaves into the army even if the Negroes wanted to fight for the Confederacy, which was by no means assured.

Several Alabamians were ready to serve as officers in the newly formed Negro regiments should they become active. Longstreet wrote to Lee's Headquarters with the recommendation that Privates Young M. Edwards and Joseph J. Dean of Company E, 15th Alabama, and a member of the 4th Alabama be appointed commissioned officers in the Negro organizations. Longstreet offered their names as a reward after they captured a deserter from the brigade who attempted to go over to the enemy. The deserter was tried and sentenced to be shot on March 31, the day after Longstreet's letter. Longstreet hoped to reduce desertion and suggested "it advisable to encourage such conduct as the above by every means in our power."[187]

"My God, General, ain't they never going to pay us any more money?"

Law's Alabamians were less occupied with affairs of state than with rations during this period of the war. In an effort to curb complaints about short bread rations, Field's Division established a bakery in Richmond. The plan proved a failure, as the ration from the bakery was three fourths of a loaf, less than the six biscuits which the men could provide themselves if given flour.[188] Although admitting there was serious complaint in the division, its inspector found no fault with the bakery. "I cannot find that there is any neglect on the part of the commissaries," he reported to Field, "who so far as I can ascertain, issue to the troops all the rations to which they are entitled under existing orders." He admitted, however, that he had no time to inspect the division during the last 30 days.[189]

The officers in the Alabama brigade decided there must be pilferage at the bakery and detailed two men to investigate. Billy Jordan and another man were sent to learn the truth. They found the bakery filled with Negro women who had to be driven out with the bayonet. Jordan told Bart Reneau, who served as the baker, that he would have to be reported for his neglect. Jordan left his comrade to guard the bakery and escorted a wagonload of bread back to the brigade. The loaves were tossed into the wagon without any wrapping or covering. As he neared brigade headquarters, Jordan was met by two officers in beautiful uniforms who were determined to have a loaf of bread. When Jordan resisted, they pulled rank but he was undaunted, telling them he would shoot one and bayonet the other if they persisted. The officers called on Major William H. Scruggs, of the brigade staff, who ordered Jordan to give each officer a loaf. Jordan did as ordered but he threatened Scruggs that if each man in the brigade did not receive his fair share, he would report Scruggs for the shortage. In this way, Jordan brought back to the brigade one and a half loaves per man.[190]

Insufficient bread rations plagued Law's Brigade throughout the last, dismal months of the war. From October 1864 until the brigade began the move toward Appomattox Court House, the Alabamians had too little bread. Sometimes, cornmeal was substituted for flour. Although rations of peas, rice, potatoes and turnips were often issued in full, bread shortages caused almost constant complaint from the troops.[191]

Despite light rations, the Alabamians did almost constant duty in the trenches, serving on picket every other night.[192] At the same time, the soldiers were deficient in clothing, shoes and blankets. In September, Law's Brigade was destitute of shoes and pants. October brought a supply of shoes but by the end of January resupply had rendered the Alabama brigade only "deficient in pants and jackets." Blankets were never in adequate number during the last winter.[193] Although Field's Division received more clothing in January than any month since the previous July and a large supply of clothing every month since October, it was not enough. On January 31, the quartermaster of the division explained the short fall by asserting the soldiers' arduous duties of "storming works and building fortifications" during the fourth quarter of 1864 made it impossible for supply to keep up with need.[194]

After November, soap was nearly unattainable. There was none in December and only four days' ration of soap was issued Field's Division in January. Living in trenches, wearing rags for uniforms, going weeks without an adequate supply of soap, it is little wonder that "camp itch" was common in the brigade.[195]

Military discipline in the brigade became lax. Besieged and living in trenches, drill was ignored. The heavy loss in the officer ranks led to looseness in discipline. The officers neglected regimental records and company books or, perhaps because they were new to the job, did not understand how to complete them.

By January 1865 there was considerable unrest in the brigade, caused by at least two factors. First, the Alabamians had not been paid in six months.[196] The Subsistence Department had been unable to supply the necessities. Because they had not been paid the men could not buy tobacco, soap or other items from the local sutlers. This neglect by the Confederate authorities created great unrest in the brigade. The payroll may have been held back because the government realized many more would desert if they had all their back pay with which to subsist until they reached their homes. On one occasion, their embarrassment caused several Alabamians to gather around a wagon full of sweet potatoes, unable to buy any of the produce. Perry, by then a general, rode up to find the cold men looking longingly at the tubers. Bryant Skipper, a boy only 17 years old when the war ended, implored of Perry, "My God, General, ain't they never going to pay us any more money?" Perry gave Skipper five dollars which bought the young man two sweet potatoes.[197]

The second cause of the unrest in the brigade was the perception of preferential treatment for its officers. They were given leave, which the privates and non-commissioned officers rarely received. Furloughs were frequently extended on some pretext. All too often, officers simply failed to return. When the new year of 1865 began Law's Brigade had more officers absent on leave than present in its regiments.[198] This was probably the situation throughout most of the army. The case of Elisha Mayo gives an indication of the deteriorating morale in the ranks and the army's course of action to correct the problem. When Mayo, after an extended absence without leave, submitted his resignation the army high command decided to take punitive action against him.

Mayo's "immediate and unconditional" resignation, dated February 17, 1865, was received the latter part of February. Captain John Ham, commanding the 47th Alabama, endorsed Mayo's resignation and forwarded it to brigade headquarters where Perry also endorsed it. But the First Corps headquarters decided to make an example of Mayo. His resignation was disapproved and forwarded to Lee's headquarters with the recommendation that "this officer should be arrested and returned, much of the dissatisfaction among the men is owing to the conduct of this kind on the part of the officers." Lee concurred. His office endorsed the recommendation and forwarded the resignation to the secretary of war with this added endorsement: "It is recommended that the name of this officer be dropped from the rolls and the Bureau of Conscript be instructed to enroll him as a conscript and assign him to some command in the army. Such an example is much needed." The War Department acted promptly. On March 7, Mayo was dropped from the officer rolls. Instructions were issued to the general commanding the reserve forces in Alabama to arrest him and send him to his regiment in Virginia as a conscript. Before the order could be carried out the war was over. Mayo remained in Alabama and was paroled June 7, 1865.[199]

Law Serves in the Cavalry

After Wade Hampton asked for Law to serve in his cavalry, Law went to South Carolina in January 1865. When Law reached South Carolina, he found the command structure in that theater very confused. Hampton arrived in South Carolina on January 28, assuming command of the cavalry division of Major General Matthew Calbraith Butler on February 7. On February 11, General Beauregard arrived in Columbia, and put Hampton in command of the Confederate troops in the surrounding area.[200] Despite his incredible exploits in the service of the Confederacy, including three wounds and having sixteen horses shot from under him, Major General Joseph Wheeler arrived from Georgia with a tarnished reputation. Beauregard wrote Lee on February 12 that Wheeler could not control such a large cavalry force, and recommended Hampton to the command. Lee agreed to the request, and Hampton was given control of all cavalry forces in South Carolina. [201]

The War Department issued orders on February 16 for Law to return to duty and report to Bragg in Wilmington, North Carolina, for orders.[202] By February 16, Law was already in Columbia, South Carolina. When he arrived in Columbia is not known and by what orders he was in Columbia is unknown. Neither is it known who Law's commanding officer was before February 16. It is known that Law was in the South Carolina capital doing his bit to oppose Sherman's advance. Columbia was filled with old men, women, children and refugees fleeing from the Federal army as it approached the city. Law dispatched scouts to report the progress of the Federals.[203] On February 15, the city was placed under martial law. Law, acting as provost marshal, was responsible for maintaining order. Southern novelist and poet, William Gilmore Simms, was in Columbia at the time and left a record of the events he witnessed. He remembered Law, "with characteristic energy, (the officer) executed his trusts and was employed day and night in the maintenance of order. This, with some few exceptions, was surprisingly maintained."[204]

On the morning of February 16, Sherman's left wing arrived at Columbia. Some of those who did not flee the advance of Sherman's army turned to looting. Among those attempting to quell the anarchy was the Assistant Professor of Mathematics and French at the Arsenal and an 1861 graduate of the Citadel, Second Lieutenant Robert Oswald Sams. Sams remembered Law called in the various detachments to perform the impossible task of stopping the looters. The cadets were lined up in front of City Hall, where Law located his headquarters. Law's military bearing impressed Sams who thought the general's "every movement showed his efficiency." By afternoon, "The street was packed with marauders, some drunk, the rest of them on horseback and loaded with booty taken from stores and residences that had been broken into. Quite a number were drunk and restless."[205]

The mounted renegades spurred their horses into the line of cadets, forcing their commander to issue the order to "Charge Bayonets" to preserve their line and protect themselves. The rioters persisted and Law was called out of his headquarters. Law took immediate control of the situation. "Opening a way through (the) ranks, his wounded arm in a sling, he went at once to the ring leader of the rabble, seized him by the shoulder, pulled him from his horse, called for a file of cadets and placed him in jail." Sams asserted Law's heroic action took the heart out of the band of "thieves and cutthroats."[206]

The Federal army was just across the Congaree River, its artillery already shelling the city. Beauregard had written on February 15 that Sherman's army was investing the capital.[207] After daylight on February 16, Hampton ordered Wheeler to withdraw his command from the eastern bank of the Congaree and retreat toward Winnsboro. He also sent a courier to Butler at Granby, five miles south of Columbia, with a message to join Wheeler. Hampton ordered Butler to destroy the Charlotte and South Carolina Railroad on his way to link up with Wheeler.[208] Beauregard informed the mayor of Columbia that all Confederate troops were to leave the city by daylight on February 17.[209] During the night of February 16, the governor, a long train of state officials and the military under Beauregard's command began to evacuate.[210]

Law wrote a short letter on February 16 in which he remarked that the "enemy is in front of Columbia. Hope to hold it."[211] That was not possible with the small number of Confederates who faced the army of Sherman. Four Federal corps invested Columbia.[212] Few people remained in the capital the next day. That night, the greater part of Columbia was burned.[213]

During the month of March, Law was occupied with retreating before Sherman, still entertaining hope of commanding an infantry division. Writing from "Headquarters, Butler's division," because headquarters was truly in the saddle, with instructions to a new member of his staff on how to find his command, Law wrote that he was temporarily commanding Butler's troops until Butler could recover from illness. "It was the intention of those in authority to give me an infantry division. I haven't taken the trouble to inquire after the matter recently and don't know how it progresses." Whether Law was still in contact with political allies in Richmond or was relying on promises made before he transferred to the Carolinas is not known.[214]

Law was issued new orders on March 4, 1865, which made official what was already fact. On that date, the adjutant and inspector general's office revoked its order assigning Law to Bragg's command and assigned him to Hampton's cavalry.[215] Law commanded a small number of poorly equipped troopers who could do little to stop the march of the Federal army through the Carolinas. Scouting the roads east of Bentonville, North Carolina, on March 20, Law encountered Federal infantry and artillery in numbers too strong for him to attack. He wrote frankly of his circumstances and asked for help. "A few regiments of infantry would check his advance, I think, very materially," wrote Law to Hampton's headquarters. "Our cavalry," he continued, "is too weak to accomplish much."[216]

After Hampton achieved command of the cavalry in the department and Law was in that command, he again recommended Law for promotion to major general to replace Butler who was absent sick. Butler, another South Carolinian, lost his right foot at Brandy Station in 1863 but continued to serve. General Joseph E. Johnston heartily recommended to Lee that he follow Hampton's suggestion and promote Law to major general.[217]

Law surrendered with Joseph Johnston's army on April 25, 1865, at Greensboro, North Carolina.[218] Apparently at a loss about what to do next, Law was at Salisbury until at least April 28. Hampton wrote to Law on that date, telling him to go home to Yorkville.

Personnel Changes Before the Spring Campaign

A number of personnel changes occurred in the officer ranks of Perry's Brigade the last week of January 1865. Six promotions were processed. Willis W. Walls, former drummer, fifer and chief musician of the 47th Alabama, was promoted to captain of Company G. Walls was always present in the regiment and first served as an officer at Gettysburg. He was rewarded for faithful service by being appointed captain in November 1864, his commission being confirmed January 25, 1865. James M. Hill had made a very favorable impression on the examining board which reviewed his application for first lieutenant of Company B, 44th Alabama. His moral character and qualities as a soldier were noted as "Good." He was judged as "Very Good" in his knowledge of tactics. Two more personnel actions were processed on March 3 when Lemuel H. Dawson and Robert Lapsley were promoted to brigade quartermasters. The last promotion in Perry's Brigade occurred on March 18 when William H. Galloway was elected junior second lieutenant of Company C, 47th Alabama.[219]

During the same period six separations occurred. Captain Joab Goodson, Company B, 44th Alabama, who had written so vividly of the charges at Chickamauga, died of disease at Richmond.[220] Two officers were dropped from the rolls for prolonged absence. Two resigned as a result of wounds sustained at the Wilderness on May 6, 1864.

There were a number of desertions in the ranks as privates decided the cause was lost. Most were like Private Carter Walls, musician of the 47th Alabama. They were good men whose fighting spirit had simply been worn down. Until his decision to desert, Walls was always present in the regiment and never given the luxury of a furlough. On March 8, Walls went over to the Federals, taking him out of the war. Walls took the Oath of Allegiance March 10 and was sent to Springfield, Illinois.[221]

In the early spring of 1865 the 48th Alabama had a number of men "laying out" in north Alabama. Perry needed these men back to fill out his badly thinned ranks. He also believed a second field officer was needed to command the regiment while Wiggenton was absent if discipline and morale were to be sustained. Perry's solution was to promote Wiggenton to lieutenant colonel and find a suitable candidate for the post of major. The solution seemed simple enough, but its implementation was complicated. Perry's application clearly explains the situation:

> "*Application is respectfully made for the appointment of Major J. W. Wiggenton, 48th Reg't Ala Vols. to the Lieut. Coloncy. Maj. Wiggenton is the only field officer with the regiment or likely to be with it. The resignation of Col. Sheffield was accepted on the 30th day of May 1864. Lieut. Col. Hardwick, while at home on furlough of disability was captured by the enemy on the 7th June last. Having been first promoted to a field officer for gallantry there can no question as to his promotion to the colonelcy on his return.*
>
> *My reasons for hoping that in this case the circumstances will justify a departure from established usage in reference to two promotions is two fold. 1st, the interest of the regiment would in my opinion be materially advanced by making Capt. Thos. L. Christian one of its field officers and this cannot be done unless Maj Wiggenton is first promoted. 2nd, The peculiar circumstances of this regiment at present make it highly important that there be two field officers with it. Having been raised in northern counties of the state about two hundred of its men who have gotten home have joined the various cavalry commands there, instead of returning to Virginia. Much of these men can be brought back if an energetic officer were sent after them clothed with authority to take them wherever found. Maj. Wiggenton is the only officer with the regiment that I regard as suitable to be sent on such a duty and, he being now the only field officer cannot be spared from the regiment.*"[222]

Perry's application was dated January 11, 1865. It was still not acted on until April 2, 1865, when Grant began his final campaign against the Army of Northern Virginia.

Chapter 17

Appomattox and Home

Richmond Is Abandoned

In late March 1865 President Abraham Lincoln left Washington and traveled to City Point, VA, to meet with his generals to ensure that his army was prepared to open the spring campaign against Richmond. He found that Grant's plan was simple: take the offensive on March 29 by initiating a turning movement around the Confederate right. The maneuver would serve a two-fold purpose. First, by turning Lee's right, Grant believed the Army of Northern Virginia would be forced to abandon the Petersburg defenses, and second, the infantry would be able to support a cavalry thrust aimed at destroying the Southside and Danville Railroad.[1] Lincoln left the meeting confident that the fall of Richmond was near. However, heavy rains on March 29–30 rendered the roads impassable, delaying the Federal move. When the weather cleared on March 31, Grant launched his offensive by sending a large cavalry and infantry force toward Dinwiddie Court House on the Confederate right flank. The Federal cavalry was driving on Five Forks when Lee dispatched Pickett's infantry and cavalry commanded by Fitz Lee to counter the Federal offensive. Pickett enjoyed early success by initially driving the Federal troopers back on Dinwiddie. But before the day was over Pickett had been forced to fall back, and with Federal infantry arriving in force by nightfall on April 1, Pickett's detachment was overwhelmed and routed. In the evening of April 1, Lee urgently ordered Longstreet to come to the Southside and bring Field's Division with him.[2] All tents and other equipment were left standing in line. Initially, two brigades were to go by rail and three by road. The corps quartermaster hastily arranged for transportation while Field's brigades crossed the James River below Richmond by pontoon bridge and marched on to the railroad station.[3] If the troops had marched to Petersburg, they would not have been in time to be of any value to Lee nor would they have been in fighting condition. A flurry of messages were sent between Lee's headquarters and the chief quartermaster of the First Corps before it was decided the other three brigades must travel by rail.[4]

Federal artillery began a massive bombardment of Petersburg about 9 p.m.[5] As Field's Division rode through the night, thunder from hundreds of guns rolled across the countryside. Flashes from the gun muzzles played around the smoke from the burning powder like lightning in a summer thunderstorm. Musketry opened along the picket lines at 1:45 a.m. on April 2.[6] The Texas brigade and Perry's Brigade followed Benning and Bratton by five hours and had not detrained before the Confederate line below Petersburg was breached.[7] The Alabamians were still on the march when, at 4:45 a.m., Grant launched the assault that broke the Confederate line.

The nine-month siege of Petersburg was over, and Lee's army was powerless to save either the besieged city or Richmond. Shortly after 10:30 on the morning of April 2, Lee informed Davis he would try to hold his position until night, but there was no certainty that could be accomplished. He planned to withdraw north of the Appomattox River and concentrate near the Richmond and Danville Railroad.[8]

Perry's Brigade arrived at the shattered line amid a scene of confusion. Federal skirmishers were so close to the lines that their shouts could be clearly heard.[9] The Alabamians entered the works just east of Indian Town Creek, a small tributary of the Appomattox. The works were due west of Petersburg and crossed the Boydton Plank Road.[10] At 7 p.m., Lee sent Davis his final message before leaving the Petersburg lines. Lee informed the president that troops from the Petersburg and Richmond defenses were being withdrawn. The president and citizens of Richmond were left to their own devices.

Successfully extricating itself from the lines would not be an easy task for the Army of Northern Virginia. Lee's engineers had little time to solve the logistics of moving the army with its full complement of wagons and artillery. The infantry and wagons had to travel over the same roads. The route of each corps was carefully worked out and orders issued. The withdrawal was ordered to begin at 8 p.m. with the artillery leaving first, followed by the infantry. Finally, the pickets were to follow at 3 a.m. on the morning of April 3.[11]

Lee's intent was to join Johnston's army in North Carolina. To do that the army would follow the Richmond and Danville Railroad to its terminus in Danville and then move into North Carolina. But first there was the issue of supplies. The men were leaving the lines with meager rations, with only a few having sufficient food for perhaps two days. Most had much less or none at all. Lee's first objective was Amelia Court House, a stop on the Danville railroad.[12] Rations and ammunition would be waiting there when the army arrived. With a day's head start on Grant, Lee felt he had sufficient time to resupply the army and still stay in front of the pursuing Federals.

Longstreet led three divisions—those of Field, Heth and Wilcox—on the retreat from Petersburg. A. P. Hill was dead and the skeletons of his once-proud divisions were placed under Longstreet's command.[13] Heth and Wilcox were pretty well used up after two days of fighting.[14] Field's Division was the largest in Lee's army and still retained the discipline exhibited in the Wilderness a year before.[15] Field's Division moved out of the works on Indian Town Creek in perfect military order and probably crossed the Appomattox at the Battersea Factory.[16] After crossing to the north side of the river, the column turned west toward Amelia Court House. Major General John B. Gordon's Second Corps withdrew across the Pocahontas and railroad bridges. Both corps took the Hickory Road, which divided a short distance northwest of Petersburg and recombined near Ferguson. Longstreet followed the left fork, known as the Appomattox or River Road.[17]

The Alabamians carried few provisions, some rations having been distributed in the days before leaving the trenches at Richmond.[18] The need for their services at Petersburg had been so urgent that little, if any, rations were brought with them. But Perry's Alabamians probably thought little of this as they left Petersburg. They were confident that "Marse Robert" would see to their provisions along the way.

Longstreet's column marched throughout the night of April 2.[19] Travel over muddy roads resulting from three days of heavy rains was exasperatingly slow.[20] All the army guns and more than 1,000 wagons jammed the too few roads needed to handle the large volume of traffic. Troops went through an endless cycle of stop and start.[21] Even with the slow pace, stragglers immediately appeared. A winter of poor rations had extracted a toll on the men's stamina. Men who were once able to march 25 miles a day found their strength gone. A brief rest was ordered near Clarence's Store. Those fortunate enough to have rations ate along the roadside while Lee and Longstreet dined at nearby Clover Hill.[22] For the others there was little cause to worry, for by now it was common knowledge that trains were bringing provisions to Amelia Court House, a day's march ahead. The column then moved on toward Bevill's Bridge, finding the approaches to the bridge under water and impassable. Longstreet turned toward Goode's Bridge, farther upstream, reaching it near sundown.[23] The remnants of the Army of Northern Virginia made camp the night of April 3–4 on the north side of the Appomattox. Perry's Alabamians crossed the river that night to watch for Federal cavalry, and early on April 4 the column resumed the march toward Amelia Court House.[24]

All Are Not with Us

When Perry's Brigade departed, many of its Alabamians were left behind. Those on detached service sought the best means of escape. The sick from the brigade were confined in hospitals around Richmond. Stragglers soon appeared.

Three of Perry's officers who were confined to hospitals in and around Richmond fell into Federal hands. First Lieutenant John F. Tweedell, Company C, 44th Alabama, was captured April 3, 1865. He had been absent over a year after being wounded severely in the right thigh at the Battle of Chickamauga. Tweedell was released on his Oath of Allegiance June 20 at Washington, D.C.[25]

Simeon W. Melton, junior second lieutenant, Company B, 47th Alabama, was a thirty–six year old who had been in and out of several hospitals during 1864 and the first months of 1865. He was captured at Howard's Grove Hospital. Melton was paroled April 23, one of the first prisoners released after the surrender.[26]

Twenty-seven-year-old Captain James H. Brown, Company F, 4th Alabama, was made a prisoner at Jackson's Hospital and transferred to Libby prison. His stay in Federal hands was also relatively short. After being turned over to the provost marshal Brown, a mechanic from Huntsville, Alabama, was paroled April 23, 1865.[27]

Most of the 51 companies of Perry's Brigade were well below one third their normal strength. Company K of the 4th Alabama had left Larkinsville four years earlier 80 strong. Its captain, Henry Lindsay, was the regiment's first officer to die in combat. When it left Petersburg, Company K was no more than 10 strong.[28] Company K, the 44th Alabama, counted eleven privates, two corporals, two sergeants and two officers present at the surrender. Typical of the soldiers in this regiment, Corporal Salathiel Clements had joined ahead of the conscript act, only two months after his eighteenth birthday. His survival owed no small debt to sickness and injury. He missed the fighting at Sharpsburg because of illness and the fighting at Chickamauga due to a wound received at Gettysburg. These battles resulted in heavy losses to his regiment. Although he waited until the draft, he served three years without a furlough, until the collapse of the Confederacy.[29] The soldiers left in the brigade by April 1865 had seen their ranks decimated by attrition and desertion but had stayed until the bitter end. These were the men who were present day after day throughout the war, doing their duty without fanfare or recognition.

In Richmond thirty-one-year-old Captain James Jones, 4th Alabama, feared for the safety of his wife and small child. Jones was in the capital on detached service with the adjutant general's office, where his primary duties were examining court-martial cases.[30] In the early morning hours of April 3 he desperately sought passage out of Richmond. By sheer luck, Jones managed to secure places for himself and his family in a boxcar that was part of a train used to transport government records. Occupants in the boxcar read like a who's who in the Confederate government. Some of the president's cabinet, including

Secretary of State Judah P. Benjamin and Postmaster General John H. Reagan were among the passengers.[31]

Pinckney Bowles joined the president's train at Danville. While on leave in Alabama, Bowles had left his sword, silver spurs and other personal items in the 4th Alabama's quartermaster wagon. During his absence the wagon was captured by Federal cavalry. As the train rolled south Secretary of War John C. Breckinridge issued Bowles a commission with orders assigning him to Lieutenant General Alexander P. Stewart's Corps. At that stage of the war Bowles was not sure how the Federals would treat a captured Confederate general. Expecting to be captured, Bowles destroyed the appointment.[32] Bowles did not join Stewart but traveled on to Alabama where he resumed the life of a lawyer at Sparta.

When Perry's Brigade withdrew from Richmond, Privates Billy Jordan and James F. Hartsfield of the 15th Alabama, were on detached service guarding the plantation of Mrs. Christian, an aunt of Captain Thomas Christian, the brigade's assistant adjutant general. The plantation was northeast of Richmond on the Chickahominy River. Perry's Brigade, which Jordan returned to several times a week for supplies and mail, was about six miles to the south. Jordan returned to the regiment on April 2 and found the lines deserted. He hurried back to the plantation without learning why the 15th Alabama had moved. In the evening a courier rode by with news that Richmond was to be evacuated. The boom of siege guns from the direction of Richmond convinced Jordan that he and Hartsfield were cut off from the army. Jordan was determined that the pair would not to be captured and plotted a course around the Federal army. He correctly believed that Lee would fall back on Danville and then try to join Johnston's army in North Carolina. Grant, Jordan realized, enjoyed superiority in numbers and fielded a better fed army than the Confederates. As he considered the situation Jordan had some doubt about Lee's ability to make it to North Carolina. Jordan was fairly confident, however, that Lee would succeed in getting the army to Danville. With provisions and a Confederate fifty dollar bill supplied by Mrs. Christian, Jordan and Hartsfield set out on April 3 to find the army.[33]

The Road West

Longstreet's First Corps passed Amelia Court House the night of April 4.[34] Perry's Alabamians reached the courthouse April 4 with the anticipation that rations were waiting there, but found none. Orders had been issued to bring provisions up from Danville but the trains had been unable to get through. The entire army was greatly demoralized. Lee had no choice but to send foragers out into the countryside seeking food. After a futile search, the foragers returned with empty wagons. In the meantime Federal cavalry continued to menace the column, threatening its flanks. Longstreet placed his infantry and artillery in position to guard against a surprise attack, but the cavalry chose to keep a safe distance.[35] Twenty-four hours after the army made camp around the courthouse, Lee put it in motion again.[36] Longstreet was still in the lead, following the railroad toward Danville. The delay to forage proved fatal.

Grant pushed his men hard and by April 5 was in position to block Lee's retreat. The one day lead that Lee enjoyed on April 3 had vanished. At Jetersville, Lee discovered Federal cavalry in force across his path. In addition, Federal infantry moving up from Burkeville cut Lee's communications with the Danville and Richmond Railroad, which he relied on for his subsistence. Rain fell throughout the morning of April 5, adding to the misery of the Confederates.[37] Once again the army prepared to engage the Federals but the Federal cavalry commander decided the Confederate position was too strong to bring on a general engagement. However, skirmishers from both sides exchanged shots throughout the afternoon.[38]

Lee was forced to change his plans.[39] A store of supplies at Lynchburg could be brought forward to Farmville, and from there he would be able to regroup and then make his escape to North Carolina. The Army of Northern Virginia turned west toward Farmville. Lee knew his only chance to elude Grant was to regain the day he had lost at Amelia Court House. The day's delay could only be regained by a night march.[40] The army's poor condition meant the night march would be a grueling experience. Nevertheless, Longstreet put his column in motion shortly after dark, traveling along the Amelia Springs and Jetersville Road.[41]

At Sayler's Creek the road to Farmville forked. One road led to High Bridge, spanning the Appomattox, the other to Rice's Station and then Farmville. Lee learned from a cavalry reconnaissance that Federals were at Rice's Station, threatening his flank. Longstreet was sent to check this force while the rest of the army moved forward on the High Bridge Road.[42]

Longstreet's men arrived a few hours ahead of the Federal infantry. Field's Division was deployed across the enemy's path and skirmishers thrown out. Construction of crude breastworks and rifle pits was hurriedly undertaken. The Confederates were still entrenching when two brigades of the First Division, XXIV Army Corps began filing into position about mid-afternoon. They advanced, driving in Field's skirmishers.[43] Longstreet sent the skirmish line back to its original position with orders to hold. Longstreet remained in front of the Federals during the afternoon of April 6, both sides content to watch each other while the Federals brought up reinforcements.[44] Longstreet's line eventually faced two divisions.[45] Federal and Confederate skirmishers were active while the Federal infantry was leisurely reinforced. Darkness settled over the field before the Federal line was ready to offer battle.[46] During the night Longstreet quietly withdrew and marched toward Farmville where it was believed rations were waiting.[47] Fitzhugh Lee's cavalry covered the rear of the First Corps.

Longstreet's column immediately ran into trouble. Marching the night of April 6, along a road that was a sea of mud, was the most difficult experience of the retreat.[48] The hungry and exhausted soldiers suffered more than usual on this difficult march. Many stumbled, fell and because they were unable to go on were left behind. These hapless individuals later became prisoners when overtaken by the Federals.[49] Private Theophilus Botsford, Company D, 47th Alabama, was among those captured. Botsford was detailed to look after two privates who suffered from night blindness. The three held hands as Botsford led his charges through the night. Their progress was slow and they fell behind. By mid-morning of April 7, Botsford knew he and his companions would soon be captured. The Alabamians stacked arms, pulled off their cartridge boxes and hung them on their rifles. The Federal XXIV Corps pushed forward to Longstreet's abandoned works at first light and continued after the retreating column.[50] When the Federals arrived, Botsford and his companions were sitting at the base of a large oak tree. The three were soon on their way to Richmond as prisoners.[51]

Longstreet's First Corps was still on the road when the forward elements of Gordon's corps filed into Farmville and began receiving rations.[52] Federal infantry soon appeared and threatened Gordon's position which necessitated the termination of ration distribution before all of the men received their issue.[53] Lee pushed on, trying to break away from Grant's relentless pursuit. He wanted to reach Appomattox Court House, then turn south toward Campbell Court House by way of Pittsylvania.[54]

The head of Longstreet's column stumbled into Farmville early on the morning of April 7. Once again the promised rations were unavailable. Fitzhugh Lee's cavalry was, at the time, fighting a rear guard action west of the Bush River. Federal infantry steadily pushed the Confederate cavalry back on Farmville while Longstreet crossed to the north

—————— William C. Jordan's Route of Travel

←—←—←—← Route of Longstreet's Corps

The Route from
Richmond to Appomattox, Virginia
April 3 - 9, 1865

Larry Erickson

side of the Appomattox.[55] It was then that Longstreet learned that Ewell and Anderson's corps and a cavalry division had been captured on the High Bridge Road.[56] The once proud Army of Northern Virginia was reduced to two pitifully small corps commanded by Longstreet and Gordon.

Longstreet's corps and the cavalry of Fitzhugh Lee became the army's rear guard. The army's wagons were placed safety between Gordon and Longstreet while Lee's cavalry protected the rear of the First Corps.[57] With the Federal cavalry constantly menacing Longstreet's flanks, Adjutant Coles went to the regimental wagons to retrieve some papers that he did not want to risk losing to the Federals. While he was there, Federal cavalry massed to charge them. Stragglers hovering around the trains and teamsters were gathered up and placed behind the wagons to defend against a charge. Though they were few in numbers, the ragged defenders made up for their inadequate strength by raising a loud racket. Fortunately for the defenders the Federals were led to believe a much larger force guarded the wagons and did not attack.[58] Longstreet's corps was soon on its way to Appomattox Court House.

Scruggs and Coles were ahead of the 4th Alabama when they discovered two of the regiment's privates sitting by the road picking feathers from two plump turkeys. Scruggs was sure the birds were stolen, and even in its current condition the army did not condone taking private property. The two were ordered back to the regiment and punished by both having to carry an extra gun. Scruggs ordered Coles to accompany the privates and moved on toward the head of the column. When the colonel was out of hearing distance, Coles told the two that each turkey was heavier than a musket. They were to hold the turkeys and wait for the regiment to come up. Coles walked a short distance away, then turned to see the pair happily picking feathers from the birds.[59]

The two 4th Alabama privates were extremely lucky to find food because Longstreet's men badly needed subsistence, but there was none to be had from the commissary. Once resolute soldiers threw away their arms, and others impeded movement of the wagon trains looking for food. Coles recalled that the men, suffering from hunger and lack of sleep, "were becoming desperate and hard to control."[60]

Saturday, April 8, was a quiet day, the first since leaving Petersburg that constant musketry and the boom of artillery was not heard.[61] The same order of march of the previous day was maintained. Federal infantry quietly followed, but did not menace the rear guard.[62] Longstreet permitted the rear guard to camp at sundown. After a hard week trying to elude the Federal army the men were able to get a good night's sleep.[63]

Gordon reached Appomattox Court House on the evening of April 8 and halted for a short rest. Federal cavalry blocked their path, and infantry was on both flanks. Longstreet's rear guard was being pressed, and though surrounded, the Army of Northern Virginia was not yet willing to succumb to superior numbers.

Gordon and Fitzhugh Lee were ordered to cut their way out of the trap. The movement was scheduled to start at 1 a.m. on April 9. Lee's plan called for Gordon and Fitzhugh Lee, after driving the Federals from their front, to wheel left and cover the passage of the wagon trains. Longstreet, still on the road from Farmville, was to replace Gordon and Fitzhugh Lee when his command came up. The position was to be held until the wagon trains passed on to safety.[64]

Federal infantry and cavalry attacks during the night caused Lee to delay Gordon's advance until dawn. Gordon moved out at 5 a.m. on April 9. Longstreet's column resumed marching at sunrise, but encountered difficulty when it found the wagon train stalled in the line of march. Wagons were halted in the road, and some were parked by the roadside.[65] After traveling about two miles Longstreet's column was forced to halt.[66] The rear of the Army of Northern Virginia rested while Gordon attempted to fight his way through the Federal lines. Gordon found forward movement was impossible. The Army of Northern Virginia's fate was sealed. Lee decided to meet Grant.[67]

The Army Is Surrendered

Lee and Grant had exchanged letters during the previous two days. In a brief note, dated April 8, Grant had suggested terms of surrender. On April 9 couriers shuttled through the lines under flags of truce, while Lee attempted to communicate with the Federal commander. Lee at first thought Grant was at the Confederate rear and sent messages in that direction. But Grant was to the front, and the better part of a day was gone before the two generals met. In the meantime the Federal army continued closing on Lee's rear, Federal skirmishers pressing to within 100 yards of the Confederate rear guard and it appeared the Federals were forming for an assault on the First Corps. Lee learned of the pending attack and requested it be delayed until Grant was contacted. The immediate Federal commander felt himself under orders to deliver the attack and pressed on.[68] Longstreet ordered his last line of battle formed in the early afternoon. Lee rode by while Perry's Brigade was filing into line. Just as the general reached the head of the 4th Alabama a shot rang out from its rear. Reining up Traveler, Lee sternly inquired: "Who fired that gun?" When told that one of the men in the rear was cleaning his gun, Lee ordered all firing to cease and rode on toward the front.[69] A short time later the Federal commander in front of Longstreet ordered his men to stand down. Both armies waited for Grant and Lee to meet.

For those in the rear there were indications that the army's demise was near as all activity ceased. Polley, historian of the Texas brigade, described the atmosphere as taking on a "death-like stillness." When men did talk it was not above a whisper. Then came rumors that truce flags had been seen, and as the reality of the army's plight began to be understood, men were overcome with grief, more than one soldier breaking down and weeping.[70] As the afternoon wore on rumors that the army was to be surrendered continued to circulate. Late in the afternoon, word reached the men of Hood's old division through teamsters that Lee had surrendered the army.[71]

Paroles were prepared April 10, a day of steady rainfall.[72] Each Confederate soldier was given a parole signed by his commanding officer. There was also a copy of an order issued by Grant's headquarters which validated the parole.[73] When the paroles were tallied Perry's Brigade was a mere shell of its original strength. During its illustrious career the aggregate strength of the five regiments numbered 6,260, though it rarely exceeded 2,000 effectives in the field. On April 12, 1865, there were only 82 officers and 891 enlisted men to answer the last roll call.[74] Even with that small number, Perry's Brigade was one of the largest in the Army of Northern Virginia.

Only seven field officers were present: one brigadier general, one colonel, two lieutenant colonels and three majors. There were 23 captains, 22 first lieutenants, 12 second lieutenants, seven junior second lieutenants, four ensigns and one adjutant. Of the 51 companies that made up the brigade, seven were commanded by non-commissioned officers. Twenty-five companies had only one officer present and of these 21 were commanded by lieutenants. At Appomattox, Perry's staff was composed of six officers. Captain Thomas Christian was the brigade's assistant adjutant general and Major Amzi Babbitt the commissary officer. Major William H. Scruggs was quartermaster and was served by two assistant quartermasters, Captain Robert Lapsley and Captain Lemuel H. Dawson. Second Lieutenant Thomas C. Pinckard was the ordnance officer.[75]

Two field officers were present in the 4th Alabama. Lieutenant Colonel Lawrence Scruggs commanded the regiment; Major Mack Robbins was the second field officer present. With a strength of 233 officers and men the gallant 4th Alabama was one of the largest regiments in the army.[76] Lowther led the 15th Alabama at its final formation. Once the largest regiment in the brigade, the 15th Alabama brought an aggregate strength of 219 to the field of surrender. Fourteen officers were present with the command.[77] Five of these, including Lowther, had recently returned from extended furloughs. Lieutenant Colonel John Jones commanded the 44th Alabama, 209 strong at Appomattox.[78] Jones's second in command was Major George Cary, who had proven fearless under fire. At the Devil's Den and the Wilderness, Cary had rushed to the front of the regiment when his commander fell. He was wounded at Fussell's Mill, but was back with the regiment by year's end.[79] Captain Eli Clower led the 47th Alabama which mustered an aggregate of 188 officers and men.[80] The 47th had been commanded by senior captains since the death of Leigh Terrell on the Darbytown Road in October 1864. Clower commanded the regiment at Chickamauga, but then spent the next 15 months in Alabama on recruiting detail for the brigade.[81] The 48th Alabama, commanded by Major James Wiggenton, was the smallest regiment in the

Alabama brigade with an aggregate strength of 136. There were 14 officers and one musician present. With only six present, Company F was the smallest company in the brigade. First Sergeant A. J. Edwards commanded two sergeants and three privates. Company C was only one man stronger. Captain H. C. Kinnebrew commanded a sergeant and five privates.[82]

Lee prepared a farewell message which was read to each regiment.[83] General Orders No. 4 began: "After four years of arduous service, marked by unsurpassed courage and fortitude, the Army of Northern Virginia has been compelled to yield to overwhelming numbers and resources." Lee assured the men his decision to surrender the Army of Northern Virginia was not the result of distrust of their ability. The terms of the agreement permitted the officers and men to return home until exchanged. Lee concluded with: "I bid you all an affectionate farewell."[84]

During the day an apple tree that Lee had rested under on April 9 was cut down and chopped into small pieces for souvenirs.[85] The tree's roots were being cut up when Private Hollis, Company K, 4th Alabama, happened by and saw the activity. Hollis investigated and on discovering the cause decided he too wanted something by which to remember the occasion. After collecting a chip Hollis was on his way.[86]

Lee told Grant his troops were hungry, and Grant graciously ordered rations passed through the Confederate lines. Federal soldiers began visiting the Confederate camps. Some came on official business, other simply came out of curiosity to see the defeated foe. Each saw the depression and shock the Confederates were experiencing. There was also widespread hunger, and to the Federal victors their former enemies were now comrades in need and many shared their own rations. A man in blue gave Hollis a cracker. It wasn't much but the hungry Confederate remembered it to be as tasty as a pound cake.[87]

Jordan's Trek Around the Army

Jordan and Hartsfield reached Lynchburg April 8, having traveled by rail and foot. After leaving Mrs. Christian's plantation, the pair followed the Chickahominy as far as the Virginia Central Railroad. From there they walked along the roadbed to Hanover Junction. Finding a spike-driven handcart, the two men laboriously propelled themselves toward Frederick Hall. Several men riding a crank-propelled handcar overtook them and pushed the smaller car into Frederick Hall. They were then fortunate to obtain a ride to Gordonsville on an engine. From there they made their way to Charlottesville and a chance encounter with General Isaac Trimble near Amherst Court House.

Jordan introduced himself and informed the general his regiment at one time was assigned to Trimble's Brigade. Trimble inquired as to his regiment. On being told Jordan's regiment was the 15th Alabama, Trimble, with tears streaming down his cheeks, replied: "Jordan, I don't say that the 15th Alabama was the best regiment from the state of Alabama, but the best regiment in the Confederate service."

After several days of hard walking and a constant threat of Federal raiding parties, Hartsfield grew weary. He became discouraged and wanted to quit the march, but Jordan convinced his companion to stick with him and assured him they were safe. He and Hartsfield reached Lynchburg April 8, rested a couple of hours and set out on foot for Pittsylvania, arriving there April 10. A band of North Carolinians brought news that Lee had surrendered the army. Jordan and Hartsfield decided to try for Johnston's army in North Carolina.[88]

The Last March

The Army of Northern Virginia laid down its arms the morning of April 12, with neither Grant nor Lee present at the formal surrender. Shortly after the proceedings concluded, Lee and his staff departed for Richmond, and Grant went to Washington, D.C., to undertake the task of dismantling an army that was costing a million dollars a day to keep in the field. The honor of receiving the surrender went to Joshua Chamberlain, now a brigadier general. His exploits against the Alabamians on Little Round Top had earned him the commission and the Medal of Honor. To take the surrender, three brigades of troops representative of the Federal army were selected and ordered drawn up in battle array at the Appomattox Court House. The entire Army of Northern Virginia, officers, men, color bearers, were to march past.[89]

Very few details of the actual surrender are known. Once proud soldiers chose to either forget or not write about the humiliation. Much of what is known was recounted primarily by Gordon and Chamberlain.

Chamberlain deployed at first light for a sunrise surrender ceremony. His brigades formed their lines near the court house, along the road leading to Lynchburg. The Confederates, still in bivouac, were located on a hill beyond a small valley. The Third Brigade drew up on one side of the road, the Second Brigade forming in the rear of the Third Brigade. The First Brigade was across the road in line of battle. All three brigades stood at order arms. Chamberlain had issued orders to salute the Army of Northern Virginia as it passed on one last review and had placed himself on the right nearest the Confederate approach.[90]

As the Army of Northern Virginia marched by, only twelve feet separated Chamberlain from the Confederates. Gordon's Second Corps led the Southern column from its last bivouac. Longstreet's First Corps came last with Field's Division, serving as the rear guard of the First Corps. The exact location of Perry's Alabamians in the column is not known. But from the sketchy information available it is believed they were either last or next to last in the line of march. Perry would have followed suite with the preceding brigades.

At the appointed place the brigade halted, turned and faced the Federal line. Company commanders took particular care to correctly dress their lines. The field and staff of each regiment took up positions between the regiment. Each general moved to the rear of his command. Bayonets were fixed and arms stacked. Cartridge boxes were then unbelted and hung on the stacks. Color bearers carefully folded their battle flags and placed them in a pile near the arms.[91]

Ensign William W. Beasley carried the 4th Alabama's colors, a brand new flag that a member of the regiment had recently procured in Richmond. On the night of April 9 the old flag had been torn into scraps for souvenirs.[92] A white cloth served as the 15th Alabama's regimental flag. Ensign John Archibald was the architect of a scheme to save his flag from an inglorious end. Before the surrender march began, Archibald removed the regiment's flag from its staff and replaced it with a large white handkerchief. Archibald then wrapped the real flag around his body to prevent its discovery and marched onto the field with the battle flag concealed beneath his shirt. In his later years Archibald vowed to be buried with the flag serving as his pillow. It was reported his pledge was carried out.[93] The 44th Alabama colors were carried by Ensign James M. Grice. Thirty-year-old Ensign David J. Smith, a resident of De Soto, Alabama, carried the 47th Alabama colors. At least two previous battle flags had accompanied the 47th Alabama into battle. In March 1865 Michael Bulger presented two tattered and bullet-torn flags to Governor Watts for safekeeping by the state. In a warm reply the governor pledged to "preserve the flags in the capital of the state, as mementos of the bravery and heroism of the noble men who compose that regiment." Forty years later Joseph Burton attempted to locate the flags and sadly discovered they were lost.[94] In May 1864, Jim Sheffield sent to Watts by courier the first battle flag of the 48th Alabama. He informed the governor that five color bearers had died carrying the regimental banner in combat.[95]

Each man in the Confederate column learned to accept the humiliation of defeat in his own way. For many the ability to fight on may have been gone, but the spirit and will to resist was as strong as ever. When his turn came to lay down his arms Private Tom Norton, 4th Alabama, carefully stacked his musket, removed his cartridge box and placed it on the stack. In one last act of defiance he then faced the Federal line and called out: "Don't you make any demonstration over this, damn you."[96] With that bit of business concluded Norton reentered civilian life.

A Sad Sight for the Alabamians

Perry's Brigade was camped along the road leading to Richmond. The 47th Alabama rested among some trees a short distance from the road. All was quiet when a low cheer arose from the direction of the court house. As the cheering grew louder Captain John Q. Burton, Company H, ran to the road to determine the cause of the cheering. Presently a squad of Federal cavalry with swords drawn, came into view. Immediately behind them, Lee rode Traveler. Another squad of cavalry, their swords also drawn, rode behind Lee. At the sight of Lee sandwiched between the Federal cavalry squads, many Confederates thought Lee a prisoner. A large number of the 47th Alabama broke down and wept uncontrollably at the thought of their beloved leader subjected to such a humiliating circumstance.[97]

Unknown to Perry's men the escort was actually a show of respect by the Federal army. Lee had been offered an escort to Richmond, which he declined. But the Federals had insisted on escorting the commander of the Army of Northern Virginia some distance from camp.[98]

The Trip Home

Terms of the surrender provided for transportation, where available, at government expense. There were three alternative routes. The land route took the Alabamians through the Carolinas, Georgia, and then to Alabama. Of the three alternatives this was the most direct route. However, much of the trip was made by walking because the Southern rail system lay in ruins as a result of Federal raids through Georgia and the Carolinas. The so-called northern route went by way of Baltimore, west through Ohio and then south to Alabama. The problem for paroled Confederates selecting this route was that they traveled through unfriendly territory most of the way. Lincoln's assassination shortly after the surrender made the trip all the more hazardous. The sea route was probably the easiest. Travelers would be deposited ashore at either Charleston, South Carolina, or Savannah, Georgia. A large part of the remaining trip could be made by rail transportation. Many of the Alabamians were uncomfortable with boats, especially since the boats were rumored to be very crowded.

Most of the Alabamians elected to take the more direct land route. The men of Companies A and C, 44th Alabama, decided it prudent to remain together for mutual protection. Captain Robert Powers and Second Lieutenants Elkanah Burson and George W. Reese led the group south toward High Point, North Carolina. They were able to secure rail transportation to Charlotte, but then they were forced to walk across South Carolina and much of

Georgia until rail transportation was found at Union Point. The group split up at West Point, which was just a few miles east of the Georgia-Alabama border. Reese was able to borrow a horse from an uncle and reached Montgomery May 3. He arrived at his home near Benton, Alabama, just after Wilson's Raid passed through. Everything but the houses had been destroyed.[99]

First Lieutenant Alvin O. Dickson, commanding Company A, 48th Alabama, kept his company together until it reached north Alabama. Dickson's actual route is conjecture but it is believed that Dickson followed essentially the same route as the Powers group. At Atlanta the band would have turned north, followed the railroad to Rome and then traveled east through the Coosa River Valley to Gadsden, Alabama. At this point they would have then been less than 50 miles from home, which was to the northwest. After climbing the southern side of Sand Mountain the last leg home would have been a relatively easy walk. Thirty days after departing Appomattox, Dickson and his men entered Blount County. It was only then that Dickson finally disbanded the company and sent the men to their homes.

Most of the 15th Alabama followed suit. Four long years ago the young men of Company H were eager for war and the adventure it brought. Led by the combative Oates, their new captain, the group had left home with his assurance that the company would be home for the fall harvest. A survivor of Company H recalled, many years later, the many hardships suffered during the war. A fitting epitaph entitled "Least We Forget" read: "After four years and 48 hard fought battles the decimated Henry County Pioneer Infantry Company of the CSA, stacked arms at Appomattox and walked back to Abbeville."[100]

Major Robbins was the first member of the 4th Alabama to leave Appomattox. Robbins mounted his horse and with tears freely flowing down his cheeks rode among the men for one last talk. He made one last, though very brief, speech which included the sentiment that "God has, certainly for some good purpose, passed us safely through all the trials and dangers which for four years we have encountered." Robbins rode out of view with head bowed.[101] Because of the desolate conditions in Alabama after the war, Robbins found it impossible to continue his law practice there. He returned to his native North Carolina and became a successful attorney in Salisbury and later moved to Statesville. Robbins became the second Confederate representative on the Gettysburg National Park Commission, replacing William H. Forney. His last years were largely devoted to the commission's activities.[102]

Of the 4th Alabama all but Scruggs, Karsner and Coles choose the land route home. They were joined by Doctor J. J. Dement, late surgeon in Heth's Division. From Appomattox they retraced their steps to Petersburg, arriving there April 16. At City Point the group took passage by water to Baltimore. The boat was crowded with Federal officers, who occupied the upper deck. Their horses were housed on the lower deck. The Alabamians were forced to stand among the horses while the Federals celebrated the Union victory. There was much relief among the Alabamians when the boat docked the next morning. The recent parolees were a motley looking bunch. All but the doctor were dressed in dark gray jeans which had not been cleaned in some time. Dement's uniform was cadet gray; his major's bars were prominently visible on his collar. Scruggs and his companions were among the first Confederates from Lee's army to reach Baltimore, and their presence drew considerable attention as they walked in search of lodging. As the group walked past a clothing store an old man beckoned from the shadows and led the men to the back of the store. They were quickly informed that a new Baltimore ordnance forbid Confederate soldiers to wear their uniforms in public. The old man gave each a duster to wear over his uniform. Later, at a hotel they bathed for the first time in weeks and ate their first decent meal in days. As the group departed the dining room an old gentleman wanted to know if they had paid for their meals. Karsner was immediately offended and emphatically replied "Yes!" The old man gently placed his hand on Karsner's shoulder and, in a very low voice, said: "Oh, I mean no offense, my desire was, if you had paid, to have it returned to you." The group refused the old man's hospitality, but at his insistence accepted a free room. News of their presence spread quickly and many sympathizers with the Southern cause came to visit. Dement went out to locate friends while Karsner and Coles went in search of Federal transportation. The doctor ran into a hostile crowd and had to be escorted back to the hotel under police protection. In the meantime Karsner and Coles were unable to secure Federal supplied transportation. Then the Alabamians' luck changed as Robert Herstein, formerly a merchant in north Alabama, came to the hotel to see if any of the Confederates were friends. They were in luck as Herstein advanced them sufficient funds to get home. Scruggs, Coles, and Karsner reached Huntsville, Alabama, only a few days before their compatriots who chose the more direct southern land route.[103]

When Jordan and Hartsfield set out for Johnston's army they quickly found the railroads cut and the way blocked. All hope of reaching Johnston was gone. Jordan found a house with an atlas and plotted a route home. Again Jordan and Hartsfield rode and walked, though most of the trip was accomplished walking. This time they added horses to their mode of transportation. After commandeering horses a short distance north of the South Carolina border they were arrested by a Confederate lieutenant and later turned loose. At Washington, Georgia, the pair intended to board a train, but did not have money nor script for the fare. Upon making the acquaintance of an Alabama captain and about a dozen men traveling with him, Jordan and Hartsfield decided to join the band. The new traveling companions all wanted to take the train but none had fare for the ticket. They decided to board the train anyway and soon after the train was under way the conductor came by collecting tickets. When he found the group was without tickets, the conductor threatened to stop the train and have the men thrown off. To a man the group rose in unison and according to Jordan, informed the conductor: "If necessary we will take control of this train. If guards come after us we shall shove them out the window as fast as they come in. We have been having a little fun for the last four years and we will not mind having a little more." The conductor permitted the group to ride unmolested. They got off at Covington. The captain was a good scribe and with an old transportation ticket proved himself an excellent forger, so that everyone in the group soon possessed a new ticket. Jordan and Hartsfield left the band near the Georgia and Alabama border and arrived at Jordan's home about noon on April 28. They beat the first arrivals from the 15th Alabama by one week. Jordan estimated he had walked around 560 miles to reach home.[104]

Parolees from Prison

When the Army of Northern Virginia surrendered, 11 officers of Perry's Brigade were in Federal prisons. Eight were confined at Fort Delaware, Maryland, and three at Johnson's Island, Ohio. Robert Wicker, 15th Alabama, Company L, at Fort Delaware and John B. Eubanks, 48th Alabama, at Johnson's Island had been imprisoned the longest. Both had been captured at Gettysburg on July 2, 1863. Eubanks was the first officer from the brigade released from prison.

Lieutenant John Eubanks was a thirty-two-year-old farmer from Blountsville, Alabama, when he entered the service in 1862. Much of his time in the prison camp had been spent thinking about his plight and contemplating alternatives to get out of prison. Escape was not practical, so he eventually decided the Confederate cause was lost and apparently concluded amnesty offered the most viable alternative. In his petition for amnesty, Eubanks stated he had always been a strong Union man and only joined the Confederate army because he was too far from the Federal lines to escape. He volunteered to join the Federal army if necessary. Eubanks closed his petition by lamenting he had not attempted an escape from the Confederate army because of the great danger of being recaptured. The Federal authorities did not believe him. Maybe it was because Eubanks had been elected by his company to the office of junior second lieutenant and then promoted to second lieutenant. It could easily be assumed his peers would not elect a strong Union sympathizer to lead them in battle. In actuality, Eubanks resided in a region with considerable Union sympathy. Had he chosen to seek sanctuary he would have been relatively safe a few miles west of his home. In any event Eubanks spent the remainder of the war a Federal prisoner. He was finally permitted to take an Oath of Amnesty May 12, 1865.[105]

Oates described Wicker as a fine soldier and as "brave as any man in the regiment."[106] His bravery, however, did not compensate for the necessary leadership qualities to fulfill the duties of captain. A Military Examining Board twice refused Wicker promotion to captain of Company L. Captain Shaaff, commanding the 15th Alabama on December 17, 1864, explains what happened afterwards:

> *"He (Wicker) was taken prisoner at the battle of Gettysburg, July 2, '63 and is still in the hands of the enemy. There being no one in the company in any way competent to fill the office of captain, an election was ordered by the brigade commander which resulted in the election of Lieutenant Hatcher of Company D. Lieutenant Wicker most cheerfully and willingly wavered his claim verbally in favor of Lieutenant Hatcher. His written waiver could be readily procured if he was not in the hands of the enemy. Lieutenant Hatcher was his own choice for a captain and he acknowledged himself not competent to fill the office."*

Wicker was released June 12, 1865, upon his Oath of Allegiance to the Union. [107]

James W. Jones, first lieutenant, Company A, 48th Alabama, was released June 12. Jones was a deserter, having been absent from the regiment since December 1862. He was arrested near Huntsville, Alabama on October 13, 1863, and sent to Johnson's Island.[108]

Joseph J. Parton, a second lieutenant in Company F, 4th Alabama, was in Huntsville recovering from a wound received at Gettysburg when he was captured. When the war began Parton had been a twenty-six-year-old mechanic in Huntsville. He was also released June 12.[109]

Lieutenant Colonel William Hardwick had been twice captured, the second time near Cedar Bluff, Alabama on June 1, 1864, while on extended sick furlough to recover from an illness that threatened blindness. He had been turned over to the provost marshal in Kingston, Georgia. From there he was forwarded to Nashville, Tennessee, and then to Johnson's Island where he spent the remainder of the war. On June 25, 1865 Hardwick became the last officer from the brigade released from prison.[110] Hardwick had enlisted in north Alabama where he had lived for a time, but on release from prison stated his residence was Eufaula, Alabama. He was able to acquire a large tract of land in Henry County south of Eufaula on which he built a large colonial-style home. Hardwick later established a general store to serve the surrounding farming country. Eventually two other stores, a saloon and post office were added. The tiny village became known as Hardwicksville in honor of its founder. Today, Hardwicksville, like the Confederacy, is a ghost of the past.[111]

Epilogue

For most of the men who served in Law's Brigade, the Civil War was a pivotal point of their lives. Had they not served in the Confederate army, it is likely that many would never have left their home counties during their lifetimes. The war took them on a grand tour through states on both sides of the Mason-Dixon line. Most returned to an agrarian life in Alabama at the end of hostilities, but some took up new pursuits after the fighting ended.

Law returned to South Carolina in May of 1865 and became a landowner and president of a small railroad by virtue of his wife's inheritance. The railroad did not prosper and Law's agricultural attempts proved futile. In 1867, he wrote to his wartime aide-de-camp, Mims Walker, that he was bankrupt after two years of hard work. He reminded Walker that he had one of Law's horses from the war and asked Walker to sell it for him.[1]

In 1872, Law returned to Alabama to farm and organize numerous chapters of the five-year-old fraternal organization of farmers, known as The Grange. One historian credits Law with the establishment of The Grange in Alabama.[2] By 1881, he had returned to South Carolina and became associate principal at the King's Mountain Military Institute, the school founded by Asbury Coward and Micah Jenkins before the war. Three years later, Law was again farming in South Carolina where he stayed until 1893 when he moved to Florida to establish a military school of his own. His school was described as "tightly run" by a former student who also attended West Point. After the school became part of the Florida college system, a misunderstanding arose between Law and state authorities in 1902. As happened nearly four decades before, Law felt his honor demanded that he submit his resignation. Most of the class of 1903 walked out with Law. Two of this class served in the Florida legislature and as secretary of state. In 1929, they pushed a bill through the state government granting a diploma to the class of 1903. One of Law's students described Law as "a fine Southern gentleman, of the highest caliber—perhaps a little sensitive—but of unquestioned integrity and fine character."[3]

In the 1880s, Law acted as the South Carolina agent of the *Battles and Leaders of the Civil War* series, though it is unlikely that the enterprise was profitable. During the last working years of his life, Law was editor of the Bartow (Florida) *Courier-Informant*, acting in that capacity into his eightieth year.

Throughout his postwar years, Law was active in veteran organizations, serving as vice president of the influential Association of the Army of Northern Virginia, and delivering the annual address in 1890.[4] Law often attended monument dedications, along with his aide-de-camp, John Cussons, and such notables as Fitzhugh Lee, Wade Hampton, and Charles Field.[5] Beginning as early as 1866, Law delivered speeches to various groups throughout the South such as the Euphradian and Cliarosophic Societies at the University of South Carolina, the annual meeting of the South Carolina Press Association and the commencement address at Virginia Military Institute in 1893.

Even though Law wrote several articles on the war, he did not become embroiled in the postwar discord that occupied a number of ex-Confederates. With the exception of the actions of the detested Longstreet before Chattanooga and Knoxville, Law did not ascribe the failure of the Southern cause to poor generalship or mean motives. He believed Lee failed at Gettysburg because he attacked the enemy where the enemy wanted him to attack, but made it clear he also believed Lee had no other option. It is odd that Law did not write more extensively and in more depth about the war. He was a newspaper editor for more than a decade and an active participant in Confederate groups, yet he left no body of papers.

Law was an unreconstructed Rebel for most of his life. Although he detailed several reasons for Confederate defeat in addresses and articles, he always attributed the major cause of the failure of the Confederacy as the direct intervention of Providence. But Law put aside the past and accepted Yankees and Confederates as brethren in the American community. In his last year, Law talked with a newspaper reporter. "For a long time I thought," admitted the old general, "that the most effective work of my life was done while I was fighting Yankees. In recent years, however, I have concluded that my best work has been for the school children of Polk County (Florida) during the past seven years and in loving the men I fought. There's no room in our country for factionalism and hatred; there's no room for nothing but unity and love."[6]

When Law died on October 31, 1920, the town of Bartow, Florida, closed its schools and businesses to honor the Confederate general. In Bartow, a memorial to Law has been erected and his Confederate coat (complete with the three stars and laurel leaves of a brigadier) is on display at the Chamber of Commerce.

Perry became a planter for two years. In 1867 Perry moved to Glendale in Hardin County, Kentucky, where he managed the local military college. He later became a professor of English and Philosophy at Ogden College in Bowling Green, Kentucky.[7] In his later years Perry wrote several articles detailing the participation of the 44th Alabama during the war. Perry's recall of events was excellent, describing with accuracy the scene of conflict and movements of the 44th Alabama and the Alabama brigade. His descriptions of Gettysburg, Chickamauga, and the Wilderness correlate well with other eyewitness accounts. Perry's map depicting the 44th Alabama's movement at Chickamauga, drawn almost 30 years after the battle, is amazingly accurate. A warm relationship developed between Oates and Perry during the war years which lasted until Perry's death in 1901. On learning of his friend's death at Bowling Green, Oates wrote a stirring tribute to his friend which was published in the Montgomery *Advertiser* on March, 2, 1902. Its opening paragraph read:

> *"When a good man dies—one whose character and life work constitute a splendid example for the young men of the state to emulate, it should be accurately reported and published to that end, and in justice to the memory of the departed; that his due and noble deeds may live after him rather than to be interred with his bones and soon forgotten. The name of my old comrade and friend who died in the 79th year of his age, was such a man."[8]*

Law had relieved Perry of command of his regiment for apparent cowardice on the battlefield and then reluctantly gave him a second chance, but the incident created a rift between the two. Their differences were intensified when Law thought Perry sided with Longstreet. Unfortunately, the rift between Law and Perry was never reconciled. In the end, Perry's tenure as commander of the brigade was longer than Law's.[9] Perry did not cut the figure of the dashing brigadier that Law projected so naturally. That is probably the reason the brigade rank and file continued to refer to it as Law's Brigade after the war. He led the brigade during its finest hour, however, for in the final analysis the brigade's fighting ability did not suffer under Perry.

After the war, Sheffield, a self-made man who rose from poverty to prominence, returned to Alabama to find himself back in dire economic straits. He had used nearly $60,000 of his own money to equip the 48th Alabama. Sheffield had served as sheriff of Marshall County, in the Alabama House of Representatives, and in the Secession Convention before the war. By 1860, he was a retired planter. Although Sheffield served in the Alabama Senate in the 1880s and ran for governor on the Greenback ticket in 1882, his lost fortune proved too much to overcome. At the time of his death, he held only a clerkship in the office of the Superintendent of Education.

Sheffield killed a doctor in 1890 because the medical man had ruined the reputation of his spinster daughter as well as supplied her with drugs. Using his hold on Sheffield's daughter, the doctor also coaxed her into criminal activity. She was caught attempting to burn down the home of a neighbor. The ex-Confederate was acquitted in a short trial. Sheffield was instrumental in sending his daughter to the state hospital for the insane, where she stayed for 30 years, to prevent her standing trial for arson.[10]

Oates became a prominent figure in the state of Alabama, serving in the state legislature, U.S. Congress and later as governor. In the Spanish-American War Oates was commissioned a brigadier general.[11] While serving in the U.S. Congress, Oates supported the bill which appropriated funds for the Gettysburg Military Park.[12] Because of his political influence Oates was able to secure his fellow Alabamian, William Forney, an appointment as the lone Confederate representative on the original commission. When Forney died Oates successfully lobbied to have his old friend, William M. Robbins, appointed to fill the vacancy.[13] In his twilight years Oates decided it was appropriate to erect a monument on the battlefield in memory of his brother and the others of the 15th Alabama who fell at Gettysburg.[14] Oates wanted the monument placed at the most advanced point reached by the 15th Alabama on Little Round Top, which violated a commission rule stipulating monuments to units should be placed where the unit formed its line of battle. Though the previous commission frequently waived the rule Robbins and his fellow commissioners decided there would be no exceptions and informed the late governor of Alabama that the monument could be placed along Confederate Avenue, a road built after the war to make the battlefield more accessible.[15] Oates's application to place the monument on Little Round Top was returned to him. Oates replied he would never consent to placing a monument to his men on Confederate Avenue.[16]

When Oates pressed the issue the Federal members deferred to Robbins to act as intermediary for the commission and explain their position. Robbins wrote Oates that he deferred to his colleagues on the commission.[17] Unfortunately, Oates incorrectly concluded Robbins was the primary obstacle to a favorable action on his request.[18] Federal commission members clearly wanted to avoid direct communication with Oates and continued to place Robbins between themselves and Oates. Colonel John P. Nicholson, Gettysburg National Military Park Commissioner, and chairman of the Gettysburg Battle Commission, went so far as to write Oates that the commission largely deferred to Robbins on Southern matters.[19] Robbins became the man caught in the middle. The North Carolinian expressed considerable displeasure to his fellow commissioners over the position in which they placed him. He felt they had incorrectly implied he was the main reason why Oates's request was refused.[20] Commission members, however, did nothing to dispel the idea. Oates, in a letter dated July 4, 1903, accused Robbins of personally blocking his application to place a monument on Little Round Top. Robbins maintained his position that the commission was not granting exceptions. A once warm relationship had soured beyond repair.

In an effort to overturn the commission's decision Oates sent a barrage of letters to commission members, U.S. congressmen, the War Department and Joshua Chamberlain.[21] Oates informed Robbins that he only "wanted to leave a little stone on the spot" where his brother was killed. He offered to use his own funds to place the monument on the mountain.[22]

The War Department deferred to the commission.[23] The commission sought Chamberlain's opinion on the matter. Chamberlain had no objection to the monument, but stated it should be correctly located. Oates contended his men pushed the Maine defenders back. In earlier years Chamberlain acknowledged the Alabamians pushed his men back almost to Hazlett's guns.[24] But as the years wore on Chamberlain's memory of the events changed and he refused to admit giving ground. He and Oates could never agree on how far the 15th Alabama advanced on that hot July day.

As he grew older, Oates did not always remember correctly the events as they occurred on Little Round Top. His quest was doomed when he wrote Secretary of War Elihu Root that the 15th Alabama had turned the 20th Maine's right and rolled up the 83rd Pennsylvania's left.[26] When he was informed of Oates's statement Chamberlain withdrew any support he may have had for Oates's request. Oates made a last futile effort to force the commission to honor his request. On November 4, 1903, Oates informed Nicholson that the Alabama legislature had "passed a joint resolution requesting the senators and nine representatives from this state to investigate and see why it is that permission is not given to me to erect the monument."[27] But the damage to Oates's cause was irreparable. The issue dragged on another two years but the commission continued to refuse Oates's request.[28] Today, the only monument to Law's Brigade stands on Confederate Avenue where Law formed his line of battle July 2, 1863.

The combative Oates died September 9, 1910, at Montgomery, Alabama. On his tombstone is an epitaph probably written by Oates himself. It reads:

> *"Born in poverty; reared in adversity, without education advantage. Yet by honest individual effort he obtained a competency and the confidence of his fellow man, while fairly liberal to relatives and to the worthy poor. A devoted Confederate soldier, he gave his right arm to the cause. He accepted the result of the war without a murmur, and in 1898–9 he was a Brigadier General of the United States volunteers in the war with Spain."[29]*

Oates's low opinion of Lowther's leadership qualities were unfounded. Lowther performed well after relieving Oates of command of the 15th Alabama. Oates also questioned Lowther's courage, which was unwarranted. After assuming command Lowther was at the front of his regiment when severely wounded at Fussell's Mill on August 16, 1864. After the surrender, Lowther returned to Alabama and assumed the occupation of planter in Russell County, Alabama.

Michael J. Bulger, lieutenant colonel of the 47th regiment, pursued a political career during the latter part of and immediately after the war. He was a candidate for governor on the Peace Party ticket in 1865. Known as "Reconstructionists," they had organized in the winter of 1864–65, maintained communications with the Federals in Alabama and attempted to reestablish government in those areas of the state occupied by the Bluecoats. The Huntsville *Advocate*, October 19, 1865, editorialized that Bulger would have the endorsement of the Johnson administration because he opposed secession and the support of the Alabama voter because he served in the 47th Alabama.[30] In 1898, at age 92, Bulger attended the Confederate Veterans Reunion in New Orleans. A reporter for the *New Orleans Picayune* identified Bulger as the oldest living officer of the Confederate army. He survived eight more years, dying September 11, 1900.

Lieutenant Colonel John A. Jones returned to Alabama where he farmed in Wilcox County, Alabama, through 1878. He then became a teacher, working at various places in Alabama until 1885. He next served as president of the Dalton Female College until 1889. Jones joined the faculty of the Central College of Lexington, Missouri, in 1889, remaining there until his death in 1896.[31]

George Cary, the 44th Alabama's dashing young major from Montevallo, Alabama, became a partner in a dry goods firm in New Orleans, remaining there until 1880. He then relocated to New York City as a cotton broker, becoming one of the better known and respected former Confederates residing in the city. It was reported that he had a unique ability to "administer a rebuke without leaving a sting." In a letter written when both men were in their twilight years, Perry wrote to his friend:

> *"To the students of my college classes to whom I often related war stories—your name is as familiar as a household word—how you scaled the cliff at Devil's Den ahead of your line and with flashing sword and blazing face landed among the artillerymen of the battery, demanding and receiving the surrender, how you seized the flag of the regiment in the Battle of the Wilderness and called upon the men to follow you as you ascended the hill beyond the little swamp from which we had driven several lines of battle; how you repeated the performance at Frazier's Farm and received what we all supposed for a time to be a mortal wound."*[32]

Cary, like many former Confederates, was active in veterans' activities in his later years. But, above all he was a respected member of the community, where he was residing at the time of his death.[33]

John Cussons left Confederate service after his parole from a Federal military prison. He felt his services as an aide were not needed as long as Law was not with the brigade. In addition, Cussons was an Englishman, not subject to Confederate conscript laws. He married and took up residence at Glen Allen, VA. Shortly after the end of the conflict, he began a publishing company and prospered. Energetic and innovative, Cussons patented the tear-off desk calendar.[34] He founded a local newspaper and wrote about the war, including a small volume entitled, *United States 'History' as the Yankee Makes and Takes It*, a tract designed to dispel the myths of Northern writers. In a pamphlet called *The Passage of Thoroughfare Gap and the Assembling of Lee's Army for the Second Battle of Manassas* it labeled Law the "true hero of Thoroughfare Gap." "The truth of Law's actions at Thoroughfare Gap will not be known, he said, until Law sets aside his modesty and gives history a full account of the facts."[35] After quarreling with his neighbors for years, Cussons died a wealthy recluse.

John W. Purifoy, 44th Alabama, became the Alabama secretary of state and Mims Walker and Nathaniel H. R. Dawson served in the state legislature. Dawson was the original captain of Company C, the 4th Alabama, whose wife was sister-in-law of Abraham Lincoln. He eventually held the powerful post of Speaker of the Alabama House of Representatives and served as United States Commissioner of Education.

Captain Isaac H. Vincent of the 47th regiment served as treasurer of Alabama for three terms. During an audit of the treasury, Vincent, who ran for office as "Honest Ike," left suddenly for Texas. Vincent was brought back to Alabama and convicted in 1887 of embezzling $250,000 of state funds. He was sentenced to ten years in the penitentiary but received a pardon from Governor Thomas G. Jones in 1893. Jones was bitterly criticized for the pardon and even burned in effigy by his political enemies in Bessemer, Alabama. Ike Vincent died in Palo Pinto County, Texas, in 1898, just about the time he would have been released from prison had he served his full term.[36]

Billy Jordan returned to his plantation near Midway, Alabama, where he had been master of 20 slaves prior to the war. Jordan was arrested in June of 1865 for failing to free his slaves. After an ugly exchange with the Federal officer serving as judge, Jordan accepted parole regulations which permitted him to reclaim his rights as a citizen. His former slaves were read the Emancipation Proclamation.

Jordan struggled to make his plantation a paying enterprise for the next three years. By 1868, Jordan decided he must resist what he viewed as Negro rule of Alabama by participating in the political process. He tried to prevent his Negro workers from voting and fired them when they went to the polls in defiance of his ultimatum. This led to a boycott of his plantation by area Negroes, and Jordan was forced to rent his land and live with relatives in 1873. By 1876, Jordan's county was freed of Republican control. Jordan, however, was briefly detained on charges of disrupting the elections before he was freed for lack of evidence. Jordan served in the Alabama legislature in 1884 and won appointment from President Grover Cleveland to the Land Office in Montgomery.[37]

Ensign William Beasley had joined the 4th Alabama in April 1861, a single, nineteen-year-old printer from Selma, Alabama. He had first borne the regimental colors at Chickamauga, then had been appointed the regimental musician in late 1863. He was once again the regimental color bearer at the Wilderness where he was shot in the chest. Most of the summer was required for Beasley's wound to sufficiently heal for him to return to service. After the war Beasley returned to Alabama but, in his later years, made his way to Louisville, Kentucky. In 1897 wounds sustained in the war rendered the old Confederate unable to walk. He managed to eke out a meager existence operating a cigar stand. A shabby derby hat and old clothing that had seen better days were his normal dress. In spite of his plight Beasley kept an eye for the ladies and was always eager to exchange pleasantries with passersby. A visitor to his stand would say: "How is business?" Beasley would reply: "Fairly good. I've no right to complain. As long as I make a dollar a day we can get the necessaries, but the luxuries—well, we can do without them."[38]

Appendix A

Brigade Field and Staff

Brigadier Generals
Evander McIver Law
William Flake Perry

Assistant Adjutant Generals[1]
James Gadsden Holmes[2]
Thomas L. Christian
Leigh Richmond Terrell
Battle O. Peterson (A[3])
Jeremiah Edwards (A)
Winns P. Becker[4]

Chiefs of Commissary
Amzi Babbitt
Gardner M. McConnico (A)
William F. Robbins (A)

Quartermasters
Joseph Warren Hudson
Robert Lapsley
Lemuel H. Dawson
William P. Golightly (A)
William H. Scruggs

Ordnance Officers
John Drake
Thomas C. Pinckard

Aides-de-Camp
John Cussons
Robert Sharp[6]
Mims Walker[7]
Thomas J. Kirkman[8]
John K. Law[9]
Joseph B. Hardwick
Thomas L. Samuels
Lewis A. Morgan (A)
William F. Robbins (A)

Couriers
Virginius S. Smith[5]
James H. Howard
Steptoe P. Chapman
E. M. Ervin
Thomas J. Sinclair[10]
Gilbert S. Nicholson[11]

(A) = Acting

Regimental Organization

4th Regiment Alabama Volunteer Infantry[1]
Organized: Dalton, Georgia, May 7, 1861

Field and Staff

Colonels
Egbert J. Jones
Evander McIver Law
Pinckney Downey Bowles

Adjutants
Joseph Hardee
Robert Thompson Coles

Assist. Chiefs of Commissary
Arthur C. Beard
John D. Brandon

Surgeons
John R. Slaughter
William E. Pegram
A. Howard Scott
William O. Hudson
James Harvey Boyd[4]
John A. Morson
C. B. Hilliard
Charles T. Taliaferro
Edwin F. Degraffenried
John B. Wortham
Elias O. Hodges[7]

Chaplains
William D. Chadick
Robert L. Frazier
W. H. Carroll[10]
C. C. Ellis

Lieutenant Colonels
Evander McIver Law
Thomas J. Goldsby
Owen Kenan McLemore
Pinckney Downey Bowles
Lawrence Houston Scruggs

Assist. Quartermasters
George Washington Jones
Joseph Warren Hudson
Barna McKinne

Assist. Surgeons
H. B. Leveritt
Henry H. Seargeant
William A. Duncan
John S. Andrews
Hugh S. Paisley[5]
Hugh C. Bradley[6]
William H. Baptist
Robert E. McNeil
W. M. McCaine
William E. Pegram
Joseph N. Boggs[8]
Levin W. Shepherd

Musicians
George Thomas Fogarty (Chief)[9]
Alexander A. Murray (Drummer)[11]
Charles T. Halsey[12]

Majors
Charles Lewis Scott
Benjamin Alston[2]
Owen Kenan McLemore
Pinckney Downey Bowles
Lawrence Houston Scruggs
Thomas K. Coleman
William McKendre Robbins

Ensigns
William W. Beasley

Color Bearers
Gilchrist R. Boulware[3]
Robert Sinclair

Sergeant Majors
John Lowe Brown

Commissary Sergeants
Patrick S. Wheelan

Quartermaster Sergeants
Thomas Morgan
Patrick S. Wheelan

Ordnance Sergeants
Frank R. Lamson

Chaplains	*Musicians*	*Hospital Stewards*
Ira E. Brown	John H. Ellms (Fifer)	Joel C. Ledbetter
A. Parker[13]	John Fried	George H. Sayre[14]
	Jacob Marshall[15]	

Organization – 4th Alabama

	Company[16]	County Raised	Date Organized
A	Governor's Guards	Dallas	April 26, 1861
B	Tuskegee Zouaves[17]	Macon	April 28, 1861
C	Magnolia Cadets	Dallas	April 25, 1861
D	Canebrake Rifles[18]	Perry, Marengo	April 26, 1861
E	Conecuh Guards	Conecuh	April 25, 1861
F	Huntsville Guards	Madison	April 26, 1861
G	Marion Light Infantry	Perry	April 24, 1861
H	Lauderdale Guards[19]	Lauderdale	April 28, 1861
I	North Alabamians	Madison	April 26, 1861
K	Larkinsville Guards	Jackson	April 27, 1861

15th Regiment Alabama Volunteer Infantry
Organized: Fort Mitchell, Alabama, Jul. 3, 1861

Field and Staff

Colonels	*Lieutenant Colonels*	*Majors*
James Cantey	James Fletcher Treutlen	John Wilhite Lewis Daniel
James Fletcher Treutlen	Isaac Ball Feagin	Alexander A. Lowther
William Calvin Oates		William Calvin Oates
Alexander A. Lowther	*Assist. Quartermasters*	
	Thomas Woolfolk	*Assist. Chiefs of Commissary*
Adjutants	Samuel J. Feagin	James Vernoy
Locke Weems	Edmond P. Head (A)	Cornelius V. Morris
DeBernie B. Waddell		
Isaac H. Parks (A)	*Assist. Surgeons*	*Sergeant Majors*
	William G. Drake	Van Marcus
Surgeons	J. J. Davis	Green C. Renfroe
Francis A Sanford		Robert Cicero Norris[20]
Alexander Rivers	*Ensigns*	
Edmund Shepherd[21]	John G. Archibald	*Musicians*
George W. Briggs	Charles Smith[22]	Robert S. Warlick (Fifer)
	James R. Edwards[23]	Joshua C. Harrell (Fifer)
Ordnance Sergeants		Julian C. Kersey
William A. Crews	*Quartermaster Sergeants*	James Cunningham[24]
T. J. Bass	M. D. Doney	James P. Harris (Drummer)
	William A. Crews	Richard Harris[25]
		James F. Newberry
Chaplains	*Commissary Sergeants*	Patrick Brannon (Drummer)
H. J. McKennon[26]	Joseph R. Breare[27]	Allan A. Kirkland

Chaplains	*Commissary Sergeants*	*Colonel's Orderlies*
Samuel B. McJunkin(A)[28]	Jeptha P. Hill	Richard Harris
Sydney Rogers	John W. Screws (A)	
D. C. Conners[29]		
	Hospital Stewards	
	S. D. Wilson[30]	

Organization – 15th Alabama

	Company	County Raised	Date Organized
A	Cantey Rifles	Russell	July 3, 1861
B	Midway Southern Guards	Barbour	July 3, 1861
C	Macon County Commissioners	Macon	July 3, 1861
D	Ft. Browder Roughs	Barbour	July 3, 1861
E	Dale County Beauregards	Dale	July 3, 1861
F	Brundidge Guards	Pike	July 3, 1861
G	Henry Pioneers	Henry	July 3, 1861
H	Glennville Guards	Barbour, Dale	July 3, 1861
I	Quitman Guards[31]	Pike	July 3, 1861
K	Eufaula Guards[32]	Barbour	July 3, 1861
L	Pike Sharpshooters	Pike	March 11, 1862

44th Regiment Alabama Volunteer Infantry
Organized: Selma, Alabama, May 16, 1861

Field and Staff

Colonels	*Lieutenant Colonels*	*Majors*
James Kent	Charles Alexander Derby	William Flake Perry
Charles Alexander Derby	William Flake Perry	John Archibald Jones
William Flake Perry	John Archibald Jones	George Walton Cary

Adjutants	*Assist. Quartermasters*	*Assist. Chiefs of Commissary*
Thomas A. Nicoll	Robert Lapsley	Gardner M. McConnico

Surgeons	*Assist. Surgeons*	*Sergeant Majors*
Benjamin F. Watkins	John F. Blevins	John H. Pettway
	William J. Pierce	Kincheon Lee Haralson[33]
Colonel's Orderly	Robert T. Merriwether	
William G. Albritton	John H. Purifoy	*Orderly Sergeant*
	Harvey O. Milton	John S. Gardner
Musicians	Hugh William Caffey[34]	
William G. Albritton[35]	J. J. Harden	*Chaplains*
Harvey O. Milton		William G. Perry
	Ordnance Sergeants	James H. Nabors
Ensigns	James J. Garrett	F. S. Petaway[36]
James M. Grice[37]		

Quartermaster Sergeants	*Commissary Sergeants*	*Hospital Stewards*
Thomas F. Smitherman	Thomas Booth	Thomas Lee
Thomas B. Somerville	Robert H. Crosswell	John A. Powers
		William J. Pierce

Organization – 44th Alabama

	Company[38]	County Raised	Date Organized
A	James M. Calhoun Guards	Lowndes, Dallas	March 17, 1862
B	Scottsville Guards	Bibb	May 15, 1862
C	Cedar Grove Guards[39]	Wilcox	March 29, 1862
D	Kenan Musketeers	Shelby	April 7, 1862
E	Sallie Ratcliffe Guards	Shelby	April 5, 1862
F	Dan Steele Guards	Bibb	March 28, 1862
G	Wash Smith Guards	Dallas, Bibb	April 18, 1862
H	Dawson Warriors[40]	Bibb	May 2, 1862
I	Aberchroche Guards	Randolph	April 24, 1862
K	Cynthia Border Greys[41]	Calhoun	May 6, 1862

47th Regiment Alabama Volunteer Infantry
Organized: Loachapoka, Alabama, May 22, 1861

Field and Staff

Colonels	*Lieutenant Colonels*	*Majors*
James McCarthy Oliver	James Washington Jackson	John Y. Johnston
James Washington Jackson	Michael Jefferson Bulger	James McDonald Campbell
Michael Jefferson Bulger	Leigh Richmond Terrell	

Adjutants	Assist. *Quartermasters*	*Assist. Chiefs of Commissary*
Henry A. Garrett	Lemuel H. Dawson	Wade A. Herren
William H. Keller		
Reuben E. Jordan	*Ordnance Sergeants*	*Sergeant Majors*
	P. F. Lawes[42]	Abel L. Robinson
		James M. P. Coker
Surgeons	*Assist. Surgeons*	George W. Knight
John R. Burton	Michael A. Ridgeway	
	J.P. Cooke	*Chaplains*
Ensigns		W. G. Starr
David J. Smith	*Musicians*	Francis T. J. Brandon
	Carter Walls (Fifer)	Thomas N. White
Color Bearers	Willis N. Walls (Drummer)	James McDonald Campbell[43]
Benjamin F.C. Russel	J. H. Campbell	

Commissary Sergeants	*Quartermaster Sergeants*	*Hospital Stewards*
Samuel C. Oliver (A)	Isaac H. Vincent	Richard L. Basset
James V. Sewell	Robert L. Mitchell	Reuben E. Jordan

Organization – 47th Alabama

	Company	County Raised	Date Organized
A	____	Tallapoosa	March 28, 1862
B	Tallapoosa Tigers[44]	Tallapoosa	April 7, 1862
C	Jeff Holly Guards	Tallapoosa	April 19, 1862
D	____	Tallapoosa	April 26, 1862
E	____	Cherokee, Calhoun	April 30, 1862
F	____	Tallapoosa	May 13, 1862
G	____	Tallapoosa, Randolph	May 14, 1862
H	____	Coosa	May 16, 1862
I	Chambers Infantry	Chambers	April, 18, 1862
K	Goldwaithe Guards	Tallapoosa	April 29, 1862

48th Regiment Alabama Volunteer Infantry
Organized: Auburn, Alabama, May 22, 1862

Field and Staff

Colonels
James Lawrence Sheffield

Adjutants
Thomas B. Harris
Thomas James Eubanks
Henry Stokes Figures
Frank N. Kitchell
Thomas J. Sinclair (Λ)

Surgeons
James Penn
James M. Lowe
John N. Doyle

Quartermaster Sergeants
W. C. Hammons[46]

Ordnance Sergeants
John Dykes Taylor

Musicians
James A. Hallet (Drummer)
E. S. Smith (Fifer)
Joseph S. Harris

Lieutenant Colonels
Abner A. Hughes
Jesse J. Alldredge
William McTyiere Hardwick

Assist. Quartermasters
Daniel C. Turrentine
William P. Golightly

Assist. Surgeons
W. S. Pinson
R. W. Cain
M. A. Butler
H. H. Seargeant

Chaplains
James B. Hall
William E. Lucy
Blackford Price

Hospital Stewards
R. W. Cain

Commissary Sergeant
Elijah S. Hardwick

Majors
Enoch Alldredge
William McTyiere Hardwick
William Calvin Oates
James W. Wiggenton

Assist. Chiefs of Commissary
William F. Robbins

Sergeant Majors[45]
William F. Robbins
James G. Brown

Ensigns
John J. Pollard

Color Bearers
J. M. Parrish[47]
S. A. Rogers[48]

Orderly Sergeants
James M. Ratliff[49]
Richard A. Yarborough

Organization – 48 Alabama

	Company	County Raised	Date Organized
A	Jackson Boys	Blount	April 7, 1862
B	Mills Valley Guards	Dekalb	April 7, 1862
C	Mountain Rangers	Marshall	April 7, 1862
D	Sheffield Guards[50]	Marshall	April 7, 1862
E	Jacksonians	Marshall	March 31, 1862
F	Jeff Davis Boys	Blount	April 10, 1862
G	Elisha King Guards[51]	Cherokee	April 10, 1862
H	Cherokee Grays[52]	Cherokee	April 29, 1862
I	Newman Pound Guards[53]	Calhoun	April 29, 1862
K	Moore Rifles	Calhoun	May 3, 1862

(A) = Acting

Roster[1] of Officers

Name	Regt	Co	Rank	Remarks
Adams, James J.	4th	A	3rd Lt[2]	Resigned Oct. 2, 1862, due to disability
Adrian, James F.	48th	F	3rd Lt	Resigned Aug. 30, 1864, due to wounds
Adrian, John D.	44th	K	Capt	Killed Oct. 7, 1864, Darbytown Rd., VA
Adrian, John G.	47th	E	2nd Lt	Killed Jul. 2, 1863, Gettysburg, PA
Alford, Pierce L.	47th	C	1st Lt	Killed May 6, 1864, Wilderness, VA
Allen, Edward L.	4th	I	2nd Lt	Resigned Oct. 1, 1862
Alldredge, Andrew Jackson	48th	A	Capt	Resigned Jul. 15, 1862, due to wounds
Alldredge, Enoch	48th	FS[3]	Maj	Resigned Sep. 21, 1862 due to wounds
Alldredge, Jesse J.	48th	FS	Lt Col	Resigned Jul. 17, 1863 due to wounds
Ambrose, Guston	44th	B	1st Lt	Resigned Apr. 15, 1863, medical
Anderson, Francis M.	4th	B	2nd Lt	Paroled at Appomattox, VA
Andrews, Milton	47th	I	1st Lt	Died of disease Sep. 29, 1862
Appleton, Thomas N.	48th	E	1st Lt	Paroled at Appomattox, VA[4]
Archibald, John G.	15th	FS[5]	Ensign[6]	Paroled at Appomattox, VA
Armistead, Heslop	4th	H	Capt	Killed Jun. 27, 1862, Gaines's Mill, VA
Arnold, Jesse H.	48th	G	1st Lt	Resigned at consolidation, Co G and H
Arnold, Preston B.	44th	F	3rd Lt[7]	Dropped from rolls Nov. 4, 1864
Babbitt, Amzi	Brgd[8]	BS[9]	Maj	Paroled at Appomattox, VA
Baker, Eli A.	47th	B	1st Lt	Killed May 26, 1864, N. Anna R., VA
Ballard, William	47th	C	Capt	Took oath Jun. 15, 1865
Barnard, Patterson Abner	48th	D	1st Lt	Resigned Feb. 20, 1863, due to wounds
Barrett, Benjamin C.	44th	H	3rd Lt	Resigned Oct. 23, 1862[10]
Barton, W. J. G.	48th	C	1st Lt	Mortally wounded Aug. 16, 1864
Bass, Washington P.	15th	A	2nd Lt	Took oath and paroled after the war[11]
Baugh, Alexander R.	15th	K	2nd Lt	Resigned Sep. 13, 1862[12]
Beard, Arthur	4th	FS	Maj	Resigned Apr. 22, 1862
Beasley, William W.	4th	FS	Ensign	Paroled at Appomattox, VA

Name	Regt	Co	Rank	Remarks
Beaty, William A.	48th	K	2nd Lt	Killed Aug. 16, 1864, Fussell's Mill, VA
Becker, Winns P.	44th	G	Capt	Took oath at Fort Delaware, MD[13]
Bedford, James M.	48th	C	Capt	Resigned Aug. 11, 1863, due to wounds
Bentley, John F.	47th	H	3rd Lt	Paroled at Appomattox, VA
Berry, Thomas D.	47th	H	1st Lt	Paroled Jun. 24, 1865, Montgomery, AL
Berry, William T.	15th	A	1st Lt	Resigned Jan. 21, 1863 for medical[14]
Bethune, William J.	15th	K	Capt	Paroled at Appomattox, VA
Billingsley, Martin T.	4th	G	1st Lt	Killed Sep. 19, 1863, Chickamauga, GA
Bonfield, J. W.	4th	K	2nd Lt	Resigned Jul. 19, 1861
Boothly, Frank L.	15th	H	1st Lt	Died of disease Dec. 15, 1865
Bowles, Pinckney Downey	4th	FS	Col	Transferred Apr. 3, 1865
Bozeman, David L.	44th	A	Capt	Mortally wounded May 8, 1864
Bradley, Jackson N.	47th	A	3rd Lt	Resigned Jul. 14, 1862
Brainard, Henry C.	15th	G	Capt	Mortally wounded Jul. 2, 1863
Brandon, Francis T. J.[15]	47th	E	Capt	Resigned Sep. 1, 1863, medical disability
Brandon, John D.	4th	I	ACS	Brigade commissary
Brazile, John H.	48th	A	2nd Lt	Dropped from rolls, prolonged absence
Breare, Joseph R.	15th	E	1st Lt	Dropped from rolls Feb. 4, 1865
Breedlove, John P.	4th	B	Capt	Parole/separation records not located[16]
Brodnax, Joseph W.	4th	A	2nd Lt	Disabled in AL at the end of war[17]
Brooks, Esaw	15th	E	Capt	Resigned Mar. 16, 1862 from wounds[18]
Brown, Baylis E.	4th	B	Capt	Killed May 6, 1864, Wilderness, VA
Brown, Bluford W.	44th	G	Capt	Resigned Dec. 9, 1862
Brown, Ira E.	4th	K	1st Lt	Resigned Apr. 22, 1862
Brown, James H.	4th	F	Capt	Paroled Apr. 23, 1865, Richmond, VA
Brown, Lewis D.	44th	B	Capt	Resigned Mar. 18, 1863
Brown, Pulaski H.	15th	K	1st Lt	Resigned Jan. 30, 1865, due to wounds[19]
Bryan, Daniel F.	15th	E	2nd Lt	Resigned Nov. 16, 1861[20]
Bryan, Lee M.	15th	L	Capt	Resigned Mar. 24, 1863
Buckelew, Seaborn B.	47th	I	1st Lt	Dropped from rolls Mar. 16, 1864
Bulger, Michael Jefferson	47th	FS	Col	Retired Feb. 14, 1865, to invalid corps
Bulger, William D.	47th	A	1st Lt	Dropped from rolls Feb. 8, 1865
Burgess, Joel F.	47th	I	1st Lt	Paroled at Appomattox, VA
Burgess, Thomas J.	48th	B	Capt	Resigned Jun. 16, 1862, medical
Burk, Francis M.	48th	G	1st Lt	Paroled at Appomattox, VA
Burns, John P.	47th	A	3rd Lt	Resigned Aug. 2, 1864, medical
Burson, Elkanah	44th	C	2nd Lt	Paroled at Appomattox, VA
Burton, Joseph Quarterman[21]	47th	H	Capt	Paroled at Appomattox, VA
Campbell, James McDonald	47th	FS	Maj	Killed May 14, 1864, Spotsylvania, VA
Cantey, James	15th	FS	Col	Transferred Jan. 8, 1863

Name	Regt	Co	Rank	Remarks
Carlisle, Standmon H.	47th	H	2nd Lt	Resigned Jan. 8, 1863, medical
Carter, John E.	15th	I	2nd Lt	Resigned Aug. 14, 1863 from wounds[22]
Cary, George Walton	44th	FS	Maj	Paroled at Appomattox, VA
Cary, Robert E.	44th	E	3rd Lt	Resigned Jan. 27, 1865, due to wounds
Chapman, Louis A.	4th	B	2nd Lt	Resigned Apr. 22, 1862
Christian, Alfred	4th	E	1st Lt	Paroled at Appomattox, VA
Christian, Thomas L.	Brgd	BS	Capt	Paroled at Appomattox, VA
Chumley, George W.	48th	B	1st Lt	Parole/separation records not located
Clarke, Richard	4th	D	Capt	Resigned Apr. 22, 1862
Clifton, Francis M.	48th	H	2nd Lt	Paroled at Appomattox, VA
Clower, Eli Daniel	47th	F	Capt	Paroled at Appomattox, VA
Cobb, Lemuel	47th	E	Capt	In AL at the end of the war
Cody, Barnett H.	15th	G	2nd Lt	Mortally wounded Jul. 2, 1863
Coggin, Ebernezer B.	47th	H	2nd Lt	Mortally wounded Sep. 19, 1863
Coker, Mason N.	44th	K	1st Lt	Paroled at Appomattox, VA
Coleman, Benjamin F.	15th	B	2nd Lt	Resigned May 15, 1862, medical
Coleman, John W.	47th	D	1st Lt	Paroled at Appomattox, VA
Coleman, Thomas K.	4th	FS	Maj	Mortally wounded Sep. 20, 1863
Coles, Robert Thompson, Jr.	4th	FS	1st Lt	Paroled at Appomattox, VA
Collins, W. W.	48th	D	2nd Lt	Paroled at Appomattox, VA
Cox, Samuel A.	48th	D	Capt	Died of disease Apr. 29, 1863
Cox, Samuel W.	48th	B	1st Lt	Dropped from rolls Dec. 7, 1864
Crosswell, Robert H.	44th	G	2nd Lt	Paroled May 20, 1865, Talladega, AL
Cullen, Hugh J.	44th	H	2nd Lt	Resigned Sep. 1, 1862, medical
Culver, Isaac Francis	15th	G	1st Lt	Resigned Feb. 26, 1862
Cussons, John	Brgd	BS	1st Lt	Transferred Jan. 7, 1865
Daniel, John Wilhite Lewis[23]	15th	FS	Maj	Resigned Jan. 24, 1862, medical
Daniel, Thomas C.	44th	G	Capt	Killed Aug. 31, 1862, Manassas, VA
Darby, James W.	4th	E	2nd Lt	Paroled at Appomattox, VA
Dawson, Lemuel H.	Brgd	BS	Capt	Paroled at Appomattox, VA
Dawson, Nathaniel H. R.[24]	4th	C	Capt	Resigned Apr. 22, 1862
DeArmond, Jerome N.	48th	B	Capt	Killed Jun. 26, 1864, Petersburg, VA
Denman, Absalom W.	44th	I	Capt	Paroled at Appomattox, VA
Derby, Charles Alexander	44th	FS	Col	Killed Sep. 17, 1862, Sharpsburg, MD
Dickson, Alvin O.	48th	A	1st Lt	Paroled at Appomattox, VA
Douglas, Thomas H.	4th	I	3rd Lt	Resigned Apr. 22, 1862
Downs, James W.	44th	K	Capt	Resigned Aug. 28, 1862, medical
Drake, Richard	Brgd	BS	Maj	Paroled Jun. 18, 1865[25]
Dryer, Thomas B.	4th	B	Capt	Resigned Apr. 22, 1862
Dudley, Richard J.	44th	A	Capt	Dropped from rolls Mar. 8, 1863

Name	Regt	Co	Rank	Remarks
Dunklin, William A.	44th	G	Capt	Killed Jul. 2, 1863, Gettysburg, PA
Edwards, Daniel B.	44th	A	Capt	In AL at the end of the war
Edwards, James R.	15th	E	3rd Lt	Paroled at Appomattox, VA
Edwards, Jeremiah	48th	F	Capt	Paroled Feb. 24, 1865
Edwards, William A.	15th	E	Capt	Resigned Sep. 2, 1863, medical
Elliott, Johnie C.	47th	K	1st Lt	Dropped from rolls Nov. 29, 1863
Ellis, Reuben	48th	F	Capt	Resigned Sep. 18, 1862, due to wounds
Ellison, James H.	15th	C	Capt	Killed Jul. 2, 1863, Gettysburg, PA
Ellison, Joseph M.	15th	C	1st Lt	Resigned Nov. 1, 1862[26]
Emmerson, F. M.	15th	L	3rd Lt	Mortally wounded Aug. 30, 1862
Eubanks, John B.	48th	F	2nd Lt	Paroled May 12, 1865
Eubanks, Thomas James	48th	D	Capt	Mortally wounded Oct. 28, 1865
Evins, James S.	4th	G	3rd Lt	Died of disease Mar. 4, 1863
Ewing, Reuben T.	48th	I	Capt	Paroled at Appomattox, VA
Farguson, John T.	47th	H	Capt	Resigned Nov. 1, 1862, medical
Fariss, Dewitt C.	4th	F	3rd Lt	Killed Aug. 29, 1862, Manassas, VA
Feagin, Isaac Ball[27]	15th	FS	Lt Col	Resigned Dec. 7, 1865, due to wound
Feagin, Noah Baxter[28]	15th	B	Capt	In AL at the end of war
Ferguson, Thomas C.	44th	E	Capt	Paroled at Appomattox, VA
Fields, Hugh	15th	A	1st Lt	Paroled at Appomattox, VA
Figures, Henry Stokes	48th	FS	1st Lt	Killed May 6, 1864, Wilderness, VA
Fletcher, James E.	4th	F	2nd Lt	Resigned Apr. 22, 1862
Fondren, John B.	44th	F	Capt	Paroled at Appomattox, VA
Fowler, Martin H.	44th	K	Capt	Paroled at Appomattox, VA
Frazer, John A.	47th	I	2nd Lt	Paroled at Appomattox, VA
Freeman, James L.	47th	G	Capt	Dropped from rolls Mar. 16, 1864
Gallaway, John H.	47th	F	2nd Lt	Resigned Jul. 28, 1863[29]
Galloway, William H.	47th	C	3rd Lt	Paroled at Appomattox, VA
Gammell, George W.	47th	K	3rd Lt	Resigned Jun. 16, 1864, from wounds[30]
Gardner, Benjamin	15th	I	Capt	Resigned Dec. 15, 1861
Gardner, John S.	44th	H	1st Lt	Resigned Sep. 1, 1864
Garmon, Albert	48th	E	3rd Lt	Court-martialed Jan. 9, 1863[31]
Garrett, Henry A.	47th	FS	Adj	Resigned Apr. 17, 1863
Gary, William P.	15th	B	2nd Lt	Paroled at Appomattox, VA
Gaskin, James A.	47th	E	Capt	Killed Sep. 30, 1864, Ft. Harrison, VA
Gibson, William T.	4th	A	3rd Lt	Died of disease Apr. 18, 1864
Gilbert, Phillip B.	48th	G	Capt	Resigned, consolidation of Co G and H
Glass, E. Jones	4th	B	Capt	Resigned Mar. 16, 1863 from wounds[32]
Glover, Henry W.	15th	B	1st Lt	Mortally wounded Oct. 13, 1864
Goldsby, Thomas Jefferson	4th	FS	Lt Col	Resigned

Name	Regt	Co	Rank	Remarks
Golightly, Robert C.	48th	H	Capt	Killed Sep. 17, 1862, Sharpsburg, MD
Golightly, William P.	48th	FS	1st Lt	Commission revoked Jun. 12, 1864
Goode, Francis M.	44th	H	Capt	Resigned Nov. 1, 1862
Goodson, Joab	44th	B	Capt	Died of disease Feb. 11, 1865
Graham, Chambers	4th	G	1st Lt	Resigned Feb. 18, 1863[33]
Graves, Randolph	48th	A	Capt	Parole/separation records not located
Gray, James H.	15th	K	2nd Lt	Mortally wounded Oct. 28, 1863
Gray, John	47th	B	1st Lt	Resigned Aug. 22, 1863[34]
Green, William N.	44th	F	Capt	Resigned Nov. 29, 1864, due to wounds
Gregory, J. J.	48th	C	3rd Lt	Resigned Jun. 7, 1862, medical
Grice, Henry Floyd	4th	C	2nd Lt	Paroled May 5, 1865, Montgomery, AL
Grice, James M.	44th	FS	Ensign	Paroled at Appomattox, VA
Grice, John G.	4th	E	1st Lt	Resigned Jun. 2, 1862, due to wounds[35]
Grimmett, William A.	47th	K	2nd Lt	Killed Aug. 30, 1862, Manassas, VA
Guerry, Lagrand L.	15th	C	Capt	In AL at the end of the war
Guerry, Nehemire D.	15th	C	1st Lt	Resigned Dec. 11, 1861, medical
Guerry, Peter V.	15th	C	Capt	Killed Jun. 27, 1862 Gaines's Mill, VA
Halsey, Orlando	4th	F	1st Lt	Resigned Aug. 24, 1863, medical
Ham, John	47th	A	Capt	Paroled
Haralson, James T.	44th	F	2nd Lt	Died of disease Dec. 24, 1862
Hardee, Joseph	4th	FS	1st Lt	Resigned Apr. 22, 1862
Hardwick, John B.	48th	H	1st Lt	Parole/separation records not located
Hardwick, Joseph B.	48th	H	1st Lt	Parole/separation records not located
Hardwick, William McTyiere	48th	FS	Lt Col	Took oath Jun. 25, 1865
Harris, Thomas B.	48th	FS	1st Lt	Resigned Sep. 21, 1862
Harris, Watkins	4th	I	Capt	In AL at the end of the war
Hart, Henry C.	15th	K	Capt	Resigned Sep. 13, 1862, medical
Harwell, William S.	4th	K	2nd Lt	Killed Jul. 2, 1863, Gettysburg, PA
Hatcher, James J.	15th	L	Capt	Paroled, Appomattox, VA[36]
Haynes, William B.	44th	A	1st Lt	Resigned Oct. 2, 1862, medical
Head, Edmond P.	15th	D	1st Lt	Killed Jul. 24, 1863, Battle Mtn., VA
Heaton, Henry A.	44th	I	2nd Lt	Paroled May 20, 1865, Talladega, AL
Heaton, John L. F.	44th	I	2nd Lt	Killed Nov. 29, 1863, Knoxville, TN[37]
Herren, James W.	47th	K	Capt	Resigned Aug. 12, 1862, medical
Herren, Wade A.	47th	FS	ACS	Dropped from rolls Sep. 1, 1863
Hill, Blanton Abram	15th	D	Capt	Mortally wounded Aug. 16, 1864
Hill, James M.	44th	B	1st Lt	Paroled at Appomattox, VA
Hill, Robert H.	15th	L	Capt	Killed Jun. 8, 1862, Cross Keys, VA
Hinds, James M.	48th	D	3rd Lt	Killed Aug. 16, 1864, Fussell's Mill, VA
Hinds, R. W. P.	48th	F	3rd Lt	Resigned Jul. 15, 1862, medical

Name	Regt	Co	Rank	Remarks
Hood, Joseph Nathaniel	47th	E	Capt	Resigned Mar. 19, 1863, due to wounds
Hooks, Daniel	15th	L	2nd Lt	Died of disease May 28, 1862
Hornbuckle, James W.	4th	G	1st Lt	Paroled at Appomattox, VA
Horton, Wylie Hill	44th	D	1st Lt	Paroled at Appomattox, VA
Howell, John H.	47th	B	3rd Lt	Resigned Aug. 16, 1862
Hubbard, John B.	48th	K	Capt	Took oath Jun. 17, 1865 and paroled
Hudson, Joseph Warren	Brgd	BS	Capt	Parole/separation records not located
Hufstutler, George W.	48th	F	2nd Lt	Died of disease Jun. 1, 1862
Hughes, Abner A.	48th	FS	Lt Col	Resigned Oct. 15, 1862, medical
Hughes, Albert F.	48th	G	1st Lt	Resigned Oct. 28, 1862
Hughes, John J.	47th	F	1st Lt	Retired Sep. 14, 1862, to invalid corps
Hughes, Robert N.	4th	F	3rd Lt	Paroled at Appomattox, VA
Hunnicutt, William R.	44th	K	1st Lt	Dropped from rolls Aug. 19, 1864
Irvine, Seymour	4th	H	2nd Lt	Resigned Mar. 10, 1863, from wounds[38]
Jackson, James Washington	47th	FS	Col	Resigned Jul. 16, 1863, medical
Jamison, William W.	47th	D	2nd Lt	Resigned Feb. 8, 1862, medical disability
Johnson, Joseph S.	44th	H	Capt	In AL at the end of the war.
Johnson, Joshua O.	44th	H	3rd Lt	Resigned Nov. 29, 1864, due to wounds
Johnston, George D.	4th	G	2nd Lt	Transferred Feb. 1862 to 25th[39]
Johnston, John Y.	47th	FS	Maj	Resigned Aug. 18, 1862
Johnston, Joseph S., Jr.	47th	B	Capt	Killed Jul. 2, 1863, Gettysburg, PA
Jones, Bush	4th	D	3rd Lt	Resigned Apr. 22, 1862
Jones, Egbert J.	4th	FS	Col	Mortally wounded Jul. 19, 1861
Jones, George Washington	4th	FS	AQM	Transferred Aug. 1, 1861, brigade QM
Jones, James Taylor	4th	D	Capt	Parole/separation records not located
Jones, James W.	48th	A	1st Lt	Dropped from rolls Apr. 23, 1863[40]
Jones, John Archibald	44th	FS	Lt Col	Paroled at Appomattox, VA
Jones, John E.	15th	E	Capt	Retired Jul. 8, 1864[41]
Jones, Met L.	44th	C	1st Lt	Dropped from rolls Nov. 26, 1863
Jones, Richard Channing[42]	44th	C	1st Lt	In AL at the end of the war
Jones, Robert P.	4th	K	Capt	Resigned Feb. 24, 1865, due to wounds
Jones, Virginius W.	44th	B	1st Lt	Killed May 6, 1864, Wilderness, VA
Jones, Watt P.	15th	B	1st Lt	Died of disease Feb. 5, 1863
Jordan, Reuben E.	47th	FS	Adj	Sick in hospital Jan. 25, 1865
Karsner, William F.	4th	H	Capt	Paroled at Appomattox, VA
Keith, James H.	4th	K	Capt	Killed Dec. 13, 1862
Kellam, James W.	47th	I	Capt	Resigned Oct. 31, 1862, medical
Keller, William H.	47th	FS	Adj	Resigned Feb. 17, 1864, medical
Kennemar, Levi	48th	E	3rd Lt	Resigned, consolidation of Co E
Kent, James	44th	FS	Col	Resigned Sep. 1, 1862, medical

Name	Regt	Co	Rank	Remarks
Kidd, Reuben Vaughan	4th	A	1st Lt	Killed Sep. 19, 1863 Chickamauga, GA
Kimball, Nathan Crawford	47th	D	1st Lt	Killed Oct. 7, 1864, Darbytown Rd., VA
King, David B.	4th	F	3rd Lt	Killed Sep. 17, 1862, Sharpsburg, MD
King, David R.	48th	B	Capt	Mortally wounded Aug. 9, 1862
King, Porter	4th	G	Capt	Resigned Apr. 22, 1862
King, William T.	44th	D	Capt	Killed Aug. 31, 1862, Manassas, VA
Kinnebrew, H. C.	48th	C	Capt	Paroled at Appomattox, VA
Kirkman, James L.	4th	H	1st Lt	Resigned Apr. 22, 1862
Kirkman, Thomas	Brgd	BS	——	Cadet at the Citadel Academy[43]
Kitchell, Frank N.	48th	FS	1st Lt	In AL at the end of the war
Knox, James H.	47th	B	1st Lt	Paroled at Appomattox, VA
Kunzie, John L.	4th	B	2nd Lt	Mortally wounded May 6, 1864
Lamar, John H.	4th	C	1st Lt	Paroled at Appomattox, VA
Langley, Edmond B.	47th	A	1st Lt	Paroled at Appomattox, VA
Lanier, Isaac A.	4th	I	1st Lt	Resigned Aug. 19, 1861, due to wounds
Lapsley, Robert	Brgd	BS	Capt	Paroled at Appomattox, VA
Larkin, George W. A.	4th	K	2nd Lt	Resigned Apr. 22, 1862
Law, Evander McIver	Brgd	BC	BG	Transferred Jan. 7, 1865
Law, John K.	Brgd	BS	——	Cadet at the Citadel Academy[44]
Lawrence, John W.	44th	G	1st Lt	In AL at the end of the war[45]
Lee, Moses	48th	K	Capt	Killed Aug. 30, 1862, Manassas, VA
Lee, William	4th	E	Capt	Killed Jul. 2, 1863, Gettysburg, PA
Leftwich, William W.	4th	F	Capt	Killed Jul. 2, 1863, Gettysburg, PA
Lewis, Benjamin H.	15th	F	Capt	Resigned Feb. 7, 1862, medical[46]
Lewis, Robert G.	4th	B	1st Lt	Resigned Feb. 24, 1863
Lindsay, Henry C.	47th	D	Capt	In AL at the end of the war
Lindsay, Lewis Ervin	4th	K	Capt	Killed Jul. 21, 1861, Manassas, VA
Lloyd, Benjamin F.	15th	C	3rd Lt	Died of disease Dec. 3, 1861
Lloyd, William P.	15th	C	1st Lt	Paroled at Appomattox, VA
Longhridge, James T.	44th	F	1st Lt	Paroled at Appomattox, VA
Love, Thomas W.	44th	E	2nd Lt	Resigned Nov. 4, 1862
Lowther, Alexander A.	15th	FS	Col	Paroled at Appomattox, VA
Lumpkin, Thomas J.	48th	H	Capt	Paroled at Appomattox, VA
Lusk, John M.	48th	I	2nd Lt	Mortally wounded Sep. 19, 1863
Malone, George Y.	15th	F	Capt	Resigned Mar. 18, 1863, due to wound
Mastin, Gustavus Boardman	4th	F	Capt	Killed May 31, 1862, Seven Pines, VA
Mathews, George A. C.	15th	I	1st Lt	Paroled Jun. 7, 1865, Montgomery, AL
Mayo, Elisha	47th	F	1st Lt	Paroled Jun. 7, 1865, Montgomery, AL
McCaghren, P. T. G.	48th	I	1st Lt	Paroled at Appomattox, VA
McClendon, William Augustus	15th	G	2nd Lt	Paroled at Appomattox, VA

Name	Regt	Co	Rank	Remarks
McConnico, Gardner W.	44th	FS	ACS	Parole/separation records not located
McCraw, S. Newton	4th	C	2nd Lt	Resigned Apr. 22, 1862
McDonald, Thomas J., Jr.	47th	B	Capt	Paroled at Appomattox, VA
McDuffie, Norman H.	48th	G	Capt	Parole/separation records not located
McFarland, Robert	4th	H	Capt	Resigned Apr. 22, 1862
McInnis, Archibald D.	4th	E	Capt	Parole/separation records not located
McIntosh, Angus A.	15th	D	3rd Lt	Killed Jun. 27, 1862
McIntosh, William C.	47th	H	1st Lt	Resigned Jan. 3, 1863, medical[47]
McKee, John V.	47th	G	Capt	Died of disease Jun. 11, 1863
McKinne, Barna	4th	FS	AQM	Transferred Mar. 1, 1863[48]
McLemore, Owen Kenan	4th	FS	Lt Col	Mortally wounded Sep. 14, 1863[49]
McLendon, Simeon K.	47th	K	1st Lt	Paroled at Appomattox, VA
Melton, Simeon W.	47th	B	3rd Lt	Paroled May 3, 1865
Menefee, Albert	47th	D	Capt	Killed Aug. 9, 1862, Cedar Run, VA
Metcalf, James H.	15th	H	2nd Lt	Resigned May 19, 1862[50]
Mills, Wesley B.	15th	E	2nd Lt	Killed Jun. 5, 1862, Cross Keys, VA
Moon, Thomas L.	48th	B	3rd Lt	Resigned Jul. 17, 1862, medical[51]
Morgan, Lewis A.	4th	D	2nd Lt	Paroled at Appomattox, VA
Moragne, John S.	48th	G	Capt	Resigned Aug. 6, 1862[52]
Morris, Cornelius V.	15th	FS	ACS	Resigned Dec. 31, 1864
Morris, Richard	15th	K	3rd Lt	Resigned Jun. 14, 1863[53]
Morrow, Thomas L.	44th	D	Capt	Resigned Jul. 12, 1864[54]
Moseley, Henry H.	4th	G	Capt	Paroled at Appomattox, VA
Murray, Alexander C.	4th	K	Capt	Killed Jul. 28, 1864, Petersburg, VA
Nabors, James H.	44th	D	2nd Lt	Resigned Aug. 12, 1862
Nance, Sterling A.	4th	H	1st Lt	Paroled at Appomattox, VA
Nation, David	48th	A	2nd Lt	Resigned Jul. 10, 1862, age 56 years
Neilson, John H.	44th	E	Capt	Killed May 8, 1864
Newbill, George H.	4th	K	3rd Lt	Paroled at Appomattox, VA
Newell, Isaac M.	47th	G	1st Lt	Died of disease Jun. 9, 1864
Newman, Martin W.	48th	B	2nd Lt	Resigned Oct. 11, 1862, medical
Newsome, William O.	4th	H	2nd Lt	Mortally wounded May 6, 1864
Nickolson, P. W.	15th	F	2nd Lt	Took oath Jun. 6, 1865 and paroled
Nicoll, Thomas A.	44th	FS	Adj	Took oath Jun. 14, 1865 and paroled
Norred, Preston B.	44th	I	3rd Lt	Killed Jul. 2, 1863, Gettysburg, PA
Nuckolls, Thomas J.	15th	A	2nd Lt	Resigned Dec. 30, 1862[55]
Nuckolls, William T.	15th	A	2nd Lt	Died of disease Nov. 4, 1861
O'Connor, Patrick	15th	K	3rd Lt	Killed Jun. 1, 1864
Oakes, John H.	44th	D	1st Lt	Retirement Nov. 2, 1864[56]
Oakes, Jonas	44th	D	Capt	Captured Jun. 3, 1863 and paroled

Name	Regt	Co	Rank	Remarks
Oakley, William D.	44th	F	1st Lt	Resigned Jun. 18, 1863; elected sheriff
Oates, John A.	15th	G	1st Lt	Mortally wounded Jul. 2, 1863
Oates, William Calvin	15th	FS	Col	Transferred Mar. 23, 1864
Ogilvie, John D.	4th	K	Capt	Died of disease Mar. 27, 1864
Oliver, James MCarthy	47th	FS	Col	Resigned Aug. 2, 1862, medical[57]
Park, Frank	15th	I	Capt	Mortally wounded Nov. 25, 1863
Parks, Isaac H.	15th	I	2nd Lt	Paroled at Appomattox, VA
Parton, Joseph J	4th	F	2nd Lt	Took oath Jun. 12, 1865 and paroled
Patterson, Allen D.	15th	E	2nd Lt	Died of disease Jan. 27, 1862
Paul, Robert	15th	L	3rd Lt	Died of disease May 25, 1862
Perry, William Flake[58]	Brgd	BC	BG	Paroled at Appomattox, VA
Peterson, Battle D.	4th	B	2nd Lt	Killed Jan. 16, 1864, Dandridge, TN
Pettit, H. L.	48th	K	Capt	Paroled at Appomattox, VA
Pettway, John H.	44th	B	3rd Lt	Dropped from rolls Feb. 29, 1864
Pinckard, Thomas C.	Brgd	BS	2nd Lt	Paroled at Appomattox, VA
Pitts, David W.	4th	D	3rd Lt	Killed Jul. 21, 1861, Manassas, VA
Pollard, John J.	48th	FS	Ensign	Paroled May 30, 1865, Talladega, AL
Porter, Fred M.	15th	K	1st Lt	Mortally wounded Sep. 19, 1863
Pounds, Richard F.	48th	I	2nd Lt	Resigned Aug. 30, 1862
Pounds, William L.	48th	I	3rd Lt	Resigned Sep. 16, 1862
Powers, Robert	44th	C	Capt	Paroled at Appomattox, VA
Price, Alfred C.	4th	C	Capt	Mortally wounded Jun. 27, 1862
Prior, Thomas J.	15th	F	1st Lt	Paroled at Appomattox, VA
Purifoy, John W.	44th	C	Capt	Resigned Feb. 2, 1863, due to wounds
Randolph, William	44th	E	1st Lt	Dismissed Apr. 14, 1863, Court-martial
Ray, Andrew	47th	E	3rd Lt	Killed Jul. 2, 1863 at Gettysburg, PA
Ray, Augustus	44th	I	3rd Lt	Killed Sep. 17, 1862, Sharpsburg, MD
Rayburn, Samuel K.	48th	E	Capt	Resigned Jun. 13, 1862
Rearden, William W.	47th	D	3rd Lt	Resigned Nov. 5, 1862, medical
Reese, George	44th	A	1st Lt	Paroled at Appomattox, VA
Renfroe, Thomas M.	15th	G	1st Lt	Retired Nov. 15, 1864
Rice, Erwin Foster	48th	K	1st Lt	In AL at the end of the war
Richardson, William A.	15th	H	Capt	Took oath Jun. 10, 1865, released
Riddle, Patrick P.	44th	K	Capt	Died of disease Aug. 3, 1862
Ridgeway, James S.	48th	D	1st Lt	Captured Jul. 8, 1863[59]
Rison, William B.	4th	F	3rd Lt	Resigned Apr. 22, 1862
Robbins, Frank C.	4th	C	Capt	Paroled at Appomattox, VA
Robbins, William McKendre	4th	FS	Maj	Paroled at Appomattox, VA
Roberts, George A.	15th	K	1st Lt	Resigned Jun. 11, 1862, medical
Robinson, William H.	4th	K	Capt	Resigned Aug. 19, 1862, due to wounds

Name	Regt	Co	Rank	Remarks
Robinson, William W. C.	47th	I	2nd Lt	Resigned Sep. 9, 1862
Roper, Henry Bently[60]	4th	I	3rd Lt	In AL at the end of the war
Rose, John	48th	E	2nd Lt	Resigned Jul. 17, 1862
Ross, Francis M.	48th	E	Capt	Resigned under arrest Jun. 1, 1862
Ross, Jesse E.	48th	B	2nd Lt	Resigned Jul. 20, 1862
Rottenberry, Henry F.	44th	H	2nd Lt	Paroled
Rowland, A. M.	4th	I	1st Lt	Transferred to a GA regt., May 1862
Russell, Joseph T.	47th	C	Capt	Resigned Jan. 8, 1864, medical
Sale, Charles C.	4th	I	Capt	Died of disease Sep. 6, 1861
Samuel, Patterson M.	4th	A	2nd Lt	Resigned Sep. 25, 1862
Samuels, Thomas L.	4th	A	3rd Lt	Retired Dec. 24, 1864, to invalid corps
Sanford, James A.	47th	K	Capt	Killed May 6, 1864, Wilderness, VA
Savage, Robert Russell[61]	47th	E	Capt	Resigned Nov. 10, 1862, medical
Scoggins, William H.	15th	E	3rd Lt	Died of disease Sep. 11, 1963
Scott, Charles Lewis	4th	FS	Maj	Resigned Jul. 23, 1862, due to wounds
Scott, David B.	4th	G	2nd Lt	Resigned Jan. 13, 1863, medical
Scott, Willis L.	48th	I	1st Lt	Resigned Oct. 6, 1862, medical
Scruggs, Lawrence Houston	4th	FS	Lt Col	Paroled at Appomattox, VA
Scruggs, William H.	Brgd	BS	Maj	Paroled at Appomattox, VA
Shaaff, Francis Key	15th	A	Capt	Paroled at Appomattox, VA
Shealy, John N.	47th	F	2nd Lt	Died of disease Sep. 10, 1862
Sheffield, James Lawrence	48th	FS	Col	Resigned May 31, 1864
Sheppard, John H.	48th	B	1st Lt	Resigned Jan. 7, 1864, due to wounds
Shortridge, George D., Jr.	4th	C	1st Lt	Resigned Apr. 22, 1862
Simmons, Henry D.	47th	B	3rd Lt	Killed Jul. 2, 1863, Gettysburg, PA
Simpson, John J.	4th	H	1st Lt	Killed Jul. 21, 1861, Manassas, VA
Sinclair, Thomas J.[62]	48th	FS	1st Lt	Paroled at Appomattox, VA
Sistrunk, Robert W.	4th	B	3rd Lt	Resigned Apr. 22, 1862
Small, Issom B.	48th	E	Capt	Died of disease Jun. 24, 1864
Smith, C. V.	15th	E	3rd Lt	Declined promotion Feb. 25, 1864
Smith, David J.	47th	FS	Ensign	Paroled at Appomattox, VA
Smith, James M.	48th	D	2nd Lt	Resigned Jun. 13, 1862, medical
Smith, Otterson	48th	G	2nd Lt	Resigned Jan. 1, 1864
Smitherman, Thomas F.	44th	H	2nd Lt	Resigned Aug. 1, 1863[63]
Snead, Henley G.	44th	F	Capt	Resigned Jun. 18, 1863
Sparks, James Thomas	48th	C	1st Lt	Resigned Dec. 29, 1862
Spraggins, Elias C.	4th	I	1st Lt	Resigned Apr. 22, 1862, Yorktown, VA
St. John, Columbus B.	48th	F	1st Lt	Retired Nov. 2, 1864, to invalid corps
Stanton, F. D.	15th	H	2nd Lt	Resigned Jun. 18, 1862, medical
Starke, A. W.	15th	I	3rd Lt	Resigned May 1, 1862, medical

Name	Regt	Co	Rank	Remarks
Stearns, John S.	4th	E	3rd Lt	Paroled at Appomattox, VA
Sterrett, Major Dowell	4th	C	Capt	Resigned Jan. 24, 1863, due to wounds
Stewart, James H.	4th	I	1st Lt	In AL at the end of the war
Stokes, John G.	4th	B	3rd Lt	Resigned May 3, 1861
Strickland, William H.	15th	I	Capt	In AL at the end of the war
Sullivan, James H.	4th	K	Capt	Killed Sep. 17, 1862, Sharpsburg, MD
Sutton, James T.	48th	G	1st Lt	Dropped from rolls Nov. 28, 1864
Swan, Joseph N.	47th	E	1st Lt	Resigned Mar. 9, 1864, due to wounds
Taliaferro, Charles T.	4th	E	2nd Lt	Resigned Oct. 9, 1862, medical
Taylor, William H.	4th	F	1st Lt	Resigned Apr. 22, 1862
Teague, John M.	44th	K	Capt	Killed Jul. 2, 1863, Gettysburg, PA
Terrell, Leigh Richmond[64]	4th	D	Lt Col	Transferred to 47th AL Infantry
Thornton, Dozier	15th	D	1st Lt	In AL at the end of the war
Thornton, Richard A.	44th	A	3rd Lt	Returned to the ranks Aug. 24, 1863[65]
Tidwell, S. R.	48th	A	1st Lt	Resigned Jun. 10, 1863, medical
Todd, James A.	47th	K	Capt	Paroled May 22, 1865, Talladega, AL
Towles, Albert	47th	I	Capt	Court-martial conviction Feb. 19, 1863
Tracey, Edward Dorr	4th	I	Capt	Transferred Aug. 1, 1861[66]
Travis, Mark B.	4th	E	3rd Lt	Resigned Apr. 22, 1862, Yorktown, VA
Treutlen, John Fletcher	15th	FS	Col	Resigned Apr. 28, 1863, medical
Turnbow, James M.	4th	G	2nd Lt	Killed Jul. 2, 1863, Gettysburg, PA
Turner, Daniel H.	4th	I	2nd Lt	Parole/separation records not located
Turner, Gasbon W.	47th	H	2nd Lt	Resigned Aug. 1, 1862
Turner, James C.	4th	F	1st Lt	Killed Jul. 21, 1861, Manassas, VA
Turner, William F.	4th	D	1st Lt	Paroled at Appomattox, VA[67]
Turrentine, Daniel C.	48th	FS	1st Lt	Resigned Jun. 25, 1863
Tweedell, John F.	44th	I	1st Lt	Paroled Jun. 20, 1865
Tyler, Spenser C.	48th	E	1st Lt	Died of disease Jun. 24, 1864
Vaughan, Paul Turner	4th	C	3rd Lt	Resigned Dec. 12, 1864
Vernoy, James	15th	FS	ACS	Transferred from the regiment
Vincent, Isaac H.	47th	I	Capt	Paroled at Appomattox, VA
Waddell, DeBernie B.	15th	G	Capt	Paroled at Appomattox, VA
Wadsworth, John N.	15th	F	3rd Lt	Paroled at Appomattox, VA
Walker, Mims	Brgd	BS	1st Lt	Transferred from 4th AL Jan. 1, 1863
Walker, William S.	48th	C	Capt	Resigned Oct. 1, 1862
Walls, Willis W.	47th	G	Capt	Paroled at Appomattox, VA
Ward, John T. C.	47th	C	2nd Lt	Resigned Mar. 16, 1864
Weems, Locke	15th	A	Capt	Killed Jun. 27, 1862, Gaines's Mill, VA
West, Jason M.	4th	A	Capt	Paroled Appomattox, VA
Whitaker, James	47th	G	Capt	Resigned Nov. 29, 1864, due to wounds

Name	Regt	Co	Rank	Remarks
Wicker, Robert H.	15th	L	3rd Lt	Took oath on Jun. 12, 1865
Wiggenton, James W.	48th	FS	Maj	Paroled at Appomattox, VA
Williams, Dekalb	15th	F	Capt	In AL at the end of the war
Williams, Thomas H.	44th	E	3rd Lt	Resigned Aug. 19, 1862
Wilson, James S.	15th	D	1st Lt	Resigned Dec. 5, 1861
Wilson, John R.	4th	C	3rd Lt	Resigned Apr. 22, 1862
Wilson, William L.	15th	H	2nd Lt	Retired Feb. 24, 1865, due to wounds
Wood, William D.	15th	H	1st Lt	Resigned Aug. 1, 1863
Woodliff, Augustus L.	48th	G	Capt	Resigned Oct. 1, 1862, medical[68]
Woolfolk, Thomas J.	15th	FS	AQM	Transferred Jan. 1, 1863
Worthington, Moses	15th	D	Capt	Resigned Oct. 21, 1861
Wright, Robert E.	15th	B	Capt	Resigned Oct. 8, 1863, due to wounds
Wykley, Remmer H.	48th	G	2nd Lt	Resigned Jul. 17, 1863
Young, Benjamin P.	47th	C	1st Lt	Resigned Aug. 15, 1862, medical[69]
Young, James Harvey	4th	K	Capt	Resigned Apr. 22, 1862
Zimmerman, William C.	4th	G	3rd Lt	Resigned Nov. 10, 1862

Appendix D

Brigade Statistics[1]

Enrollment[2]

Reg't	Officers	Enrolled Men	Aggregate	Officers	Surrendered[3] Men	Aggregate
4th	98	1324	1422	21	202	223
15th	78	1555	1633	15	204	219
44th	63	1031	1094	17	192	209
47th	66	1000	1066	16	171	188
48th	70	975	1045	13	122	135
Totals	375	5885	[4]6260	82	891	[5]973

Brigade Casualties

Reg't	Officers	Killed Men	Aggregate	Officers	Died of Wounds Men	Aggregate
4th	26	160	179	7	47	54
15th	17	168	177	8	72	80
44th	12	97	105	2	28	30
47th	14	92	102	4	25	29
48th	10	99	105	4	37	41
Totals	79	614	668	25	209	234

Other Deaths and Prisoners of War

Reg't	Officers	Died of Disease Men	Aggregate	Officers	Absent/Captured Men	Aggregate
4th	4	77	81	1	53	54
15th	8	430	438	5	131	136
44th	3	189	192	2	64	66
47th	4	162	166	1	37	38
48th	3	158	161	2	57	59
Totals	22	1016	1038	11	342	353

Other Separations[6]

Reg't	Resigned	Retired	Discharged	Transferred	Deserted
4th	38	9	389	119	72
15th	29	21	183	46	51
44th	20	15	95	47	69
47th	25	12	132	76	64
48th	41	3	91	34	77
Totals	153	60	890	323	333

Appendix E

Battles and Skirmishes

Event	Date	Participating Regiments
Manassas, VA	Jul. 21, 1861	4th [1]
Rappahannock River, VA	Apr. 1862	15th[2]
Eltham's Landing, VA	May 7, 1862	4th
Front Royal, VA	May 23, 1862	15th
Winchester, VA	May 25, 1862	15th
Seven Pines, VA	May 31, 1862	4th
Cross Keys, VA	Jun. 8, 1862	15th
Port Republic, VA	Jun. 9, 1862	15th
Gaines's Mill, VA[3]	Jun. 27, 1862	4th, 15th
Malvern Hill, VA	Jul. 1, 1862	4th, 15th
Cedar Run, VA[4]	Aug. 9, 1862	15th, 47th[5], 48th[6]
Rappahannock River, VA	Aug. 12, 1862	15th
Hazel River, VA	Aug. 22, 1862	4th, 15th
Warrenton Springs, VA	Aug. 26, 1862	4th
Groveton, VA[7]	Aug. 28, 1862	15th, 47th, 48th
Manassas, VA[8]	Aug. 29, 1862	4th, 15th, 47th, 48th
Manassas, VA[9]	Aug. 30, 1862	4th, 15th, 44th, 47th, 48th
Chantilly, VA[10]	Sep. 1, 1862	15th, 47th, 48th
Boonsboro, MD[11]	Sep. 14, 1862	4th
Harpers Ferry, VA	Sep. 14, 1862	15th, 47th, 48th
Harpers Ferry, VA	Sep. 15, 1862	15th, 47th, 48th
Sharpsburg, MD	Sep. 16, 1862	4th
Sharpsburg, MD	Sep. 17, 1862	4th, 15th, 44th[12], 47th, 48th
Shepherdstown, MD	Sep. 19, 1862	15th
Fredericksburg, MD	Dec. 13, 1862	4th, 15th, 44th, 47th, 48th
Fort Huger, VA	Apr. 19, 1863	44th
Suffolk, VA	Apr. 28, 1863	15th, 44th
Suffolk, VA	Apr. 30, 1863	15th
Suffolk, VA	May 2, 1863	15th
Suffolk, VA	May 3, 1863	4th, 15th
Gettysburg, PA	Jul. 2, 1863	4th, 15th, 44th, 47th, 48th
Gettysburg, PA	Jul. 3, 1863	4th, 15th, 44th, 47th, 48th
Falling Waters, MD	Jul. 14, 1863	4th
Thoroughfare Gap, VA[13]	Jul. 23, 1863	4th
Battle Mountain, VA	Jul. 24, 1863	15th
Thorton River, VA[14]	Jul. 24, 1863	4th

Event	Date	Participating Regiments
Hazel River, VA	Jul. 27, 1863	4th
Port Royal, VA	Aug. 23, 1863	48th
Chickamauga, GA	Sep. 19, 1863	4th, 15th, 44th, 47th, 48th
Chickamauga, GA	Sep. 20, 1863	4th, 15th, 44th, 47th, 48th
Brown's Ferry, TN	Oct. 28, 1863	15th
Wauhatchie, TN[15]	Oct. 28, 1863	4th, 15th, 44th, 47th, 48th
Loudon, TN[16]	Nov. 14, 1863	4th
Campbell's Station, TN	Nov. 16, 1863	4th, 15th, 44th, 47th
Knoxville, TN	Nov. 25, 1863	4th, 15th, 48th
Knoxville Heights, TN	Nov. 29, 1863	4th, 15th, 44th, 47th
Knoxville, TN	Dec. 1, 1863	4th
Bean's Station, TN	Dec. 23, 1863	4th, 15th
Dandridge, TN	Jan. 16, 1864	4th, 15th, 44th, 47th, 48th
Dandridge, TN	Jan. 17, 1864	47th
Wilderness, VA	May 6, 1864	4th, 15th, 44th, 47th, 48th
Spotsylvania, VA	May 8, 1864	4th, 15th, 44th, 47th, 48th
Spotsylvania, VA	May 10, 1864	4th, 15th, 44th, 47th, 48th
Spotsylvania, VA	May 12, 1864	4th, 15th, 44th, 47th, 48th
Hanover Junction, VA	May 25, 1863	4th, 15th, 47th, 48th
Ashland, VA	May 31, 1864	15th
Mechanicsville Rd., VA	Jun. 1, 1864	4th, 15th, 44th, 48th
Cold Harbor, VA	Jun. 3, 1864	4th, 15th, 44th, 47th, 48th
Chester Station, VA[17]	Jun. 17, 1864	4th, 15th, 44th, 47th, 48th
Petersburg, VA	Jun. 18 – Jul. 25, 1864	4th, 15th, 44th, 47th, 48th
Deep Bottom, VA[18]	Aug. 14, 1864	4th, 15th, 48th
Fussell's Mill, VA	Aug. 16, 1864	4th, 15th, 47th, 48th
Fort Gilmer, VA	Sep. 29, 1864	4th, 15th, 48th
Fort Harrison, VA	Sep. 30, 1864	4th, 15th, 44th, 47th, 48th
Darbytown, Rd., VA	Oct. 7, 1864	4th, 15th, 44th, 47th, 48th
Darbytown, Rd., VA	Oct. 13, 1864	4th, 15th, 44th, 47th, 48th
Darbytown, Rd., VA[19]	Oct. 27, 1864	4th, 15th, 44th, 47th, 48th
Darbytown, Rd., VA	Dec. 10, 1864	4th, 15th, 44th, 47th, 48th
Appomattox Court House, VA	Apr. 9, 1865	4th, 15th, 44th, 47th, 48th

Appendix F

Casualties from Selected Battles

Battle of Gettysburg, PA – Jul. 2, 3, 1863

Regt	Strength Officers	Men	Aggregate
4th	39	298	337
15th	35	452	487
44th	31	288	319
47th	36	254	290
48th	35	240	275
Brigade	6	0	6
Totals	182	1532	1714

Reg't	Killed Off	Men	Ag	Wounded[1] Off	Men	Ag	Missing Off	Men	Ag	Aggregate Off	Men	Ag
4th	4	14	18	4	45	49	3	20	23	11	79	90
15th	4	18	22	1	65	66	3	81	84	8	164	172
[2] 44th	3	22	25	2	62	64	0	5	5	5	89	94
47th	4	6	10	1	39	40	2	15	17	7	60	67
48th	0	10	10	7	61	68	2	22	24	9	93	102
Brigade	0	0	0	0	0	0	1	0	1	1	0	1
Totals	15	70	85	15	272	287	11	143	154	41	485	526
								Percent:		23	32	31

Battle of Chickamauga, GA – Sep. 19, 20, 1863

Reg't	Strength Officers	Men	Aggregate
4th	24	225	249
15th	24	349	373
44th	28	248	276
47th	26	257	283
48th	25	251	276
Brigade	5	0	5
Totals	132	1330	1462

Reg't	Killed Off	Men	Ag	Wounded Off	Men	Ag	Missing Off	Men	Ag	Aggregate Off	Men	Ag
4th[3]	3	9	12	4	41	45	1	0	1	8	50	58
15th[4]	1	10	11	5	116	121	0	0	0	6	126	132
44th[5]	0	10	10	6	65	71	0	8	8	6	83	89
47th[6]	1	6	7	5	51	56	0	7	7	6	64	70
48th[7]	1	18	19	7	60	67	0	1	1	8	79	87
Brigade	0	0	0	0	0	0	0	0	0	0	0	0
Totals	6	53	59	27	333	360	1	16	17	34	402	436
									Percent:	26	30	30

Battle of Wilderness, VA – May 6, 1864

Reg't	Strength Officers	Men	Aggregate
4th	22	181	203
15th	20	278	298
44th	26	254	280
47th	23	219	242
48th	18	153	171
Brigade	4	0	4
Totals	113	1085	1198

Reg't	Killed Off	Men	Ag	Wounded Off	Men	Ag	Missing Off	Men	Ag	Aggregate Off	Men	Ag
4th[8]	3	10	13	6	43	49	0	7	7	9	60	69
15th	0	5	5	2	24	26	1	12	13	3	41	44
44th	1	5	6	7	29	36	0	5	5	8	39	47
47th	2	14	16	2	47	49	1	16	17	5	77	82
48th	1	4	5	2	11	13	0	8	8	3	23	26
Brigade	0	0	0	0	0	0	0	0	0	0	0	0
Totals	7	38	45	19	154	173	2	48	50	28	240	268
									Percent:	25	22	22

Note: Off   =   Officers

        Ag   =   Aggregate

     Reg't   =   Regiment

Appendix G

The Resignation of E. M. Law

Brigade Headquarters
December 17, 1863

General,[1]

I have the honor to tender my resignation of the position of Brigadier General in the Provisional Army, and to make the following explanatory statement.

As senior Brigadier of Hood's Division, I commanded it during the greater portion of two days at the Battle of Gettysburg– General Hood being disabled by wounds– during the retreat from Pennsylvania and on the 19th and 20th of September at Chickamauga. For the manner in which my duties as Division Commander were discharged, in camp and on the field during that most eventful period in the history of the Division, I refer to those who alone have a right to sit in judgment, my superior officers. And, as an additional evidence, I would call attention to the opinion of those who have served under my command, as expressed to the President, by the Brigade Commanders for themselves, their officers and men.

Immediately after the Battle of Chickamauga, Brigadier General Jenkins was assigned to Hood's Division, and, by virtue of an older commission (being six or seven weeks my senior) assumed command of the Division. Although not identified with it by association or service on a single battlefield of the war, and in opposition to the expressed wishes of the officers, he has been nominated as permanent Division Commander by the Lieutenant General commanding the Corps.

Aside from the individual injustice done in such cases, if the prospect of promotion which is the only manner in which our government recognizes faithful and efficient service in our army, is taken away from its officers, however fine and lofty the patriotism which animates them, they must lose much of that interest and enthusiasm which renders military service most effective.

This resignation is not tendered in a spirit of resentment or pique but under the deliberate conviction that in the unsatisfactory and unpleasant situation in which I am placed by the circumstances that have been stated, I cannot serve the country with that intense enthusiasm which she has right to demand from all of her sons. From the Battle of Chickamauga until now, I have summated quietly to what I could not but consider as injustice, and have performed my duties without complaining because I felt that the exigencies of our situation demanded it. Now that the campaign has closed and the purpose no longer exists, I desire to place myself in some other (though much humbler) position in which I may render service to my country with satisfaction to myself.

I am General,
Very Respectfully
E. M. Law
Brigadier General

General S. Cooper
Adjutant & Inspector General[2]

Endnotes

Introduction

1. Among the original officers of the 4th Alabama, 22% listed their occupation as lawyer, 17% were planters, there was one military instructor and one "gentleman." 4th AL Inf, ADAH.
2. Richmond *Times-Dispatch*, Aug. 20, 1905.
3. Yorkville (SC) *Enquirer,* Jul. 8, 1858.
4. Richard M. McMurry, *John Bell Hood*, 76.
5. *CV*, v20, n11, 1912. A quarter of the officers of Law's brigade were killed or disabled. Twenty-eight percent of the brigade officers received at least one wound.
6. The brigade attacked at Gettysburg, Chickamauga, the Wilderness, Fort Harrison, Fussell's Mill, First Darbytown and Second Darbytown. In Lookout Valley (twice), Cold Harbor and Spotsylvania they withstood assaults.
7. Oates, *The War*, 492.
8. G. Moxley Sorrel, *Recollections of a Confederate Staff Officer*, 230.
9. Law, *B&L*, v3, 319.
10. Sommers, *Richmond Redeemed*, xii, xiii.
11. Law, "The Fight for Richmond in 1862," 649.
12. Ibid., 723.

Chapter 1 – Law Earns His Commission

1. Moore, *Alabama and Her People*, v1, 412–413, 418.
2. Garrett, *Public Men in Alabama*, 720.
3. Moore, *Alabama and Her People*, v1, 511–512.
4. Smith, *History and Debates*, 118–119.
5. Bulger, Surname File, ADAH.
6. Smith, *History and Debates*, 108–109.
7. Bulger, Surname File, ADAH.
8. Smith, *History of Debates*, 356–358.
9. McIver is pronounced "Ma-Keev-er." Although

known as McIver, Law's cousin and classmate at the Citadel, Tom Law, called him "Keever." Thomas Law, *Citadel Cadets*, 22.

10. J. Law, *Adger-Law Notebook*, 85. Society Hill was a satellite community of Darlington, SC.
11. Law, Surname File, ADAH.
12. Law's Oath of Allegiance, signed Sep. 12, 1865, in Darlington County Historical Commission; Interview with Law's granddaughter, Jane Law Norvell, Feb. 1, 1993.
13. Thomas Law, *Citadel Cadets*, 23, 302. The military manuals were Winfield Scott, *Infantry–Tactics; Or, Rules for the Exercise and Manoeuvers of the United States Infantry* (3 vols., New York, 1852) and William J. Hardee, *Rifle and Light Infantry Tactics; for the Exercise and Manoeuvers of Troops when acting as Light Infantry or Riflemen* (2 vols., Philadelphia, 1855).
14. Quoted in Thomas Law, *Citadel Cadets*, 10–11.
15. Law got 92 demerits during the year. Two hundred demerits were grounds for dismissal. OROC at the SCMA, Nov., 1856, 7, 12–13.
16. Thomas Law, *Citadel Cadets*, 36–39. John Francis Lanneau, later captain of cavalry in the Hampton Legion and president of several colleges, including Wake Forest, graduated first in the class of 1856. J. A. Scott left the Citadel Sep. 19, 1856, with an honorable discharge. H. D. Moore served as chaplain of the 12th AL, was president of two colleges and an ordained minister. R. M. Sims was a captain in the 6th SC of Micah Jenkins's Brigade. A member of Longstreet's staff, Sims carried the flag of truce which ended hostilities at Appomattox. According to Law family legend, Judge Law had to make several trips to the Citadel to speak on McIver's behalf after the youngster got into scrapes.
17. Thomas Law, *Citadel Cadets*, 65–69; OROC of the SCMA, Nov. 1856, 7, 12–13.

18. The SCMA furnished 193 officers to the Confederacy out of 224 living graduates through the class of 1863. Thirty-nine were killed in action and four died while in the service. Freeman, *Lee's Lts*, v1, 710. Law met cadets at the Citadel who figured prominently in his military career, particularly in East Tennessee in 1863.

19. Dawson to Elodie Todd, letters of May 10, 1861, and May 13, 1861, NDP.

20. Marion *Star*, Dec. 16, 1856.

21. 8th U.S. Census, 1860.

22. Law, Surname File, ADAH.

23. ADAH; Citadel Alumni Office Records; *Dictionary of American Biography*, v11, 38–39. Law's partner in the school was Robert Parks.

24. Law's Oath of Allegiance, Sep. 12, 1865.

25. Yorkville *Enquirer*, Feb. 7, 1861.

26. Coles, "Company Sketches," 3, 5–6.

27. Bowles, Surname File, ADAH; *Memorial Record*, v1, 703–705; *CMH*, v8, 393; Pinckney Bowles to Marcus Wright, Oct. 5, 1886, WRHS.

28. Jones, "First Blood," 36; Porter King Diary, Apr. 24, 1861, USAMHI.

29. SG 11139 #5, ADAH. The flag was presented to the state archives in 1957 by the surviving daughter of Robert N. Smith, Co. D, 4th AL.

30. Selma *Reporter*, Apr. 25, 1861.

31. Pierrepont, *Reuben Kidd*, 267.

32. SG 11139#5, ADAH. The flag was presented to the State of Alabama on Nov. 14, 1907 by Pinckney Bowles and James W. Durby.

33. Anderson, "War Diary"; Coles, "Company Sketches," 9.

34. Brewer, *Public Men*, 530.

35. "Reminiscences of the Fourth Alabama," Marion *Commonwealth*, Sep. 6, 1866, 4th AL Inf, ADAH, indicates McFarland opposed Law; Alphine Sterrett Scrapbook, 4th AL Inf, ADAH, reported Law was unanimously elected.

36. Chestnut, *Chestnut's Civil War*, 25, 213.

37. Alphine Sterrett Scrapbook, 4th AL Inf, ADAH.

38. Porter King Diary, May 14, 1861, USAMHI.

39. *OR*, v2, 470 gives the organization of the Third Brigade at the First Battle of Manassas as the 4th Alabama, 2nd Mississippi, 11th Mississippi, 1st Tennessee, and Imboden's Battery.

40. Dawson to Elodie Todd, May 10, 1861, NDP.

41. Coles, "The First Manassas Campaign," 18.

42. Dawson to Elodie Todd, May 29, 1861, NDP.

43. Owen, *Alabama Dictionary*, v4, 920; Coles, "The First Manassas Campaign," 18–19.

44. Dawson to Elodie Todd, Jun. 25, 1861, NDP.

45. The time is given by Capt. Goldsby, "Official Report," Huntsville *Democrat*, Aug. 7 and 21, 1861; Coles, "The First Manassas Campaign,"

4; *OR*, v2, 473–474.

46. Huntsville *Independent*, Aug. 10, 1861.

47. Huntsville *Democrat*, Aug. 7, 1861.

48. Coles, "The First Manassas Campaign," 7; HMR Co. D, 4th AL Inf, ADAH; "Heroes of Manassas," 4th AL Inf, ADAH. The four charges were led by Brigadier General Samuel P. Heintzelman who identified the regiments as the 11th NY (Fire Zouaves), 1st MN, 1st MI and 11th Brooklyn (38th NY), *OR*, v2, 403; Hudson, "General Bee," and Coles, "The First Manassas Campaign," 6–9, reported the fight, was 1¹⁄₂ hours; Hollis, 4th AL Inf, ADAH, recalled the fight was 1 hour and 20 minutes, and was at close range. . . .

49. Russell, *Lowndes Court House*, 114.

50. Huntsville *Tribune*, Nov. 29, 1900; Huntsville *Democrat*, Aug. 7, 1861; Huntsville *Independent*, Aug. 10, 1861.

51. Huntsville *Democrat*, Aug. 7, 1861.

52. Ibid., Aug. 21, 1861; Coles, "The First Manassas Campaign," 9, identifies the unknown regiment as the 27th New York, Goldsby indicated there were two regiments, but does not identify either, REC, Co. G, 4th AL Inf, NA, indicates the 4th Alabama was ordered back to avoid capture; Huntsville *Independent*, Aug. 10, 1861, reported Scott's wound was to the left leg.

53. The incident is described by Hudson, "General Bee"; Coles, "The First Manassas Campaign," 11; Hollis, 4th AL Inf, ADAH; Goldsby, Huntsville *Democrat*, Aug. 21, 1861.

54. *CV*, v30, n5, May 1922, 197.

55. Three eyewitness accounts of the battle say essentially the same thing. Coles, "The First Manassas Campaign," 11, quoted Bee as: "Come with me and go yonder where Jackson stands like a "stone wall"; Hudson, "General Bee," quoted Bee as saying: "Follow me, let us support Jackson. See, he stands like a stone wall." It is not clear from the accounts if either Cole or Hudson actually heard Bee; Hollis, 4th AL Inf, MDAH, refers to Jackson as "standing like a stone wall." The phrase stuck and Jackson became Stonewall Jackson. His brigade of Virginians became the Stonewall Brigade.

56. Huntsville *Democrat*, Aug. 21, 1861.

57. Coles, "The First Manassas Campaign," 12.

58. *OR*, v2, 470.

59. CSR, 4th AL Inf, NA; 8th U.S. Census, 1860, Lauderdale County, Alabama; Warren, *Lauderdale County, Alabama*, 200; Garrett, *Lauderdale County History*, 175.

60. Mobile *Advertiser & Register*, Aug. 21, 1861; Jackson was prominent in the organization of the 27th AL in the winter of 1861, Brewer, *Public Men*, 633.

61. Coles, "The First Manassas Campaign," 13.
62. "Heroes of Manassas," 4th AL Inf, ADAH.
63. *OR*, Series IV, v1, 710.
64. Pierrepont, *Reuben Kidd*, 297.
65. Jones's wounds were serious. One leg was shattered, the other was mangled by a bullet that entered his hip and traveled down through his leg.
66. Horsman, *Josiah Nott*, 261, 264.
67. Huntsville *Democrat*, Sep. 4, 1861; Huntsville *Independent* Sep. 14, 1861; Huntsville *Democrat*, Sep. 11, 1861.
68. Porter King Diary, Oct. 28, 1861, USAMHI; Maj. Benjamin Alston, a West Point graduate and cavalryman in the old army, was his lone opponent, and received four votes. He had been assigned temporary command of the 4th AL after First Manassas and had failed in his attempts to instill discipline in the 4th AL.
69. Selma *Reporter*, Nov. 25, 1861; Porter King Diary, Nov. 6, 1861, USAMHI; Dawson to Todd, Nov. 7, 1861, NDP.
70. Porter King Diary, Apr. 21, 1862, USAMHI.
71. CSR, 4th AL Inf, NA; Letters received by the Confederate A&IG, M474, v67, NA.
72. Ritter, *American Legislative Leaders*, 170.
73. *B&L*, v2, 219.
74. W. L. Yancey to Jefferson Davis, Apr. 17, 1862; Law to Watts, Apr., 23, 1862, GO.
75. Third Brigade Officers to Randolph, Jun. 2, 1862; Lee to Davis, Jun. 10, 1862, GO.
76. Davis's statement on distributing the regiments to the brigades of the several states refers to the idea of establishing brigades with all regiments from the same state, an idea that Davis heavily favored. This idea will be addressed in considerable detail later.
77. Law, "Fight for Richmond in 1862," 651–652.
78. Ibid., 657.
79. Coles, "Seven Days Battles," 7.
80. *B&L*, v2, 363; Griffith, *Battle Tactics*, 142; In Trimble's Brigade, which was in the Confederate center, Private Frank D. Champion, Co. D, 15th AL, grabbed a horse and rode along the line to rally the men who thought he was an officer, Freeman, *R. E. Lee*, v2, 152. In the charge, the 15th AL was to the right of Hood and the 4th TX. This was the first time the two Alabama regiments fought together.
81. *B&L*, v2, 363.
82. Coles, "Seven Days Battles," 7.
83. REC, 4th AL Inf, NA.
84. Davis, *Chaplain Davis*, 77.
85. *OR*, v2, pt2, 555–556.
86. Smith, *Confederate War Papers*, 326–327.
87. Freeman, *Lee's Lts*, v1, 119–120.

88. Warner, *Generals In Gray*, 334.
89. Col. Leroy Stafford commanded Starke's Fourth Brigade, Jackson's Division, Jackson's Command, on Law's immediate left. Brigadier General William Starke commanded Brigadier General Charles S. Winder's (Jackson's) division, *OR*, v12, pt2, 548. The Confederate left was commanded by Major General Thomas J. Jackson.
90. *OR*, v12, pt2, 623.
91. Coles, "Second Manassas Campaign," 11; *OR*, v12, pt2, 623.
92. *OR*, v12, pt2, 623.
93. Ibid., 605.
94. Ibid., 565; Ibid., 624; Coles, "Second Manassas Campaign," 17–18.
95. *OR*, v12, pt2, 624; Coles, "Second Manassas Campaign," 18.
96. *OR*, v12, pt2, 625.
97. *CV*, v10, n8, Aug. 1902, 367– 368.
98. ECPLC.
99. *OR*, v9, pt2, 937; Nolan, *Iron Brigade*, 140
100. *OR*, v19, pt1, 937, Coles, "Maryland Campaign," 15; Robbins to Gould, Mar. 25, 1891, DC.
101. Robbins to Gould, Mar. 25, 1891, DC; Coles, "Maryland Campaign," 15–16.
102. *OR*, v19, pt1, 938.
103. Robbins to Gould, Mar. 25, 1891, DC.
104. *OR*, v19, pt1, 923.
105. Ibid., 811.
106. Coles, "Maryland Campaign," 22; *OR*, v19, pt1, 957; CSR, 4th AL Inf, NA.
107. *CV*, v10, n8, Aug. 1902, 367–368; *West Point Graduates*, 250
108. Clopton to Davis, Jul., 23, 1862; Dargan to Randolph, Jul. 24, 1862, CGSO.
109. Watts to Randolph, Aug. 2, 1862, CGSO.
110. Hood to Randolph, Jun. 30, 1862; CSR, CGSO.
111. Officers' petition to Randolph, about Sep. 1, 1862, CGSO
112. Officers' petition to Randolph, about Sep. 20, 1862, CGSO
113. *Journal Confederate Congress*, v2, 414.
114. *OR*, v19, pt2, 719.
115. CSR, 4th AL Inf, NA.
116. *Northern Alabama*, 342; 8th U.S. Census, 1860, Madison County, Alabama, 215; Williams, *Huntsville Directory*, 81.
117. Coles, "Company Sketches," 5.
118. CSR, 4th AL Inf, NA.
119. Longstreet, *Manassas to Appomattox*, 290, 299; REC, CSR, 44th AL Inf, NA.
120. Goodson, "Goodson Letters," 131.
121. Freeman, *Lee's Lts*, v2, 236–238, 250; *OR*, v19, pt1, 803–807.

122. *OR*, v19, pt2, 683.

123. *OR*, v21, 1033.

124. Ibid., 624.

Chapter 2 – The Alabamians

1. Beauregard to Davis, Oct. 22, 1861, BPDU; Rowland, *Jefferson Davis*, v5, 141, Davis to Beauregard, Oct. 16, 1861; Beauregard's words would prove prophetic when Virginia suffered from the wholesale destruction of Picket's Virginia division on Jul. 3, 1863.

2. *OR*, v5, 893–895.

3. Govan, *Joseph E. Johnston*, 83, 88. The War Department ordered brigades formed according to state organization but Johnston resisted the order as dangerous to his command, *OR*, v5, 913–914, 985.

4. LRCAI, M474, rolls 33, 54, NA.

5. Freeman, *Lee's Lts*, v1, 270.

6. *OR*, v21, 1031, 1099.

7. Oates, *The War*, 174. Although it was an executive order, Oates believed the Confederate Congress had passed a law to brigade by state.

8. Feagin to his sisters, Jan. 30, 1863, 15th AL Inf, ADAH.

9. Taylor, *48th Alabama*.

10. Daniel to his wife, Jan. 24, 1863, DCSU.

11. Oates, *The War*, 174.

12. 15th AL Inf, ADAH.

13. *CMH*, v8, 397; Cantey, Surname File, ADAH.

14. Oates, *The War*, 68.

15. Daniel, Surname File, ADAH; 8th U.S. Census, 1860, Barbour County, Alabama, 600.

16. Oates, *The War*, 69–70.

17. Ibid., 74, 76.

18. 15th AL Inf, ADAH; CSR, 15th AL Inf, NA; Oates, *The War*, 86.

19. Oates to S. Cooper, Jul. 20, 1864, CSR, 15th AL Inf, NA; John M. Richy to the secretary of war, Mar. 3, 1864, CSR, 15th AL Inf, NA; Oates, *The War*, 87.

20. Oates, *The War*, 87.

21. John M. Richy to the secretary of war, Mar. 3, 1864, CSR, 15th AL Inf, NA.

22. Oates, *The War*, 760.

23. Ibid., 88–92.

24. Oates, *The War*, 102; CSR, 15th AL Inf, NA.

25. Oates, *The War*, 102.

26. Ibid., 104–105.

27. Lowther to S. Cooper, Jul. 12, 1862, CSR, 15th AL Inf, NA.

28. *CWTI*, v23, n3, 24; Oates, *The War*, 136–137.

29. Oates, *The War*, 137

30. Ibid., 144, 145.

31. *OR*, v19, pt1, 976.

32. Ibid., 958, 976.

33. McClendon, *Recollections*, 143–144; Oates, *The War*, 589–590; *OR*, v19, pt1, 977.

34. *OR*, v19, pt1, 973.

35. Oates, *The War*, 168. Oates did not identify which of the two men received the shoes.

36. CSR, 15th AL Inf, NA.

37. Warner, *Generals in Gray*, 43.

38. CSR, 15th AL Inf, NA.

39. Dawson to Elodie Todd, Apr. 2, 1861, NDP.

40. Oates, *The War*, 375.

41. Kent, Surname File, ADAH; 8th U.S. Census, 1860, Dallas County, Alabama, 807; 44th AL Inf, Brewer, *Public Men*, 654–655; Selma *Reporter*, Jun. 18, 1862.

42. 44th AL Inf, ADAH.

43. Selma *Reporter*, May 26, 1862.

44. Ibid., Jun. 18, 1862.

45. Griffin to M. A. Griffin, Jun. 26, 1862, WAGL.

46. Ibid.

47. REC, Regimental Return, 44th AL Inf, NA.

48. Selma *Reporter*, Jul. 3, 1862; REC, Co. A, 44th AL Inf, CSR, NA.

49. *OR*, v11, pt2, 487.

50. REC, Co. B, I, K, 44th AL Inf, NA; HM, Co. C, 44th AL Inf, ADAH.

51. Goodson, "Goodson Letters," 127.

52. *OR*, v12, pt3, 686; CSR, 44th AL Inf, NA.

53. Selma *Daily Reporter*, Mar. 23, 1864.

54. Kent, Surname File, ADAH. When the Federal raider, General James Wilson, lay siege to Selma in Mar. 1865, Kent resumed the soldier's duty one last time. He fought in the city's fortifications until Selma surrendered. Kent moved to Birmingham in 1876. His health caused him to retire in the late 1870s. Kent relocated to Shades Mountain where he died May 5, 1881.

55. Owen, *Alabama Dictionary*, v3, 934; Jones, Surname File, ADAH; 8th U.S. Census, 1860, Scottsville, Bibb County, Alabama, 776.

56. 44th AL Inf, ADAH.

57. *CMH*, v8, 435; 44th AL; *CWTI*, v10, n36; Oates, "Perry and His Career"; 44th AL Inf, ADAH.

58. 44th AL Inf, ADAH; CSR, 44th AL Inf, NA.

59. 8th U.S. Census, 1860, Tallapoosa County, AL.

60. 47th AL Inf, ADAH; Brewer *Public Men*, 659, 660; Burton, *47th Alabama*; 8th U.S. Census, 1860, Tallapoosa County, AL, 178.

61. Mrs. James Jackson to Thomas Owens, Jul. 16, 1902, 47th AL Inf, ADAH.

62. John Rayburn to Samuel K. Rayburn, Nov. 1861, RFP, ADAH.

63. Ibid., Jan. 30, 1862.
64. Rayburn was president of the Tennessee and Coosa Railroad Co. and served on Governor Moore's staff in early 1862. Duncan, *Marshall County*, 49. John Rayburn was killed at Sharpsburg.
65. John Rayburn to Samuel K. Rayburn, Jan. 30, 1862, RFP, ADAH.
66. Ibid.
67. Ibid., Feb. 22, 1862.
68. Owen, *Alabama Dictionary*, 156; Duncan, *Marshall County*, 51; *Northern Alabama*, 619.
69. Duncan, *Marshall County*, 44; *Northern Alabama*, 405.
70. John Rayburn to Samuel K. Rayburn, Feb. 22, 1862, RFP, ADAH.
71. Jacksonville *Republican*, May 15, 1862.
72. Duncan, *Marshall County*, 50–51; *Northern Alabama*, 619.
73. Alldredge, Surname File, ADAH.
74. Co. E and H, 47th AL Inf, ADAH.
75. *OR*, v12, pt2, 648; 47th AL Inf, ADAH, 48th AL Inf, ADAH; Daniel to Mat, Jun. 27, 1862, DCSU.
76. CSR, 47th AL Inf, NA; 47th AL Inf, ADAH.
77. Daniel to his wife, Aug. 14, 1862, DCSU.
78. *OR*, v12, pt2, 207.
79. 47th AL Inf, ADAH; *OR*, v12, pt2, 209.
80. *OR*, v12, pt2, 208.
81. Ibid., 206.
82. 47th AL Inf, ADAH; *OR*, v12, pt2, 209; to wife, Aug. 14, 1862, DCSU.
83. Col. Joshua Stover stated the 10th VA was on the brigade's extreme left and on the left of the road and the other regiments on the right. Lt. Col. Samuel T. Walton reported the 23rd VA was sent to the right to support Pegram's battery (Purcell Virginia Artillery) an hour before and indicated the 23rd advanced on the right of the 37th Virginia. Maj. H. C. Wood confirmed the 37th Virginia was to the left of the 23rd Virginia, which was on the brigade's extreme right. Wood indicated the 47th and 48th AL was on his left, but does not indicate the order. When the brigade's line later gave way due to an attack from the left 47th AL sustained the most casualties, the 48th AL and the 37th VA sustained the second and third most respectively. The casualty count for the 47th indicates it took the brunt of the Federal onslaught. Casualties were correspondingly less further to the right. Therefore, it is concluded the 47th and 48th AL were on the line's left. *OR*, v12, pt2, 210–212.
84. Ibid., 212.
85. Ibid., 208.
86. *CMH*, v8, 503.
87. 47th AL Inf, ADAH.
88. Jacksonville *Republican*, Aug. 28, 1862.
89. *OR*, v12, pt2, 212.
90. Ibid., 208.
91. Ibid., 208; Daniel to his wife, Aug. 14, 1862, DCSU.
92. *OR*, v12, pt2, 208; Ibid., 211.
93. Ibid., 208.
94. CSR, 47th AL Inf, NA.
95. BSF, ADAH; *CMH*, v8, 502, 503.
96. Rice, *Civil War Letters*, 15–18.
97. Ibid., 19.
98. *OR*, v12, pt1, 166.
99. Oates, *The War*, 145.
100. Burton, *47th Alabama*; Taylor, *48th Alabama*.
101. 47th AL Inf, ADAH.
102. Burton, *47th Alabama*.
103. Taylor, *48th Alabama*.
104. ECPLC.
105. *OR*, v19, pt1, 905. Figures for the 47th and 48th do not include slightly wounded. Therefore the percent of the force engaged was probably much higher.
106. Taylor, *48th Alabama*.
107. Burton, *47th Alabama*.
108. Daniel to his wife, Sep. 22, 1862, DCSU.
109. Douglas, *I Rode with Stonewall*, 183; McKee to Martha, Sep. 22, 1862; ML.
110. Douglas, *I Rode with Stonewall*, 192.
111. Alldredge's son, David, claimed the elder Alldredge sent seven sons and two sons-in-law to the Confederate military, Alldredge, Surname File, ADAH. The five sons entering the service with Enoch were: Andrew J., Jesse J., John P., Van B., and Nathan, CSR, 48th AL Inf, NA. The son-in-laws were Alvin O. Dickson of the 48th AL and William Suttles, Co. B, 19th AL.
112. CSR, 48th AL Inf, NA.
113. Ibid ; Alldredge, Surname File, ADAH.
114. CSR, 48th AL Inf, NA
115. Alldredge, Surname File, ADAH.
116. CSR, 48th AL Inf, NA; Warren, *Henry's Heritage*.
117. Taylor, *48th Alabama*.
118. Daniel to his wife, Dec. 23, 1862, DCSU.
119. Ibid.
120. Coles, "Fredericksburg," 1.
121. Oates, *The War*, 172.
122. Ibid.; Crowder to family, Jan. 13, 1863, JPCL; Cody, "Cody Letters," 366–367; Daniel to his wife, Jan. 5, 1863, DCSU.
123. Coles, "Fredericksburg," 1; Taylor, *48th Alabama*; Goodson, "Goodson Letters," 136–137.

124. Coles, "Siege of Suffolk," 1–2.

125. Simpson, *Texas Brigade*, 206–207.

126. Feagin to his sisters, Jan. 30, 1863, 15th AL Inf, ADAH.

127. Simpson, *Texas Brigade*, 206.

128. Goodson, "Goodson Letters," 138–139. Goodson thought the whole affair was great fun, but wrote home "none of your school–childrens' snowballings for me."

129. Feagin to his sisters, Jan. 30, 1863, 15th AL Inf, ADAH.

130. Simpson, *Texas Brigade*, 207.

131. Feagin to his sisters, Jan. 30, 1863, 15th AL Inf, ADAH.

132. Blackford, *Letters From Lee's Army*, 165–166.

133. Special Order #28, Headquarters, Army of Northern Virginia, Jan. 28, 1863, M921, NA; Cody, "Cody Letters," 367, 368.

134. Freeman, *Lee's Lts*, v1, 268, said of Harvey Hill, "If he admired conduct on the field, no compliment was too extravagant; where he distrusted or disapproved, condemnation was complete."

135. General Order #7, Jan. 21, 1863, General Order #22, Feb. 18, 1863, CSR, 15th AL Inf, NA.

136. *OR*, v19, pt1, 976–978.

137. CSR, 44th AL Inf, NA.

138. Special Orders #7, Jan. 21, 1863 and #128, Nov. 25, 1862, Army of Northern Virginia, CSR, 15th AL Inf, NA; *Army Regulations*, Article #85 mandated the publication of name, crime, etc., near the residence of any officer convicted of cowardice or fraud.

139. CSR, 47th AL Inf, NA.

140. Special Orders #7, Jan. 21, 1863 and #123, Oct. 28, 1862, Army of Northern Virginia, CSR, 15th AL Inf, NA.

141. James Cantey, colonel; Thomas Woolfolk, quartermaster; and James Vernoy, commissary officer, transferred from the 15th AL CSR, 15th AL Inf, NA.

142. A year earlier John Rayburn had questioned Sheffield's ability to instill discipline.

Chapter 3 – The Siege of Suffolk

1. Seddon, a Virginia politician, replaced George W. Randolph as secretary in the Nov. of 1862.

2. *OR*, v19, pt2, 679, v21, 1084.

3. *OR*, v18, 876.

4. HMR, Co. A, 4th AL Inf, ADAH; *OR*, v18, 880.

5. Daniel to his wife, Feb. 13, 1863, DCSU.

6. Taylor, *48th Alabama*, 14. Taylor estimated the snowfall of the seventeenth at twelve inches; Vaughan, "Vaughan Diary," 573; HMR, Company A, 4th AL Inf, Co. B, C, E and K, 44th AL

Inf, ADAH; McDaniel to Hester Felker, Feb. 26, 1863, McDaniel, *With Unabated Trust*, 133, described this march as the most severe of the war for his Georgia brigade.

7. Daniel to his wife, Feb. 13, 1863, DCSU.

8. Ibid., Feb. 6, 1863.

9. *OR*, v18, 882, 884.

10. Jones, *War Clerk's Diary*, 261.

11. McDaniel to Hester Felker, Feb. 26, 1863, McDaniel, *With Unabated Trust*, 133.

12. Daniel to Companion, Feb. 13, 1863 (misdated), DCSU.

13. Vaughan, "Vaughan Diary," 573.

14. Daniel to Companion, Feb. 24, 1863 (misdated), DCSU.

15. Vaughan, "Vaughan Diary," 572, 573.

16. Ibid., 575.

17. Ibid.

18. McDaniel to Hester Felker, Mar. 21, 1863, McDaniel, *With Unabated Trust*, 140.

19. Jones, *War Clerk's Diary*, 276.

20. Oates, *The War*, 175.

21. Ibid., 737.

22. *OR*, v18, 927.

23. Almost twelve inches of snow fell on Richmond and its environs during the night of Mar. 19. Younger, *Inside the Confederate Gov.*, 45; Mims Walker to Mary Gray Pitts, Apr. 4, 1863, CGP. By Apr. Mims Walker could write that rain and snow fell for 30 days with only scarce sunshine; McDaniel to Hester Felker, Mar. 21, 1863, McDaniel, *With Unabated Trust*, 141, 143. McDaniel reported two occasions when snow was 10 and 12 inches on the ground.

24. Coles, "Suffolk," 2.

25. Coles, "Suffolk," 2.

26. McClendon, *Recollections*, 170, 171, 176.

27. Coles, "Suffolk," 2.

28. Crowder to his brother, Mar. 22, 1863, JPCL.

29. *OR*, v18, 883.

30. *OR*, v51, pt2, 681.

31. *OR*, v18, 871.

32. Ibid., 950, 970, 996.

33. Ibid., 943, 953.

34. Walker to Mary Gray Pitts, Apr. 4, 1863, CGP.

35. HMR, Co. A, and Co. C and H, 4th AL Inf, ADAH; Goodson, "Goodson Letters," 140, 141; McClendon, *Recollections*, 171.

36. Law, Surname File, ADAH.

37. 8th U.S. Census, 1860. York County, SC real estate owned by William Latta had a value of $47,000 and his personal estate was valued at $105,000; Interviews with Law's granddaughter, Mrs. Jane Law Norvell of Columbia, SC,

Feb. 2, 1993, and Law's grand niece, Mrs. Louise Law Wilson, Baytown, TX, Jan. 10, 1993.

38. Walker to Mary Gray Pitts, Apr. 4, 1863, CGP.

39. Dawson to Todd, Oct. 16, 1861, NDP.

40. Vaughan, "Vaughan Diary," 577; McDaniel to Hester, Apr. 6, 1863, McDaniel, *With Unabated Trust*, 149.

41. Walker to Mary Gray Pitts, Apr. 4, 1863, CGP.

42. Hanson, *Virginia Place Names*, 2.

43. Coles, "Suffolk," 3, 4.

44. Vaughan, "Vaughan Diary," 578.

45. Ibid.

46. Ibid., 579.

47. Coles, "Suffolk," 4.

48. *OR*, v18, 910.

49. Ibid., 967, 968.

50. *ORN*, v8, 729, 733, 739.

51. *OR*, v18, 332, 333.

52. Ibid., 943, 944.

53. HMR, Company A, 4th AL Inf, ADAH; James B. Daniel, 47th AL, dated his letters of Apr. 17 and 25, 1863 to his Companion as "In ditch near Suffolk, VA," DCSU.

54. Daniel to Companion, Apr. 25, 1863, DCSU.

55. Coles, "Suffolk," 5.

56. Ibid.

57. Warner, *Generals in Blue*, 364, 365; *OR*, v18, 597.

58. *ORN*, v8, 713, 716, 717; *OR*, v18, 597. Admiral Lee was a cousin of General Robert E. Lee.

59. Stevens, "The Siege of Suffolk," MHSM, 205.

60. *Dictionary of American Naval Fighting Ships*, v6, 618; *ORN*, v8, 713, 714, 716, 717.

61. *ORN*, v8, 722–725.

62. Ibid. This was artillery of Hood's Division, commanded by Major M. W. Henry, batteries unknown.

63. Sands, "Brilliant Career," 10.

64. *ORN*, v8, 721.

65. Ibid., 722–725.

66. *OR*, v18, 988.

67. Ibid., 995, 996. (Special Orders, #2, Headquarters, French's Command, Apr. 16 (or 17), 1863). Interestingly, French assigned Stribling's battery to Pickett's Division, even though he had relieved one of Henry's batteries at Ft. Huger—in the heart of Hood's command—with Stribling's on the night of Apr. 15.

68. French, *Two Wars*, 160, 160n, 161.

69. *OR*, v18, 325. The battery was later known as Co. E, 18th Battalion Heavy Artillery, Virginia Artillery.

70. Ibid., 998.

71. Ibid., 997.

72. Oates, *The War*, 619.

73. Latrobe Diary, VHS.

74. McDaniel to Hester Felker, Apr. 16, 1863 and Apr. 23, 1863, McDaniel, *With Unabated Trust*, 151–154; Vaughan, "Vaughan Diary," 579.

75. *OR*, v18, 336, 989.

76. *ORN*, v8, 731–733; Getty's Third Division was held at Suffolk when the IX Corps was sent west. Getty's detachment was the Federal response to Longstreet's transfer south of Richmond, *OR*, v18, 884, 890, v25, pt2, 630–632; *ORN*, v8, 731–733.

77. *OR*, v18, 336; *ORN*, v8, 759–762.

78. *OR*, v18, 336, 337. This infantry is unidentified.

79. Coles, "Suffolk," 7, 8.

80. *OR*, v18, 324; *ORN*, v8, 733, 734. The wooden hulled *Teaser*, a tug, was one of the first in any navy to serve as an observation balloon ship and mine layer.

81. *OR*, v18, 336, 337.

82. *ORN*, v8, 731–734.

83. Ibid., 738–741.

84. *OR*, v18, 336, 337; HMR, Co. B, 44th AL Inf, ADAH.

85. *OR*, v18, 331.

86. Chesterman, "Duels and Duellists."

87. Oates, *The War*, 176, 177; Tyler, *Men of Mark*.

88. Law, "A Night in the Enemy's Lines."

89. *OR*, v18, 325.

90. Ibid., 328, 331, 336.

91. Vaughan, "Vaughan Diary," 580.

92. *OR*, v18, 336.

93. HMR, 44th AL Inf, ADAH. Memorandum of Joab Goodson, (probably dated Jan. 1865).

94. *OR*, v18, 1001.

95. Ibid., 325, 328.

96. Ibid., 325, 328, 332.

97. Ibid., 338–340.

98. Stevens, "Siege of Suffolk," 212, 213, MHSM.

99. *OR*, v18, 304.

100. *ORN*, v8, 746, 747; Stevens " Siege of Suffolk," 214, MHSM.

101. *ORN*, v8, 746, 747.

102. Ibid., 746, 747.

103. *OR*, v18, 336, 337.

104. Sands, "Brilliant Career," 13.

105. Ramey, *Years of Anguish*, 193.

106. *OR*, v18, 304.

107. Stevens, " Siege of Suffolk," 215, 216, MHSM.

108. HMR, 44th AL Inf, ADAH. Memorandum of Joab Goodson; *ORN*, v8, 755, 756, 759–762.

109. HMR, Company B, 44th AL Inf, ADAH. Remarks on the muster listed Harkey as "killed in

110. Stevens, "Siege of Suffolk," 215, 216, MHSM; Butts, "Reminiscences of Gunboat Service," 42, 43.
111. *OR*, v18, 337.
112. The strength of the two companies was 128 officers and men, including those on detail, furlough, absent sick and absent wounded but only 72 were in the fort. The five officers captured were Capt. David L. Bozeman, Lt. Daniel B. Edwards, Sec. Lt. George Reese, Third Lt. Richard A. Thornton of Co. A and Sec. Lt. Joab Goodson of Co. B.
113. Chesterman, "Duels and Duellists."
114. French, *Two Wars*, 162. Lt. George Reese, 44th AL, captured at Ft. Huger on Apr. 19, recalled in 1897 that the distance from camp to the fort was two miles.
115. Chesterman, "Duels and Duellists."
116. *OR*, v18, 338, 339.
117. Richmond *Enquirer*, Apr. 24, 1863, from the Petersburg *Daily Express*, Apr. 23, 1863. The description of the greeting by the "secesh" ladies is confirmed by Goodson's memorandum, HMR, 44th AL Inf, ADAH.
118. Richmond *Enquirer*, Apr. 24, 1863.
119. 44th AL Inf, NA.
120. *OR*, v18, 339; Ibid., 1002.
121. Ibid., 332.
122. French, *Two Wars*, 162, 163.
123. *OR*, v18, 1002.
124. Vaughan, "Vaughan Diary," 580, 581.
125. Stevens, "Siege of Suffolk," 216, MHSM.
126. *OR*, v18, 305.
127. *ORN*, v8, 749, 751, 752, 752–754, 756–758, 759–762. Admiral Lee had considered the removal of the gunboats from the upper reaches of the river as early as Apr. 18, *ORN*, v8, 740.
128. *OR*, v18, 331, 332. Shumaker placed the time of these reports at 1 p.m.
129. Coles, "Suffolk," 7, 8.
130. Figures to his mother, Apr. 17, 1863, FC.
131. *OR*, v18, 1002.
132. Ibid., 1016.
133. Ibid., 337.
134. Ibid., 326, 327.
135. Ibid., 1014.
136. Ibid., 1016.
137. Ibid., 327.
138. McDaniel to Hester Felker, Apr. 23, 1863, McDaniel, *With Unabated Trust*, 154.
139. The easy resolution of the challenge once the two camps began talking is strong evidence that Terrell believed the 55th NC was either in place or under orders to support the battery or both

until he heard the facts.
140. Belo, *Memoirs of Belo*, 25. After the war, Belo went to TX, where he answered an ad for a bookkeeper at the Galveston *News*. Ten years later, he owned the newspaper. He eventually owned the Dallas *Morning News*, as well. Belo was a hunting companion of President Grover Cleveland and owned the first telephone in TX.
141. Oates, *The War*, 176, 178.
142. Clark, *North Carolina Regiments*, v3, 291, 292.
143. Oates, *The War*, 177.
144. Chesterman, "Duels and Duellists." Cussons identified Tom Goldsby as his second, but Goldsby was not with the brigade at that time. Goldsby, whom Cussons called "Glorious Tom Goldsby," was a wealthy, cosmopolitan planter with an Ivy League education.
145. *CV*, v31, n12, 1923.
146. Belo, *Memoirs of Belo*, 25.
147. "The Gallant Belo," Ward Collection, MDAH; Coles, "Suffolk," 9; Pierrepont, *Reuben Kidd*, 320.
148. "The Gallant Belo," Ward Collection, MDAH.
149. Ibid.
150. Ibid.
151. Clark, *North Carolina Regiments*, v3, 292; Oates, *The War*, 178.
152. Chesterman, "Duels and Duellists."
153. "The Gallant Belo," Ward Collection, MDAH.
154. Ibid. Oates, *The War*, 178, wrote that Cussons said, "Major, this is d——d poor shooting we are doing today. If we don't better than this we will never kill any Yankees." Oates may have combined the remarks for the sake of a good story.
155. Clark, *North Carolina Regiments*, v3, 292; Oates, *The War*, 178.
156. "The Gallant Belo," Ward Collection, MDAH.
157. Belo, *Memoirs of Belo*, 26.
158. Chesterman, "Duels and Duellists." Cussons wrote about the duel on Dec. 5, 1908, in response to an inquiry by Chesterman.
159. "The Gallant Belo," Ward Collection, MDAH.
160. *Army Regulations*. Article 25 prescribes that any officer who issues or accepts a challenge to duel or serves as a second shall be cashiered from the service.
161. Wilson, *Code of Honor*, 13–17.
162. Chesterman, "Duels and Duellists"; French, *Two Wars*, 162.
163. *ORN*, v8, 754.
164. Ibid., 773, 777, 779, 781.
165. Ibid., 781, 782.
166. Ibid., 781–783.
167. Ibid., 783.
168. McDaniel to Hester Felker, May 1, 1863, McDaniel, *With Unabated Trust*, 157, 158.

169. Ibid., 158; *OR*, v18, 311.
170. McDaniel to Hester Felker, Apr. 23, 1863, McDaniel, *With Unabated Trust*, 154.
171. John M. Richy to the secretary of war, Mar. 4, 1864, CSR, 15th AL Inf, NA; Law to War Department, Sep. 20, 1863, CSR, 15th AL Inf, NA.
172. *OR*, v18, 658.
173. Ibid., 667.
174. Ibid., 1024, 1025.
175. Ibid., 1029, 1032. When Davis served as U.S. secretary of war, he had known Cooper as the adjutant general of the U.S. Army.
176. Ibid., 1037; *OR*, v18, 684.
177. Ibid., 306, 319, 320; Stevens, "Siege of Suffolk," 221, MHSM.
178. *OR*, v18, 1040.
179. Ibid., 319.
180. Jordan, *Events*, 36; Coles, "Suffolk," 10. The other six companies of the 4th AL were under heavy shelling by the batteries in Suffolk as Peck sought to support his reconnaissance in force.
181. *OR*, v18, 319.
182. Jordan, *Events*, 37, 38. Two other members of Co. B were killed in the fighting of May 3: Frank B. Calloway and Neal A. McCaskill.
183. *OR*, v18, 319, 320.
184. Coles, "Suffolk," 10.
185. Jordan, *Events*, 37.
186. Montgomery *Daily Mail*, May 15, 1863; CSR, 44th AL Inf, NA.
187. *OR*, v18, 1038.
188. Vaughan, "Vaughan Diary," 583; Coles, "Suffolk," 10, 11; McClendon, *Recollections*, 174.
189. Coles, "Suffolk," 11.

Chapter 4 – The Route to Gettysburg

1. REC, Co. D, Co. E, CSR, 48th AL Inf, NA.
2. *OR*, v27, pt2, 284.
3. Ibid., pt3, 880–881.
4. Ibid., pt3, 305, 868.
5. Alexander, *Fighting for the Confederacy*, 221.
6. Daniel to his wife, Jun. 8, 1863, DCSU.
7. Wise, *Long Arm of Lee*, 581.
8. CSR, 48th AL Inf, NA.
9. 48th AL Inf, ADAH; 4th AL Inf, ADAH; CSR, 4th AL Inf, NA; CSR, 47th AL Inf, NA.
10. 44th AL Inf, ADAH; CSR, 44th AL Inf, NA.
11. 48th AL Inf, ADAH; CSR, 48th AL Inf, NA.
12. A. A. Lowther to S. Cooper, Oct. 15, 1863, CSR, 15th AL Inf, NA. The protest was personally delivered by J. P. McQuire.
13. CSR, 9th AL Inf, NA; John Rayburn to Samuel K. Rayburn, Feb. 22, 1862, RFP, ADAH;

Duncan, *Marshall County*, v1, 65; LRCAI, roll 56, NA; CSR, 48th AL Inf, NA.
14. Biography, FC.
15. CSR, NA; 4th AL Inf, ADAH.
16. Longstreet, *Manassas To Appomattox*, 335–337.
17. *OR*, v27 pt2, 357; "Coles, Gettysburg Campaign," 1; REC, Co. D, CSR, 48th AL Inf; Co. A, CSR, 47th AL Inf, NA; Vaughan, "Vaughan Diary," 585.
18. Coles, "Gettysburg Campaign," 1, refers to Washington as Little Washington; Vaughan, "Vaughan Diary," 585.
19. Vaughan, "Vaughan Diary," 585, 586; *OR*, v27, pt2, 428.
20. REC, Co. D, CSR, 47th AL Inf, NA; Coles, "Gettysburg Campaign," 2; Youngblood, "Unwritten History," 312.
21. Youngblood, "Unwritten History," 313.
22. Coles, "Gettysburg Campaign," 2; Vaughan, "Vaughan Diary," 586.
23. Coles, "Gettysburg Campaign," 2; REC, Co. E, CSR, 4th AL Inf, NA; Vaughan, "Vaughan Diary," 586; McDaniel to Hester Felker, Jun. 21, 1863, McDaniel, *With Unabated Trust*, 175.
24. McDaniel to Hester Felker, Jun. 21, 1863, McDaniel, *With Unabated Trust*, 175; Figures to his mother, Jun. 21, 1863, FC.
25. Coles, "Gettysburg Campaign," 3.
26. Ibid.; Vaughan, "Vaughan Diary," 587.
27. Coles, "Gettysburg Campaign," 3; Vaughan, "Vaughan Diary," 587.
28. Youngblood, "Unwritten History," 313.
29. REC, Co. B, CSR, 44th AL Inf, NA; Vaughan, "Vaughan Diary," 587.
30. Coles, "Gettysburg Campaign," 4; Vaughan, "Vaughan Diary," 587 indicates they were four miles from the Potomac River.
31. Vaughan, "Vaughan Diary," 587.
32. Sturgis, "War Record," ADAH
33. Ward, "Incidents," 345.
34. Polley, *Hood's Texas Brigade*, 146–147.
35. Sturgis, *War Record*, ADAH.
36. REC, Co. D, CSR, 44th AL Inf, NA; Vaughan, "Vaughan Diary," 587.
37. Coles, "Gettysburg Campaign," 5; Reese, "Family Sketch," 111.
38. Co. H, HM, 44th AL Inf, ADAH.
39. Coles, "Gettysburg Campaign," 5; Vaughan, "Vaughan Diary," 587.
40. Pierrepont, *Reuben Kidd*, 329.
41. Daniel to Mat, Jun. 28, 1863, DCSU.
42. Figures to his parents, Jul. 18, 1863, FC.
43. Ward, "Incidents," 345.
44. REC, Co. C, 44th AL Inf, Co. D, CSR, 47th

AL Inf, NA; Coles, "Gettysburg Campaign," 5; Vaughan, "Vaughan Diary," 587.

45. Ward, "Incidents," 345.

46. Ibid.

47. Ibid., 346.

48. Vaughan, "Vaughan Diary," 587.

49. Coles, "Gettysburg Campaign," 6.

50. Ward, "Incidents," 346.

51. Yeary, *Reminiscences*, 451; Love, a 22-year-old resident of Madison Station, AL, was wounded three times during the war. He transferred to the 4th AL Cavalry in Feb. 1865, CSR, 4th AL Inf, NA. Love, Henry B. (fn 51)

52. Daniel to Mat, Jun. 28, 1863, DCSU.

53. Coles, "Gettysburg Campaign," 6; Longstreet, "Lee's Invasion," 250; Longstreet, *Manassas to Appomattox*, 346–347; *OR*, v27, pt1, 358; Sorrel, *Recollections*, 155.

54. REC, Co. E, H, CSR, 48th AL Inf, NA; Figures to his parents, Jul. 18, 1863, FC.

55. Figures to his sister, Jul. 18, 1863, FC.

56. CSR, 48th AL Inf, NA.

57. Figures to his parents, Jul. 18, 1863, FC.

58. Coles, "Gettysburg Campaign," 7.

59. Law, "Round Top," 319; Vaughan, "Vaughan Diary," 588; Coles, "Gettysburg Campaign," 7.

60. 15th AL Inf, ADAH.

61. Oates, *The War*, 649.

62. Ibid., 632; 15th AL Inf, ADAH.

63. Oates, "Gettysburg," 173.

64. Ibid., 173; Vaughan, "Vaughan Diary," 588.

65. CSR, 4th AL Inf, NA; Bowles to E. P. Alexander, AP. The nature of the sentence is unknown.

66. Law's Pension Application, 1909.

67. Brigade strength is estimated from analysis of CSR, NA and HMR, ADAH.

68. Stevens was a Pennsylvania congressman, uncompromising abolitionist and leader of the Radical Republicans, a group he helped organize, Boatner, *Civil War Dictionary*, 797.

69. Purifoy, "Horror of War," 254; Ward, "Incidents," 346; Longstreet, *Manassas to Appomattox*, 365; *OR*, v27, pt2, 394.

70. Oates, *The War*, 206.

71. Longstreet, *Manassas to Appomattox*, 365.

72. Coles, "Gettysburg Campaign," 7; Law, "Round Top," 319; *OR*, v27, pt2, 394.

Chapter 5 – Attack on the Federal Left

1. Purifoy, "Horror of War," 254; Perry, "Devil's Den," 161.

2. Purifoy, "Horror of War," 254.

3. Georg, "Principal Loss," 1.

4. Ward, "Incidents," 346.

5. Ibid.

6. Figures to his parents, Jul. 18, 1863, FC.

7. *OR*, v27, pt2, 308, 318.

8. Ibid.; Pfanz, *Second Day*, 113.

9. *OR*, v27, pt2, 308, 318.

10. Longstreet, *Manassas to Appomattox*, 365; Alexander, "Artillery at Gettysburg," 358; *OR*, v27, pt2, 318.

11. McLaws, "Gettysburg," 68.

12. Longstreet, "Lee's Right at Gettysburg," 30; McLaws, "Gettysburg," 68, was an eyewitness to the conversation between Lee and Longstreet. For detailed analyses of this issue and Longstreet's subsequent behavior see, for example, Pfanz, *Second Day*, Chapter 6; Coddington, *Gettysburg Campaign*, Chapter 14; and Freeman, *Lee's Lts*, v3, Chapter 7.

13. *OR*, v27, pt2, 308. *See also* Pfanz, *Second Day*, 28, for a discussion.

14. Longstreet, *Manassas to Appomattox*, 365.

15. Alexander, "Artillery at Gettysburg," 358, 359.

16. McLaws, "Gettysburg," 69.

17. Law, "Round Top," 320.

18. *OR*, v27, pt2, 396.

19. McLaws, "Gettysburg," 69.

20. *See* Pfanz, *Second Day*, 120, for the route from Herr Ridge to the Emmitsburg Rd.

21. *OR*, v27, pt2, 396, 397.

22. McLaws, "Gettysburg," 71.

23. *OR*, v27, pt2, 367.

24. Longstreet, *Manassas to Appomattox*, 366.

25. McLaws, "Gettysburg," 70.

26. Longstreet, "Lee's Right Wing at Gettysburg," 340, 341; Longstreet, *Manassas to Appomattox*, 367; Hood "Letter From General John B. Hood," 149. *See also* Pfanz, *Second Day*, 113, for a discussion of Lee's orders.

27. *OR*, v27, pt2, 367.

28. Hood, *Advance and Retreat*, 58.

29. Ibid., 57.

30. Ibid., 58

31. Law, "Round Top," 323; *OR*, v27, pt2, 412.

32. McLaws, "Gettysburg," 73.

33. *OR*, v27, pt2, 407; Law, "Round Top," 320.

34. Law, "Round Top," 320.

35. *OR*, v27, pt2, 404, 414.

36. Ibid., 428; Coles, "Gettysburg Campaign," 8; Ward, "Incidents," 347.

37. Alexander, "Artillery at Gettysburg," 359.

38. Coles, "Gettysburg Campaign," 8; *OR*, v27, pt2, 428.

39. Oates, "Gettysburg," 174.

40. Bulger to Law, BSF.
41. Coles, "Gettysburg Campaign," 14.
42. Coles, "Gettysburg Campaign," 13, 14.
43. *OR*, v27, pt2, 391.
44. Norton, *Attack and Defense*, 263.
45. Purifoy, "Lost Opportunity," 217.
46. Norton, *Attack and Defense*, 263; Purifoy, "Lost Opportunity," 217, 218.
47. Smith, "4th Battery," 1290.
48. *OR*, v27, pt1, 515.
49. Steven's, *Berdan's Sharpshooters*, 2.
50. Kurtz, "Berdan's Sharpshooters," 15.
51. *OR*, v27, pt1, 518, 519.
52. Bulger to Law, BSF.
53. Law, "Round Top," 321.
54. Ibid., 321, 322.
55. Hood, *Advance and Retreat*, 58.
56. Ibid., said he sent his adjutant general, Col. Henry Sellers. Law, "Round Top," 322, identified the officer as Hamilton.
57. Law, "Round Top," 322; McLaws, "Gettysburg," 72.
58. Ward, "Incidents," 346.
59. Law, "Round Top," 322. Law never knew if his protest was passed on to Lee but from the brief time that elapsed between Hamilton's departure and return, Law suspected it was not.
60. Oates, *The War*, 207.
61. Ward, "Incidents," 347.
62. Bulger to Law, BSF.
63. Ward, "Incidents," 348.
64. Law, "Round Top," 323, remembered years later that the time was 5 p.m., but other accounts agree it was about 4 p.m. *OR*, v27, pt2, 407–408, 412; Sorrel, *Recollections*, 159. Sheffield, *OR*, v27, pt2, 395, does not give the time, but reported the 48th was in position about one-half hour before advancing, which is consistent with the brigade being in line between 3 and 3:30 p.m.; Oates, *The War*, 207.
65. Ward, "Incidents," 348.
66. Hood, *Advance and Retreat*, 59.
67. Texas Troops Folder, GNMP, indicates Hood was with the 1st Texas and wounded after a few paces; Hood, *Advance and Retreat*, 59, said he was wounded 20 minutes after reaching the Peach Orchard. What is important is that he was wounded a short time after the charge began.
68. *OR*, v27, pt2, 391; Robertson to Bachelder, Apr. 20, 1876, NHHS.
69. Ward, "Incidents," 347; Bulger to Law, BSF.
70. Ward, "Incidents," 347.
71. *OR*, v27, pt2, 404; Robertson to Bachelder, Apr. 20, 1876, NHHS.
72. Georg, "Principal Loss," 4.
73. Texas Troops Folder, GNMP.
74. Ward, "Incidents," 347.
75. Ibid.
76. Ibid.; CSR, 4th AL Inf, NA.
77. CSR, Co. K, 48th AL Inf, NA; Anderson to E. P. Anderson, Jul. 17, 1863, APJSU.
78. Neal, *Record of Confederate Burials*, GNMP. Turnbow was buried near the Slyder house.
79. *OR*, v27 pt2, 392; Oates, *The War*, 622.
80. Lindsay, 47th AL Inf, ADAH; Dickson, 48th AL Inf, ADAH; Oates, *The War*, 207.
81. Coles, "Gettysburg Campaign," 8; Zach Landrum, Texas Troops Folder, GNMP.
82. Ward, "Incidents," 347; Coles, "Gettysburg Campaign," 8; Zach Landrum, Texas Troops Folder, GNMP.
83. Norton, *Attack and Defense*, 256.
84. *OR*, v27 pt2, 391; Coles, "Gettysburg Campaign," 8.
85. Coles, "Gettysburg Campaign," 9.
86. Ward, "Incidents," 347; Coles, "Gettysburg Campaign," 9. Halsey was a musician, deserted in Feb. 1865, took the oath to the U.S. and moved to Boston, MA, CSR, 4th AL Inf, NA.
87. *OR*, v27, pt2, 392.
88. Bulger to Law, BSF.
89. *OR*, v27, pt1, 518.
90. Ibid., pt2, 393.
91. Oates *The War*, 208.
92. *OR*, v27 pt2, 393; Perry, "Devil's Den," 161.
93. *OR*, v27 pt2, 392.
94. Bulger to Law, BSF.
95. This conclusion would appear to conflict with the regimental history and other correspondence by Oates after the turn of the century when he stated: "General Law rode up to me as we were advancing, and informed me that I was then on the extreme right of our line and for me to hug the base of Great Round Top and go up the valley between the two mountains, until I found the left of the Union line, to turn it and do all the damage I could," Oates, *The War*, 211. Similar statements were made in correspondence. This implies that when the entire line was still in Plum Run Valley Law knew the Federal flank rested on Little Round Top and not as they, at first believed, extended nearly to Round Top. Therefore, it does not seem reasonable that Law would, at that time, order a turning movement around Little Round Top. Lt. Charles F. Sawyer of the 4th Maine reported that Little Round Top was not occupied until the attack on his position by the 44th and 48th was well under way, *OR*, v27, pt1, 509. Unfortunately Oates,

in his last years, all too often contradicted previous statements. This appears to be one of them.

96. Oates, "Gettysburg," 175; Oates to Robbins, Feb. 14, 1903, OC.

97. Bulger to Law, BSF.

98. 47th AL Inf, ADAH. Lindsay commanded the battalion from the 47th AL; Dickson, 48th AL Inf, ADAH, identifies the 48th AL companies; Oates, *The War*, 207.

99. Walker to Bachelder, Jan. 6, 1886, NHHS.

100. *OR*, v27 pt1, 509.

101. Walker to Bachelder, Jan. 6, 1886, NHHS.

102. *OR*, v27 pt1, 161.

103. Ibid., 509.

104. Perry, "Devil's Den," 161–162; Purifoy, "Horror of War," 254.

105. *OR*, v27 pt2, 394.

106. Ibid., pt1, 510.

107. Walker to Bachelder, Jan. 6, 1886, NHHS.

108. *OR*, v27, pt2, 395, 396.

109. Ibid., 396.

110. Ibid., 414, 415.

111. Ibid., 396.

112. Ibid., 405.

113. Law, "Round Top," 324.

114. *OR*, v27 pt2, 424.

115. Walker to Bachelder, Jan. 6, 1886, NHHS.

116. Perry, "Devil's Den," 161.

117. 44th AL Inf, ADAH.

118. Law, "Round Top," 324.

119. Purifoy, "Longstreet at Gettysburg," 293.

120. *OR*, v27 pt2, 396.

121. Perry, "Devil's Den," 162.

122. Walker to Bachelder, Jan. 6, 1886, NHHS.

123. "New York at Gettysburg," 1291.

124. *OR*, v27 pt2, 396.

125. Figures to his parents, Jul. 8, 1863, FC.

126. *OR*, v27, pt2, 396.

127. Pullen, *20th Maine*, 109.

128. Norton, *Attack and Defense*, 281–285; Warner, *Generals in Blue*, 527–528.

129. Judson, *83rd Pennsylvania*, 67.

130. Norton, *Attack and Defense*, 265.

131. Chamberlain to Nicholson, Aug. 14, 1903, OC; Nash, *44th New York*, 143; *OR*, v27, pt1, 616; Norton, *Attack and Defense*, 265.

132. Nash, *44th New York*, 146.

133. Pullen, *20th Maine*, 110.

134. Ibid.; Judson, *83rd Pennsylvania*, 67.

135. *OR*, v27, pt1, 616.

136. Warner, *Generals in Blue*, 76–77; Boatner, *Civil War Dictionary*, 135.

137. Norton, *Attack and Defense*, 265; Nash, *44th New York*, 143; Chamberlain to Nicholson, Aug. 14, 1903, OC, indicated Vincent said "hold at all costs."

138. *OR*, v27, pt1, 623; Chamberlain to Nicholson, Aug. 14, 1903, OC.

139. Chamberlain to Nicholson, Aug. 14, 1903, OC.

140. Nash, *44th New York*, 144.

141. Judson, *83rd Pennsylvania*, 66.

142. *OR*, v27, pt1, 623.

143. Morrill to Chamberlain, Jul. 8, 1863, NHHS.

144. *OR*, v27, pt1, 623.

145. Judson, *83rd Pennsylvania*, 67; *OR*, v27, pt1, 626.

146. Nash, *44th New York*, 144.

147. Judson, *83rd Pennsylvania*, 67.

148. Ward, "Incidents," 347.

149. Robbins to Nicholson, Feb. 26, 1903, OC.

150. *OR*, v27, pt2, 412.

151. Ward, "Incidents," 348; Montgomery *Advertiser*, Jan. 6, 1864.

152. *OR*, v27, pt1, 617; Nash, *44th New York*, 151; Judson, *83rd Pennsylvania*, 67.

153. Coles, "Gettysburg Campaign," 20.

154. Nash, *44th New York*, 145.

155. *OR*, v27, pt2, 411–412.

156. Norton, *Attack and Defense*, 258.

157. Barziza, *Adventures of a POW*, 45.

158. Coles, "Gettysburg Campaign," 11, 12.

159. Ibid., 12; Norton, *Attack and Defense*, 259; Judson, *83rd Pennsylvania*, 67.

160. *OR*, v27, pt2, 392.

161. Oates, "Gettysburg," 174; Norton, *Attack and Defense*, 256–257; *OR*, v27, pt1, 519.

162. Oates, *The War*, 212.

163. Oates, "Gettysburg," 174–176.

164. Bulger to Law, BSF.

165. Chamberlain to Nicholson, Aug. 14, 1903, OC. In earlier correspondence, Chamberlain said the "Rebels burst upon the 20th Maine with a shout," Chamberlain to Bachelder, n.d., NHHS.

166. Bulger to Law, BSF.

167. Ibid. This was Bulger's third serious wound in less than a year. Robbins Diary, Jul. 1, 1899, RPSHC, placed Bulger's position about ten yards east of Sykes's Avenue where it just descends to the foot of Little Round Top "nearly opposite the southern end of the wing wall of the avenues."

168. *OR*, v27, pt2, 395.

169. Oates, "Gettysburg," 176; Norton, *Attack and Defense*, 261.

170. Oates, "Gettysburg," 176; Oates, *The War*, 214, 221.

171. Judson, *83rd Pennsylvania*, 68.
172. Spear to Bachelder, Nov. 15, 1892, NHHS.
173. *OR*, v27, pt1, 623.
174. Judson, *83rd Pennsylvania*, 68.
175. Spear to Bachelder, Nov. 15, 1892, NHHS; Chamberlain to Bachelder, n. d., NHHS; Chamberlain to Nicholson, Aug. 14, 1903, OC; Nash, *44th New York*, 146; *OR*, v27, pt1, 623.
176. Oates, "Gettysburg," 176.
177. *OR*, v27, pt1, 623.
178. Ibid., pt2, 392.
179. Oates, "Gettysburg," 176, 177.
180. *OR*, v27, pt1, 623, pt2, 392.
181. Ibid., pt2, 392; Oates, "Gettysburg," 176.
182. Oates, "Gettysburg," 176.
183. *OR*, v27, pt1, 623.
184. Chamberlain to Bachelder, n.d., NHHS.
185. Rittenhouse, *Battle of Gettysburg*, Rittenhouse Papers, LC.
186. Oates, "Gettysburg," 177.
187. *OR*, v27, pt1, 624.
188. Chamberlain to Bachelder, n.d., NHHS.
189. *OR*, v27, pt2, 392.
190. Oates, *The War*, 755.
191. CSR, 15th AL, Inf, NA; 15th AL, Inf, ADAH.
192. Chamberlain to Bachelder, n.d., NHHS; Chamberlain to Nicholson, Aug. 14, 1903, OC.
193. Judson, *83rd Pennsylvania*, 68. The 83rd PA reported the enemy kept pressing left and got in the rear of the regiment. This was probably Waddell and his men.
194. Judson, *83d Pennsylvania*, 67.
195. Norton, *Attack and Defense*, 210.
196. Leeper's Statement, Apr. 28, 1883, NHHS.
197. *OR*, v27, pt2, 411; Norton, *Attack and Defense*, 259, 260.
198. *OR*, v27 pt2, 394.
199. Perry, "Devil's Den," 162.
200. Anderson to E. P. Anderson, Jul. 17, 1863, APJSU.
201. Oates, "Gettysburg," 177; *OR*, v27, pt2, 392; Chamberlain to Nicholson, Aug. 14, 1903, OC. Oates later wrote the Federals on his left were dismounted cavalry. They were probably the small body of Stoughton's sharpshooters that Norton, *Attack and Defense*, 257, reported moved to the 47th AL's left as Oates chased Stoughton up Round Top.
202. Morrill to Chamberlain, Jul. 8, 1863, NHHS.
203. Oates, "Gettysburg," 178.
204. Chamberlain to Bachelder, n.d., NHHS.
205. *OR*, v27, pt1, 624.
206. Ibid., 624, pt2, 395. Oates never elaborated as

to how he prepared to withdraw. Chamberlain specifically reported two lines. Since Oates was seriously considering withdrawing it seems reasonable he would throw out a skirmish line to cover his rear. This is the same conclusion drawn by Pfanz, *Second Day*, 235.
207. *OR*, v27, pt1, 624.
208. Spear to Bachelder, Nov. 15, 1892, NHHS.
209. Oates, "Gettysburg," 176.
210. Morrill to Chamberlain, Jul. 8, 1863, NHHS; Oates, "Gettysburg," 178.
211. Oates, *The War*, 221, 717.
212. Spear to Bachelder, Nov. 15, 1892, NHHS; Oates, *The War*, 221.
213. *OR*, v27, pt1, 624; Oates, *The War*, 771, 772.
214. Oates, *The War*, 221.
215. *OR*, v27, pt1, 624; Judson, *83rd Pennsylvania*, 68.
216. *OR*, v27, pt1, 624.
217. Bulger to Law, BSF.
218. *OR*, v27, pt1, 625. It is impossible to identify the number of prisoners taken during the sweep because the captured tabulated from the CSR, NA and HMR, ADAH include wounded left in field hospitals. Federal accounts greatly overstate the actual number captured, however. Chamberlain placed the number at 400, Chamberlain to Nicholson, Aug. 14, 1903, OC. Total captured from Law's Brigade was 154 and from Robertson's 120, *OR*, v27, pt2, 339.
219. Morrill to Chamberlain, Jul. 8, 1863, NHHS.
220. Judson, *83rd Pennsylvania*, 68. The 83rd Pennsylvania historian described the incident, but was unable to identify the officer. The Confederate officer's identity, therefore, is based on the process of elimination. Four line officers from Law's Brigade were captured. The circumstances under which three were captured are known. Oates and Barnett were severely wounded and left disabled where they fell. Wicker was captured by Chamberlain and identified by Oates, *The War*, 771, 772. Breare is therefore the officer referred to in the account.
221. *OR*, v27, pt1, 626; CSR, 15th AL Inf, NA; 15th AL Inf, ADAH.
222. Giles, *Rags and Hope*, 180.
223. Fletcher, *Rebel Private*, 60
224. Giles, *Rags and Hope*, 180.
225. Judson, *83rd Pennsylvania*, 68; The Confederate's identity is not known. However, from the description of the incident the wounded man was probably a Texan or Alabamian.
226. Law, "Round Top," 326; *B&L*, v3, 394.
227. Coles, "Gettysburg Campaign," 20.
228. *OR*, v27, pt1, 625.

229. Judson, *83rd Pennsylvania*, 69.
230. *OR*, v27, pt1, 618.
231. Nash, *44th New York*, 326
232. Ibid., 153.
233. *OR*, v27, pt2, 395.
234. Bulger to Law, BSF.
235. Judson, *83rd Pennsylvania*, 69.
236. Bulger to Law, BSF; Barziza, *Adventures of a POW*, 54, reported the Confederate wounded were well treated when they were brought into the lines. The wounded Rebels were placed right beside the Federal wounded.
237. Chamberlain to Nicholson, Aug. 14, 1903, OC. Oates first mentioned the incident in his article, Oates, "Gettysburg," 181,182, but Chamberlain did not take issue with Oates at that time.
238. *OR*, v27, pt1, 625.
239. Bulger was obviously one, the second was Col. R. M. Powell, 4th TX.
240. Norton, *Attack and Defense*, 113.
241. Montgomery *Advertiser*, Jan. 6, 1864.
242. William Brown to his brother, Jul. 7, 1863, *83rd Pennsylvania* Folder, GNMP.
243. Oates, *The War*, 597.
244. Ward, "Incidents," 348.
245. Nash, *44th New York*, 151.
246. Law, "Round Top," 326; Judson, *83rd Pennsylvania*, 69; *OR*, v27, pt1, 625.

Chapter 6 – Farnsworth's Charge

1. Tyler, *Men of Mark in Virginia*, 103.
2. Montgomery *Advertiser*, Jul. 26, 1863.
3. Coles, "Gettysburg Campaign," 21.
4. Ibid., 22.
5. Parsons, "Farnsworth's Charge," map, 394.
6. Law, "Round Top," 326.
7. Dedication, 86.
8. Law, "Round Top," 326.
9. Ibid., 327.
10. Ibid., referred to the house as the Kern house. It is shown variously as the Kern or Currens house. The name used here is the Currens house after the battlefield survey of 1868 and 1869.
11. Ibid.; *Dedication*, 86.
12. Parsons, "Farnsworth's Charge," 393.
13. Purifoy, "Farnsworth's Charge," 307.
14. *OR*, v27, pt2, 397.
15. Law, "Round Top," 327; Purifoy, "Farnsworth's Charge," 307.
16. *OR*, v27, pt2, 402.
17. Ibid.; Law, "Round Top," 328; *Dedication*, 87; Purifoy, "Farnsworth's Charge," 308.

18. Parsons, "Farnsworth's Charge," 396n.
19. Farnsworth made a reconnaissance of the area and returned convinced an attack could not succeed, King, "Hugh Kilpatrick," 127.
20. Parsons, "Farnsworth's Charge," 394. The second battalion had been thrown out as skirmishers.
21. Parsons, "Farnsworth's Charge," 394.
22. Jane Law Norvell Collection.
23. Law, "Gaines's Mill," 364; McWhiney, *Attack and Die*, 128, reported 60 percent of the 250 Union cavalry were felled in the charge at Gaines's Mill.
24. Coles, "Gettysburg Campaign," 24, 25.
25. Parsons, "Farnsworth's Charge," 395.
26. New York *Times*, Jul. 21, 1863; Parsons, "Farnsworth's Charge," 395. Parsons did not identify where the group entered the Union lines. However, from the probable location at the time the logical route would be over ground occupied by the left of Law's Brigade and then around the northern end of Round Top.
27. *Dedication*, 124.
28. Coles, "Gettysburg Campaign," 26.
29. Parsons, "Farnsworth's Charge," 395; Botsford, *Memories*, 9.
30. Coles, "Gettysburg Campaign," 25.
31. Oates, *The War*, 236.
32. *Dedication*, 125.
33. Oates, "Gettysburg," 182.
34. Oates, "Gettysburg," 182; Oates, *The War*, 237; Parsons, "Farnsworth's Charge," 396n; Coles, "Gettysburg Campaign," 26.
35. Coles, "Gettysburg Campaign," 26, 27. Nix transferred to Co. C, 31st AL as sec. lt., CSR, 4th AL Inf, NA.
36. *Dedication*, 93.
37. Ibid., 90.
38. McLaws, "Gettysburg," 87– 88.
39. Ibid., 88.
40. McLaws to I. R. Pennypacker, Jul. 31, 1888, Philadelphia *Weekly Press*.
41. *OR*, v27, pt2, 416–417. The exact location of the hill, or rise, described by Benning is not known. McLaws line was north of the Devil's Den, under cover of woods, and extended almost to the intersection of the Emmitsburg Road and the Wheatfield Road, McLaws, "Gettysburg," 79.
42. McLaws to I. R. Pennypacker, Jul. 31, 1888, Philadelphia *Weekly Press*.
43. *OR*, v27, pt2, 423.
44. Law, "Round Top," 330.
45. Oates, *The War*, 237–239.
46. *OR*, v27, pt2, 392.

47. Ibid., 395.
48. Ibid., 396; There is no record that St. John was actually appointed maj. Apparently Sheffield appointed him acting major prior to the battle.
49. CSR, 15th AL Inf, NA.
50. Oates, *The War*, 709.
51. *OR*, v27, pt2, 482, 483.
52. Alexander, *Fighting for the Confederacy*, 236.
53. Survivors Association, *History of the 118th Pennsylvania Volunteers*, 261, 262; William Brown to his brother, Jul. 7, 1863, *83rd Pennsylvania* Folder, GNMP.
54. *CV*, v5, n9, Sep. 1897, 470.
55. Ibid., n10, Oct. 1897, 514.
56. The effective date of Christian's promotion was Nov. 17, 1863, CSR, 4th AL, NA.
57. LRCAI, 1861–1865, M474, roll 101.
58. CSR, 4th AL Inf, NA.
59. *CMH*, v8, 488, 489.
60. *The Medical and Surgical History*, pt2, v2, 81.
61. *CMH*, v8, 488, 489; CSR, 4th AL Inf, NA.
62. CSR, 4th AL Inf, NA.
63. *CMH*, v8, 488, 489.
64. CSR, 48th AL Inf, CSR, 15th AL Inf, NA.
65. CSR, 15th AL Inf, NA.
66. Oates, *The War*, 634, recalled cavalry raised in the conscript department were not considered very effective and were referred to as "Buttermilk Rangers."
67. CSR, 47th AL Inf, CSR, 15th AL Inf, CSR, 4th AL Inf, NA.
68. CSR, 4th AL Inf, NA.
69. CSR, 47th AL Inf, NA; 47th AL Inf, ADAH; three of the four brothers perished in the war, which could also be said of many southern families.
70. Imboden, "Retreat From Gettysburg," 423–425.
71. *OR*, v27, pt2, 214, 280, 437, 655; Hudson, "Soldier Boys," 64.
72. CSR, 48th AL Inf, NA.
73. Coles, "Gettysburg Campaign," 29; REC, Co. D, CSR, 44th AL Inf; REC, Co. E, CSR, 44th AL Inf, NA.
74. *CV*, v19, n5, May 1911. Thomas had been promoted to sergeant for "gallant and meritorious service" in early 1863. He was on detached service in Alabama seeking clothing for the 4th Alabama when the Confederacy collapsed, CSR, 4th AL Inf, NA.
75. Coco, *A Vast Sea of Misery*, 143.
76. Vaughan, "Vaughan Diary," 588; Coles, "Gettysburg Campaign," 29; Purifoy, "Battle Array," 372.
77. Vaughan, "Vaughan Diary," 589–590; REC, Co. C and K, CSR, 44th AL Inf, NA.
78. Purifoy, "Battle Array," 372; Vaughan, "Vaughan Diary," 590; REC, 4th AL Inf, NA.
79. *OR*, v27, pt2, 323, 428.
80. Coles, "Gettysburg Campaign," 32; Vaughan, "Vaughan Diary," 590.

Chapter 7 – On the Rappahannock

1. *OR*, v27, pt1, 324.
2. McClendon, *Recollections*, 179; Jordan, *Events*, 46, 47; Goodson, "Goodson Letters," 144–147.
3. Simpson, *Texas Brigade*, 294.
4. Newell to Martha McKee, Jul. 24, 1863, ML.
5. Ibid.
6. Reuben Kidd to Sue, Jul. 17, 1863, Pierrepont, *Reuben Kidd*, 330.
7. Daniel to M. A. Daniel, Jul. 27, 1863, DCSU.
8. *OR*, v27, pt2, 324, 362.
9. Ibid., pt1, 999, 1000, pt2, 324, 362; Vaughan, "Vaughan Diary," 591.
10. *OR*, v27, pt2, 362.
11. Ibid.
12. Wise, *17th Virginia*, 160–162; *OR*, v27, pt2, 362, pt1, 945.
13. *OR*, v27, pt1, 937.
14. Ibid., pt2, 362; Coles, "From Falling Waters to Fredericksburg," 1.
15. *OR*, v27, pt2, 417.
16. Wise, *17th Virginia*, 160.
17. Vaughan, "Vaughan Diary," 591.
18. *OR*, v27, pt2, 362.
19. Ibid., 417, 418.
20. Ibid., 489, 490.
21. Ibid., 417, 418.
22. Coles, "From Falling Waters to Fredericksburg," 2; Vaughan, "Vaughan Diary," 591.
23. Oates, *The War*, 250, 251.
24. Ibid.
25. Ibid.
26. Ibid., 251; Jordan, *Events*, 48.
27. *OR*, v27, pt2, 419.
28. Newell to Martha McKee, Jul. 24, 1863, ML.
29. *OR*, v27, pt1, 999, 1004, pt2, 418.
30. Ibid., pt2, 419.
31. Ibid., pt1, 1004, pt3, 753, 754, 805.
32. Ibid., pt1, 1004; Richmond *Dispatch*, Aug. 4, 1863.
33. Oates, *The War*, 251; McClendon, *Recollections*, 181.
34. Oates, *The War*, 251.

35. Richmond *Dispatch*, Aug. 4, 1863.
36. Oates, *The War*, 251.
37. *OR*, v27, pt2, 419.
38. Richmond *Dispatch*, Aug. 4, 1863.
39. *OR*, v27, pt1, 1004.
40. Coles, "From Falling Waters to Fredericksburg," 3, 4.
41. Taylor, *48th Alabama*; Vaughan, "Vaughan Diary," 592.
42. McClendon, *Recollections*, 181, placed the troops at seven or eight miles from town, while Goodson, "Goodson Letters," 144–147, located them five miles south and three miles from their winter quarters.
43. Vaughan, "Vaughan Diary," 593.
44. Taylor, *48th Alabama*.
45. Ibid.
46. Newell to Martha McKee, Jul. 26, 1863, ML.
47. Mrs. Jackson to Thomas Owen, Jul. 16, 1902, 47th AL Inf, ADAH.
48. Campbell to James A. Seddon, Dec. 29, 1863, CSR, 47th AL Inf, NA.
49. Law to Campbell's Examining Board, Jul. 30, 1863, CSR, 47th AL Inf, NA.
50. Campbell to James A. Seddon, Dec. 29, 1863, CSR, 47th AL Inf, NA.
51. Company and regimental commanders to examining board, Jul. 29–31, 1863, CSR, 47th AL Inf, NA.
52. Law to examining board, Jul. 30, 1863, CSR, 47th AL Inf, NA. The text quoted is Law's entire testimony, for clarity the original text has been modified to spell out abbreviations and add punctuation marks.
53. 47th Alabama company commanders to R. E. Lee, Aug. 7, 1863, CSR, 47th AL Inf, NA.
54. 47th AL company commanders to Cooper, Nov. 22, 1863, CSR, 47th AL Inf, NA.
55. Opinion of Campbell's examining board, undated, CSR, 47th AL Inf, NA.
56. Campbell to James A. Seddon, Dec. 29, 1863, CSR, 47th AL Inf, NA.
57. Seddon, Jan. 18, 1864, CSR, 47th AL Inf, NA.
58. James T. Jones to F. S. Lyon, Apr. 21, 1864, CSR, 47th AL Inf, NA.
59. Terrell's application, May 4, 1864, CSR, 47th AL Inf, NA.
60. James Taylor to Georgia Taylor, Aug. 30, 1863, CGP; Goodson, "Goodson Letters," 148.
61. Vaughan, "Vaughan Diary," 593–594.
62. Ibid.
63. Taylor, *48th Alabama*.
64. Crowder to family, Aug. 26, 1863, JPCL. This is corroborated by Daniel to wife, Aug. 26,

1863, DCSU. Both members of the 47th, they seemed delighted that the 48th had been driven right back across the river.
65. *OR*, v29, pt2, 38, 89, 90, 93; Taylor, *48th Alabama*; Vaughan, "Vaughan Diary," 594.
66. Goodson, "Goodson Letters," 147, 148.
67. Figures to his mother, Aug. 26, 1863, FC.
68. Shingleton, *Sea Ghost*, 88.
69. *OR*, v29, pt2, 111, 112.
70. Richmond *Dispatch*, Sep. 7, 1863.
71. *OR*, v29, pt2, 104; King, "Hugh Kilpatrick," 141, 142.
72. *OR*, v29, pt1, 98.
73. Ibid.
74. Richmond *Dispatch*, Sep. 7, 1863; Andrews, *South Reports the War*, 550, identifies "Bohemian" as Dr. William G. Shepardson, who also wrote under the name de plum of "Evelyn."
75. *OR*, v29, pt1, 98.
76. Richmond *Dispatch*, Sep. 7, 1863.
77. Burton, *47th Alabama*.
78. Jones, *Christ in the Camp*, 312; Romero, *Religion in the Rebel Ranks*, 98.
79. Vaughan, "Vaughan Diary" 591, 593; Jordan, *Events*, 49–50; *Southwestern Baptist*, Dec. 3, 1863.
80. Ibid.
81. Ibid; Oates, *The War*, 602.
82. Vaughan, "Vaughan Diary" 594; *Southwestern Baptist*, Dec. 3, 1863.
83. *Southwestern Baptist*, Dec. 3, 1863.
84. Vaughan, "Vaughan Diary" 594; Jordan, *Events*, 50.
85. Jordan, *Events*, 50.
86. *Southwestern Baptist*, Dec. 3, 1863.

Chapter 8 – Fighting along the Chickamauga

1. Freeman, *Lee's Lts*, v3, 220–221.
2. Longstreet, *Manassas to Appomattox*, 433–437.
3. *OR*, v29, pt2, 7106, 713, 714; Longstreet, *Manassas to Appomattox*, 467, claimed that Jenkins was transferred to the First Corps upon application of Hood. Since Hood was recovering from his wound the more plausible scenario is that presented by Freeman, *Lee's Lts*, v3, 223.
4. *OR*, v29, pt2, 719–720.
5. New York *Herald*, Sep. 9, 14, 1863.
6. *OR*, v30, pt1, 34–36, 186, 187–189, 191.
7. Alexander, *Military Memoirs*, 448–449; *OR*, v30, pt2, 592.
8. Longstreet, *Manassas to Appomattox*, 436; Alexander, *Military Memoirs*, 448–449; *OR*, v30, pt2, 592; Black, *Railroads*, 185.
9. *OR*, v29, pt2, 706; Taylor, *48th Alabama*; HM, Co. E, 4th AL Inf, ADAH.

10. Vaughan, "Vaughan Diary," 595; HM, Co. D, 47th AL Inf, ADAH.

11. Hood, *Advance and Retreat*, 55; Simpson, *Texas Brigade*, 299, 300.

12. Black, *Railroads*, 191.

13. Goodson, "Goodson Letters," 149–150; Vaughan, "Vaughan Diary," 595.

14. Jones, *War Clerk's Diary*, 277. Throughout the summer and fall, Holden had editorialized for a negotiated settlement of the war.

15. Freeman, *Lee's Lts*, v3, 218; Yearns, *North Carolina Documentary*, 292–299. Holden later served two terms as governor, though he lost the 1864 election to Zebulon Vance for the governorship of North Carolina; Amis, *Historical Raleigh*, 139. Members of the 48th NC strongly denounced the *Standard's* views in an article in the Richmond *Dispatch*, Sep. 1, 1863.

16. Amis, *Historical Raleigh*, 139; a rival newspaper loaned the *Standard* sufficient equipment to be back in operation the next day; Richmond *Daily Dispatch*, Sep. 11, 1863.

17. Jones, *War Clerk's Diary*, 277.

18. *OR*, v27, v29, pt2, 710; Jones, *War Clerk's Diary*, 277.

19. Richmond *Daily Dispatch*, Sep. 11, 1863; Jones, *War Clerk's Diary*, 277, refers to the *State Journal* as ultra secessionist.

20. Vaughan, "Vaughan Diary," 595.

21. *OR*, v29, pt2, 710.

22. Vaughan, "Vaughan Diary," 595; *OR*, v51, pt2, 764–765.

23. Jordan, *Events*, 50; Bond, *South Carolinians*, 83–84; Jordan, *Events*, 50.

24. CSR, 48th AL Inf, NA.

25. Bond, *South Carolinians*, 84.

26. Longstreet, *Manassas to Appomattox*, 437.

27. Coles, "Chickamauga," 1.

28. Goodson, "Goodson Letters," 149–150.

29. Vaughan, "Vaughan Diary," 596; Taylor, *48th Alabama*.

30. Coles, "Chickamauga," 2.

31. Taylor, *48th Alabama*.

32. Coles, "Chickamauga Campaign," 2.

33. Oates, *The War*, 253.

34. HMR, 48th AL Inf, ADAH. The regimental rolls show at least ten soldiers left in this manner.

35. Martin, *Desertion of Alabama Troops*, 45, 46, 56, 128.

36. Richmond *Enquirer*, Sep. 8, 1863.

37. Martin, *Desertion of Alabama Troops*, 25.

38. HMR, 44th AL Inf, ADAH.

39. HMR, 44th and 47th AL Inf, ADAH. "Outlying"

was an Alabama colloquialism used when a deserter hid in the woods, usually near his home, Martin, *Desertion of Alabama Troops*, 24.

40. HMR, 47th AL Inf, ADAH.

41. Vaughan, "Vaughan Diary," 596; Taylor, *48th Alabama*; HM, Co. E, 4th AL Inf, ADAH.

42. Taylor, *48th Alabama*.

43. Hood, *Advance and Retreat*, 62.

44. Coles, "Chickamauga," 3.

45. Ibid., 2.

46. Vaughan, "Vaughan Diary," 596; *OR*, v30, pt2, 451; HM, Co. E, 4th AL Inf, ADAH.

47. Jordan, *Events*, 50.

48. Oates, *The War*, 676.

49. Ibid.; Burger, "Episcopal Clergy," 66.

50. The Confederate organization is from *OR*, v30, pt2, 11–20.

51. The Federal organization is from *OR*, v30, pt1 41–147.

52. The description and location of the battlefield is from *B&L* v3, 670, and Longstreet, *Manassas to Appomattox*, 443; Chickamauga Creek is identified as West Chickamauga Creek or West Chickamauga River, Davis, *Atlas*, map 46. It is referred to here by its more commonly used name of the Chickamauga. The La Fayette-Rossville Rd. is the present day U.S. Highway 27.

53. Huntsville *Daily Confederate*, Oct. 17, 1863; CSR, 47th AL Inf, NA.

54. Estimated strengths are based on analysis of regimental muster rolls.

55. Perry to Carman, Oct. 16, 1893, ECP.

56. *OR*, v30, pt2, 453.

57. Oates, *The War*, 253.

58. The organization of Longstreet's left wing is from *OR*, v30, pt2, 16–18.

59. Goodson, "Goodson Letters," 152.

60. Jordan, *Events*, 51; Huntsville *Daily Confederate*, Oct. 17, 1863.

61. Oates, *The War*, 745–746.

62. The four divisions represented along this part of the Union line were those of Reynolds, Palmer, Van Cleve and Jefferson C. Davis.

63. Oates, *The War*, 254.

64. Coles, "Chickamauga," 5.

65. *OR*, v30, pt2, 453.

66. Ibid.

67. Ibid., 383, 510.

68. Coles, "Chickamauga," 3–4.

69. *OR*, v30, pt2, 510–511, 517–518.

70. Perry to Carman, Oct. 16, 1893, ECPLC.

71. Ibid; Coles, "Chickamauga," 4.

72. Coles, "Chickamauga," 4.

73. Perry to Carman, Oct. 16, 1893, ECPLC.

74. Goodson, "Goodson Letters," 150.

75. Perry to Carman, Oct. 16, 1893, ECPLC.

76. Ibid.

77. Goodson, "Goodson Letters," 150; Coles, "Chickamauga," 5, recounted that in the rapid rush through the timber the 44th was entirely lost. According to Oates, *The War*, 254, the 44th became "entirely disconnected" from the brigade.

78. Perry to Carman, Oct. 16, 1893, ECPLC.

79. Oates, "Perry and His Career." This lengthy obituary is perhaps the only account of this incident on Sep. 19.

80. *OR*, v30, pt2, 384, 395.

81. Oates, *The War*, 254; Oates to A. P. Stewart, Dec. 23, 1890, ECP.

82. Oates, "Perry and His Career."

83. Tucker, *Chickamauga*, 123.

84. Figures to mother, Sep. 26, 1863, USAMHI; *OR*, v30, pt1, 815.

85. Oates, *The War*, 254.

86. Clark, *125th Ohio*, 92–95.

87. Oates, *The War*, 745, 754.

88. Coles, "Chickamauga," 6.

89. Pierrepont, *Reuben Kidd*, 268, 336, 384.

90. Coles, "Chickamauga," 4.

91. Oates, *The War*, 254–255.

92. Coles, "Chickamauga," 4–5.

93. CSR, 4th AL Inf, NA.

94. Oates, *The War*, 254–255; Coles, "Chickamauga," 5.

95. Stewart and Fulton had fought troops of Beatty and Dick of Van Cleve and King of Reynolds and the 92nd IL.

96. *OR*, v30, pt1, 632.

97. Ibid., pt2, 455.

98. Negley, supported by Brannan recaptured most the ground lost west of the La Fayette Rd.

99. *OR*, v30, pt1, 474. Turchin had met Alabamians before. In 1862, a court-martial sentenced him to be dismissed from the army for the sack of Athens, AL. Abraham Lincoln ignored the court's findings and promoted Turchin to brig. gen.

100. ECPLC.

101. Perry to Carman, Oct. 16, 1893, ECPLC.

102. *OR*, v30, pt2, 392.

103. Perry to Carman, Oct. 16, 1893, ECPLC.

104. Hinman, *The Sherman Brigade*, 422, 423.

105. Hampton, *Dark Days*, 31.

106. Turchin, *Chickamauga*, 187.

107. CSR, 44th AL Inf, NA.

108. *OR*, v30, pt2, 412.

109. Burton, *47th Alabama*.

110. HMR, 47th AL Inf, ADAH; CSR, 47th AL Inf, NA.

111. Savage, *Piedmont Alabama*, 76.

112. Jordan, *Events,* 51; Bushrod Johnson thought they were 600 yards east of the road, *OR*, v30, pt2, 456.

113. Hood, *Advance and Retreat*, 62.

114. Coles, "Chickamauga," 5.

115. Oates, *The War*, 255.

116. Coles, "Chickamauga," 6.

117. Oates, *The War*, 255.

118. Oates, "Perry and His Career."

Chapter 9 – Charge through the Federal Center

1. Oates, "Perry and His Career."

2. Law and Perry remained at odds for the remainder of the war. Mary Gray Pitts to Mims Walker, Apr. 12, 1864, CGP.

3. Hill, *B&L*, v3, 652.

4. Longstreet, *Manassas to Appomattox*, 439.

5. Hunter, *82nd Indiana*, 3, CCNMP; McNeil, *Personal Recollections*, 16; Otto, *11th Indiana Battery*, 38.

6. Longstreet, *Manassas to Appomattox*, 440.

7. *OR*, v30, pt2, 456.

8. Ibid., 516.

9. Ibid., 456. Col. Sugg assumed brigade command the previous afternoon when Brig. Gen. John Gregg was wounded, ibid., 17.

10. Coles, "Chickamauga Campaign," 8; Goodson, "Goodson Letters," 151; Oates, *The War,* 258.

11. *OR*, v30, pt2, 511, 518.

12. Estimated strengths and officers present are based on analysis of regimental muster rolls.

13. Perry to Carman, Oct. 16, 1893, ECP.

14. *OR*, v30, pt2, 41.

15. Ibid., pt1, 402, 409.

16. Ibid., 402, 408.

17. Battery D is also referred to as 4th Michigan by Brannan ibid., 406, and by Lt. Marco Gary of Battery C, 1st OH Light Artillery, ibid., 426. Capt. Josiah Church, commanding the battery in question, referred to the guns in his report as Battery D, 1st MI Light Artillery; but then signed the report as commanding officer of the 4th MI Battery, ibid., 415. The battery will be referred to hereafter as the 4th MI Battery.

18. Ibid., 694. Wood's Second Brigade was stationed in Chattanooga.

19. *Harper's Pictorial Civil War History*, 546.

20. *OR*, v30, pt1, 983–984.

21. Ibid., 409.

22. *B&L*, v3, 653.

23. Longstreet, *Manassas to Appomattox*, 447.

24. *Harper's Pictorial Civil War History*, 544.

25. Longstreet, *Manassas to Appomattox*, 447.

26. *OR*, v30, pt1, 635.

27. Ibid., pt1, 42, pt2, 15.

28. Ibid., pt1, 500. Lytle commanded the First Brigade, Laiboldt commanded the Second Brigade, Third Division, XX Corps.

29. Ibid., pt2, 457, 495.

30. Ibid., pt2, 495.

31. Ibid., pt1, 409. Connell used "flying" to describe the movement of his right regiment.

32. *Indiana at Chickamauga*, 231, 82nd IN Folder, CCNMP.

33. *OR*, v30, pt1, 414.

34. Ibid., pt1, 414.

35. Ibid., pt2, 495. Sugg talked with McNair before moving forward through his ranks; therefore McNair must have been wounded after Sugg passed his line.

36. Ibid., pt1, 423, 425.

37. *Tenth Indiana Volunteer Infantry*, 234, 10th IN Folder, CCNMP; *OR*, v30, pt1, 420, 406.

38. Ibid., 420; *Tenth Indiana Volunteer Infantry*, 233–234, 10th IN Folder, CCNMP.

39. Perry to Carman, Oct. 16, 1893, ECPLC.

40. Oates, *The War*, 255; Bennett, *36th Illinois*, 468.

41. Goodson, "Goodson Letters," 151.

42. Perry to Carman, Oct. 16, 1893, ECPLC.

43. Goodson, "Goodson Letters," 151.

44. The accepted location is just about where the Law's Brigade marker now stands on U.S. 27, north of the Brotherton house.

45. *OR*, v30, pt2, 407, 414.

46. Coles, "Chickamauga," 7.

47. Based on analysis of the Compiled Service Records available from the National Archives and the Alabama Department of Archives and History. The records indicate only four captains from the 4th AL were present that day. Karsner was the senior officer present.

48. *OR*, v30, pt2, 518.

49. *Tenth Indiana Volunteer Infantry*, 233, 10th IN Folder, CCNMP.

50. *OR*, v30, pt1, 44–45.

51. Crittenden indicated his objective was to cover retiring troops should reverses be experienced, Ibid., 610.

52. Ibid., 851, Livingston used the word "circuitous" to describe his movement.

53. Ibid., 623.

54. Ibid., 820.

55. Ibid., 800; ibid., 623, reported the fighting was quite heavy in front when the 8th IN and Battery H, 4th U.S. Artillery fell back. Cushing did not come into the battery line until the enemy appeared from the woods.

56. Ibid., 1, 678.

57. 7th IN Battery Folder, CCNMP; *OR*, v30, pt1, 678.

58. *OR*, v30, pt1, 610, 611.

59. Burton, *47th Alabama*.

60. *OR*, v30, pt1, 851. Livingston reported two Confederates guns were brought to bear on his position. Coles, "Chickamauga," 7–8 reported Bragg's batteries moved in line with them as they charged through the woods.

61. Coles, "Chickamauga," 7.

62. *OR*, v30, pt1, 678.

63. Joseph Breuling Letter, dated Sep. 29, 1863, 3rd Wisconsin Battery Folder, CCNMP.

64. Huntsville *Daily Confederate*, Oct., 17, 1863.

65. Burton, *47th Alabama*.

66. Perry to Carman, Oct. 16, 1893, ECPLC.

67. CSR, 47th AL Inf, NA.

68. Botsford, *Memories*, 18.

69. *OR*, v30, pt2, 495.

70. Ibid., 836.

71. *3rd Battery, Wisconsin Light Artillery*, 31.

72. Burton, *47th Alabama*; Clark, *North Carolina Regiments*, 713.

73. HMR, 48th AL Inf, ADAH.

74. Ibid.

75. *3rd Battery, Wisconsin Light Artillery*, 31.

76. Coles, "Chickamauga," 8.

77. *OR*, v30, pt1, 851, 623.

78. Ibid., pt2, 495, 498.

79. *CV*, v30, n8, 1900; *OR*, v30, pt2, 458.

80. Perry to Carman, Oct. 16, 1893, ECPLC.

81. Huntsville *Daily Confederate*, Oct. 17, 1863.

82. *OR*, v30, pt2, 511.

83. Ibid.

84. Perry to Carman, Oct. 16, 1893, ECPLC.

85. Botsford, *Memories*, 12. Thirty-year-old Anderson Glaze began his military career with 15th GA Infantry, enlisting, as a substitute for Houston Glaze, in Lincoln County GA on Jul. 14, 1861. He transferred to the 47th AL on Jun. 30, 1862 when it arrived in Richmond. Glaze was later declared permanently disabled and retired from military service on Dec. 3, 1864. He returned to Opelika, AL. CSR, 47th AL Inf, NA.

86. Clark, *North Carolina Regiments*, 714. The North Carolinians felt the issue was settled in their favor by the Chickamauga Commission in Nov. 1893.

87. *OR*, v30, pt2, 497, 498.

88. Ibid., 458.
89. The marker is on the northeast side of the Dyer field pointing to the capture of "the nine guns."
90. Ibid., 17. The 39th NC was attached to McNair's Brigade.
91. Ibid., 498.
92. Oates, *The War*, 255, 256.
93. Ibid., 256, *OR*, v30, pt2, 330.
94. Oates, *The War*, 256, 258, 259.
95. Otto, *11th Indiana Battery*, 42.
96. Oates, *The War*, 256.
97. *OR*, v30, pt2, 334.
98. Oates, *The War*, 256.
99. Bennett, *36th Illinois*, 469.
100. Oates, *The War*, 258, 259.
101. Ibid., 259; Jordan, *Events*, 52. There is no evidence the 15th AL actually overran the guns.
102. Oates, *The War*, 259.
103. *OR*, v30, pt2, 504; Oates, *The War*, 260, believed he was between the 7th and 3rd SC.
104. Jordan, *Events*, 52.
105. Oates, *The War*, 260–262.
106. Ibid., 262.
107. Jordan, *Events*, 53.
108. Law to McLaws, Apr. 29, 1864, MPSHC; Montgomery *Advertiser*, Oct. 13, 1863.
109. *OR*, v30, pt2, 215–216, 229, 256, 270, 287, 343, 356, 360, 370, 382, 411–412, 448.
110. Perry to Carman, Oct. 16, 1893, ECPLC.
111. Jordan, *Events*, 53.
112. Perry to Carman, Oct. 16, 1893, ECPLC.
113. HMR of the five Alabama regiments in ADAH; CSR of the five Alabama regiments, NA. The missing officer was Lt. Battle "Batt" D. Peterson, Co. B, 4th AL, who was captured on Sep. 20. He escaped the Federal prison, but was killed Jan. 16, 1864 at Dandridge, TN.
114. HMR of the five Alabama regiments in ADAH; CSR of the five Alabama regiments, NA.
115. Oates, *The War*, 264.
116. Huntsville *Daily Confederate*, Oct. 17, 1863.
117. CSR, Co. I, 47th AL Inf, NA; HMR, 47th AL Inf, ADAH.
118. Crowder to his mother, Sep. 27, 1863, JPCL.
119. "Chickamauga," *Military Medicine*, 389.
120. E. P. Anderson to Anderson, Oct. 10, 1863, APJSU.
121. Huntsville *Daily Confederate*, Oct. 5, 1863.
122. Jacksonville *Republican*, Jan. 25, 1868.

Chapter 10 – Affair in Lookout Valley

1. Oates, *The War*, 264–265.
2. Longstreet, *Manassas to Appomattox*, 462; *OR*, v30, pt2, 287–292.
3. Longstreet, *Manassas to Appomattox*, 463.
4. Alexander, *Military Memoirs*, 466.
5. CGSO, M331, NA. Watts was the Confederate attorney general until his election as governor of Alabama in Aug. 1863.
6. CGSO, M331, NA.
7. Ibid.
8. *B&L*, v3, 329.
9. Thomas, *SC Military Academy*, 542.
10. Freeman, *Lee's Lts*, v3, 223–224.
11. Jenkins, CSR, NA; H. C. Conner to Ellen, Mar. 16, 1863, H. C. Conner Papers, SCL; James Longstreet to Micah Jenkins, Jan. 20, 1863, MJP; Micah Jenkins to James Longstreet, Jan. 21, 1863, John Jenkins Papers, SCL; Freeman, *Lee's Dispatches*, 34.
12. Goree, *Goree Letters*, 162; Piston, "Tarnished Lieutenant," 299–300, quotes from a letter of T. J. Goree, Longstreet's staff, in which Jenkins was described as the "perfect model of a Christian hero."
13. Thomas, *Micah Jenkins*, 6.
14. Freeman, *Lee's Lts*, 223–224, 249–250; Freeman, *Lee's Dispatches*, 33–34.
15. Warner, *Generals in Gray*, 155, 174.
16. Bond, *The South Carolinians*, 83.
17. Jenkins to his wife, Dec. 29, 1863, MJP.
18. McMurray, *Hood*, 76.
19. In Law's handwriting, labeled "exact copy of the original paper submitted to General Longstreet" in possession of Jane Law Norvell.
20. Polley, *Hood's Texas Brigade*, 213–214.
21. Taylor, *48th Alabama*. Law used every effort in his power," Taylor continued, "to have his brigade transferred to some other field of action."
22. Freeman, *Lee's Lts*, v3, 223–224; Longstreet, *Manassas to Appomattox*, 467–468.
23. Oates, *The War*, 338.
24. John T. Darby (for Hood) to Jenkins, Oct. 5, 1863, John Jenkins Papers, SCDAH.
25. J. B. Hood to Custis Lee, Oct. 14, 1863, Jenkins CSR, NA.
26. Longstreet, *Manassas to Appomattox*, 467–468.
27. *OR*, v52, pt2, 555.
28. Longstreet, *Manassas to Appomattox*, 463.
29. Philadelphia *Times* Clipping, n.d., RPSHC.
30. Vaughan, "Vaughan Diary," 596–597.
31. Ibid., 597.
32. Crowder to his mother, Sep. 29, 1863, JPCL.
33. Houghton, *Two Boys*, 38.
34. Vaughan, "Vaughan Diary," 597.
35. *OR*, v30, pt3, 931.

36. Oates, *The War*, 269; Goodson, "Goodson Letters," 152–153.

37. Daniel to Mrs. M. A. Daniel, Sep. 29, 1863, DCSU.

38. Vaughan, "Vaughan Diary," 597.

39. *OR*, v31, pt1, 216. Vaughan and Longstreet agree the date was Oct. 9, 1863; Law, in his report, written on Nov. 3, 1863, gives the date as "about Oct. 8."

40. Coles, "Lookout Valley," 1, 6, 7; Law, "From Chickamauga to Chattanooga." Law believed that the sharpshooters came from division. He estimated their number at eight to ten; McClendon, *Recollections*, 188–189, said Sergeant Phinias K. McMiller, Co. K, 4th AL, was one of the scouts. In the estimate of his comrades, a "gallant and meritorious" solider, McMiller was severely wounded at Knoxville and captured in Dec. 1863; Oates, *The War*, 699, said Green C. Renfroe, of Co. G, 15th AL, was also a sharpshooter armed with a Whitworth.

41. Philadelphia *Times* Clipping, n.d., RPSHC.

42. Coles, "Lookout Valley," 2–3; Alexander, *Military Memoirs*, 467, claimed the Confederate blockade "was fully enforced" and the wagons stopped as of Oct. 9.

43. Jordan, *Events*, 55; Oates, *The War*, 270. When the three remaining regiments followed is not known. It is known they were in the valley by the Oct. 15 by Vaughan's diary entry reporting the 4th AL was relieved from the bluffs overlooking Haley's Trace by the 48th AL. They spent a few days encamped on Lookout Mountain but soon took up their old position along the Tennessee River. Vaughan, "Vaughan Diary," 598–599.

44. Vaughan, "Vaughan Diary," 597, 598; Jordan, *Events*, 55.

45. *OR*, v31, pt1, 224.

46. Coles, "Lookout Valley," 2.

47. ECPLC; Law, "From Chickamauga to Chattanooga"; Alexander, *Military Memoirs*, 466, concurred with Law's opinion that a division was required to secure Lookout Valley.

48. Law, "From Chickamauga to Chattanooga."

49. ECPLC; Law, "From Chickamauga to Chattanooga"; Coles, "Lookout Valley," 2.

50. *OR*, v52, pt2, 543; Austin, *Blue and Gray*, 109.

51. Law, "From Chickamauga to Chattanooga"; Oates, *The War*, 271, 273, describes one of these reconnaissance.

52. Alexander, *Military Memoirs*, 467.

53. Vaughan, "Vaughan Diary," 598. Cut off by the swollen Chickamauga Creek, out of its banks by three to four hundred yards, and suffering for rations for forty-eight hours, South Carolinians of Jenkins's Brigade built a raft to float supplies to their positions opposite Chattanooga. Bratton, *Bratton Letters*, 118; Lewis, *Camp Life*, 62.

54. Coles, "Lookout Valley," 7.

55. Houghton, *Two Boys*, 39.

56. ECPLC; Hood, *Advance and Retreat*, 65.

57. *OR*, v31, pt1, 224; Law published the order from R. M. Sims to Sheffield, commanding the brigade in Law's absence, Law, "From Chickamauga to Chattanooga."

58. Law, "From Chickamauga to Chattanooga." Law estimated the strength of these regiments at 1,000.

59. Law, "From Chickamauga to Chattanooga."

60. *OR*, v31, pt2, 224.

61. Alexander, *Military Memoirs*, 466.

62. *OR*, v31, pt1, 216; Goodson, "Goodson Letters," 152.

63. *OR*, v31, pt1, 77, 79.

64. Ibid., 77–79, 82, 86.

65. Oates, *The War*, 276.

66. Jordan, *Events*, 56.

67. Oates, *The War*, 275.

68. Ibid.; Jordan, *Events*, 57–58.

69. Jordan, *Events*, 58.

70. Ibid.; Oates, *The War*, 275–276.

71. *OR*, v31, pt1, 224.

72. Ibid., 85.

73. Oates, *The War*, 276.

74. McClendon, *Recollections*, 194; Oates, *The War*, 275–276.

75. *OR*, v31, pt1, 225; Oates, *The War*, 277–279.

76. Coles, "Lookout Valley," 8–9.

77. Ibid., 8–9.

78. Ibid., 8–9; ECPLC.

79. Oates, *The War*, 279–280; Law, "From Chickamauga to Chattanooga."

80. Law, "From Chickamauga to Chattanooga." 6,000 was Law's estimate; Maj. Robbins, of the 4th AL, later remarked that Hooker's column came "into our presence with the suddenness of an apparition." He assumed it was a surprise to the Confederate command for he believed Hooker could have been defeated before he linked up with the lodgment at Brown's Ferry. Philadelphia *Times* Clipping, n.d., RPSHC.

81. *OR*, v31, pt1, 78, 80.

82. Law, "From Chickamauga to Chattanooga." In this article Law recalled telling Longstreet that "the ounce of prevention which had been neglected rendered any amount of this sort of cure worthless."

83. *OR*, v31, pt1, 225.

84. Ibid., 220–222.

85. *OR*, v52, pt2, 550–551.

86. *OR*, v31, pt1, 56.

87. Ibid., 40, 117, 119, 217.

88. *OR*, v52, pt2, 556.

89. Ibid.

90. *OR*, v31, pt1, 219.

91. Ibid., 227.

92. About 220 feet high and several hundred feet long, these ridges were very narrow at the crest, suggesting the shape of a hog's back.

93. Thomas, *Micah Jenkins*, 17.

94. Copy of Jenkins Report, Nov. 2, 1863, SCL.

95. *OR*, v31, pt1, 225–226.

96. Ibid., 227. This contradicts the report Jenkins wrote of the operation. Jenkins stated positively that the rest of the division joined Law's Brigade at 10 p.m. In addition, Jenkins said Bratton moved when Law reported he was in position.

97. Huntsville *Daily Confederate*, Nov. 9, 1863. This article was authored by "W. F. R.," an unidentified Alabama soldier. Jenkins, in his report, Nov. 2, 1863, gave the time that Law began his movement as 7 p.m.

98. *OR*, v31, pt1, 228–229.

99. Ibid., 234.

100. Coles, "Lookout Valley," 13.

101. *CV*, v17, n3, Mar. 1909. The breastworks were no more than knee high but veterans knew there was protection in such fortifications, Philadelphia *Times* Clipping, n.d., RPSHC.

102. *OR*, v31, pt1, 229.

103. Ibid., 111, 112.

104. Taylor, *48th Alabama*; Huntsville *Daily Confederate*, Nov. 9, 1863. Written by a member of the 48th AL, this article claimed Eubanks's death "caused more universal sorrow and regret among his acquaintances" than any he saw during the war.

105. Coles, "Lookout Valley," 14.

106. *OR*, v31, pt1, 231.

107. Ibid., 113; ECP. The adjutant of the 137th NY claimed in a letter dated Nov. 1, 1863, that the regiment had been ordered to sleep with "shoes and stockings and all [his] equipment on for we shall doubtless be attacked before morning."

108. *OR*, v31, pt1, 123.

109. Ibid., 113, 114, 132, 133. Brig. Gen. John W. Geary, Capt. Milo B. Eldredge, commanding the 137th NY and Lt. Col. Charles B. Randall, 149th NY, agreed on the time of the attack.

110. This compares the returns published in the *OR*. However, in a letter to Ezra Carman, John Bratton believed his "acting force" at Wauhatchie was only about 1,250 rifles because of a large picket detail. ECPLC.

111. Eddie Geary became sec. lt. of Knapp's Battery in the fall of 1861, at the age of 16, one of the Civil War's true "boy Lieutenants."

112. *OR*, v31, pt1, 94, 96.

113. Ibid., 227, 229, 234, ECPLC; Coles, "Lookout Valley," 13.

114. Alexander, *Military Memoirs*, 470.

115. *OR*, v52, pt2, 89.

116. Philadelphia *Times* Clipping, n.d., RPSHC.

117. *OR*, v31, pt1, 227, 229.

118. Ibid., 108.

119. Hurst, *73rd Ohio*, 88. Maj. Robbins, of the 4th AL, Philadelphia *Times* Clipping, n.d., RPSHC, also believed most of the Alabamians' fire went over the enemy's heads until they got close.

120. *OR*, v31, pt1, 104, 109.

121. Ryder, *Three Years Service*, 43.

122. ECPLC.

123. Philadelphia *Times* Clipping, n.d., RPSHC.

124. Ibid.

125. *OR*, v31, pt1, 227. Jamison was in Jenkins's class at the Citadel.

126. Ibid., 228.

127. ECPLC.

128. *OR*, v31, pt1, 234.

129. Ibid.

130. Ibid., 230.

131. Underwood, *33rd Mass*, 167, quoting an 1876 letter from Waddell to Carman, thought to be the missing portion of Waddell's letter in the ECPL, quoted below.

132. Undated letter from Waddell to Carman, ECPL. Regrettably, only a portion of the letter was in the Carman Papers.

133. Philadelphia *Times* Clipping, n.d., RPSHC.

134. Underwood, *33rd Mass*, 168.

135. Ibid., 167, quoting a letter from Lowther to Carman in 1877.

136. *OR*, v31, pt1, 230.

137. Polley, *Hood's Texas Brigade*, 217.

138. Jordan, *Events*, 65–66.

139. Ibid. One Union report mentioned the scattered debris left by the withdrawal, *OR*, v31, pt1, 107.

140. Houghton, *Two Boys*, 40; Oates, *The War*, 283, blamed the retreat of the 15th AL on Lowther. Oates claimed the regiment was "demoralized" when Lowther was in command.

141. Oates, *The War*, 283–284.

142. Underwood, *33rd Mass*, 168, quoting a letter from Bowles to Carman in 1876.

143. Daniel to M. A. Daniel, Nov. 3, 1863, DCSU.

144. *OR*, v31, pt1, 106.

145. Ibid., 109.
146. Jordan, *Events*, 65.
147. *CV*, v17, n3, Mar. 1909.
148. ECPLC.
149. *OR*, v52, pt2, 556.
150. Ibid., 218–219, 557, 558. In his report, Jenkins also remarked about the problems inherent in night engagements, claiming the division was slow getting into place.
151. *OR*, v31, pt1, 217, 219.
152. Bragg realized the consequences of the Federal occupation of Lookout Valley: "We have thus lost our important position on the left, and the enemy holds the railroad within six miles of Chattanooga, and from there, by dirt road and pontoon bridge, to the rear of his position." *OR*, v52, pt2, 556.
153. Ibid.
154. Bratton, *Bratton Letters*, 124.
155. Copy of Jenkins Report, Nov. 2, 1863, SCL.
156. Hoyt, "Palmetto Riflemen," 33–34.
157. Vaughan, "Vaughan Diary," 599.
158. McClendon, *Recollections*, 195.
159. *CV*, v18, n11, Nov. 1910. Coker was a neighbor of Law's from Society Hill, South Carolina. He was in the Citadel Class of 1856, but left in Sep. of 1855 before graduating. In his later years, Coker was a philanthropist and founded Coker College.
160. Charleston *Daily Courier*, Nov. 7, 1863. Since no reporter was an actual witness to the fighting in Lookout Valley, "Personne" based his story on interviews in the Confederate camp.
161. Howard, *Oliver Otis Howard*, 465–466.
162. Thomas, *Micah Jenkins*, 17.
163. ECPLC.
164. *OR*, v52, pt2, 557–558; Robertson, *Touched with Valor*, 48–49.
165. *OR*, v31, pt1, 466–467.
166. Robertson, *Touched With Valor*, 13–15.
167. Law to Sellers, Nov. 2, 1863, SCDAH.
168. Jenkins to Latrobe, Jan. 4, 1864, SCDAH.
169. Ibid. Apparently, Jenkins's report was lost a second time.
170. Jenkins to Latrobe, Jan. 4, 1864, SCDAH.
171. Jamison's statement, Jan. 18, 1864, SCDAH. He was probably referring to Capt. T. A. Hamilton of the 5th TX who served on Robertson's staff.
172. *OR*, v31, pt1, 227.
173. Oates, *The War*, 281.
174. Bond, *The South Carolinians*, 90–91. If Law did make the remark, it is the only public criticism he made of Jenkins.
175. Copy of Jenkins Report, Nov. 2, 1863, SCL.
176. Ibid. The numbers of the opposing forces was a problem for Jenkins. He initially thought the Federal force at Wauhatchie was about 1,000. He was told by prisoners that he was attacking the entire XII Corps. By the time of his report, he counted the Federals as a division of the XII Corps.
177. Copy of Jenkins Report, Nov. 2, 1863, SCL.
178. *OR*, v31, pt1, 219.
179. *OR*, v52, pt2, 89–90.
180. Ibid.
181. Alexander, *Military Memoirs*, 470.
182. *OR*, v31, pt1, 121, 126, 132, 134.
183. Ibid., 150, 158, 186–187.
184. Ibid. , 150.
185. Ibid., 188.
186. Ibid., 159, 172.
187. Bancroft, *Carl Schurz*, 63.
188. *OR*, v31, pt1, 228, 234.
189. Polley, *Hood's Texas Brigade*, 220–221.

Chapter 11 – Campaigning in East Tennessee

1. *OR*, v30, pt2, 65–66, pt4, 705–706.
2. *OR*, v52, pt2, 554–555. Longstreet's detachment occurred more than a month after the Battle of Chickamauga. By then, the Federals had reinforced the army facing Bragg.
3. Longstreet, *Manassas to Appomattox*, 485.
4. Coles, "Knoxville Campaign," 1; Vaughan, "Vaughan Diary," 600; Jordan, *Events*, 66.
5. REC, Co. E, CSR, 4th AL Inf, NA; Vaughan, "Vaughan Diary," 600.
6. REC, Co. E, CSR, 4th AL Inf, NA; Coles, "Knoxville," 1.
7. REC, Co. E, CSR, 4th AL Inf, NA; Alexander, *Military Memoirs*, 481.
8. Law, "Burnside and Longstreet in East Tennessee."
9. *OR*, v31, pt1, 476–477.
10. Ibid., 215.
11. McClendon, *Recollections*, 196.
12. Vaughan, "Vaughan Diary," 600; Coles, "Knoxville," 1; McClendon, *Recollections*, 196; Jordan, *Events*, 66.
13. *OR*, v31, pt3, 76.
14. *B&L*, v3, 695.
15. Vaughan, "Vaughan Diary," 600.
16. Jordan, *Events*, 66.
17. Vaughan, "Vaughan Diary," 600.
18. Brearly, *East Tennessee Campaign*, 4; Fink, "Battle of Knoxville," 93.
19. *OR*, v31, pt1, 481.
20. Ibid.
21. Coles, "Knoxville," 1.

22. Law, "Burnside and Longstreet in East Tennessee."
23. Ibid.
24. Jordan, *Events*, 66.
25. Committee of the Regiment, *36th Massachusetts*, 94; Cutcheon, *20th Michigan*, 73.
26. *OR*, v31, pt1, 457, 525.
27. Ibid., 458.
28. Ibid., 525.
29. Ibid., 274, 350.
30. Committee of the Regimental Association, *35th Massachusetts*, 181.
31. *OR*, v31, pt1, 274.
32. Ibid., 482.
33. Ibid., 362, 525.
34. Davidson, "Michigan and Defense," 31.
35. Osborne, *29th Massachusetts*, 263; Committee of the Regimental Association, *35th Massachusetts*, 181.
36. Davidson, "Michigan and Defense," 31.
37. Fink, "Battle of Knoxville," 93.
38. *OR*, v31, pt1, 526.
39. Ibid., 483, 526.
40. Ibid., 458.
41. Ibid., 483, 526. Years later, Law asserted it was his idea to flank the Federal line, claiming he offered his suggestion to Jenkins in Longstreet's presence. Law, "Burnside and Longstreet in East Tennessee."
42. Ibid., 274, 458, 483, 526; Committee of the Regiment, *36th Massachusetts*, 95, 96; Committee of the Regimental Association, *35th Massachusetts*, 183; Thompson, *112th Illinois*, 134; Todd, *79th New York*, 361.
43. In his report, McLaws, *OR*, v31, pt1, 483, correctly assessed Burnside's plan to retreat, expressing his belief that the Union commander never intended to stand against the larger Confederate force.
44. Law, "Burnside and Longstreet in East Tennessee."
45. Coles, "Knoxville," 2.
46. *OR*, v31, pt1, 526–527.
47. Ibid., 527.
48. Longstreet, *Manassas to Appomattox*, 494–495.
49. Alexander, *Fighting for the Confederacy*, 316–317.
50. Law, "Burnside and Longstreet in East Tennessee."
51. *OR*, v31, pt1, 466–467, Longstreet asserted Robertson had been complained of frequently, presumably by Jenkins.
52. Freeman, *Lee's Lts*, v3, 285, described Hood's Division as "probably the finest combat force in the Army of Northern Virginia," before dis-

sension tore it apart.
53. Oates, *The War*, 334.
54. Coles, "Knoxville," 2.
55. Coles, "Knoxville," 2–3.
56. *OR*, v31, pt1, 456.
57. Coles, "Knoxville," 3.
58. Jordan, *Events*, 67.
59. Cutcheon, *20th Michigan*, 79; *OR*, v31, pt1, 363; Philadelphia *Times* Clipping, n.d., RHSHC.
60. Cutcheon, *20th Michigan*, 80; Coles, "Knoxville," 4; Philadelphia *Times* Clipping, n.d., RPSHC.
61. Philadelphia *Times* Clipping, n.d., RHSHC.
62. Cutcheon, *29th Michigan*, 78.
63. *OR*, v31, pt1, 519.
64. Woodford, *Father Abraham's Children*, 72, 82.
65. *OR*, v31, pt1, 337–38, 349, 352, 366–367.
66. Coles, "Knoxville," 4; Cutcheon, *20th Michigan*, 80.
67. *OR*, v31, pt1, 366; Robertson, *Michigan in the War*, 197.
68. Cutcheon, *20th Michigan*, 80.
69. *OR*, v31, pt1, 519; Coles, "Knoxville," 4; Philadelphia *Times* Clipping, n.d., RHSHC. Robbins remembered the rifle pits curved so the Alabamians could also enfilade the Michiganders as they ran into a near cul-de-sac.
70. Coles, "Knoxville," 4. Coles did not believe the 2nd Michigan knew of the presence of his company until it opened fire; Robertson, *Michigan in the War*, 205.
71. Robertson, *Michigan in the War*, 205; Hodge, *Mayo Letters*, 244; *OR*, v31, pt1, 519.
72. Robertson, *Michigan in the War*, 205.
73. Davidson, "Michigan and Defense," 39.
74. John S. Maltman, letter to his brother, Nov. 21, 1863 (misdated), quoted in Davidson, "Michigan and Defense," 39.
75. Robertson, *Michigan in the War*, 199, 404.
76. Hodge, *Mayo Letters*, 244.
77. Philadelphia *Times* Clipping, n.d., RHSHC; CSR, NA; Bowles also believed a sergeant of the 44th AL was bayoneted to death at the Battle of Wauhatchie. Underwood, *33rd Mass*, 168; Little, *A Year of Starvation*, 8, counted eight other members of the 44th AL with him in Federal prison, including Sergeant Byington, although misspelled as Pyington.
78. Latrobe Diary, VHS, 27; *OR*, v31, pt1, 307; Joyce, *Checkered Life*, 94; Co. E, 4th Alabama was across the river on Nov. 23, HMR, 4th AL Inf, ADAH. It is possible that elements of the brigade were back on the north side to observe the assault against Ft. Sanders on Nov. 29, McClendon, *Recollections*, 197–198. That part

of the river was then known as the Holston River and is often referred to as such.

79. *OR*, v31, pt1, 479; Law, "From Chickamauga to Chattanooga."

80. Jordan, *Events*, 67; Joyce, *Checkered Life*, 94; Cameron's brigade was composed of the 65th IL, 24th KY, 103rd OH, supported by an Indiana battery.

81. Law, "From Chickamauga to Chattanooga."

82. Ibid. Law did not identify these two regiments but the 44th and 47th AL did not take part in the demonstration.

83. Joyce, *Checkered Life*, 95.

84. McClendon, *Recollections*, 197; Latrobe Diary, VHS, 28; Taylor, *48th Alabama*.

85. Jordan, *Events*, 67.

86. Joyce, *Checkered Life*, 95; Jordan, *Events*, 67, recalled reaching to 150 or 200 yards of the Federal works, while Joyce believed the Confederates made their advance to within 50 yards of the breastworks.

87. McClendon, *Recollections*, 197.

88. Ibid.

89. Jordan, *Events*, 69; Oates, *The War*, 725.

90. CSR, 15th AL Inf, NA.

91. Todd, *79th New York*, 404.

92. CSR, 15th AL Inf, NA.

93. Houghton, *Two Boys*, 18. Frank L. Boothly left the theatrical group to join the 15th AL with Wilson. Both became officers in Co. H. Boothly died in Dec. 1864 from the effects of a gun shot wound to the head, CSR, 15th AL Inf, NA.

94. Latrobe Diary, VHS, 28.

95. Law, "From Chickamauga to Chattanooga."

96. Ibid. The text of Longstreet's note, as printed in the paper: "Headquarters, Nov. 27, 1863. General: I wish you would make a careful reconnaissance tonight of the position that you found the enemy in the other day (25th), and be ready with your own and General Robertson's Brigades to renew the attack there tomorrow morning. I will be over as early as I can get the two brigades of Buckner's Division and two brigades of cavalry over, when I desire to bring on a fight in the same way as you made it the other day. Be prepared but do not begin the affair till I arrive. What artillery will best there, and how much can be used? Most respectfully, J. Longstreet, Lt Gen, Com"

97. Law to McLaws, Apr. 29, 1864, McLaws Papers, SHC. Law enclosed a copy of the note to McLaws, not the original.

98. Law, "From Chickamauga to Chattanooga." Law's attack would precede McLaws's and the Federal commander might think the attack on the south side was the main assault if he be-

99. Law, "From Chickamauga to Chattanooga."

100. Ibid.

101. Ibid.

102. *OR*, v31, pt1, 475; Taylor, *48th Alabama*. It is not known what portion of Law's Brigade was engaged on the 29th.

103. Jordan, *Events*, 69.

104. Oates, *The War*, 605; Jordan, *Events*, 69.

105. *OR*, v31, pt1, 466.

106. Sketch of Longstreet's operations taken from Freeman, *Lee's Lts*, v3, 295–297. In a newspaper article, Law offered his opinion that Longstreet failed while detached from Bragg for three reasons: first, the slow move from Chattanooga to Loudon; second, allowing Burnside to escape from Lenoir's Station to Knoxville; third, the twelve day delay in attacking Burnside at Knoxville and then assaulting the enemy's strongest point, Law, "From Chickamauga to Chattanooga."

107. Polley, *Hood's Texas Brigade*, 223; Longstreet, *Manassas to Appomattox*, 511; Alexander, *Military Memoirs*, 490.

108. Coles, "Knoxville," 8; Alexander, *Military Memoirs*, 490.

109. Taylor, *48th Alabama*.

110. Sorrel, *Recollections*, 209.

111. Longstreet, *Manassas to Appomattox*, 526; Alexander Porter, "Longstreet at Knoxville," *B&L*, v3, 750.

112. Longstreet, *Manassas to Appomattox*, 521, 526.

113. Goodson, "Goodson Letters," 217.

114. *OR*, v32, pt3, 638; Longstreet, *Manassas to Appomattox*, 521.

115. Longstreet, *Manassas to Appomattox*, 524, noted Dec. was cold but by New Year's the temperature had fallen to zero and held there for two weeks.

116. Coles, "East Tennessee Campaign," 6.

117. Alabama soldiers missed receiving badly needed clothing from home because of their detachment to East Tennessee. The Quartermaster General of Alabama, Col. W. R. Pickett, arrived in Dalton, GA, in Jan., 1864, with clothing for Alabama troops in the Army of Tennessee. Pickett distributed a circular requesting Alabama units send their quartermasters to pick up the clothing, but by Jan. Law's Brigade was with Longstreet, shivering in Tennessee. *Records of the Confederate States Army*, 1861–1865, v111, 112, LC.

118. *OR*, v32, pt2, 508–509.

119. McClendon, *Recollections*, 201.

120. Crowder to family, Jan. 15, 1864, DCSU.

121. *OR*, v32, pt2, 633.

122. Goodson, "Goodson Letters," 215.

123. Longstreet, *Manassas to Appomattox*, 514.

124. Coles, "Knoxville," 8, 9. Coles noted the two brigades arrived at Bean's Station completely exhausted by their duty escorting the wagons over the muddy roads.

125. Longstreet, *Manassas to Appomattox*, 514.

126. Coles, "Knoxville," 9.

127. *OR*, v31, pt1, 464.

128. Coles, "Knoxville," 9–10.

129. HMR, Company C, 44th AL Inf, ADAH.

130. Longstreet, *Manassas to Appomattox*, 520.

131. Coles, "East Tennessee Campaign," 2; McClendon, *Recollections*, 201.

132. Coles, "East Tennessee Campaign," 3; Goodson, "Goodson Letters," 215; Crowder to his family, Jan. 15, 1864, JPCL.

133. Coles, "East Tennessee Campaign," 3; Crowder to his family, Jan. 15, 1864, JPCL.

134. Coles, "East Tennessee Campaign," 3–4.

135. Ibid., 3; Goodson, "Goodson Letters," 215; McClendon, *Recollections*, 201.

136. Goodson, "Goodson Letters," 215.

137. *OR*, v31, pt1, 462–463.

138. Ibid., 463.

139. Jordan, *Events*, 70.

140. Coles, "East Tennessee Campaign," 1.

141. Goodson, "Goodson Letters," 218–220.

142. Ibid.

143. HMR, 4th AL Inf, ADAH; CSR of Former Confederates Who Served in the 1st through 6th U.S. Volunteer Infantry Regiments, 1864–1866, M1017, roll 25, NA.

144. Coles, "East Tennessee Campaign," 2. Coles incorrectly identified Matthew as Mathis.

145. Sanger, *James Longstreet*, 244.

146. Lewis, *Camp Life*, 74, 77.

147. *OR*, v31, pt1, 464, 475.

148. Oates, *The War*, 281.

149. Law's resignation, Dec. 17, 1863. In the possession of Jane Law Norvell. Law referred to the petition written by Benning, Robertson, and Sheffield, found in *OR*, v31, pt1, 471. The complete text of Law's resignation is found in Appendix G.

150. Law's resignation, Dec. 17, 1863.

151. Ibid.

152. Ibid.

153. Law's 30-day leave was dated Dec. 20, 1863, near Bean's Station, Special Orders, #28, by Sorrel for Longstreet and extended an additional 20 days on Dec. 26, LCRAI, M474, roll 72, NA; Oates, *The War*, 338.

154. Richmond *Enquirer*, Nov. 20, 1863. Smith had resigned his major generalcy in Jan. 1863. He then served as major general in the Georgia militia.

155. Oates, *The War*, 338; *OR*, v31, pt1, 471.

156. Oates, *The War*, 339.

157. S. W. Melton to wife, Dec. 26, 1863, MPSCL.

158. Petition of Lt. Col. John A. Jones, Commanding the 44th AL, Maj. William M. Robbins, commanding the 4th AL, Maj. Alexander A. Lowther, commanding the 15th AL, Lt. Col. William Hardwick, commanding the 48th AL and Capt. Henry Lindsay, commanding the 47th AL to Cooper, Dec. 19, 1863, LRCAI, M474, roll 57, NA.

159. Longstreet's endorsement of petition, Dec. 21, 1863, LRCAI, M474, roll 57, NA.

160. Jones, Robbins, Hardwick and Lindsay to Longstreet, Dec. 26, 1863, near Morristown, TN, LRCAI, M474, roll 57, NA.

161. A. A. Lowther to James Longstreet, Dec. 26, 1863, LRCAI, M474, roll 57, NA.

162. James Longstreet to S. Cooper, Jan. 5, 1864, Longstreet Order Book, CAH, Austin, TX.

163. *OR*, v31, pt3, 859, 866–867.

164. Ibid., 867.

165. Ibid.

166. Ibid.

167. LRCAI, M474, roll 57, NA.

168. Col. Pinckney D. Bowles, Lt. Col. John A. Jones, Capt. F. Key Shaaff, Capt. H. C. Lindsay, and Capt. J. W. Wiggenton signed the petition to Cooper, Jan. 28, 1864, WFPP.

169. Ibid.

170. William P. Chilton, Jabez L. M. Curry, David Clopton, Thomas J. Foster, James L. Pugh, John P. Ralls and Edmund S. Dargan recommended Perry to Davis, Feb. 9, 1864, WFPP.

171. *OR*, v31, pt3, 866–867.

172. LRCAI, M474, roll 124, NA.

173. Alabama brigade officers' petition to Cooper, February 12, 1864, LRCAI, M474, roll 57, NA.

174. *OR*, v32, pt2, 726.

175. Warner, *Generals in Gray*, 87. His varied post–war career included two years' service in the employ of the Khedive Ismail of Egypt.

176. Freeman, *Lee's Lts*, v3, 310.

177. Longstreet tried indirect means to promote Jenkins to command of Hood's Division following Field's appointment. *See* Freeman, *Lee's Lts*, v3, 310–312 and Piston, *Lee's Tarnished Lieutenant*, 300–301, 310–311.

178. LRCAI, M474, roll 124, NA; Law had received two extensions of his leave of Dec. 20.

179. *OR*, v31, pt1, 471.

180. Oates, *The War*, 339.

181. *OR*, v52, pt2, 633, 634.

182. The exact date of Law's arrest is unknown. It was after his return from leave and before Mar. 8, 1864, when Longstreet left TN for a meeting in Richmond.

183. *OR*, v32, pt3, 617.

184. Latrobe's Diary, quoted in Freeman, *Lee's Lts*, v3, 308; *OR*, v32, pt3, 618, 622.

185. *OR*, v32, pt3, 652.

186. *OR*, v31, pt1, 471.

187. A. Moxley Sorrel to Law, Mar. 22, 1864, Longstreet Order Book, CAH, Austin, TX.

188. *OR*, v31, pt1, 472.

189. Oates, *The War*, 339.

190. *OR*, v31, pt1, 472–473.

191. Ibid., pt1, 474.

192. Dowdey, *Lee's Wartime Papers*, 703.

193. Freeman, *Lee's Lts*, v3, 315.

194. *OR*, v32, pt3, 793.

195. Law to McLaws, Apr. 29, 1864, MPSHC.

196. *OR*, v31, pt1, 474–475.

197. Longstreet wrote to Lee on Apr. 27, declaring his intention to rearrest Law. Law wrote to McLaws on the 29th, telling of his rearrest.

198. *OR*, v31, pt1, 473.

199. Piston, *Tarnished Lieutenant*, 309.

200. *OR*, v31, pt1, 473.

201. Ibid., 473–474; Oates, *The War*, 339, claimed Davis was fully informed about Hood's meeting with Seddon. Seddon made Richmond's position clear to Lee for the general wrote the secretary, that "The circumstances as explained by you have changed my opinion as to the conduct of General Law," *OR*, v52, pt2, 672.

202. *OR*, v31, pt1, 473–474; Oates, *The War*, 339.

203. *OR*, v52, pt2, 633–634.

204. Piston, *Tarnished Lieutenant*, 307; Law to McLaws, Apr. 29, 1864, MPSHC.

205. Lafayette McLaws to Lizzie Ewell, Feb. 24, 1864, quoted in Freeman, *Lee's Lts*, v3, 300–301.

206. Law to McLaws, Apr. 29, 1864, MPSHC.

207. Ibid.

208. Freeman, *Lee's Dispatches*, 182.

209. Piston, *Tarnished Lieutenant*, 312–313.

Chapter 12 – Fighting Alone in the Wilderness

1. Alexander, *Fighting for the Confederacy*, 343; Field, "Campaign of '64 & '65," 542; Jordan, *Events*, 73.

2. Daniel to M. A. Daniel, Apr. 21, 1864, DCSU.

3. Coles, "Wilderness," 1, remembered the trains were dilapidated; Goodson, "Goodson Letters," 220, described the cars as "old and leaky"; Jordan, *Events*, 73.

4. Taylor, *48th Alabama*; Daniel to Mrs. M. A. Daniel, Apr. 25, 1864, DCSU.

5. Goodson, "Goodson Letters," 220.

6. Goodson, "Goodson Letters," 220; Oates, *The War*, 340, and Taylor, *48th Alabama*; Daniel to Mrs. M. A. Daniel, Apr. 25, 1864, DCSU.

7. Daniel to M. A. Daniel, Apr. 25, 1864, DCSU.

8. Royal, *Some Reminiscences*, 28.

9. Longstreet, *Manassas to Appomattox*, 548.

10. Grant defeated Johnston and Beauregard at Shiloh, TN; Lt. Gen. John C. Pemberton at Vicksburg, MS; and Bragg at Chattanooga, TN.

11. Law, "Wilderness to Cold Harbor," 142.

12. Simpson, *Texas Brigade*, 388, cites Pomeroy, *War Memoirs*, 72; Bowles, "Wilderness."

13. Crowder to his mother and brothers, May 4, 1864, JPCL.

14. Daniel to M. A. Daniel, May 2, 1864, DCSU.

15. Bowles, "Wilderness."

16. Crowder to his mother and brothers, May 4, 1864, JPCL; Taylor, *48th Alabama*.

17. Simpson, *Texas Brigade*, 389; *Rebel Diary*, 19, and Goodson, "Goodson Letters," 220, indicates a division review was held, but gives the date as Apr. 28; Longstreet, *Manassas to Appomattox*, 548; Daniel to Mrs. M. A. Daniel, May 2, 1864, DCSU, describes the event as a "big review."

18. Goodson, "Goodson Letters," 220.

19. Dickert, *Kershaw's Brigade*, 340; Alexander, *Fighting for the Confederacy*, 346; *Rebel Diary*, 19, thought it was a nine gun salute; Goodson, "Goodson Letters," 220.

20. Alexander, *Fighting for the Confederacy*, 346; Jordan, *Events*, 73, remembered General Lee's daughter was with him.

21. Simpson, *Texas Brigade*, 389; Dickert, *Kershaw's Brigade*, 341.

22. Dickert, *Kershaw's Brigade*, 340.

23. Goodson, "Goodson Letters," 220–221.

24. Alexander, *Fighting for the Confederacy*, 345.

25. Dickert, *Kershaw's Brigade*, 341.

26. Bowles, "Wilderness."

27. Oates, *The War*, 340.

28. Oates, "Perry and His Career"; Oates, *The War*, 340; Longstreet Order Book, CAH, Austin, TX.

29. Oates, *The War*, 340.

30. Bowles, "Wilderness"; Montgomery *Daily Advertiser*, Jun. 4, 1864.

31. Stevens, "The Sixth Corps in the Wilderness," 186; Webb, "Through the Wilderness," 153; *OR*, v36, pt1, 305; Pyne, *Ride to War*, 183, 185.

32. Descriptions are from Law, "Wilderness to Cold Harbor," 119, 122, and Longstreet, *Manassas to Appomattox*, 555, 556; Sorrel, *Recollections*,

226; Stevens, "The Sixth Corps in the Wilderness," 187; Schaff, *Battle of the Wilderness*, 57; Bowen, *37th Mass*, 278. The Orange Turnpike is referred hereafter as the Turnpike; the Orange Plank Rd. is referred hereafter as the Plank Rd.

33. The Brock Rd. is sometimes referred to as the Culpeper Plank Rd.

34. Longstreet, *Manassas to Appomattox*, 556; Sorrel, *Recollections*, 229.

35. Estimated brigade strength is based on analysis of muster rolls, CSR, NA and HMR, ADAH.

36. Based on analysis of the CSR, NA and HMR, ADAH. Capt. John W. Wiggenton commanded the *48th Alabama*.

37. Coles, "Wilderness," 6; *B&L*, v4, 153; Alexander, *Fighting for the Confederacy*, 350; *Rebel Diary*, 20, indicates the time was 11 p.m.

38. Coles, "Wilderness," 6; Sorrel,*Recollections*, 229.

39. Coles, "Wilderness," 7. A report from the battlefield placed the bivouac of May 5 at approximately 12 miles from the battlefield, Montgomery *Daily Advertiser*, Jun. 4, 1864

40. Bowles, "Wilderness."

41. Black, "Presentments in Battle," 52.

42. Alexander, *Fighting for the Confederacy*, 350; Sorrel, *Recollections*, 230.

43. A report from the battlefield indicates the column moved out at 2 a.m., Montgomery *Advertiser*, Jun. 4, 1864; Sorrel, *Recollections*, 231, puts the time at 1 a.m.

44. Longstreet, *Manassas to Appomattox*, 559.

45. Bowles, "Wilderness."

46. Longstreet, *Manassas to Appomattox*, 559; Coles, "Wilderness," 8.

47. Longstreet, *Manassas to Appomattox*, 559; Coles, "Wilderness," 8.

48. Alexander, *Fighting for the Confederacy*, 350; Field, "Campaign of '64 & '65," 543.

49. Coles, "Wilderness," 8.

50. Perry, "Campaign of '64," 50.

51. Coles, "Wilderness," 8.

52. *OR*, v36, pt1, 682; Craft, *141st Pennsylvania*, 180. The four divisions were those commanded by Brig. Gens. John Gibbon, Gershom Mott, and George W. Getty.

53. *OR*, v36, pt1, 321.

54. Perry, "Campaign of '64," 50; Bowles, "Wilderness."

55. Bowles, "Wilderness."

56. It should be recalled that on the second day of fighting Longstreet exploited a large gap in the Federal center and started a rout of the Federal army.

57. Clark, *North Carolina Regiments*, 665.

58. Coles, "Wilderness," 8.

59. Bowles, "Wilderness."

60. Law, "Wilderness to Cold Harbor," 125.

61. Chamberlin, *150th Pennsylvania*, 211.

62. Oates, "Perry and His Career."

63. Oates, *The War*, 344.

64. Perry, "Campaign of '64," 52.

65. Oates, *The War*, 344; Coles, "Wilderness," 10.

66. Simpson, *Texas Brigade*, 396.

67. Bowles, "Wilderness."

68. Ibid.

69. Law, "Wilderness to Cold Harbor," 125. Law's description is largely about the 4th and 47th AL, but it is indicative of the struggle of the other regiment in the brigade.

70. Perry, "Campaign of '64," 52.

71. Ibid.

72. Bowles, "Wilderness."

73. Coles, "Wilderness," 10, 11; Bowles, "Wilderness."

74. Oates, "Perry and His Career."

75. Perry, "Campaign of '64," 52–53.

76. Ibid., 53–54.

77. Because of the disorganization resulting from previous fighting between Wadsworth and the Confederates, it is difficult to locate exactly Wadsworth's units. Approximate locations are deduced from Federal eyewitness accounts, such as Page, *14th Connecticut*, 235; Curtis, *24th Michigan*, 234, 235; Norton, "In the Wilderness," and discussions with Battle of Wilderness researcher and author, John M. Priest, Boonsboro, MD.

78. Cowtan, *10th New York*, 248; Grant, "In the Wilderness." The location of Grant is based on discussions with Battle of the Wilderness researcher John M. Priest.

79. *OR*, v36, pt1, 115.

80. *B&L*, v4, 181.

81. *OR*, v36, pt1, 609.

82. Myerhoff, "The Wilderness"; Sawyer, *8th Ohio*, 162; Bowles, "Wilderness."

83. *OR*, v36, pt1, 108.

84. Ibid., 446–447; Sawyer, *8th Ohio*, 162.

85. Steere, *Wilderness Campaign*, 318.

86. Bowles, "Wilderness." Bowles had mistakenly assumed the works belonged to the Federals. The works had been abandoned by the Confederates earlier in the morning.

87. Galwey, *Valiant Hours*, 199.

88. Ibid.

89. Myerhoff, "The Wilderness."

90. Norton, " In the Wilderness."

91. Ibid.

92. Chamberlin, *150th Pennsylvania*, 211, 215; Curtis, *24th Michigan*, 235; Nesbit, "Cross Roads in the Wilderness"; *OR*, v36, pt1, 611. Stone was injured May 5. His brigade was commanded by Lt. Col. Irvin, 149th PA, Chamberlain, *150th Pennsylvania*, 235; Survivors Association. *121st Pennsylvania*, 71; *OR*, v36, pt1, 611.

93. *OR*, v36, pt1, 477.

94. Haynes, "Medal of Honor"; Page, *14th Connecticut*, 238.

95. Bowles, "Wilderness," implies he cut a hole in the Federal line. At his farthest point of penetration both flanks were in the air. This is borne out by Federal accounts, Chamberlin, *150th Pennsylvania*, 211, 215–216 and Curtis, *24th Michigan*, 235

96. Cowtan, *10th New York*, 250, 251.

97. Ibid., 250.

98. Page, *14th Connecticut*, 237, 243; Carroll, *OR* v36, pt1, 447, reported only the 10th NY, holding his right, was hard pressed.

99. Grant, "In the Wilderness"; *OR*, v36, pt1, 689.

100. Warner, *Generals in Blue*, 532, 533.

101. Chamberlin, *150th Pennsylvania*, 211.

102. Coles, "Wilderness," 12.

103. Ibid.

104. Chamberlin, *150th Pennsylvania*, 215.

105. Perry, "Campaign of '64," 56.

106. *OR*, v36, pt1, 682.

107. Bowles, "Wilderness"; Coles, "Wilderness," 13.

108. Oates, "Perry and His Career."

109. Jordan, *Events*, 74.

110. Ibid., 74.

111. Ibid., 74–75.

112. Perry, "Campaign of '64," 53.

113. Ibid., 54.

114. Perry to the secretary of war, Jan. 11, 1865, Christian, CSR, 4th AL Inf, NA.

115. Oates, "Perry and His Career."

116. Chamberlin, *150th Pennsylvania*, 215–216.

117. Bowen, *37th Massachusetts*, 278–280.

118. Chamberlin, *150th Pennsylvania*, 216.

119. Webb, "Through the Wilderness," 160; *OR*, v36, pt1, 438.

120. Webb, "Through the Wilderness," 160; *OR*, v36, pt1, 437, 438.

121. Bowles, "Wilderness" contends the 4th AL killed Wadsworth. But, the Federal accounts placed his fatal wounding later in the day, see specifically, Monteith, "Wilderness," 414 and Monteith, "Battle in the Wilderness," 413; *OR*, v36, pt1, 615.

122. Perry, "Campaign of '64." 56; Bowles, "Wilderness."

123. Field, "Campaign of '64 & '65," 544, reported the same ground was fought over at least a half dozen times. Law "Wilderness to Cold Harbor," 125, said the battle passed several times over the same ground. Perry, "Campaign of '64," 55, recalled Heth's wounded counted six or seven Federal lines of battle which were driven back by a single line of Alabamians. Heth's men were referring to Bowles's command.

124. Robbins to Thomas Owen, 4th AL Inf, ADAH; Coles, "Wilderness," 14.

125. Coles, "Wilderness," 15.

126. Yeary, *Reminiscences*, 695.

127. Bowles, "Wilderness"; CSR, 4th AL, NA.

128. Perry, "Campaign of '64," 57.

129. Bowles, "Wilderness"; Perry, "Campaign of '64," 57.

130. Perry, "Campaign of '64," 57.

131. Law, "Wilderness to Cold Harbor," 125–126.

132. Sorrel, *Recollections*, 231–232.

133. Field, "Campaign of '64 & '65," 544.

134. Sorrel, *Recollections*, 232; Perry, "Campaign of '64," 59.

135. Field, "Campaign of '64 & '65," 544, 545.

136. Ibid., 545.

137. Law, "Wilderness to Cold Harbor," 126; Perry, "Campaign of '64," 59.

138. Perry, "Campaign of '64," 60.

139. Major General Ambrose Burnside, Commanding the IX Corps, *OR*, v36, pt1, 113; ibid., 908.

140. Brig. Gen. Robert Potter's Sec. Division consisted of two brigades: the First Brigade under Col. Zenas Bliss and the Second Brigade under Col. Simon Griffin, Ibid., 113.

141. Perry, "Campaign of '64," 60.

142. Oates, "Perry and His Career."

143. Coles, "Wilderness," 18.

144. Oates, *The War*, 349.

145. Coles, "Wilderness," 19.

146. Oates, *The War*, 350.

147. Perry, "Campaign of '64," 60.

148. Ibid., 61.

149. Oates, *The War*, 350.

150. Perry, "Campaign of '64," 61.

151. 44th AL Inf, ADAH, indicates Perry was on a courier's horse.

152. Oates, "Perry and His Career."

153. Coles, "Wilderness," 19.

154. Bowles, "Wilderness."

155. Avery, "In the Wilderness," 440. Avery surrendered with his company at Appomattox, CSR, 47th AL, NA.

156. Bowles, "Wilderness."

157. Perry, "Campaign of '64," 61–62.
158. Oates, *The War*, 350.
159. Coles, "Wilderness," 29–20.
160. Perry, "Campaign of '64," 62; Coles, "Wilderness," 20.
161. Bowles, "Wilderness."
162. Perry, "Campaign of '64," 55.
163. Ibid., 58.
164. Capt. Baylis Brown, Co. B, 4th AL; Lt. Virginius Jones, Co. B, 44th AL; Lt. Alford Pierce, Co. C, 47th AL; Lt. James Sanford, Co. K, 47th AL; Lt. Henry Figures, Adj., 48th AL.
165. Johnson, *Maple Hill Cemetery*, 1.
166. F. K. Shaaff to S. Cooper, Sep. 8, 1864, CSR, 15th AL Inf, NA.
167. Houghton, *Two Boys*, 37.
168. Black, "Presentments in Battle," 52. In 1926 David and William Abernathy were two of three known survivors of Co. I, 47th AL, *CV*, v34, n10, Oct. 1902.
169. *The Tribune*, Nov., 1900; Williams, *Huntsville Directory*, 63; 8th U.S. Census, 1860 Madison County, AL, 201; CSR, 4th AL Inf, NA.
170. Bowles, "Wilderness."
171. Chamberlin, *150th Pennsylvania*, 219.
172. Freeman, *Lee's Lts*, v3, 374.
173. Warner, *Generals In Gray*, 8; Boatner, *Civil War Dictionary*, 14.
174. Sorrel, *Recollections*, 239. Sorrel recalled that Lee was considering Maj. Gens. Jubal A. Early, Edward Johnson, and Richard H. Anderson.
175. Oates, "Perry and His Career."

Chapter 13 – On the Confederate Right at Spotsylvania

1. Alexander, *Fighting for the Confederacy*, 366, places the time at 10:00 p.m.; Pendleton, *OR*, v36, pt1, 1041, thought the column moved out at 11:00 p.m.
2. Freeman, *Lee's Lts*, v3, 380.
3. Ibid.
4. Matter, *If It Takes All Summer*, 45.
5. Oates, *The War*, 354.
6. Ibid.
7. Ibid.
8. Curtis, *24th Michigan*, 240.
9. Oates, *The War*, 354.
10. Ibid.
11. Field, "Campaign of '64 & '65," 547.
12. Oates, "Perry and His Career."
13. Oates, *The War*, 355, 575.
14. Oates, "Perry and His Career."
15. *OR*, v36, pt1, 109. These were elements of Brig.
16. Somerville to Mrs. Bozeman, Jun. 16, 1864, Bozeman Letters.
17. Field, "Campaign of '64 & '65," 547.
18. Oates, *The War*, 355, 356.
19. Jordan, *Events*, 77.
20. Coles, "Spotsylvania," 2; Oates, *The War*, 355.
21. Coles, "Spotsylvania," 4.
22. CSR, 4th AL Inf, NA. Love was slightly wounded at First Manassas and Fredericksburg. He transferred to the 4th AL Cav in Feb. 1865.
23. Somerville to Mrs. Bozeman, May 11, 1864, Bozeman Letters.
24. Ibid., May 11, May 16, Jun. 16, 1864.
25. CSR, 44th AL NA; HMR, 44th AL, ADAH.
26. Somerville to Mrs. Bozeman, Jun. 16, 1864, Bozeman Letters.
27. Ibid., Bozeman was buried next to Maj. James Campbell who was killed in the battle.
28. Lt. Col. Jones to Mrs. Bozeman, May 19, 1864, Bozeman Letters.
29. CSR, 15th AL Inf, NA.
30. Oates, *The War*, 355; Tevis, *14th Militia*, 120.
31. Coles, "Spotsylvania," 4.
32. Webb, "Through the Wilderness," 167.
33. Wise, *The Long Arm of Lee*, v2, 782; Curtis, *24th Michigan*, 240.
34. Coles, "Spotsylvania," 3.
35. Law, "Wilderness to Cold Harbor," 129; Coles, "Spotsylvania," 4.
36. Nash, *44th New York*, 224.
37. Law, "Wilderness to Cold Harbor," 129; Wise, *The Long Arm of Lee*, v2, 782, puts the final assault of the day at 7 p.m.
38. Tevis, *14th Militia*, 121–122.
39. Coles, "Spotsylvania," 4.
40. Tevis, *14th Militia*, 122.
41. Ibid.
42. Law, "Wilderness to Cold Harbor," 129; Wise, *The Long Arm of Lee*, v2, 782.
43. Tevis, *14th Militia*, 122.
44. Coles, "Spotsylvania," 3–4.
45. Law, "Wilderness to Cold Harbor," 129; Curtis, *24th Michigan*, 241, remembered the rain was the first since the Army of the Potomac crossed the Rapidan.
46. Oates, *The War*, 356.
47. Ibid, 357.
48. Jordan, *Events*, 78–79.
49. Coles, "Spotsylvania," 6.
50. Oates, *The War*, 357.
51. Jordan, *Events*, 79

Gen. Cutler's (formerly Wadsworth's) division. *See also* Matter, *If It Takes All Summer*, 355, 356.

52. Oates, *The War*, 756–757.

53. *See* Matter, *If It Takes All Summer*, pt3, for a description of the fighting in the salient; *Rebel Diary*, 23, indicates it rained all day.

54. Curtis, *24th Michigan*, 241, reported the Iron Brigade made its fourth and last assault against Law's Brigade May 12, but counted a demonstration on the morning of May 10 as an assault; Law's men also counted four attacks because they included the same demonstration on May 10 as an assault, Coles, "Spotsylvania," 3–4, 6.

55. Tevis, *14th Militia*, 124; Curtis, *24th Michigan*, 241.

56. Matter, *If It Takes All Summer*, 231.

57. *Rebel Diary*, 23–25.

58. Coles, "Spotsylvania," 7.

59. *Rebel Diary*, 24, puts the time about noon.

60. Brandon, "Killed in Battle."

61. Rice, *Civil War Letters*, 24.

52. *CV*, v16, n6, Jun. 1918, 277; Brandon, "Killed in Battle."

63. *CV*, v16, n6, Jun. 1918, 277.

64. Rice, *Civil War Letters*, 7.

65. *OR*, v36, pt1, 1057.

66. Ibid.

67. Coles, "Spotsylvania," 9.

68. James T. Jones to F. S. Lyon, Apr. 21, 1864, CSR, 47th AL Inf, NA.

69. L. R. Terrell to F. S. Lyon, May 4, 1864, CSR, 47th AL Inf, NA.

70. 47th Alabama Officers' Petition to J. A. Seddon, Jun. 8, 1864, CSR, 47th AL Inf, NA.

71. W. F. Perry's endorsement, Jun. 8, 1864, CSR, 47th AL Inf, NA.

72. James M. Campbell, CSR, 47th AL Inf, NA.

73. Ibid.

74. CSR, 47th AL Inf, NA; Bulger to Law, BSF.

75. Coles, "Spotsylvania," 8; Coles does not provide the exact date. But from the description it is surmised the event occurred near the Crutchfield Farm.

Chapter 14 – A Bloody Day at Cold Harbor

1. Daniel to M. A. Daniel, May 23, 1864, DCSU.

2. *OR*, v36, pt2, 812.

3. Sturgis, "One of Lee's Scouts," 119; 44th AL Inf, ADAH.

4. Sturgis, "One of Lee's Scouts," 119.

5. *OR*, v36, pt2, 833.

6. Daniel to M. A. Daniel, May 23, 1864, DCSU.

7. *OR*, v31, pt1, 1058; *Rebel Diary*, 25, 26.

8. Coles, "Spotsylvania," 9.

9. Bowles, "Wilderness."

10. Oates, *The War*, 363.

11. *OR*, v31, pt1, 1058.

12. Oates, *The War*, 363.

13. McClendon, *Recollections*, 208–209.

14. Law, "Wilderness to Cold Harbor," 137.

15. *OR*, v36, pt1, 1058.

16. Law, "Wilderness to Cold Harbor," 138.

17. Bowles, "Cold Harbor."

18. McClendon, *Recollections*, 210.

19. *OR*, v36, pt1, 1021; Law, "Wilderness to Cold Harbor," 138.

20. Oates, *The War*, 365.

21. Law, "Wilderness to Cold Harbor," 139.

22. Clark, *18th Army Corps*, 65.

23. Smith, "18th Corps," 225; Law, "Wilderness to Cold Harbor," 139.

24. Bowles, "Cold Harbor."

25. Ibid.; CSR, 4th AL Inf, NA.

26. Bowles, "Cold Harbor."

27. Coles, "Spotsylvania," 12.

28. Law, "Wilderness to Cold Harbor," 139. Law used wooden stakes to mark the line.

29. Ibid.

30. Bowles, "Cold Harbor;" Coles, "Spotsylvania," 14.

31. Coles, "Spotsylvania," 14.

32. *OR*, v36, pt1, 1021; Law, "Wilderness to Cold Harbor," 139; *OR*, v51, pt1, 1254.

33. Bowles, "Cold Harbor."

34. Oates, *The War*, 366.

35. *OR*, v36, pt1, 1021.

36. Oates, *The War*, 366.

37. Law, "Wilderness to Cold Harbor," 129–132.

38. Oates, *The War*, 365, indicates he was on the brigade's extreme left and the 4th was on his right. Bowles, "Cold Harbor," states the 44th AL was on his right. The order of the 47th and 48th is based on analysis.

39. Bowles, "Cold Harbor."

40. Oates, *The War*, 366.

41. Coles, "Spotsylvania," 14.

42. Bowles, "Cold Harbor."

43. Law, "Wilderness to Cold Harbor," 139.

44. Griffin to Martha, Jun. 5, 1864, WAGL.

45. Bowles, "Cold Harbor."

46. Clark, *18th Army Corps*, 65.

47. Coles, "Spotsylvania," 14.

48. Smith, "18th Corps," 225. Presumably the general meant he intended to charge the Confederate works and see what might develop.

49. *OR*, v36, 1, 1254. According to Derby, "Charge of the Light Brigade," 362, the First Brigade was known as the Star Brigade.

50. Vallentine, *23rd Massachusetts*, 121.

51. Clark, *18th Army Corps*, 66.
52. Bowles, "Cold Harbor."
53. *OR*, v51, pt1, 1254.
54. Law, "Wilderness to Cold Harbor," 139; *OR*, v27, p1, 1254.
55. Law, "Wilderness to Cold Harbor," 139.
56. Clark, *18th Army Corps*, 66.
57. Derby, "Charge of the Light Brigade," 364; Bowles, "Cold Harbor"; *OR*, v27, p1, 1254.
58. Bowles, "Cold Harbor."
59. *OR*, v51, pt1, 1254; Smith, "18th Corps," 225.
60. Bowles, "Cold Harbor."
61. *OR*, v51, pt1, 1254.
62. Ibid.
63. Smith, "18th Corps," 226.
64. Bowles, "Cold Harbor."
65. Griffin to Martha, Jun. 5, 1864, WAGL.
66. Bowles, "Cold Harbor."
67. Ibid.
68. Law, "Wilderness to Cold Harbor," 141.
69. Daniel to Martha, Jun. 7, 1864, DCSU.
70. Valentine, *23rd Massachusetts*, 122.
71. Daniel to Martha, Jun. 7, 1864, DCSU.
72. Bowles, "Cold Harbor."
73. Coles, "Spotsylvania," 16.
74. Denny, *25th Mass*, 318.
75. Ibid., 317.
76. Oates, *The War*, 367; Cole, "Spotsylvania," 17.
77. *OR*, v36, pt1, 1059. Anderson counted 14 attacks against the First Corps before 8 a.m.
78. Law, General and Staff Officers, CSR, NA.
79. Law to Mims Walker, Jun. 23, 1864, CGP.
80. Melton to wife, Jun. 4, 1864, MPSCL.
81. CSR, 4th AL Inf, NA.
82. Ibid.
83. CSR, 47th AL Inf, NA.
84. Ibid.
85. *OR*, v51, pt2, 982–983.
86. Denny, *25th Mass*, 318–319.
87. Bowles, "Cold Harbor."
88. Coles, "Spotsylvania," 18; Bowles, "Cold Harbor."
89. Bowles, "Cold Harbor"; CSR, 4th AL Inf, NA. Bowles incorrectly identified Newbill as a lieutenant and Harris as Harrison.
90. Derby, "Charge of the Star Brigade," 309; Cary was not mentioned by name, but he was the only major present in Law's Brigade.
91. Coles, "Spotsylvania," 19.
92. CSR, 15th AL Inf, NA.
93. Cooper to the secretary of war, Jun. 24, 1864, 15th AL Inf, NA.
94. J. L. Pugh to Jefferson Davis, Jun. 10, 1864, CSR, 15th AL Inf, NA.
95. Perry to Cooper, Jun. 15, 1864, 15th AL Inf, NA.
96. Field's endorsement of Perry's application for Oates, Jun. 15, 1864, CSR, 15th AL Inf, NA.
97. Hood to Cooper, Jun. 24, 1864, CSR, 15th AL Inf, NA.
98. Oates to Cooper, Jul. 20, CSR, 15th AL Inf, NA.
99. Lt. Col. William Hardwick was then a prisoner of the United States government.
100. Perry to Cooper, Jun. 28, 1864, 15th AL Inf, NA.
101. Order of General Robert E. Lee, Jul. 2, 1864, 15th AL Inf, NA.
102. Oates to Cooper, Jul. 20, 1864, 15th AL Inf, NA.
103. CSR, 15th AL Inf, NA.
104. CSR, 44th AL Inf, NA ; CSR, 15th AL Inf, NA.

Chapter 15 – Richmond and Petersburg Besieged

1. CSR, 4th, 15th, 44th, 47th, and 48th AL Inf, NA.
2. Coles, "Siege of Richmond and Petersburg," 1; *OR*, v36, pt1, 1059–1060.
3. *OR*, v36, pt1, 1060.
4. *OR*, v40, pt2, 657.
5. Lykes, "Petersburg National Military Park," 4, 6. This pamphlet lists nine major roads and five railroads converging at Petersburg. Lee early decided that he would use the rail line between the cities to shuttle troops back and forth. He wrote the president in Jun. that if he could "maintain the road from Petersburg to Richard in running order, I think we shall be able to meet any attack the enemy may make upon the latter place." Freeman, *Lee's Dispatches*, 251.
6. Lee had told Jubal Early in early Jun. that if Grant trapped the Army of Northern Virginia in a siege, it was "a mere question of time" before the Confederacy was defeated. Quoted in Freeman, *R. E. Lee*, v3, 398.
7. Freeman, *Lee's Dispatches*, 244.
8. *OR*, v40, pt1, 760.
9. Freeman, *Lee's Dispatches*, 244.
10. *OR*, v51, pt2, 1079.
11. Oates, *The War*, 368–369. This may have been members of the 9th NJ, 23rd MA and 48th NY. Drake, *9th New Jersey*, 224.
12. Field, "Campaign of '64 and '65," 549.
13. Freeman, *R. E. Lee*, v3, 416.
14. Jordan, *Events*, 85.
15. *OR*, v40, pt1, 749. Lee wrote Davis the men were in position at 10.30 a.m.; Eden, *Sword and the Gun*, 21.
16. Freeman, *Lee*, v3, 418.
17. *OR*, v51, pt2, 1019, 1020.
18. Freeman, *Lee*, v3, 418.

404   *Endnotes for pages 282 to 289*

19. *OR*, v40, pt1, 749; Jordan, *Events*, 85–86.

20. Jordan, *Events*, 86.

21. Ibid.

22. Jordan, *Events*, 86; Oates, *The War*, 604; Posey was considered a good soldier but was burdened with poor health most of his service.

23. *OR*, v51, pt2, 1019–1020.

24. Freeman, *Lee*, v3, 418–419.

25. Oates, *The War*, 369.

26. Ibid., also placed Law and Hood on field's front line with Anderson and Benning in support; Coles, "Siege of Richmond and Petersburg," 3, 5.

27. Venable, "Campaign of '64 and '65," 539.

28. Jordan, *Events*, 86.

29. *OR*, v40, pt1, 761.

30. Ibid., pt2, 668. Benning's and Jenkins's Brigades had to march to Petersburg because Law's; Anderson's and Gregg's Brigades filled the available cars, letter of 21 Jun., 1864, Dr. Lee Papers, DU; Coles, "Siege of Richmond and Petersburg," 5.

31. Coles, "Siege of Richmond and Petersburg," 5–6.

32. Coles, "Siege of Richmond and Petersburg," 5.

33. HMR, 4th AL Inf, ADAH.

34. Ibid.

35. Law to Walker, Jun. 23, 1864, CGP.

36. Ibid.

37. Law to Walker, Jul. 4, 1864, CGP.

38. Ibid.

39. Ibid.

40. Ibid.; Orders and Circulars Issued by the Army of Northern Virginia, CSA, 1861–1865, Special Orders, #210, Paragraph II, M901, roll 4, NA.

41. Field's Division was called out of the trenches to support Hoke's Division in a Jun. 24 attack near the Appomattox River. It was a failure and, though he did not participate, some in Hoke's Division criticized Field. *See* Freeman, *Lee*, v3, 554 ff. and *OR*, v40, pt1, 797–805.

42. Corbin, "Letters to Europe," 51.

43. Venable, "Campaign of '64 and '65," 549; *OR*, v40, pt1, 787. Pegram's battery had four guns, supported by the 18th and 22nd SC of Elliott's Brigade, hence the area was also known as Elliott's Salient.

44. Freeman, *Lee*, v3, 464.

45. *OR*, v40, pt1, 761–762, ibid., pt3, 290, 292, 293, 298.

46. Ibid., pt2, 1161; Jordan, *Events*, 87.

47. Montgomery *Daily Mail*, Aug. 31, 1864. This short article was written on Jul. 17 by "Soldier," a member of Law's Brigade.

48. Richmond *Dispatch*, Jul. 7, 8, 1864; Saval, *City Under Siege*, 39.

49. *OR*, v40, pt3, 458–459; Bratton, Bratton Letters, LC, 166; HMR, Co. C, 4th AL Inf, ADAH.

50. Hagood, *Memoirs of the War*, 284.

51. Ibid.

52. Williams to Laura, Jan. 1, 1865, WWL.

53. *OR*, v40, pt2, 675.

54. Hagood, *Memoirs of the War*, 284.

55. Coles, "Siege of Richmond and Petersburg," 7.

56. Hagood, *Memoirs of the War*, 284. Work on the trench system had to be done at night to avoid the Federal sharpshooters.

57. Goodson, "Goodson Letters," 224.

58. Ibid., 224–225.

59. Ibid., 225.

60. Coles, "Siege of Richmond and Petersburg," 7.

61. Hagood, *Memoirs of the War*, 286–287; Montgomery *Daily Mail*, Aug. 28, 1864. In this article, entitled, "Letter from Virginia," the trenches are described as "infested by an accumulation of filth" and malodorous.

62. Jordan, *Events*, 87.

63. Coles, "Siege of Richmond and Petersburg," 6; Manuscript of Nicholas Pomeroy, 82; Letter of Aug. 13, 1864, Felder Letters, HC.

64. Corbin, "Letters to Europe," 54. Corbin's well appointed saddle and uniform, especially his French boots, elicited sarcasm from the soldiers of Field's Division. Some would taunt him with remarks such as, "Come out of them boots, I say, mister; I see your head a-peeping out."

65. *OR*, v40, pt1, 762.

66. McCarty Diary, CAH, Austin, TX.

67. *OR*, v40, pt3, 814.

68. Jordan, *Events*, 90.

69. McCarty Diary, CAH, Austin, TX; *OR*, v40, pt1, 767, Rice Station was also known as Rice's Turnout; *OR*, v40, pt1, 762, 767.

70. *OR*, v40, pt3, 592–593.

71. McCarty Diary, CAH, Austin, TX; *OR*, v40, pt1, 767.

72. Freeman, *Lee's Lts*, v3, 466.

73. *OR*, v42, pt2, 35.

74. Venable, "Campaign of '64 and '65," 550.

75. *OR*, v42, pt2, 1156.

76. Venable, "Campaign of '64 and '65," 551.

77. Montgomery *Daily Mail*, Aug. 12 and 16, 1864.

78. McClendon, *Recollections*, 215; Richmond *Daily Enquirer*, Aug. 31, 1864.

79. HMR, Co. G, 4th AL Inf, ADAH.

80. Bratton, Bratton Letters, LC, 173.

81. HMR, 4th AL Inf, ADAH. The five conscripts were Calvin Cassady, J. Luny Chapman, James K. Davies, James M. Frazier and Ephraim Hawkins, all of Co. H.

82. Oates, *The War*, 373.

83. *NOR*, v10, 351–352; *OR*, v42, pt2, 1164–1165, 1168, 1181–1182.

84. *NOR*, v10, 348.

85. Jordan, *Events*, 90; Oates, *The War*, 373. Oates noted a lieutenant of the 48th Alabama was buried by the explosion of a shell. He was hurriedly uncovered by his men before he suffocated only to be killed on Aug. 16 at Fussell's Mill. Two lts. of the 48th were killed on Aug. 16: Sec. Lt. William A. Beaty and Third Lt. James M. Hinds. Which of the two was buried is unknown.

86. Oates, *The War*, 373. Perry's furlough, with permission to extend if necessary, was issued on a surgeon's certificate of disability, dated Aug. 20, 1864. Orders and Circulars Issued by the Army of the Potomac and the Department of Northern Virginia, CSA, 1861–1865, M921, NA.

87. Venable, "Campaign of '64 and '65," 551.

88. *OR*, v42, pt2, 136.

89. Venable, "Campaign of '64 and '65," 551.

90. Maxfield, *11th Maine*, 237.

91. White, Wyman Diary, 145–146.

92. CSR, 48th AL Inf, NA; U.S. Army Commands Misc Rolls, Deserters, POW and Refugees, NA.

93. Letters Received by A&IG, roll 119, NA.

94. Ibid.

95. Ibid.

96. CSR, Co. K, 15th AL Inf, NA.

97. LRCAI, roll 119, NA.

98. Ibid.

99. *OR*, v42, pt1, 216–217, 241, pt2, 150.

100. Maxfield, *11th Maine*, 238–239.

101. Ibid., 239.

102. *OR*, v42, pt1, 698; Richmond *Daily Enquirer*, Aug. 31, 1864.

103. Maxfield, *11th Maine*, 239.

104. *OR*, v42, pt1, 878.

105. Richmond *Daily Enquirer*, Aug. 31, 1864.

106. *OR*, v42, pt1, 878.

107. Maxfield, *11th Maine*, 239.

108. Oates, *The War*, 373; Corbin, "Letters to Europe" 57–58.

109. Venable, "Campaign of '64 and '65," 551–552; Richmond *Daily Enquirer*, Aug. 31, 1864.

110. Bond, *The South Carolinians*, 149–150.

111. McClendon, *Recollections*, 214.

112. Venable, "Campaign of '64 and '65," 552; Richmond *Daily Enquirer*, Aug. 31, 1864; *OR*, v42, pt1, 878.

113. Griffith, *Battle Tactics*, 129, quoting the memoirs of William T. Sherman.

114. Venable, "Campaign of '64 and '65," 552.

115. Corbin, "Letters to Europe," 58–59.

116. Venable, "Campaign of '64 and '65," 552–553.

117. Ibid., 553.

118. *OR*, v42, pt1, 699.

119. Ibid., 688, 700.

120. Ibid., pt2, 1156–1157.

121. Venable, "Campaign of '64 and '65," 553; Corbin, "Letters to Europe," 59. In a letter to England, dated Aug. 26, 1864, Corbin named only the two units. Field remembered, in 1886, asking for every available man from his division—not just two brigades—ordering Gregg to leave only a skirmish line to man New Market Heights.

122. Richmond *Daily Enquirer*, Aug. 31, 1864; Caldwell, *Recollections*, 177.

123. Venable, "Campaign of '64 and '65," 553.

124. Bond, *The South Carolinians*, 150–151; Jordan, *Events*, 91; Venable, "Campaign of '64 and '65," 553; Richmond *Daily Enquirer*, Aug. 31, 1864; Corbin, "Letters to Europe," 60.

125. Venable, "Campaign of '64 and '65," 553; Oates, *The War*, 374.

126. *OR*, v42, pt1, 364, 747.

127. Jordan, *Events*, 91; McClendon, *Recollections*, 215.

128. Columbus (Georgia) *Daily Sun*, Sep. 1, 1864; Jordan, *Events*, 92. Shaaff believed the detachment numbered 75 men.

129. Columbus (Georgia) *Daily Sun*, Sep. 1, 1864. Report of strengths and casualties by Capt. F. Key Shaaff, Corroborating Shaaff's numbers, Jordan, *Events*, 92, gave the strength of the 15th AL as 140. In addition, a count of the muster roll for Aug. 16, 1864, tallied 210 present for all eleven companies or 152 for eight companies.

130. Columbus (Georgia) *Daily Sun*, Sep. 1, 1864.

131. Oates, *The War*, 377.

132. Ibid. Oates believed the Federal battle line was nearly a mile long.

133. Ibid., 374–375.

134. Jordan, *Events*, 92; CSR, 15th AL Inf, NA.

135. McClendon, *Recollections*, 215.

136. Oates, *The War*, 375.

137. Ibid., 375–376.

138. Ibid., 376.

139. Richmond *Daily Enquirer*, Aug. 31, 1864.

140. McClendon, *Recollections*, 215.

141. Ibid.; Jordan, *Events*, 91. McClendon estimated 18 soldiers of Co. B and G and two lieutenants were wounded at this time.

142. Richmond *Daily Enquirer*, Aug. 31, 1864.

143. Maxfield, *11th Maine*, 246.

144. Ibid., 245–246; Richmond *Daily Enquirer*, Aug. 31, 1864; *OR*, v42, pt1, 747–748, 766; Jordan, *Events*, 91.

145. Richmond *Daily Enquirer*, Aug. 31, 1864.

146. Columbus (Georgia) *Daily Sun*, Sep. 1, 1864.

147. Richmond *Daily Enquirer*, Aug. 31, 1864.

148. Corbin, "Letters to Europe," 60; Jordan, *Events*, 93.

149. Oates, *The War*, 380, believed Defnall died because of over exertion from carrying water for his wounded colonel; McClendon, *Recollections*, 215–216; Jordan, *Events*, 92. Defnall and Jordan were made color sergeants in Jun., while in the Petersburg trenches. "Old Man" John G. Archibald was ensign on Aug. 16, 1864 but was absent wounded, Jordan, *Events*, 87, 92.

150. McClendon, *Recollections*, 215–216. Although his company muster lists McClendon as sec. lt. commanding the company in 1863, his rank as lieutenant dates from Aug. 30, 1864.

151. *OR*, v42, pt2, 224–225, 1180. All fighting ended by 4 p.m.

152. CSR, 44th AL Inf, NA.

153. The only mention of the remaining eight companies of the 44th is found in the report Oates provided E. Porter Alexander after the war for Alexander's unfinished history of the First Corps. In this statistical report of the 15th regiment, Oates claimed the 44th AL supported the 15th and 48th regiments, AP.

154. List of Casualties During the Campaigns of 1864, M836, roll 7, NA; HMR, 4th AL Inf, ADAH.

155. *OR*, v42, pt2, 1228.

156. Corbin, "Letters to Europe," 62.

157. Ibid., 61.

158. Jordan, *Events*, 92.

159. Venable, "Campaign of '64 and '65," 555.

160. Ibid., 554.

161. *OR*, v42, pt1, 220.

162. Montgomery *Daily Mail*, Jul. 31, 1864. The unidentified Alabamian wrote under the nom de plum of "Soldier." His letter was dated Jul. 17, 1864.

163. Montgomery *Daily Mail*, Aug. 26, 1864, letter from Special Correspondent, "Soldier," dated Aug. 17, 1864.

164. E. M. Law to Mims Walker, Jul. 4, 1864, CGP. By the time Law's leave expired, he would have known that Longstreet was on the mend. One newspaper reported Longstreet was riding along the lines at the Battle of Darbytown Rd., Oct. 13, even though his arm was in a sling, Columbia (GA) *Daily South Carolinian*, Oct. 23, 1864.

165. McCarty Diary, CAH, Austin, TX; Montgomery *Daily Mail*, Aug. 28, 1864.

166. *OR*, v42, pt2, 334. This information was furnished to the Federals by a deserter from the 44th Alabama who put his regimental strength at 100 rifles.

167. *OR*, v42, pt2, 334.

168. Ibid., 1192–1193; Bratton, Bratton Letters, LC, 175.

169. *OR*, v42, pt2, 1193.

Chapter 16 – Guarding the Roads to Richmond

1. *OR*, v42, pt2, 1193, 1201; Venable, "Campaign of '64 and '65," 555.

2. *OR*, v42, pt2, 1192–1193; REC, Co. G, 44th AL Inf, NA; McCarty Diary, CAH, Austin, TX.

3. Corbin, "Letters to Europe," 62; Coles, "Siege of Richmond and Petersburg," 10.

4. Corbin, "Letters to Europe," 63; Montgomery *Daily Mail*, Sep. 4, 1864.

5. Remarks of W. Perry, commanding brigade, Jan. 27, 1865, Brigade Inspection Report, M935, NA.

6. Reports of Aug. 29 and Sep. 8, 1864; Brigade Inspection Report, M935, NA.

7. Montgomery *Daily Mail*, Aug. 28, 1864.

8. Report of Sep. 20, 1864, Brigade Inspection Report, M935, NA. The brigade assistant inspector general was Capt. Thomas L. Christian.

9. The four staff present were: Maj. Amiz Babbitt, chief of commissary; Capt. Thomas L. Christian, inspector; Lt. Richard Drake, ordnance officer; and Maj. William H. Scruggs, QM. Report of Aug. 29, 1864, Brigade Inspection Report, NA.

10. *OR*, v42, pt1, 879, pt2, 628, 630, 683.

11. Ibid., pt2, 683, 740, 758.

12. Sommers, *Grant's Fifth Offensive*, RU, 700.

13. Bratton, Bratton Letters, LC, 176.

14. Report of Sep., 1864, Brigade Inspection Report, M935, NA.

15. Bratton, Bratton Letters, LC, 176; Montgomery *Daily Mail*, Sep. 4, 1864, reported quiet conditions for the brigade on Aug. 23 and Aug. 25. Sep. was the longest period of quiet for the Alabamians since the summer of 1863.

16. Walker to Mary Gray Pitts, Sep. 11, 1864, CGP.

17. Mims Walker to Mary Gray Pitts, Sep. 11, 1864, CGP. Despite his observations, Walker wrote with optimism that if Southerners will make up their minds to "remain firm and undaunted" they would yet see their independence.

18. Natchez *Weekly Courier*, Dec. 11, 1862, Talladega *Democratic Watchtower*, Sep. 28, 1863, quoted in Gates, *Agriculture and the Civil War*, 38–40.

19. Martin, *Desertion of Alabama Troops*, 132–133.

20. Paul Turner Vaughan Papers, SHC.

21. Martin, *Desertion of Alabama Troops*, 132.
22. Ibid., 133.
23. *OR*, Series IV, v2, 258.
24. Ibid., v2, 576.
25. Ibid., v3, 1043.
26. Law, "Round Top," 319; Oates, *The War*, 154.
27. *OR*, v42, pt2, 1302–1303.
28. Venable, "Campaign of '64 and '65," 555. It would be almost eight hours before the Alabama soldiers could reach Ft. Gilmer on the north side, a distance of only slightly more than twenty miles.
29. Hollis, *Confederate Veteran*, 20.
30. Venable, "Campaign of '64 and '65," 555.
31. Hollis, *Confederate Veteran*, 20.
32. *OR*, v42, pt2, 1303.
33. Coles, "Siege of Richmond and Petersburg," 11; Venable, "Campaign of '64 and '65," 556.
34. Coles, "Siege of Richmond and Petersburg," 11. The Federal attack was by the X Corps. *See* Sommers, *Grant's Fifth Offensive*, for details of the Federal attack before Bowles arrived at Ft. Gilmer.
35. McClendon, *Recollections*, 213. Also inside Ft. Gilmer was the 25th VA Battalion, led by Lt. Col. Wyatt M. Elliott. The fort mounted two guns, manned by Thomas Gathright's Goochlanders. Sommers, *Richmond Redeemed*, 17, 65.
36. The *Daily Richmond Enquirer* of Nov. 22, 1864, incorrectly credits the Alabama brigade with repulsing the right of the charging Negro troops.
37. McClendon, *Recollections*, 214.
38. Corbin, "Letters to Europe," 68, 82.
39. McClendon, *Recollections*, 214.
40. Hollis, *Confederate Veteran*, 21.
41. Venable, "Campaign of '64 and '65," 556.
42. Hollis, *Confederate Veteran*, 21–22.
43. Venable, "Campaign of '64 and '65," 556; Coker, 9th SC, 158; *OR*, v42, pt1, 879–880.
44. Venable, "Campaign of '64 and '65," 556. By the time the Confederates attacked, elements of the XVIII Corps had thrown up a defense line of earth and logs across the gorge of Ft. Harrison, *OR*, v42, pt1, 675, 800.
45. Freeman, *Lee's Lts*, v3, 591.
46. Coles, "Siege of Richmond and Petersburg," 13–14.
47. Venable, "Campaign of '64 and '65," 557.
48. Freeman, *Lee's Lts*, v3, 591, puts the number of guns at 24; but Sommers, *Grant's Fifth Offensive*, 511, counts 40 guns.
49. Venable, "Campaign of '64 and '65," 557.
50. Ibid.
51. Hollis, *Confederate Veteran*, 22.
52. Venable, "Campaign of '64 and '65," 557.
53. Corbin, "Letters to Europe," 82.
54. *OR*, v42, pt1, 818.
55. *Daily Richmond Enquirer*, Nov. 22, 1864.
56. Hollis, *Confederate Veteran*, 23–24; *OR*, v42, pt1, 880, 938. The cries of the dying who were too close to the fort to be removed were kept up all night.
57. *Daily Richmond Enquirer*, Nov. 22, 1864.
58. Freeman, *Lee*, v3, 507.
59. Botsford, *Memories*, 20.
60. CSR, 47th AL Inf, NA.
61. Ibid., pt2, 1121, 1144.
62. Ibid., pt2, 1144.
63. Ibid., pt1, 876.
64. Freeman, *Lee*, v3, 507.
65. Venable, "Campaign of '64 and '65," 557.
66. The description of the attack plan is taken from Freeman, *Lee*, v3, 507–508.
67. Coles, "Siege of Richmond and Petersburg," 15.
68. CSR, 47th AL Inf, NA.
69. Botsford, *Memories*, 20.
70. Ibid.
71. CSR, 47th AL Inf, NA.
72. McClendon, *Recollections*, 218.
73. Ibid., 219.
74. Venable, "Campaign of '64 and '65," 557; Coles, "Siege of Richmond and Petersburg," 16; *Daily Richmond Enquirer*, Nov. 22, 1864.
75. McClendon, *Recollections*, 220. The Georgia col. was probably Col. Joseph Walker, whose SC regiment held the left of Bratton's brigade.
76. Jordan, *Events*, 94–95.
77. Venable, "Campaign of '64 and '65," 558; *Daily Richmond Enquirer*, Nov. 22, 1864. In *Lee's Lts*, v3, 593, Freeman notes no reason was ever given for Hoke's failure to attack. He asserts Hoke failed to cooperate in assaults on four other occasions: May 16, at Drewry's Bluff; Jun. 1, at Cold Harbor; Jun. 24, along the banks of the Appomattox; and Sep. 30, at Ft. Harrison. Hagood, *Memoirs of the War*, 309, recalled officers in Field's Division believed Hoke was derelict in his duty when he failed to attack.
78. *OR*, v42, pt1, 881.
79. The Texans suffered so grievously from their first time under the fire of repeater rifles that McCarty, McCarty Diary, CAH, Austin, TX, described the brigade as "pretty well used up."
80. *OR*, v42, pt1, 731.
81. Ibid., 731.
82. Ibid., 731–732; CSR, 44th AL Inf, NA.
83. *OR*, v42, pt1, 852.
84. Coles, "Siege of Richmond and Petersburg," 16. Gregg was a native of Lawrence County, AL and had many friends among Law's Brigade.

85. *OR*, v42, pt1, 876.

86. Hagood, *Memoirs of the War*, 309; Venable, "Campaign of '64 and '65," 558.

87. *OR*, v42, pt3, 1144.

88. Ibid., pt1, 876.

89. Ibid., pt3, 182–183, 186; McCarty Diary, CAH, Austin, TX, notes the work began on Oct. 10.

90. Venable, "Campaign of '64 and '65," 558.

91. *OR*, v42, pt3, 183–184, 188.

92. Ibid., 189–190.

93. Coles, "Siege of Richmond and Petersburg," 16. The construction was aided by entrenching tools captured on Oct. 7.

94. Trumbull, *Knightly Soldier*, 310.

95. *OR*, v42, pt1, 690, 706, 722.

96. Venable, "Campaign of '64 and '65," 558. The Alabamians' location is based on the fact that the Texans were already in place and the Union brigade which struck their position held the right of the attacking line.

97. McClendon, *Recollections*, 222.

98. Oates, *The War*, 595–596.

99. CSR, 15th AL Inf, NA.

100. Ibid.

101. *OR*, v42, pt3, 218–219. One Federal officer remarked of the Confederate position that "It was altogether an ugly looking chance for a charge," ibid., pt1, 733.

102. Ibid., pt3, 213.

103. Ibid., pt1, 682.

104. Ibid., pt3, 219.

105. Ibid., pt1, 682.

106. McClendon, *Recollections*, 222.

107. Ibid.

108. *OR*, v42, pt1, 690.

109. Ibid.

110. McClendon, *Recollections*, 222.

111. *OR*, v42, pt1, 740.

112. Ibid., 690.

113. McClendon, *Recollections*, 222.

114. Ibid., 223.

115. Trumbull, *Knightly Soldier*, 318.

116. *OR*, v42, pt1, 690.

117. Ibid., 146–147, 690.

118. Ibid., 690.

119. Ibid., 686.

120. Clark, *29th Illinois*, 226. Clara Barton assisted the Union surgeons after the battle. Barton had been nursing Federal soldiers since a mob attacked the 6th MA in Baltimore in Apr. 1861. She took medical supplies to field hospitals throughout the war.

121. *OR*, v42, pt1, 741.

122. CSR, 47th AL Inf, NA.

123. Mobile *Evening News*, Oct. 31, 1864.

124. McClendon, *Recollections*, 223; Botsford, *Memories*, 20.

125. The events surrounding the Dutch Gap canal and prisoners of war is taken from Sommers, "Dutch Gap Affair," 51–64. The names of the three Alabamians came from Sommers's personal library.

126. *OR*, v42, pt1, 871.

127. Ibid., pt3, 366–367.

128. Ibid., pt1, 872.

129. Oates, *The War*, 571, 781, 786, 797.

130. *OR*, v42, pt1, 877.

131. Ibid., pt3, 1260. This was part of a larger demonstration of the First Corps.

132. *OR*, v42, pt3, 1262.

133. Corbin, "Letters to Europe," 88.

134. *OR*, v42, pt3, 1262; Jones, *War Clerk Diary*, 458; Jordan, *Events*, 100.

135. Jordan, *Events*, 100. Jordan called this reconnaissance the Battle of Williamsburg.

136. *OR*, v42, pt1, 825–826, pt3, 949.

137. Corbin, "Letters to Europe," 89.

138. Martin, *Desertion of Alabama Troops*, 34; *OR*, v43, pt2, 890, 907–908.

139. The Mobile *Advertiser and Register*, Feb. 16, 1864, printed governor's appeal that women and children evacuate the city before it is attacked.

140. The Alabama Legislature appropriated $3 million in Dec. 1863, $2 million in Oct. 1864, and $3 million in Dec. 1864 for aid to indigent families. *Acts of Alabama, 1863*, 81–82, 85, *Acts of Alabama, 1864*, 5–7, *Acts of Alabama, 1864*, 58–61. "Family" was defined as mothers, sisters and daughters of indigent soldiers who could prove they attempted to support themselves by honest means.

141. *OR*, v42, pt3, 1213, Lee's statement was made upon learning 100 men convicted of desertion in Pickett's command had been reprieved. Either from a change of heart or because the policy failed, Lee offered an amnesty to deserters in Feb., 1865.

142. CSR, 4th AL Inf, NA.

143. Hollis, *Confederate Veteran*, 17–18.

144. Ibid., 18.

145. Freeman, *Lee's Lts*, v3, 622.

146. Oates, *The War*, 429. In 1901, Oates estimated 5–10 percent of Confederates deserted. He later declared that estimate was much lower than the true number.

147. Owen, "Fowler's Work," 190; Oates, *The War*, 634, makes an unconfirmed claim that another Alabamian was shot for desertion.

148. CSR, 4th AL Inf, NA. These two conscripts were Eli W. Meggs and J. O. Owens, both of Co. H.

149. Martin, *Desertion of Alabama Troops*, 18. Citing the Fowler reports, Martin listed Co. H, I, K of the 44th AL and Co. C, D, E, I of the 48th AL as particularly lax in this regard.

150. CSR, 44th AL Inf, NA.

151. *OR*, v46, pt2, 1228, 1230.

152. Oates, *The War*, 584.

153. McClendon, *Recollections*, 224–225. The three men who accompanied McClendon were Cicero Kirkland, James R. Watts and Cincinnatus Harper, who was only 18 years old in 1865.

154. LTCAIG, 1861–1865, roll 6 (v43, 90), NA.

155. LRCAI, roll 126, NA. Just what this legal maneuver was is unknown.

156. Dowdey, *Wartime Papers*, 868.

157. LRCAI, roll 126, NA.

158. Ibid.

159. Ibid.

160. Ibid.

161. Ibid.

162. Ibid.

163. Ibid.

164. WFPP.

165. Ibid.

166. Ibid.

167. Ibid.

168. Dowdey, *Lee*, 451.

169. LTCAIG, 1861–1865, roll 6 (v43, 273), NA.

170. WFPP.

171. LRCAI, roll 126, NA.

172. *OR*, v33, 1315.

173. LRCAI, roll 126, NA.

174. *OR*, v46, pt2, 1019.

175. CSR, 4th AL Inf, NA; CSR, 44th AL Inf, NA.

176. *OR*, Series II, v8, 69; LRCAI, roll 115, NA.

177. LRCAI, roll 158, NA.

178. Eckenrode, *Lee's War Horse*, 279–281.

179. Freeman, *Lee's Lts*, v3, 555

180. Address to Army of Northern Virginia Association, May 28, 1890; Philadelphia *Weekly Press*, Oct., 1897 and Nov. 2, 1887.

181. This discussion is based in large measure on Durden, *Debate on Emancipation*.

182. *OR*, Series IV, v2, 767.

183. Oates, *The War*, 496–497.

184. Corbin, "Letters to Europe," 90, 93.

185. *OR*, v46, pt2, 1229.

186. Ibid., 1236. In his memoirs, Oates, *The War*, 500, asserted that all three of Lee's corps favored the use of Negroes in the army.

187. *OR*, v46, pt3, 1367. It is not known if this unidentified deserter was executed.

188. Jordan, *Events*, 100–101.

189. Report of Nov. 30, 1864, Division Inspection Report, M935, NA.

190. Jordan, *Events*, 101–102. The bakery was discontinued because the men preferred the biscuits they could make over the bakery's production.

191. Reports of Nov. 30, 1864 and Jan. 27, 1865, Division Inspection Report, M935, NA. During this time period, bacon and salt pork rations were at about one third but no complaint was mentioned in the inspection reports.

192. Jordan, *Events*, 100; *OR*, v42, pt3, 1311.

193. Reports of Sep. 8, 1864, Oct. 30, 1864, Jan. 27, 1864, Division Inspection Report, M935, NA.

194. Report of Jan. 31, 1865, ibid. The quartermaster issued 3572 pants, 2831 jackets, 5177 drawers, 4553 shirts, 6088 socks, 4504 blankets, 6398 shoes since Oct. Field's Division did not muster for inspection more than 4,000 aggregate during this period.

195. Report of Jan. 31, 1865, ibid.

196. Report of Dec. 27, 1864, ibid.

197. McClendon, *Recollections*, 224.

198. Based on examination of brigade CSR, NA.

199. CSR, 47th AL Inf, NA; Maj. Gen. Jones M. Withers was commander of the reserve forces in AL at the time, Warner, *Generals in Gray*, 343.

200. *OR*, v47, pt1, 1047. Beauregard commanded the forces of Hardee, Hampton, Stevenson and Wheeler; *OR*, v47, pt2, 1157.

201. Ibid., 1204; Warner, *Generals in Gray*, 40–41.

202. Ibid., 1204.

203. Ibid., 1071.

204. Simms, *The Sack and Destruction of the City of Columbia*, 33. William G. Simms, Jr., entered the Citadel in 1862. The elder Simms was appointed to the school's Board of Visitors in 1864. Baker, *Cadets in Gray*, 14, 201.

205. R. O. Sams Manuscript, SCL, 3–4.

206. Ibid., 4.

207. *OR*, v47, pt2, 1194.

208. Lucas, *Sherman and the Burning of Columbia*, 70.

209. Ibid., 69.

210. Simms, *Sack and Destruction of Columbia*, 34.

211. *OR*, v47, pt2, 1207.

212. Ibid., 1193.

213. Slocum, *B&L*, v4, 686.

214. Law to Maj. John Stokes, Mar. 24, 1865, VHS.

215. *OR*, v47, pt1, 1320.

216. Ibid., pt1, 1129, 1443.

217. Ibid., pt3, 737. The first recommendation was on Jan. 17, 1865, the second was on Apr. 1, 1865.

218. Law's Pension Application, 1909.

219. CSR, 47th AL Inf, 44th AL Inf, NA.

220. CSR, 44th AL Inf, NA,

221. CSR, 47th AL Inf, NA.

222. CSR, 48th AL Inf, NA. Capt. Thomas Christian was, at the time of the application, the brigade's assistant adjutant general. He was well known to the men of the 48th AL and had amply demonstrated his leadership qualities in combat at the Wilderness when he rode among the 48th AL and rallied a faltering line. It can logically be assumed that Christian supported the application and welcomed the chance at field command.

Chapter 17 – Appomattox and Home

1. Bevin, "Fall of Richmond," 40.

2. Longstreet, *Manassas to Appomattox*, 602.

3. Ibid.

4. *OR*, v46, pt1, 1372–1373.

5. Ibid., 1285.

6. Ibid., 1285.

7. Burton, *47th Alabama*; Longstreet, *Manassas to Appomattox*, 606; *OR*, v46, pt3, 1374.

8. *OR*, v46, pt1, 1264.

9. Botsford, *Memories*, 17–18.

10. Davis, *Atlas*, Map 77, 2.

11. *OR*, v46, pt1, 1379.

12. Ibid., 1265.

13. Hill's Third Corps had taken the brunt of Grant's assault. His troops were badly scattered.

14. Freeman, *Lee*, v4, 58.

15. Freeman, *Lee's Lts*, v3, 690.

16. Freeman, *Lee's Lts*, v3, 684; Freeman, *Lee*, v4, 57 fn; *OR*, v46, pt1, 1379.

17. *OR*, v46, pt1, 1379; Davis, *Atlas*, Map 74, 1.

18. Freeman, Lee, v4, 11.

19. Longstreet, *Manassas to Appomattox*, 609; Coles, "Petersburg to Appomattox," 1.

20. *OR*, v46, pt1, 53.

21. Freeman, *Lee's Lts*, v3, 687.

22. *See* Davis, *Atlas*, Map 78, 1 for location of the store. Freeman, *Lee's Lts*, v3, 687, identified Cox Plantation at Clover Hill as the place Longstreet and Lee ate breakfast.

23. Freeman, *Lee*, v4, 61.

24. Longstreet, *Manassas to Appomattox*, 609.

25. CSR, 44th AL Inf, NA.

26. CSR, 47th AL Inf, NA.

27. CSR, 4th AL Inf, NA.

28. "Paroles of the Army of Northern Virginia," *SHSP*, v15, 144–160.

29. CSR, 44th AL Inf, NA.

30. CSR, 4th AL Inf, NA. Jones was lawyer by profession and was placed on detached service when severely wounded in the Wilderness. He had ap-

plied to be appointed a judge of one of the military courts on Mar. 29, 1865, but his application had not been acted on when Richmond fell, Taylor to Breckenridge, Mar. 29, 1865, CSR, 4th AL Inf, NA.

31. 4th AL Inf, ADAH.

32. Bowles to Wright, Oct. 5, 1886, WRHS; Bowles, Surname File, ADAH. Stewart commanded Polk's old corps of the Army of Tennessee then in NC.

33. Jordan, *Events*, 111–113.

34. *OR*, v46, pt1, 1301.

35. Longstreet, *Manassas to Appomattox*, 609.

36. *OR*, v46, 1, 1265.

37. Freeman, *Lee*, v4, 71.

38. Longstreet, *Manassas to Appomattox*, 609.

39. *OR*, v46, pt1, 1265; Longstreet, *Manassas to Appomattox*, 609–610.

40. Freeman, *Lee*, v4, 76.

41. Longstreet, *Manassas to Appomattox*, 610.

42. Ibid., 611.

43. *OR*, v46, pt1, 1174, 1178, 1180, 1186.

44. Longstreet, *Manassas to Appomattox*, 612, 616.

45. *OR*, v46, pt1, 1180, 1215. The two divisions were Brig. Gen. Robert S. Foster's First Division and Brevet Maj. Gen. John W. Turner's Independent Division.

46. Alexander, *Fighting for the Confederacy*, 524; *OR*, v46, pt1, 1174.

47. Longstreet, *Manassas to Appomattox*, 616; Alexander, *Fighting for the Confederacy*, 524.

48. Alexander, *Fighting for the Confederacy*, 524.

49. Rufus Hollis to Thomas Owen, Jun. 18, 1921, 24, 4th AL Inf, ADAH.

50. *OR*, v46, pt1, 1174, 1180.

51. Botsford, *Memories*, 18.

52. Freeman, *Lee's Lts*, v3, 715.

53. *OR*, v46, pt1, 1266.

54. Ibid., 1266.

55. Alexander, *Fighting for the Confederacy*, 525; Longstreet, *Manassas to Appomattox*, 616; *OR*, v46, pt1, 1180, 1303.

56. Longstreet, *Manassas to Appomattox*, 614; *OR*, v46, pt1, 1266.

57. *OR*, v46, pt1, 1303.

58. Coles, "Petersburg to Appomattox," 1, 2.

59. Ibid., 2.

60. Ibid., 3, 4.

61. Alexander, *Fighting for the Confederacy*, 528.

62. *OR*, v46, pt1, 1303.

63. Alexander, *Fighting for the Confederacy*, 530.

64. *OR*, v46, pt1, 1266.

65. Longstreet, *Manassas to Appomattox*, 620.

66. Alexander, *Fighting for the Confederacy*, 530.
67. *OR*, v46, pt1, 1266.
68. Freeman, *Lee*, v4, 129, presents a detailed discussion of the situation on Longstreet's front just before the surrender talks began.
69. Coles, "Petersburg to Appomattox," 6.
70. Ibid., 5.
71. Polley, *Hood's Texas Brigade*, 277.
72. Freeman, *Lee*, v4, 149; Coles, "Petersburg to Appomattox," 7.
73. Alexander, *Fighting for the Confederacy*, 541.
74. *OR*, v46, pt1, 1277, lists an aggregate of 983, composed of 91 officers and 892 men; "Paroles of the Army of Northern Virginia," *SHSP*, v15, 144–160, the aggregate identified in the text does not include surgeons, assistant surgeons and chaplains. The brigade surrendered four surgeons, five assistant surgeons and one chaplain. Considering these the aggregate surrendered was 983.
75. "Paroles of the Army of Northern Virginia," *SHSP*, v15, 144.
76. CSR, 4th, AL Inf, NA; "Paroles of the Army of Northern Virginia," *SHSP*, v15, 144, 146–149.
77. CSR, 15th AL Inf, NA; "Paroles of the Army of Northern Virginia," *SHSP*, v15, 144, 149–152.
78. CSR, 44th AL Inf, NA; "Paroles of the Army of Northern Virginia," *SHSP*, v15, 144, 152–155.
79. CSR, 44th AL Inf, NA; 44th AL Inf, ADAH.
80. CSR, 47th AL Inf, NA; "Paroles of the Army of Northern Virginia," *SHSP*, v15, 144, 155–158.
81. CSR, 47th AL Inf, NA.
82. "Paroles of the Army of Northern Virginia," *SHSP*, v15, 144, 158–160.
83. Coles, "Our Return Home," 1.
84. *OR*, v46, pt1, 1267.
85. Alexander, *Fighting for the Confederacy*, 538.
86. Rufus Hollis to Thomas Owen, Jun. 18, 1921, 24, 4th AL Inf, ADAH.
87. Ibid.
88. Jordan, *Events*, 114–116, 120, 122, 126. The North Carolinians had left the army before the formal surrender ceremonies and were making their way home.
89. Chamberlain, "Last Salute," 360.
90. Ibid., 361, 362; Chamberlain, *Passing of the Armies*, 261.
91. Chamberlain, "Last Salute," 362; Chamberlain, *Passing of the Armies*, 261.
92. Coles, "Petersburg to Appomattox," 6.
93. H. C. Yelverton, Feb. 11, 1927, Co. H, 15th AL Inf, Regimental Flags (SG 11139), ADAH.
94. Watts to Bulger, Mar. 1, 1865, AGC, 205; Joseph Burton to Thomas Owen, Jun. 15, 1905,

Regimental Flags (SG 11139), ADAH.
95. T. H. Watts to James L. Sheffield, May 25, 1864, AGC, 149.
96. Coles, "Petersburg to Appomattox," 7.
97. Burton, *47th Alabama*.
98. Freeman, *Lee*, v4, 158.
99. Reese, "A Sketch of His Family," 112.
100. 15th AL Inf, ADAH.
101. Coles, "Our Return Home," 2.
102. 4th AL Inf, ADAH.
103. Coles, "Our Return Home," 2–5.
104. Jordan, *Events*, 134, 138–142.
105. 44th AL Inf; ADAH; CSR, 44th AL Inf, NA.
106. Oates, *The War*, 771.
107. The text is an excerpt from Shaaff's letter seeking Hatcher's appointment and confirmation. Hatcher was elected captain of Co. D Jun. 2, 1863, CSR, 15th AL Inf, NA. Apparently at that time no one had thought to get a written statement of Wicker's waiver.
108. CSR, 48th AL Inf, NA.
109. CSR, 4th AL Inf, NA.
110. CSR, 48th AL Inf, NA. The conclusion that Hardwick was the last officer from the brigade released from prison is based on examination of CSR for the brigade.
111. Warren, *Henry's Heritage*, 57.

Epilogue

1. Law to Walker, Nov. 14, 1867, CGP. For reasons now obscure, Law's mare was at Cedar Grove plantation. Charles Walker did not believe Law could recover her, so he told Mims to offer Law $1000 for her. Charles Walker to Mims Walker, May 1, 1864, CGP.
2. Beginning with Tuskegee, Law set up 78 local Granges in AL in less than three years and served as state secretary from 1873 to 1876. Rogers, "Alabama State Grange," 105.
3. Gray, R. A. "I Saw A General Cry," Orlando (Florida) *Sentinel*, Dec. 29, 1963; Gray, *My Story*, 38–39, 42.
4. Law, "The Confederate Revolution."
5. *SHSP*, v17, 266; *SHSP*, v22, 347, 351.
6. Clipping of unknown Columbia, SC newspaper, undated. Law said he was already 83 years old, so the interview was between Aug. 1919 and his death on Oct. 31, 1920.
7. *CMH*, v8, 435–436; Warner, *Generals in Gray*, 237. Perry was residing in Bowling Green, KY at the time of his death.
8. Oates, "Perry and His Career."
9. This time is measured from the creation of Law's Alabama Brigade in Jan. 1863.

10. Hughes, *The Letters of a Victorian Madwoman*, 14–19.

11. Owen, *Alabama Dictionary*, 1293.

12. Oates to Nicholson, Feb. 11, 1903, OC.

13. Oates to Elihu Root, Jun. 2, 1903, OC.

14. Oates to Nicholson, Feb. 11, 1903, OC.

15. Robbins to Nicholson, Feb. 20, 1903, OC.

16. Robbins Diary, Dec. 19, 1903, RPSHC.

17. Ibid.

18. Robbins to Nicholson, Feb. 11, 1903; Oates to Robbins, Jul. 4, 1903, OC.

19. Robbins Diary, December 19, 1903, RPSHC.

20. Robbins to Nicholson, February 11, 1903, Robbins to Nicholson, February 26, 1903, Robbins to Oates, June 20, 1903, OC; Robbins Diary, December 19, 1903, RPSHC.

21. Robbins Diary, December 19, 1903, RPSHC.

22. Oates to Robbins, February 14, 1903, OC.

23. Root to Oates, January 22, 1904, OC; Robbins Diary, December 19, 1903, RPSHC.

24. Chamberlain to Bachelder, n.d., NHHS.

25. Oates to Robbins, July 18, 1904; Chamberlain to Nicholson, August 14, 1903; Oates to Nicholson, December 29, 1904; Oates to Nicholson, March 1, 1905; Chamberlain to Oates, May 18, 1905, OC; Chamberlain to Nicholson, March 16, 1905, OC.

26. Oates to Root, June 2, 1903, OC.

27. Oates to Nicholson, November 3, 1903, OC.

28. In Oates's last known correspondence to the commission he still maintained the 15th Alabama drove the 20th Maine's right flank back, Oates to Nicholson, March 1, 1905, OC.

29. Oates, Surname File, ADAH.

30. Cook, *Restoration and Innovation*, 7, 36–37.

31. 44th AL Inf, ADAH.

32. *CV*, v17, n5, May 1909, 242; CSR, 44th AL Inf, NA; 44th AL Inf, ADAH, Perry was incorrect regarding Cary's wound, which occurred August 16, 1864 at Fussell's Mill.

33. New York *Times*, March 17, 1907.

34. *Official Gazette*, v19, #7, February 15, 1881, 399.

35. Cussons, *The Passage of Thoroughfare Gap*, 30.

36. Rogers, *The One-Gallused Rebellion*, 236; Griffith, Alabama, 520–521.

37. Sterkx, "William C. Jordan," 61–73.

38. Williams, "One of the Real Heroes."

Appendix A – Brigade Field and Staff

1. Unless otherwise noted brigade staff officers are from Law's and Perry's Staff, M 311, RG 109, NA.

2. Crute, Confederate Staff Officers, 111.

3. Indicates serving in acting capacity.

4. Replaced Terrell after Law was wounded Jun. 3, 1864, 44th AL Inf, ADAH.

5. Killed at Fredericksburg, Virginia, Dec. 13, 1862, acting as courier for Colonel Law.

6. Transferred from Hampton's South Carolina Legion, Law's and Perry's Staff, M 311, RG 109, NA.

7. Served as courier before assignment as ADC.

8. Thomas Kirkman, a cadet from the Citadel, was on temporary duty, assigned to Law's and Perry's staff, MC 311, RG 109, NA.

9. E. M. Law's younger brother, a cadet from the Citadel, was on temporary duty, assigned to Law's staff, ibid.

10. Sinclair and Ervin were couriers and acting aides-de-camp. Sinclair was also on brigade commissary detail for a period of time, CSR, 4th AL, NA.

11. Disabled May 5, 1864.

Appendix B – Regimental Organization

1. Data, except, as noted, is from CSR, NA and Regimental Folders, ADAH.

2. Major, P.A.C.S., assigned temporary by the war department.

3. Severely wounded Fredericksburg, VA, Dec. 13, 1862, CSR, 4th AL Inf, NA; given position of color bearer Jun. 8, 1863; severely wounded Sep. 20, 1863.

4. Ward master at Richmond by order of secretary of war.

5. Served as dentist in the regiment; ordered to Richmond as assistant surgeon.

6. Assigned to a Richmond hospital.

7. Assigned to sec. AL Hospital at Richmond.

8. Assigned to third AL Hospital in Richmond.

9. Captured at Gettysburg, PA.

10. Vaughan, "Vaughan Diary," 595.

11. Elected junior second lieutenant Aug. 25, 1862.

12. Deserted Feb. 1865, took oath, moved to Boston, MA.

13. Index to CSR, of Confederate Soldiers Who Served From the State of Alabama.

14. Detached service as hospital steward at College Hospital, Lynchburg, VA.

15. Discharged 1862, underage, 15 years old when enlisted.

16. Company names are from Coles, "Company Sketches," 4th AL Inf, ADAH.

17. Also known as the "Alabama Zouaves," ibid.

18. Also known as the "Canebrake Rifle Guards," ibid.

19. Also known as the "Lauderdale Volunteers," ibid.
20. Elected lieutenant 60th AL Inf, Oates, *The War*, 666; *CV*, v21, n11, 1913, 547.
21. Oates, *The War*, 80.
22. Color Sergeant.
23. Oates, *The War*, 640.
24. Age 14 at enlistment, drummer.
25. Ibid., 734; enlisted at Bull's Gap, TN, Mar., 1864, age 15.
26. Index to CSRs of Confederate Soldiers who served in Organizations Raised Directly by the Confederate Government and of Confederate General and Staff Officers and Non-Regimental Enlisted Men.
27. Elected junior second lieutenant Jun. 5, 1862.
28. Vaughan, "Vaughan Diary," 595.
29. Index to CSR, of Confederate Soldiers Who Served From the State of Alabama.
30. Oates, *The War*, 671.
31. Also called "City Light Guards."
32. Also know as "Eufaula Zouaves," 15th AL Inf, ADAH.
33. *CV*, v36, n4, Apr. 1928, 145, gives his middle name as Lee.
34. *CV*, v28, n2, Feb. 1920, 66, identifies his middle name.
35. Drummer; wounded Jun. 18, 1864 at Bermuda Hundred, VA.
36. Norton, *Rebel Religion*, 128.
37. Wounded Oct. 7, 1864.
38. Company names from the Selma *Reporter*, Jun. 18, 1862.
39. Also called "Cedar Creek Guards," 44th AL Inf, ADAH.
40. Company was named in honor of Nathaniel H. R. Dawson, former captain in the 4th AL. Dawson returned the compliment with a $500 donation for the care and relief of company sick, Selma *Reporter*, Jun. 17, 1862.
41. Also called "Sallie Border's Boys," 44th AL Inf, ADAH.
42. Also listed as Laws.
43. *Journal of Confederate Congress*, v1, 609.
44. Also known as "Tallapoosa Light Infantry," REC, 47th AL Inf, NA.
45. Botsford, *Memories*, 4.
46. Also listed as Hammonds.
47. Mortally wounded Jul. 2, 1863, died Jul. 26, 1863.
48. Color bearer at the Battle of Chickamauga, GA; remarks on HMR, 48th AL Inf, ADAH read "killed while planting his flag on the enemy battery line."
49. Killed Sept. 20, 1863.

50. Also know as "Sheffield Rifles."
51. Original Co. G was commanded by Capt. Phillip B. Gilbert. This company was consolidated with Co. E on Jul. 17, 1862. New Co. G was commanded by John S. Moragne.
52. Also known as "Cherokee Guards," SG 11125#1, ADAH.
53. Also known as "Lee County Guards," Amann, *Personnel of the Civil* War, 84.

Appendix C – Roster of Officers

1. Unless otherwise noted sources are CSR, NA and HMR, ADAH.
2. Entry is highest rank held
3. Indicates individual was in regimental command structure.
4. Appleton was wounded May 10, 1864; two fingers were amputated; he returned to service in Jun. 1864.
5. Indicates individual was assigned to a regiment's field and staff.
6. Ensign carried the rank of second lieutenant; the individual holding the commission was the regimental color bearer.
7. The rank of third lieutenant was also referred to by the rank of brevet second lieutenant.
8. Indicates individual was a member of the brigade command or staff structure.
9. Indicates individual was assigned to the brigade staff.
10. Barrett stated his resignation was "tendered unconditional and immediate for means known to myself." Col. William Perry, commanding the regiment, endorsed Barrett's resignation with "it would be in the best interest of this regiment to have an officer in place of Barrett who has been thus far worthless."
11. Entry on HMR reads: "One of the best." Bass was sent from Federal prison to Morris Island, SC, where he was one of 600 prisoners placed under Confederate fire in retaliation for Federal prisoners being placed under fire in Charleston during bombardment of the city.
12. Resigned when denied promotion. Major Alexander Lowther, commanding the regiment, noted in his endorsement of Baugh's resignation: "The interest of the service will suffer less by the acceptance of this resignation. The officer promoted is all together the superior of the two."
13. Though he was a New Yorker by birth and listed his residence as the state of NY, Becker had an exemplary record as a Confederate officer.
14. Surgeon's certificate stated Berry suffered from "rheumatism, neuralgia and general stability resulting from typhoid fever."
15. Full name was Francis Thomas Jefferson. Became

chaplin of the 47th AL after his resignation.

16. Sent from Federal prison to Morris Island, SC, where he was one of 600 prisoners placed under Confederate fire in retaliation for Federal prisoners being placed under fire in Charleston during bombardment of the city.

17. Wounded Jul. 2, 1863 at Gettysburg, PA; not present in the command afterwards.

18. The surgeon's statement indicated Brooks suffered from medical disability caused by lung disease. Brooks stated his resignation was due to "the consequence of protracted illness and the infirmation of old age."

19. Took Oath of Allegiance Jun. 7, 1865.

20. Col. William Oates stated Bryan was "exceedingly careless and negligent, . . . , a poor disciplinarian and in my judgment is mentally and physically incapable of performing the duties of an officer."

21. Burton, Surname File, ADAH.

22. Because Carter was financially independent he was described by his commanding as a "man of affluent circumstance and able to live without the pay of an officer."

23. Daniel, Surname File, ADAH.

24. His full name was Nathaniel Henry Rhodes Dawson.

25. Transferred to First Corps Headquarters Feb. 22, 1862 as chief ordnance officer. Captured Apr. 5, 1865 at Amelia Court House, VA.

26. Ellison was passed over for promotion on recommendation by Maj. Alexander Lowther, commanding the regiment.

27. Feagin, Surname File, ADAH.

28. Ibid. Studied under Lee after the war.

29. Gallaway tendered his resignation unconditionally. Col. James Jackson's endorsement read, in part, "I believe it is his intention never to do any more service. I believe it should be accepted and that his name should be reported to the Office of Conscripts."

30. Severely wounded in the arm Sep. 15, 1862 at Sharpsburg, MD, resulting in permanent paralysis of the arm.

31. Resigned Jan.9, 1863.

32. Jones's resignation stated he intended to join the cavalry. No record of his cavalry service has been located.

33. Returned to the ranks at his own request. Graham noted, "I find the function of a private much more agreeable to me than that of a commissioned officer."

34. Col. James Sheffield's endorsement read in part: "appeared before an examining board at camp near Fredericksburg for promotion to captain. He was denied promotion because he did not answer regarding the school of the soldier, com-

pany or battalion."

35. Grice's left leg was amputated due to a wound received Aug. 30, 1862.

36. Captain Francis Shaaff, commanding regiment, noted that Hatcher was "an intelligent officer and a good disciplinarian."

37. An examining board for second lieutenant found Heaton to be "Very Good" in the character of a soldier, "Good" in moral character and "Very Good" in his knowledge of tactics. Heaton was passed unanimously.

38. Irvine's resignation stated his intention to join the cavalry. No record of his cavalry service has been located.

39. Johnston rose to colonel of the 25th AL and was appointed brigadier general Jul. 26, 1864, Warner, *Generals in Gray*, 160, 161.

40. Captured near Huntsville, AL, Oct. 18, 1863. Took oath Jun. 12, 1865 and paroled.

41. Crippled for life from wounds of Sep. 19, 1863.

42. Jones, Surname File, ADAH.

43. On temporary assignment to Law's staff.

44. On temporary assignment to Law's staff.

45. Lawrence applied for retirement because of a severe wound to the leg May 6, 1864.

46. A surgeon's examination found him "in a physical and mental condition which disqualifies him for performance of duties as a soldier."

47. McIntosh suffered from a severe wound inflicted Aug. 9, 1862 at Cedar Run, VA. The surgeon's statement read in part: "wound in the left thigh area causes the muscle of the leg to contract so much he cannot get his foot to the ground."

48. Promoted QM Chief of Law's Brigade.

49. McLemore was a West Point graduate, class of 1856, ranking 39th out of 49. Of the seven of his class who joined the Confederacy, McLemore was the single fatality from the war, *Former Cadets*, 245.

50. His commanding officer, Maj. Alexander Lowther, wrote "the service benefited from his resignation."

51. Metcalf was found to have a disease of the kidneys and suffering from general disability.

52. Moragne's wounds were inflicted by the explosion of a cannon. He was 48 years old.

53. Morris's commanding officer, Col. William Oates, wrote "the good of the service requires that his resignation be accepted."

54. Col. William Perry recommended Morrow's resignation be accepted. Perry noted Morrow had been absent for seven months previous and was not a good officer when present. Perry further noted that Morrow was "believed to be harbored by the hospital at Montevallo and prefers to have a contract from the government to make whiskey."

55. Maj. Alexander Lowther, commanding the regiment, recommended the resignation be accepted because that was the "shortest means of ridding the service of a worthless officer."

56. Severely wounded Apr. 29, 1863 which necessitated the amputation of the left foot.

57. Oliver was found to suffer from neuralgia of the face and scalp and chronic disease of the liver.

58. Tucker, *Burrell Perry*, 19–20.

59. Exchanged Oct. 1, 1864; no further record has been located.

60. *Northern Alabama*, 285, identifies his middle name.

61. Savage, *The Story of Piedmont*, v2, 30, identifies the full name.

62. Transferred from 4th AL.

63. Smitherman tendered his resignation with intent to accept an appointment as Register of the Chancery for the 25th District, Middle Chancery Division, State of Alabama. His resignation was at first refused. Governor Thomas Watts intervened on his behalf and Smitherman's resignation was then accepted.

64. See Safakis, *Who was Who in the Civil War*, 644, for his full name.

65. Returned to the ranks by order of Col. Sheffield.

66. Promoted brig. gen.; killed July 1, 1863 at Port Gibson, MS.

67. Muster roll entry reads "gallant and meritous."

68. Woodliff claimed his bad health was caused by dyspepsia and chronic diarrhea.

69. The surgeon stated Young suffered from permanent enlargement of the heart, making him incapable of performing his duties.

Appendix D – Brigade Statistics

1. Statistics cover each regiment's organization to surrender.

2. Statistics, except as noted, are from Owen, *TAHS*, 190, 191; statistics on officers are from CSR, NA and HMR, ADAH.

3. Surrendered at Appomattox, Virginia, *SHSP*, v15, 144–160.

4. Aggregate does not include surgeons, assistant surgeons and chaplains. The five regiments contained during their existence included 21 surgeons, 29 assistant surgeons and 14 chaplains. Inclusion of surgeons and chaplains makes the aggregate 6324.

5. Aggregate does not include surgeons, assistant surgeons and chaplains. The brigade surrendered four surgeons, five assistant surgeons and one chaplain. Inclusion of surgeons and chaplains makes the aggregate surrendered was 983.

6. Owen, *TAHS*, 191, lists one death by execution. He was a private in the 4th AL.

Appendix E – Battles and Skirmishes

1. Unless otherwise noted battles and skirmishes engaged in by the 4th AL are from CSR, 4th AL Inf, NA; *see also* Oates, The *War*, 780, 781.

2. Unless otherwise noted battles and skirmishes engaged in by the 15th AL are from 15th AL Inf, ADAH; *see also* Oates, The *War*, 569–571.

3. Also known as First Cold Harbor, VA.

4. Also known as Cedar Mountain, Slaughter Mountain and Southwest Mountain.

5. Unless otherwise noted battles and skirmishes engaged in by the 47th AL are from 47th AL Inf, ADAH; *see also* Oates, The *War*, 791, 792.

6. Unless otherwise noted battles and skirmishes engaged in by the 48th AL are from 48th AL Inf, ADAH; *see also* Oates, The *War*, 796, 797.

7. Frequently included as part of Battle of Second Manassas, VA.

8. Also known as Second Manassas, VA.

9. Also known as Second Manassas, VA.

10. Also known as Ox Hill, VA.

11. REC, 4th AL Inf, NA. Also known as South Mountain and Crampton's Gap.

12. Unless otherwise noted battles and skirmishes engaged in by the 44th AL are from 44th AL Inf, ADAH; *see also* Oates, The *War*, 785, 786.

13. REC, 4th AL Inf, NA.

14. Ibid.

15. Also known as Lookout Valley, TN.

16. REC, 4th AL Inf, NA.

17. Also known as Howlett's House, VA.

18. Also known as New Market Heights, VA.

19. Also known as Williamsburg Rd., VA.

Appendix F – Casualties from Selected Battles

1. Number wounded, except for the 47th AL, is from *OR*, v27, pt2, 330.

2. Number killed, wounded and captured/missing are from the Montgomery *Advertiser*, Jul. 26, 1863.

3. Number killed and wounded are from the Huntsville *Daily Confederate*, Oct. 14, 1863.

4. Number killed and wounded are from Oates, *The War*, 264.

5. Number killed and wounded are from the Mobile *Evening Register*, Sep. 30, 1863.

6. Number killed and wounded are from the Montgomery *Advertiser*, Sep. 30, 1863.

7. Number killed and wounded are from the Huntsville *Daily Confederate*, Oct. 15, 1863.

8. Number killed and wounded are from the Montgomery *Daily Advertiser*, May 27, 1864.

Appendix G – The Resignation of E. M. Law

1. Longstreet's endorsement:
    Headquarters, Bean's Station
    December 17, 1863
    Respectfully forwarded. This officer's services
    are well known to the government. His reasons
    can be better decided upon by the government
    than by myself.
    J. Longstreet
    Lieutenant General

2. Law's resignation is in the possession of Jane
    Law Norvell.

Bibliography

Books, Articles and Pamphlets

Albaugh, William A., III. *Confederate Faces, A Pictorial Review*. Wilmington, North Carolina: Broad Publishing Company, 1993.

Alexander, E. Porter. *Military Memoirs of a Confederate*. New York: Charles Scribner's Sons, 1907.

————. *Fighting for the Confederacy*. Chapel Hill, North Carolina: The University of North Carolina Press, 1989.

————. "The Great Charge and Artillery Fighting at Gettysburg." *Battles & Leaders of The Civil War*. Vol. 3. New York: The Century Company, 1888.

Amann, William Frayne, Editor. *Personnel of the Civil War*. 2 Vols. New York: Thomas Yoseloff, 1961.

Amis, Moses N. *Historical Raleigh with Sketches of Wake County and Its Important Towns*. Raleigh, North Carolina: Commercial Printing Co., 1913.

Anderson, George, T. "War Diary of George T. Anderson." Huntsville (Alabama) *Democrat*, September 11, 1861.

Andrews, J. Cutler. *The South Reports the Civil War*. Princeton, New Jersey: Princeton Press, 1970.

Army Regulations, Adopted for the Use of the Army of the Confederate States, Also, Articles of War for the Government of the Army of the Confederate States of America. Richmond, Virginia: West and Johnston, 1861.

Austin, John P. *The Blue and the Gray, Sketches of a Portion of the Unwritten History of the Great American Civil War*. Atlanta, Georgia: Franklin Printing, 1899.

Avery, Sanders. "In the Battle of the Wilderness." *Confederate Veteran*, vol. 7, no. 9 (September 1899).

Axford, Faye A. *The Journal of Thomas Hobbs*. University, Alabama: The University of Alabama Press, 1976.

Baker, Gary R. *Cadets in Gray*. Columbia, South Carolina: Palmetto Bookworks, 1989.

Bancroft, Frederic, and William A. Dunning. *The Reminiscences of Carl Schurz*. 3 vols. New York: The McClure Co., 1908.

Barziza, Decimus et Ultimus. Edited by R. Henderson Shuffler. *The Adventures of A Prisoner of War 1863–1864*. Austin, Texas: University of Texas Press, 1964.

Belo, Alfred H. *Memoirs of Alfred Horatio Belo*. Introduction by Charles Peabody. Boston: Alfred Mudge and Company, 1904.

Bennett, L. G., and William M. Haigh. *History of the, Thirty-Sixth Regiment Illinois Volunteers, During the War of the Rebellion*. Aurora, Illinois: Knickerbocker & Hodder, Printers and Binders, 1876.

Bevin, Ken. "The Fall of Richmond, Driving Dixie Down." *America's Civil War*, vol. 8, no. 2, n.d.

Black, George H. "Presentments in Battle Realized." *Confederate Veteran*, vol. 6, no. 2 (February 1898).

Black, Robert C., III. *The Railroads of the Confederacy*. Chapel Hill, North Carolina: University of North Carolina Press, 1952.

Blackford, Charles M. *Letters from Lee's Army, or Memoirs of Life In and Out of the Army of Northern Virginia During the War Between the States*. Compiled by Susan L. Blackford. Edited by Charles M. Blackford III. New York: Charles Scribner's Sons, 1947.

Boatner, Mark M. *The Civil War Dictionary*. New York: David McKay Company, Inc., 1959.

Bond, Natalie Jenkins, and Osmun Latrobe Coward. *The South Carolinians, Colonel Asbury Coward's Memoirs*. New York: Vantage Press, 1968.

Botsford, Theophilus F. *Memories of the War of Secession*. Montgomery, Alabama: The Paragon Press, 1911.

Bowen, James L. *History of the Thirty-Seventh Regiment Mass. Volunteers in the Civil War of 1861–1865*. Holyoke, Massachusetts and New York: Clark W. Bryan and Company, 1882.

Bowles, Pinckney. "Battle of the Wilderness." Philadelphia *Weekly Press*, October 4, 1884.

———. "Battle of Cold Harbor." Philadelphia *Weekly Press*, January 31, 1885.

Brandon, Francis T. J. "Killed in Battle." *Southern Christian Advocate*, June 9, 1864.

Brearly, William H. *Recollections of the East Tennessee Campaign*. Detroit: Tribune Book and Job Office, 1871.

Brewer, Willis. *Alabama, Her History, Resources, War Record and Public Men from 1540 to 1872*. 1872. Reprint, Spartanburg, South Carolina: The Reprint Publishers, 1975.

Burger, Nash K., and Charlotte Copers. "Episcopal Clergy of Mississippi, 1790–1940." *Journal of Mississippi History* (April 1946).

Butts, Frank B. "Reminiscences of Gunboat Service on the Nansemond." *Personal Narratives of Events in the War of the Rebellion, Being Papers Read Before the Rhode Island Soldiers and Sailors Historical Society*, 3rd ser., no. 8 (1884). Providence, Rhode Island: Soldiers and Sailors Historical Society.

Caldwell, James Fitz James. *The History of a Brigade of South Carolinians, Known first as "Gregg's," and Subsequently as "McGowan's Brigade."* Philadelphia: King and Baird Printers, 1866.

Campbell, Birdie. *The Names of People Buried in Maple Hill Cemetery That Were Not Born in Huntsville, Alabama, (1867–1918)*. Compiled for the Huntsville-Madison County Public Library, Huntsville, Alabama, 1940.

Chamberlain, Joshua L. *The Passing of the Armies, An Account of the Final Campaign of the Army of the Potomac, Based Upon Personal Reminiscences*. New York: G. P. Putnam & Sons, The Knickerbocker Press, 1915.

Chamberlin, Thomas. *History of the One Hundred and Fiftieth Regiment Pennsylvania Volunteers, Second Regiment, Bucktail Brigade*. Philadelphia: F. McManu & Company, Printers. 1905. Reprint, Baltimore, Maryland: Butternut and Blue, 1986.

Chambers, C. C. "The Coahoma Invincibles." *Confederate Veteran*, vol. 31, no. 12 (December 1923).

Chestnut, Mary. *Mary Chestnut's Civil War*. C. Vann Woodward, Editor. New Haven, Connecticut: Yale University Press, 1981.

Clark, Charles M. *The History of the Thirty-Ninth Regiment, Illinois Volunteer Veteran Infantry*. Chicago: Veteran Association, 1889.

Clark, Charles T. *The Opdycke Tigers, 125th O.V.I.* Columbus, Ohio: Spahr and Glenn, 1895.

Clark, Harvey. *My Experience with Burnsides Expedition and 18th Army Corps*. Gardner, Massachusetts, n.p., 1914.

Clark, Walter. *Histories of the Several Regiments and Battalions from North Carolina in the Great War, 1861–1865*. 5 vols. Raleigh and Goldsboro, North Carolina: Nash Bros., Book and Job Printers, 1901.

Coco, Gregory A. *A Vast Sea of Misery, A History and Guide to the Union and Confederate Field Hospitals at Gettysburg, July 1–November 2, 1863*. Gettysburg, Pa.: Thomas Publications, 1988.

Coddington, Edwin B. *The Gettysburg Campaign, A Study in Command*. New York: Charles Scribner's Sons, 1968.

Cody, Barnett H. "Letters of Barnett Hardeman Cody and Others, 1861–1864." Edited by Edmund Cody Burnett. *Georgia Historical Quarterly*, vol. 23 (1939).

Coker, James Lide. *History of Company G, Ninth S.C. Regiment, Infantry, S.C. Army and of Company E, Sixth S.C. Regiment, Infantry, S.C. Army.* Greenwood, South Carolina: Attic Press, 1979.

Commager, Henry S. *The Blue and the Gray.* New York: The Fairfax Press, 1991.

Committee of the Regimental Association, *History of the Thirty-Fifth Regiment Massachusetts Volunteers, 1862–1865.* Boston: Mills, Knight and Company, 1884.

Committee of the Regiment, *History of the Thirty-Sixth Regiment Massachusetts Volunteers, 1862–1865.* Boston: Rockwell and Churchill, 1884.

Confederate Miltary History, Clement A. Evans, Editor. "Alabama-Mississippi," vol. 7 (1899). Reprint, vol. 7, "Alabama," with "Additional Sketches Illustrating the Services of Officers and Patriotic Citizens of Alabama." Wilmington, North Carolina: Broadfoot Publishing Company, 1987.

Cook, Marjorie Howell. "Restoration and Innovation: Alabamians Adjust to Defeat, 1865–1867." Ph.D. dissertation. University of Alabama, 1968.

Corbin, Richard W. "Letters of a Confederate Officer to His Family in Europe During the Last Year of the War of Secession." *The Magazine of History*, no. 24 (1913). New York.

Cormier, Steven A. "The Siege of Suffolk." Masters thesis. Old Dominion University, 1982.

Cowtan, Charles W. *Services of the Tenth New York Volunteers (National Zouaves) in the War of the Rebellion.* New York: Charles W. Ludwig, Publisher, 1882.

Craft, David. *History of the One Hundred Forty-First Regiment Pennsylvania Volunteers, 1862–1865.* Towanda, Pennsylvania: Reporter-Journal Printing Company, 1885.

Crute, Joseph H. *Confederate Staff Officers, 1861–1865.* Powhatten, Virginia: Derwent Books, 1982.

Curtis, O. B. *History of the 24th Michigan of the Iron Brigade, Known as the Detroit and Wayne County Regiment.* Gaithersburg, Maryland: Old Soldier Books, Inc., 1988.

Cussons, John. *The Passage of Thoroughfare Gap and the Assembling of Lee's Army for the Second Battle of Manassas.* York, Pennsylvania: Gazette Print, 1906.

———. *United States "History" as the Yankee Makes and Takes It.* Glen Allen, Virginia: Cussons, May & Co., 1900.

Cutcheon, Byron M. *The Story of the Twentieth Michigan Infantry, July 15th, 1862 to May 30th, 1865.* Lansing, Michigan: Robert Smith Printing Co., 1904.

Davidson, James F. "Michigan and the Defense of Knoxville, Tennessee, 1863." *The East Tennessee Historical Society's Publications.* Knoxville: East Tennessee Historical Society, 1963.

Davis, George B., Editor. *The Official Atlas of the Civil War.* New York: Arno Press, 1978.

Davis, Jefferson. *Jefferson Davis, Constitutionalist, His Letters, Papers and Speeches.* Dunbar Rowland, Editor. 10 vols. Jackson, Mississippi: 1923.

Davis, Nicholas A. *Chaplain Davis and Hood's Texas Brigade.* Edited and with an introduction by Donald E. Everett. San Antonio, Texas: Principa Press of Trinity University, 1962.

Dedication of the Statue to Brevet Major–General William Wells and the Officers and Men of the First Regiment Vermont Cavalry, July 13, 1913. Privately printed, n.d.

Denny, J. Waldo. *Wearing of the Blue in the Twenty-Fifth Mass Volunteer Infantry, with Burnsides Coast Division, 18th Army Corps and Army of the James.* Worchester, Massachusetts: Putnam & Davis Publishers, 1879.

Derby, W. P. "Charge of the Star Brigade." *Camp and Field: Sketches of Army Life by Those Who Followed the Flag.* Compiled by W. F. Hinman. Cleveland: N. G. Hamilton Publishing Company, 1892.

Dickert, D. Augustus. *History of Kershaw's Brigade, With Complete Roll of Companies, Biographical Sketches, Incidents, Anecdotes, Etc.* 1899. Reprint, with an introduction by W. Stanley Hoole. Dayton, Ohio: Press of Morningside Bookshop, 1973.

Dictionary of American Naval Fighting Ships. 4 Vols. Naval Historical Division, Department of the Navy, Washington, D.C., 1969.

Douglas, Henry Kyd. *I Rode with Stonewall.* New York: Fawcett Publications, Inc., 1961.

Dowdey, Clifford. *Lee.* New York: Bonanza Books, 1965.

Dowdey, Clifford, Editor, and Louis H. Manarin, Associate Editor. *The Wartime Papers of R. E. Lee.* New York: Bramhall House, 1961.

Drake, J. Madison. *The History of the Ninth New Jersey Veteran Volunteers.* Elizabeth, New Jersey: Journal Printing House, 1889.

Duncan, Katherine M., and Larry J. Smith. "Prehistory to 1939." *The History of Marshall County, Alabama*, vol. 1. Albertville, Alabama: Thompson Printing, 1969.

Durden, Robert F. *The Black and the Gray: The Confederate Debate on Emancipation*. Baton Rouge: LSU Press, 1972.

Eckenrode, H. J., and Bryan Conrad. *James Longstreet, Lee's War Horse*. Chapel Hill, North Carolina: University of North Carolina Press, 1936.

Eden, R. C. *The Sword and the Gun: A History of the 37th Wisconsin Volunteer Infantry*. Madison, Wisconsin: Atwood and Rublee, 1865.

Edwards, Chris, and Faye Axford. *The Lure and Lore of Limestone County*. Tuscaloosa, Alabama: Portals Press, published for the Limestone Historical Society, 1978.

Fairchild, C. B. *History of the 27th Regiment N.Y. Vols*. Bingham, New York: Carl & Matthews, Printers, 1888.

Farinholdt, B. L. "Escape From Johnson's Island." *Confederate Veteran*, vol. 5, no. 9 (September 1897).

———. "Battle of Gettysburg–Johnson's Island." *Confederate Veteran*, vol. 5, no. 10 (October 1897).

Field, Charles W. "Campaign of 1864 and 1865." *Southern Historical Society Papers*, vol. 14 (1886). Edited by Rev. J. William Jones. Richmond, Virginia.

Fink, Harold S. "The East Tennessee Campaign and the Battle of Knoxville in 1863." *The East Tennessee Historical Society's Publications*. Knoxville: East Tennessee Historical Society, no. 29 (1957).

Fleming, Walter L. *Civil War and Reconstruction in Alabama*. New York: Columbia University Press, 1905.

Fletcher, William Andrew. *Rebel Private, Front and Rear*. Beaumont, Texas: Press of the Greer Print, 1908.

Freeman, Douglas S., Editor. *Lee's Dispatches: Unpublished Letters of General Robert E. Lee, C.S.A. to Jefferson Davis and the War Department of the Confederate States of America, 1862–65*. New York: G. P. Putnam's Sons, 1957.

———. *Lee's Lieutenants, A Study In Command*. 3 Vols. New York: Charles Scribner's Sons, 1942.

———. *R. E. Lee, A Biography*. 4 Vols. New York: Charles Scribner's Sons, 1935.

French, General Samuel G. *Two Wars: An Autobiography*. Nashville: Confederate Veteran, 1901.

Galway, Thomas Francis. *The Valiant Hours*. Edited by W. S. Nye. Harrisburg, Pennsylvania: The Stackpole Company, 1961.

Garrett, Jill K. *A History of Lauderdale County, Alabama*. n.p., 1964.

Garrett, William. *Reminiscences of Public Men in Alabama for Thirty Years*. 1872. Reprint, Spartanburg, South Carolina: The Reprint Company, Publishers, 1975.

Gates, Paul W. *Agriculture and the Civil War*. New York: Alfred A. Knopf, 1965.

Georg, Kathleen. "Our Principal Loss Was in this Place." *The Morningside Notes*, June 12, 1984. Dayton, Ohio: Press of Morningside Bookshop.

Giles, Val C. *Rags and Hope: The Memoirs of Val C. Giles, Four Years with Hood's Brigade, Fourth Texas Infantry, 1861–1865*. Compiled and edited by Mary Lasswell. New York: Coward-McCann, Inc., 1961.

Goodson, Joab. "The Letters of Captain Joab Goodson, 1862–1864. Edited by W. Stanley Hoole. *The Alabama Review*, vol. 10 (April 1957).

Goree, Thomas Jewett. *The Thomas Jewett Goree Letters: vol. 1, The Civil War Correspondence*. Edited and annotated by Langston James Goree. Bryan, Texas: Family History Foundation, 1981.

Govan, Gilbert E., and James W. Livingood. *A Different Valor: The Story of General Joseph E. Johnston, C.S.A*. Indianapolis: Bobbs Merrill, 1956.

Grant, Lewis A. "In the Wilderness." *National Tribune*, January 28, 1897.

Gray, R. A. *My Story: Fifty Years in the Shadow of the Near Great*. Privately printed, n.d.

Griffith, Lucille. *Alabama: A Documentary History to 1900*. University, Alabama: University of Alabama Press, 1968.

Griffith, Paddy. *Battle Tactics of the Civil War*. New Haven, Connecticut: Yale University Press, 1989.

Guernsey, Alfred, and Henry M. Alden. *Harper's Pictorial History of the Civil War*. New York: The Fairfax Press, 1866.

Hagood, Johnson. *Memoirs of the War of Secession*. Columbia, South Carolina: State Company, Columbia, 1910.

Hampton, Noah J. *An Eyewitness to the Dark Days of 1861–65, or A Private Soldier's Adventures and Hardships During the War*. Nashville: n.p., 1898.

Hanson, Raus McDill. *Virginia Place Names, Derivations and Historical Uses*. Verona, Virginia: McClure Press, 1969.

Haynes, Asbury F. "How Haynes Won His Medal of Honor." *National Tribune*, October 21, 1926.

Hill, Daniel H. "Chickamauga—The Great Battle of the West," *Battles & Leaders of The Civil War*. Vol. 3. New York: The Century Company, 1888.

Hinman, Wilbur F. *The Story of the Sherman Brigade*. Alliance, Ohio: Press of The Daily Review, 1897.

Hodge, Robert W., Editor. *The Civil War Letters of Perry Mayo*. East Lansing, Michigan: Michigan State University, 1967.

Hollis, Rufus. *Confederate Veteran*. Scotsboro, Alabama: Press of the Scotsboro Citizen, n.d.

Hood, John Bell. *Advance and Retreat: Personal Experiences in the United States and Confederate States Armies*. Edited by Richard Current. Bloomington, Indiana: Indiana University Press, 1959.

———. "Letter From General John B. Hood." *Southern Historical Society Papers*, vol. 4 (1876). Reprint, Millwood, New York: Kraus Reprint Company, 1977.

Horsman, Reginald. *Josiah Nott of Mobile, Southern Physician and Racial Theorist*. Baton Rouge: Louisiana State University Press, 1987.

Houghton, W. R., and M. B. Houghton. *Two Boys in the Civil War and Afterwards*. Montgomery, Alabama: The Paragon Press, 1912.

Howard, Oliver Otis. *Autobiography of Oliver Otis Howard*. 2 vols. New York: Baker and Taylor, 1907.

Hoyt, James A. "The Palmetto Riflemen: Co B, Fourth Regiment South Carolina Volunteers, Co C, Palmetto Sharpshooters, Historical Sketch (an address delivered at the reunion July 21, 1885)." Greenville, South Carolina: Hoyt and Keyes, 1886.

Hudson, Travis. "Soldier Boys in Gray." *Atlanta Historical Journal*, vol. 23, no. 1 (Spring 1979).

Hughes, John S., Editor. *The Letters of a Victorian Madwoman*. Columbia: South Carolina, University of South Carolina Press, 1993.

Hurst, Samuel H. *Journal-History of the Seventy-Third Ohio Volunteer Infantry*. Chillicothe, Ohio, 1866.

Imboden, John D. "The Confederate Retreat From Gettysburg." *Battles & Leaders of The Civil War*. Vol. 3. New York: The Century Company, 1888.

Johnson, Dorothy S. *Maple Hill Cemetery Sexton's Records*. Compiled for the Huntsville-Madison County Public Library, Huntsville, Alabama, 1982.

Johnson, John L. *University Memorial-Biographical Sketches of Alumni of University of Virginia Who Fell in the Confederate War*. Baltimore: Turnbull Brothers, 1880.

Jones, J. B. *A Rebel War Clerk's Diary at the Confederate State Capital*. Earl Schenck, Editor. New York: Sagamore Press, 1958.

Jones, Rev. J. William. *Christ in the Camp or Religion in Lee's Army*. Richmond, Virginia: B. F. Johnson, 1887.

Jones, Kenneth W. "The Fourth Alabama Infantry: First Blood," *The Alabama Historical Quarterly*, vol. 36, no. 1 (1974). Montgomery, Alabama: Alabama Department of Archives and History.

Jordan, William C. *Some Events and Incidents During the Civil War*. Montgomery, Alabama: Paragon Press, 1909.

Journal of the Congress of the Confederate States of America, 1861–1865, 7 vols. (1905).

Joyce, John A. *A Checkered Life*. Chicago: S. P. Rounds, Jr., 1883.

Judson, A. M. *History of the Eighty-Third Regiment Pennsylvania Volunteers*. Erie, Pennsylvania: B. F. H. Lynn, Publisher, 1865.

King, George Wayne. "The Civil War Career of Hugh Judson Kilpatrick." Masters thesis. University of South Carolina, 1969.

Kurtz, Henry I. "Berdan's Sharpshooters: Most Effective Union Brigade?" *Civil War Times Illustrated*, vol. 1, no. 10 (February 1963).

Law E. McIver. "The Struggle for Round Top." *Battles & Leaders of The Civil War*. Vol. 3. New York: The Century Company, 1888.

————. "On the Confederate Right at Gaines's Mill." *Battles & Leaders of The Civil War.* Vol. 2. New York: The Century Company, 1888.

————. "From the Wilderness to Cold Harbor." *Battles & Leaders of The Civil War*. Vol. 4. New York: The Century Company, 1888.

————. "The Fight for Richmond in 1862." *The Southern Bivouac,* vol. 2, no. 12 (1887). Louisville, Kentucky: The Southern Historical Association of Louisville: Courier Journal Job Rooms.

————. "From Chickamauga to Chattanooga " Philadelphia *Weekly Press*, July 11, 1888.

————. "Burnside and Longstreet in East Tennessee." Philadelphia *Weekly Press*, July 18, 1888.

————. "From Chickamauga to Chattanooga." Philadelphia *Weekly Press*, July 25, 1888.

————. "A Night in the Enemy's Lines." Richmond *Dispatch*, May 22, 1894.

————. "The Confederate Revolution." *Southern Historical Society Papers*, vol. 17 (1886). Edited by Rev. J. William Jones. Richmond, Virginia.

Law, John Adger. *Adger-Law Ancestral Notebook.* Spartanburg, South Carolina: Jacob Graphic Arts Company, 1936.

Law, Thomas Hart. *Citadel Cadets: The Journal of Cadet Tom Law.* John Adger Law, Editor. Clinton, South Carolina: P. C. Press, 1941.

Lewis, Richard. *Camp Life of a Confederate Boy.* Charleston, South Carolina: The News and Courier Book Presses, 1883.

Little, R. H. *Year of Starvation Amid Plenty.* Waco, Texas: Facsimile Press, 1966.

Longstreet, James. *From Manassas to Appomattox: Memoirs of the Civil War in America.* Secaucus, New Jersey: The Blue and Grey Press, 1985.

————. "Lee's Invasion of Pennsylvania." *Battles & Leaders of The Civil War*. Vol. 3. New York: The Century Company, 1888.

————. "Lee's Right Wing at Gettysburg." *Battles & Leaders of The Civil War*. Vol. 3. New York: The Century Company, 1888.

Lucas, Marion Brunson. *Sherman and the Burning of Columbia.* College Station, Texas: Texas A & M University Press, 1976.

Lykes, Richard Wayne. "Petersburg National Military Park, Virginia." Washington, D.C.: *National Park Service Historical Handbook*, ser. 13. 1951. Reprint, 1961.

Maine at Gettysburg: Report of the Maine Commissions. Maine Gettysburg Commission. Portland, Maine: Lakeside Press, 1898.

Martin, Bessie. *Desertion of Alabama Troops from the Confederate Army: A Study in Sectionalism.* New York: Columbia University Press, 1932.

Mathis, Ray. *In the Land of the Living: Wartime Letters of Confederates from the Chattahoochee Valley of Alabama and Georgia.* Troy, Alabama: Troy State University Press, 1981.

Matter, William D. *If It Takes All Summer: The Battle of Spotsylvania.* Chapel Hill: The University of North Carolina Press, 1988.

Maxfield, Albert. *The Story of One Regiment: The Eleventh Maine Infantry Volunteers in the War of the Rebellion.* New York: Press of J. J. Little & Co., 1896.

McClendon, William A. *Recollections of War Times By an Old Veteran While Under Stonewall Jackson and Lieutenant General James Longstreet: How I Got In and How I Got Out.* Montgomery, Alabama: Paragon Press, 1909.

McDaniel, Major Henry. *With Unabated Trust.* Edited by Anita B. Sams. Monroe, Georgia: The Historical Society of Walton County, Inc., 1977.

McLaws, Lafayette. "Gettysburg." *Southern Historical Society Papers*, vol. 7 (1879). Reprint, Millwood, New York: Kraus Reprint Company, 1977.

McMurry, Richard M. *John Bell Hood and The War For Southern Independence.* Lexington, Kentucky: University of Kentucky Press, 1982.

McNeil, Samuel A. *Personal Recollections of Service in the Army of the Cumberland and Sherman's Army, from August 17, 1861 to July 20, 1865.* Richwood, Ohio: n.p., 1910.

McWhiney, Grady, and Perry D. Jamieson. *Attack and Die: Civil War Military Tactics and the Southern Heritage.* University, Alabama: University of Alabama Press, 1982.

The Medical and Surgical History of the War of the Rebellion. 3 vols. Washington, D.C.: Government Printing Office, 1877.

Memorial Record of Alabama, 2 vols. (1893). Reprint, Spartanburg, South Carolina: The Reprint Company, Publishers, 1976.

Moneith, Robert. "Battle of the Wilderness, and Death of General Wadsworth." *War Papers, Being Read Before the Commandery of the State of Wisconsin Military of the Loyal Legion of the U.S.*, vol. 1 (1993).Wilmington, North Carolina: Broadfoot Publishing Company.

Moore, Albert B. *History of Alabama*. University, Alabama: University Supply Store, 1934.

———. *History of Alabama and Her People*. 3 vols. Chicago and New York: The American Historical Society, Inc., 1927.

Myerhoff, Charles H. "The Wilderness, The Charge of Carroll's Celebrated Brigade." *National Tribune*, October 23, 1890.

Nash, Eugene A. *A History of the Forty-Fourth Regiment New York Volunteer Infantry in the Civil War, 1861–1865*. Chicago: R. R. Donnelly & Sons, 1911.

New York Monuments Commission for the Battlefields of Gettysburg and Chattanooga, Final Report for the Battlefield of Gettysburg, vol. 3. "New York at Gettysburg." Albany, New York: J. B. Lyon, 1902.

Nolan, Alan T. *The Iron Brigade*. New York: The Macmillan Co., 1961.

Northern Alabama, Historical and Biographical. 1888. Reprint, Spartanburg, South Carolina: The Reprint Company, Publishers, 1976.

Norton, F. M. "That Tangle in the Wilderness." *National Tribune*, June 13, 1913.

Norton, Herman. *Rebel Religion: The Story of Confederate Chaplins*. St. Louis: The Bethany Press, 1961.

Norton, Oliver W. *The Attack And Defense Of Little Round Top*. 1913. Reprint, with an introduction by John J. Pullen. Dayton, Ohio: Press of Morningside Bookshop, 1983.

Oates, William C. *The War Between the Union and Confederacy and Its Lost Opportunities with a History of the 15th Alabama Regiment and the Forty-Eight Battles in Which It was Engaged*. 1905. Reprint, with an introduction by Robert K. Krick. Dayton, Ohio: Press of Morningside Bookshop, 1985.

———. "Gettysburg –The Battle on the Right." *Southern Historical Society Papers*, vol. 6 (1876). Reprint, Millwood, New York: Kraus Reprint Company, 1977.

———. "General William F. Perry and Something of his Life in War and Peace." *Montgomery Advertiser*, March 2, 1902.

Official Gazette of the United States Patent Office, vol. 19, no. 7. Washington, D.C.: Government Printing Office, February 15, 1881.

Official Records of the Union and Confederate Navies in the War of the Rebellion. Washington, D.C.: U.S. Government Printing Office, 1894–1922.

Osborne, William H. *The History of the Twenty-Ninth Regiment of Massachusetts Volunteer Infantry, in the War of the Rebellion*. Boston: Albert J. Wright, 1877.

Otto, John. *History of the 11th Indiana Battery*. Fort Wayne, Indiana: W. D. Page, Printer and Publisher, 1894.

Owen, Thomas M. *History of Alabama and Dictionary of Alabama Biography*. 4 Vols. 1921. Reprint, with an introduction by Milo B. Howard. Spartanburg, South Carolina: The Reprint Publishers, 1978.

Owen, Thomas M. "The Work of William Henry Fowler as Superintendent of Army Records, 1863–1865." Tuscaloosa, Alabama: *Transactions of the Alabama Historical Society, vol. 2, 1897–1898*.

Page, Charles D. *History of the Fourteenth Regiment Connecticut Vol. Infantry*. Meriden, Connecticut: The Horn Printing Co., 1906.

"Paroles of the Army of Northern Virginia." *Southern Historical Society Papers*, vol. 15 (1887). Millwood, New York: Kraus Reprint Company, 1977.

Parsons, H. C. "Farnsworth's Charge and Death." *Battles & Leaders of The Civil War*. Vol. 3. New York: The Century Company, 1888.

Perry, William F. "The Devil's Den." *Confederate Veteran*, vol. 9, no. 4 (April 1901).

———. "Reminiscences of the Campaign of 1864 in Virginia." *Southern Historical Society Papers*, vol. 7 (1879). Reprint, Millwood, New York: Kraus Reprint Company, 1977.

Pfanz, Harry W. *Gettysburg, The Second Day*. Chapel Hill, North Carolina: The University of North Carolina Press, 1987.

Pierrepont, Alice V. D. *Reuben Vaughan Kidd:Soldier of the Confederacy*. Petersburg, Virginia: Violet Bank, 1947.

Piston, William Garrett. "Lee's Tarnished Lieutenant: James Longstreet and His Image in American Society." Ph.D. dissertation. University of South Carolina, 1982.

Polley, J. B. *Hood's Texas Brigade: Its Marches, Its Battles, Its Achievements*. New York: Neale Publishing Company, 1910.

Pullen, John J. *The Twentieth Maine: A Volunteer Regiment in the Civil War*. Dayton, Ohio: Press of Morningside Bookshop, 1980.

Purifoy, John. "The Lost Opportunity at Gettysburg." *Confederate Veteran*, vol. 31, no. 6 (June 1923).

———. "The Battle of Gettysburg, July 2." *Confederate Veteran*, vol. 31, no. 7 (July 1923).

———. "Longstreet's Attack at Gettysburg, July 2, 1863." *Confederate Veteran*, vol. 31, no. 8 (August 1923).

———. "The Battle of Gettysburg." *Confederate Veteran*, vol. 31, no. 11 (November 1923).

———. "Farnsworth's Charge and Death at Gettysburg." *Confederate Veteran*, vol. 32, no. 8 (August 1924).

———. "The Horror of War." *Confederate Veteran*, vol. 33, no. 7 (July 1925).

———. "In Battle Array at Williamsport and Hagerstown." *Confederate Veteran*, vol. 33, no. 10 (October 1925).

Pyne, Henry R. *Ride to War: The History of the First New Jersey Cavalry*. Earl Schenck Miers, Editor. New Brunswick, New Jersey: Rutgers University Press, 1961.

Ramey, Emily G., and John K. Gott. *The Years of Anguish: Fauquier, Virginia, 1861–1865*. Warrenton, Virginia: Fauquier Democrat, 1965.

Rice, Edmond L. *Civil War Letters of James McDonald Campbell, of the 47th Alabama Infantry, with a Brief Sketch of His Life*. Privately printed, n.d.

Riley, Benjamin F. *History of Conecuh County, Alabama*. Blue Hill, Maine: Weekly Packet, 1964.

Ritter, Charles F., and Jon L. Wakelyn. *American Legislative Leaders, 1850–1910*. New York: Greenwood Press, 1989.

Robertson, James I., Jr. *General A. P. Hill, The Story of A Confederate Warrior*. New York: Random House, 1987.

Robertson, Jerome B. *Touched with Valor*. Edited by Colonel Harold B. Simpson. Hillsboro, Texas: Hill Junior College Press, 1964.

Robertson, John, Editor. *Michigan in the War*. Lansing, Michigan: W. S. George & Co., 1882.

Rogers, William Warren. "The Alabama State Grange." *The Alabama Review,* (April 1955).

———. *The One-Gallused Rebellion: Agrarianism in Alabama, 1865–1896*. Baton Rouge, Louisiana: State University Press, 1970.

Romero, Sidney J. *Religion in the Rebel Ranks*. New York: University Press of America, 1983.

Royal, William F. *Some Reminiscences*. New York and Washington, D.C.: The Neale Publishing Company, 1909.

Russell, Mildred. *Lowndes Court House, A Chronicle of Hayneville, An Alabama Black Belt Village*. Montgomery, Alabama: Paragon Press, 1951.

Ryder, John J. *Reminiscences of Three Years Service in the Civil War*. New Bedford, Massachusetts: Reynolds Printing, 1928.

Sands, Francis P. B. "The Brilliant Career of Lieutenant Roswell H. Lamson, U. S. Navy." *Loyal Legion of the United States Commandery of the District of Columbia*, (January 6, 1909).

Sanger, Donald B., and Thomas R. Hay. *James Longstreet: Soldier, Politician, Officeholder and Writer*. Baton Rouge: LSU Press, 1952.

Savage, Robert Haynes. *The Story of Piedmont, Alabama*, 2 vols. Centre, Alabama: Stewart University Press, 1979.

Saval, Wallace Michael. "Montage of a City Under Siege: Petersburg, 1864 to 1865." Masters thesis. Virginia State College, 1971.

Sawyer, Franklin. *Military History of the 8th Regiment Ohio Vol. Inf'y: Its Battles, Marches and Army Movements*. Cleveland: Fairbanks & Co. Printers, 1881.

Schaff, Morris. *The Battle of the Wilderness*. Boston and New York: Houghton Mifflin Company, 1910.
Shingleton, Royce Gordon. *John Taylor Wood, Sea Ghost of the Confederacy*. Athens, Georgia: University of Georgia Press, 1979.
Sifakis, Stewart. *Who was Who in the Civil War*. New York: Facts on File Publications, 1988.
Simms, William Gilmore. *The Sack and Destruction of the City of Columbia, South Carolina*. Edited by A. S. Salley. Oglethorpe University Press, 1937.
Simpson, Harold B. *Hood's Texas Brigade: Lee's Grenadier Guard*. Waco, Texas: Texian Press, 1970.
Slocum, Henry W. "Sherman's March from Savannah to Bentonville." *Battles & Leaders of The Civil War*. Vol. 4. New York: The Century Company, 1888.
Smith, General Gustavus W. *Confederate War Papers: Fairfax Courthouse, New Orleans, Seven Pines, Richmond and North Carolina*. New York: Atlantic Publishing and Engraving Company, 1884.
Smith, James E. "The Fourth Battery at Gettysburg." New York Monuments Commission for the Battlefields of Gettysburg and Chattanooga, Final Report on The Battlefield of Gettysburg, *New York at Gettysburg*, vol. 3. Albany, New York: J. B. Lyon Company, Printers, 1900.
Smith, William F. "The Eighteenth Corps At Cold Harbor." *Battles & Leaders of The Civil War*. Vol. 4. New York: The Century Company, 1888.
Smith, William R. *The History and Debate of the Convention of the People of Alabama*. 1861. Reprint, Spartanburg, South Carolina: The Reprint Company, Publishers, 1975.
Sommers, Richard J. "The Dutch Gap Affair: Military Atrocities and Rights of Negro Soldiers." *Civil War History*, vol. 21 (March 1975).
———. *Richmond Redeemed: The Siege at Petersburg*. Garden City, New York: Doubleday and Company, 1981.
———. "Grant's Fifth Offensive at Petersburg, A Study in Strategy, Tactics, and Generalship: The Battle of Chaffin's Bluff, The Battle of Poplar Spring Church, The First Battle of the Darbytown Road, The Second Battle of the Squirrel Level Road, The Second Battle of the Darbytown Road." Ph.D. Dissertation. Rice University, 1971
Sorrel, G. Moxley. *Recollections of a Confederate Staff Officer*. Bell Irvin Wiley, Editor. Jackson, Tennessee: McCowat–Mercer Press, 1958.
Steere, Edward. *The Wilderness Campaign*. Harrisburg, Pennsylvania: The Stackpole Company, 1960.
Steiner, Paul, M.D. "Head Wounds—Fragments of Civil War History." *Military Medicine*, vol. 118 (1956). Washington, D.C.: The Association of Military Surgeons of the U.S.
Sterkx, H. E. "William C. Jordan and Reconstruction in Bullock County, Alabama." *Alabama Review* (January 1962).
Stevens, C. A. *Berdan's U.S. Sharpshooters in the Army of the Potomac*, 1861–1865. Reprint, Dayton, Ohio: Press of the Morningside Bookshop, 1972.
Stevens, Hazard. "The Sixth Corps in the Wilderness." *Papers of the Military Historical Society of Massachusetts*, vol. 4 (1895–1918). Boston: Cadet Armory.
———. "The Siege of Suffolk, April 11–May 3, 1863." *Military Historical Society of Massachusetts Papers, vol. 9: Operations on the Atlantic Coast, 1861–1865*, (1912). Boston: Military Historical Society of Massachusetts.
Sturgis, H. H. "From One of General R. E. Lee's Scouts." *Confederate Veteran*, vol. 16, no. 3 (March 1908).
———. "Humor and Pathos In The Army." *Confederate Veteran*, vol. 16, no. 6 (June 1908).
Survivors Association. *History of the 118th Pennsylvania Volunteers, Corn Exchange Regiment, From Their First Engagement at Antietam to Appomattox*. Philadelphia: J. L. Smith, Map Publisher, 1905.
Survivors Association. *History of the 121st Pennsylvania Volunteers*. Philadelphia: Press of Buck and McFetridge Co., 1893.
Tancig, W. J. *Confederate Military Land Units*. Cranbury, New Jersey: Thomas Yoseloff, 1967.
Taylor, John Dykes. "History of the 48th Regiment, Alabama Infantry, C.S.A." Montgomery (Alabama) *Advertiser*, March 9, 1902.
Tevis, C. V. *The History of the Fighting Fourteenth*. Brooklyn: Brooklyn Eagle Press, 1911.
Thomas, John Peyre. *The History of the South Carolina Military Academy*. Charleston, South Carolina: Walker, Evans and Cogswell, 1893.

————. *The Career and Character of General Micah Jenkins, CSA*. Columbia, South Carolina: The State Co., 1908.

Thompson, B. F. *History of the One Hundred Twelfth Regiment of Illinois Volunteer Infantry in the Great War of the Rebellion, 1862–1865*. Toulon, Illinois: Stark County News Office, 1885.

Todd, William. *The Seventy-ninth Highlanders, New York Volunteers in the War of the Rebellion, 1861–1865*. Albany, New York: Brandow, Barton & Co., 1886.

Trumbull, Chaplain H. Clay. *The Knightly Soldier: A Biography of Major Henry Ward Camp, 10th Connecticut Volunteers*. Boston: Nichols and Noyes, 1865.

Tucker, Elsie Perry. *Burrell Perry Descendants and Ancestors*. Tomball, Texas: Genealogical Publications, 1978.

Tucker, Glenn. *Chickamauga*. Dayton, Ohio: Morningside Bookshop, 1976.

Turchin, John B. *Chickamauga*. Chicago: Fergus Printing Company, 1888.

Underwood, Adin B. *The Three Years Service of the Thirty-Third Massachusetts Infantry Regiment, 1862–1865*. Boston: A. Williams & Co., 1881.

Valentine, Herbert E. *Story of Co. F 23rd Massachusetts Volunteers in the War for the Union, 1861–1865*. Boston: W. B. Clarke & Co., 1896.

Vaughan, P. Turner. "Diary of Turner Vaughan, Co. "C" 4th Alabama Regiment, CSA. Commenced March 4th, 1863, and Ending February 12, 1864." *Alabama Historical Quarterly*, vol. 18 (1956).

Venable, Charles S. "Campaign of 1864 and 1865." *Southern Historical Society Papers*, vol. 14 (1886). Edited by Reverend J. William Jones, Richmond, Virginia.

The War of the Rebellion: A Compilation of the Official Records of the Union and Confederate Armies. Washington, D.C.: U.S. Government Printing Office, 1880–1901.

Ward, William C. "Incidents and Personal Experiences on The Battle Field at Gettysburg." *Confederate Veteran*, vol. 8, no. 8 (August 1900).

Warner, Ezra J. *Generals In Blue, Lives of the Union Commanders*. Baton Rouge: Louisiana State University Press, 1964.

————. *Generals In Gray, Lives of the Confederate Commanders*. Baton Rouge: Louisiana State University Press, 1959.

Warren, Dr. Hoyt M., Compiler. *Henry's Heritage, A History of Henry County, Alabama*. Abbeville, Alabama: Henry County Historical Society, 1978.

Warren, Polly. *Lauderdale County, Alabama, Civil War Record, 1860 Census*. Columbia, Tennessee: P-Vine Press, 1970.

Webb, Alexander S. "Through the Wilderness." *Battles & Leaders of The Civil War*. Vol. 4. New York: The Century Company, 1888.

Wesson, Kenneth R. "Evolution of a Soldier." *The Huntsville Review*, vol. 6, nos. 3, 4 (1976). Huntsville, Alabama: The Huntsville-Madison County Historical Society.

West Point Alumni Foundation. *Register of Graduates and Former Cadets of the U.S. Military Academy*. Cullum Memorial Edition, 1970.

White, Wyman S. *The Civil War Diary of Wyman S. White, First Sergeant of Company F of the 2nd U.S. Sharpshooter Regiment (New Hampshire Men) in the Army of the Potomac, 1861–1865*. Baltimore: Butternut and Blue, 1991.

Williams Huntsville Directory, City Guide and Business Mirror, vol. 1 (1859–1860). Huntsville, Alabama: Strowe Publishing Co., 1972.

Williams, Nannie. "One of the Real Heroes." *Confederate Veteran*, vol. 5, no. 4 (April 1897).

Wilson, John Lyde. *The Code of Honor: or Rules for the Government of Principals and Seconds in Duelling*. Charleston, South Carolina: James Phinney, 1858.

Wise, George. *History of the Seventeenth Virginia Infantry, CSA*. Baltimore, Maryland: Kelly, Pilt & Co., 1870.

Wise, Jennings C. *The Long Arm of Lee, or the History of the Artillery of the Army of Northern Virginia*. 2 Vols. Lincoln, Nebraska: University of Nebraska Press, 1991.

Woodford, Frank B. *Father Abraham's Children: Michigan Episodes in the Civil War*. Detroit: Wayne State University Press, 1961.

Yearns, W. Buck, and John G. Barrett, Editors. *North Carolina Civil War Documentary*. Chapel Hill, North Carolina: University of North Carolina Press, 1980.

Yeary, Mamie, Compiler. *Reminiscences of the Boys in Gray, 1861–1865*. 1912. Reprint, with an introduction by Robert Krick. Dayton, Ohio: Morningside House, Inc., 1986.
Youngblood, William. "Unwritten History of the Gettysburg Campaign." *Southern Historical Society Papers*, vol. 38 (1977). Millwood, New York: Kraus Reprint Company.
Younger, Edward, Editor. *Inside the Confederate Government, The Diary of Robert Garlick Hill Kean*. New York: Oxford Press, 1975.

Manuscript Sources

Alabama Department of Archives and History, Montgomery, Alabama
  Confederate Muster Rolls Collection
    4th Alabama Infantry Regiment, Box 2, Folders 13–23
      Robert T. Coles. "History of the 4th Regiment Alabama Volunteer Infantry, C.S.A., Army of Northern Virginia"
      Field and Staff
      Historical Muster Rolls
      Turner Vaughan Diary
      "Reminiscences of the Fourth Alabama," *Marion Commonwealth*, September 6, 1866
      Alphine Sterrett Scrapbook
    15th Alabama Infantry Regiment, Box 8, Folders 12–23
      Field and Staff
      Historical Muster Rolls
      Noah B. Feagin to his sisters, January 30, 1863
    44th Alabama Infantry Regiment, Box 36, Folders 1–11
      Field and Staff
      Historical Muster Rolls
      H. H. Sturgis, "War Record of H. H. Sturgis"
    47th Alabama Infantry Regiment, Box 39, Folders 1–11
      Field and Staff
      Historical Muster Rolls
      Henry C. Lindsay, "Sketch of Gettysburg"
      Mrs. James W. Jackson Letter
      Untitled account of the 47th Alabama
    48th Alabama Infantry Regiment, Box, Folders 1–11
      Field and Staff
      Historical Muster Rolls
  Manuscript Collection
    Rayburn Family Papers, Box 206, 7S#6
  Surname File
  Regimental Flags (SG 11139)
  Alabama Governors' Correspondence, May, 1863–April, 1864 (SG 5687)
Auburn University, Ralph B. Draughn Library, Auburn, Alabama
  Joseph Q. Burton, "Sketch of the 47th Regiment Alabama Volunteers"
Birmingham Public Library, Department of Archives and Manuscripts, Birmingham, Alabama
  Cedar Grove Plantation Papers, 1833–1964, Collection #390 (microfilm)
Bowdoin College Library, Brunswick, Maine
  Elisha Coon Manuscript and Folder
    Account of Colonel William C. Oates, 15th Alabama
Chickamauga and Chattanooga National Military Park, Chickamauga, Georgia
  3rd Wisconsin Battery Folder
  7th Indiana Battery Folder
    7th Indiana Battery
  10th Indiana Infantry Folder
    10th Indiana Infantry

82nd Indiana Infantry Folder
    Morton C. Hunter Account of "82nd Indiana Participation in Battle of Chickamauga"
    Indiana at Chickamauga
The Citadel Archives, Charleston, South Carolina
  Alumni Office Records
  Official Register of the Officers and Cadets of the SCMA, 1853–1856
Darlington County Historical Commission, Darlington, South Carolina
    Law's Oath of Allegiance, September 12, 1865
Dartmouth College Library, Hanover, New Hampshire
  Antietam Collection
  William M. Robbins to John M. Gould, March 25, 1891
  Map, Returned and Marked by William M. Robbins, March 25, 1891
Duke University, Special Collections Library, Durham, North Carolina
  Pierre G. T. Beauregard Papers
  Micah Jenkins Papers
  Dr. Lee Papers
Emory University, Robert W. Woodruff Library, Special Collections, Atlanta, Georgia
  The James Preston Crowder Letters (microfilm)
Florida State Archives, R. A. Gray Building, Tallahassee, Florida
  E. M. Law Pension Application
Gettysburg National Military Park, Gettysburg, Pennsylvania
  4th Maine Folder
  Berdan's Sharpshooters Folder
    Berdan's Sharpshooters
  83rd Pennsylvania Folder
  John W. C. Neal, M.D., *Record of Confederate Burials*
  William C. Oates Correspondence (copy)
  Texas Troops Folder
Hill College, Harold B. Simpson Confederate Research Center, Hillsboro, Texas
  Rufus K. Felder Letters
  Nicholas Pomeroy Manuscript
  Watson D. Williams Letters
Huntsville-Madison County Public Library, Zeitler Room, Huntsville, Alabama
  Figures Collection, 82–1, Box 1
    File 2, Copy of Henry Figures Letters
    File 11, Biography
  Historical Collection
    Edward Dorr Tracey Letters
Jacksonville State University, Houston Cole Library, Jacksonville, Alabama
  William E. and Nelda Simpson (Compilers). "The Correspondence of John M. Anderson, Private, CSA"
Library of Congress, Manuscript Division, Washington, D.C.
  John Bratton Letters to His Wife, February, 1861–July, 1865. Transcribed by the North Carolina Historical Records Survey, 1942.
  Ezra Ayers Carman Papers
  R. W. York, "Death of General Bee"
  Joshua L. Chamberlain Papers
  Records of the Confederate States Army, 1861–1865, vol. 111, 112
  Benjamin F. Rittenhouse Papers
    "The Battle of Gettysburg, as Seen From Little Round Top"
  History of the Services of the Third Wisconsin Battery
Mississippi Department of Archives and History, Jackson, Mississippi
  Ward Collection
  Dr. B. F. Ward, "The Gallant Belo, Story of His Duel With Coussins Told By An Eye-Witness."

Memphis *Commercial Appeal*, May 1, 1901
Museum of the Confederacy, Eleanor S. Brockenbrough Library, Richmond, Virginia
  G. Moxley Sorrel Diary
  Rebel Diary, Covering the Battles of Wilderness, Spotsylvania, Cold Harbor, etc., Found in
  Richmond, May 1865
National Archives, Washington, D.C.
  Record Group 94, The Adjutant General's Office
    Compiled Service Records of Former Confederates Who Served in the 1st through 6th U.S.
    Volunteer Infantry Regiments, 1864–1866, M1017, roll 25
  Record Group 109, War Department Collection of Confederate Records
    Compiled Service Records of Confederate Soldiers Who Served in Organizations From
    Alabama, M311
      4th Alabama Infantry, rolls 118–132
        Record of Event Cards
        Compiled Service Records
      7th Alabama Infantry, rolls 169–170
        Compiled Service Records
      9th Alabama Infantry, rolls 182–190
        Compiled Service Records
      15th Alabama Infantry, rolls 241–250
        Record of Event Cards
        Compiled Service Records
      44th Alabama Infantry, rolls 407–415
        Record of Event Cards
        Compiled Service Records
      47th Alabama Infantry, rolls 423–431
        Record of Event Cards
        Compiled Service Records
      48th Alabama Infantry, rolls 432–437
        Record of Event Cards
        Compiled Service Records
  Compiled Service Records of Confederate Generals and Staff Officers and Nonregimental
  Enlisted Men, M331
    Jefferson Davis Papers, Papers J–M, roll 99
    General and Staff Officers
      William F. Perry Papers, Box 227
  Letters Received by the Confederate Secretary of War, M437, rolls 94, 115, 136
  Letters Received by the Confederate Adjutant and Inspector General, 1861–1865, M474, rolls
  33, 54, 57, 72, 101, 115, 119, 124, 126, 156, 158
  Letters and Telegrams Sent by the Confederate A&IG, 1861–1865, M627, roll 6, (v43, 90),
  (v43, 273)
  Index to CSR, of Confederate Soldiers Who Served From the State of Alabama, M374, 49
  Rolls
  Index to CSRs of Confederate Soldiers Who Served in Organizations Raised Directly by the
  Confederate Government and of Confederate General and Staff Officers and Non-Regimental
  Enlisted Men, M818, roll 26.
  List of Casualties During the Campaigns of 1864, M836, roll 7
  General Orders and Circulars of the Confederate War Department, 1861–1865, M901, roll 1
  Orders and Circulars Issued by the Army of Northern Virginia, CSA, 1861–1865, M921, rolls
  1–4
  Brigade Inspection Reports, M935
  Division Inspection Reports, M935
  U.S. Army Commands Misc Rolls, Deserters, POW and Refugees, entry 199

New Hampshire Historical Society, Concord, New Hampshire
    John B. Bachelder Papers
New York Public Library, Rare Books and Manuscripts Division, New York, New York
    Ezra Ayers Carman Papers
Personal Collections
    Gordon T. Carter, Montgomery, Alabama
        James Barrett Daniel Letters
    Jess Henson, Terre Haute, Indiana
        William Alexander Griffin Letters
    Gwendolyn Gross Hicks, Athens, Alabama
        John V. McKee Letters
    George Jones, Princeton, New Jersey
        David L. Bozeman Letters
    Jane Law Norvell, Columbia, South Carolina
        Evander McIver Law Resignation
        Copy of Petition of Alabama Officers to Longstreet, September 22, 1863
Samford University Library, Birmingham, Alabama
    Special Collection
        Letters of James Barrett Daniel
Smiley Public Library, Archives/Special Collections
    Lafayette McLaws to I. R. Pennypacker, Philadelphia *Weekly Press* (copy)
South Carolina Department of Archives and History, Columbia, South Carolina
    John Jenkins Papers
        Micah Jenkins Folder (RG 5000)
United States Army Military History Institute, Carlisle Barracks, Pennsylvania
    The Civil War Miscellaneous Collection
        Porter King Diary (copy)
        Henry Figures Letter (synopsis)
University of North Carolina, Southern Historical Collection, Chapel Hill, North Carolina
    Edward Porter Alexander Papers
    Nathaniel H. R. Dawson Papers
    Lafayette McLaws Papers
    William McKendree Robbins Papers
    Paul Turner Vaughan Papers
University of South Carolina, South Caroliniana Library, Columbia, South Carolina
    Henry Calvin Conner Papers
    John Jenkins Papers
    Samuel W. Melton Papers
    Robert Oswald Sams Manuscript
University of Texas, Center for American History, Austin, Texas
    James Longstreet Order and Letter Book, 1861–1864
    Thomas L. McCarty Diary
Virginia Historical Society, Richmond, Virginia
    Evan R. Chesterman, "Duels and Duellists of Bygone Virginia Days." *Richmond Evening Journal*, n.d.
    Osmun Latrobe Diary
    E. M. Law to John G. Stokes Letter (MSS2L4109al)
        Lyon G. Tyler. *Men of Mark, Biographical Outlines of American Life.* N.d., n.p.
Western Reserve Historical Society, Cleveland, Ohio
    Pinckney Bowles to Marchus J. Wright, October 5, 1886

Newspapers

Columbus (Georgia) *Daily Sun*
Daily Richmond Enquirer
Huntsville (Alabama) *Daily Confederate*
Huntsville (Alabama) *Democrat*
Huntsville (Alabama) *Independent*
Huntsville (Alabama) *Tribune*
Jacksonville (Alabama) *Republican*
Marion (Alabama) *Commonwealth*
Marion (Alabama) *Star*
Memphis *Commercial Appeal*
Mobile *Advertiser & Register*
Mobile *Evening News*
Montgomery *Daily Advertiser*
Montgomery *Daily Mail*
Natchez (Mississippi) *Weekly Courier*
New York *Herald*
New York *Times*
Orlando (Florida) *Sentinel*
Petersburg *Daily Express*
Philadelphia *Daily Evening Bulletin*
Philadelphia *Weekly Times*
Richmond *Daily Dispatch*
Richmond *Dispatch*
Richmond *Enquirer*
Richmond *Times-Dispatch*
Selma (Alabama) *Daily Reporter*
Southern Christian Advocate
Southwestern Baptist
Talladega (Alabama) *Democratic Watchtower*
Washington, D.C. *Evening Star*
Yorkville (South Carolina) *Enquirer*

Secondary Sources

Albaugh, June Middleton. *Collirene, The Queen Hill*. Montgomery, Alabama: Herff Jones–Paragon Press, 1977.
Alexander, Bevin. *Lost Victories: The Military Genius of Stonewall Jackson*. New York: Henry Holt and Company, 1992.
Alleman, Mrs. Tillie (Pierce). *At Gettysburg or What a Girl Saw and Heard of the Battle*. New York: W. Lake Borland, 1889.
Amos, Harriet E. *Cotton City: Urban Development in Antebellum Mobile*. University, Alabama: University of Alabama Press, 1985.
Barney, William L. *The Secession Impulse: Alabama and Mississippi in 1860*. Princeton: Princeton University Press, 1974.
Barker, Eugene, Editor. "The Confederate Exodus to Latin America." *Southwestern Historical Quarterly*, vol. 39 (July 1935–April 1936). Austin, Texas: The Texas State Historical Association.
Beringer, Richard E., Herman Hattaway, Archer Jones and William N. Still, Jr. *Why the South Lost the Civil War*. Athens, Georgia: University of Georgia Press, 1986.
Bill, Alfred Hoyt. *The Beleaguered City: Richmond, 1861–1865*. New York: Alfred A. Knopf, 1946.
Boucher, Ann Williams. "Wealthy Planter Families in Nineteenth-Century Alabama." Ph.D. dissertation. University of Connecticut, 1978.
Boyd, Charles E. *The Devil's Den: A History of the 44th Alabama Volunteer Infantry Regiment Confederate States Army (1862–1865)*. Privately printed, 1987.

Brown, Kent Masterson. "Lee at Gettysburg, The Man, The Myth, The Recriminations." *Civil War*, vol. 11, no. 1 (January–February 1993).

Bruce, Dickson D., Jr. *Violence and Culture in the Antebellum South*. Austin, Texas: University of Texas Press, 1979.

Carter, Kit C., and Jerry C. Oldshue. "N. H. R. Dawson: Soldier, Statesman, and U.S. Commissioner of Education." *The Alabama Review*, vol. 34, no. 3 (1981).

Childs, James Rives. *Reliques of the Rives (Ryves)*. Lynchburg, Virginia: J. P. Bell Company, 1929.

Collier, Calvin L. *They'll Do to Tie To! The Story of the Third Regiment Arkansas Infantry C.S.A.* Major James D. Warren, Publisher.

Connelly, Thomas L., and Barbara L. Bellows. *God and General Longstreet: The Lost Cause and the Southern Mind*. Baton Rouge: Louisiana State University Press, 1982.

Cornish, Dudley Taylor. *The Sable Arm: Black Troops in the Union Army, 1861–1865*. Lawrence, Kansas: University Press of Kansas, 1987.

Cunningham, H. H. *Doctors in Gray: The Confederate Medical Service*. Baton Rouge: Louisiana State University Press, Second Edition, 1960.

Davis, Charles S. *The Cotton Kingdom in Alabama*. Montgomery, Alabama: Alabama State Department of Archives and History, 1939.

Dawson, Francis W. *Reminiscences of Confederate Service, 1861–1865*. Bell I. Wiley, Editor. Baton Rouge: Louisiana State University Press, 1980.

Dolton, John. "Chickamauga." *Confederate Veteran*, vol. 1, no. 12 (December 1893).

Dorman, Lewy. "Party Politics in Alabama From 1850 Through 1860." *Publication of the Alabama State Department of Archives and History, Historical and Patriotic Series,* no. 13. Wetumpka, Alabama: Wetumpka Printing Company, 1935.

Dowdey, Clifford. *Lee's Last Campaign: The Story of Lee and His Men Against Grant-1864*. Boston: Little Brown and Company, 1960.

———. *The Seven Days—The Emergence of Robert E. Lee*. New York: The Fairfax Press, 1978.

Duckworth, Peggy Jane. "The Role of Alabama Black Belt Whigs in the Election of Delegates to the Secession Convention." Masters thesis. University of Alabama, 1961.

Farmer, Margaret Pace, Compiler. "Record of Confederate Soldiers, 1861–1865, Pike County, Alabama." Troy, Alabama: *Pike County Civil War Centennial Commission Publications*, 1962.

Fletcher, William A. *Rebel Private, Front and Rear*. Austin, Texas: University of Texas Press, 1954.

Floyd, Fred C. *History of the Fortieth (Mozart) Regiment, New York Volunteers*. Boston, Massachusetts: F. H. Gilson Co., 1909.

Foscue, Virginia O. *Place Names in Alabama*. Tuscaloosa, Alabama: University of Alabama Press, 1989.

Frisbie, Louise. *Peace River Pioneers*. Miami, Florida: E. A. Seemann Publishing Company, 1974.

Gallagher, Gary W., Editor. *The Third Day at Gettysburg and Beyond*. Chapel Hill, North Carolina: The University of North Carolina Press, 1994.

Griggs, William Clark. *The Elusive Eden: Frank McMullan's Confederate Colony in Brazil*. Austin, Texas: University of Texas Press, 1987.

Hagerman, Edward. *The American Civil War and the Origins of Modern Warfare*. Bloomington and Indianapolis: Indiana University Press, 1988.

Hamilton, D. H. *History of Company M, First Texas Volunteer Infantry, Hood's Brigade, Longstreet's Corps, Army of the Confederate States of America*. Waco, Texas: W. M. Morrison, 1962.

Hardie, Joseph. "Confederate Brothers and Cousins." *Confederate Veteran*, vol. 20, no. 7 (July 1912).

Harter, Eugene C. *The Lost Colony of the Confederacy*. Jackson, Mississippi: University Press of Mississippi, 1985.

Hennessy, John. "The Fight for Henry Hill, Manassas, Virginia, July 21, 1861." *The Morningside Notes*. Dayton, Ohio: Morningside Bookshop, 1986.

Hesseltine, William B., and Hazel C. Wolff. *The Blue and the Gray on the Nile*. Chicago: University of Chicago Press, 1961.

Hetherington, M. F. *History of Polk County, Florida: Narrative and Biographical*. Chuluota, Florida: Mickle House, Publishers, 1971.

Horn, John. *The Destruction of the Weldon Railroad: Deep Bottom, Globe Tavern and Reams Sta-*

tion, August 14–25, 1864. Lynchburg, Virginia: H. E. Howard, Inc., 1991.

Hudson, James G. "A Story of Company D, 4th Alabama Infantry Regiment, CSA." *Alabama Historical Quarterly*, vol. 23, nos. 1, 2 (Spring 1961). Montgomery, Alabama: State Department of Archives and History.

Jamieson, Perry D. "The Development of Civil War Tactics." Ph.D. dissertation. Wayne State University, 1979.

Johns, John E. *Florida During the Civil War*. Gainesville, Florida: University of Florida Press, 1963.

Jones, Kenneth. "The Fourth Alabama Infantry: A Fighting Legion." *Alabama Historical Quarterly*, vol. 38, no. 3 (Fall 1976). Montgomery, Alabama: State Department of Archives and History.

Kelley, Dennis. "The Second Battle of Manassas." *Civil War Times Illustrated*, vol. 22, no. 3 (May 1983).

Kelley, O. H. *Origin and Progress of the Order of the Patrons of Husbandry in the United States; A History from 1866 to 1873*. Philadelphia: J. A. Wagenseller, 1875.

Krick, Robert K. *Lee's Colonels, A Biographical Register of the Field Officers of the Army of Northern Virginia*. Dayton. Ohio: Press of the Morningside Bookshop, 1979.

———. *Stonewall Jackson at Cedar Mountain*. Chapel Hill, North Carolina: University of North Carolina Press, 1990.

LeGrand, Phyllis LaRue. "Destitution and Relief of Indigent Soldiers' Families of Alabama During the Civil War." Masters thesis. Auburn University, 1964.

Linderman, Gerald F. *Embattled Courage: The Experience of Combat in the American Civil War*. New York: The Free Press, 1987.

Mahon, John K. "Civil War Infantry Assault Tactics." *Military Affairs*, vol. 25, no. 2 (1961): 57–68.

McDonough, James Lee. *Chattanooga: A Death Grip on the Confederacy*. Knoxville: University of Tennessee Press, 1984.

McLaws, Lafayette. "After Chickamauga," in *Addresses Delivered before the Confederate Veteran Association of Savannah, Georgia, to Which is Appended the President's Annual Report*. Savannah, Georgia: Braid and Hutton, printers, 1898.

McMurray, W. J. "The Gap of Death at Chickamauga." *Confederate Veteran*, vol. 2, no. 8 (August 1894).

Mickle, William E. *Well Known Confederate Veterans and Their War Records*. New Orleans, Louisiana, 1907.

Morris, Roy, Jr. "I Am Dying Egypt, Dying." *Civil War Times Illustrated*, vol. 25, no. 6 (October 1986).

Nelson, Dr. Henry Lee, Jr. "A Dream Not Realized: The Story of Captain Cussons and "Forest Lodge." *The Henrico County Historical Society Magazine*, vol. 10, no. 1 (1986).

Nesbit, John W. *General History of Company D 149th Pennsylvania Volunteers and Personal Sketches of the Members*. The Oakdale Printing and Publishing Co., 1908.

Norton, Oliver W. "Strong Vincent and His Brigade at Gettysburg, July 2, 1863." *The Gettysburg Papers*, vol. 2. Compiled by Ken Brady and Florence Freeland. Dayton, Ohio: Press of Morningside Bookshop, 1978.

Oldshue, Jerry C. "The Secession Movement in Tuscaloosa County, Alabama." Masters thesis. University of Alabama, 1961.

Pfanz, Harry W. "The Gettysburg Campaign after Pickett's Charge." *The Morningside Notes* (1982). Dayton, Ohio: Morningside Bookshop.

Pomfret, John E., Editor. "Letters of Fred Lockley, Union Soldier, 1864–1865." *The Huntington Library Quarterly*, vol. 26, no. 1 (1952): 75–107.

Priest, John Michael. *Antietam: The Soldiers' Battle*. New York: Oxford University Press, 1993.

Pullen, John J. "Effects of Marksmanship." *The Gettysburg Magazine*, no. 2 (January 1990). Dayton, Ohio: Morningside Press.

Ray, O. P. "Hindman's Successful Strategy." *Confederate Veteran*, vol. 30, no. 8 (August 1922).

Rittenhouse, Benjamin F. "The Battle of Gettysburg as Seen From Little Round Top." *The Gettysburg Papers*, vol. 2 (1978). Compiled by Ken Brady and Florence Freeland. Dayton, Ohio: Press of Morningside Bookshop.

Ross, Fitzgerald. *Cities and Camps of the Confederate States*. Edited by Richard B. Harwell. Urbana, Illinois:University of Illinois Press, 1958.

Scott, Robert G. *Into the Wilderness with the Army of the Potomac*. Bloomington, Illinois: Indiana University Press, 1985.

Seabourne, J. Gay. "The Battle of Cedar Mountain." *Civil War Times Illustrated* (December 1966).

Sears, Stephen W. *Landscape Turned Red: The Battle of Antietam*. New Haven, Connecticut: Ticknor and Fields, 1983.

"Sketch of the Late Major Robbins." *The Gettysburg News*, September 12, 1905.

Smith, A. P. *History of the Seventy-Sixth Regiment New York Volunteers*. Cortland, New York: J. P. Davis & Speer, 1867.

Stackpole, Edward J. "The Battle of Gettysburg." Special Gettysburg Edition. *Civil War Times Illustrated*, n.d.

Steele, Matthew F. *American Campaigns*. 2 vols. Washington, D.C.: Bryon S. Adams, 1909.

Steere, Edward. *The Wilderness Campaign*. Harrisburg, Pennsylvania: The Stackpole Company, 1960.

Suderow, Bryce A. "An Automobile Tour of Hancock's Second Expedition North of the James, August 14–20, 1864," unpublished manuscript.

Trudeau, Noah Andre. *The Last Citadel: Petersburg, Virginia, June 1864–April 1865*. Boston: Little, Brown and Company, 1991.

———. *Bloody Roads South, The Wilderness to Cold Harbor, May–June 1864*. Boston, Toronto, London: Little, Brown and Company, 1989.

Tucker, Glenn. *High Tide at Gettysburg*. Dayton, Ohio: The Press of Morningside Bookshop, 1973.

Vincent, Boyd. "The Attack and Defense of Little Round Top, Gettysburg, July 2, 1863." *The Gettysburg Papers*, vol. 2 (1978). Compiled by Ken Brady and Florence Freeland. Dayton, Ohio: Press of Morningside Bookshop.

Welch, Richard F. "Gettysburg Finale." *America's Civil War*, vol. 6, no. 3 (July 1993).

Wert, Jeffry D. "Gettysburg: The Full Story of the Struggle." *Civil War Times Illustrated*, vol. 27, no. 4 (Summer 1988).

West, John C. *A Texan in Search of a Fight*. Waco, Texas: Texian Press, 1969.

Winkler, Mrs. A. V. *The Confederate Capital and Hood's Texas Brigade*. Austin, Texas: Eugene Von Boeckmann, 1894.

Wright, B. F. "From the Wilderness to Richmond to Cold Harbor." Minnesota Commandery of *MOLLUS*, 1887–1889 (1890). St. Paul, Minnesota: St. Paul Book and Stationary Co.

Wright, James R. "Time on Little Round Top," *The Gettysburg Magazine*, no. 2 (January 1990). Dayton, Ohio: Morningside Press.

Yearns, Wilfred Buck. *The Confederate Congress*. Athens, Georgia: University of Georgia Press, 1960.

Index

A

Abbeville, AL, 20, 337
Abernathy, David H. B., 234, 254, 401
Abernathy, William F., 234, 254, 401
Adams, James Young, 216
Adrian, James F., 134
Adrian, John D., 116, 308
Alabama and Tennessee Railroad, 29
Alabama Artillery
    S. H. Dent's Battery, 158, 171
Alabama Infantry
    4th, xiv, 4, 5, 6, 14, 25, 38, 40, 47, 125, 128, 129,
        134, 175, 272, 274, 275, 276, 301, 302, 305, 308,
        314, 320, 332, 335, 336, 337
        assigned to Third Brigade, Whiting's division, 9
        attempt to destroy Raleigh *Standard*, 141
        Battle Mountain, VA, skirmish, 130
        camp life, 5
        captains oppose Col. Jones, 5
        casualties, 8, 14, 16, 18, 121, 297
        Chickamauga, GA, 144, 145, 146, 151, 158, 164,
        167, 390
        Co. A, Governor's Guards, 4, 9, 50
        Co. B, Tuskegee Zouaves, 2, 3, 4
        Co. C, Magnolia Cadets, 4
        Co. D, Canebrake Rifles, 4
        Co. E, Conecuh Guards 3, 4
        Co. G, Marion Light Infantry, 4, 5
        Co. H, Lauderdale Guards, 5
        Co. I, North Alabamians, 4, 50
        Co. K, 283, 328
        Cold Harbor, VA, 269, 270, 274, 276
        Deep Bottom, VA, 288
        deserters, 288, 314
        East TN, 202, 208, 209, 210, 211, 212, 215, 217
        enroute to Gettysburg, 70, 75, 76
        Fussell's Mill, VA, 296
        Gaines's Mill, VA, 10, 11
        Gettysburg, PA, 79, 82, 85, 87, 88, 90, 91, 98, 99,
        101, 106, 109, 114, 116, 118, 125

        inducted into Confederate service, 5
        Jackson christened Stonewall, 8
        last line of battle, 333
        Lookout Valley, TN, 181, 182, 183, 184, 185, 188,
        189, 190, 191, 392
        Manassas, VA, Aug. 29–30, 1862, 13, 14
        Manassas, VA, July 21, 1861, 6, 8
        military bearing, 18
        military instruction, 5, 6
        North Anna River, VA, 267
        occupations, 372
        officer ranks depleted, xvi
        organization, xvi, 4, 9,
        Peninsula Campaign, 10
        Petersburg, VA, 283, 287
        Sharpsburg, MD, 16
        Spotsylvania, VA, 257, 262
        strength, 8
        Suffolk, VA, 48, 50, 51, 53, 55, 59, 64, 65, 380
        surrender, 333
        Wilderness, VA, 234, 237, 238, 240, 241, 243,
        244, 247, 248, 251, 252, 400
    7th, 28, 37
        Lafayette Guards, 28
    9th, 2, 29
    14th, 16
    15th, xiv, 20, 23, 24, 25, 35, 38, 40, 46, 63, 67,
        296, 342
        Battle Mountain, VA, 129, 130
        casualties, 121, 405
        Cedar Run, VA, 23
        Chester Station, VA, 281, 282
        Chickamauga, GA, 144, 145, 148, 149, 158,
        164, 171, 172, 173, 174, 334, 335, 337, 338,
        339
        Co. A, 100, 129, 184
        Co. B, 20, 65, 172, 184, 211
        Co. C, 295
        Co. D, 295
        Co. E, 76, 295
        Co. F, 295

Co. G, 103, 143, 184, 211, 305
Co. H, 337
Co. I, 295
Co. K, 184, 295, 309
Co. L, 23, 295, 339
Co. L, Pike sharpshooters, 23
Cold Harbor, VA, 274
Cross Keys, VA, 23
deserters, 142, 315
East TN, 202, 209, 211, 213
Fredericksburg, VA, Dec. 13, 1862, 24
Fussell's Mill, VA, 287, 292, 293, 295
Gettysburg, PA, 82, 88, 90, 99, 100, 101, 103,
    104, 106, 107, 108, 109, 116, 118, 119, 384
Henry County Pioneer Infantry Company, 337
Lookout Valley, TN, 180, 181, 182, 184, 185, 189,
    190, 191, 193, 194, 195, 393
Manassas, VA, Aug. 29–30, 1862, 24
North Anna River, VA, 267
officer ranks depleted, xvi
order of seniority, 21
organization, 21
Sharpsburg, MD, 24
Spotsylvania, VA, 257, 260
strength, 405
Suffolk, VA, 53, 64
surrender, 333
transferred to Virginia, 21
Wilderness, VA, 238, 245, 248, 251, 252
19th, 171
44th, xiv, 27, 38, 39, 91, 134, 266, 270, 286, 320,
    328, 335, 336, 341
assigned to Wright's Brigade, 27
camp of instruction, 25
casualties, 28, 121, 154, 166
Chickamauga, GA, 144, 146, 148, 151, 154, 156,
    158, 164, 170, 389
Co. A, 54
Co. A captured, 56
Co. B, 54, 146, 216, 286
Co. B captured, 56
Co. E, 27
Co. G, 28
deserters, 27, 142, 284, 312
East TN, 27, 216, 396
Gettysburg, PA, 82, 87, 90, 91, 94, 99, 105, 109
Lookout Valley, TN, 185, 189, 190, 191, 193, 194
organization, 25
return to VA from East TN, 230
Sharpsburg, MD, 28
Spotsylvania, VA, 256, 257
strength, 28, 406
Suffolk, VA, 54, 55, 56, 57
surrender, 333
transferred to Law's Brigade, 18
transferred to Virginia, 27
Wilderness, VA, 234, 238, 241, 243, 244, 246,
    251, 252

47th, xiv, 1, 20, 28, 34, 37, 38, 39, 40, 72, 132,
    133, 134, 136, 231, 266, 297, 305, 320, 336
casualties, 35, 121
Cedar Run, VA, 31, 32
Chickamauga, GA, 144, 148, 158, 164, 167
Co. I, 214
deserters, 142, 312, 324
East TN, 214, 396
Gettysburg, PA, 82, 85, 87, 88, 90, 96, 99, 100,
    101, 103, 108, 109, 116
Lookout Valley, TN, 185, 189, 190, 193
Manassas, VA, Aug. 29–30, 1862, 34
organization, 28
receives new battle flag, 230
return to VA from East TN, 230
Sharpsburg, MD, 35
Spotsylvania, VA, 257, 258
strength, 35, 76
surrender, 333, 335
transferred to Law's Brigade, 20
transferred to Virginia, 31
Wilderness, VA, 234, 238, 240, 241, 243, 244,
    246, 248, 251, 252, 270, 401
48th, xiv, 2, 20, 37, 38, 39, 40, 134, 136, 270,
    289, 320, 336, 342
casualties, 35, 121, 299
Cedar Run, VA, 31, 32, 34
Chickamauga, GA, 143, 144, 148, 158, 164
Co. C, 334
Co. E, 295
Co. F, 334
Co. K, 32, 290, 291
deserter punished, 131
deserters, 324
East TN, 211
enroute to Gettysburg, 72, 74, 75
Fussell's Mill, VA, 293, 295, 296
Gettysburg, PA, 82, 87, 90, 93, 94, 105, 109, 382
Lookout Valley, TN, 185, 188, 189, 190, 392
Manassas, VA, Aug. 29–30, 1862, 34
military appearance, 75
organization, 29
return to VA from East TN, 230
Sharpsburg, MD, 35
Spotsylvania, VA, 257
strength, 35, 76
Suffolk, VA, 57
surrender, 333
transferred to Law's Brigade, 20
transferred to Virginia, 31
Wilderness, VA, 234, 238, 241, 244, 246, 251
Alexander, E. Porter, 79, 82, 112, 121, 138, 186, 189,
    199, 206, 208, 213, 214, 303, 312
Alldredge, Andrew J., 376
Alldredge, Enoch, 35, 376
elected maj. 48th AL, 31
resigns commission, 67
sketch, 31, 37

Alldredge, Jesse J., 376
  promoted lt. col. 48th AL, 37
  resigns commission, 67
Alldredge, John P., 376
Alldredge, Nathan, 376
Alldredge, Van B., 376
Alston, Benjamin, 374
Amelia Court House, VA, 329
Ames, Adelbert, 308, 309, 310
Amherst Court House, VA, 334
Amissville, VA, 129
Anderson, George Thomas 'Tige', 38, 50, 53, 66, 271, 272, 303, 305
Anderson, John M., 87, 105
Anderson, Richard H., 27, 254, 255, 331, 401
  commanding First Corps, 281, 282, 289, 303
Anderson's Brigade, 77. *See* Brigades, Army of Northern Virginia, Army of Tennessee
Appleton, Thomas, 174
Appomattox Campaign
  Amelia Court House, 329, 330
  Amelia Springs and Jetersville Rd., 330
  Appomattox Court House, 332
  Clarence's Store, 327
  Farmville, 330
  Field ordered to Petersburg, 326
  Field's Division evacuates Petersburg, 327
  Indian Town Creek works, 327
  Lee surrenders, 333
  Lee's farewell message, 334
  Lee's planned evacuation route, 327
  Longstreet forms his last line of battle, 333
  paroles, 333
  Perry's Brigade
    strength, 333
  Rice's Station, 330
  Richmond and Danville Railroad, 329
  River Rd., 327
  surrender ceremonies, 335
Appomattox Court House, VA, 335, 337
Archibald, John G., 335
  color bearer at Gettysburg, 104
  sketch, 253
Arkansas Artillery
  1st Battery, 154
Arkansas Infantry
  3rd, 82, 87, 145, 188, 189, 190
Army of the Cumberland, 201
  Brigades
    First, Third Division, XIV Corps, 159
    First, Third Division, XX Corps, 390
    Second, Third Division, XIV Corps, 159
    Second, Third Division, XX Corps, 390
  Corps
    XI, 183, 185, 190, 195, 196
    XII, 183, 185, 394
    XIV, 143, 151
    XX, 143

    XXI, 143, 148, 151
  Divisions
    First, XXI Corps, 148
    Fourth, XIV Corps, 151, 159
    Second, XXI Corps, 151
    Third, XI Corps, 159, 190
    Third, XIV Corps, 159
    Third, XXI Corps, 148, 159
  organization, 143
Army of the James, 280, 308, 312
  Brigades
    First, First Division, X Corps, 291, 293
    Third, First Division, X Corps, 291
  Corps
    X, 289, 291, 292, 293, 302, 308, 309, 312, 407
    XVIII, 313, 407
  Divisions
    First, X Corps, 291, 308
    First, XXIV Corps, 330
    Third, X Corps, 308
Army of Northern Virginia, 18, 47, 63, 66, 80, 255, 294, 301, 308, 328, 330, 338
  Artillery
    German (South Carolina) Artillery, 112, 116
    Hart's (South Carolina) Artillery, 113
    Pegram's Battery, 284
    Rowan's (North Carolina) Artillery, 82, 85, 112, 116, 118
  Brigades
    Anderson's, 38, 53, 62, 70, 82, 96, 112, 128, 269, 270, 271, 288, 299, 303, 404. *See also* G. T. Anderson
    Benning's, 82, 91, 93, 96, 119, 121, 128, 129, 130, 141, 143, 235, 288, 293, 296, 326, 404. *See also* H. L. Benning
    Bratton's, 303, 326
    Bryan's, 271
    Elliott's, 404
    First or Texas Brigade, 9, 10
    Gregg's, 235, 236, 257, 281, 301, 404. *See also* J. Gregg
    Henagan's, 256
    Hood's, 282
    Humphreys's, 256
    Jenkins's, 138, 235, 250, 404. *See also* M. Jenkins
    Lane's, 293
    Law's. *See* Law's Brigade
    McGowan's, 293
    Perry's, 318. *See also* Law's Brigade
    Provisional, 304
    Robertson's, 81, 82, 93, 128, 131, 145. *See also* J. B. Robertson
    Third, Jackson's Division, 31. *See also* W. B. Taliaferro, W. E. Starke
    Third, Whiting's division, 9, 10, 13, 16
    Trimble's, 24, 39, 304
    Wofford's, 270
    Wright's, 18, 27

Cavalry
  F. Lee's Division, 289, 330. *See also* F. Lee
Corps
  First, xvi, 18, 47, 52, 68, 71, 75, 76, 79, 80, 81,
    82, 120, 123, 127, 128, 130, 138, 139, 230, 231,
    234, 235, 236, 253, 254, 255, 267, 269, 276,
    280, 281, 284, 286, 300, 304, 315, 320, 322,
    326, 329, 330, 331, 332, 335
  Jackson's, 37
  Longstreet's, 20, 27
  Second, 18, 20, 66, 68, 123, 126, 230, 327, 335
  Third, 66, 68, 71, 123, 129, 230, 236, 287, 299.
    See also A. P. Hill
Divisions
  Anderson's, 27, 250
  Ewell's, 24
  Field's, 43, 66, 230, 235, 236, 248, 255, 263,
    281, 282, 284, 286, 287, 289, 293, 297,
    305, 313, 326, 327, 404, 407, 409. *See also*
    C. W. Field
  Heth's, 235, 236, 287, 327, 337. *See also* H.
    Heth
  Hoke's, 269, 404
  Hood's, 24, 38, 45, 46, 47, 48, 50, 51, 52, 53, 58,
    65, 66, 68, 76, 77, 79, 80, 81, 82, 85, 91, 95,
    109, 111, 119, 128, 134, 143, 144, 154, 158,
    378. *See also* J. B. Hood
  Johnson's, 283
  Kershaw's, 230, 235, 236, 240, 255, 269, 289.
    See also J. B. Kershaw
  Mahone's, 299
  McLaw's, 16, 38, 66, 80. *See also* L. McLaws
  Pickett's, 45, 47, 53, 66, 230, 269, 281, 282, 283,
    378. *See also* G. E. Pickett
  Whiting's, 10, 11, 13
  Wilcox's, 235, 293, 327
  organization, 13, 18, 66, 230, 327
  position, April 1864, 230, 231
  surrender, 335
  unit designations, xvii
Army of Northern Virginia, Association of, 340
Army of the Ohio, 201
  Artillery
    2nd New York Light Artillery, 209
    2nd U.S. Artillery, 209
  Corps
    IX, 202, 204, 209
    XXIII, 204, 211
  Divisions
    First, IX Corps, 205, 209
    Second, IX Corps, 209
    Second, XXIII Corps, 204, 205
Army of the Potomac
  Artillery
    4th New York Battery, III Corps, 82, 83, 85, 87,
      94
    Independent Artillery Brigade, 240

Brigades
  First (Iron Brigade), Fourth Division, V Corps, 240
  First, Second Division, II Corps, 240
  First, Second Division, IX Corps, 250, 400
  First, Second Division, XVIII Corps, 271
  Second, Second Division, V Corps, 240
  Second, Second Division, VI Corps, 240
  Second, Second Division, IX Corps, 250, 251,
    400
  Second, Second Division, XVIII Corps, 271
  Second, Fourth Division, V Corps, 240
  Third, Third Division, 91, 95
  Third, Fourth Division, II Corps, 240
  Third, Second Division, II Corps, 240
Cavalry
  First Brigade, Third Division, 113
  Reserve Brigade, First Division, 113
  Second Brigade, Third Division, 129
Corps
  II, xiv, 235, 240, 287, 289, 291, 297
  III, 83
  V, xiv, 91, 95, 256, 271, 284
  VI, 246, 271
  IX, 250
  XVIII, 271
  XXIV, 330
Divisions
  First, XXIV Corps, 83, 91
  Fourth, V Corps, 235, 240
  Second, II Corps, 240, 291
  Second, IX Corps, 250
  Second, XVIII Corps, 271
  Third, II Corps, 235, 297
Army of the Shenandoah, 5
  Third Brigade, 5
Army of Tennessee, 396
  Brigades
    Anderson's, 205
    Bate's, 144, 151
    Benning's, 158, 164, 170. *See also* H. L.
      Benning
    Brown's, 144, 146, 151, 154
    Clayton's, 146, 151
    Deas's, 158, 161, 171, 172
    Fulton's, 148, 151, 158
    Gregg's, 158
    Humphreys's, 215. *See also* B. G. Humphreys
    Jenkins's, 178, 186, 204, 223, 392
    Kershaw's, 170
    Law's. *See* Law's Brigade
    McNair's, 158, 162
    Robertson's, 158, 170, 185, 188, 191, 193, 200,
      211, 212, 213, 215, 396. *See also* J. B.
      Robertson, Robertson's Brigade, Gregg's
      Brigade, Hood's Brigade, Army of Northern
      Virginia
  Corps
    Buckner's, 144
    First, 177, 179, 195, 219, 221, 222

Longstreet's, 158
Divisions
  Buckner's, 396
  Hindman's, 161
  Hood's, 173, 177, 178, 179, 181, 197, 206,
    395. *See also* J. B. Hood
  Johnson's, 144, 158, 161
  McLaws's, 205, 206, 223
  Pickett's, 177
  Stewart's, 144, 148, 154
  organization, 143, 157
Arsenal Academy, 2
Ashby's Gap, VA, 127
Ashland, VA, 47, 269
Atlanta, GA, 27, 174, 337
Atlee's Station, VA, 269
Atwell, James A., 186
Auburn, AL, 28, 29
Augusta, GA, 27, 142, 174, 219
Austin, John P., 185
Avery, Sanders, 252, 400

B

Babbitt, Amzi, 333, 406
Bachman, William K., 75, 113, 116
Bachman's batteries. *See* William K. Bachman; *see also*
  German Artillery, South Carolina Artillery
Baker, Eli A., 267
Baker, Myron, 170
Ballard, William, 168
Baltimore and Ohio Railroad, 35
Baltimore, MD, 37, 122, 336, 337
Bane, John P., 105
Barker, John F., 55
Barnes, Sidney, 159, 161, 166
Bartow, Florida, 341
Bartow (Florida) *Courier-Informant*, 340
Barziza, Decimus Ultimus, 99
Bass, Washington P., 251
Bate, William B., 144, 148, 151
Batey, Thomas, 174
Battery Rosecrans, 48
Battle Mountain, VA
  skirmish at, 129
Battles and Leaders of the Civil War, 340
Baxter, Henry, 240, 243, 248
Bean's Station, TN, 215
  skirmish at, 215
Beasley, William W., 335, 345
Beatty, Jesse E., 141
Beatty, Samuel, 151, 166, 389
Beatty, Thomas K., 48
Beaty, William, 405
Beaumont, Fletcher, 170, 171
Beauregard, Pierre G. T., 9, 19, 139, 280, 281, 317, 322,
  323
Becker, Winns P., 28, 119

Bee, Bernard Elliott, 6
  Jackson christened Stonewall, 8
Belle Fonte, AL, 283
Belo, Alford H., 55
  issued challenge to duel, 60
  participated in duel, 60, 61
  sketch, 379
Benjamin, Judah P., 320, 329
Benning, Henry Lewis, 66, 128, 129, 130, 132, 133,
  149, 154, 178, 186, 196, 198, 199, 200, 385
  attorney for Law, 221
Benning's Brigade, 66. *See* Brigades, Army of North-
  ern Virginia, Army of Tennessee. *See also* H. L.
  Benning
Benton, AL, 337
Bentonville, NC, 324
Berdan, Hiram, 83
Bibb County, AL, 28, 65
Billingsley, Martin, 174
Birney, David B., 235, 236, 243, 291, 293
Birney, William, 308
Birtwistle, James, 52
Black, John L., 113
Blain's Cross Roads, TN, 215, 216
Bledsoe County, TN, 31
Bliss, Zenas R., 250, 400
Blount County, AL, 29, 337
Blountsville, AL, 338
Boggs, Francis J., 58
Bond, Frank S., 159
Boonsboro Gap, MD, 14, 16
Boothly, Frank, 257, 258, 396
Botsford, Theophilus F., 168, 170, 330
  compiled history of 4th AL, xvii
  Lookout Valley, TN, 181, 184
Bowles, Pinckney Downey, 9, 217, 265
  Cold Harbor, VA, 270, 271, 272, 274, 275
  commanding Law's Brigade, 289, 290, 300, 302,
    407
  Darbytown Rd., 305, 307, 309, 310, 312
  Ft. Harrison, 303, 304
  issued brig. gen. commission, 329
  orders execution, 314, 315
  promoted col. 4th AL, 18
  signs petition to Cooper, 397
  sketch, 3
  under arrest, 76
  Wilderness, VA, 237, 238 240, 241, 243, 244, 245,
    246, 247, 248, 250, 252, 253, 254
Bowling Green, KY, 341
Bozeman, David L., 54, 55, 59, 257, 258, 379
  burial, 401
  sketch, 257
Bradford, W. D., 54
Bragg, Braxton, 138, 139, 142, 143, 144, 145, 156, 157,
  161, 176, 178, 180, 183, 185, 186, 194, 195, 196,
  201, 213, 222, 223, 316, 322, 394
Bragg, Edward, 257

Brainard, Henry C., 67, 103
Brandon, Francis Thomas Jefferson, 34, 37, 132
Brannan, John M., 159, 161, 162, 164
Brannan's division. *See* J. M. Brannan
Brannon, Robert W., 145
Bratton, John, 186, 188, 189, 190, 195, 196, 198, 199, 202, 205, 223, 288, 291, 292, 299, 303, 305, 307
Brazile, John H., 174
Breare, Joseph, 108, 123, 384
Breckenridge, John C., 195, 329
Breedlove, John P., 122, 125
Bridgeport, AL, 182, 183
Bristol, TN, 230
Brown, Baylis, 248, 401
Brown, James H., 328
Brown, Jep, 257
Brown, John C., 144, 154
Brown, Pulaski, 278
Brown's Ferry, TN, 181, 183, 185, 186, 188, 189
    captured by the Federals, 183
Bryan, Goode, 271, 272
Buckner, Simon B., 143, 144, 221
Buell, George P., 161, 166
Bulger, Michael Jefferson, 40, 132, 133, 263, 265, 288, 335, 343
    Gettysburg, PA, 85, 90, 96, 100, 109
        attack on Little Round Top, 101
        captured on Little Round Top, 107, 109, 110
        commanding 47th, 88
        opposed to secession, 1, 288
        reported dead, 122
        wounded, 101, 383
    promoted lt. col. 47th AL, 34
    wounded, Cedar Mountain, 32
Bull's Gap, TN, 230
Bunker Hill, VA, 16, 127
Burk, Francis, 119
Burnside, Ambrose E., 182, 201, 202, 204, 205, 206, 208, 213, 216, 223, 250
Burson, Elkanah, 336
Burton, Joseph Quarterman, 336
    compiled history of 47th AL, xvii
Butler, Benjamin F., 280, 281, 308, 309, 312
Butler, Matthew Calbraith, 322, 324
Byington, Cornelius, 209, 210

C

Calhoun County, AL, 29
Callaway, William, 245
Calloway, Frank B., 380
Cameron brigade, 396
Cameron, Daniel, 211
Camp, Henry, 310, 312
Camp life, 5, 8, 25, 37, 46, 71, 72, 231, 232, 234, 236
    enroute to Gettysburg, 74, 75, 76
    great snowfall fight, 38
    Potomac River, 71
    return to VA from PA, July 1863, 127
    snowfall enroute to Suffolk, VA, 47
    whiskey issued, 71
    winter quarters, 20, 37, 38, 313
        1863–1864, 117, 215, 396, 397
        1864–1865, 321, 322, 409, 409
Campbell Court House, VA, 330
Campbell, James McDonald, 32, 37, 40, 109, 119, 125,
    burial, 401
    commanding 47th AL, 101, 230, 238, 244, 252
    confrontation with Col. Oliver, 34
    elected capt., 34
    elected maj. 47th AL, 34
    killed, 262, 263
    minister to the troops, 137
    petitions War Dept. for promotion, 133
    promotion opposed by Law, xv, 132
    seeks promotion to lt. col., 132, 133
    wounded, 32
Campbell's Station, TN, 202, 204, 205, 206, 208, 223
Cantey, James, 21, 23, 40
    elected col. 15th AL, 21
    transferred from 15th AL, 25
Carman, Ezra Ayers, 151
Carolina Infantry
    2nd, 296
Carroll, Samuel S., 240, 241, 243, 244, 248
Carroll, W. H., 137
Carter, Thomas, 126
Cary, George Walton, 94, 119, 246, 262, 270, 271, 275, 276, 333
    commanding 44th AL, 148
    wounded, 297
Cary, Robert E., 174
Cashtown, PA, 76
Cassady, Calvin, 404
Catoosa Station, GA, 143
Cedar Bluff, AL, 339
Cedar Grove, AL, 283
Cedar Run, VA, 23, 31. *See also* 15th, 47th, 48th AL
Central Female College, 28
Chamberlain, Joshua Lawrence, 95, 96, 101, 103, 104, 106, 107, 108, 109, 110, 111, 335
    capture of Bulger, 385
    captures Wicker, 384
    charges 15th AL, 107
        prisoners, 384
    extends line to meet 15th AL, 103
    orders charge against 15th AL, 106, 384
    sketch, 95
    views advance on Little Round Top, 103
    withdraws support for Oates's petition, 343
Chambersburg, PA, 75
Champion, Frank D., 374
Chancellorsville battlefield, 232
Chapman, Frank G., 138
Chapman, J. Luny, 404

Charleston *Evening News*, 2
Charleston, SC, 122, 336
Charlotte and South Carolina Railroad, 323
Charlotte, NC, 27, 141
Charlottesville, VA, 221, 230, 334
    General Hospital, 275
Chattanooga and Nashville Railroad, 186
Chattanooga, TN, 139, 211, 213
Cherokee County, AL, 34, 37, 263
Chester, SC, 178, 315
Chester Station, VA, 281
Chestnut, Mary, 5
Chickamauga, GA. *See also* Law's Brigade, 4th AL,
    15th AL, 44th AL, 47th AL, 48th AL, B. Bragg,
    D. Coleman, J. M. Connell, J. T. Croxton, J. B.
    Hood, E. M. Law, J. Longstreet, E. McNair, W.
    C. Oates, W. F. Perry, J. T. Reynolds, W. S.
    Rosecrans, C. Sugg, T. J. Wood
    battlefield description, 143, 164, 388
    First Corps route from Virginia, 139
    Sep. 19, 1863
        44th AL position, 151
        Brock field, 154
        Brotherton house, 148
        casualties, 154
        Confederate positions, 144
        LaFayette Rd., 143, 144, 145, 146, 148, 149, 151,
            154, 156
        Snodgrass Hill, 144
    Sep. 20, 1863
        attack on Lytle Hill, 171
        Brotherton house, 159, 161, 164, 171
        Confederate center, 158
        Confederate positions, 158
        controversy over the captured guns, 170
        Dyer Field, 161, 162, 164, 166, 167, 170, 171,
            172, 173
        Federal flank crumbles, 161
        Federal guns are overrun, 167, 168
        Federal right, 159
        Federals leave a gap, 158
        LaFayette Rd., 157, 158, 159, 161, 162, 164, 171
        Snodgrass Hill, 162, 166, 167, 170, 172, 173
        spoils of war, 170, 174
Chilton, Robert Hall, 18, 28, 177
Chilton, William P., 397
Christian, Thomas L., 101, 109, 122, 246, 329, 333, 406,
    397, 410
    exchanged, 122
    recommended for field commission, 325
Church, Josiah, 159, 162, 164, 389
Citadel Academy, 2
City Point, VA, 122, 300, 337
Clanharty, Charles W., 188
Clark, Dr., 110
Clark's Mountain, VA, 232
Claysville, AL, 31
Clayton, Henry D., 144

Clements, Salathiel, 328
Cleveland, TN, 201
Clopton, David, 16, 177, 316, 397
Clower, Eli Daniel, 134, 167, 333
    sketch, 144
Cobb, Lemuel, 304
Cody, Barnett H., 67, 103
Coffee County, AL, 301
Coggin, Ebernezer B., 174
    sketch, 156
Coker, James L., 195
    sketch, 394
Cold Harbor, VA, 270, 271, 272, 274, 275. *See also*
    P. D. Bowles, E. M. Law, J. H. Martindale, W. C.
    Oates, W. F. Smith, Law's Brigade
    Jun. 1, 1864, 269
    Jun. 2, 1864
        Kershaw's position, 269
        Law's Brigade constructs fortifications, 270
        sharpshooting, 275, 276
    Jun. 3, 1864
        25th MA charges Law's position, 274
        Anderson's position, 270
        Federal attack on Law's position, 271, 272, 274
        Federal wounded in front of Law's position, 275
        Law's position, 270
        Martindale's first assault, 272, 276
        Martindale's first repulse, 272
        Martindale's second assault, 272
        Martindale's second repulse, 274
    sharpshooting, 275
    truce to bury Federals, 276
Coleman, David, 170, 171
    commanding McNair's Brigade, 162, 166, 167, 168,
        170
Coleman, Thomas K., 9, 53, 124, 132, 174, 175
    commanding 4th AL, 88, 98, 99, 146, 164
    mortally wounded, 164
    promoted maj., xv
    promoted maj. 4th AL, 18
Coles, Robert Thompson, 8, 48, 53, 59, 70, 71, 72,
    88, 98, 99, 105, 114, 130, 141, 142, 145, 156,
    158, 181, 184, 208, 209, 214, 217, 230, 235, 236,
    244, 248, 251, 252, 257, 260, 265, 274, 276, 282,
    283, 302, 331, 332, 337, 395
    compiled history of 4th AL, xvii
Columbia, SC, 27, 48, 141, 322, 323
Columbus, GA, 63
Confederate Ships
    CSS *Richmond*, 50
    CSS *Virginia*, 54
Confederate Veteran, xvii
Connally, John K., 52, 55, 57, 59, 60
Connecticut Infantry
    6th, 291
    8th, 56
    10th, 291, 307, 310, 311
    14th, 243

Connell, John M., 159, 161, 162, 164, 166
Connell's brigade. *See* John M. Connell
Conner, James, 293
Conscript Act, 25
Cooke, Dr. J. P., 136
Cooper, Samuel, 64, 138, 214, 219, 220, 221, 222, 277, 316, 317
Corbin, Richard W., 287, 292, 293, 313, 320
    taunted by Field's division, 404
Corse, Montgomery D., 128
Court-martials, 39, 67
Covington, GA, 142, 338
Coward, Asbury, 3, 178, 296, 340
Crittenden, Thomas, 143, 166, 167
Croxton, John T., 159, 162, 164, 173
Croxton's brigade, 159. *See* J. T. Croxton
Crowder, James Preston, 134, 174, 180, 231
Cruft, Charles, 151, 154
Culpeper, VA, 66, 127, 129, 130
Cumberland Gap, TN, 139
Cunningham, George A., 55, 58
Curry, Jabez L. M., 397
Cushing, Harry, 166, 167, 390.*See also* 4th U.S.Artillery
Cushing, William B., 51, 54
Cussons, John, 54, 57, 62, 318, 340
    captured, Gettysburg, 112
    challenged to duel, 60
    coolness under fire at Gettysburg, 109
    exchanged, 122
    Federal prisoner, 122
    opinion on relations between Law and Longstreet, xv
    participated in duel, 60, 61
Custer, George A., 128, 129, 130
Cutler, Lysander, 240, 243, 248, 258, 260, 262, 401

D

Dadeville, AL, 28
Dale County, AL, 301
Dalton, GA, 4, 213
Dandridge, TN, 214
    skirmish at, Jan. 16–17, 1864, 216
Daniel, James Barrett, 35, 37, 46, 50, 75, 127, 180, 230, 231, 266, 274
Daniel, John Wilhite Lewis, 21
    elected maj. 15th AL, 21
Danville, VA, 329
Darbytown Rd., VA
    Oct. 7, 1864
        Gregg mortally wounded, 307
        Law's Brigade attack on Federal right, 305, 307
    Oct. 13, 1864
        10th CT attack on Law's Brigade, 310
        Federal attack, 309
        Law's Brigade, 309
        strength, 310
    Oct. 27, 1864
        casualties, 313

Dargan, Edmund S., 16, 397
Darlington, SC, 275
Darwin, John Taylor, 87
Davies, James K., 404
Davis, Jefferson C., 161, 388
Davis, President Jefferson, 9, 10, 45, 138, 141, 177, 186, 194, 201, 213, 217, 220, 221, 222, 224, 277, 298, 305, 310, 314, 315, 316, 317, 318, 319, 327, 398
    disagreement with Longstreet, 219
    favors Law for maj. gen., 179
    favors state brigades, 13, 19, 374
    position on charges against Law, 222
    rebukes Longstreet for charges against Law, 222
Dawson, Lemuel H., 333
Dawson, Nathaniel H. R., 9
Dawson, T. H., 154
Dean, Joseph P., 320
Deas, Zachariah C., 9, 158, 161, 171
Defnall, William J., 406
    color bearer at Fussell's Mill, 297
    sketch, 297
De Fontaine, Felix G., 195
DeKalb County, AL, 29
Dell, James O., 211
Dement, J. J., 337
Dent, Staunton H., 158
Department of North Carolina (Confederate), 47
Department of North Carolina and Southern Virginia (Confederate)
    Divisions
        Hoke's, 303, 305
Department of Richmond (Confederate), 47, 292
    Brigades
        Hughs's, 288
    Cavalry
        Gary's, 293, 297, 305
Derby, Charles A., 28
    elected lt. col. 44th AL, 25
    promoted col. 44th AL, 28
Deserters, 131, 141, 143, 142, 284, 288, 290, 301, 307, 312, 313, 314, 315, 320, 324, 339, 397, 408
    Lee offers amnesty, 315
    punishment, 39
Dexter, Charles T., 27
Dick, George F., 151
Dickson, Alvin O., 102, 337, 376, 383
Dinwiddie Court House, VA, 326
Downsville, VA, 125
Drake, Richard, 406
DuBose, Dudley M.
    commanding Benning's Brigade, 296, 301, 302
Dunklin, William, 121
Dutton, Arthur H., 64, 65

E

Early, Jubal A., 31, 232, 289, 297, 401

East Alabama Female Institute, 28
East Tennessee and Virginia Railroad, 208, 216
Edwards, A. J., 334
Edwards, Daniel B., 379
Edwards, James R., 295
Edwards, Jeremiah, 119, 123
Edwards, John F., 223
Edwards, Oliver, 247
Edwards, William A., 76
Edwards, Young M., 320
Elliott, Stephen, 404
Elliott, Wyatt, 407
Ellison, James H., 103
Elzey, Arnold, 47
Emmitsburg, MD, 84
Estep, George, 166, 167, 168. *See also* 8th Indiana
    Battery
Eubanks, John B., 338
Eubanks, Thomas James, 67, 94, 119, 186
    commanding 48th, Gettysburg, 105
    killed, Lookout Valley, TN, 188, 393
Eufaula, AL, 63, 339
Eustis, Henry L., 246
Evergreen, AL, 67
Ewell, Richard S., 24, 230, 234, 288, 308, 331
Ewing, Reuben, 119
Executions, 314

F

Fairfax, John Walter, 84
Farmville, VA, 330
Farnsworth, Elon J., 113, 114, 116, 118, 385
    death, 118. *See also* Gettysburg, PA, July 3, 1863
        Farnsworth's Charge
Fayetteville, NC, 28, 75
Fayetteville, PA, 75
Feagin, Isaac Ball, 24, 25, 63, 67, 277, 297
    appointed lt. col. 15th AL, 63, 277
    arrested, 39
    organization of 15th AL, 21
    wounded, 24, 87
Feagin, Noah Baxter, 20, 65, 184
Federal armies
    unit designations, xvii
Federal prisons
    Ft. Delaware, MD, 291, 338
    Hampton, VA, 211
    Johnson's Island, OH, 122, 123, 211, 338, 339
Ferguson, Thomas C., 297
Ferrero, Edward, 205, 209
Field hospitals, 236
Field, Charles William, 221, 256, 260, 266, 267, 271,
    277, 281, 282, 283, 287, 288, 289, 290, 293, 295,
    296, 298, 299, 300, 302, 303, 304, 307, 308, 309,
    312, 313, 317, 321, 327, 330, 340. *See also* Field's
    Division, Army of Northern Virginia
    assigned command of Hood's Division, 220

Chester Station, VA, 281, 282
Fussell's Mill, VA
    complimented by Lee, 297
    moves toward North Anna River, 266
    reviews division, 231
    sketch, 220
    Wilderness, VA
        commanding division, 235, 238, 248, 250
Figures, Henry Stokes, 59, 68, 71, 72, 74, 75, 79, 94,
    148, 214, 253
Flags
    4th AL, 4, 269, 335
    15th AL, 335
    44th AL, 335
    47th AL, 230, 335
    48th AL, 336
Flint Hill, VA, 128
Florence, AL, 8
Florence, SC, 139
Forney, William, 337, 342
Forte, James L., 94
Fortykins, xiv, 25, 142
Foster, Robert A., 291, 296
Fowler, Henry Fowler, xvii
Franks, Rufus B., 85, 98
Frazer, John W., 139
Frazier, Robert L., 137
Frederick Hall, VA, 66
Fredericksburg, VA, 18, 38, 131, 134, 136, 232
French, Samuel G., 47, 48, 52, 55, 58, 59, 62, 64,
    178
Front Royal, VA, 128
Ft. Delaware, MD, 122
Ft. Gilmer, VA, 302
Ft. Harrison, VA, 303
    captured by Federals, 301, 302
    Confederate attempt to recapture, 303, 304
    Confederate forces, 303
    description of the fort, 302
Ft. McHenry, MD, 37, 122
Ft. Mitchell, AL, 21
Ft. Monroe, VA, 37, 122
Ft. Pulaski, GA, 122
Fulton, John S., 148, 149, 158
Fussell's Mill, VA, 287
    Aug. 14, 1864
        Confederate defensive positions, 291
        Field's line, 292
        Law's Brigade, 292
        New Market Rd., 292
    Aug. 16, 1864
        15th and 48th AL counterattack, 293, 295
        attack on Field, 293
        Confederate positions, 293
    Charles City Rd., 292, 293
    Deep Bottom, 295
    Four Mile Creek, 291, 292
    James River, 292

Kingsland Rd. 291
New Market Heights, 292, 293, 297
New Market Rd., 292

G

Gadsden, AL, 337
Gaines Cross Roads, VA, 128, 129
Gaines's Mill, VA, 10, 11
Galloway, William H.
  last promotion in Perry's Brigade, 324
Gaplin, Charles R., 210
Gardner, Benjamin, 21
Garfield, James A., 159
Garmon, Albert, 39
Garnett, Thomas S., 31, 32
Gary, Martin W., 288, 293, 297, 305, 308, 312
Gaskin, James L., 304
Gathright, Thomas, 407
Geary, Edward R., 189, 393
Geary, John W., 185, 186, 188, 189, 190, 194, 196
Georgia Infantry
  Anderson's Brigade, 205
    1st, 34
    3rd Battalion Sharpshooters, 209, 210
    7th, 113
    8th, 113, 292
    9th, 113, 116, 293
    11th, 11, 113, 223, 293
    15th, 296
    17th, 296
    18th, 11
    20th, 296
    21st, 14, 16
    37th, 151, 154
    59th, 113, 292
    64th, 284
Getty, George Washington, 53, 54, 55, 56, 57, 64, 240, 246, 399
Gettysburg National Military Park, 337, 342
Gettysburg, PA, 76, 78, 127. See also Law's Brigade, 4th AL, 15th AL, 44th AL, 47th AL, 48th AL, L. Chamberlain, E. M. Law, R. Lee, J. Longstreet, L. McLaws, W. C. Oates, W. F. Perry, J. E. Smith, S. Vincent, E. Walker
  Jul. 2, 1863
    15th AL attacks 20th ME, 101, 103, 104
    20th ME charges 15th AL, 106, 107
    47th AL attacks 20th ME, 101
    attack on Devil's Den, 91, 93, 94
    attack on Vincent's center, 96
    attack on Vincent's right, 105
    battlefield description, 78
    Bushman house, 79, 85
    casualties, 111
    Chamberlain charges 15th AL, 106, 107, 108
    Currens house, 113
    deployment on Federal left, 82, 91

Devil's Den captured, 93
Emmitsburg Rd., 78, 79, 80, 81, 82, 83, 84, 87, 93, 95, 113
Houck Ridge, 78, 82
John E. Planck farm, 111
Little Round Top, 79, 80, 95, 96, 98, 99, 104, 105, 106, 109
Pickett's Charge, 112
Round Top, 76, 78, 81, 82, 83, 84, 85, 88, 90, 91, 93, 94, 95, 96, 99, 100, 101, 108, 109
Slyder house, 76, 78, 79, 83, 88, 90
strength, 76
Warfield Ridge, 78, 79, 80, 82
  Jul. 3, 1863
    Bushman house, 113
    Currens house, 113
    Emmitsburg Rd., 113, 118, 119
    Farnsworth's Charge, 113, 116, 385, 385
    Hood's Division withdraws to Emmitsburg Rd., 119
    Kern house, 385
    Pickett's Charge, 118
    Round Top, 116
    Slyder house, 114
  Jul. 5, 1863
    Confederates withdraw, 123
    treatment, captured wounded, 385
Gibbon, John, 240, 399
Girardey, Victor J. B., 293
Glass, E. Jones, xv, 18
Glaze, Anderson, 170
Glen Allen, VA, 122
Glover, Henry W., 309
Goggin, James M., 223
Goldsby, Thomas J., 6, 9
  elected lt. col. 4th AL, 9
  sketch, 379
Golightly, Robert C., 35
  commanding 47th, 35
Goodson, Joab, 27, 38, 146, 158, 164, 174, 183, 214, 231, 286, 324, 379
Goodson, Rufus 'Rufe', 142, 287
Gordon, John B., 327, 330, 331, 332, 335
Gordonsville, VA, 139, 223, 230
Grant, Lewis A., 240, 244
Grant, U. S., 185, 202, 213, 231, 232, 250, 255, 266, 269, 271, 280, 286, 289, 297, 300, 301, 304, 308, 309, 312, 313, 325, 326, 327, 329, 330, 332, 333, 334, 335
Graves, Randolph, 87
Greencastle, PA, 72
Greensboro, NC, 324
Greenville, AL, 301
Greenville, GA, 28, 131
Gregg, John, 235, 282, 288, 289, 293, 299, 303, 307, 308. See also Gregg's Brigade, Army of Northern Virginia, Army of Tennessee
Grice, James M., 335

Grice, John G., 67
Griffin, Simon G., 250, 400
Griffin, William Alexander, 27, 272
Grose, William, 151, 154
Guerry, Lagrand L., 295

H

Hagerstown, MD, 125
Halleck, Henry W., 136, 139, 185
Halsey, Charles T., 88, 382
Ham, John, 252, 322
Hamilton, James, 84, 197
Hamilton, T. A., 394
Hamilton's Crossing, VA, 38
Hampton, VA, 9, 211
Hampton, Wade, 318, 322, 323, 324, 340
Hancock, Winfield S., 235, 250, 288, 289, 290, 292, 293, 296, 297, 298
Hanover Junction, VA, 45, 334
Haralson, Frank, 6
Hardee, Joseph, 9, 195
Hardee, William J., 316
Hardships
   Mobile Bread Riots, 301
   shortages in Alabama, 301
Hardwick, William McTyiere, 40, 119, 132, 136, 144, 278, 339, 403
   captured, 325
   last officer of Law's Brigade released from prison, 339
   promoted maj. 48th AL, 37, 67
   signs petition to transfer Law's Brigade, 397
Hardwicksville, AL, 339
Harker, Charles G., 148, 149, 161, 170, 172
Harkey, Reuben C., 56, 57
Harper, Cincinnatus, 409
Harpers Ferry, VA, 24
Harris, T. A., 51
Harrison, Jesse, 11
Hart, J. F., 113
Hartranft, John F., 204, 206
Hartsfield, James F., 329, 334, 338
Harvie, Edwin J., 18
Hatcher, James J., 237, 339
Hawkins, Ephraim, 404
Hazen, William B., 183, 184
Hazlett, Charles, 98, 104
Head, Edmond P., 130
Hecker, Frederick, 199
Henagan, John W., 256
Henry County, AL, 339
Henry, M. W., 378
Hentz, Robert Eugene, 254
Herstein, Robert, 338
Heth, Henry, 234, 252, 287, 327, 337, 400
High Point, NC, 336
Hill, Ambrose Powell, 1, 66, 129, 130, 230, 234, 235, 327

Hill, Blanton Abram, 106
   commanding 15th AL, Gettysburg, 108
   mortally wounded, 295
Hill, Daniel H., 24, 39, 47, 143, 201
Hill, James M., 324
Hill, Robert H., 23
Hilliard's Legion, 21
Hindman, Thomas Carmichael, 157, 158
Hinds, James M., 405
Hocutt, Lorenzo W., 297
Hogg, Samuel, 76
Hoke, Robert F., 43, 270, 303, 307, 308, 312, 315, 404, 407
Holden, William W., 141
Hollis, Rufus, 302, 314, 334
Hood, John Bell, 10, 11, 13, 14, 16, 18, 66, 70, 71, 120, 277, 387
   Chickamauga, GA, 144, 145, 156
   commanding First Corps, 143
   commanding Longstreet's Corps, 158, 161
   joins troops in Richmond, 139
   severely wounded, 170
   supports Jenkins for maj. gen., 179
   supports Law for maj. gen., 179
   Gettysburg, PA, 79, 80, 81, 82, 84, 85, 87
      deploys for battle, 81
      protests plan of attack, 81, 84, 85
      severely wounded, xv, 85
      wounded, 382
   promoted maj. gen., 18
   Suffolk, VA, 45, 52, 53, 55, 58, 59, 62, 63, 64
Hood, Joseph Nathaniel, 34, 156
Hood's Brigade. *See* Brigades (First or Texas), Army of Northern Virginia
Hood's Division. *See* Divisions, Army of Northern Virginia, Army of Tennessee
Hooker, Joseph E., 63, 64, 66, 68, 71, 183, 185, 186, 199
Hornbuckle, James, 267
Houck, John, 78
Houghton, Mitchell B., 180, 193
Howard, Oliver O., 196
Howard's Grove Hospital, 263, 307, 328
Howell, Henry, 314, 315
   executed for desertion, 314
Hubbard, John B., 267, 290
   accused of deserting, 290
   dropped from the rolls, 291
   Federal prisoner, 291
Hudson, William O., 61, 184
Huff's Ferry, TN, 202
Huger, Benjamin, 50, 53
Hughes, Abner A., 29, 35
   elected lt. col. 48th AL, 29
   resigned commission, 37
Hughs, John M., 288, 292
Hughes, John W., 261
Humphrey, William., 209

Humphreys, Benjamin G., 215
Humphreys, John T., 154
Hundley's Corner, VA, 269
Hunter, Morton C., 162
Huntsville, AL, 4, 9, 68, 74, 75, 123, 253, 254, 276,
    328, 338, 339
Huntsville (Alabama) *Democrat*, 68

I

Illinois Infantry
    39th, 310
    65th, 396
    74th, 180
    92nd, 389
Imboden, John D., 123
Indiana Infantry
    10th, 164, 170
    14th, 241
    82nd, 159, 162, 164
Indiana Artillery
    7th Battery, 166
    8th Battery, 166, 390
Indigent families, 142, 408
Infantry Tactics
    Hardee's *Manual*, 2, 3
    Scott's *Infantry Tactics*, 2
Irvin, John, 240

J

Jackson, AL, 21, 175
Jackson, James
    sketch, 8
Jackson, James Washington, 31, 32, 35, 40, 119, 131
    commanding Taliaferro's brigade, 35
    elected lt. col. 47th AL, 28
    Gettysburg, PA, 85, 88
    resigns commission, 131
    sketch, 28
Jackson, Thomas J. "Stonewall," 8, 11, 13, 23, 24, 66
    christened Stonewall, 8
    promoted maj. gen., 18
Jackson's Gap, Alabama, 265
Jackson's Hospital, 328
Jacksonville, AL, 29, 309
Jamison, D. R., 190, 197
Jasper County, GA, 37
Jefferson, VA, 27
Jemison, Robert, 283
Jenkins, Micah, 39, 52, 177, 178, 179, 180, 182, 185,
    186, 189, 190, 193, 194, 195, 196, 197, 198, 199,
    231, 250, 318, 340
    commanding Hood's Division, 205
    complains about Robertson, 395
    East TN
        censures Law, 206
        commanding Hood's division, 201, 202, 204,

    205, 208, 213, 215, 218, 219, 220, 224
        endorses Perry for brig. gen., 220
        quarrel with Law, 206, 218
    Longstreet's protégé, xv
    Lookout Valley, TN, 394
    rivalry with Law, xv, 178, 197
    sketch, 391
Johns, William N., 111
Johnson, Bushrod R., 144, 145, 157, 166, 171, 172,
    173, 213, 283, 288
Johnson, Joseph S., 65, 278
Johnson, President Andrew, 3
Johnson's Crook, TN, 185
Johnston, George D., 9
Johnston, John Y., 34
    elected maj. 47th AL, 28
Johnston, Joseph E., 5, 9, 324, 327, 334
    opposed state brigades, 375
Johnston, Joseph S., Jr., 111, 123, 131
Jones, Egbert J., xvi
    death, 9
    discord with troops, 5
    elected col. 4th AL, 4
    Manassas, VA, July 21, 1861, 6
    officers request his resignation, 5
    popular with troops, 8
    wounded, 374
Jones, James Taylor, 114, 263, 328
Jones, James W., 339
Jones, John Archibald, 40, 119, 215, 246, 258, 333
    commanding 44th AL at Chickamauga, 158
    commanding 44th AL at Suffolk, 57
    promoted maj. 44th AL, 28
    signs petition to Cooper, 397
    signs petition to transfer Law's Brigade, 397
Jones, John E., 174
    sketch, 28
Jones, Virginius, 401
Jordan, William C. "Billy", xvi, 64, 65, 129, 137, 172,
    173, 183, 184, 193, 202, 204, 209, 211, 213, 245,
    261, 282, 297, 307, 321, 329, 334, 338

K

Karsner, William F., 149, 337
    commanding 4th AL, 164
Kautz, August V., 305, 308, 309
Keils, John, 107
Keith, James H., 283
Keller, W. H., 119
Kennedy, Alsop, 87
Kent, James, 25
    attempt to eliminate alcohol, 25
    elected col. 44th AL, 25
    resigns commission, 28
Kentucky Cavalry (Confederate)
    9th, 182, 185
Kentucky Infantry (Federal)
    9th, 148

Kershaw, Joseph Brevard, 80, 81, 158, 172, 213, 250, 255, 270, 283, 287
Kershaw's Brigade. *See* Brigades, Army of Northern Virginia, Army of Tennessee
Kershaw's Division. *See* Divisions, Army of Northern Virginia
Keyes, Erasmus Darwin, 51
Kidd, Reuben Vaughan, 8, 9, 72, 127, 149, 174
Kilpatrick, Judson, 113, 114, 129, 134, 136
Kimball, Nathan Crawford, 305
King, Edward A., 159
King George Courthouse, VA, 136
    skirmish at, 134
King, James David, 175
King, Porter, 9
Kings Mountain Military Institute, 178, 340
Kingston, GA, 339
Kingston, TN, 202
Kinnebrew, H. C., 334
Kirkland, Cicero, 409
Kitching, J. Howard, 240, 245, 248
Knoxville, TN, 139, 208
    Ft. Dickerson, 208
    Ft. Higley, 208
    Ft. Sanders, 208, 209, 212, 213
    Ft. Stanley, 208
    Mabry's Hill, 212
    Military Hospital, 211
Kornegay, S. Pratt, 39
Kunzie, John L., 248

L

Lafayette, AL, 28
La Fayette, GA, 143
Laiboldt, Bernard, 161
Lamar, John, 6
Lamson, Roswell H., 51, 52, 53, 54, 55, 56, 62
Lane, David, 209
Lane, James H., 293. *See also* Lane's Brigade, Army of Northern Virginia
Lanneau, John Frances, 3
    sketch, 372
Lapsley, Robert, 324, 333
Latrobe, Osmun, 197, 211, 317
Latta, Elizabeth, 48
Latta, William A., 48
    sketch, 377
Law, Evander McIver, 2, 9, 14, 19, 29, 39, 40, 63, 67, 70, 120, 127, 267. *See also* Law's Brigade
    attempt to transfer his brigade, 391
    Chickamauga, GA
        Sep. 19, 1863, 144, 145, 148, 154, 156
        Sep. 20, 1863, 157, 158, 173
    claims right to command Hood's Division, 178
    Cold Harbor, VA
        Jun. 2, 1864, 269, 270
        ordered to reinforce line, 269

    repairs salient, 270
    Jun. 3, 1864, 272, 274, 275
    commanding Hood's Division, xvi, 128, 131, 138
    commanding Third Brigade, 9
    convalescent leave, 9, 283
    East TN, 201, 204
        arrested by Longstreet, 181, 221, 222, 398
        condemns Longstreet for failure against Burnside, 396
        Bean's Station, 215
        Campbell's Station, 205, 206, 395
        censured by Longstreet, 219, 220
        Knoxville, TN, 212, 213, 396
        lobbies for maj. gen. commission, 218
        Longstreet prefers charges, 221
        ordered to join Field's Division, 221
        quarrel with Jenkins, 218
        quarrel with Longstreet, 213, 217, 218, 221, 222, 223, 283, 284
        resigns commission, 217
        under arrest, 221, 222
    elected col. 4th AL, 9
    elected lt. col. 4th AL, 5
    first view of Lee, 10
    Gaines's Mill, VA, 10, 11
    Gettysburg, PA
        Jul. 2, 1863, 82, 83, 84, 85, 87, 90, 93, 109, 112, 113, 120
        Jul. 3, 1863, 113, 114, 118, 119
        Lookout Valley, TN, 181, 182, 183, 185, 186, 189
        accused of disobedience, Oct. 28, 1863, 197, 198
        engagement at Wauhatchie, Oct. 28, 1863, 190, 191, 193, 196
        position Oct. 28, 1863, 189
    Manassas, VA, July 21, 1861, 6
    Manassas, VA, Aug. 29–30, 1862, 13, 14
    military education, 2, 3
    opposes Campbell's promotion, xv, 132
    ordered to Gettysburg, 76
    popular with troops 5, 6
    post war, 340
        agent for *Battles and Leaders*, 340
        death, 341
        editor, 340
        establishes military school, 340
    promoted brig. gen., 16
    quarrel with Longstreet
        Cooper's ultimatum, 317
        officially relieved of brigade command, 318
        quarrel with Longstreet, xv
        refuses to serve under Longstreet, xv, 317
        resigns from brigade command, 317
        seeks transfer, 315, 316
        under arrest, 232
    quarrel with Perry, xv
    recommended for brig. gen. commission, 16
    relationship with Hood, 10
    rivalry with Jenkins, xv, 179

seeks brig. gen. commission, 10
seeks maj. gen. commission, 177, 179
service in the cavalry, 322, 323
Sharpsburg, MD, 14, 16
sketch, xiv, 2
Suffolk, VA, 53, 58, 59, 62, 64
    visited by his wife, 48
support for maj. gen. commission, 177, 178
surrendered with Johnston, 324
views on state brigades, 20
views on the war, xviii
volunteered for service, 3
wounded, 6
Law, Ezekiel Augustus, 2
Law, Sarah Elizabeth McIver, 2
Law, Thomas Hart, 372
Lawrence, John E., 18, 312
Law's Brigade, 18, 27, 38, 40, 45, 63, 66, 127, 130, 131,
    266, 269, 276, 278, 280, 281, 289, 290, 292, 299,
    300, 302, 304, 305, 311, 312, 314, 316, 318, 320,
    321, 322. *See also* Law's Brigade, 4th AL, 15th
    Al, 44th Al, 47th AL, 48th AL, J. B. Hood, E. M.
    Law, J. Longstreet, W. C. Oates, W. F. Perry
Alabama Brigade created, 19
assaults, 372
Ashby's Gap, 68
camp at Culpeper, VA, 66
camp at Millwood, 71
camped at Chambersburg, PA, 75
casualties, 267
Chattanooga, siege of, 180
Chattanooga, TN, 181
Chester Station, VA, 281, 282
    Howlett Line, 283
Chickamauga, GA
    arrives North GA, 143
    camps on the battlefield, 143
    casualties, 174
    charges artillery, 166, 167, 168, 171
    departs Chickamauga battlefield, 176
    route from Virginia, 139, 141, 142
    Sep. 19, 1863, 144, 145, 146, 148, 151, 154, 156
    Sep. 20, 1863, 157, 158, 159, 161, 171, 174
Cold Harbor, VA
    Jun. 2, 1864, 269
    Jun. 3, 1864, 270, 271, 272, 274, 275, 276
    Jun. 7, 1864, 276
Court-martials, 39
East TN, 201, 208, 211, 214, 215
    Campbell's Station, 205, 206
    departs Chattanooga, 201
    Knoxville, TN, 211, 213, 214
    officers petition for commander of choice, 219
    officers petition for transfer, 218
    officers support for Jenkins, 220
    officers support for Perry, 219
    ordered to Army of Northern Virginia, 222
    ordered to Buckner's Corps, 221

ordered to rejoin First Corps, 222
skirmish at Dandridge, Tennessee, 216
strength, 280
winter quarters, 215, 217
Fussell's Mill, VA, 291, 292, 293
    casualties, 297
Gettysburg, PA
    approach to the battlefield, 80
    casualties, 122
    deployment, 81, 82
    Gettysburg, battlefield monument, 342
    joins Hood's Division, 77
    Jul. 2, 1863, 79, 80, 82, 84, 85, 87, 90, 91, 93,
        105, 108, 109, 111
    Jul. 3, 1863, 119, 385
    Jul. 5, 1863, 125
    return to VA from PA,
        arrives Fredericksburg, 131
        Chester Gap, 128
        Manassas Gap, 128
        Warrenton Rd., 129
    strength, 76
    withdraws from the battlefield, 123
    withdraws to Emmitsburg Road, 119
Great Revival, 137
Greencastle, PA, 71, 72
Lookout Valley, TN, 183, 185
    engagement at Wauhatchie, Oct. 28, 1863, 186,
        188, 191, 199
New Guilford, PA, 75
New Market Heights, 288, 298
North Anna River, VA, 267
    astride Richmond and Fredericksburg Railroad,
        267
    march to the North Anna River, 266
Petersburg, VA, 283, 284, 287
    deserters, 284
Plum Run Valley, 88
Port Royal, VA
    48th AL skirmishes Kilpatrick, 134
    guarding forage trains, 134
    Kilpatrick attacks 48th AL, 136
    Law reviews brigade, 134
promotions, 67, 143, 263, 318
resignations, 63, 67, 265, 278, 318, 325
return to VA from East TN, 230
Spotsylvania, VA, 255, 258, 260, 262
    approach to the battlefield, 255
    assaults by Cutler, 402
    position near Crutchfield farm, 266
Suffolk, VA, 45
    casualties, 65
    constructing fortifications, 50
    departs Richmond, 46, 47
    fighting behind breastworks, 258
    Ft. Huger captured, 56
    May 3, 1863, skirmish, 64
    moves to Crutchfield farm, 263

occupies Ft. Huger, 53
  position on upper Nansemond, 53
  returns to Lee from Suffolk, 63
Wilderness, VA, 232, 237, 245, 250, 252, 253
  approach to the battlefield, 234, 235
  assault against Federals, xiv
  brigade line of battle, 238
  casualties, 253
  deploys for battle, 238
  the brigades finest hour, xvi
  retires from the field, xvi, 252
  strength, 234
  winter quarters, 38, 40
Lawton, Alexander R., 14, 24
Lee, Fitzhugh, 330, 331, 340
Lee, George Washington Curtis, 179
Lee, Moses, 29, 32, 35
Lee, Robert E., 10, 11, 14, 16, 39, 40, 45, 50, 63, 64,
    66, 68, 71, 72, 74, 75, 125, 221, 222, 230, 280,
    281, 283, 286, 289, 291, 292, 297, 298, 299, 301,
    312, 319, 320, 326, 329, 330, 333, 335, 403
  commander, Army of Northern Virginia, 10
  creates Law's Alabama Brigade, 19
  Darbytown Rd., VA, 305, 308
  desires to retain Law's Brigade, 222
  encourages Law's Brigade, xiv, 237
  evacuates Petersburg, 327
  Ft. Harrison, 301, 303
  Gettysburg, PA, 79, 80
  orders amnesty for deserters, 315
  position on Law, 318
  position on Oates's commission, 278
  position on state brigades, 19
  reorganizes army, 13, 18
  reviews First Corps, 231
  sends army toward North Anna, 266
  Spotsylvania, VA, 255, 263
  Wilderness, VA, 234, 235, 236, 254
Lee, Samuel P., 51, 52, 62
Leech, Mrs. F. J., 139
Leftwich, William W., 111, 123
Leggett, Pervical S., 136
Lenoir's Station, TN, 202, 204, 208, 223
Lewis, John, 274
Libby prison, 328
Lincoln, President Abraham, 1, 309, 326, 336, 389
Lindsay, Henry C., 32, 87, 275, 328, 383
  commanding 4th AL, 397
  signs petition to cooper, 397
  signs petition to transfer Law's Brigade, 397
Lindsay, Lewis Ervin, 283
Little, Francis H., 223
Livingston, Courtland, 166, 167, 168. *See also* 3rd
    Wisconsin Battery
Loachapoka, AL, 28, 127, 305
Local Defense Forces (Confederate), 305
Longstreet, James, xv, 13, 14, 18, 45, 46, 47, 66, 68,
    71, 75, 77, 123, 127, 128, 138, 143, 176, 178,

180, 230, 231, 234, 298, 312, 313, 317, 320, 326,
    327, 329, 330, 335, 378, 406
Chickamauga, GA, 157, 158, 161
complains about Bragg, 201
East TN, 214, 217
  advance on Knoxville, 202
  Bean's Station, 215
  Campbell's Station, 205, 206
  censures Law, 221
  crisis in the command, 206
  Knoxville, TN, 213
  quarrel with Bragg, Law, McLaws, Robertson,
    206
  quarrel with Law, 217, 218, 219, 220, 222, 223
  quarrel with McLaws, 224
  rebuked by Davis, 222
  returns to VA, 230
  siege of Knoxville, 212
  winter quarters, 215
  withdraws from Knoxville, 213
forms last line of battle at Appomattox, 333
Gettysburg, PA, 80, 81, 84, 85, 112, 118
  opposes Lee's plan of attack, 79
  praises Law for handling of troops, 118
given corps command, 13
ignores order for Campbell's examining board, 133
petitioned to promote Law, 178
promoted maj. gen., 18
requests Jenkins's Brigade, 177
returns from convalescence leave, 312, 406
Suffolk, VA, 47, 48, 50, 51, 52, 55, 58, 59, 63, 64, 65
Wauhatchie, TN, 182, 183, 185, 186, 195, 197
  blames Law for failure, 194, 198
Wilderness, VA, 235, 250
  seriously wounded, 250
Lookout Valley, TN, 181
  Brown's Ferry
    captured by the Federals, 183
    consequence of Federal occupation, 394
  engagement at Wauhatchie, Oct. 28, 1863, 186
    Federal strength, 394
    Jenkins's Brigade strength, 393
    Smith's Hill, 188, 189, 190, 191, 193, 194
      Law's position, 189
    Tyndale's Hill, 188
Louisa Court House, VA, 27, 66
Love, Henry B., 22, 74, 257, 381
Lowndes County, AL, 6
Lowther, Alexander A., 24, 40, 63, 67, 282, 315, 320,
    333
  appointed major, 23
  commanding 15th AL, 193
  Fussell's Mill, VA, 295, 296
  ordered removed from rolls, 63
  organization of 15th AL, 21
  promoted col. 15th AL, 277
  protests promotions, 67
  quarrel with Oates, xv

tendered resignation, 23
wounded, 275, 296
Lumpkin, Thomas J., 290
Lusk, John M., 174
Lynchburg, VA, 5
Lyon, F. S., 316
Lytle, William H., 161, 171, 172

M

Madison County, AL, 9, 74
Mahone, William, 299
Maine Infantry
3rd, 243
4th, 83, 91, 93, 94, 105, 121
10th, 16
11th, 291, 293, 307
20th, 95, 96, 99, 101, 103, 104, 108, 109
attacked by 15th AL, 105
charges 15th AL, 107
strength, Gettysburg, 108
Maltman, John S., 210
Manassas Gap Railroad, 68, 128
Manassas, VA
Jul. 21, 1861, 6
Buck Hill, 6
casualties, 8
August 29–30, 1862, 13, 14, 24, 27, 34
Warrenton Turnpike, 13
Manigault, Arthur M., 161
Marietta, GA, 174
Markham Station, Va,
Marshall County, AL, 1, 29, 31, 301, 342
Marshall News (Marshall County, AL), 67
Marshall, William O. "Billy", 87
Martin, Captain, 58, 174
Martindale, James H., 271, 272, 274
Martinsburg, VA, 127
Maryland Cavalry
1st (Dismounted), 291
Mason, Daniel Murray, 57
Massachusetts Infantry
6th, 408
20th, 247
23rd, 274
24th, 292
25th, 212, 274, 275
27th, 276
33rd, 190, 191, 193, 194
37th, 247
Matthews, Thomas L., 217
Maury, D. H., 316
Mayo, Elisha, 322
McArdle, Barney, 267
McCaghren, Robert A., 263
McCalley, Bolivar, 50
McCalley, John, 50
McCandless, William, 119

McCaskill, Neal A., 380
McClellan, George B., 9
McClendon, William Augustus, 195, 267, 297, 305, 307, 310, 315, 406, 409
compiled history of 15th AL, xvii
McCook, Alexander M., 143, 159
McDaniel, Henry, 63
McDonald, Jack, 261
McDuffie, Norman H., 188
McFarland, Robert, 5
McGowan, Samuel, 238, 293. *See also* McGowan's Brigade, Army of Northern Virginia
McGraw, J. J., 312
McIntosh, John, 282
McJunkin, Samuel B., 137
McKee, John V., 67, 127, 131
McLaws, Lafayette, 16, 66, 202, 205, 213, 215, 223, 395, 396
Gettysburg, PA, 12, 118, 119, 381, 385
quarrel with Longstreet, 223
McLaws's Division. *See* Divisions, Army of Northern Virginia, Army of Tennessee
McLemore, Owen Kenan
candidate for lt. col., 9
commanding 4th AL, 9
elected lt. col. 4th AL, 9
Gaines's Mill, VA, 11
mortally wounded, 14
sketch, 16
McLeod, John, 211
McMiller, Phinias K., 392
McNair, Evander, 158, 164
wounded, 390
McQuire, J. P., 380
McSpadden, S. K., 171
Meade, George G., 75, 79, 82, 113, 127, 136, 138, 231, 301, 304
Meggs, Eli W., 409
Melton, Simeon W., 218, 328
Mendenhall, John, 166, 167, 168
Menefee, Albert, 32
Merritt, Wesley, 113
Michigan Artillery
4th Battery, 159, 162, 389
Michigan Cavalry
5th, 128, 129
6th, 128, 129
Michigan Infantry
1st, 129, 130
2nd, 209, 210, 395
5th, 129, 130
16th, 95, 96, 98, 105, 106
17th, 209, 210
20th, 209, 210
Milford Station, VA, 136
Military appearance
47th AL, 231
48th Alabama, 75

Hood's Division, 18
   Law's Brigade, 299, 300
Military reviews
   cavalry, 66
   Law's Brigade, 134
   Lee reviews First Corps, 231
Mississippi Infantry
   2nd, 9, 10, 13, 14
   11th, 9, 10, 11, 13, 14, 60
   13th, 270
   16th, 19
Millwood, VA, 127
Mobile, AL, 301
Montague, Edgar B., 304
Monterey Springs, PA, 125
Montgomery, AL, 29, 337
Montgomery (Alabama) *Advertiser*, 341
Montgomery *Daily Mail*, 286
Moore, Governor Andrew B., 1, 3, 5, 8
Moore, H. D., 2, 372
Morrill, Walter G., 96, 106, 107, 108
Morristown, TN, 215, 220
Mosely, John W., 98, 109, 110
Mossy Creek, TN, 216
Motes, O. J., 46
Mott, Gershom, 399
Moulton, Orson, 274, 275
Moxley, G. Sorrel, 81, 118
Murphy, Steve, 270
Murray, Alexander A., 283

N

Nash, Eugene, 96, 99
Nashville and Chattanooga Railroad, 182
Nashville, TN, 339
National Tribune, xvii
Negley, James Scott, 159, 389
Nellis, Joseph, 109
Nelson, John, 104
Newbill, George H., 276
Newby's Cross Roads, VA, 129
Newell, Isaac M., 127, 131
New Guilford, PA, 75
New Hampshire Infantry
   3rd, 310
   13th, 51
New Jersey Infantry
   6th, 94
   9th, 403
New Market, TN, 219
New Orleans Picayune, 344
Newport News, VA, 45
Newsome, William O., 149
New York Artillery
   2nd, 209
   4th Battery, 83. *See also* James E. Smith
   15th, 240, 245

New York Cavalry
   1st, 123
New York *Herald*, 138, 139
New York Infantry
   10th, 243, 400
   14th State Militia (84th), 258, 260
   40th, 94
   44th, 95, 98, 109
   48th, 403
   76th, 240, 241, 243
   79th, 209, 211
   84th (14th State Militia), 258, 260
   89th, 56
   99th, 51
   100th, 291, 307
   117th, 62, 64
   124th, 83
   136th, 191, 194
   137th, 393
   140th, 105
   141st, 188
New York, NY,
Nicholson, John P., 110
Nicoll, Thomas A., 313
Nix, Reuben, 118
Noble, William, 210
Norfolk and Petersburg Railroad, 65
Norris, Robert Cicero, 106
North Anna River, VA, 266
North Carolina Artillery
   Rowan Artillery, 82. *See also* James Reilly
North Carolina Infantry
   6th, 9, 10, 13, 14, 18
   39th, 162, 171
   55th, 52, 55, 57, 59, 60, 62, 379
Norton, Oliver W., 110
Norton, Tom, 336
Nott, Josiah, 9

O

Oakley, William D., 67
Oates, John 67, 123
   mortally wounded, 103
Oates, William Calvin, 20, 21, 23, 24, 25, 39, 40, 46,
   63, 67, 76, 90, 128, 129, 130, 132, 143, 144, 145,
   148, 149, 151, 154, 156, 180, 256, 257, 260, 261,
   262, 267, 270, 282, 283, 289, 301, 307, 309, 314,
   319, 337, 339
   accepts maj. commission, 278
   appointed col. 15th AL, 63
   attorney for Law, 221
   capt. 15th AL, 20
   Chickamauga, GA, 157, 158, 171, 172, 173, 174
   Cold Harbor, VA, 274
   commanding Law's Brigade, 148, 156
   compiled history of 15th AL, xvi
   Fussell's Mill, VA, 292, 295, 296, 297

severely wounded, 295
Gettysburg, PA, 82, 88, 90, 96, 99, 100, 103, 104,
106, 107, 108, 110, 114, 116, 118, 119, 123, 205,
382, 384, 385, 393
    attack on Vincent's left, 105
    attacks 20th ME, 101, 103
    falls out from exhaustion, 108
    Plum Run Valley, 383
    proposes new plan of attack, 100
    withdraws from Little Round Top, 107, 108
    Lookout Valley, TN, 176, 183, 184, 185, 197
post war, 341, 342
    petition for Gettysburg monument, 342
organization of 15th AL, 21
quarrel with Lowther, xv
reduced in rank, xv, 277
U.S. brigadier, 342
Wilderness, VA, 232, 238, 240, 244, 245, 248, 251,
252, 253
    view of Lee, 237
O'Connor, Patrick, 104
Ogilvie, John D., 283
Ohio Artillery
    First Ohio Light Artillery, 389
Ohio Infantry
    8th, 241
    17th, 159, 162, 164
    18th, 185
    31st, 159, 162
    62nd, 310
    73rd, 190, 193, 194
    74th, 164
    103rd, 396
Oliver, James McCarthy, 34
    elected col. 47th AL, 28
    resigns commission, 31
Opelika, AL, 278
Orange & Alexandria Railroad, 230
Orange Court House, VA, 8, 66, 231, 232
Orion, AL, 46, 314
O'Rorke, Patrick H., 105
Otis, John L., 311
Owens, J. O., 409

P

Palmer, John M., 388
Palo Pinto County, Texas, 345
Panther Springs, TN, 215, 216
Park, Frank, 46, 106
Parsons, H. C., 114, 116, 118
Parton, Joseph J., 339
Peck, John, 51, 53, 54, 58, 63, 64
Pegram's battery, 376
Pemberton, John C., 292
Pennsylvania Artillery, 166
    26th Battery, 154, 166

Pennsylvania Infantry
    83rd, 95, 96, 98, 101, 103, 104, 107, 109, 110
    85th, 310
    111th, 16
    118th, 121
    143rd, 243, 244, 246
    143th, 244
    149th, 243, 244
    150th, 243, 244, 246, 247
Penny, Riley, 123
Penny, William, 123
Perrin, Abner, 250
Perry, Edward A., 250
Perry, William Flake, 40, 119, 121, 132, 144, 146, 148,
241, 277, 278, 315, 317, 322, 324, 333
    Chickamauga, GA, 146, 151, 154, 156, 157, 158,
    164, 167, 168, 170, 171, 173
    relieved of command, 148
    commanding Law's Brigade, 164, 232, 238, 240,
    246, 248, 251, 253, 275, 280, 313
    death, 341
    East TN
        commanding Law's Brigade, 218
    elected maj., 25
        supported by brigade officers, 316
        supports Oates for colonel, 278
    Gettysburg, PA, 78, 90, 91, 93, 94, 99, 105
    injured, 289, 405
    post war, 341
    promoted brigadier, 318
    promoted col. 44th AL, 28
    promoted lt. col. 44th AL, 28
    quarrel with Law, 341
    recommended for brigadier's commission, 220, 317
    sketch, 28
    Spotsylvania
        commanding Law's Brigade, 256, 257, 258, 260,
        262, 263
    succeeded Law as brigade commander, xiv, 318
    support of the brigade officers, 316
    Wilderness, VA
        commanding Law's Brigade, 236, 238, 240, 244,
        245, 246, 248, 250, 251, 252, 253
        view of Lee, 237
        wounded, 252
Perry, William G., 287
Perry's Brigade, 329. *See also* Law's Brigade
    Appomattox Campaign, 328
        Amelia Court House, 329
        arrives Petersburg, 327
        forms last line of battle, 333
        Goode's Bridge, 328
        strength, 333
        surrender ceremonies, 335, 336
    Perry made official commander, 318
    promotions, 324
    resignations, 324
Peters, Silas B., 76

Petersburg (Virginia) *Daily Express*, 57
Petersburg, VA, 27, 65, 283, 286, 326, 327, 332, 337
  defenses, 280
  siege of, 280
    Boydton Plank Rd., 327
    Chimneys, 284
    Elliot's Salient, 284
    Field's Division, 284
    Indian Town Creek, 327
    Jerusalem Plank Rd., 284, 287
    Lee withdraws, 327
    opposing positions, 284
    rations, 287
    sniping, 286
    trench conditions, 286, 404
Peterson, Battle D., 391
Pettit, H. L., 290, 291
Philadelphia *Weekly Press*, xvii
Pickett, George E., 45, 48, 51, 52, 53, 66, 111, 128, 179, 326
  Chester Station, VA, 281, 282
Pickett, W. R., 396
Pierce, Alford, 401
Pinckard, Thomas, 333
Pitts Folly, AL, 300
Pitts, John Davidson, 300
Pitts, Mary, 300
Pittsylvania, VA, 330, 334
Plackett, William, 168
Planck, John E., 125
Pleasant Hill, Alabama, 258
Pleasonton, Alfred, 113, 136
Plimpton, Homer A., 310
Point Lookout, MD, 122
Polk County Florida, 341
Polk, Leonidas, 138, 143, 157, 161, 176, 201
Polley, Joseph B., 71, 178, 333
Pond, Francis B., 293, 310
Pope, John, 24, 27
Port Royal, VA, 134, 136
Porter, Fred, 149, 174
Posey, John W., 282
Potter, Robert, 250, 251, 400
Powell, Ephraim, 269
Powell, R. M., 385
Powell, William A., 142
Powers, Robert, 336, 337
Preston, William, 157
Pruett, Jacob, 149
Pugh, J. L., 277, 397
Purifoy, John W., 344

Q

Quinley, Stephen, 167, 248

R

Raccoon Mountain, TN, 182
Raleigh, NC, 27, 131, 141

Raleigh (North Carolina) *Standard*, 141
Ralls, John P., 397
Randolph County, AL, 301
Randolph, George W., 377
Randolph, William, 10, 16, 39, 68, 83
Ransom, Robert, Jr.
  proposed to command Hood's Division, 219
Rappahannock Academy, 134
Ray, Andrew, 123
Ray, Augustus, 28
Rayburn, John, 29, 67, 376
Rayburn, Samuel K., 29, 301, 376
Reagan, John H., 329
Reams Station, VA, 299
Reese, George W., 336, 379
Reid, Harrison Preston, 125
Reilly, James, 82, 85, 113, 116
  defends guns against Farnsworth, 118
Reilly's battery. *See* James Reilly; *see also* Rowan Artillery, North Carolina Artillery
Religious services
  gospel meetings, 37
  Great Revival, 137
Reneau, Bart, 321
Renfroe, Green C., 392
Renfroe, Thomas M., 143, 171
Resaca, GA, 300
Reynolds, Joseph J., 151, 159, 161, 162, 173
Reynolds's division. *See* Joseph J. Reynolds
Rhode Island Infantry
  4th, 64
Rhodes, James M., 261, 305
Rice, Erwin Foster, 290, 291
Rice, James C., 95, 96, 109, 110, 240, 241, 248
  mortally wounded, 260
Rice Station, VA, 288
Richardson, William N., 193
Richmond and Danville Railroad, 327, 329
Richmond and Fredericksburg Railroad, 267
Richmond and Petersburg Railroad, 45, 65, 280, 281
Richmond City Battalion, 288
Richmond *Enquirer*, 296, 320
Richmond, Fredericksburg & Petersburg Railroad, 45
Richmond, Fredericksburg and Potomac Railroad, 136
Richmond, VA, 9, 11, 13, 21, 27, 31, 45, 46, 47, 48, 221, 327, 328, 335
  defenses
    Bermuda Hundred Line, 281
    Cornelius Creek, 308
    exterior line, 286, 302, 303, 304, 308
    Ft. Gilmer, 303
    Ft. Harrison, 308
    Howlett Line, 281
    intermediate line, 308
    New Market line, 303
  roads
    Charles City Rd., 281
    Darbytown Rd., 281, 304, 305, 308

New Market Rd., 281
Nine Mile Rd., 313
Osborne Turnpike, 280
vicinity of
Bermuda Hundred, 281
Camp Holly, 313
Chaffin's Bluff, 280, 288
Chaffin's farm, 304
Charles City Rd., 312
Clay farm, 281. *See also* Chester Station, VA
Deep Bottom, 281. *See also* Fussell's Mill, VA
Drewry's Bluff, 288, 289, 302
Dutch Gap, 312
Four Mile Creek, 289
Ft. Gilmer, 302
Ft. Harrison, 301. *See also* Ft. Harrison
James River, 287
Jerusalem Plank Rd., 300
New Market Heights, 281, 288
Port Walthall Junction, 281
White Oak Swamp, 280
Richmond (Virginia) *Dispatch*, 122, 136, 388
Richmond (Virginia) *Enquirer*, 142, 388
Ridgeway, James S., 123, 136
Ringgold, GA, 213
Rittenhouse, Benjamin, 104
Robbins, William McKendre, 14, 16, 98, 99, 125, 191, 209, 210, 248, 305, 333, 337, 392, 393, 395
Gettysburg National Military Park Commissioner, 342
Robertson, Felix H., 118
Robertson, Jerome Bonaparte, 58, 66, 120, 131, 132, 143, 145, 149, 186, 190, 194, 196, 213, 395, 396. *See also* Brigades, Army of Northern Virginia, Army of Tennessee
censured by Longstreet, 208
Gettysburg, PA, 82, 87, 93, 112
supports Law for maj. gen., 177
Robertson's Brigade, 77. *See* Brigades, Army of Northern Virginia, Army of Tennessee, J. B. Robertson
Robinson, John C., 240
Robinson, William H., 283
Rodes, Robert E., 126
Roemer, Jacob, 209
Rogers, John, 168
Rogersville, TN, 213, 215, 216
Root, Elihu, 343
Roper, Henry B., 125
Rosecrans, William S., 138, 139, 143, 145, 158, 159, 176, 180, 201
Ross, Francis V., 67
Rowe, Frederick A., 51
Rucker, F. Pope, 315

S

Salem, VA, 27
Salisbury, NC, 337

Sams, Robert Oswald, 323
Samuels, Thomas L., 275
Sanders, John C. C., 293
Sandusky, Ohio, 122
Sanford, James, 401
Satterfield, E. Fletcher, 60
Sauls, Thomas, 275
Savage, Robert Russell, 34
Savannah, GA, 336
Sawyer, Charles F., 383
Sayler's Creek, VA, 330
Schurz, Carl, 185, 190, 199
Scotland, PA, 75
Scott, Charles Lewis, 5, 6, 9, 18
elected maj. 4th AL, 5
sketch, 5
Scott, J. A., 3
Scottsville, AL, 28
Scruggs, Lawrence Houston, 14, 48, 50, 51, 88, 119, 125, 141, 144, 191, 245, 262, 308, 321, 332, 333, 337
commanding 4th AL, 76, 128
Gettysburg, PA, 112
promoted lt. col. 4th AL, 18
wounded, 146
Scruggs, William H., 321, 406
Secession
Alabama votes to secede, 1
Baptist convention position, 1
Convention, 342
Cooperationists, 1
Methodist convention position, 1
Opposition in Alabama, 1
Secessionists, 1
Seddon, James A., 133, 222, 316, 319
opinion about Law's conduct, 398
Sellers, Henry, 382
Selma, AL, 25
Selma (Alabama) *Reporter*, 25, 54
Seven Pines, VA, 10
Shaaff, Francis Key, 24, 101, 107, 108, 129, 184, 251, 256, 295, 296, 339, 397
Shady Grove Church, VA, 255
Sharpsburg, MD, 14, 24, 28, 35
Dunker Church, 14
East Woods, 14
West Woods, 35
Sheffield, James Lawrence, 29, 35, 37, 40, 67, 68, 72, 119, 132, 134, 139, 142, 143, 144, 145, 188, 189, 181, 193, 278, 301, 336, 387
commanding Law's Brigade, 112, 131, 128, 134, 143, 144, 145, 157
elected col. 48th AL, 29
Gettysburg, PA, 82, 85, 90, 93, 94, 96, 105
injured, 148
opposition to secession, 1
post war, 342
raises regiment with own funds, 29

sketch, 2, 31, 342
Shenandoah Valley, VA, 5, 127, 289
Shepherd, J. H., 148
Shepherdstown, VA, 14
Sherman, William T., 202, 213, 314, 322, 323
Shorter, Governor John Gill, 177
Shumaker, L. M., 55, 58
Simmons, Henry D., 112
Simms, William Gilmore, 323
  sketch, 409
Sims, Robert M., 3, 319
  sketch, 372
Sinclair, Robert R., 6
Skinkers Neck, VA, 38
Skipper, Bryant, 172, 322
Slavery
  issue of arming slaves, 319, 320
Small, A. W., 137
Smith, David J., 335
Smith, Francis M., 248
Smith, Gustavus W., 218
Smith, James, 39
Smith, James E., 83, 85, 87, 90, 91, 93, 94, 99
Smith, Joseph T., 151
Smith, Maurice T., 55
Smith, Orland, 190
Smith, William F., 271, 272
Smoot, David L., 52, 58
Smoot's battery, 53, 54. *See also* Alexandria Light Artillery, Virginia Artillery
Society Hill, SC, 2
Somerville, Thomas B., 257, 258
Sorrel, G. Moxley, 52, 221, 232, 250
South Carolina Artillery
  German Artillery, 75. *See also* William K. Bachman
  Hart's Battery, 113
South Carolina Cavalry
  1st, 113
South Carolina Infantry
  5th, 296
  7th, 172
  15th, 172
  18th, 404
  22nd, 404
  23rd, 13
South Carolina Military Academy, 2, 3
South Carolina Press Association, 341
Southern Historical Society, xvii
Southside and Danville Railroad, 326
Southside Railroad, 301
Sparta, AL, 3, 4, 329
Spear, Ellis, 103, 106, 107
Spenser, G. E., 87
Spotsylvania County, VA, 50
Spotsylvania Court House, VA, 232
Spotsylvania, VA
  Confederates leave the Wilderness battlefield, 255
  May 8, 1864
    Field arrives Laurel Hill, 256

Field's route from the Wilderness, 255
Law's Brigade engages the Federals, 257
positions on Confederate left, 257
May 10, 1864
  Cutler's attack on Law's Brigade, 260
  Cutler's demonstration against Law's Brigade, 258
May 12, 1864
  attack on the Confederate right, 262
  Cutler attacks Law's Brigade, 262
May 15, 1864
  Grant moves toward Richmond, 263
Spring Garden, AL, 156
St. John, Columbus B., 119, 386
  acting maj., 386
  commanding 48th, 35
Stafford, Leroy, 374
Stanard, Robert C., 130
Stanley, Timothy R., 185
Stannard, George, 271
Starke, William E., 24, 34
Starr, W. G., 230
State brigades, 11, 19
  Law's Alabama brigade created, 20
Statesville, NC, 337
Statistics
  casualties
    2nd MI, 210
    4th AL, 8, 14, 16, 18, 297
    10th CT, 310
    15th AL, 108, 121, 174, 184, 405
    20th ME, 108
    44th AL, 28, 121, 154, 166, 297
    47th AL, 121
    48th AL, 35, 121
    82nd IN, 162
    Field's Division, 313
    Law's Brigade, 65, 76, 111, 121, 122, 174, 253, 278, 313
    U.S. Navy, Suffolk, 52
  strength
    4th AL, 76, 328, 333, 390
    10th CT, 310
    15th AL, 76, 174, 333, 405, 405
    44th AL, 328, 333, 406
    47th AL, 76, 333
    48th, 76, 300, 333
    Federal strength, 394
    Field's Division, 409
    Jenkins's Brigade, 393
    Law's Brigade, 76, 144, 234, 280, 299
    Longstreet at Suffolk, 47
    Perry's Brigade, 333
    Wauhatchie, TN, 394
Stedman, Griffin, 271, 272
Steinwehr, Adolph, 185
Sterling, Dump, 47
Stevens, Alanson, 166, 168

Stevens, Hazard, 55, 56, 58
Stevens, Thaddeus, 76
Stevenson, AL, 176
Stewart, Alexander P., 144, 145, 154, 157, 158, 161, 329
Stewart, John, 72
Stone, J. B., 149
Stone, Roy, 240, 243, 244, 248
Stoughton, Homer R., 83, 90, 384. *See also* 2nd U.S. Sharpshooters
Stoughton's Sharpshooters. *See also* 2nd U.S. Sharpshooters, Homer R. Stoughton
Strasburg, VA, 5
Strawberry Plains, TN, 213
Stribling, Robert M., 53, 54, 55, 56, 57
Stribling's battery, 57, 58, 59, 62. *See also* Fauquier Artillery, Virginia Artillery
Strickland, William H., 21, 173, 295
Stuart, James Ewell Brown, 66, 68, 255
Sturgis, Henry H., 71, 194, 262
    compiled history of 44th AL, xvii
Suffolk, VA, 47, 48, 51, 55, 57
    siege of
        44th AL occupies Ft. Huger, 55
        Blackwater River, 48
        Cahoon Point, 56
        campaign objectives, 47
        casualties, 65
        constructing fortifications, 50
        description of Suffolk, 48
        Doctor Council's Landing, 56
        duel, 60, 61
        earthworks, 50
        Federals capture Ft. Huger, 56
        Ft. Huger, 50, 52, 53, 54, 58, 62, 64
        Hill's Point, 50, 54, 57, 64
        Hood engages the gunboats, 51
        Hood engages the naval landing force, 53
        Hood withdraws to the Blackwater, 64
        Hood's position on the Nansemond, 50
        Law's Brigade arrives, 48
        Law's Brigade on Upper Nansemond, 53
        Reed's Ferry Rd., 58
        skirmish of May 3, 1863, 64
        stalemate on the river, 62
        U.S. naval force, 51
Sugg, Cyrus, 162, 164, 166, 167, 168, 170, 171, 389, 390
Sugg's Brigade. *See* Cyrus Sugg
Sullivan, James H., 283
Summerfield, AL, 301
Summit, AL, 37
Swallow, George, 166, 168. *See also* 7th Indiana Battery
Swan, Joseph, 174

T

Taliaferro, William B., 20, 31, 34, 35

Talladega, AL, 28, 288, 301
Tallapoosa County, AL, 1, 288
Taylor, John Dykes, 178, 188, 214, 391
Taylor, Walter H., 304
Tennessee and Virginia Railroad, 139
Tennessee Infantry
    1st (Consolidated), 158
    15th, 148
    18th, 154
    37th, 148
    50th, 158, 171
Terrell, Leigh Richmond, 57, 60, 85, 88, 100, 133, 143, 173, 184, 191, 238, 250, 251, 263, 284, 305, 333
    burial with military honors, 312
    challenged to duel, 60
    leads charge against Federal artillery, 167, 168
    mortally wounded, 312
Terry, Alfred H., 291, 293, 305, 307, 309, 312
Texas Infantry
    1st, 11, 18, 87, 88, 113, 114, 118, 188, 189, 193, 211
    4th, 11, 18, 85, 87, 90, 91, 98, 105, 108, 188, 191, 193
    5th, 11, 14, 16, 82, 87, 88, 90, 91, 98, 109, 158, 188, 191
    7th, 158
The Grange, 340
Thielberg, Henry, 52
Thomas, George H., 125, 143, 159, 161, 166
Thompson, Allen, 142
Thompson, Hugh S., 2
Thompson, T. P., 172
Thompson, Theo P., 211, 213
Thornton, Dozier, 295
Thorton, Richard A., 379
Tibbett, William H., 312
Towles, Albert, 39
Townes, W. H., 60
Tracey, Edward Dorr, 6
Trench Warfare, 284
Treutlen, James Fletcher, 23
    elected lt. col. 15th AL, 21
    promoted col. 15th AL, 25
    resigns commission, 63
Trimble, Isaac R., 21, 23, 24, 334
Trimmer, William, 87
Trion, AL, 56
Troy, AL, 211
Trumbull, Clay, 310
Turchin, John B., 151, 154, 183, 389
Turnbow, James M., 87
Turner, Daniel H., 53
Turner, John W., 410
Turner, William F., 130, 208
Tuskegee, AL, 16, 28, 122
Tuskegee Military High School, 2, 3
Tweedell, John F., 328

Tyler, R. C., 148
Tyler, Spencer C., 67
Tyndale, Hector, 188, 190, 199. *See also* Tyndale's
   Hill, Lookout Valley, TN
Tyner's Station, TN, 201

U

U.S. Artillery
   2nd
      Battery M, 129
   4th
      Battery H, 166, 390
U.S. Cavalry
   5th, 114
U.S. Infantry
   1st Sharpshooters, 83
   1st Volunteer, 397
   2nd U.S. Sharpshooters, 87, 88, 91, 99, 290
   6th Volunteer, 397
   8th, 16
   Colored Troops
      5th, 312
      7th, 312
      22nd, 302
      30th, 312
U.S. Navy
   North Atlantic Blockading Squadron, 51
Uniontown, AL, 9
*United States 'History' as the Yankee Makes and
   Takes It*, 344
United States ships
   USS *Agawam,* 289
   USS *Alert,* 51, 54
   USS *Coeur de Lion,* 54
   USS *Cohasset,* 51
   USS *Commodore Barney,* 52
   USS *Mount Washington,* 51, 52, 56
   USS *Smith Briggs,* 51
   USS *Stepping Stones,* 51, 53, 56, 58
   USS *Teaser,* 54, 378
   USS *West End,* 52

V

Van Cleve, Horatio Phillips, 63, 151, 159, 161, 388, 389
Vance, Governor Zebulon B., 141, 388
Vaughan, Paul Turner, 46, 48, 55, 58, 59, 68, 75, 131,
   134, 180, 195, 202, 270, 308
Venable, Charles S., 282
Vermont Cavalry
   1st, 113, 114
Vermont Infantry
   4th, 244
Vernoy, James, 377
Vicksburg, VA, 127
Vincent, Isaac H., 132, 345

Vincent, Strong, 91, 93, 96, 99, 105, 109, 110
   attacked by 44th and 48th AL, 105
   attacked by 4th AL, 4th, 5th TX, 98
   deploys on Little Round Top, 95, 96
   mortally wounded, 105
   sketch, 95
Vincent's brigade. *See* S. Vincent
   brings in wounded at Gettysburg, 109
   strength at Gettysburg, 95
Virginia Artillery
   12th Battalion, 58
   Alexandria Light Artillery, 52, 53
   Fauquier Artillery, 52, 53. *See also* Robert M.
      Stribling, Stribling's battery
Virginia Central Railroad, 288, 334
Virginia Infantry
   10th, 31, 32
   17th, 128
   23rd, 31
   25th Battalion, 407
   37th, 31, 32
Virginia Military Institute, 341
Volunteer Companies
   departing ceremonies, 4

W

Waddell, DeBernie B., 104, 106, 107, 108, 184, 191,
   194, 211, 261, 267, 295, 297, 384
   elected capt., 143
   sketch, 143
Wade, E. B., 114
Wadsworth, James S., 235, 236, 240, 243, 244, 246, 247,
   400
Walke, John P., 38
Walker, Elijah, 83, 91, 93, 94, 96
Walker, James, 39
Walker, John Marshall, 300
Walker, Mims, 48, 157, 232, 283, 284, 300, 318, 340,
   344
Wallis, David, 274
Walls, Carter, 324
Walls, Willis W., 324
Walnut Grove Church, VA, 269
Wappen, VA, 128
Ward, Benjamin J., 61
Ward, Durbin, 162
Ward, Edward J. J., 307
Ward, John Henry Hobart, 83, 91, 240, 243, 248
Ward, William C., 71, 72, 85, 87, 98, 111
Warfield Ridge, 78
Warren, E. T. H., 37
Warren, Gouverneur K., 82, 85, 95, 105, 256, 258, 262
Warren, Thomas V., 275
Washington, D.C., 335
Washington, GA, 338
Washington, VA, 68
Watts, Governor Thomas H., 10, 16, 177, 301, 335

Wauhatchie, TN, 188, 189. *See also* Lookout Valley, TN
  engagement Oct. 28, 1863, 199, 200
Webb, Alexander S., 247
Weldon, NC, 27, 139
Weldon Railroad, 289, 297, 313
Wells, William, 114, 116
Wesley, Mills, 23
West, Jason M., 267
West Point, 16
West Point, GA, 337
West Virginia Cavalry
  1st, 114
West Virginia Infantry
  7th, 241
Westminister, MD, 122
Whatley, Leonidas, 257
Wheaton, Frank, 240, 244, 245
Wheeler, Joseph, 201, 322, 323
White, W. W., 80, 205, 260, 261
White, Wyman S., 290
Whiting, W. H. C., 9, 11, 317
  opposes state brigades, 11
  proposed to command Hood's Division, 219
Whiting's division. *See* Whiting's division, Army of Northern Virginia
Wicker, Robert H., 123, 338, 339
  captured on Little Round Top, 107
Wiedrich, Michael, 240, 245
Wigfall, Louis T., 10
Wiggenton, James W., 234, 324, 333
  signs petition to Cooper, 397
Wilcox, Cadmus M., 234, 235, 293, 327
Wilderness, VA. See also Law's Brigade, 4th AL, 15th AL, 44th AL, 47th AL, 48th AL, D. Birney, S. S. Carroll, C. W. Field, J. B. Kershaw, E. M. Law, R. E. Lee, J. Longstreet, W. C. Oates, W. F. Perry, R. Potter, J. S. Wadsworth
  description of the battlefield, 232
  May 6, 1864
    4th and 47th AL attack along Plank Road, 241
    4th and 47th AL charge the Federals, 246
    4th and 47th AL engage the 150th PA, 244
    15th AL engages 15th NY, 245
    44th and 48th AL engage the Pennsylvanians, 246
    Brock Rd., 234, 238, 240, 243, 250
    Burnside's attack, 252
    charge of the 37th MA, 247
    charge of the Texans, 236
    Federal line breaks, 241
    Heth's Division overrun, 236
    Law's Brigade retires from the field, 253
    McGowan works, 243
    Orange Plank Rd., 235, 236, 237, 238, 240, 241, 243, 244, 245, 246, 247, 248, 250, 252, 253
    Perry engages Stone's brigade, 244
    Widow Tapp farm, 238, 240, 244, 245
Willis, James, 64

Wilmington, NC, 13, 139, 316, 318, 322
Wilson, Andrew J., 234, 254
Wilson, Bryant, 261
Wilson, W. B., 3
Wilson, William L., 211
Winchester, VA, 5, 16, 18, 68, 127
Winder, Charles S., 374
Winston, Governor John A., 4
Wisconsin Infantry
  6th, 257
Wisconsin Artillery
  3rd Battery, 166, 167
Withers, Jones Mitchell, 409
Wofford, William T., 252, 269, 270
Wood, H. C., 32
Wood, John Taylor, 134
Wood, Thomas J., 148, 159
Wood, William D., 119
Woodham, Eugene B., 53
Wood's division. *See* Thomas J. Wood
Woodward, Orpheus S., 103, 104
Woolfolk, Thomas, 377
Wright, Ambrose R., 27
Wright, Horatio G., 271
Wright, Tommy, 173

Y

Yancey, William Lowndes, 10
Yorkville, SC, 3, 178, 283, 324
Young, James H., 283
Young, John W., 74, 112
Youngblood, William, 70, 71

Z

Zahn, Joseph H., 276
Zoellner, Frank, 210